BATHING AT THE EDGE OF THE EMPIRE

Bathing at the Edge of the Empire

Roman Baths and Bathing Habits in the North-Western Corner of Continental Europe

SADI MARÉCHAL

BREPOLS

THE ARCHAEOLOGY OF NORTHERN EUROPE
VOLUME 2

British Library Cataloguing in Publication Data
A catalogue record for this book is available from the British Library.

D/2023/0095/158
ISBN: 978-2-503-60066-6
e-ISBN: 978-2-503-60067-3

DOI: 10.1484/M.TANE-EB.5.129940

Printed in the EU on acid-free paper.

To Aisha

Table of Contents

List of Illustrations

6. Building Material and Decoration

7. Bathing and Society

Catalogue

Key to All Plans

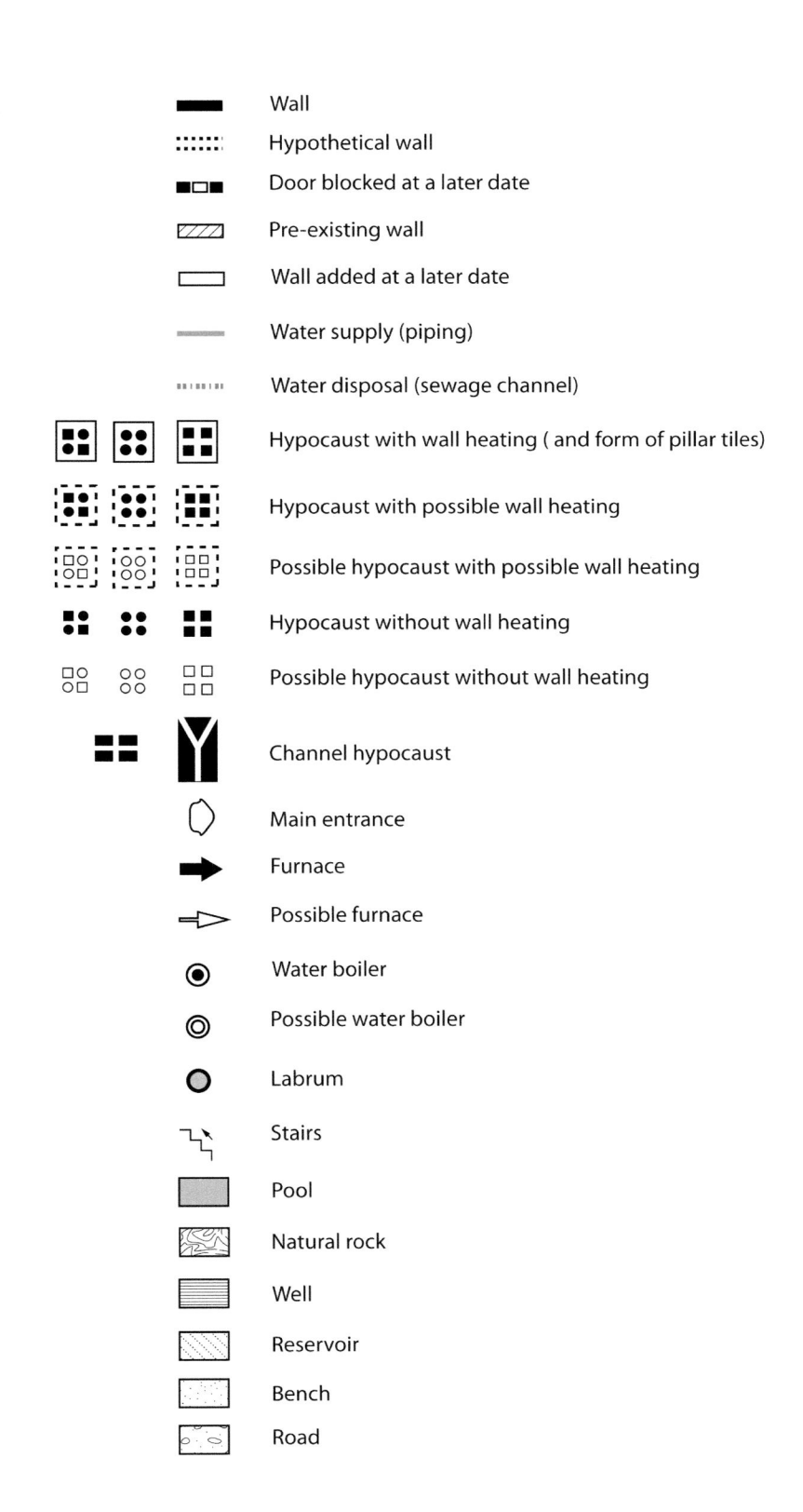

▬		Wall
┈┈		Hypothetical wall
■□■		Door blocked at a later date
▨		Pre-existing wall
▭		Wall added at a later date
━		Water supply (piping)
┉		Water disposal (sewage channel)

Hypocaust with wall heating (and form of pillar tiles)

Hypocaust with possible wall heating

Possible hypocaust with possible wall heating

Hypocaust without wall heating

Possible hypocaust without wall heating

Channel hypocaust

Main entrance

Furnace

Possible furnace

Water boiler

Possible water boiler

Labrum

Stairs

Pool

Natural rock

Well

Reservoir

Bench

Road

Preface

This book is the result of a postdoctoral research project (October 2018–October 2022), funded by the Research Foundation — Flanders (FWO-Vlaanderen, 12I9619N) and carried out at the department of Archaeology at Ghent University (Belgium). The project benefitted from the expertise of the Historical Archaeology Research Group (HARG), led by Prof. Dr Wim De Clercq, as well as from close collaboration with colleagues of the Mediterranean Research Unit (MARU), led by Prof. Dr Frank Vermeulen. I wish to express my sincere gratitude to both for supporting this project and providing much appreciated insights and feedback. I would also like to extend this gratitude to Dr Nathalie de Haan (Radboud University Nijmegen, the Netherlands), who has been my intellectual mentor ever since I started working on Roman baths, and whose advice, feedback, and friendship have been fundamental throughout my academic career. A special word of thanks also goes to my colleagues of the Historical Archaeology Research Group for all the stimulating meetings and coffee breaks. In particular, I would like to thank my 'north-western' colleagues Dr Sibrecht Reniere, Dr Sofie Vanhoute, Dr Vince Van Thienen, Dr Maxime Poulain, Dr Jan Trachet, Dr Dimitri Teetaert, Dr Ewoud Deschepper, Dante De Ruijsscher, Michiel Dekoninck, and Tim Clerbaut. I also express my gratitude to my 'Mediterranean' colleagues Dr Dimitri Van Limbergen, Dr Devi Taelman, Dr Lieven Verdonck, Dr Adeline Hoffelinck, Dr Wieke De Neef, and Sophie Dralans for the numerous discussions, at the department or online. Many thanks also go to Prof. Dr Guy De Mulder for numerous bibliographical references and Prof. Dr Arjan Zuiderhoek (History Department) for the interesting theoretical discussions. And I certainly cannot forget to thank Ariane Raman and Debby Van den Bergh for making sure the administration of this project ran as smoothly as possible, even during successive lockdowns.

An important part of the research was carried out during the exceptional circumstances of the covid pandemic. Inevitably this had an important impact on data gathering, site visits, and collaboration with colleagues. The closure of archives, libraries, and research institutions proved to be problematic for accessing non-digitized reports, plans, and photos, which means that this book is less illustrated than I initially wanted it to be. However, thanks to the formidable efforts of the library staff at Ghent University, almost all relevant publications were traced and digitized on-demand. During these exceptional times, this research could simply not have been possible without them. I must also thank a number of national and international colleagues who were so kind as to provide me with information, publications, plans, and photos. In no particular order, I would like to thank Alain Vanderhoeven, Ruben Pede, Karen Jeneson, Lacey Wallace, Arne De Graeve, Paul Johnson, Patrizio Pensabene, Michel Polfer, Arne Verbrugghe, Cécile Evers. I am also indebted to two anonymous reviewers for their interesting additions, corrections, and remarks. My sincere appreciation also for the editors of The Archaeology of Northern Europe (TANE) series at Brepols, Dr Paul Johnson and Dr Sam Turner, and publishing manager Dr Rosie Bonté, for their tireless assistance. All remaining errors are my own.

To conclude, I wish to thank my family, family-in-law, and friends for their continuing love and support, especially during the very trying pandemic. A special thanks goes to Jan, Arne, Thomas, and Dimitri, for roaming the Belgian Ardennes together from our hub in Givry, in search of Roman sites. Most of all, I thank my wife Nathalie, whose energy, love, and support pulled us through the pandemic, and my little star Aisha, who was born during this project, and who has enriched our lives ever since. I dedicate this book to her.

Sadi Maréchal
Ghent, July 2022

Introduction

Aims and Structure of the Book

The aim of this book is to present an understudied corpus of Roman baths in a peripheral region of the Roman Empire, namely the north-western corner of continental Europe, and use this corpus to study socio-cultural transformations and societal change in this part of the Roman world. Roman bathhouses are very recognizable buildings, representing not only the advances of Roman architecture and technology, but also a very 'classical' view on health and the human body, and an important concern with appearance. The introduction, adoption, and adaption of this very Roman building and its associated socio-cultural connotations can hence be used as a proxy to study the interaction between indigenous and Roman cultural spheres. As the indigenous inhabitants were unacquainted with a very specific building for communal bathing, when, where, and how such a building was adopted can reveal when, where, and how a Roman way of life penetrated new territory. When are the first Roman-style baths built and what can this tell us about the Roman conquest? Are Roman baths found mainly in urban contexts, as in the Mediterranean, or is there a different distribution pattern in this region with few antecedents in urbanism? Was the architecture, decoration, and technology simply copied or can we detect local preferences and changes that can reveal an indigenous attitude towards the underlying Roman bathing culture? Such important questions address wider debates on long-term cultural change and intercultural negotiation, social networking and social mobility, identity self-redefinition, or technological innovation, lifting the book beyond a mere architectural study with an illustrated catalogue.

Up till now, there has been no regional overview of Roman bathhouses in this part of the Empire. Furthermore, there has been an important increase in both the quantity and quality of the archaeological dataset in the last three decades. Development-led archaeology, the most common context for excava-tions in Belgium, the Netherlands, northern France, and western Germany, is continuously generating an ever-growing archaeological dataset, but is also rapidly revolutionizing archaeological fieldwork, digitalizing data during the excavations and including natural sciences (palynology, archaeozoology, etc.) in post-excavation research strategies. This has led to a high-resolution dataset, covering also many more aspects of the past (e.g. on the environment, the climate), but on the downside the ever-accelerating pace of excavations has also created an ever-increasing gap between generated data and scientific analysis and synthesis. Another important development in archaeological research has been the widespread implementation of GIS, following the emergence of freely available datasets. Soil maps, geological maps, Lidar data, and georeferenced historical maps can be overlain and linked to archaeological datasets in the same digital environment, enabling a series of computational calculations and spatial analyses. Furthermore, in Flanders (Central Archaeological Inventory) and the Netherlands (Archis), an exhaustive online archaeological dataset enables researchers to rapidly assemble large datasets, comprising both old and recent data, through targeted queries. These important developments, in combination with the increasing amount of unprocessed data, create very inviting circumstances to endeavour a multi-source and polyfocal study.

Chapter 1 gives an introduction to the history of communal bathing and bathhouses. It is not another overview of the general evolution of baths, but rather highlights some important aspects of Roman bathing culture which are crucial in understanding and contextu-alizing the 'export' of this typically Roman phenomenon to the provinces. Five key elements are discussed: the genesis of Roman-style bathhouses, the underlying motives for the popularity of baths and bathing, the blurred line between private and public bathing, the special case of thermal baths, and the spread of baths across the Empire. Chapter 2 presents a state-of-the-art on research on Roman baths in the north-west of the Empire. It breaks down into subchapters on the research tradition in north-western Europe (the first excavations, the first archaeological services, and the rise of rescue excavations and contract archaeology), on how baths of north-western continental Europe were incorporated into general works on Roman bathing and on previous specific studies on the baths in the research area. Chapter 3 zooms in on the balance between private and public baths in the research area and their spread throughout the three *civitates* forming the study region. Especially for baths in rural contexts, such as villa baths, the location of the site is examined by looking at both environmental (soil, geographic relief, waterways) and human features (roads, settlement patterns). Chapter 4 is the more traditional overview of the architecture of the baths in the study area. It looks at the typology of the plans, the size, and the different rooms of the bathhouses, making a distinction between the public and private buildings. This chapter builds upon the architectural data and the re-examined plans compiled in the catalogue at the end of this book. Besides providing a synthesis of the catalogued data, this part of the book also compares the dataset to baths in the cradle of this bathing culture in the Mediterranean. Chapter 5 focuses on the technology of the Roman bath, including subchapters on the furnaces, the hypocaust, the wall heating, the water supply, and the waste water disposal, while maintaining a division between public and private baths. As for the architecture, the technology of the baths in the dataset is compared to the technology of baths in the Mediterranean part of the Empire. Chapter 6 is devoted to the decoration and the building materials of the catalogued baths. The subchapters examine different types of building stone, bath-specific ceramic building materials (hypocaust tiles, *tubuli, tegulae mammatae*), marbles and other decorative stones, mosaics, wall paintings, and other types of decoration (stucco mouldings, *opus signinum*). Special attention is paid to the provenance of both building and decorative stones and the occurrence and spread of stamps on ceramic building materials, insofar as this data has been published. Chapter 7 then incorporates the results of all the previous chapters to examine the wider socio-cultural and societal implications of the introduction of baths to the research area. The subchapters focus subsequently on the initial phase of introduction of bathhouses, on the classical ideas about body, health, and appearance that migrated together with baths, on the way in which local elites gradually adopted the Roman bathing habit and used baths in intra-elite competition, and eventually on how accessibility to bathhouses reveals phenomena of cultural change and social exclusion. In the conclusions, the results of this study on baths are used in the broader

narrative about how a rural peripheral region was culturally integrated in the larger Empire, despite the absence of a pre-existing urban culture and a very low degree of urbanization even under Roman rule, both often considered to have been essential prerequisites for a successful integration.

At the end of the book, there is a catalogue of all studied baths. The different bathhouses are arranged alphabetically following the modern topographical name where the baths were found. An ID-number is also allotted to each bath, which can be linked to the general map with locations of the baths (Map 1). For each bathhouse, a data summary is compiled. The structure of each summary is loosely based on similar summaries found in the catalogues by Nielsen (1993), Thébert (2003), or Fournet, Redon, and Vanpeene (2017). Important information on current location (under 1), research history (2), type of baths (3), dating (4), level of confidence to interpret as baths (5), plan and rooms (6), technology (7), decoration (8), figures (9), and relevant bibliography (10) are thus concisely presented. More detailed information on these summaries can be found in the introduction to the catalogue. Whenever possible, the plans of the baths are also given, reproduced following a special key created by the author to present a uniform and clear corpus of plans that enables easy comparison. This key is also used for redrawn plans of baths not included in the catalogue and can be found after the list of figures (see above).

Methodology

The corpus of baths was assembled on the basis of published old and modern excavation data. For a small number of recently excavated baths, the unpublished excavation reports were consulted due to the absence of published data. Existing overviews formed a good starting point for the data collection: the work on Roman villas in Belgium by Robert De Maeyer (1937; 1940; 1979), a synthesizing article by Xavier Deru on Roman baths in the *civitas Tungrorum* (1994), an overview of public baths in small towns in Gaul by Alain Bouet (2003a), and the recent magnum opus on Roman Wallonia under the direction of Raymond Brulet (2008).[1] The corpus of bath sites that was compiled

---

1   As this study focuses on three *civitates* that only partially overlap with the territory of modern-day Belgium, several baths that are included in these earlier works are not catalogued in this book. It concerns the public baths of *Orolaunum* (Arlon; Loes 1909) and of Virton/Saint-Mard (Defosse and Mathieu 1983–1984) and the villa baths of Habay-la-Vieille (Anonymous 2000), Lacuisine/ Florenville (Mignot, Henrotay, and Bossicard 1997), Robelmont

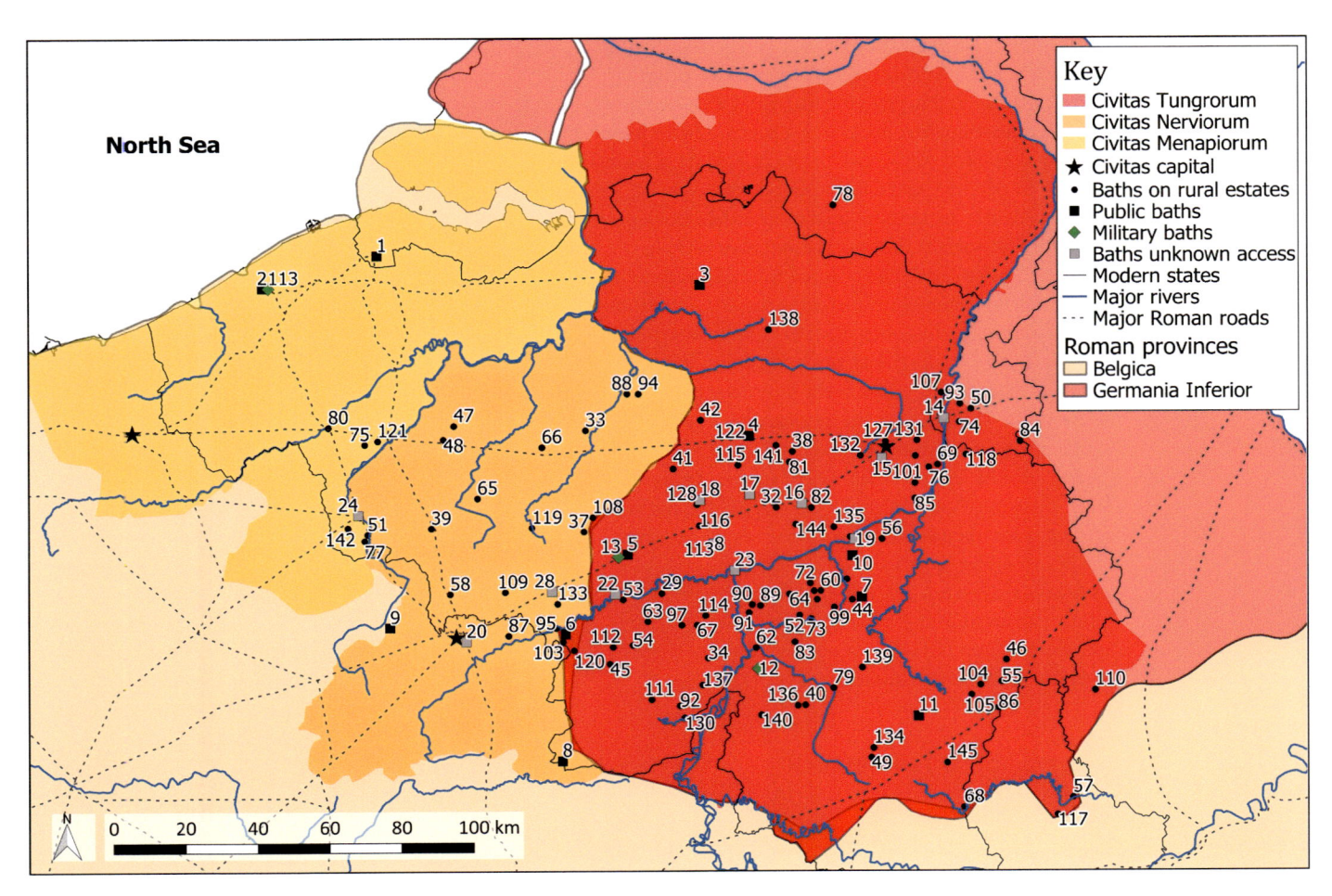

Map 1. Delimitation of the research area with location of the different baths. Map by author.

on the basis of these studies was complemented by sites found through targeted searches in the Central Archaeological Inventory (CAI) of the Flemish Heritage Agency and the Archaeological Information System (Archis) of the Dutch Agency for Cultural Heritage. Additional data was retrieved by a systematic search through relevant journals, especially those publishing yearly round-ups of all (Roman) excavations (e.g. *Archéologie, Archaeologica Belgica, Journée d'Archéologie Romaine, Signa, Chronique de l'archéologie Wallonne, Bilan Scientifique, Revue du Nord, Berichten van de Rijksdienst voor het Oudheidkundig Bodemonderzoek*, etc.). Only Roman baths known through excavations were included in this study. Possible bathhouses identified during prospection, by aerial photography, by remote sensing,

or geophysical prospection have not been studied. It is also important to note that the available archaeological evidence does not always allow a clear identification as a bathhouse. For several sites, excavators and scholars used the presence of a hypocaust to identify a bath, but the occurrence of heated living rooms makes such interpretations questionable. For this research, the archaeological evidence was rated with an A to C system:

A. Building/rooms that can unquestionably be inter-preted as baths: at least one pool identified with certainty, or strong evidence for the presence of a pool or *labrum* (e.g. *exedra*, water adduction channel, sewage channel, hydraulic mortar) in combination with at least one room heated by a hypocaust.

B. Building/rooms that can be identified with a high probability as bath: strong evidence of a pool in combination with a (nearby) room on a hypocaust, or two or more adjacent rooms with a hypocaust heating.

C. Building/rooms that can possibly be identified as baths: evidence for a pool, or two or more adjacent

(Bonenfant 1987), Rulles (Halbardier and Thomas 1987), Sainte-Marie-sur-Semois (Mignot 1994a), and Torgny (Bossicard 1994). Robert De Maeyer (1940) mentions possible bath suites in the villas of Heckbous – Rue de Girsch (p. 189), Fouches (p. 192) and Breuvanne (p. 222). All these remains are located in the *civitas Treverorum*.

rooms with a hypocaust heating or one round room with hypocaust heating (presumed *laconicum*). Although the catalogue of baths does not pretend to be exhaustive, few excavated examples will have been overlooked. Only the unpublished data from sites in northern France have been more difficult to access. For the arguments in this research, however, it is more important that a representative sample (i.e. 145 bathhouses) could be studied in order to test the hypothesis and attempt to answer the research questions. The bibliography has been updated until the summer of 2021. In the catalogue at the end of this book, the original excavation plans have been restudied and redrawn on the basis of the primary and secondary publications, and when possible, observations on site. Unfortunately, the vast majority of studied baths have been destroyed or reburied. The size of the baths is always given in relation to a scale bar of 5 m, except for the unusually large baths, where an additional scale bar of 10 m is also given. Once the database was compiled, all the entries were also inserted in a GIS-environment, which was then linked back to the database through the individual object identifiers (ID).

Geographical Framework

The research area for this study comprises the continental north-west of the Empire. After Julius Caesar's conquest, the province of *Gallia Belgica* was created during the reign of Augustus, somewhere between 27 and 13 BC. The area along the Rhine was detached from *Belgica*, first on a military level by Tiberius, then on an administrative level under Domitian, creating the provinces of *Germania Inferior* and *Germania Superior* between AD 82 and AD 90 (Schön 2006). Within these provinces, a further administrative subdivision was made in *civitates*. This administrative unit was created around a central city or *civitas* capital, taking into account but not strictly following the territories of pre-Roman communities and tribes (Wightman 1985, 29–31). North-western Gaul was hence divided into the *civitas Menapiorum*, the *civitas Nerviorum*, and the *civitas Tungrorum*. The latter was probably originally a part of *Belgica*, but was later added to *Germania Inferior* (Brulet 2008, 48). In Late Antiquity, the administrative reforms of the Tetrarchy split up *Gallia Belgica* in *Belgica Prima* and *Belgica Secunda*. *Germania Inferior* was rebaptized *Germania Secunda* and still comprised the *civitas Tungrorum*. However, the *civitates* in *Gallia Secunda* were reorganized: the *civitas Menapiorum* was transformed into the *civitas Turnacensium*, while the *civitas Nerviorum* was enlarged with the area around Cambrai, becoming the *civitas Camarcensium* (Wightman 1985, 202–06).

For the territorial boundaries of the *civitas Menapiorum*, this book follows the delimitations by De Laet (1961), with the exception of the northern boundary with the *civitas Frisiavionum*, where the delimitation proposed by Bogaers (1971) is followed. The territory thus delimited stretches from the North Sea in the west, to the Easterscheldt in the north, the Scheldt in the east, and the valleys of the rivers Scarpe, Deule, Lys, and Aa in the south. The capital during the High Empire was *Castellum Menapiorum*, modern Cassel (France). In Late Antiquity, *Turnacum* (Tournai, Belgium) took over the role as main city. In modern geopolitical terms, the *civitas* encompassed a large part of Flanders in Belgium, part of the 'Département du Nord' in France and part of the Zeeland province in the Netherlands.

The possible boundaries of the *civitas Nerviorum* have been delimited by Faider-Feytmans (1952), more recently complemented with archaeological data by Deru (2009). The northern and western border with the *civitas Menapiorum* was formed by the river Scheldt, while the eastern border with the *civitas Tungrorum* consists of the rivers Hantes, Sambre, Piéton, Lasne, Dyle, and Ruppel. The southern limit coincides with the upper course of the Scheldt and the sources of the Oise and the Sambre. This entire southern side was delimited from east to west by a chain of forests (*Atrewasia Silva*, *Teoracia Silva*, and *Fania Silva*). The original capital of the *civitas* was *Bagacum* (Bavay, France), being replaced by *Camaracum* (Cambrai, France) after the Tetrarchic reforms. The *civitas* included modern-day central-Belgium and the northern part of the 'Département d'Ardennes' in France.

The largest of the three *civitates*, the *civitas Tungrorum*, was originally part of *Gallia Belgica* according to several ancient authors (e.g. Ptol. *Geog.* II.9.5). However, the discovery of an altar-inscription (CIL XIII.3599) in *Atuatuca* (Tongeren) mentioning the *Mun(icipium) Tung(rorum)* implies that the *civitas* later became part of *Germania Inferior* (Raepsaet-Charlier 1995). For the boundaries of the *civitas*, we follow the delimitations proposed by the 'Mapping the *civitas* Tungrorum' project, a collaboration between the Gallo-Roman Museum of Tongeren and the department of archaeology of Ghent University (Van Thienen, Creemers, and De Clercq 2019). This delimitation is based on an assumed 'maximal area', taking as base the proposed boundaries by Raepsaet-Charlier (1994). The western border has already been described when delimiting the *civitas Nerviorum* (see above). The north-western section bordering the *civitas Menapiorum* is a bit problematic, as the course of the Scheldt has changed over time. The northern border is even more problematic as an inscription mentioning the *civitas Batavorum* (CIL XIII.8771) has been found at Sint-Michielsgestel, south of the river Meuse (Raepsaet-Charlier 1994, 54–55). To have a maximal area, a hypothetical line south of and parallel with the Meuse has been drawn. The eastern border in its northern part is delimited by the river Meuse, until just north of Maastricht where we should probably follow the river Geul to the east (Raepsaet-Charlier 1994, 56). From the Geul, a theoretical line must be drawn south of Aachen following more or less the Belgian–German border, possibly down to the river Prum until Lunebach. From here, a theoretical line must be drawn to the river Our, forming the border between the Great Duchy of Luxembourg and Germany, and then to the river Sûre, including the territory around Diekirch and Ettelbruck. The southern border probably followed the Sûre to the east, until more or less the border with Belgium, running east–west across Belgium's Luxembourg province (excluding Neufchâteau) until the Semois river, which it then followed west until its confluence with the Meuse at Monthermé (France). From here, a straight east–west line can be imagined following some small streams until the sources of the rivers Oise or Wartoise (Raepsaet-Charlier 1994, 58). In modern geographical terms, the *civitas* comprised roughly Antwerp, Limburg, the eastern part of Flemish Brabant, and Wallonia, excluding Hainaut and the southern part of Luxembourg provinces, in Belgium, parts of the provinces of Limburg and northern Brabant in the Netherlands, the Eifelkreis Bitbürg-Prüm district in Germany's Rhineland-Palatinate province, the cantons of Clervaux, Wiltz, Diekirch, and Vianden in the Grand Duchy of Luxembourg and the northern part of the Département d'Ardennes in France.

Chronological Framework

The Roman period in the research area is delimited by two important historical events: Julius Caesar's conquest of Gaul beginning in 57 BC and the withdrawal of the military troops along the Rhine and along the Bavay–Cologne road in the early fifth century. Yet, this starting and end point are more a modern scholarly convention than strict cultural caesuras. The campaigns of Caesar can obviously not be seen as a period of permanent settlement. Between 58 and 51 BC, the Roman presence in north-western Gaul consisted of temporary army camps, of which little archaeological evidence has come to light so far (Brulet 2008, 35). Even for the subsequent Augustan-Tiberan era, the archaeological data for construction activity is mainly restricted to the cities, such as *Atuatuca* (Tongeren), as the rural sites at this time still display all the characteristics of the indigenous culture. It is only after the development of a road network between the reigns of Claudius and the Flavian dynasty that the number of towns and small towns sharply increased, while Roman building techniques and technologies found their way to the countryside. The so-called 'villa landscapes' of the Roman north only start to emerge from the middle of the first century AD.

The end of the Roman period is even less clear-cut, as early fifth-century events were the result of processes that were already in motion during the later third and fourth century. In the second half of the third century, several raids by Germanic tribes into north-western Gaul seem to have had a severe impact on rural estates and small towns (Brulet 2008, 231). Even after some stability was achieved with the administrative reforms of the Tetrarchy and during the reign of Constantine, violence once again flared up in the 350s and 360s with usurper Silvanus declaring the independence of Gaul, forcing commander Julian to rely on Germanic auxiliaries to restore order (Hunt 1998, 28). The fact that these troops declared Julian emperor in AD 360 demonstrated the growing discontent with Rome in Gaul. Raids of the Alamanni and Franks in the 360s prompted Emperor Valentinian I to reside in Trier (Curran 1998, 84). Fragile peace treaties did not hold, with sieges on Cologne and Trier in the final decades of the fourth century, resulting in the transfer of the imperial court to Arles in AD 392 (Brulet 2008, 262). With the withdrawal of the troops along the *limes* and the Bavay–Cologne road, Roman command of the region was handed over to the Franks, who had taken over northern Gaul. After several battles and peace treaties, the Frankish king Childeric was entrusted with the administrative powers over *Belgica Secunda* by the emperor (Wightman 1985, 304–05).

A Note on Names and Terminology

The place names in this book refer to the ancient Latin names when known (e.g. *Atuatuca*) and modern topographical names, as for the majority of villa sites no Latin or indigenous place names are known. Only for a minority of central places (city, *vicus*, or smaller centre) is the Latin name known. Some modern place names are known for having more than one Roman villa, e.g. Maillen. In this case, the different villa sites are designated by the local toponyms where the villa was found, e.g. Maillen – Al Sauvenière, Maillen – Ronchine, and Maillen – Arches. If more than one bathhouse was present on a villa site, the different buildings are simply labelled 'Bath 1' and 'Bath 2', if possible in chronological order according to construction date, e.g. Haccourt 'Bath 1' as the oldest bathhouse attached to the first phase of the first villa. The personal names of well-known ancient authors and emperors are given in their standard English form, following the Oxford

Classical Dictionary (edition 1996). Furthermore, the titles of the ancient literary works and modern epigraphic corpora are abbreviated following the same reference work.

For the chronological terminology, the standard subdivision pertaining to the Imperial period is used: the early Imperial period (27 BC–AD 68), the High Empire (AD 69–284) and Late Antiquity (AD 285–476, for the Western Roman Empire). The term Late Antiquity is preferred over 'late Roman' or 'later Roman', as it expresses a certain independence from the previous periods, yet also stresses the unmistakable continuity. It is also a more neutral chronological indication than the more culturally charged 'Roman' equivalents, pointing to an era with new socio-cultural developments that were not necessarily Roman. The label 'Roman' should also be understood as a chronological indication, i.e. pertaining to the period of Roman rule in the research area, without necessarily implying a cultural connotation. The term 'Romanization' is used in its meaning as modern theoretical debate about the nature of the Roman conquest, not to designate an historic reality of Roman culture 'colonizing' and 'civilizing' new territories.

The bath-related terminology in this book follows the glossary in the previous work by the author (Maréchal 2020a, 456–60). It is important to repeat that the Latin terms designating the separate rooms of the baths, architectural elements, or building materials are the result of modern scholarly conventions, rather than reflecting an historic 'standard' terminology. The terms 'bath', 'baths', and 'bathhouse' are used as synonyms in this book, while the Latin terms *thermae* and *balneum/balnea* are used as Latin umbrella terms to cover the whole range of Roman baths, as there is still some debate on their specific use in ancient texts (on the differences, see Maréchal 2012; 2015). The specification 'private bath' is used in its modern meaning, i.e. a bath belonging to a house, without necessarily implying that its use was restricted to the inhabitants of the house (see Chapter 6). Throughout the book, the term 'elite' is used to indicate the powerful and wealthy layer of society, without implying a cultural background. Occasionally, a further specification 'indigenous' is added, to stress the background of the elite, or 'local', which does not imply specific roots or cultural background but stresses the fact this elite was negotiating its power and identity on a local scale. The term 'villa' is also used according to the modern scholarly convention for designating a Roman-period rural domestic building with evidence for investment of a considerable level of surplus wealth in its construction (Hingley 1989, 21). The word 'city' is only used in a general context of the Roman Empire, denoting the large urban centres such as Rome, Lyon, or Trier, and for the *civitas* capitals in the study area. The term 'central place' or 'small town' is preferred above the Latin term *vicus* to denote smaller urban centres, as the exact definition of *vicus* is still debated (Brulet 2008, 90). Although in the research area, such 'small towns' (or 'agglomérations secondaires' in French) are still often labelled *vici*, the term 'central place' is more neutral and does not imply a certain size or hierarchical order. It can be used for centres of all kinds of functions, including administrative, economic, military, or religious centres. For permanent military camps, the specification *castellum* will be used. Stop-overs consisting of a single building on the road are designated as 'relay stations', while 'road station' denotes a settlement of a few buildings along the road.

For measurements, the following abbreviations are used throughout the book: km for kilometre(s), m for metre(s), cm for centimetre(s), and m² for square metre(s). For geometric terms, the following abbreviations are used: 'l.' for length, 'w.' for width, 'h.' for height, 'diam.' for diameter, 'r' for radius, and 's' for side. The dimensions given in this book are those published in the original excavation reports. No new measurements were taken. When certain dimensions of rooms or surfaces were not explicitly mentioned in the publications, approximations were made using the published plans. The number of decimals after the decimal point indicate the precision of the measurement. For graphs, N refers to the total number of entries taken into account.

CHAPTER 1

Communal Baths — a Roman Phenomenon?

The following chapter is not meant to present yet another overview on the evolution of Roman bathhouses and bathing habits. It merely aims to highlight some of the important aspects of Roman bathing culture which are crucial in contextualizing and understanding the export of this 'typically Roman phenomenon' beyond the Italian Peninsula and into the far corners of the Empire. Five key elements will be discussed: the genesis of Roman-style bathhouses, the underlying motives for the popularity of baths and bathing, the blurred line between private and public bathing, the special case of thermal baths, and the spread of baths across the Empire.

How Roman Are Baths?

Most scholars now agree that Greek-Hellenistic bathhouses and bathing habits had a profound influence on the development of 'a peculiarly Roman cultural phenomenon with few parallels' (DeLaine 1999a, 7). In fact, the first public bathhouses in the Mediterranean were built in the Classical Greek period.[1] Important constituents of the Roman *thermae* and *balnea* including communal heated pools and a basic type of floor heating sometimes called proto-hypocaust originated in the Greek-Hellenistic cultural sphere, especially in Sicily (Broise and Jolivet 1991; Broise 1994; Lucore 2013). The Greek-Hellenistic *balaneion* hence paved the way for its Roman successor, introducing public bathing infrastructure for the first time in large parts of the Mediterranean (Yegül 2013).

Besides the obvious impact of Greek-Hellenistic baths on Roman bathing culture, several authors also pointed to the tradition of building a small bath room (*lavatrina*) next to the kitchen in the Italian Peninsula

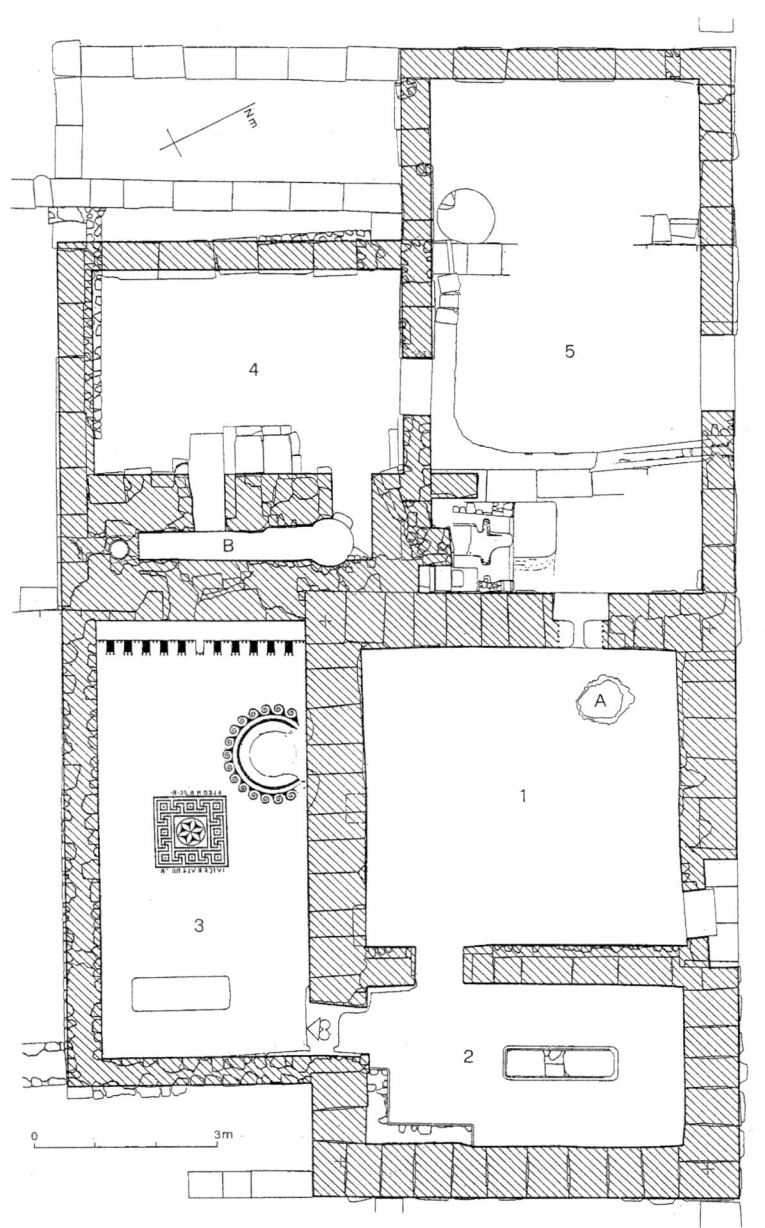

Figure 1. Plan of the baths of Musarna (central Italy), late second century BC. Figure in Broise 1994, 31, fig. 19.

---

1 The standard work on Greek public baths remains Ginouvès 1962. More recently, see Hoffmann 1999; Trümper 2009; 2014; and the contributions in Lucore and Trümper 2013. For the Greek-Hellenistic influence on the development of Roman baths, see among others Brödner 1983, 6–18; Heinz 1983, 36–51; DeLaine 1989; Yegül 1992, 6–29; Nielsen 1993a, 6–12; Fagan 2001.

(Fabbricotti 1976; Yegül 1992, 50–55). However, few archaeological remains of such bath rooms have been found (de Haan 2010, 20–21). In central Italy, a crossover between Italic bath rooms and Greek-Hellenistic-style private baths developed in the third and second century BC, in which we can find two or three rooms with waterproof flooring, Greek-style hip baths, immersion tubs which could be heated by an underlying furnace channel, wash basins (*labra*), and an occasional *laconicum* (Broise and Jolivet 1991; Lafon 1991; de Haan 2010, 21–22). The parallel development of bathing technology in both public and private facilities in central Italy, with Greek-Hellenistic and Italic influences, resulted in a 'basic' layout for Roman-style baths. A heated room (*caldarium*) with a heated pool (*alveus*) and a *labrum* was preceded by a tepid room (*tepidarium*). The latter was indirectly heated by connection to the *caldarium* by a simple doorway (Fig. 1).

During the second century BC, possibly in central Italy, the Greek-Hellenistic proto-hypocaust was improved into a fully functional hypocaust system. By the end of the first century BC, rooms with a hypocaust were also equipped with wall heating. Tiles with protruding knobs (*tegulae mammatae*) were attached to the wall with iron T-shaped nails, creating a hollow space in which hot gasses of the hypocaust could rise. By the end of the first century AD, the *tegulae mammatae* were replaced by the more heat-efficient system of box tiles (*tubuli*) (Adam 1984, 292; Degbomont 1984, 140–46). The improved heating system could reach higher temperatures and heat larger volumes (Schiebold 2010, 22; Lehar 2012, 181–82). The round sweat rooms (*laconica*) heated by a central brazier were no longer included in newly built baths, while existing *laconica* in public baths were often transformed into cold pools. The addition of the cold room with cold pool (*frigidarium*) to the bathing rooms happened during the first century BC and first century AD (Gros 1996, 393–94). When Vesuvius covered the Central Baths in Pompeii in AD 79, this public bathhouse was still in construction (Fig. 2). We find here a well-dated example of a late first-century bath which included a sporting ground (*palaestra*) with open-air swimming pool (*natatio*), a dressing room (*apodyterium*), a cold room (*frigidarium*) with cold pool (*piscina*), a tepid room (*tepidarium*), a sweat room with hypocaust (*sudatorium*), and a hot room (*caldarium*) with two heated pools (*alveus*, pl. *alvei*) but no wash basin (*labrum*). Near an entrance was a latrine, flushed by the drain of the swimming pool. The main rooms, with the exception of the *sudatorium*, were rectangular in plan and lay on a single axis. This type of layout, with the basic rooms following each other in a gradation of heat from cold to hot, grouped in a simple linear articulation, became very popular in the Italian Peninsula, as well as in the provinces, for both public and private baths (Nielsen 1999). Especially for baths in military contexts, inside the camp or in the *canabae* (civilian settlements) close to the camp, the simple linear plan with basic rooms remained popular throughout the Roman period (Nielsen 1993a, 76–80). The preference for semicircular, polygonal, or round shapes in bathhouse architecture increased from the Trajanic-Hadrianic period onwards (Nielsen 1993a, 59; Gros 1996, 402).

The Popularity of Roman Baths

There are several aspects that can account for the popularity of bathhouses and bathing in the Roman period. Perhaps the most obvious reason is that taking a hot bath was simply very pleasurable. Ancient literature and inscriptions abound with references to the pleasures of bathing (Dunbabin 1989, 6–8; Busch 1999, 35–83; Fagan 1999, 75–76). It is amply clear from the written evidence that one went to the baths not only to wash away the dirt, but foremost to meet up with friends, hear the latest gossip, or get invited to a dinner party. The social role of baths within Roman society can hardly be overestimated. Wealthy citizens, not least the emperor, vying for political support and fully understanding the popularity of baths, competed with their rivals to offer the people the most splendid and well-equipped baths (Fagan 1999, 104–75). For the common man who could not afford a private bath, large *thermae* and *balnea* offered a taste of luxury, besides an essential scrub after a hard days' work.

In addition to a shared pastime, bathing was also considered to be beneficial for health. Romans did not have our modern notion of hygiene. In fact, the whole concept was different, as knowledge of bacteria and how these were transmitted was absent. Instead, prevailing medical ideas were much more interwoven with a general vision on the nature of the human body (Nutton 2004, 39–52). In a nutshell, the widely spread Hippocratic teachings presented the body as a combination of *humores* or bodily fluids, the most important of which are blood, phlegm, yellow and black bile. The balance of these fluids was crucial for maintaining good health (Nutton 2004, 77–79). If one of the *humores* increased or decreased, such imbalance had to be corrected. It was the firm belief that this could be achieved by subjecting the body to specific combinations of heat or cold and moisture or dryness. Thus bathing (or refraining from it) was justified by medical theories, but also grew out to be an essential act in maintaining good health (Villard 1994; Flemming 2013; Blonski 2014a, 99–117). The essential rooms of a Roman bathhouse reflect the obligatory steps in keeping the body in balance: acclimatizing

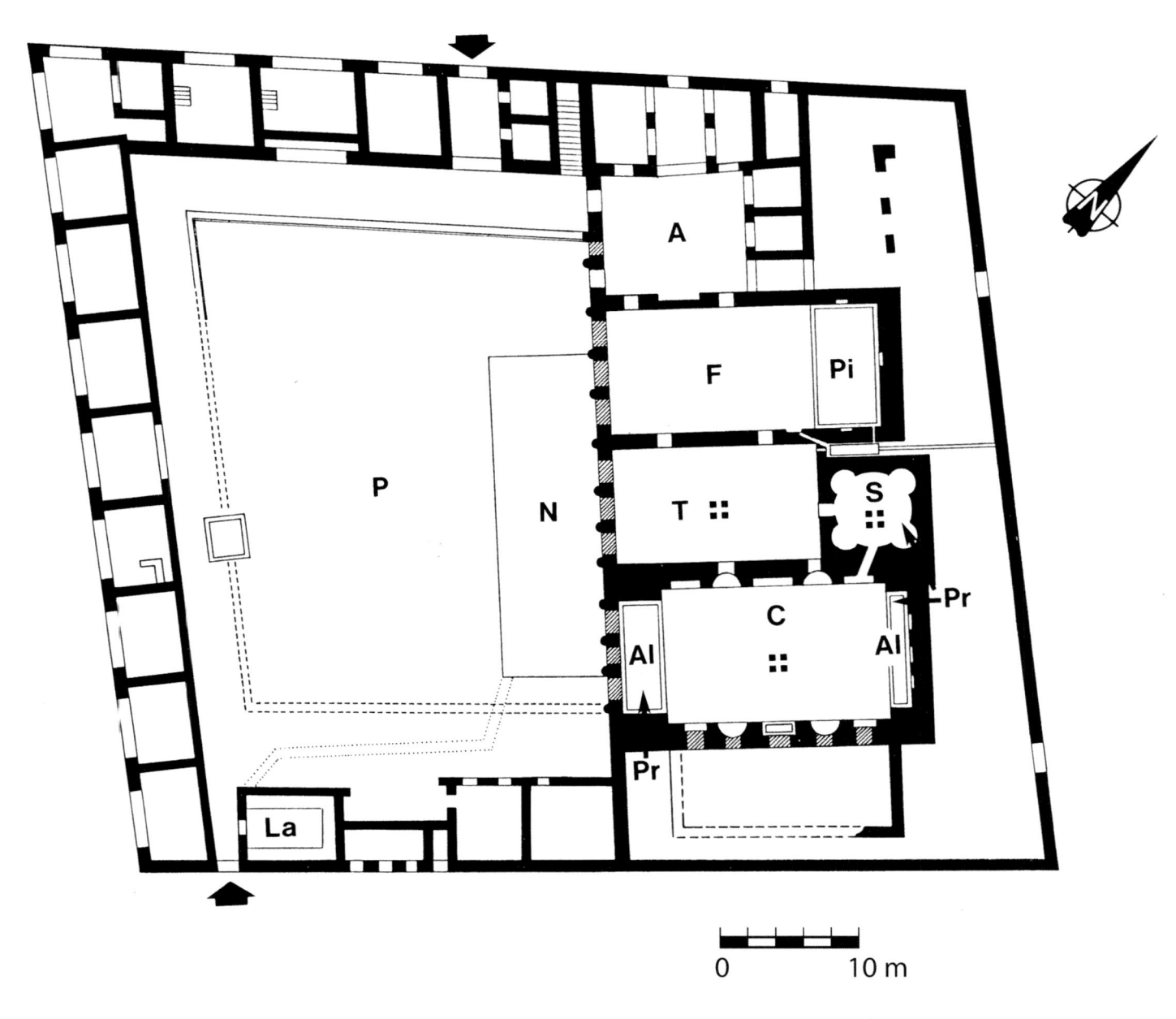

Figure 2. Plan of the Central Baths in Pompeii (Italy), under construction in AD 79. Figure after Nielsen 1993b, 98, fig. 75.

to the heat in the *tepidarium*, sweating out the bad bodily fluids by opening the pores in the *caldarium* (or separate *sudatorium*), relaxing the body in the hot water of the *alveus*, and at last closing the pores again in the cold pool of the *frigidarium*. The persistence of these classical medical theories, originating in the Greek-Hellenistic period, ensured the survival of the basic plan of the Roman bathhouse, even into Late Antiquity (Maréchal 2020a, 189–90).

A visit to the baths was not only pleasurable and good for your health, it also was considered a civil duty (*officium*) to be presentable and look your best. Being dirty or neglecting your appearance implied a withdrawal from civilized society, only to be tolerated in special circumstances such as mourning (Blonski 2014a, 159–69). The city, where one could find public baths, was the location *par excellence* for a civilized lifestyle, in contrast to the wild and disordered countryside. Hence baths became a symbol of a civilized way of life, of *humanitas*, which could certainly be found inside the city, but also on the well-equipped villas of the elite (de Haan 2010, 130–34). The latter took their lifestyle with them when they retreated from the city. The equation of baths equalling city life should rather be replaced by baths equalling civilized life in the Roman mind; this could mainly — but not exclusively — be found in cities. This is an important nuance that has escaped most modern studies on baths.

To summarize, Roman bathhouses offered their users a facility to wash away the dirt, a pleasurable pastime, a place for social interaction, an opportunity to maintain one's health and appearance, a chance to partake in a civilized lifestyle, and a place to enjoy and show off wealth and luxury all at the same time. The architecture, plan, technology, and decoration of the bath building ensured that all of these expectations could be met.

Private Baths

As briefly outlined above, private bathhouses developed simultaneously with public baths. Already in the Greek-Hellenistic period, wealthy citizens had equipped their houses with a bathroom that boasted waterproof mortar with plinths shaped in a quarter circle on the transition to the walls, bath tubs, and sewage systems (Trümper 2010). The first examples of such private bathrooms in Sicily and southern Italy appear in the fourth century BC (de Haan 2010, 14–19). With the introduction of larger pools heated by an underlying channel and the disappearance of hip baths in favour of wash basins (*labra*), private bathrooms became more elaborate and hence counted several rooms. It is not always easy to know whether a certain technological innovation first appeared in public baths and was then copied in private houses or whether private experimentation caught on and was subsequently adapted in public buildings. For the case of the communal pool heated by a hypocaust, however, it seems that private baths played an important role in the development phase, paving the road for adaptation in public baths (de Haan 2010, 37–38). By the second century BC, private bathrooms were also found in central Italy, e.g. in the houses of Cosa (Broise and Jolivet 1991). Besides simple rooms with (portable) tubs and hydraulic mortar floors often located next to the kitchen, some villas in *Latium* already had fixed hip baths, sweat rooms (*laconica*), and wash basins (Lafon 1991). By the end of the Republic, a private bath seems to have been an indispensable commodity for a wealthy house owner, both in the city and in the countryside. For Pompeii, some 30 out of 400 houses (*c.* 7.5 per cent) had a private bath (de Haan 1997, 206). In Rome, private baths must also have been a standard commodity for rich houses, even if the archaeological evidence is rather limited (Papi 1999). A better water supply through aqueducts and the widespread use of hypocaust systems in the second half of the first century BC enabled the construction of more and larger public baths (de Haan 1996; Manderscheid 1996). Subsequently, the construction of new private baths, especially in urban contexts, seems to have dwindled, as these small private facilities could not compete with the sumptuous new public baths. In suburban and rural villas, private baths remained a necessity, ensuring a civilized lifestyle even in the countryside. Especially during the second century AD, several maritime and rural villas were equipped with baths, or existing baths were restored and enlarged (Marzano 2007, 43, 190).

Just like their public counterparts, private baths had the quintessential cold, tepid, and hot room with at least one cold and one heated pool (Kolodziejczyk 2001; Marzano 2007, 43). Additional rooms, such as heated dressing rooms, sweat rooms, or extra pools of different sizes could be included according to the budget, available space, and personal preferences of the commissioner. In contrast to public baths, exercise courts (*palaestra*) were absent due to a lack of space. In urban houses, the size, shape, and layout of the bathing rooms often depended on the available space within the house. Simple linear arrangements of the rooms, or cropped together as a block, were most common (Fig. 3; de Haan 2010, 116). In maritime and rural villas, the baths were often larger and from the late first century AD onwards increasingly built as attached or freestanding buildings (Marzano 2007, 190). The trend is also observable outside the Italian Peninsula, in southern Gaul or *Hispania*. These early private baths can often be linked to villas with a material culture consisting mainly of imports from the Italian Peninsula, pointing to an occupation by Roman settlers rather than an indigenous elite adopting Roman habits (Bouet 2000, 36). In *Gallia Narbonnensis*, the number of private baths increased after 50 BC. These often consisted of a 'Vitruvian', also called 'Pompeian' *caldarium* with one semicircular short end accommodating the *labrum* (or the *schola labri*) and opposite a straight end against which the *alveus* was located (Fig. 3). The *frigidarium* was the last room to be added to the layout, around the middle of the first century AD (Bouet 2000, 37–38). In *Hispania*, the large boom of villa baths occurred in the second century AD. As in southern Gaul, the plans were often of the simple linear type, with more intricate plans and additional rooms appearing in the late second and third century (García-Entero and Arribas Domínguez 2000, 88).

Owning a private bath was a sign of wealth. Even if somewhat small in size or limited in number of rooms or pools, constructing, operating, and maintaining a private bath was always a heavy investment of money, people, and resources. Water had to be provided, stored, and disposed of, special fire and waterproof building materials had to be bought (hypocaust tiles, *tubuli*, hydraulic mortar), specialized construction workers had to be hired, enough fuel had to be supplied, and a trained staff who could not attend other duties while working there, had to be present (to fire and oversee the furnace, to clean the bath, etc.). Literary passages

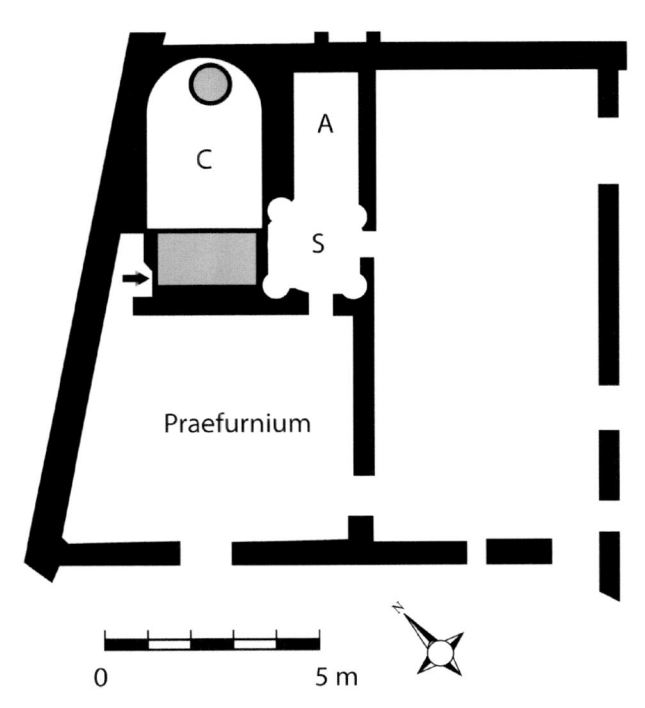

Figure 3. Plan of the private bath of the Casa del Cryptoportico in Vulci (central Italy) with 'Vitruvian' *caldarium* (C), end of the second century BC. Figure by author after de Haan 2010, Tafel XXIV, plan 29.

describing the daily villa life in the Italian Peninsula make clear that the master of the house invited friends, family, and colleagues to join him in his private bath, eager to impress and demonstrate their civilized lifestyle, even outside the city (de Haan 2010, 129–30). It is evident that a master should prepare his private baths when receiving friends or relatives, as is testified by numerous passages in the letters of Cicero (e.g. Cic. *Att.* 11.3). Pliny the Younger was even comforted by the fact that a small village lay close to his villa, as the three public baths there could be used in case anything went wrong with his own private bath (Plin. *Ep.* 2.17.26). It seems that a good host was expected to offer his visitors a bath. Unsurprisingly, wealthy villa owners tried to impress their peers with ever larger and more luxurious baths. Seneca (*Ep.* 86.6–7) laments the excess of luxury in contemporaneous villa baths, compared to the functional baths once used by Scipio Africanus.

At nunc quis est, qui sic lavari sustineat? Pauper sibi videtur ac sordidus, nisi parietes magnis et pretiosis orbibus refulserunt, nisi Alexandrina marmora Numidicis crustis distincta sunt, nisi illis undique operosa et in picturae modum variata circumlitio praetexitur, nisi vitro absconditur camera, nisi Thasius lapis, quondam rarum in aliquo spectaculum templo, piscinas nostras circumdedit, in quas multa sudatione corpora exinanita demittimus, nisi aquam argentea epitonia fuderunt. Et adhuc plebeias fistulas

loquor; quid, cum ad balnea libertinorum pervenero? Quantum statuarum, quantum columnarum est nihil sustinentium, sed in ornamentum positarum inpensae causa! Quantum aquarum per gradus cum fragore labentium! Eo deliciarum pervenimus, ut nisi gemmas calcare nolimus.

(But who in these days could bear to bathe in such a fashion? We think ourselves poor and mean if our walls are not resplendent with large and costly mirrors; if our marbles from Alexandria are not set off by mosaics of Numidian stone, if their borders are not faced over on all sides with difficult patterns, arranged in many colours like paintings; if our vaulted ceilings are not buried in glass; if our swimming-pools are not lined with Thasian marble, once a rare and wonderful sight in any temple—pools into which we let down our bodies after they have been drained weak by abundant perspiration; and finally, if the water has not poured from silver spigots. I have so far been speaking of the ordinary bathing-establishments; what shall I say when I come to those of the freedmen? What a vast number of statues, of columns that support nothing, but are built for decoration, merely in order to spend money! And what masses of water that fall crashing from level to level! We have become so luxurious that we will have nothing but precious stones to walk upon.) (trans. by Gummere 1920, 313)

Not only in the Italian Peninsula, but also in the Iberian Peninsula, the villa baths increased in size and became more luxurious in the second half of the second and mainly in the third century (García-Entero and Arribas Domínguez 2000, 92). In southern Gaul, the main building activity took place in the last quarter of the first century AD, with some renewed activity in the fourth century, especially in *Aquitania* (Bouet 2003b, 328, 342). By this time, more and more baths were also completely freestanding from the house (Gros 2001, 329–31).

A Special Case: Thermal Baths

Studies about Roman thermal baths have been a separate field of research, as their location, architecture, and use are inherently different from regular bathhouses. The use of thermal sources often predated the Roman era and continued long after Roman rule had ended, even until today (Guérin-Beauvois and Martin 2007). In the Italian Peninsula, the volcanic area west of the Bay of

Naples known as the *Campi Flegrei* counted several hot springs and fumaroles (Guérin-Beauvois 2015, 103–05). Some early Italian scholars even proposed that the exceptional natural conditions inspired the Romans to invent the hypocaust system (Sgobbo 1929; Di Capua 1940; 1941; Crova 1956). The presence of natural hot water and steam spurred the construction of a large thermal resort at *Baiae*, arguably the most famous thermal site in the Empire, which continued to attract visitors long after the Roman period (Russo Mailer 1988; Yegül 1992, 93–110; Guérin-Beauvois 2015, 127–92; Nieberle 2020).

Thermal baths were located near natural springs, so unlike regular baths, they could not be constructed wherever there was a need. Furthermore, the infrastructure was built around the natural resources, adapting the architecture to the springs and fumaroles. Accordingly, thermal baths did not have a specific typology (DeLaine 2007, 27; Köhler 2016, 192). Recurrent features include sweat chambers making use of fumaroles, large warm water pools, which could be rectangular (ratio 2/1) or round (up to 8 m in diameter) and were often accessible by steps from all sides, and several small single-person pools for personal use (Brödner 1983, 163–79; Köhler 2006; Guérin-Beauvois 2015, 355–61). Sometimes, several rooms of a regular bathhouse, such as a *caldarium*, *sudatorium*, or *frigidarium* were added to enable bathers to follow a traditional bathing routine besides the special water treatments (Yegül 1992, 111; Köhler 2012, 58). The warm water was captured at the source and then piped directly to the pools, to a *castellum divisorium* or to several cisterns where the water was allowed to cool down, creating water of different temperatures, before being piped to the appropriate pools (Köhler 2012, 61).

The clientele of the thermal baths was also different from regular baths. Several ancient texts and inscriptions point to the curative properties of natural springs (Yegül 1992, 92–93). Thermal baths were mainly health resorts, where the wealthy went to cure whatever ailed them. Not everyone could afford to make the trip (Guérin-Beauvois 2015, 13). Medical texts do not seem to recommend a visit to thermal baths, but only mention the different benefits of the different types of water (Guérin-Beauvois 2007; 2015, 39–48). This may have been the result of the very simple nature of the remedies on offer: submerging or showering in the water, or even drinking it, did not require the specialist aid of a physician (Köhler 2012, 57). Furthermore, thermal sources were linked to a local deity, often a nymph, which gave the curative properties of the water a divine undertone (Guérin-Beauvois 2015, 369–79). The votive offerings that have frequently been found in or near such springs demonstrate a persistence of folk religion. Local deities were also 'reinterpreted'

as Roman equivalents, a striking example being *Sulis Minerva* in Bath (England), linking up local traditions with the Roman conversion of the sites.

Just as in the Mediterranean, several thermal sources in the later north-western provinces were already in use before the Roman conquest. The above-mentioned example of Bath in *Britannia* is perhaps the best known. In around AD 80, legions built two bathhouses near the hot sulphurous springs of modern-day Aachen (Germany), then called *Aquae Granni* (Schaub 2012). In the three Gauls, several thermal sites were converted into thermal bath resorts during the High Empire, including *Aquis Calidis* (Vichy, France) (Bouet 2018). In the research area, no examples of thermal baths have yet been discovered. The thermal sources of Spa (Liège province, Belgium), the place name which has been used as a synonym for thermal bath ever since the eighteenth century, are not naturally hot, but are famous for their high level of iron. The waters only seem to have been used for medicinal bathing since the sixteenth century (Jacob 1968). At Flines-lez-Râches (France, Département du Nord) the so-called 'Mer des Flines' source produces sulphite-rich (cold) water. Votive deposits from the La Tène and Roman Imperial period show that the source was well known and associated with healing, but no bath-related structures were found in the vicinity (Delmaire and others 1996, 249–52). The only naturally heated sources in the research area are located at Chaudfontaine (Liège province, Belgium), literally meaning 'hot fountain'. However, no remains of Roman occupation were found here.

The Spread of Roman Baths to the Provinces

Bathhouses found their way to the eastern shores of *Hispania* and *Gallia Narbonensis* even before the building type was fully developed in the Italian Peninsula (Mora 1981; Nielsen 1993a, 67–70; Bouet 2000; Nola 2000; Peréx and others 2014). In the Herodian period in *Judaea*, several palaces and rich houses were equipped with simple baths (Hoss 2005, 45–49). These early baths, dating to the second century BC and early first century AD, had a simple linear plan for articulating the basic rooms *apodyterium-frigidarium*, *tepidarium*, and *caldarium* (Nielsen 1999, 36; Fig. 4). Other early 'characteristics' include the use of *tegulae mammatae*, *alvei* heated by a subterranean furnace channel, a *labrum* in the *caldarium*, the presence of *laconica* and the absence of a *piscina* (see above). The material culture associated with some of the sites of these early provincial bathhouses consists almost exclusively of imported wares, pointing to Roman 'colonists' who brought their culture with them (Bouet 2003b, 321).

The military seems to have played an important role in the spread to and construction of bathhouses in the newly conquered provinces. The size and monumentality of military baths, found both inside military installations and outside their walls, could vary significantly. Small *castella* often had small baths of a very simple design, with a linear plan and only the basic rooms (Nielsen 1993a, 76–80; Fig. 5). These were mainly found outside of the defences, as auxiliary troops adopted bathing somewhat later (from the Flavian period onwards), at a time when their forts had already taken shape (Bidwell 2009, 55). Conversely, legionaries had brought bathing with them from the start, incorporating baths in the initial design of their forts. Small baths with wooden floors and walls made by timber uprights and clay infilling, seem to have been part of the legionary fortresses as early as the Augustan and Tiberian period (Bidwell 2002). The only masonry elements would have been a furnace for heating the bath water in a boiler and an apse for lodging a *labrum*.[2] As early as the Neronian period, larger more permanent forts could have large, monumental baths with (semi) symmetrical plans and numerous 'additional' rooms (extra heated rooms, lofty halls, etc.), equalling the size and architecture of urban public baths (Bidwell 2009, 60). The legions themselves were involved in the construction and restoration of the baths, as inscriptions prove.[3] Tiles bearing military stamps have also been found in numerous baths throughout the Empire, confirming the military was at least involved in large-scale brick production for large construction sites (Nielsen 1993a, 75). For Egypt, there is papyrological evidence that mentions soldiers being deployed to guard baths and ensure water and fuel supply, and even perform basic tasks within the baths (Redon 2009, 411–13). In the Libyan desert fort of *Golaia* (Bu Njem), between three and five soldiers were employed daily at the baths (Marichal 1992, 93), while in Dura Europos (Syria), a soldier was in charge of the firewood (PDur 82, coll. II.9). We can reasonably assume that the military baths acted as models for public baths built in neighbouring *canabae*, although

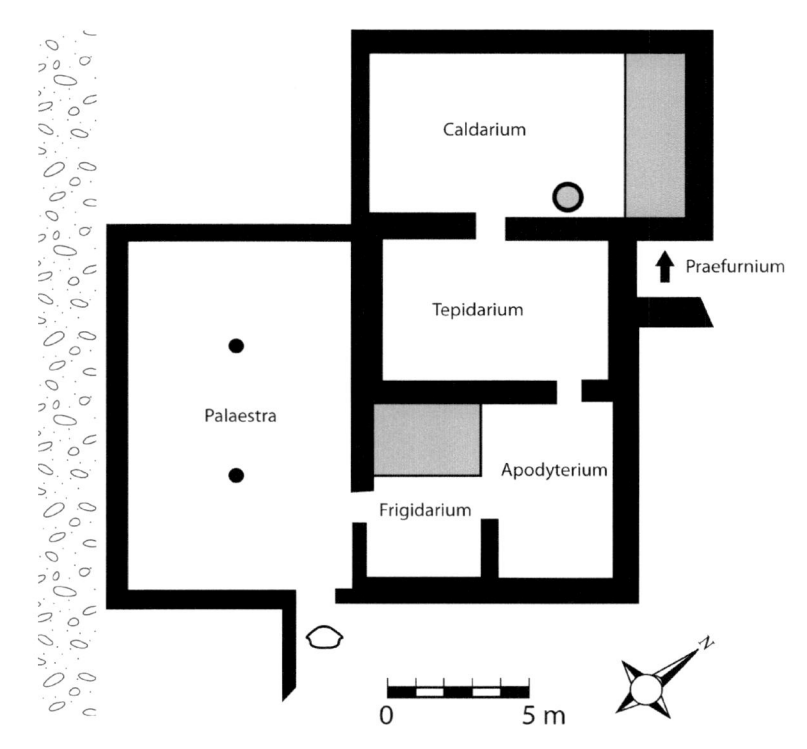

Figure 4. Plan of baths of *Baetulo* (Badalona, Spain), early first century AD. Figure by author after Nielsen 1993b, 121, fig. 116.

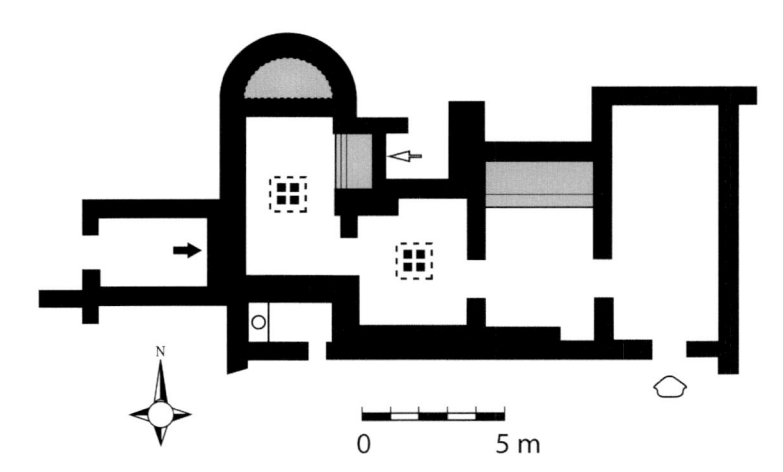

Figure 5. Plan of the Valetudinarium Baths in *Vetera* I (Xanten, Germany), Flavian period. Figure by author after Dodt 2003, 383, fig. 95.

the earliest examples of baths in auxiliary forts seem to have been inspired by the type of small public baths commonly found in urban settings (Bidwell 2009, 61). This way, the military baths may indeed have acted as conduits to introduce bath architecture in newly conquered regions. It cannot be ruled out that the military was actively involved in the construction of such public baths, especially in an early phase of conquest,

---

2 The *caldarium* and perhaps *tepidarium* of these baths were probably heated with braziers (Bidwell 2002, 470). The use of hypocausts made out of wood is rather unlikely, due to fire hazard and the transmission of toxic smoke through the floorboards (Lehar 2015, 262–67).

3 An early third-century inscription from *Lambaesis* (Algeria) quoted how the third legion Augusta restored 'their *balneum*' after it had collapsed of old age ('legio III Aug(usta) eorum balneum vetustate conlapsum restituit', CIL VIII.2706). In *Vindolanda* (UK), eighteen soldiers were possibly charged with restoring the baths ('s[tr]uctores ad balneum', Bowman and Thomas 1983, 78). An inscription from Walldürn (Germany) specifies that the soldiers paid for the restoration themselves ('de suo restit ler(unt)', CIL XIII.6592).

when architectural and technological know-how was not widely available yet. Army veterans, sometimes indigenous auxiliaries, settling in the countryside must also have been inspired by military baths when they commissioned private baths for their villas (Nielsen 1993a, 74; Black 1994).

The spread of Roman baths did not unfold as smoothly as the numerous baths all over the Empire seem to suggest. In some regions, there seems to have been a cultural resistance to the Roman bathing habit. In *Judaea*, the early introduction of Roman-style baths in the palaces and rich houses of the Herodian period was not followed by a widespread adoption of the bathhouse in the subsequent decades (Hoss 2005, 52). On the contrary, Jewish religion, which had its own ritual bath (*miqveh*), seems to have tempered the demand of public baths (Hoss 2010, 165–66). The scarce first- and second-century examples have been found in cosmopolitan trade centres like *Scythopolis* (Hoss 2010, 167; 2012). In Egypt, Greek-style baths remained popular until as late as the second century AD, occasionally borrowing new Roman technology. Roman-style baths mainly appeared in forts and large cities (Redon 2017). In Greece and Asia Minor, Roman-style baths were only slowly adopted, possibly due to continued popularity of Greek-style baths and bathing habits (Nielsen 1985, 83). In North Africa, the archaeological and epigraphic evidence for early Roman baths (before the late first century AD) is scarce. However, badly published (early) excavations and continued building activity on important sites,

burying or destroying earlier phases, may account for this state of the art (Thébert 2003, 406–07). All the above-mentioned regions had been acquainted with (public) bathhouses through Hellenism. The initial reluctance to construct Roman-style baths eventually disappeared, with important bath construction following in the second and third century, or even later in Egypt and the Middle East (fourth–fifth centuries). Eventually, Roman-style baths would survive well into Late Antiquity in these regions (Maréchal 2020a).

In regions with no prior influences of the Greek-Hellenistic bathing tradition, such as the northern border provinces and *Britannia*, the first bathhouses appear in early Roman settlements and military forts (Nielsen 1993a, 60). Villa baths in the countryside appear somewhat after the initial conquest. For *Germania Inferior*, the first villa baths seem to appear in the second half of the first century AD (Koethe 1940, 106; Dodt 2006, 71), while military baths already appeared in the Neronian-Flavian era (Hanel 2000). In south-eastern Britain, the earliest villa baths appear in the second half of the first century AD, but the main construction phase can be dated to the second and third century (Reyes Hernando 2000). The earliest public baths are Neronian in date, e.g. at Silchester. The very basic layout is reminiscent of baths in military forts, such as the Neronian fortress baths of Exeter. In these northern provinces, Roman-style bathhouses disappeared completely after the fifth century, if not earlier (Scholz 2018).

CHAPTER 2

Earlier Research on Roman Bathing in the North-West

The Research Tradition in the Roman North-West

The research on Roman baths in the northern part of the Empire is inextricably linked to the research on Roman antiquities in the different modern nations, and in particular on Roman cities and rural villas. For the territories of modern-day Belgium, the first antiquarian collections date from the early nineteenth century, even before Belgian independence in 1830, but mainly assembled Roman coins and some museum-worthy chance finds (De Bast 1804). By the middle of the same century, the boundaries of the Low Countries had been redrawn, and the creation of the Kingdom of Belgium inspired historians to bestow the newly founded nation state with a national history. Books such as Henri Moke's *La Belgique ancienne* (1854) showed an historical interest in the Roman 'conquest' of Belgium, albeit mainly based on classical literature and with little or no attention for archaeological evidence. Antoine Guillaume Bernard Schayes's impressive four volume *La Belgique et les Pays-Bas, avant et pendant la domination romaine: Tableau historique, géographique, physique, statistique et archéologique de la Gaule septentrionale, jusqu'au VIᵉ siècle* (1858–1877) looked beyond newly created boundaries and seemingly included archaeological data. However, the main focus for the Roman period (vol. 2) lies on the only two Roman cities 'worthy of this name', i.e. *Atuatuca* (Tongeren) and *Turnacum* (Tournai), for which the author admitted a lack of archaeological evidence to attempt any reconstruction (Schayes 1858, 346). The archaeological dataset, however, was soon to be enriched by a spectacular rise in archaeological digs.

The second half of the nineteenth century saw the creation of a number of local historical and archaeological societies, not only in Belgium, but also in France and the Netherlands. These societies assembled people with a passion for local history, often architects, priests, and professors, and raised funds to excavate presumed archaeological sites. Before the start of scientific excavations by universities, museums, or governmental institutions, the reports published in the journals of these societies, often entitled as *bulletins* or *annales*, are the only information we have on some of the large Roman sites in the research area. In Belgium, the archaeological societies of Namur (founded in 1845), Liège (1856), Charleroi (1863), and Brussels (1887) in particular were very active in the excavations of Roman rural villas. Important sites such as Anthée, Aiseau, Maillen, Mettet, or Jemelle were discovered in this period. In the Netherlands, the publications by the historical and archaeological society of the duchy of Limburg (*Société historique et archéologique dans le Duché de Limbourg*), already founded in 1834, is of interest for the research area. In northern France, the *Commission historique du Nord* was founded in Lille in 1839. The results of the excavations published in the society journals were brought together in a gazetteer Roman of sites as an appendix in Camille Van Dessels's work on Roman roads in Belgium (Van Dessel and Schuermans 1877, 31–230).

With the first publications of villa excavations, the first interest in Roman bathhouses also developed (Fig. 6). In 1875, the authors of a report on the villa of Gerpinnes talked about the rarity of finding a Roman private bathhouse outside the Mediterranean area (De Glymes, Henseval, and Kaisin 1875). The remains were interpreted on the basis of bath-related passages in Juvenal, Horace, and Martial, identifying rooms as specific and hard to recognize as a *sphaeristerium* (room for ball games). In their opinion the local peasants (i.e. villa owners) did not have the slaves for every part of the bathing ritual, which usually resulted in softness and debauchery.[1] The contrasting opinion of baths as both 'civilizing' and 'demoralizing' is also encountered in

---

[1] 'nos campagnards n'avaient pas le luxe d'esclaves pour tout faire, nécessaires à la molesse et à la débauche romaine' (De Glymes, Henseval, and Kaisin 1875, cviii).

Figure 6. Drawing of the excavations of the bathhouse in Arquennes in 1872. Figure in Cloquet 1873, pl. II.

Kaisin's elaboration on the baths of Aiseau (Kaisin 1878).[2] The author then assures his readers that Christianity abolished such an immoral custom, just as it had with gladiatorial games. Reverting to ancient literature, including amongst others Sidonius Apollinaris (*Ep.* 2.2.4–9) and Seneca (*Ep.* 86.6–7), but especially book five of Vitruvius's *De architectura*, was a very recurrent *modus operandi* for these early researchers, as the corpus of excavated baths was still very limited. In the absence of comparative material, some authors turned to sites such as Pompeii — as was the case for the analysis of the villa baths of Lemiers by Braat (1934) or Maillen 'Ronchinne' by Bequet (1897) — or closer to home, villa sites in England or Switzerland — as proposed for the villa baths of Meersen by Habets (1871). By the end of the nineteenth century, the number of baths in the Low Countries had increased enough to entice Habets to compare the villa baths of Heer with similar sites in Limburg and in Belgium more generally (Habets 1895, 273). Bequet compared the baths he excavated in Chastrès with the military baths of Furfooz and concluded that the bathing habit disappeared after

the invasion of the Franks, who preferred to bathe in rivers rather than in warm baths (Bequet 1900a, 32).

In 1903, the Royal Museum of Art and History in Brussels started an archaeological service, which mapped and excavated several Roman sites in Belgium during the first half of the twentieth century. The first descriptive catalogue of the national collection was published in 1937 (de Loë 1937). In the Netherlands, the Dutch National Museum of Antiquities in Leiden, which had existed since 1818, conducted several excavations of Roman villa sites in the southern part of the country. The growing dataset of Roman villas, and hence also baths, resulted in several review articles and books. In Belgium, Robert De Maeyer (1937) finished a doctoral thesis on the Roman villas in Belgium. Some general conclusions about the location, the functioning, and the architecture of villa baths were put forward (De Maeyer 1937, 165–90). His archaeological inventory of Roman villa sites was published some years later (De Maeyer 1940). In Germany, Harald Koethe (1940) published a seminal article on the Roman baths in Trier's hinterland. The German scholar, who had previously worked with bath specialist Daniel Krencker in Syria, examined thirty-two baths belonging to villas, framing his dataset within the degree and speed of the Romanization process (Koethe 1940, 43). Besides the

---

2   'Les bains utiles comme mesure hygiénique, devinrent une cause de démoralisation pour le peuple romain' (Kaisin 1878, 186).

baths in the surroundings of Trier, Koethe also briefly describes a select number of baths in neighbouring countries, including several sites in Belgium, France, Luxemburg, and Switzerland (Koethe 1940, 115–31). In France, it was not until 1945 that archaeological excavations were organized by law. Up until then, interested 'archaeologists', including both amateurs and researchers, negotiated with landowners to start an excavation.

The first decades of the second half of the twentieth century saw a relative setback in the number of studies. In Belgium, few archaeological excavations had been carried out after the First World War, while the seminal study by De Maeyer and subsequently the Romanization debate in general were shunned by the next generation of researchers due to the latter's German sympathies during World War Two. In the Netherlands, the national excavation service (*Rijksdienst voor het Oudheidkundig Bodemonderzoek* or *ROB*) was founded in 1946. Besides urban renewal projects in city centres such as Maastricht, the ROB also conducted several excavation campaigns in the countryside, mainly in the 1970s and 1980s along the Rhine and the eastern riverine area. The excavation reports were published in the service's journal (*Berichten van de Rijksdienst voor het Oudheidkundig Bodemonderzoek*, 1950–2002). The newly found villa sites, although small in number, did not spark specific bath-related research. The Romanization debate was, in contrast to Belgium, put on the agenda by scholars such as Jan Slofstra and Nico Roymans.[3] In Belgium, it was not until 1963 that the first autonomous national excavation service was founded (*Nationale Dienst voor Opgravingen, NDO* or *Service national des fouilles, SNF*). Its activities, directed by Héli Roosens and Joseph Mertens, complemented an archaeological scene that still included local (amateur) societies, museums, and universities. The results were published in the *Archaeologia Belgica* series (1949–1987). An overview of all archaeological work carried out by the different institutions was to be found as short notices in the journal *Archeologie* (1938–1990). In 1988 archaeology became a jurisdiction of the separate Flemish and Walloon governments. With the dissolution of the *NDO/SNF* and the discontinuation of *Archaeologia Belgica*, the heritage agencies, renamed *Instituut voor het Archeologisch Patrimonium* (*IAP*) in Flanders and *Service des fouilles de la Région wallonne* in Wallonia, published excavations in journals such as *Archeologie in Vlaanderen* (1991–2001) and *Chronique de l'archéologie wallonne* (1993–present). From the plethora of publications, Xavier Deru (1994) gathered all excavations of

Roman baths to compose the first and only inventory of public and private baths in the *civitas Tungrorum*. In France, the national archaeological service (*Association pour les fouilles archéologiques nationales* or *Afan*) was launched in 1973. A special fund for rescue archaeology (*fonds d'intervention pour l'archéologie de sauvetage*) was available a year later.

In the wake of the Convention of La Valetta in 1992 concerning the protection of archaeological heritage in Europe, the number of rescue excavations dramatically increased. In France, the national institute for preventive archaeology (*Institut National de Recherches Archéologiques Préventives* or *INRAP*) was created in 2001. In Flanders, the archaeological service was reorganized as *Vlaams Instituut voor het Onroerend Erfgoed* (*VIOE*) in 2004 and again in 2011 as *Agentschap Onroerend Erfgoed* (*AOE*). In the Netherlands, the former ROB was reorganized and named *Rijksdienst voor Archeologie, Cultuurlandschap en Monumenten* (*RACM*) in 2006, followed by a name change in 2009 to *Rijksdienst voor het Cultureel Erfgoed* (*RCE*). In both Flanders and the Netherlands, private archaeological companies were allowed to submit tender for rescue excavations, leading to a 'commercialization' of archaeology. A recent report shows that 90 per cent of all excavations carried out in the Netherlands in 2018 were done by private archaeological firms.[4] In Wallonia, archaeology is still a jurisdiction of the government. However, the high number of rescue excavations does not necessarily imply a high number of Roman baths being discovered, at least in the countryside. The limited areas that actually need to be investigated only rarely revealed a villa, let alone the bath. Ever since urban renewal projects started after the 1950s, a lot of hypocaust systems have come to light in cities such as Tongeren, Tournai, or Bavay. Again, the limited size of the excavated areas only rarely permitted to link a hypocaust to a bathhouse.

North-Western Continental Europe in General Works on Roman Baths

In general works on Roman baths and bathing habits, the bathhouses in north-western continental Europe have scarcely been included. This is partly due to the fact that few (large) public baths have been discovered in this part of the Empire, while it is exactly on these buildings that most of these studies focus. One of the first overview studies about Roman baths, Ernst Pfretzschner's doctoral thesis 'Die Grundrissentwicklung der römischen Thermen' (1909), only included public facilities and focused mainly on examples in Italy, North Africa, and Asia Minor. The obvious emphasis throughout the study lies on the typology of the plans, with little attention to differences between geographic zones. Only the impact of the climate on the balance between cold and hot rooms is briefly touched upon (Pfretzschner 1909, 33). In his catalogue of sites, the only bath inventoried for *Germania Inferior* is Aachen, while the four sites for *Gallia Belgica* are all located in southern France (Pfretzschner 1909, 69–70). The study that remained the standard work for Roman baths until the later decades of the twentieth century, was Daniel Krencker's publication on the imperial baths (*Kaiserthermen*) in Trier (Krencker and Krüger 1929). Besides an exhaustive report on the excavation of the large complex, Krencker included a comparative study of Roman public baths throughout the Empire. The focus still lay on the typology of the plans, even if decoration and technology (heating and water management) were also touched upon. The catalogue of baths is ordered according to modern nations instead of Roman provinces. For Germany, only military baths along the Rhine *limes* are included, apart from the Kaiserthermen and Barbarathermen in Trier. For France, none of the thirteen public baths are found in the north. Belgium and the Netherlands are not included in the catalogue. Another early general work on Roman baths was written by Guglielmo De Angelis d'Ossat (1943), but his mainly architectural study is limited to Italy.

New research on Greek public baths, masterfully assembled in a seminal work by René Ginouvès (1962), sparked renewed interest in the origins of Roman public baths. Especially Hans Eschebach's research on the Stabian Baths in Pompeii presented researchers with a more or less linear evolution from individual Greek-style bath tubs to Roman-style hypocausted baths with communal pools (Eschebach 1979). Subsequently, two more general books on Roman baths came out by the hand of German scholars during the 1980s. Krencker's student Erika Brödner (1983) wrote a comprehensive overview of bathing in the Roman world, paying attention not only to the architectural evolution, but to bathing culture in general, including intangible aspects such as opening hours, temperature inside the baths, or bathing routines. The section dedicated to private baths is still rather limited and mainly relies on the evidence of very large *villae* and some letters by Pliny the Younger (Brödner 1983, 186–97). The north-western part of the Empire, with the exception of Trier, plays only a minor role in the study, only appearing in the section on military baths (Brödner 1983, 179–86). Werner Heinz's richly illustrated book *Römische Thermen: Badewesen and Badeluxus im Römischen Reich* (1983)

covered a wide range of aspects, the main focus still lying on architecture and decoration. However, Heinz made some important remarks about villa baths, noting how these would sometimes be detached from the residence (Heinz 1983, 27, 156). No bathhouses in the north-west are discussed, but some of the military baths along the Rhine and the imperial baths in Trier are included (Heinz 1983, 26, 98–101, 118–20). In 1984, Jean-Marie Degbomont chose the northern provinces, *Belgica* in particular, as a research area for investigating hypocaust construction in private residences in the Roman Empire (Degbomont 1984). Several villa baths of the *civitas Tungrorum* and *Nerviorum* are presented as examples. The study, however, focuses only on this technical aspect of the baths. The edited exhibition catalogue *Terme romane e vita quotidiana* (Pasquinucci 1987) covers both bathing architecture and life at the baths, but mainly concerns the Mediterranean.

In the 1990s several important monographs on Roman baths were published. Inge Nielsen's *Thermae et balnea* (1990, revised in 1993) is still considered a standard work on Roman baths, combining an impressive dataset of archaeological, literary, and epigraphic evidence from every corner of the Empire to give a very comprehensive picture of Roman bathing habits. The work nevertheless focuses on public baths, resulting in a rather limited dataset for the northern part of the Empire. *Gallia Belgica* is discussed together with the western provinces, including Italy, the Iberian peninsula, and southern France (Nielsen 1993a, 65). The specific context of the northern *civitates*, for which Romanization took on a different form, is therefore lost. *Germania Inferior* is counted among the northern border provinces, together with *Britannia, Germania Superior*, and the eastern European border provinces (Nielsen 1993a, 73). Even if none of the discussed public baths falls within the limits of the research area, Nielsen makes some important points about recurring patterns in the plans of the northern baths. The very functional plans, often consisting of the main three bath rooms (*frigidarium — tepidarium — caldarium*) in a simple linear succession, seem to have been influenced by the layout of military baths, which presumably were the first Roman-style baths to be built in this part of the Empire (Nielsen 1993a, 73–74, 83–84). Furthermore, the presence of 'heat traps' between *frigidarium* and *tepidarium*, the round *laconica* in a peripheral position, and the absence of *palaestra* are linked to the military roots of baths (Nielsen 1993a, 78–81).[5] Nielsen also

---

5   The fact that the northern provinces fell outside the Greek-Hellenistic cultural sphere could also explain why the tradition of sport was never fully adopted in this part of the Empire (Nielsen 1993a, 82).

remarks how the colder climate could have inspired architects to include more heated rooms, such as heated *apodyteria*, and smaller cold sections without open-air *natationes* (Nielsen 1993a, 82–83). Fikret Yegül's monograph *Baths and Bathing in Classical Antiquity* (1992), as well as the revised and abridged version *Bathing in the Roman World* (2010), almost exclusively focuses on public baths in the Mediterranean world. Pierre Gros's chapter on baths in volume 1 of *L'architecture romaine du début du IIIe siècle av. J.-C. à la fin du Haut-Empire* (1996) discusses the baths in the three Gauls together with those in *Britannia*. Like Nielsen, he underlines the popularity of the linear succession of rooms and points to the highly axial plans of the northern baths (Gros 1996, 406–08). In volume 2, Gros focuses on private architecture, making some general remarks on the villa baths in greater Gaul (Gros 2001, 329–31). In *Antike Badekultur* (1996), Marga Weber pays some attention to private baths, even if the chapter mainly looks at the evidence from the Vesuvian cities (Weber 1996, 101–17). She notes how some villa baths in Germany were detached from the house, without going into further detail (Weber 1996, 106). Garrett Fagan's *Bathing in Public in the Roman World* (1999) contains a wealth of literary and epigraphic data on Roman baths, but subsequently remains silent on regions where no such data is available, such as north-western Gaul.

In 2010, Nathalie de Haan published the first general monograph on Roman private baths (*Römische Privatbäder: Entwicklung, Verbreitung, Struktur und sozialer Status*). As the subtitle announces, the book goes beyond an architectural study, covering almost every aspect related to private bathing culture. Even though the archaeological dataset is restricted to Italy, Britain, and North Africa, some interesting general conclusions are put forward. De Haan argues how innovations in bathing technology and architecture are often first 'tested' in private baths, before being adopted on a wider scale in public facilities (de Haan 2010, 37). The structure of the bath itself obviously shows recurrent features, yet climatic conditions may account for changes in the balance between heated and cold rooms (de Haan 2010, 91). The spread of private baths throughout the Empire is closely linked to processes of 'acculturation' and 'imitation' between the Roman and indigenous cultural sphere. The speed and success of such processes is different for each region (de Haan 2010, 52–54). Whether in Italy or in the provinces, constructing a private bath was not just about attending to one's personal hygiene, it was above all a display of wealth and a statement about adhering to a 'civilized' lifestyle directed towards one's peers, who were frequently invited to these baths (de Haan 2010, 134–35).

Specific Studies on Baths in the Roman North-West

Studies specifically focusing on baths in the Roman North-West are scarce. Robert De Maeyer was one of the first to dedicate specific attention to private baths in a chapter of his doctoral thesis (De Maeyer 1937, 165–90). The author discusses the functioning of a Roman bathhouse through examples in his research area. He groups the baths not in public or private facilities, but in freestanding and attached buildings (De Maeyer 1937, 174, 181). The chapter is limited to detailed descriptions of specific buildings, without presenting more general conclusions. In 1940, Harald Koethe published an article examining thirty-one private baths in the hinterland of Trier. The dataset did not include baths located in the *civitas Tungrorum*, but in an appendix at the end of the article, several baths in Belgium and the Netherlands are used as a comparative framework (Koethe 1940, 115–31). The author is struck by the large size of some of the baths in Trier's hinterland, taking up large parts of the total surface of villas (Koethe 1940, 43). The sample showed that the majority of baths were attached to a villa in a later phase, often along one of the small sides. Only three bathhouses were completely freestanding. According to Koethe, the location was chosen to facilitate the water supply (Koethe 1940, 104). A recurrent typological feature is the presence of a large, often square, heated room in connection to the cold section. This may have been a heated *apodyterium* or alternatively a heated living room that did not belong to the bathhouse (Koethe 1940, 112).

In 1960, Albert Grenier published the fourth volume of the *Manuel d'Archéologie gallo-romaine* on water structures. In the section about baths, the archaeological evidence from *Gallia Belgica* and *Gallia Lugdunensis* is treated together. Thirteen public bath buildings are discussed in the text, but not one of them is located in the *civitas Nerviorum* or in the *civitas Menapiorum*. After the architectural descriptions of the separate buildings, the author refrains from distilling any regional characteristics (Grenier 1960, 384). It was not until 1994, that a first overview of the baths, both private and public, in the *civitas Tungrorum* was published (Deru 1994). This catalogue comprises sixty-three baths, but we must take into account that new research has changed our knowledge of the borders of the *civitas*. Several baths included by Deru, especially in the Netherlands and Germany, are now thought to fall outside of the *civitas*.[6] The study focuses on architecture, building

---

6 These are the baths in Aachen (Wirtz 1993), Hoensbroek (Habets 1887), Ravenbosch (Remouchamps 1924), Vlengendaal (Goossens 1916), and Voerendaal (Braat 1953).

techniques, heating and water technology, decorative programme, and location. Besides some important general observations, including the popularity of the linear row type and the block type, Deru searches for explanations for recurrent features by looking at the local context (terrain elevation, natural water sources, proximity of building stone, etc.). Paul Van Ossel briefly discussed villa baths in his synthesis on late antique rural sites in northern Gaul, but admits his dataset only shows results for the Rhineland (*civitas Treverorum*) for the period between AD 260 and AD 476 (Van Ossel 1992, 127–28). No newly built baths were identified for this time frame in the other *civitates* of north-western Gaul.

After 2000, several studies were published about baths in greater Gaul, but the main body of evidence mainly consisted of sites in *Narbonnensis*, *Lugdunensis*, and *Aquitania*. Especially the work by Alain Bouet (2000; 2003a; 2003b; 2007) has focused on the baths in greater Gaul. The differences in bath architecture between the north and the south has nevertheless been pointed out, as Alain Bouet (2000, 43) underlined the fact that *Narbonnensis* had been conquered much earlier than *Belgica*, resulting in different types of baths that had been imported. The symmetrical plan, which became popular in the first century AD, is more widespread in the north than in the south of Gaul, but is absent in the area under research here (Bouet 2003a, 716). Villa baths have only rarely been the focus of research, in contrast to urban baths (Coquelet 2000; 2011, 158–65, 210–11, 278; Bouet 2003a; 2007), *castrum* baths (Boudeau 2011), sanctuary baths (Hartz 2018), and thermal baths (Bouet 2018). In the overview *Les romains en Wallonie*

(Brulet 2008), all known Roman urban and rural sites in Wallonia were discussed, including over a hundred villa sites with private baths. In the general chapter on rural estates, a passage is dedicated to private bathhouses, remarking how these were often added to the villa in a later phase. The plans are described as very basic, with the traditional rooms lying on a single axis (Brulet 2008, 140–43). The baths in *Germania Inferior*, both private and public, have been examined by Michael Dodt (2003; 2006; 2007; 2010). However, the boundaries of the province that were followed for his study omit the *civitas Tungrorum* (Dodt 2003, 8). The dataset consisted of twenty-six baths of *villae rusticae*, four private baths of urban *domus*, six public baths, and five military baths. The majority of baths were clustered in an area between Cologne and Aachen, near Bonn, and in the region of Ahr-Vingxtbach, where considerably more excavations have been conducted (Dodt 2006, 67). The military baths along the *limes* have recently been re-examined by Scholz (2018).

In summary, only the public baths (Bouet 2003a) and the baths in the *civitas Tungrorum* have been examined to some extent. The studies by Deru (1994) and Bouet (2003a), however, already date from twenty to thirty years ago. Several new baths have come to light since and research has taken some interesting new turns. The baths in *civitas Nerviorum* have been included in the works by De Maeyer (1937), Van Ossel (1992), and Brulet (2008), although none of these studies actually focuses on baths. The baths of the *civitas Menapiorum* have been overlooked ever since the work by De Maeyer (1937).

CHAPTER 3

The Roman Continental North-West, a Blank Spot for Baths?

The Share of Public and Private Baths

When looking at a distribution map of Roman baths within the research area, there is a striking discrepancy between the low number of public baths and the high number of private baths (Map 1). Considering the limited degree of urbanization of the north-western continental region, especially the sandy areas north of the river Meuse, the absence of 'city baths' should not come as a surprise (Map 2). There were very few large cities: the *civitas* capitals *Atuatuca* (Tongeren), *Bagacaum* (Bavay), and *Castellum Menapiorum* (Cassel) were monumentalized, while some larger central places such as *Turnacum* (Tournai), *Fanum Martis* (Famars), Clavier-Vervoz, Fontaine-Valmont, or Liberchies seem to have been equipped with sizeable public and administrative buildings, including public baths. The small public baths found in Amay, Braives, Grobbendonk, or Tienen confirm that smaller central places could also be equipped with basic public infrastructure. The settlements that formed near Roman military forts could also offer basic bath facilities to their inhabitants, as the examples in Aardenburg and Oudenburg confirm. Only thirteen confirmed examples out of a total of 145 bath buildings (i.e. 9 per cent) can be labelled as public baths. These are three bathhouses of a military fort, two bathhouses connected to possible road stations, and eight public bathhouses in an urban context. For another fifteen baths that were found in urban contexts, the excavated part is simply too small to confirm whether the bath was accessible to the general public. Even if the share of public baths in the research area is restricted, we can assume that this number must have been higher as the larger Roman cities still lie buried under their modern counterparts. The evidence for public baths is problematic in *Atuatuca* and *Bagacum*, while no bathhouse has been discovered yet in *Castellum Menapiorum*. Several other central places that obviously had some regional importance, such as Wervik, Velzeke,

Asse, or *Cortoriacum* (Kortrijk), have not yielded remains of baths yet, but probably also had small baths such as those found in Tienen. Nevertheless, it is highly probable that larger central places, and perhaps even the cities, only had one bathhouse, instead of the high numbers found in Mediterranean cities. Public buildings seem to have been limited to a functional minimum, not only in *Gallia Belgica* and *Germania Inferior*, but also in *Britannia*. In contrast to the Mediterranean, where elite families competed for political power by investing in public infrastructure and civic embellishment, intra-elite competition in the north-west may not have been played out in urban centres, but rather in private (rural) domestic architecture (see Chapter 7). The social organization of the indigenous societies possibly continued into the Roman period, fixing wealth and power to a small oligarchy who felt little need to invest in public infrastructure (Millett 1990, 82).

The number of private baths is directly linked to the high number of rural villas that have been excavated in the research area (Map 2). Evidence of private baths in an urban context was only found in five cities, namely in *Atuatuca*, *Bagacum*, *Turnacum*, Maastricht, and Namur. If we consider the total sample of baths, the private baths account for some 81 per cent (or 118 out of 145). Considering the fact that several villas were only partially excavated, it is difficult to assess what percentage of villas were equipped with baths. Several bathhouses were also completely freestanding, which means that the absence of a bath in the main villa building does not automatically imply the absence of a bath on the villa estate. Damage due to ploughing, especially since the second half of the twentieth century, and stone robbing in post-Roman phases can also cloud the identification of baths. For several villas, the presence of a bath has been proposed on the basis of building material (hypocaust tiles, *tubuli*, hydraulic mortar), but could not be ascertained (see below). This issue of the representativity of the archaeological data is important

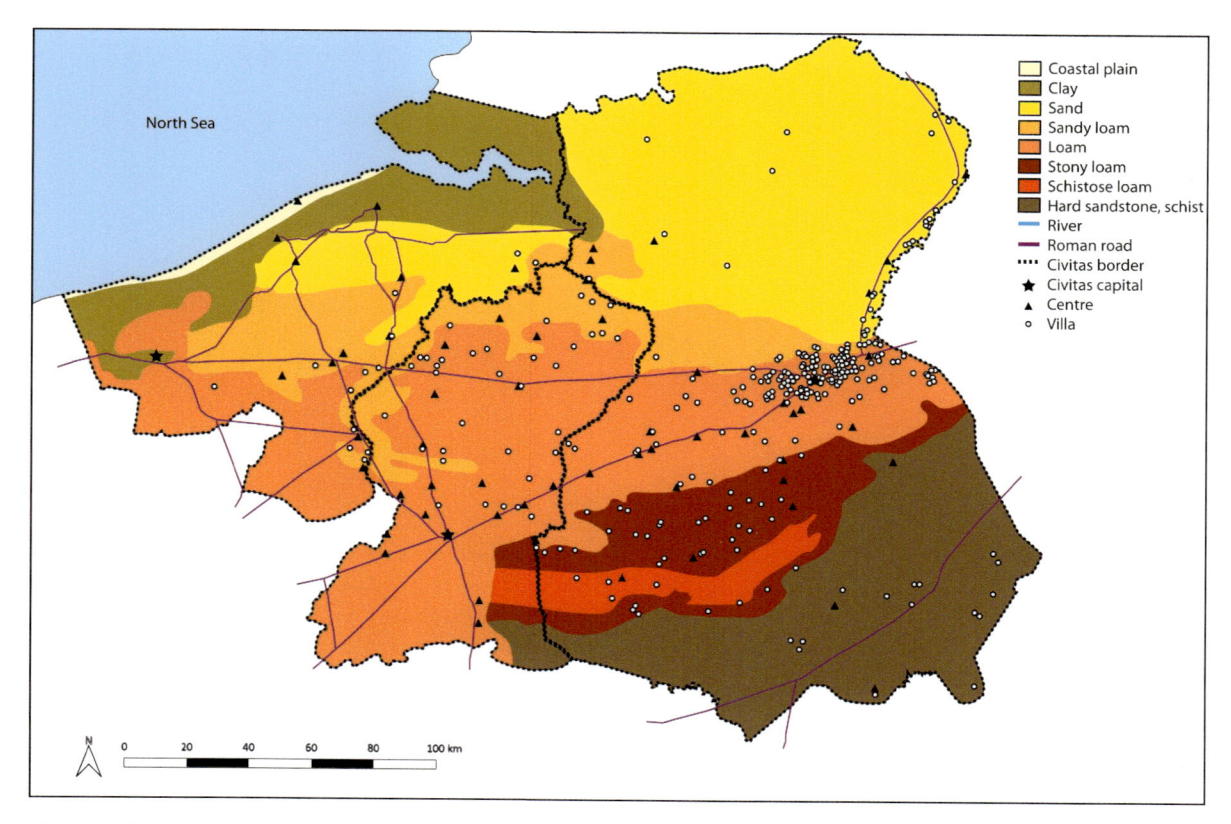

Map 2. Soil map of the research area with indication of the main Roman roads and the distribution of villas and civic centres. Map by author.

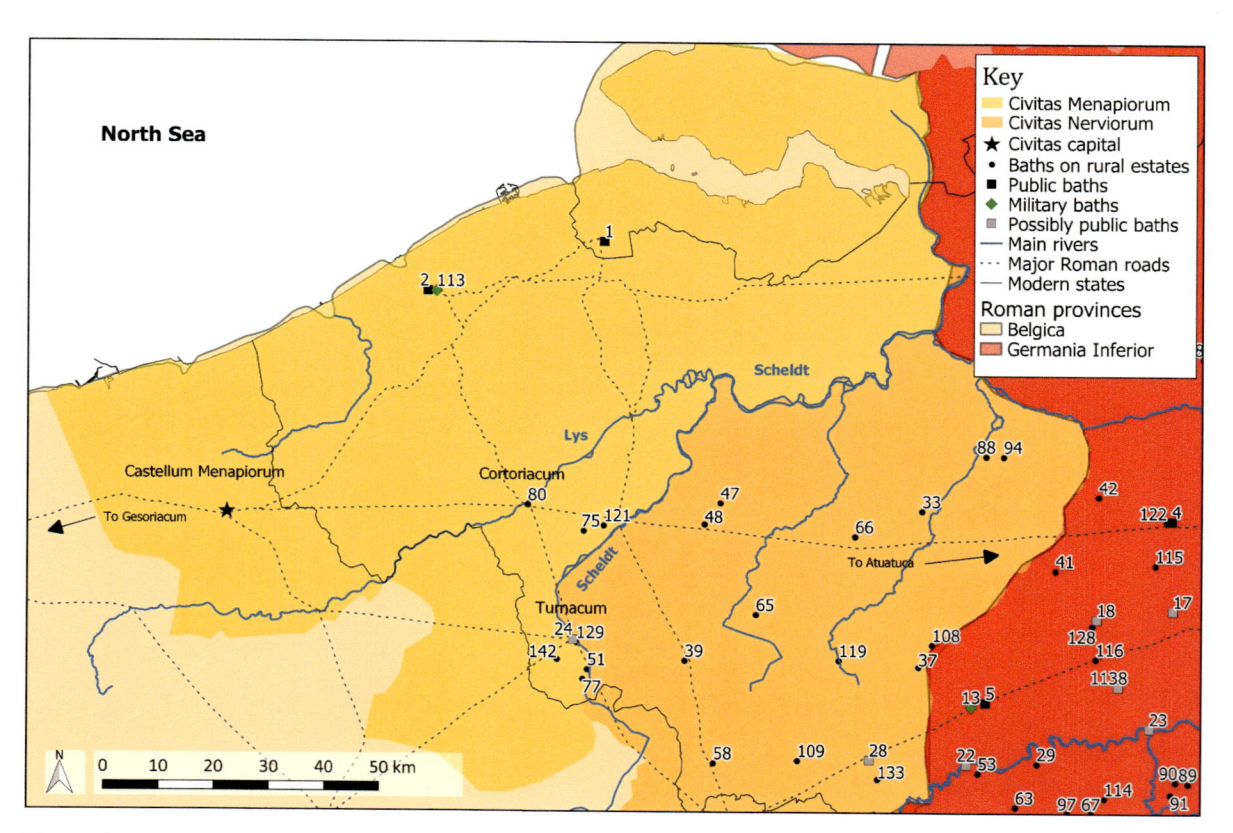

Map 3. The *civitas Menapiorum* with location of the baths, main civic centres, Roman roads, and rivers. Map by author.

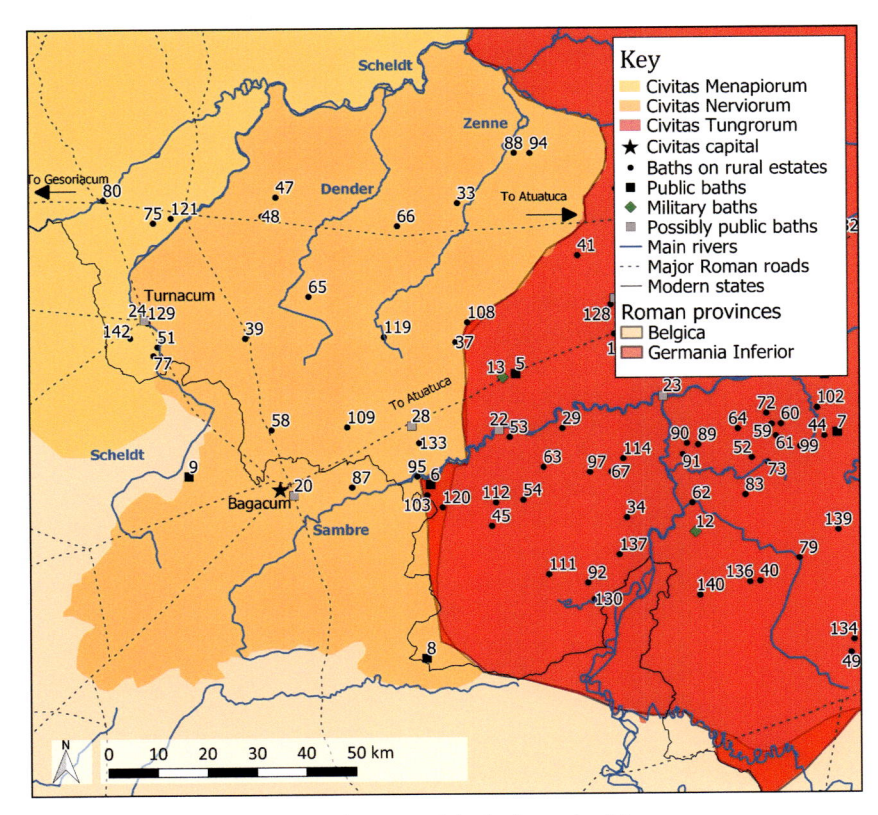

Map 4. The *civitas Nerviorum* with location of the baths, main civic centres, Roman roads, and rivers. Map by author.

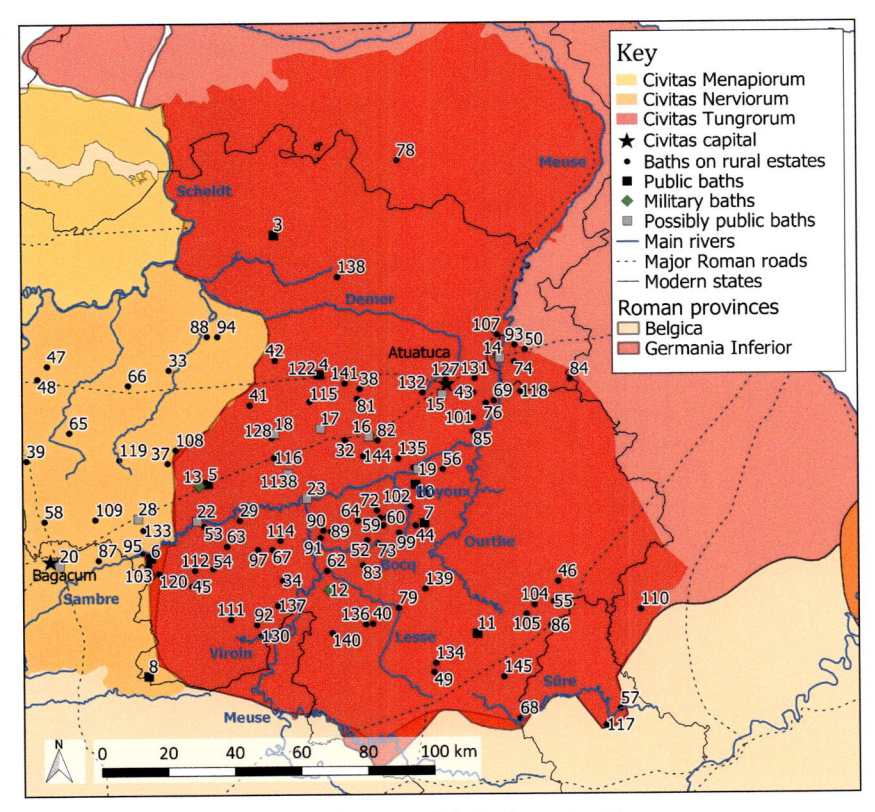

Map 5. The *civitas Tungrorum* with location of the baths, main civic centres, Roman roads, and rivers. Map by author.

when looking at the numbers below. Only the villa sites which have been (partially) excavated were taken into consideration. Villas that were identified using aerial photography or by prospection have not been included. Freestanding baths or bath suites without evidence for a villa were also left out, as it cannot be excluded that such small buildings were part of a road station or small central place. Of the twenty-one villa sites in the *civitas Menapiorum*, five had a bathhouse (24 per cent). In the *civitas Nerviorum*, forty-five villa sites yielded eighteen bathhouses (40 per cent). For the *civitas Tungrorum*, the high number of 260 villa sites on the fertile loam soils gave an equally high number of ninety-five baths (36 per cent).[1] These percentages lie in the order of the 33 per cent calculated by Dodt (2006, 29) for the province of *Germania Inferior* (excluding the *civitas Tungrorum*) in the same timespan (first–third century AD), also excluding villas known only through aerial photography or prospection. A comparison with the more urbanized regions of the Mediterranean is difficult, as less research has focused on the rural hinterland than in the densely populated northern Europe. However, a catalogue of Roman villas in *Latium* (Italy) by Marzano (2007) identified sixty-nine bathhouses for a total of 384 sites (18 per cent). She also excluded villas known only through aerial photography, prospection, and poorly documented sites. The chronological scope, however, spans the second century BC to the fifth century AD.

Spread of the Baths throughout the *civitates*

Civitas Menapiorum

The number of baths (fifteen) in the *civitas Menapiorum* is low (Map 3). Three public baths can be linked to military presence, namely two at the *castellum* of Oudenburg and one near the *castellum of* Aardenburg. Furthermore several possible baths in urban context (private or public) and five villa baths have been identified. The low degree of urbanization and the few Roman-style villas can be understood from an economical perspective, as the relatively poor sandy soils were certainly not attractive for agriculture, as well as from a cultural perspective. The coastal plain in Roman times lay more inland than today and consisted of salt marshes and higher sand ridges on older peat, criss-crossed by tidal gullies and creeks. Habitation, it

seems, was only possible on the dry sand ridges and on artificially raised peat platforms, with economic activity limited to mixed agriculture (barley), salt production, and pastoral activities (De Clercq 2011, 247). The rural settlement in the *civitas*, especially on the poor sandy soils in the north, continued to display indigenous traditions of house building, material culture, and funerary rites well into the Roman period (De Clercq 2011, 254). The villas that have been identified were located on the more fertile sandy loam and loam soils in the southern part of the *civitas*, mainly in the alluvial plain of the river Scheldt (Map 2). The important road between *Gesoriacum* (Boulogne-sur-Mer) and *Atuatuca* (Tongeren), passing *Cortoriacum* (Kortrijk), must have been of great importance to the villas of Heestert and Tiegem (Map 3). The villas of Willemeau, Hollain, and Bruyelle lay in the southern hinterland of *Turnacum* (Doornik), close to the roads coming from *Nemetacum* (Arras) and the Nervian capital of *Bagacum* (Bavay). The proximity of urban centres, the sea, (navigable) rivers, and roads were already mentioned by Cato when discussing the best locations for villas, enabling a fast and easy export of produce (*Agr.* 1.3).

The central places in the *civitas* have so far only yielded five baths in *Turnacum*, two of which may have been public, a possible bathhouse in *Cortoriacum*, a public bath in Aardenburg along the road leading up to the *castellum*, and two baths at Oudenburg, one which probably belonged to the settlement of the camp (*canabae*), and one within the walls of the late antique fort. The presence of baths in central places and in or near forts is not surprising, as such sites were pivotal locations of commerce and trade, attracting people from the wider area. Furthermore, this centralizing function ensured a supply of (ceramic) building materials, while the necessary skilled labour and manpower for construction would also have been present. Both specialized building teams and stone and ceramic building materials were certainly difficult to come by in the more remote rural areas of the *civitas*. Small towns that seem to have had some central function for a wider area, mainly consisted of buildings and structures in indigenous vernacular architecture. Sites such as Aartrijke, Destelbergen, Harelbeke, Kerkhove, Kruishoutem, Merendree, Torhout, Waasmunster, Wenduine, or *Viroviacum* (Wervik) have not yielded any evidence of baths yet. For some villa sites and settlements that were only partially excavated, the presence of hypocaust tiles and *tubuli* could point to a bath, even if the presence of heated living rooms was widespread in the entire research area (Table 1).

---

1   For the *civitas Tungrorum*, the number of villa sites is derived from the database of the project 'Mapping the *civitas* Tungrorum', a joint research project by the Department of Archaeology at Ghent University and the Gallo-Roman Museum of Tongeren.

Table 1. Roman sites in the *civitas Menapiorum* with hypocaust tiles and/or *tubuli* for which the presence of a bathhouse could not be ascertained (CAI: ID-number in the central archaeological inventory of the Flemish Heritage Agency, database for professional archaeologists accessible online through cai. onroerenderfgoed.be; CAGN: carte archéologique de la Gaule 59 — le Nord, see Delmaire and others 1996; CAGP: carte archéologique de la Gaule 62 — Le Pas-de-Calais, see Delmaire, Jacques, and Acquart 1994).

Site	Hypocaust tiles	*Tubuli*	Bibliography
Aalter – Lostraat		×	CAI 159815
Aix-en-Pévèle (area)	×		CAGN p. 87
Bailleul – ZAC des Collines	×	×	Anonymous 2009
Bavikhove (area)	×		CAI 70253
Belsele – Steenwerk		×	CAI 32656
Beveren – Steenakker		×	CAI 70232
Beveren – Tomberg		×	CAI 76043
Bossuit – Doorniksesteenweg	×		CAI 73819
Dourges – les Vingt-Huits	×		CAGP p. 816
Harnes – Chemin du Brûlé		×	CAGP p. 515
Houplin-Ancoisne – rue Gabriel Péri		×	CAGN p. 284
Koksijde – Steendam I		×	CAI 71204
Kuurne (area)	×		CAI 71106
Lille – Palais Rameau	×		CAGN p. 308
Marcq-en-Baroeul – Ermitage du Quesne	×	×	CAGN p. 333
Nevele – Kerrebroek		×	CAI 971550
Nieuwpoort – Steendam		×	CAI 70680
Pittem (area)	×		CAI 71150
Roeselare – Populierstraat		×	CAI 75166
Templemars – Fond de Vendeville	×		CAGN p. 412
Tielrode – Steenakker	×		CAI 32724
Villeneuve d'Ascq – Rue Charles le Bon	×		CAGN p. 93
Wortegem-Petegem – Moreghemkouter		×	CAI 502714

Civitas Nerviorum

In the territory of the *Nervii*, twenty-three baths have been identified (Map 4): a public bathhouse in *Fanum Martis* (Famars) and possibly in *Vodgoriacum* (Waudrez), two possible baths (presumably public) in *Bagacum* (Bavay) and nineteen villa baths. The fertile loam soils and undulating plains of central Belgium were very attractive for agriculture (Map 2). In the northern part of the *civitas*, on the sandy loam soils, rural settlement patterns strongly resemble those found in the *civitas Menapiorum* (Brulet 2008, 113). Only a few villas with baths have been found here: in Machelen and Melsbroek. The blank spot in the south of the *civitas* probably reflects a different research history, with fewer sites being discovered and published, than an historic reality. A large part of this region is also a nature reserve with forested areas (forêt de Mormal).[2] However, aerial photography, chance finds, and targeted prospections published in the Carte Archéologique de la Gaule (Delmaire and others 1996) show important activity in this part of the *civitas*. The majority of the villas have been found along important traffic arteries, such as the villas of Brakel-Zegelsem or Gooik along the *Gesoriacum–Atuatuca* road or Élouges and Aubechies along the *diverticulum* coming from *Bagacum* (Map 4). The villas of Mabeuge and Merbes-le-Chateau lay near the Sambre river, Ghislenghien/Meslin-l'Évêque near the Dender, Soignies, Anderlecht, and Machelen near the Zenne. The number of public baths is limited to the large baths in Famars and the remains of possible

---

2 The same blank spot can be remarked in the catalogue of late antique rural settlements by Van Ossel (1992).

baths near the forum of *Bagacum*. Several other remains of hypocaust systems have been found in the Nervian capital, but none could be identified as baths. Their modest size, the absence of water-related features, and the fact that only one room was heated would suggest heated living rooms rather than bath rooms. The exception is the hypocaust found in a pasture (Mandron-Peyron), which was quite large (8.9 × 3.2 m), may have consisted of two rooms judging from a wall dividing the hypocaust, and was embellished with a mosaic floor and wall paintings (Biévelet 1950, 85–86). In *Vodgoriacum* (Waudrez), the size and the location of a bathhouse in the city centre could point to a public facility rather than to a private bath. The identification of a building with hypocaust as a bath in Blicquy, near the sanctuary of Ville d'Anderlecht, is more problematic, as no pools have been identified. Central places such as Asse, Avesnes, Bléharies, Elewijt, Flobecq, Givry, Hofstade, Kester, *Pons Scaldis* (Escautpont), Pommerœil, or Velzeke have not yielded public baths (yet). In Asse, Blicquy, Elewijt, and Velzeke, hypocaust systems have been identified, although these seem to have belonged to houses (Table 2). Similarly, on several villa sites, only elements of a hypocaust were found, e.g. in Denderwindeke, Dilbeek, Heldergem, Jette, Wambeek. Several other sites without stone buildings also yielded (reused?) hypocaust-related ceramic building materials.

Civitas Tungrorum

The *civitas* of the *Tungri* was the largest of the three discussed in this book and also yielded the most baths (Map 5): a total of 114 baths included seven public baths (6 per cent), another seven could have been public, two baths were found near military forts, two baths are associated with an alleged road station, and ninety-five baths belonged to a villa (83 per cent). The concentration of both villas and central places can be located in the central part of the *civitas*, on the fertile loam soils (Map 2). This also coincides with the major roads running from *Bagacum* to *Atuatuca* and from *Gesoriacum* to *Atuatuca*, as well as with the river valleys of the Meuse and Sambre. A high concentration of villas lay in the direct hinterland of *Atuatuca*, although few seem to have been equipped with a bathhouse. Two areas seem particularly well equipped with villas boasting a bath: the area delimited by the rivers Meuse (west and north), the Hoyoux (east), and the Bocq (south) and the area between the rivers Sambre (north) and Viroin (south) (Map 5). The northern part of the *civitas*, the so-called Meuse-Demer-Scheldt area, is particularly low on Roman-style villas and central places. The landscape of the region is dominated by cover sands, lower-lying wet stream valleys, and swamps and bogs. The settlement was characterized by simple rural settlements with predominating timber construction (Creemers, De Clercq, and Hiddink 2015). The villa baths of Vorst/Laakdal and Hoogeloon-Kerkakkers are the only examples in this vast area found so far. The *vicus* of Grobbendonk was the only settlement with a small public bath. The southern part of the *civitas* coincides with the Ardennes mountain range. Few villas and central places have been identified. They concentrate along the river valleys, as dense forest covered the uninhabitable rugged ridges. Several villa sites are located close to the Ourthe river. The villas of Grumelange, Diekirch, and Schieren lie in the Sûre valley.

The existence of public baths can be assumed in the capital *Atuatuca* (Tongeren), although no remains as impressive as in Xanten or Trier have been found. However, a part of a large cold pool was discovered at the Schaetzengaerde site, perhaps indicating the existence of such a bath. The remaining evidence of hypocausts could just as easily have belonged to private rich houses (*domus*). In Namur, an important civic centre in Roman times, the baths in the rue des Echasseurs are of a size that they could either have belonged to a (very large) *domus* or might have been a public bath in their own right. The same doubt clouds our understanding of the baths in Maastricht and Amay-Ombret. In the *vicus* of Liberchies, one public bath has come to light, located in the centre along the *Bagacum-Atuatuca* road. A hypocaust built as a separate building at the back of one of the street-oriented houses cannot be identified as a bath due to the absence of water-related amenities. Also at the *vicus* of Clavier, at least two houses were equipped with a room on hypocaust, added during a later phase. The public baths were located along the main road connecting *Atuatuca* (Tongeren) to *Orolaunum* (Arlon) in the *civitas Treverorum*. Just north of the baths another possibly public building was excavated. Due to the basilical plan and the hypocaust heating, it is sometimes interpreted as an assembly hall. The modest public baths in Tienen and Grobbendonk were located amidst houses and close to the main traffic arteries. The sanctuary site of Fontaine-Valmont, located on the border with the *civitas Nerviorum*, was equipped with large baths, underlining the importance of this central place. In Tourinnes-St-Lambert, a small freestanding building with two heated rooms can possibly be interpreted as a bath, rather than as a 'potter's house' (according to Dens and Poils 1911, 293). The identification of a bathhouse in Braives is problematic due to the absence of evidence for pools. Some (large) baths that may have belonged to a villa or a small centre include Charleroi – Marchienne au Pont, Ramillies/ Autre-Église, and Soignies. Other central places such as Antwerp, Ciney, Couvin, Dilsen-Stokkem, Dinant, Huy, Jupille-sur-Meuse, Kinrooi, Kontich, Rumst, Taviers, Theux, or Vodecée have not yielded public baths yet.

Site	Hypocaust tiles	*Tubuli*	Bibliography
Asse – Steenveld	×	×	CAI 112
Avesnes-les-Sec – Barnava		×	CAGN p. 107
Bavay – Pature des Cense	×		Biévelet 1950
Bavay – Pature Mandron-Peyron	×	×	Biévelet 1950
Bavay – Route de Valenciennes	×		Biévelet 1950
Bavay – Salle des fêtes	×		Biévelet 1950
Bavay (area)	×		Biévelet 1950
Beauvois-en-Cambrésis – N43	×		CAGN p. 127
Bléharies – Les Zelvas	×		Bru 34
Blicquy – Camp romain	×		Bru 58
Blicquy – Ville d'Anderlecht	×		Bru 59
Boussières-en-Cambrésis – Champ Lefranc	×		CAGN p. 141
Denderwindeke – Kerkveld	×		CAI 30670
Dilbeek – Wolsemveld	×	×	T. Clerbaut (pers. comm.)
Dooren – Puursstraat	×		Van den Vonder 2008
Elewijt – Waversebaan	×		CAI 1232
Estinnes-au-Mont – Terre-à-Pointes	×		Bru 48
Etikhove – Buiksveld	×		CAI 500152
Froyennes (area)	×		Bru 72
Grosage (area)	×		Bru 42
Heldergem – Ninofse Waterval	×		CAI 30587
Houdeng-Goegnies – Bois de La Louvière	×		Bru 56
Huldenberg – Neerpoorten	×		CAI 423
Iwuy – Champ d'Honneur	×		CAGN p. 289
Jette – villa du Bois de Laerbeek	×	×	Van Bellingen 2011
Kester – Tomberg/Pattettestraat		×	CAI 207458
Le Nouvion-en-Thiérache – Grand Orne	×		CAGA p. 340
Leest – Kapellebaan	×		CAI 102246
Les Rues-des-Vignes – Zone sportif	×		CAGN p. 371
Meldert – Zelemsebaan		×	CAI 150512
Muizen – Heerweg	×		De Cock 1987
Outer- Stuypenberg	×		A. Degraeve (pers. comm.)
Roisin – Les Trentes Saules		×	DM p. 92
Ruien – Rosalinde		×	Verbrugge and others 2021
St-Lievens-Esse – Essenbos	×		CAI 502683
Tournai, Place S-Pierre	×		Bru 74
Tournai, rue des Choraux	×		Bru 74
Tournai, rue Madame	×		Bru 74
Tournai, vieux marché au beurre	×		Bru 74
Velzeke – Steenbeke	×		CAI 500001
Velzeke – Terracottastraat	×	×	CAI 500019
Villers-Outréaux – routes d'Arlansart/Montécouvez	×	×	CAGN p. 429
Wambeek – Langestraat	×		CAI 156974
Wemmel – Steenweg	x	x	Matthys and Wouters 1978
Zottegem – Spelaan	×		R. Pede (pers. comm.)

Table 2. Roman sites in the *civitas Nerviorum* with hypocaust tiles and/or *tubuli* for which no bathhouse could be ascertained (CAI: ID-number in the central archaeological inventory of the Flemish Heritage Agency, database for professional archaeologists accessible online through cai.onroerenderfgoed.be; CAGN: carte archéologique de la Gaule 59 — le Nord, see Delmaire and others 1996; CAGA: carte archéologique de la Gaule 8 — les Ardennes, see Nicolas and Chosserot 2011; Bru: site number in Brulet 2008; DM: see De Maeyer 1940).

In Jupille-sur-Meuse and Vodecée, hypocausts inside houses could not be linked to bathing. The baths of the forts of Liberchies – Brunehaut and Furfooz date to Late Antiquity (fourth century AD). The former is located outside of the actual fort but inside the wider defensive structure, while the latter lies outside the fortified hilltop. The bath at Outrelouxhe can be interpreted as belonging to a road relay, while the possible baths at Wyompont belonged to a somewhat larger settlement that can be described as a road station. In a building of the road station at Bergilers, a hypocaust was excavated, but further evidence for a bath is missing. Several other (villa) sites yielded evidence for hypocausts in the form of hypocaust tiles or *tubuli* (Table 3).

Table 3. Roman sites in the *civitas Tungrorum* with hypocaust tiles and/or *tubuli* for which no bathhouse could be ascertained (CAI: ID-number in the central archaeological inventory of the Flemish Heritage Agency, database for professional archaeologists accessible online through cai.onroerenderfgoed.be; Bru: site number in Brulet 2008; DM: page number in De Maeyer 1940; DM+: page number in De Maeyer 1979).

Site	Hypocaust tiles	*Tubuli*	Bibliography
Acosse (area)	×		DM p. 122
Attenhoven – Kloosterhof	×		CAI 3479
Bergilers – Malpas	×		Bru 109
Bergilers – Road station	×		Bru 109
Bergilers, villa de Basse Voie	×		Bru 109
Broekom – Sassenbroekberg	×		CAI 50128
Chastres – le Gau	×		DM p. 241
Cherain – Retigny	×		Bru 143
Ciney (area)	×		Bru 170
Clavier – Vervoz	×		Bru 87
Cobreville (area)	×		DM p. 211
Fauvillers – Hahnebour	×		DM p. 186
Fexhe-le-Haut-Clocher – E Pelho	×	×	DM p. 140
Grandru – Château des Templiers	×	×	DM p. 198
Hatrival – Champ des Monts	×		Bru 160
Hives – villa de Mémont	×		Bru 152
Hoegaarden – Blotenberg	×		CAI 3166
Hollange – Bois Lambay-Chênet	×		DM p. 195
Hollange – Le Montet	×		DM p. 195
Hollange – Thier de Hustat	×	×	DM p. 195
Hotton – Viez	×		DM p. 200
Jodoigne – Dongelberg	×		Bru 6
Jodoigne – Les Fonds de Jodoigne	×		Bru 7
Jupille-sur-Meuse – Gît-le-Coq	×		Bru 104
Lanaken – Ducatonweg	×		CAI 55505
Landelies – La Plate-Roque		×	DM p. 76
Le Roux-lez-Fosses – villa Vigetaille	×		Bru 181
Liberchies – Vicus House	×		Demanet and Vilvorder 2016
Lissoir (area)		×	DM p. 258
Longchamps – Terre à la l'Agauche	×		DM p. 266
Marche-en-Famenne (area)	×		DM p. 204
Martelange – In der Mecher	×		DM p. 207
Massul – Aux Mairies	×		DM+ p. 119

Site	Hypocaust tiles	*Tubuli*	Bibliography
Meeffe – Villa de Meeffe	×		DM p. 152
Meux (Saint-Denis) – Nausipont	×		De Boe 1979
Montenau (area)	×		DM p. 125
Montignies-sur-Sambre – Neuville		×	DM p. 83
Morsain – Villa du Champ de Présenne	×		DM p. 16
Neerlanden – Panbrugge	×		CAI 3478
Neuville – villa des Machenées	×		Bru 200
Nivelles – Clarisse	×		Bru 10
Sainte-Marie-Chevigny (area)	×		DM p. 216
Saint-Hubert – villa de l'abbaye	×		Henrotay 2011
Saint-Rémy (area)		×	DM p. 94
Sombreffe (area)	×		DM+ p. 44
Strée, Enclos du Tilleul	×		Bru 106
Taviet – Bois Joli	×		DM p. 226
Tintange – Warnach	×		Bru 139
Tongeren – Beukenbergweg	×		CAI 51955
Tongeren – Clarissenstraat	×		CAI 51391
Tongeren – Kielenstraat	×		CAI 51800
Tongeren – Kogelstraat	×		CAI 700391
Tongeren – Regulierenplein	×		CAI 52230
Tongeren – Sint-Truidersteenweg	×		CAI 159501
Vaux-et-Borset – A Vì Chesia	×		Bru 120
Vechmaal – Piringen	×		CAI 52392
Vedrin – villa Berlacomines	×		Bru 194
Verlaine – Campagne du Vivier	×		Bru 118
Vierset-Barse – Bonne	×		DM p. 167
Vodecée – Crayats des Sarrasins	×		Bru 202
Walshoutem – Hemelrijk	×		CAI 5321
Walshoutem – Kleine Hamberg		×	CAI 3497
Waremme – Haute Wegge		×	DM p. 133
Warnach – Bôlicht	×		DM p. 220
Werpin – Pierreux	×		DM p. 199
Wisembach – Rameschberg	×		DM p. 184
Wyompont – Habitations	×		Bru 162

CHAPTER 4

The Architecture of the Baths

Typology

Public Baths

The most impressive and grand layout for Roman baths has been called the 'imperial type' by modern scholars (V on Fig. 7), as this type first appeared in the early Imperial period when the emperor himself paid for large palace-like baths, especially in Rome (Nielsen 1993a, 45–48). Nevertheless, this modern terminology does not automatically imply imperial involvement. It rather pertains to the large size and symmetrical arrangement of the rooms, often in two mirrored circuits culminating in a communal *caldarium*. No imperial-type baths have been found in the three *civitates*. As the number of large cities is low, this is not surprising. The *civitas* capitals would be the most likely candidates to have such large symmetrical baths, as for example the 'Barbarathermen' (Fig. 8) and 'Kaiserthermen' in Trier (Krencker and Krüger 1929). However, no such grand structures have survived in the urban fabric in

Tongeren or Bavay. The large cold pool and the broad sturdy walls of the Schaetzengaerde site are the only remains that are suitable to have been part of large *thermae* in Tongeren. In Bavay, several heated rooms underneath Saint-Peter's church, close to the forum, may have belonged to a large bathhouse, although the absence of pools remains problematic. In Cassel, a much smaller centre than Tongeren or Bavay, no remains of (public) baths have been found.

The public baths that have been found in the smaller centres belonged to the row or the block type (I /II and III on Fig. 7, respectively). In Famars, Macquenoise, and Oudenburg 'Vicus Bath', the bath rooms are closely grouped together to form a 'block'. This layout, already described by Pfretzschner (1909, 25–29), is also frequently encountered for private baths. In Aardenburg (military context), Clavier, Fontaine-Valmont, Grobbendonk, Liberchies, and Tienen, the main rooms lay on a single axis. The advantage of such row types lies in the possibility of a single furnace at the end of this axis heating consecutive rooms

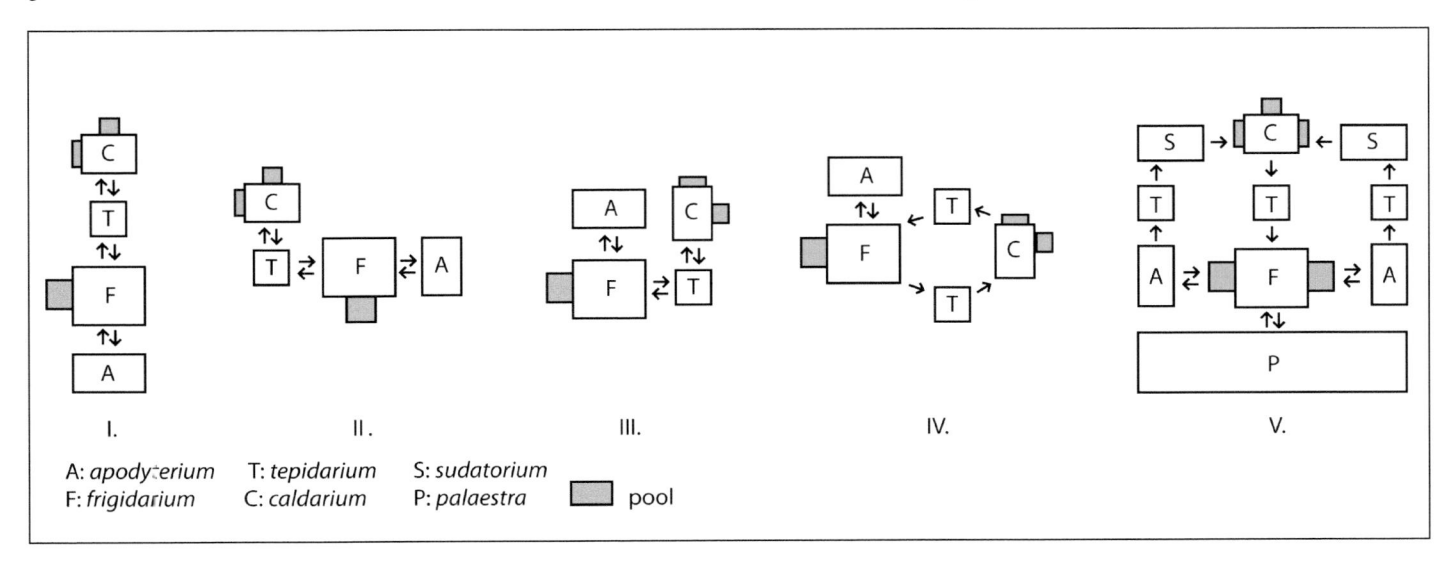

A: *apodyterium*   T: *tepidarium*   S: *sudatorium*
F: *frigidarium*   C: *caldarium*   P: *palaestra*   ▢ pool

Figure 7. Schematic overview of modern plan typologies of Roman baths (I. Linear row type; II. Angular row type; III. Block type; IV. Ring type; V. Imperial type). Figure by author after Nielsen 1993b, 51–52, fig. 1.

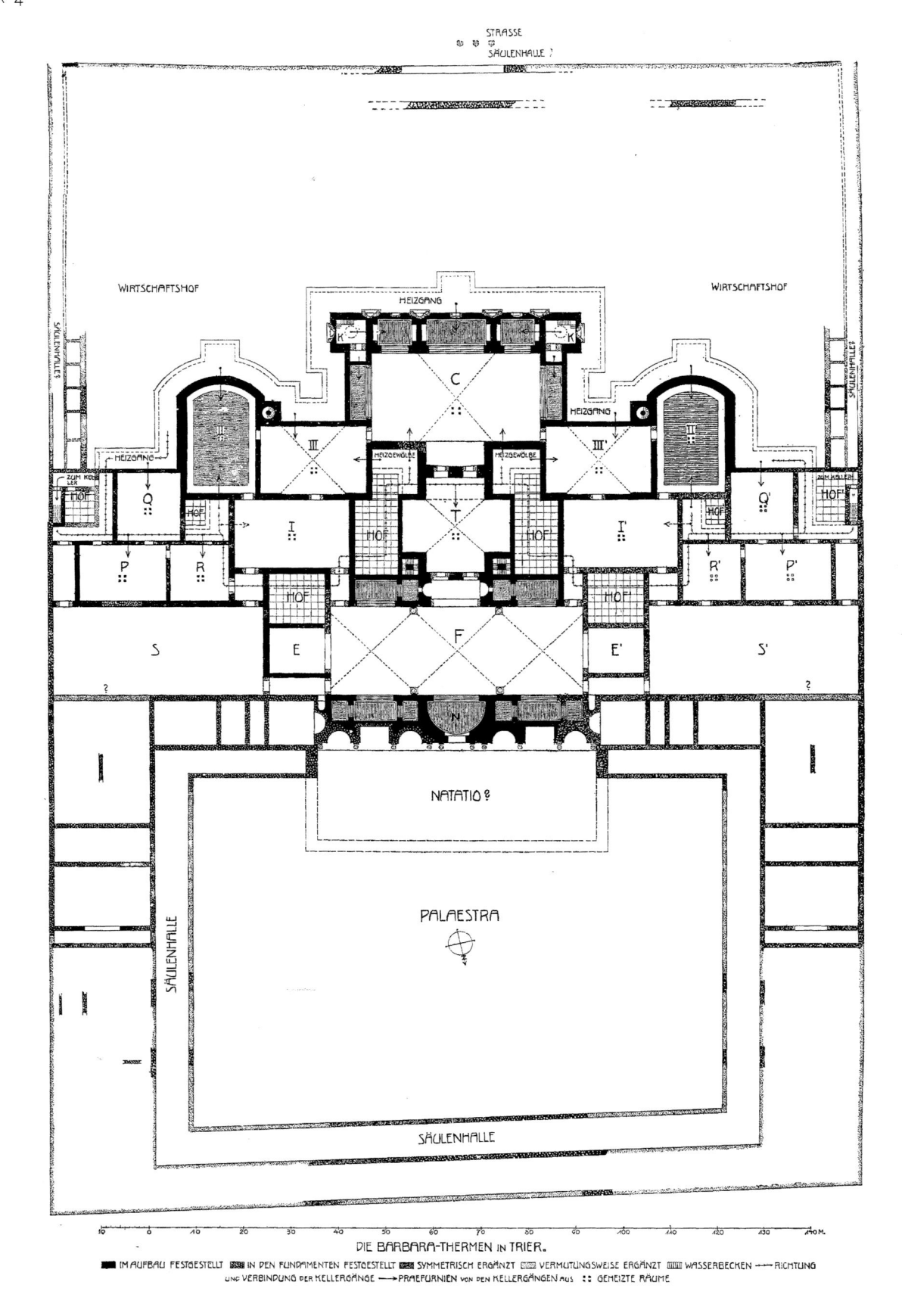

Figure 8. Plan of the imperial-type Barbara Thermen in Trier (Germany). Figure in Krencker and Krüger 1929, 242, fig. 359.

(*caldarium-tepidarium*). This focus on axiality implies a 'backtracking' itinerary, meaning the bathers had to retrace their steps to exit the baths once they had arrived in the *caldarium*. A 'circular' itinerary, where a shortcut linked the *caldarium* to the cold section (IV on Fig. 7), seems rather exceptional in the research area. Ouderburg 'Vicus Bath', located within a military context near the *castellum*, is the only example for which such an itinerary may be imagined. Unfortunately, for most baths the walls were razed down to the foundation level, making it difficult to reconstruct the location of the doorways between the different rooms.

Two baths belong to alleged relays or road stations. The baths of Outrelouxhe only consisted of a single heated room with a heated pool, added in a later stage to a large hall-type building. The direct access from the Roman road has prompted the excavators to label the compound as a road relay (Witvrouw and Witvrouw 1998, 95). At Wyompont, a building had two rooms with a hypocaust forming the entire western wing. The southernmost room had a rectangular *exedra* which probably housed an *alveus*. The two successive rooms lay on the same axis. The location of several buildings near the crossing of the Roman road over the river Ourthe, could identify the structures as part of a road station (Brulet 2008, 492). Just outside the research area, in the Belgian province of Luxembourg, a building at Anlier, along the *Orolaunum–Atuatuca* road, with a wide entrance leading into an inner courtyard was interpreted as part of a road station (Corbiau 1982). Several rooms, one of which was heated, lay around the court, including also a small bath suite (Corbiau 1983). The simple layout is comparable to the examples in the research area. A small *caldarium* possibly had an *alveus* above the furnace. However, at Anlier, this

heated room was preceded by a *frigidarium* with a small *piscina* (Fig. 9).

With some other bathhouses, it is uncertain whether they were public or private. The type of plans, however, do not change the picture sketched above. No imperial-type baths can be identified, and the block and row type are most common. The block type is represented by the baths at Amay-Ombret, Maastricht, Namur, and Tourinnes-St-Lambert. The row type can be identified for the baths in Autre-Église (phase 1), Chastrès, Soignies, and Waudrez. The remains of the baths in Tournai-Quai Luchet d'Antoing and Quai Vifquin, or Braives, are too limited to make any identification of the type of plan.

Military Baths

The bath of the *castellum* of Oudenburg was the only bath building to be found *intra muros*. Even if the plan is only partially clear due to intensive robbing and recent disturbance of the site, it is obvious that the rooms are arranged on a single axial row. The bath of the fort of Furfooz was located *extra muros*, some 50 m north of the wall, and consisted of only two rooms, making a linear configuration inevitable. The small building north-east of the *castellum* of Liberchies has also been interpreted as a bathhouse. The three rooms, each with an *exedra* on the south side, lay on the same axis. In contrast to the baths at Furfooz and Liberchies, the baths outside of the camps of Oudenburg, the so-called Vicus Bath, and Aardenburg (Gasfabriek site) probably also served civilian communities that formed around the camps. They can therefore also be drawn into the discussion of public baths. The Aardenburg bath, severely disturbed by modern activities, possibly had an axial linear plan,

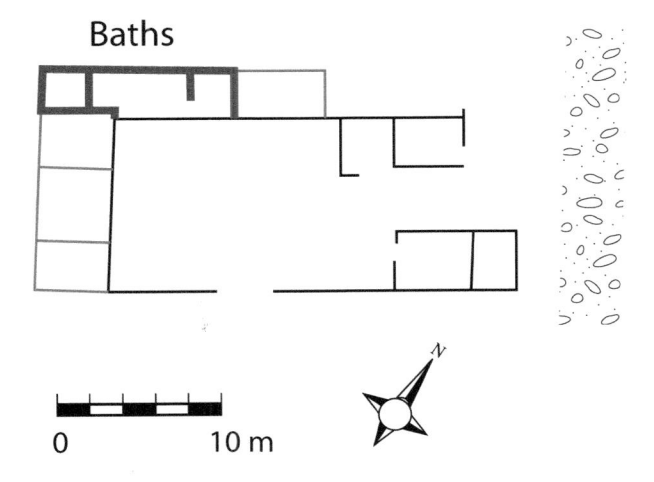
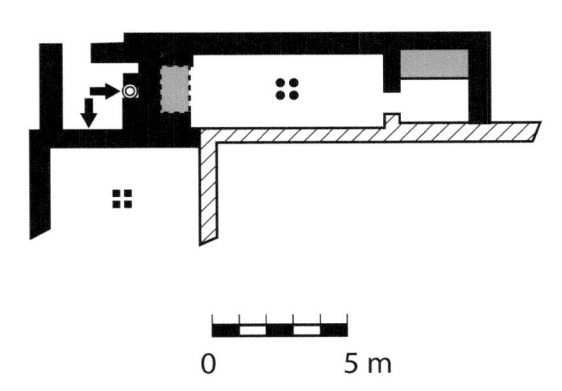

Figure 9. Plan of the road station at Anlier (Belgium) with detail of the bathhouse (right). Figure by author after Corbiau 1997, 305, unnumbered fig.

while the Oudenburg 'Vicus Bath', also badly preserved, seems to have had a block plan (perhaps with circular itinerary?).

Private Baths

The vast majority of private baths have a block-type plan: fifty-five out of 126 baths (or 44 per cent). Thirty-nine baths were of the row type (31 per cent), but ten of these only consisted of two consecutive rooms, making a plan on a linear axis more or less inevitable. At least three private baths also consisted of a single room (Attenhoven, Heestert, Vissoul). A ring-type plan is only possible at a single site: the second and third phase of the baths of Bruyelle may have belonged to that type, although the plan is far from clear due to the lack of identifiable doorways. For twenty-eight private baths (22 per cent), the excavated remains were too poorly preserved to make any conclusions about the type of plan. As mentioned above, some baths are difficult to identify as private or public. Of these twenty-one baths, five had a block-type plan, six a row type (one of which only consisting of two rooms), and of ten too little is known to make any conclusions. There is no real distinction between villa or *domus* baths. The baths in the central places of Amay-Ombret, Maastricht, Namur, and Tournai – Vieux Marché aux Jambons seem to have been of the block type, while the remains of other baths in Tongeren, Tournai, and Waudrez were too badly preserved to make any conclusions.

Recurring Plans

As has often been remarked for Roman baths, and for private baths in particular, there are a wide variety of plans (DeLaine 1988, 17; de Haan 2007, 37), even if there is a more or less 'standard set' of rooms that is present in almost all baths. The cold, tepid, and hot room (*frigidarium-tepidarium-caldarium*) forms the spine of basically every Roman bath. Although we can group the plans in broad categories on the basis of the succession of the main rooms (e.g. block type, row type, etc.), the specific articulation of the rooms (position of doorways) and the location of constituent elements (pools, *exedrae*, *labra*, etc.) vary from bath to bath, making clear that there was not one standard blueprint underlying each Roman bath. The majority of baths in the Roman empire were rather small and modestly decorated with plans that were dictated by the available building plot and the individual wishes of the commissioner (DeLaine 1992, 267–74; 1999b, 160; de Haan 2007, 45). Furthermore, the long lifespan of some baths could result in important alterations of the original plan. Identifying the different alterations can be difficult, especially with early excavations that did not pay

attention to the phasing of the building. Keeping these important caveats in mind, we do find some recurring plans in the dataset of the research area.

A first recurring plan is the succession of a rectangular *frigidarium*, *tepidarium*, and *caldarium* on a single linear axis, with two opposite semicircular *exedrae* protruding out of the *caldarium*. This plan can be recognized in the small public bath of Tienen (first century AD) and 'Bath 1' at Haccourt (late first century AD). A similar plan can possibly be reconstructed for phase 1 of the (public?) bath at Autre-Église (second century?), but unfortunately the southern part of the *caldarium* was destroyed by modern construction activity. A second semicircular *exedra* opposite the northern *exedra* would have given the *caldarium* a symmetrical design. All three sites were located within the *civitas Tungrorum* and date from the early Roman period. The villa at Haccourt lies some 50 km east of the *vicus* of Tienen as the crow flies. Ramillies lies some 20 km to its south. Besides the plan, there are no other elements, such as tile stamps, that connect these baths.

A second recurring plan also consists of the main rooms on a linear axis, but has two *exedrae* protruding out of the main building block on one of the long sides, one from the *frigidarium* and one from the *caldarium*, and one rectangular *exedra* protruding on a short side (*caldarium*). The *exedrae* are mainly rectangular, although semicircular shapes do occur. The advantage of having all the *exedrae* (for pools and *labri*) on the same side, is an easier water supply and disposal, as well as a better internal flow of the bathers (one side of the room for bathing, the other as passage between rooms). Such a plan also makes perfect sense when attached to an existing side of a house, forcing the *exedrae* on the 'free' sides of the bathing block. This plan can be recognized for the freestanding bath of Chastrès (second century?) and Soignies (middle of the second century), the fort bath of Furfooz (fourth century?), and the integrated or attached villa baths of Flostoy (second century?), Hoogeloon (second half of the second century?), Haillot (undated), Vechmaal (third century), and possibly Wange (second century). Some plans only slightly differ by adding an extra *exedra* on the long sides, e.g. in Gemechenne (second century?), Hamois (late second century), or Leignon (undated), by adding an *exedra* on the other long side (yet not obstructing the flow as it is located in the last room), e.g. in the public baths of Grobbendonk (early second century), or simply by contracting the plan to a block type, e.g. Miécret 'Bath 1' (undated). The plan seems to be in use from the early second century onwards, until the fourth century, and spread throughout the centre of the research area. As many baths remain undated, it is difficult to find contemporary clusters.[1] Most examples are located in the *civitas Tungrorum*, but at least one bath (Soignies) lies in the *civitas Nerviorum*. There are no other elements that connect these baths, such as the use of tiles from the same workshop. Tiles with the stamp HAMSIT were only found in the bath of Leignon.

On the one hand, the similarities in plan could point to the popularity or success of a basic design: a linear succession of the main bath rooms, necessitating only a single furnace. Such basic plans also remained in use over a long period of time. On the other hand, similar plans could point to a communal model, perhaps even designed by the same architect or constructed by the same specialized team. From Aulus Gellius, a second-century author writing in Rome, we know that *fabri aedium* ('builders') could present several plans of baths, drawn on parchment, to the commissioners (Gell. *NA* XIX.10.1–3). For a region with a limited number of cities or civic centres, and a high demand for a very specialized type of building such as a bath, it is not unthinkable that some of the contemporary villa owners living in the same area consulted the same architects/contractors. In the absence of written sources, such as personal letters or receipts, this hypothesis will remain difficult to prove.[2] The occurrence of the same tile stamps could at least point to the same supplier of building material, but the evidence for the sites above is unfortunately inconclusive. The similarity between the plans of the villa bath at Haccourt ('Bath 1') and the public bath at Tienen also demonstrate that the same models could be used for both public and private facilities. As precise construction dates cannot be identified, we cannot verify if the villa baths copied a public design, or perhaps even vice versa. For the type of plan found at Chastrès, Furfooz, and other sites, there is as yet no 'public' counterpart found in one of the nearby civic centres, with the exception of the slightly altered plan of Grobbendonk.

Size of the Baths

Almost half of all excavated remains of baths have only been partially uncovered, making it difficult to assess the entire surface of the bathhouses. Especially when only (part of) a pool or a hypocaust was found during

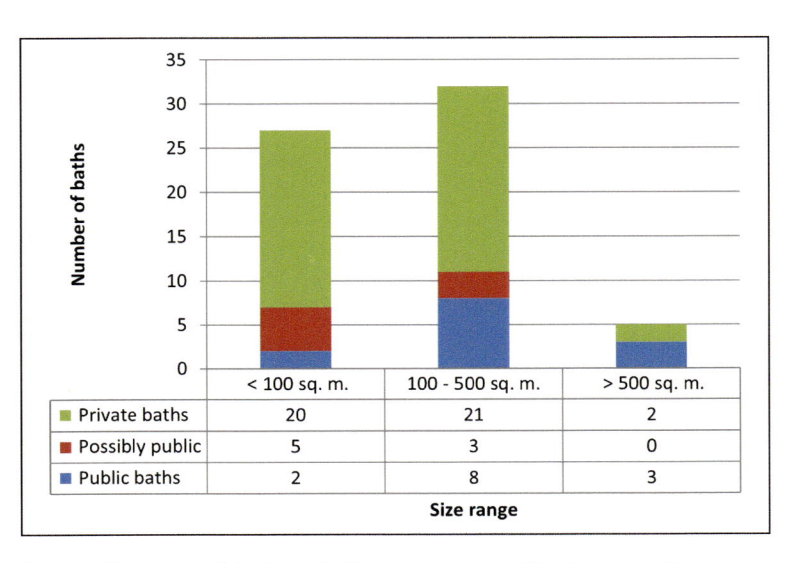

Graph 1. Size range of the baths in the research area with a known surface.

	< 100 sq. m.	100 - 500 sq. m.	> 500 sq. m.
Private baths	20	21	2
Possibly public	5	3	0
Public baths	2	8	3

rescue excavations, we have no idea of the total extent. The baths that were entirely excavated widely differ in surface, with private baths as small as 12 m² (Heestert) or public baths as large as 2600 m² (Famars).[3] There is obviously a difference in size between private and public baths, but also within these categories there are important variations.

Due to the absence of imperial-type baths, often covering several thousand square metres, the share of public baths surpassing 1000 m² is rather limited (Graph 1). Only the public baths in Famars (2600 m²) and Fontaine-Valmont (1500 m²) can be named. The majority of the public baths in central places have a total surface between 100 and 500 m², with several buildings covering around 200 m². The baths of which it is uncertain whether they were public or not have a surface area of around 100 m², although the buildings in Amay-Ombret, Charleroi, Maastricht, Namur, and Ramillies/Autre-Église (phase 2) certainly exceeded this size. If we look at the fort baths, we find both small and somewhat larger examples: the *extra-muros* bath of Furfooz only covers some 75 m², while the Castellum Bath of Oudenburg surpasses 100 m² and the *extra-muros* bath of Liberchies even 200 m². The number of possible users probably dictated the size. The bath suites connected to the possible relay and road stations are also rather limited in size, with the bath at Outrelouxhe covering only 34 m² and the possible bath of Wyompont only attaining 90 m².

For the private baths, we can make a distinction between the baths of urban *domus* and villa baths. None of the possible *domus* baths in Bavay, Namur, Tongeren,

---

1 Wange and Vechmaal only lie some 25 km apart, but the contemporaneity of both sites cannot be ascertained. The same is true for the clusters Haillot, Flostoy, and Miécret and Gemechenne, Leignon, and Furfooz, both within a radius of 7 km of each other.

2 As a general remark, Roman architects remain mostly anonymous, as they are only rarely mentioned in texts or inscriptions. Only some thirty Roman architects are known by name for the entire empire and the entire Roman period (Höcker 2006).

3 For the calculation of the size of each separate bathhouse, all rooms including service rooms, were taken into account.

or Tournai were entirely excavated. The interpretation as private bath of a house as well as an evaluation of the total size is therefore problematic. The only reliable data thus comes from the villa baths. These only rarely exceed 500 m². Only the luxurious third bathhouse at Haccourt (phase 2: 658.5 m²; phase 3: 665 m²) is a case in point. However, several villa baths easily attain a size of 300 m² (e.g. Anthée Bath 3, Basse-Wavre, Emptinne-Champion, Lemiers), thus exceeding the size of some public baths (e.g. Grobbendonk, Macquenoise, Oudenburg – *vicus*, or Tienen). The group of villa baths with a surface between 100 and 500 m² even surpasses the baths with a surface below 100 m² (Graph 1). For the latter group, the smallest baths only cover a surface of *c.* 10 m² (Ambresin, Tiegem?) or 20 m² (Mabeuge, Miécret Bath 1). These baths consisted of one or two rooms integrated in the house. But some of the freestanding baths also had only a limited size, between 10 and 40 m² (e.g. Anderlecht, Bierbeek, Gooik, Heestert, Vissoul).

It might be interesting to compare the size of the private baths to the entire surface of a house or villa, in order to examine the portion of the house allotted to bathing. This could point to the importance of the bath as a functional unit within the house and to the importance of the bathing culture for the owner. However, such a comparison is problematic for several reasons. First of all, not all private baths were integrated in the house. Some were attached or even completely freestanding, enabling the construction of much larger baths because there was no predefined space in which the baths had to be inserted.[4] Secondly, to make such a comparison, we need reliable data on the size of both the bathhouse and the villa. Unfortunately, the majority of the sites have only been partially excavated, with only eighteen sites in the dataset providing us with sizes of both villa and bath. The sample size is thus rather limited. Thirdly, the results of the excavations present us with a palimpsest, i.e. all different phases of the building combined into one plan. It is not always clear to which phase the baths belonged and which other parts of the house/villa were in use at the same time.[5] The presence of a second floor, which is not always clear, would also alter the total surface of the house, and thus the share of the bath in relation to the total living space. A final remark concerns the articulation of bath and other rooms, as it is not always clear which rooms belonged

to the baths and which not. For a villa of only some hundred square metres, two or three additional rooms can make a difference if a bath was actually 10 or 20 per cent of the entire surface. The table below thus only presents us with a cautious indication of the share of the baths in their final stage in relation to the ground floor at its maximum extension (Table 4).

There are two groups to be discerned: the baths that make out around 5–6 per cent of the total surface and baths that cover between 10–15 per cent. The first group has a median of 6 per cent with a low of 6 per cent and a high of 7 per cent. The second group has a median of 13 per cent with a low of 9 per cent and a high of 18 per cent. The baths of the 6 per cent group are found in villas of the hall-type (Flostoy, Mabeuge, Vesqueville, Vodelée) as well as in larger row-type villas (Ambresin, Matagne-la-Petite). The baths of the 13 per cent group are also found in both modest hall-type villas (Graux, Haillot, Hamois, Hoogeloon, Mont-lez-Houffalize, Oberüttfeld, Roly, Treignes) and larger row-type villas (Jemelle, Maillen-Ronchine, Merbes-le-Château, Saint-Gérard). It is striking that some smaller villas such as Haillot (*c.* 390 m²) or Graux (*c.* 550 m²) had a proportionally large bath suite (15 per cent and 18 per cent, respectively), while larger villas such as Matagne-la-Petite (1300 m²) could have a proportionally small bath (7 per cent). Even if we should be very cautious with these percentages, it at least shows us that the private baths could make up between 5 to perhaps 20 per cent of the ground floor. A similar study of twenty-one villa baths in *Germania Inferior* (excluding the *civitas Tungrorum*) by Michael Dodt also showed a similar range between 4 and 21 per cent (Dodt 2003, 126–27). The fact that most baths were enlarged, most strikingly at Emptinne-Champion, Gesves, or Haccourt 'Bath 3', or that internal baths were later supplemented by a larger attached or freestanding bathhouse, such as at Merbes-le-Château or Miécret, points to the fact that sometimes baths could be deemed too small or inadequate for the villa. Conversely, baths could also be reduced in size, perhaps when the costs of restorations or maintenance became too burdensome, or if the villa diminished in size. Examples in the research area are lacking, but the practice is known from other parts of the Empire (see Scholz 2018 for *Germania Inferior*).

As a general conclusion regarding the size of baths, we can remark that the only public baths discovered so far are rather small, especially since no large public *thermae* have been identified in the larger cities such as *Atuatuca*, *Bagacum*, *Castellum Menapiorum*, or *Turnacum*. The type of small public baths in minor central places, such as Tienen, Grobbendonk, or Macquenoise, covering between 100 and 500 m², can also be found in other regions of the Roman Empire (Staccioli 1958; Yegül 1979). Fort baths could have a similar size, or

---

4   The reasons for opting for an integrated, detached, or freestanding private bath will be examined in Chapter 7.

5   A case in point is the villa of Merbes-le-Chateau: 'Bath 1' belonged to the second phase of the villa, which covered around 790 m² (bath = 10 per cent). The entire villa as it was excavated, excluding the attached bath, was 1620 m², meaning the bath became proportionally half as small (5 per cent).

Table 4. Comparison of villa size and bath size.

Site	Name	*Civitas*	Villa in m²	Bath in m²	Percentage
Ambresin	Villa d'Ambresin	CT	200	11	6%
Flostoy	Villa de Lizée	CT	960	55	6%
Graux	Villa romaine de Graux	CT	550	100	18%
Haillot	Villa de Matagne	CT	390	60	15%
Hamois	Villa de Hody	CT	840	77	9%
Hoogeloon	Kerkakkers	CT	900	120	13%
Jemelle	Villa de Malagne	CT	2053	250	12%
Mabeuge	Villa au Bois Brûlé	CN	360	20	6%
Maillen	Villa de Ronchinne	CT	1572	200	12%
Matagne-la-Petite	Villa Aux Murets	CT	1300	90	7%
Merbes-le-Château	Villa de Champ St-Eloi — Bath 1	CN	790	80	10%
Mont-lez-Houffalize	Villa de Fin de Ville — Bath 2	CT	552	90	16%
Oberüttfeld	Villa	CT	417	60	14%
Philippeville (Roly)	Villa de la Crayellerie	CT	432	65	15%
Saint-Gérard	Villa du Try-Hallot	CT	1700	225	13%
Treignes	Villa des Bruyères	CT	1123	100	9%
Vesqueville	Corps de logis de Vesqueville	CT	496	32	6%
Vodelée	Villa romaine de Vodelée	CT	782	50	6%

were very small. The baths of relays and road stations seem to have been very small, basic facilities. For all these public facilities, the main factor for determining the size may well have been the potential number of bathers that could make use of the facility. For private baths in urban contexts, the dataset is too limited to draw any conclusions. The difference in size between villa baths is important. Unsurprisingly, the largest baths belonged to the largest and most luxurious villas. The financial power of the villa owner could play an important role here. In comparison to the total surface of the villa, integrated baths could make up 5 to 20 per cent of the ground floor.

Rooms of the Baths

Palaestra

Open-air exercise courts or *palaestrae*, often with a large open-air swimming pool or *natatio*, are predominantly found in public baths, as their main target group was the (male) youth (Nielsen 1993a, 57–58, 163–64). The small number of public baths found in the research area and the fragmentary remains of alleged baths in the larger cities such as *Atuatuca* or *Bagacum*, have yielded very few examples of such *palaestrae*. This is true for greater Gaul, especially in the northern part with its cold and wet climatic conditions (Bouet 2003a, 710). The most convincing evidence in the research area comes from the bath of Fontaine-Valmont. The large open space north of the bath rooms, incorporating also two large *natationes*, can certainly be interpreted as an exercise court. The presence of two such pools remains unexplained. These are also the only examples of *natationes* found in the research area at the time of writing. Another possible *palaestra* might be recognized in the bath of Clavier-Vervoz. The area south of the bath rooms was certainly an open space, but no traces of a portico or *natatio* have been identified. The relation to the rooms to the west is also unclear. A third possible example, albeit even more problematic, is the bathhouse near the fort of Aardenburg. The area north-west of the bath rooms was very badly damaged, and the reconstruction of a rectangular space here remains speculative (van Dierendonck and Vos 2013, 105). We could imagine that the larger bathhouses in *Bagacum* or *Atuatuca*, perhaps at the Schaetzengaerde site, may have had a *palaestra*, much like the modestly sized city baths in neighbouring regions such as the baths of *Coriovallum* (Heerlen, most recently Jeneson and Vos 2020). The smaller public baths of secondary centres, such as at Grobbendonk, Macquenoise, or Tienen did not have an exercise yard. The original layout of the baths in Famars might have included a *palaestra* east or south of the bath rooms (Beaussart 1980, 821; Bouet 2003a, 676), but the later reorganization and the fragmentary documentation of the excavations do not allow a definite interpretation.

We cannot rule out that some exercises or sports also preceded bathing on villa estates. There is some indirect evidence from the Mediterranean, such as the well-known mosaics of the bath in the villa of Piazza Armerina in Sicily depicting women competing in all sorts of sports (Wilson 1983, 41). However, sports were a popular theme in bath decoration (Manderscheid 1994, 65) and it was not necessarily implied that these were actually performed on site. The archaeological evidence does not reveal enclosed courtyards attached to villa baths. At the villa bath of Emptinne-Champion, an open space west of the bath rooms, which was enlarged in the second phase, fits the description. There is no conclusive evidence to identify this area as an exercise court, nor to dismiss it as one. In 'Bath 3' at Haccourt, an area outside the bathhouse proper, between the western *calida piscina* and the *piscina* received a mortar floor in the second phase of the bath (De Boe 1976, 20), perhaps serving as an exercise area.

Apodyteria

Changing rooms are not always easily discernible as they have few fixed features (Nielsen 1993a, 153; Weber 1996, 55). Furniture such as benches and cupboards for storing clothes was mainly in wood. It is often a room's position at the start of the bathing itinerary, and hence often in connection to the *frigidarium*, that has been used to identify dressing rooms. We can reasonably assume that bathers undressed in the first room of the bath upon entering. Hence the room preceding the *frigidarium* has been labelled *apodyterium* in for example the public bath of Clavier-Vervoz or Grobbendonk, and in the villa baths of Broekhem, Emptinne-Champion (phase 1), Clermont-sous-Huy, Gemechenne, Jemelle, or Modave. Other activities such as massages, anointing, or epilation may also have been performed in these rooms, combining several non-bathing activities which would have been allocated to specific rooms, sometimes called *unctorium*, *elaeothesium*, or *aleipterion*, in larger baths (Yegül 1992, 38–39; Nielsen 1993a, 161, 165). In some small baths, even a separate dressing room can be absent. In this case, the *frigidarium* must have functioned as such. In the research area, several such examples have come to light, in public baths, e.g. in Tienen and possibly Aardenburg, in military baths, e.g. in Furfooz, Liberchies, and possibly Oudenburg, and in private baths, e.g. in Chastrès, Flostoy, Haccourt 'Bath 1', Haillot, Maillen – Arches, Miécret Bath 1, Milmort, Oberüttfeld, Soignies, Vechmaal, and possibly Tongeren – Vrijthof and Waha. Several baths also have a heated room at the beginning of the bathing itinerary, often near or connected to the *frigidarium*, where one would

expect an *apodyterium*. Such rooms, often heated by their own furnace, have sometimes been interpreted as heated *apodyteria*, or winter *apodyteria* (Nielsen 1993a, 79). The cold climate in the northern provinces may have necessitated a heated dressing room during the cold seasons, especially if other non-bathing activities such as massages and anointing also took place there.

When the baths are integrated in a villa, it is sometimes difficult to confirm if such, often large, heated rooms were actually part of the bathhouse, or if these rooms should rather be interpreted as heated living or dining rooms (Koethe 1940, 112–13), conveniently located near the baths to make use of the same *praefurnium* or at least the firewood storage. Such a problematic location can be seen in the villas of Aiseau (integrated bath), Grumelange, Hoogeloon, Mont-lez-Houffalize – Fin de Ville, Saint-Jean-Geest, or Thirimont. When the baths form a separate entity to the villa, the inclusion of such a heated room at the start of the bathing itinerary seems less problematic. However, the fact that most of these rooms are heated by their own furnace, has prompted some researchers to interpret them as stand-alone *sudatoria*, enabling a short sweat session without going through the entire bathing itinerary (Nielsen 1993a, 78). Such *sudatoria* would be reminiscent of the solitary round sweat rooms (*laconica*) found in some (early) villas, e.g. in the villa of Ambresin (undated), in the villa of Rognée (undated), or in the last villa of Haccourt (first half of the second century). These, in turn, may have been inspired by round sweat rooms sometimes encountered in early military baths (Black 1994, 104). The connection to the *frigidarium* is also consistent with the location of *laconica*/*sudatoria* in early public baths, as exemplified in the Stabian Baths and the Forum Baths in Pompeii, and the Central Baths in Herculaneum, but also closer to the research area in *Germania Inferior*, e.g. Heerlen (Fig. 10), Rottweil, the Castellum Baths in Saalburg, the Castellum Baths in Stockstadt, or the City Baths in Xanten, and in *Britannia*, e.g. the Castellum Baths in Collen or the Early City Baths in Wroxeter (plans in Nielsen 1993b, 134–47). The round room of the Vicus Bath in Oudenburg could probably also be interpreted as a *laconicum*. However, most of the examples in the research area are quite large in comparison to the other heated rooms (*tepidarium*, *caldarium*) and are often not equipped with wall heating, pointing to rather tepid room temperatures. In examples such as Autre-Église, Boirs, Boussu-lez-Walcourt, Bruyelle, Emptinne-Champion (phase 2–3), Miécret Bath 2, or Saint-Jean-Geest these rooms were probably multifunctional heated *apodyteria*. Only in the cases of Basse-Wavre and Treignes is this room quite small and hence better suited to act as sweat room.

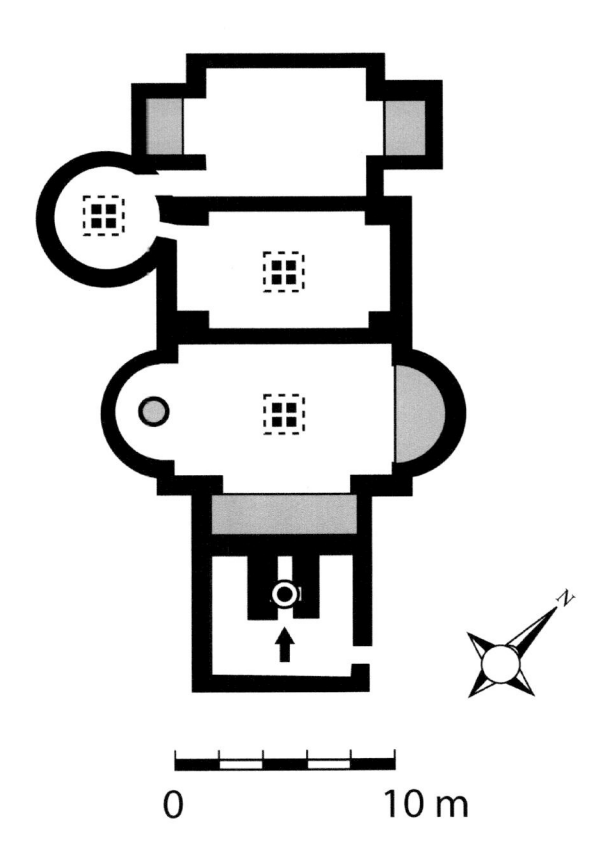

0   10 m

Figure 10. Plan of the public bath in *Coriovallum* (Heerlen), first phase (AD 65–73). Figure by author after Jeneson and Vos 2020, 80, fig. 4.25.

Frigidaria

The cold rooms in public baths all seem to be rectangular in shape, with only one cold pool (*piscina*), often located in a recess on one of the lateral sides. However, we can imagine that the cold rooms of larger public baths in for example Tongeren or Bavay may have had two *piscinae*, as was the case just outside the research area in the baths of Heerlen or Zülpich. The smallest *frigidarium* measures *c.* 8 m² (Macquenoise) while the largest measures 110 m² (Famars).[6] The median of the known surfaces (N = 8) is 13.6 m² (or 16 m² if we include the possible public bath in Maastricht, see Table 10 in the Appendix). The *piscinae* are mainly rectangular in shape. The large *piscina* of the 'Vicus Bath' of Liberchies was almost square in shape. In the bath of Clavier-Vervoz the *piscina* has a trapezoidal shape with rounded sides. In the bath of Maastricht, which may have been public, a semicircular *piscina* was constructed in one

of the later phases. The original *frigidarium* has not been identified. In Tongeren, part of a large *piscina* (or perhaps *natatio*?) was found on the Schaetzengaerde site. In Tournai, parts of *piscinae* were discovered on the Quai Vifquin and the Quai Luchet d'Antoing, but neither could be investigated entirely. These pools probably belonged to public baths. The bad state of preservation of the public baths in Fontaine-Valmont and Oudenburg have impeded the identification of the *frigidarium*. In Tienen, the *frigidarium* was identified by its location at the start of the bathing rooms and by a drainage channel running from the centre of the room and joining the drainage channel of the heated pools outside the north-east corner of the bath. A *piscina* was hypothetically reconstructed in the north-east corner of the room, in analogy with the very similar 'Bath 1' of the villa of Haccourt (Vanderhoeven, Vynckier, and Wouters 1998, 143–44). The small 'Vicus Bath' of Tourinnes-St-Lambert does not seem to have had a cold room. The size of the *piscinae* in public baths varies between 3.92 m² (Macquenoise) and 26 m² (Liberchies), while the median is 9 m² (N = 7; see Table 11 in the Appendix).[7] If we count around 1 m² per person to ensure a comfortable physical distance, this subsequently gives an idea about how many people could actually bathe at the same time. In a military context, we only have the bath of Furfooz and the presumed bath of Liberchies as examples. The *frigidarium* of the Furfooz bath is quite small in comparison to the heated room. The *frigidarium* in Liberchies was about the same size as the *tepidarium* and *caldarium*. Both *frigidaria* also had a semicircular pool in an *exedra* for one (Liberchies) or two persons (Furfooz) to bathe at the same time. The cold section of the 'Castellum Bath' at Oudenburg was unfortunately too damaged to identify the *piscina* (Vanhoutte 2018, 167).

Just as for the cold rooms of public baths, the *frigidaria* of private baths are all rectangular in shape. At the time of writing, no round or hexagonal cold rooms have been identified with certainty, in contrast to examples found in the Mediterranean (Brödner 1983, 245–46; Gros 1996, 401–02). The surface of the *frigidaria* could be as small as 1.7 m² (Miécret Bath 1) or as large as 128.5 m² (Lemiers). The median (N = 52) is 9 m² (see Table 10).[8] The *piscinae*, however, are sometimes semicircular in shape, or have an apsidal end, e.g. in Aiseau ('integrated baths'), Basse-Wavre, Boirs, Bovigny, Broekhem, Emptinne-Champion (phase 1),

---

6 For the sake of uniformity, all surfaces of the rooms include the pools, as it is sometimes unclear whether an *exedra* housed a pool or not.

7 The median is 5.46 m², if we add the 'baths of unknown access' (N = 14).

8 If we take into account the 'baths of unknown access' (N = 56), the median is 8.62 m². If we omit the 'possible' *frigidaria* (* in Table 10) and the *frigidaria* of which the dimensions are uncertain (with '?' in Table 10) (N = 35), the median is 10.35 m².

Grumelange, Landen 'Betzveld', Latinne, Liège, Milmort, Tongeren 'Schaetzengaerde', Vellereille, Vodelée, and Wancennes. A small pool, perhaps belonging to the bathhouse of a villa in Aubechies, did have an hexagonal shape, although it cannot be excluded that the basin was actually a fountain (Demarez and Henton 1995, 113). The majority of *piscinae* were, however, rectangular, with some examples tending towards a square shape, e.g. in Arquennes, Emptinne-Champion (phase 3), Flostoy, Haillot, Leignon, Modave, and Mont-lez-Houffalize – Fin de Ville (freestanding and internal baths). Octagonal *piscinae*, as for example in *Britannia*, have not been found, possibly because these were mainly an architectural development of the late third and fourth century (Walters 1996). The internal steps are not always preserved. In the few surviving examples, we can see that they ran along the entire side of the pool, e.g. in Clermont-sous-Huy, Jemelle, Maillen – Arches, Marchienne-au-Pont or Vodelée, or that they were confined to one of the corners, e.g. in Arquennes, Bruyelle, Emptinne-Champion (phase 1 and 3), Évelette – Résimont, Flostoy, Gesves (phase 1), Grumelange, Maillen – Al Sauvenière, Treignes, and Vechmaal. In Évelette and Vechmaal, the steps formed a quarter of a circle. Only in the large semicircular *piscina* of Basse-Wavre, there were steps in both corners. If wide enough, the steps could also be used as benches for sitting in the pool (Nielsen 1993a, 154). In Marchienne-au-Pont, a bench ran along the entire eastern side of the pool. The surface of the *piscinae* varies between 0.88 m² (Grumelange) and 40 m² (Haccourt Bath 3).[9] The median surface is 3.7 m² (N = 55; see Table 11).[10] The average depth is difficult to reconstruct, as few pools have been preserved to a sufficient height. A depth of around 0.60 to 0.70 m is fairly common in the few known examples (e.g. Chastrès, Tournai – Vieux Marché aux Jambons, Tournai – Quai Luchet d'Antoing, Aiseau 'Bath 1', Graux, Oberüttfeld, Vechmaal), although depths up to 1.3 m have also been recorded (e.g. Emptinne-Champion (phase 3), Haccourt 'Bath 3'). The shallow *piscinae* were probably used for quick submersions and for pouring water over oneself whilst standing knee-deep (presuming the pools were not filled to the brim), while the deeper (and unsurprisingly larger) pools enabled bathers to swim. The *frigidaria* are also often smaller

than most of the heated rooms (compare the *frigidaria* and *tepidaria-caldaria-sudatoria* in Table 10). In some baths, a cold room is absent all together, as is the case in Anderlecht, Attenhoven, Bierbeek, Heestert, Vissoul, and possibly Évelette – Clavia (see Chapter 7).

Tepidaria

The tepid rooms are often identified by their location, located between the *frigidarium* and *caldarium*. Furthermore, the *tepidaria* were often indirectly heated by connection with the hypocaust of the *caldarium*, rather than by their own furnace. Often, there was no wall heating either. A third characteristic is the frequent absence of pools (Brödner 1983, 100). In the public baths in the research area, some of the *tepidaria*, all rectangular in plan, could be quite large in comparison to the *caldaria*, such as at Aardenburg, Famars, and the possibly public bath of Maastricht (compare the *tepidaria* and *caldaria* in Table 10). The surface varies between 7 m² (Macquenoise) and 212 m² (Famars). The median is 24 m² (see Table 10).[11] In Famars, the large room in the centre of the building, the only one not heated by its own furnace, was about the same size as the *caldarium* and *sudatoria* combined (Beaussart 1980, 808). The large size of these tepid rooms can be explained by their multifunctional use: this is where people met up and relaxed (as Lucian, *Hippias*, 6 informs us), acclimatizing to the heat, getting a massage, or anointing with oil. Also in the presumed bath of the road station at Wyompont, the large room that was heated by one furnace, possibly combined the function of *tepidarium* and *apodyterium*. In the *vicus* of Tourinnes-St-Lambert, the small bath seems to have had a large *caldarium* and small *tepidarium*. When the *tepidarium* did not have a hypocaust, and was thus only heated through a large doorway by the heat in the *caldarium*, the room becomes difficult to identify, certainly in a block plan. For the public baths in Clavier-Vervoz, Fontaine-Valmont, and Oudenburg, the *tepidarium* cannot be identified among the different bath rooms. Some smaller public baths do not seem to have had a *tepidarium*. If we look at the plans of Grobbendonk, Macquenoise, or Outrelouxhe, we can only identify a large *caldarium*. Possibly, this *caldarium* combined the function of *caldarium* and *tepidarium*. Furthermore, a partition wall that was not visible in the hypocaust may once have delimited a *tepidarium*, as has been found in Tongeren-Sint-Truiderstraat (Huybrigts 1904, 313) and could have been the case in Modave and Flostoy,

---

9   The interpretation of this *piscina* is contested, however. The *piscina* of Mettet Bath 2 is also contested. The *piscina* at Marchienne-au-Pont is 14.4 m², but it is unknown whether this bath belonged to a villa or was a small public bath. The *piscina* of Basse-Wavre is 14.13 m² and is definitely part of a private bathhouse.

10 If we include the 'baths of unknown access' (N = 62), the median is 3.65 m². If we omit 'contested' *piscinae* and *piscinae* of which the dimensions are uncertain (N = 46), the median is 3.8 m².

11 Including the 'baths of unknown access' the median is 24 m². If we omit the 'possible' *tepidaria* and the *tepidaria* of which the dimensions are uncertain, the median is 23.2 m².

where a reinforcement of a lateral row of hypocaust pillars probably served to support a partitioning wall at floor level. Examples of such walls, made of *tubuli*, have been found in Pölich (Germany) (Koethe 1940, 111). A different solution can be found in the road relay of Outrelouxhe, where only half of the heated room had a hypocaust floor. The unheated, larger western part of the room could hence act as *tepidarium/apodyterium*. The fort bath of Furfooz did not have a separate *tepidarium*. In Liberchies, the *tepidarium* in the alleged fort bath was about the same size as the *frigidarium* and the *caldarium*. It had a rectangular *exedra*, which did not house a pool, in contrast to the *exedrae* of the cold and hot room (Mertens and Brulet 1974, 36–40). The *tepidarium* of the 'Castellum Bath' in Oudenburg was quite large. It had no pools and did not have a furnace heating its hypocaust.

The tepid rooms in private baths are also almost exclusively rectangular in plan, although some examples have one apsidal ending, e.g. in Boirs and the presumed *tepidaria* in Heure-le-Romain, Vellereille, and Saint-Jean-Geest. When several rooms have a hypocaust, it is not always easy to identify the *tepidarium*, e.g. in Bruyelle (phase 2 and 3), Kumtich, Saint-Gérard, Neerharen-Rekem, or Val-Meer. If the only heated room besides the *caldarium* does have a separate furnace, it could be a *sudatorium* rather than a *tepidarium*, e.g. in Anthée 'Bath 3', Clermont-sous-Huy, or Graux. The large size at Clermont-sous-Huy, however, might still point to a *tepidarium*. As in public baths, the absence of a hypocaust in the *tepidarium* complicates their identification. In Latinne, Maillen-Ronchinne, Marchienne-au-Pont, Merbes-le-Château ('Bath 2', phase 2), and Meslin-l'Évêque, it is unclear which room functioned as *tepidarium*. A lot of private baths do not seem to have had a separate tepid room, e.g. Anderlecht, Attenhoven, Broekhem, Emptinne-Champion (phase 1 and 3), Chastrès, Évelette – Clavia, Grumelange, Haillot, Hamois, Heestert, Mabeuge, Maillen – Arches, Mont-lez-Houfallize (freestanding bath), Milmort, Miécret (both Bath 1 and Bath 2), Mettet 'Bath 2', Oberüttfeld, Roly, Soignies, or Tongeren – Vrijthof. Some *caldaria* might actually have been split up by a wall on the walking level of the room, as has been suggested for some of the public baths above. Such partition might well have been the case in Bruyelle (phase 1), Flostoy, Hoogeloon, Matagne-la-Petite, Modave, Treignes, Vodelée, or Waha. In Leignon, the southern *exedra* of the *caldarium* might in fact have been use as *tepidarium*. In Jemelle, the *tepidarium* seems to have preceded the *sudatorium* (with probably a *schola labri*) rather than the *caldarium*. In the second phase of baths of Emptinne-Champion, the large heated pool (*calida piscina*), an exceptional feature even for luxurious public baths (Manderscheid 1996, 110; Bouet

2003a, 713), seems to have been accessible from the *tepidarium*. In surface, the *tepidaria* could be as small as 2 m² (Vechmaal, perhaps rather to be labelled a heat trap) or as large as 36 m² (Anthée 'Bath 3'). The median size is 15.84 m² (N = 39, see Table 10), which is actually larger than the median size of *caldaria* (13.15 m², see below).[12]

Sudatoria/laconica

The only round heated room (*laconicum*) found in the public baths in the research area, was probably a later addition to the original plan of the 'Vicus Bath' in Oudenburg. The bad state of preservation and the incomplete publication complicate our understanding of this room. So-called *sudatoria*, smaller heated rooms without pools but with their own furnace and often connected to the *caldarium*, can possibly be discerned in the public bath of Fontaine-Valmont (surface of 6 m²) and in the (public?) bath of Amay-Ombret (surface of 14.85 m²). In the public bath of Famars, the small rooms north and south of the central heated room should possibly be identified as sweat rooms (both *c.* 44 m²) rather than as *tepidaria* (as proposed by Beaussart 1980, 810). In the public bath of Liberchies, two rooms with hypocaust and heated by their own furnace both had an *alveus*. It seems as if the *sudatorium* was equipped with a pool here. In the small public baths, such as Grobbendonk, Tienen, or Tourinnes-St-Lambert, no *sudatorium* was present. No sweat rooms have been found in the military baths or in the baths of road stations either.

A round heated room was found in the villa of Ambresin, in the villa of Rognée and in the luxurious last-phase villa of Haccourt. In the latter, there was a round heated room in the villa and one as part of the bathing rooms in the large bathhouse. 'Stand-alone' *laconica* are also known from Republican and early Imperial houses and villas in Italy, e.g. the Villa dei Misteri in Pompeii (de Haan 2010, 234). As mentioned above (p. 26), they found their way into the earliest public baths as well (before being transformed into cold pools). Round sweat rooms were reminiscent of the oldest domestic baths in central Italy, closely linked to popular belief in a sweat cure (Yegül 1992, 50). These *laconica* enabled a basic sweat session, perhaps complemented by a quick wash in a portable tub or at a *labrum*. Their diameter varies from 2.75 m (Ambresin) to 5.15 m (Rognée), giving surfaces between 5.9 m² and

---

12 If we add the *tepidaria* of the 'baths of unknown access' (N = 43), the median is still 15.84 m². If we omit the 'possible' *tepidaria* and the *tepidaria* of which the dimensions are uncertain (N = 19), the median is 15.12 m².

22 m², respectively. The semicircular niches, as found in the examples of Rognée and Haccourt 'Bath 3', probably housed benches to accommodate the individual bathers. Only in the larger bathhouses, have *sudatoria* been identified, e.g. in Anthée 'Bath 2', Basse-Wavre, Bruyelle, Emptinne-Champion (phase 2), Graux, Kumtich, Jemelle, Maillen – Ronchinne, Merbes-le-Château 'Bath 2', Mettet 'Bath 1', Vellereille-les-Brayeux, Willemeau, and possibly Gerpinnes and Neerharen-Rekem. The surfaces of these sweat rooms varied from 8 or 9 m² (Anthée 'Bath 2', Maillen – Ronchinne) to 26 m² (Autre-Église), with a median of 11.74 m² (N = 14; see Table 10).[13] The bath of Treignes is smaller but does seem to have a separate sweat room. It has already been pointed out that the distinction between a *tepidarium* and *sudatorium* is sometimes difficult to make. The room that has been interpreted as a *sudatorium* in the bath of Jemelle had a *schola labri*.

Caldaria

The hot room or *caldarium* was the foremost important room of the bathhouse. It was the architectural end point of the bathing itinerary, where bathers immersed in the warm water pool (*alveus*). The importance of this room is confirmed by comparing the median sizes of *caldaria* (public baths: 26.25 m²; private baths: 13.15 m²) in comparison to *frigidaria* (public baths: 20 m²; private baths: 8 m²) and *tepidaria* (public baths: 23.6 m²; private baths: 16.42 m²). A *caldarium* was always heated by its own furnace and had one or more *alvei*, often located above these furnaces to benefit from direct heat of the flames. In the public baths in the research area, the *caldarium* had a rectangular shape, sometimes with one, two, or exceptionally three *exedrae* to lodge pools and sometimes a *labrum*. The surfaces ranged between 8.28 m² (Aardenburg) and 106.25 m² (Famars), with a median of 24 m² (N = 13; see Table 10).[14] More elongated *caldaria*, such as in Amay-Ombret, Clavier-Vervoz, Grobbendonk, or Macquenoise, may have been divided by a thin wall into a *tepidarium* and *caldarium* (Bouet 2003a, 720). Such a partitioning wall would have been built directly onto the *suspensura*, without leaving a trace on the hypocaust level. Evidence of such walls was discovered in Tongeren – Sint-Truiderstraat (Huybrigts 1904, 313).

The pools were mainly rectangular in shape, although if there were two, one pool could be semicircular, e.g. in Tienen and the presumed public bath in Autre-Église and Maastricht. In the bath of Tienen, one of the semicircular *exedrae* housed a *labrum* rather than a pool, judging from the thickness of the *exedra* wall and the absence of a water outlet (Vanderhoeven, Vynckier, and Wouters 1998, 144). The *caldarium* of Grobbendonk had three *exedrae*, all to lodge rectangular *alvei* it seems. The *caldaria* of fort baths were obviously the most important rooms of the baths. In Furfooz, it had two *alvei*: one semicircular above the furnace and a single trapezoidal one. In Oudenburg, the 'Castellum Bath' had one or probably two rectangular *alvei*. The evidence for Liberchies is again unclear, but it seems there must have been at least one rectangular *alveus* in an *exedra*, mimicking the *exedrae* of the *tepidarium* and *frigidarium*. In the baths of relays and road stations, the small *caldaria* had at least one (rectangular) *alveus*, e.g. in Outrelouxhe or Wyompont. The surface of the *alvei* in public baths — including fort baths and road stations — ranged from 2.1 m² (Furfooz) to 14 m² (Grobbendonk).[15] The median surface size is 3.86 m² (N = 16; see Table 11).[16] The heated pools are on average obviously smaller than the cold pools (median: 9 m²), as the latter could be filled directly with water from the reservoir or aqueduct, whereas *alvei* were filled with water heated in small boilers.

The *caldaria* of the private baths have mainly a rectangular plan, often with one or two *exedrae* protruding out of the bathing block to lodge pools or *labra*. Some *caldaria* have three protruding *exedrae*, giving them a cruciform shape, e.g. in Bruyelle and Miécret 'Bath 2'. Two early bathhouses have a round *caldarium*: phase 1 of Emptinne-Champion and 'Bath 2' at Haccourt. Both have a rectangular *alveus* in a rectangular *exedra* above the furnace. The *laconicum* in Ambresin might also have been a round *caldarium* perhaps with an *alveus*, but unfortunately the excavation data is too tenuous to make any conclusions. The surfaces of the *caldaria* vary between 4.4 m² (Vechmaal and Miécret 'Bath 1') and 52.4 m² (Haccourt 'Bath 3'), while the median is 13.26 m² (N = 80; see Table 10).[17] Just as

---

13   If we add the *sudatoria* of the 'baths of unknown access' (N = 17), the median is 13 m². If we omit the 'possible' *sudatoria* and the *sudatoria* of which the dimensions are uncertain (N = 6), the median is 10.89 m².

14   If we add the baths that may have had public access (N = 21), the median is 23.52 m². If we omit all *caldaria* with uncertain identification or uncertain dimensions (N = 12), the median is 22.7 m².

15   If we omit the fort baths, the smallest *alveus* is found in Fontaine-Valmont (3 m²), or Maastricht (1.9 m²) if we include baths with possibly public access.

16   If we add the baths that may have had public access (N = 26), the median is 4 m². If we omit all *alvei* with uncertain identification or uncertain dimensions (N = 14), the median is 4.4 m².

17   If we add the *caldaria* of the 'baths of unknown access' (N = 88), the median is 13.38 m², but the largest *caldarium* would be that of Amay-Ombret (c. 73 m²). If we omit the 'possible' *caldaria* and the *caldaria* of which the dimensions are uncertain (N = 62), the median is 14.3 m².

for some public baths, more elongated *caldaria* may have been divided into a *tepidarium* and *caldarium* by light walls at *suspensura* level, but the absence of foundation walls at hypocaust level makes it difficult to validate this hypothesis. Outside of the research area, such a light wall made entirely out of *tubuli* was found between the *tepidarium* and *caldarium* of the villa baths of Pölich (Koethe 1940, 111). Possible examples include the elongated *caldaria* in Attenhoven, Bierbeek, Bruyelle (phase 1), Chastrès, Clermont-sous-Huy, Flostoy, Gemechenne, Haillot, Hoogeloon, Leignon, Maillen – Ronchinne, Milmort, Modave, Oberüttfeld, Soignies, Treignes, Waha, and Wange.

The *alvei* in private baths are often located above the furnace, for maximum profit from the heat, although some *alvei* are located opposite the *praefurnium*, e.g. in Anderlecht, Attenhoven, Bierbeek, Heestert. These are all baths that consisted of a single heated room. There are several examples of semicircular *alvei*, often also housed in semicircular *exedrae*, e.g. in Aiseau 'internal bath', Anthée 'Bath 2' and 'Bath 3' (as only *alveus*), Boirs (only *alveus*?), Haccourt 'Bath 1', Merbes-le-Château 'Bath 2' (as only *alveus*?), Milmort, Saint-Jean-Geest (as only *alveus*?), and possibly in Treignes and Vodelée. In Jemelle, an *alveus* added at a later date had the shape of a rectangle with a semicircular apse in its western side. The same shape can be found in the two opposed *alvei* in the bath of Meersen. A very popular layout of the *alvei* seems to have been in an angle of 90° to each other, e.g. in Aiseau 'Bath 1' and 'Bath 2', Bruyelle (phase 1), Évelette – Résimont, Clermont-sous-Huy, Chastrès, Emptinne-Champion (phase 3), Flostoy, Gemechenne, Haccourt 'Bath 3', Haillot, Hamois, Heure-le-Romain, Hoogeloon, Latinne, Leignon, Limerlé, Maillen – Al Sauvenière, Maillen – Ronchinne, Mettet 'Bath 2', Miécret 'Bath 1', Modave, Soignies, Vechmaal, Vorst, Waha, Wange, and possibly Marcinelle. The surface of the *alvei* ranged from 0.8 m² (Hamois) to 12.5 m² (Meslin-l'Évêque), with a median of 2.4 m² (N = 102; see Table 11).[18] Only in 'Bath 3' in Anthée, the depth of the *alveus* could be measured (1.1 m).

The bad preservation of the remains or an incomplete excavation report make it sometimes difficult to decide whether an *exedra* housed an *alveus* or rather a *labrum*. For an *alveus*, the walls of an *exedra* certainly need to be sturdier, as these have to withstand more pressure due to the extra weight of the water (Deru 1994, 34). For Kumtich 'Bath 2', Lemiers, Haccourt 'Bath 1', Vodelée, and possibly Maillen – Al Sauvenière

and Milmort, a semicircular *exedra* was used to lodge a *labrum*. In the *caldarium* of Bruyelle, a rectangular *exedra* that was added to the original plan may have housed a *labrum*, as its walls were less sturdy than the other *exedrae* which possibly housed *alvei* (Ansieau and Bausier 2018, 111–12). The *caldarium* of 'Bath 3' at Haccourt gave access to an almost square *calida piscina*. A second heated swimming pool was also located east of the heated rooms, accessible by a small heat trap from the *tepidarium* and *laconicum*. The presence of two such pools points to the exceptional luxury of the bathhouse (and hence the villa). Only the sumptuous bath of Emptinne-Champion (phase 2–3) had a similar pool (see above).[19]

Praefurnia

The term *praefurnium*, literally meaning 'before the furnace', is used in modern research to denote the service room containing the furnace or furnaces itself that heated the warm rooms of the baths. In this book, the former definition is preferred. The technical aspects of the service rooms, such as boilers and the actual furnace, will be discussed below (see Chapter 5). Here, the room itself is the main focus. In the public baths, the *praefurnium* was often a room in line with the *caldarium*, e.g., Clavier-Vervoz, Grobbendonk, or in the presumed public baths of Amay-Ombret. In Tienen, Aardenburg, and the presumed public bath of Maastricht, the *praefurnium* was also a separate room attached to the main bathing block. In Fontaine-Valmont, Macquenoise, and Famars, it was an integral part of the bathing block, serving several heated rooms. At Famars, the central furnace was flanked on either side by a short flight of steps descending into additional underground furnace rooms that heated the *sudatoria*. At the 'Vicus Bath' Tourinnes-St-Lambert, there does not seem to have been a room around the furnace. Perhaps the service area was fenced off with perishable materials (wattle-and-daub walls) or was only covered by a roof resting on two posts, as in the villa bath of Soignies (see below). The absence of a service room can also be seen in the military baths, e.g. in Oudenburg, Liberchies, or Furfooz. At the latter, however, a wall was built parallel to the cliffside against which the baths were built to delimit a (covered?) service area. In the road relay of Outrelouxhe, the furnace was fired from within the main building. In the road station at Wyompont,

---

18   If we add the *alvei* of the 'baths of unknown access' (N = 112), the median is also 2.4 m². If we omit the 'possible' *alvei* and the *alvei* of which the dimensions are uncertain (N = 86), the median is 2.6 m².

19   The excavators of the villa bath of Bruyelle (phase 3) carefully suggested that one of the new heated rooms might have been a *calida piscina* (erroneously called *solium* in the publication), although the lack of a boiler near the room or the absence of a drainage channel makes this hypothesis unlikely (Ansieau and Bausier 2018, 120).

the *praefurnium* was an integral part of the building, servicing two heated rooms.

Villa baths have similar constructions for their *praefurnia*. The furnace room could be part of the building, often servicing several rooms at the same time, e.g. Aiseau 'Bath 2', Amay, Anthée 'Bath 3', Boussu-lez-Walcourt, Bruyelle, Hamois, Marchienne-au-Pont, Merbes-le-Château 'Bath 2', Meslin-l'Évêque, Mettet Bath 1, Oberüttfeld, Sauvenière, Vellereille, Vesqueville, and Vorst. The *praefurnium* could be built in line with the *caldarium*, e.g. in Broekhem, Emptinne-Champion (phase 2), Chastrès, Gemechenne, Gesves (phase 1), Haccourt 'Bath 2', Heure-le-Romain, Kumtich 'Bath 2', Lemiers, Limerlé, Maillen – Arches, Mettet 'Bath 1', Milmort, Modave, Roly, Treignes, and Vechmaal. When a bath was added at a later date to the villa, one of the rooms might have been sacrificed to create a *praefurnium*, e.g. in Flostoy, Hoogeloon, or Mabeuge. In the third phase of Emptinne-Champion the old phase 2-*caldarium* was reused (Van Ossel and De Poorter 1992, 214). If the furnace room was not built in continuation with the room it heated or as part of the building, it could be abutting the baths, hence protruding out of the main bathing block, e.g. in Anthée 'Bath 1', Arquennes, Bruyelle (phase 3), Évelette – Clavia, Gerpinnes, Gesves (phase 2), Maillen – Ronchinne, Miécret 'Bath 2', Treignes, or Vodelée. In the case of Bruyelle (phase 3) and Haccourt 'Bath 3', a new *praefurnium* was dug into the virgin soil, the walls directly built against the loam (Ansieau and Bausier 2018, 117; De Boe 1976, 18). In some cases, only a wall, presumably to protect against the prevailing wind, fenced off the furnace, e.g. in Anderlecht, Basse-Wavre, Jemelle, Leignon, Maillen – Al Sauvenière, Mont-lez-Houffalize ('Bath 1' and 'Bath 2'), Saint-Jean-Geest, and Waha. Finally, there seem to have been furnace areas that were not fenced off in any way, e.g. Bierbeek, Boirs, Froyennes, Grumelange, Haccourt 'Bath 1', Heestert, Miécret 'Bath 2', Saint-Jean-Geest, or Tongeren – Vrijthof. However, the careful excavation of the bath in Soignies has demonstrated that an awning covered the furnace area, as two post holes to support a (slanted?) roof (in perishable materials?) were found in line with the walls of the *caldarium* (Deramaix and Sartieaux 1995, 52). It is possible that similar screens or fences in perishable materials delimited the furnace areas in other baths as well.

Other Rooms

The larger public baths, such as at Famars, Fontaine-Valmont, or Clavier-Vervoz, had several rooms that could not be interpreted due to the lack of specific features. We can imagine that some rooms might have been specific rooms for massages, for anointing (*unctoria*), for scraping off the dirt with *strigiles* (*districtaria*), or simply service rooms. For the public bath of Famars, it is unclear whether the rooms east of the bathing rooms, flanking the entrance to the building, had a bathhouse-related function. It cannot be excluded that the building also offered other services, such as preparation of meals or beds for the night. Such rooms are known from better preserved baths in the Mediterranean, such as at an upper floor in the Central Baths in Herculaneum (Maiuri 1958, 91) or by the account of Seneca, who lived above a bathhouse in *Baiae* in the gulf of Naples (*Ep.* 86).[20] The oblong room east of the *frigidarium* at Famars, with portico on its north side, might have been a type of exercise court (*basilica thermarum*). A similar portico can be identified south of the *palaestra* in Fontaine-Valmont. Such a portico could be used for walking and chatting, and has sometimes been labelled a *xystus* or *ambulatio*, although these terms are rather rare in Latin texts and inscriptions (Nielsen 1993a, 162–63). Evidence for latrines has only been confirmed in the villa bath of Oberüttfeld, where they were flushed by the waste water of the *piscina* (Faust 1999, 162), and Jemelle (last phase), where they were also flushed by the waste water of the *piscina* and of one of the *alvei* (Mignot 1994c, 148). Both latrines were only accessible from outside the baths. The small room north of the *piscina* in Gemechenne might likewise have been a latrine.[21] So far, no latrines have been found in public baths, although the drainage channel of the *piscina* in Liberchies was used to flush a large (public) freestanding latrine some 30 m north of the baths (Brulet and Demanet 1997, 14). Other remarkable rooms in baths include a large room connected to the heated section, delimited by a thin wall in Mettet 'Bath 1'. As it was oriented to the south-east, it may have been a lounge-type room, sometimes called *heliocaminus* or *solarium* (Nielsen 1993a, 161). In the villa bath of Vorst, a small room connected the *caldarium* to the *frigidarium*, serving possibly as heat lock or exit-*tepidarium*. In 'Bath 3' (phase 2) at Haccourt, a similar small heated room connected the *frigidarium* with the eastern *calida piscina*. In the 'Bath 1' at Kumtich as well as in the later and larger 'Bath 2' that replaced it, the number of heated rooms (respectively four and five) allowed for specific functions such as heated *apodyteria* or *unctoria*. In the bath of Bruyelle, the newly added heated rooms of phases 2 and 3 were interpreted by the excavators as possible *unctorium/ districtarium* (Ansieau and Bausier 2018, 120).

---

20   Similarly, up until the nineteenth century, hammams in North Africa offered rooms to stay the night for travelers and peasants from out of town coming to the markets (Carlier 2000, 1311).

21   The absence of latrines near villa baths has also been remarked in *Britannia*, see Perring 2002, 175.

Wall Elevations, Vaulting, and Roof Construction

The reconstruction of wall elevations is difficult, as for most remains, only the foundations have been preserved. Post-abandonment spoliation of building materials, sometimes including the foundations, often impede even a basic understanding of wall construction or the locations of doorways. The scarcity of stone and ceramic building material in especially the northern and western part of the research area (see below, Chapter 6) stimulated reuse, but also limited their use to the foundations and the lower parts of the walls. At some sites, the low number of building stones and the presence of burnt loam make clear that the upper parts of the walls were in half-timber with loam infilling, e.g. in Antoing/Bruyelle (Ansieau and Bausier 2018, 101), Arquennes (Cloquet 1873, 78–79), or Bierbeek (De Clerck 1987, 69). The use of timber and loam is a continuation of existing pre-Roman building techniques, and must have been widespread in the research area, especially in the sandy and loamy regions where little good quality building stone was available. When such stone was available, for example in the southern part of the *civitas Tungrorum*, walls could be made entirely in *petit appareil*, with the occasional levelling layer of tiles or bricks (*opus vittatum*). Unsurprisingly, the location of windows is also difficult to reconstruct. The presence of glass panes is attested in the public bath of Macquenoise and the fort bath of Liberchies, as well as in several villa baths, namely Amay 'Integrated Baths', Bois-et-Borsu, Boussu-lez-Walcourt, Broekhem, Clermont-sous-Huy, Évelette – Résimont, Gerpinnes, Haccourt 'Bath 1' and 'Bath 2', Haillot, Heestert, Hoogeloon, Kumtich 'Bath 1' and 'Bath 2', Liège, Maillen – Al Sauvenière, Marcinelle, Mettet 'Bath 1', Miécret, Mont – Sommerain, Mont – Fin de ville 'Bath 2', Neerharen-Rekem, Nouvelles, Saint-Jean-Geest, Schieren, 's Gravensvoeren, Soignies, Tiegem, Val-Meer, and Vechmaal. In the bath of the villa of Meerssen, fragments of *lapis specularis* were found (Habets 1871, 390), which could be used in wall decoration, but also as glazing for small windows (Fontaine and Foy 2005, 161). Only some excavation reports mention the exact location of these glass panes within the baths. In Clermont-sous-Huy, the fragments were found in the *piscina* (Witvrouw 1988, 37), in Heestert, Marcinelle, and in Schieren in the *caldarium* (Janssens 1984, 20; Lejeune 1973; Biver and Groetembril 2017, 9), in Haillot in the *praefurnium*, probably originating from the adjacent *caldarium* (Lefert 2002, 244), in Soignies around the western *alveus* (Deru 1991, 7), in Miécret 'Bath 2' in the drainage channel of the *alveus* (Materne 1969, 81), in Kumtich 'Bath 1' in the small northern heated room (Cramers 1984, 116), and in Haccourt in

all of the rooms of 'Bath 1' and 'Bath 2' (De Boe 1974, 20, 26). We can assume that most, if not all rooms would have been equipped with at least a small window for illumination. The southern and western sides may have been favoured to catch the maximum amount of sunlight and some of the afternoon heat, as was recommended by authors such as Vitruvius (1.2.7) or Palladius (1.39.1). Furthermore, windows in the walls above pools, as in Clermont-sous-Huy and Soignies, or above *labra* (see Vitr. v.10.4) would cast direct sunlight onto the water, resulting in a much-appreciated glittering effect. 'Quod grata lavacra nitescunt' (because the gracious pools glitter) is how Venantius Fortunatus praised the villa bath of a friend (*De Praemiaco, villa Burdegalensi* 12; see also de Haan 2006). In the neighbouring *civitas Treverorum*, the villa baths at Wasserliesch and Pölich were sufficiently preserved to identify the lower parts of small rectangular windows above the *alvei* (Deru 1994, 14).

The use of vaults in the baths of the research area is only conjectural, as no hard evidence of vaulting has been recognized in the archaeological dataset. As the use of *opus latericium* or *opus caementicium* was rather limited, with walls mainly built in half-timber and loam or entirely in natural stone, preference was probably given to timber roof constructions. This would also have been the traditional way of roof construction in pre-Roman vernacular architecture. The many attestations of charcoal layers and nails in the destruction layers of the baths, too numerous to enlist here, also point in this direction. No voussoir stones or any elements of arches were identified. There is some evidence of *tubuli cuneati* or voussoir tiles for the larger research area (see below, Chapter 6), but none have been found within baths. We could imagine semicircular *exedrae* or round rooms (such as *laconica*) being covered by domes and half-domes, although hard evidence is lacking. An indication of vaults or domes could be found in painted ceiling plasters. An example in Emptinne-Champion, found collapsed on the floor of the *frigidarium*, did not follow the curve of a vault, but was only slightly concave (Van Ossel and De Poorter 1992, 227). The plaster seems to have been attached to ceramic tiles, perhaps *tubuli* or *tubuli cuneati*, which would imply a light structure to protect the timber roof beams from moisture, much as those proposed by Vitruvius (v.10.3). The armchair voussoirs that were sometimes used to create vaulting ribs in baths (Lancaster 2015, 156–72), have not been found, or at least have not been recognized, in the archaeological remains.

The most common roof construction of baths in the research area must have been the timber frame covered with *tegulae* and *imbrices*. These ceramic building materials have been found in both (possibly) public baths, e.g. Amay-Ombret, Fontaine-Valmont (in the portico), Maastricht, Outrelouxhe, Tienen, Tongeren – Schaetzengaerde, and in villa baths, e.g. in Bierbeek, Clermont-sous-Huy, Heer, Marchienne-au-Pont, Mettet, and Sauvenière. It can be assumed that the majority of baths were covered with this type of roof, but the nineteenth- and early twentieth-century excavation reports only rarely mention building materials, and certainly not their location or context. Alternatively, the roofs could have been covered with slabs of thin schist or slate, recognizable by a perforation to attach the tiles with a nail to the rafters. Tiles of schist have been found in Mont-lez-Houffalize – Fin de ville, Autre-Église, and Limerlé, while slate tiles were recovered from the 'Vicus Bath' in Tourinnes-St-Lambert. To protect the timber roof truss from moisture and to improve insulation, the ceilings inside the baths would have been made of wood or terracotta tiles (or *tubuli cuneati*) covered by plaster.

General Remarks

The plans and the shape of the rooms in the research area are rather modest and inconspicuous, compared to the elaborate and dynamic plans of interlocking polygonal, round, and oval rooms sometimes encountered in the Mediterranean. Complex designs such as encountered in the (public) baths in Italy (Medri and Pizzo 2019) or in the public baths in North Africa (Yegül 1992, 184–249; Thébert 2003) or Asia Minor (Yegül 1992, 250–313; Farrington 1995), are absent. The same basic plans with standard rectangular rooms with an occasional apsidal pool are also the norm in *Britannia* (Rook 1992) and *Germania Inferior* (Dodt 2003). The slow spread of new architectural trends has been identified as a possible reason for this apparent 'conservatism' in bathing architecture in more peripheral regions (Nielsen 1999, 43). In general, most 'experimental' plans and room shapes date from the late second–early third

century AD or later, both in public and private bath architecture (Maréchal 2020a, 16–19). A good case in point is the Iberian Peninsula or southern France, where the more rigid plans that often dated back to the first century BC and first century AD are gradually replaced by larger and bolder designs from the third century AD onwards (Mora 1981; Reis 2004; Peréx and others 2014). In the research area, few new constructions have been identified from the third century onwards. Furthermore, regions without a tradition of large public infrastructure are even less inclined to closely follow the latest trends. Mediterranean regions, on the other hand, had a long history of innovative building. When the first bathhouses in newly conquered regions were built, these were obviously built following the examples of contemporaneous Mediterranean baths. For the research area, the majority of baths were built in the second half of the first century AD, and the first half of the second century AD. Contemporaneous baths in the Mediterranean core region still had a 'Vitruvian' plan at this time, characterized by linear plans and rectangular rooms. The more 'experimental' shapes of rooms and more intricate plans developed from the reign of Hadrian onwards (Gros 1996, 400–02). It should then not come as a surprise that the baths in the northern regions, which had just been built a generation earlier, were not immediately transformed according to the latest Mediterranean trends. Furthermore, the construction of public baths (and public buildings and space more in general) did not follow the same pace as in the Mediterranean, possibly because local elites felt less need to compete among each other through munificence (see above, Chapter 3). This observed 'conservatism' in plan and room shape may thus be the result of a slow spread of new architectural ideas, in combination with an elite that was not eager to continuously invest in public buildings and with an historical background with no tradition in innovative stone building construction.

CHAPTER 5

Technology of the Baths

Heating

The Furnaces

The furnaces were lit from the *praefurnium* and heated the hypocausts. They consisted of a hearth, where the actual fire was lit, a furnace arch above it to reduce the pressure of the overlying wall, and often a furnace tunnel that could protrude into the hypocaust and/or into the *praefurnium* (Degbomont 1984, 74–96; Nielsen 1993c). On top of the furnace tunnel in the *praefurnium*, a boiler could be mounted to supply the hot water for the *alvei* (Fig. 11 and Fig. 12). The walls of this tunnel were then reinforced, often following the circular shape of the bottom of the boiler (Manderscheid 2000, 496–97). Furnace tunnels protruding into the hypocaust created additional support to carry the weight of *alvei*. Furthermore the furnace tunnel could also have supported a *testudo alvei*, a semicylindrical metal vessel located directly above the fire and open to the bottom of the pool on one side (Manderscheid 2000, 498–99; Schiebold 2010, 26–27). Very few boilers and *testudines* have been found, as such metal containers were some of the first elements to be torn out and recycled once the baths fell out of use.[1] The air flow to the furnace could be influenced by opening or closing the furnace mouth with metal doors or a stone or terracotta hatch (Adam 1984, 289). It was important that the furnace was constructed in fire resistant materials, such as brick or basalt, as softer stone (limestone, sandstone) would crack under the intense heat (Degbomont 1984, 67–70).

Several public baths in the research area were insufficiently preserved to make any observations on the furnaces, e.g. in Aardenburg, Grobbendonk, or Oudenburg. The early excavations of the public baths

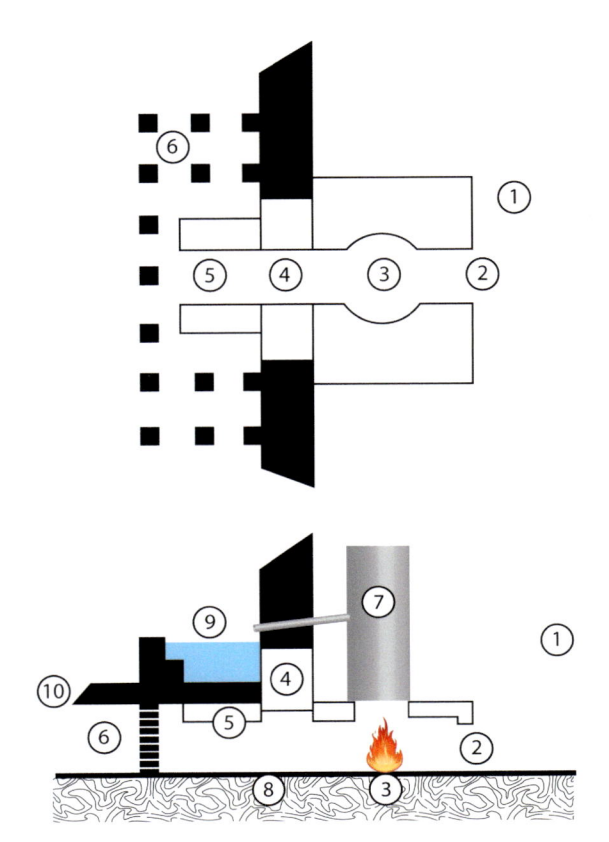

1. *Praefurnium*
2. Furnace mouth
3. Hearth
4. Furnace arch
5. Furnace tunnel
6. Hypocaust
7. Boiler
8. Tunnel floor
9. *Alveus*
10. *Suspensura*

Figure 11. Schematic drawing of a furnace in plan and in section with indication of the main constituent parts. Figure by author.

of Famars did not pay much attention to the furnaces, although the presence of two subterranean *praefurnia* is quite rare. In Tienen, the hearth and the furnace tunnel floor consisted of several layers of tiles, which may point to successive restoration phases (Vanderhoeven, Vynckier, and Wouters 1998, 143). Tiles were also used for the hearth in the possibly public baths of Braives, Macquenoise, and Maastricht. In the former, the tunnel extended underneath the hypocaust (Brulet 1981, 54), in the latter an iron grate was present above the hearth, possibly to support a boiler (Leemans 1843, 41). In Tourinnes-St-Lambert, the hearth of the 'Vicus Bath' only consisted of mortar, while the tunnel (l.: 2.5 m) was made of brick (Dens and Poils 1911, 294) and may

---

1   An extraordinary find of a boiler still *in situ* in the *praefurnium* of a villa bath in Saint-Pathus (northern France) demonstrates that such devices were certainly not restricted to public baths (Hurard and others 2016).

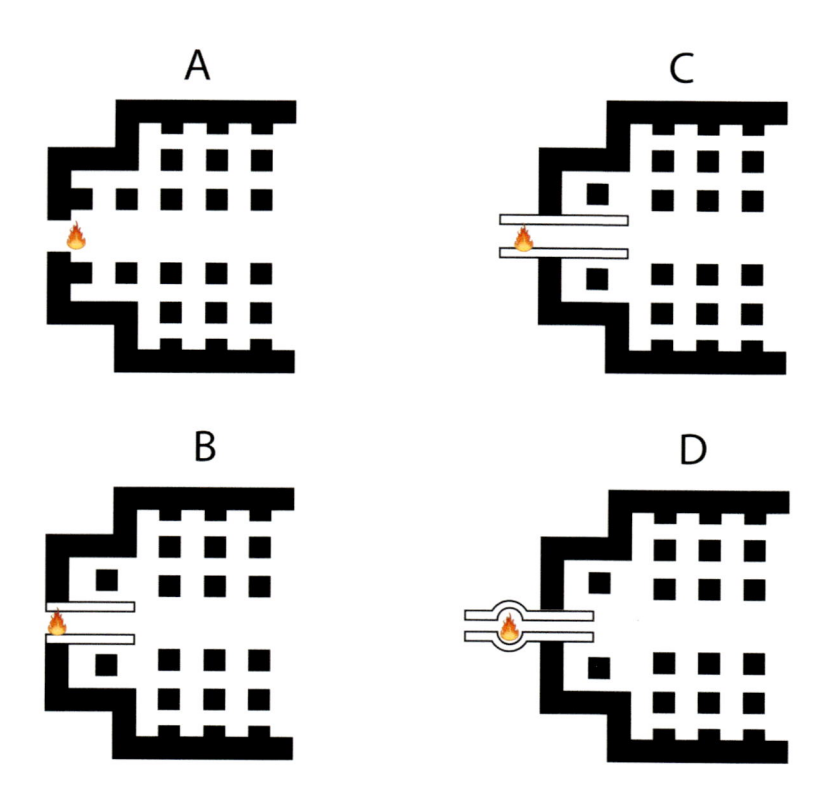

Figure 12. Schematic plans of furnace types frequently found in the research area (A: without tunnel; B: with tunnel protruding into the hypocaust; C: with tunnel protruding into the *praefurnium* and the hypocaust; D: with tunnel supporting a boiler and protruding into the *praefurnium* and the hypocaust). Figure by author after Degbomont 1984, 62, fig. 86.

have supported a boiler. Likewise, the south-western furnace of the possibly public baths of Amay-Ombret was reinforced, pointing to the presence of a boiler (Witvrouw 1986, 105). The width of the furnaces fluctuated between 0.4 m (e.g. Amay-Ombret) and 0.9 m (e.g. Maastricht).

In private baths, bricks and tiles were also commonly used to construct the hearths and the tunnel, e.g. in Anderlecht, Attenhoven, Autre-Église, Bierbeek, Bruyelle, Évelette – Clavia, Gesves (also using local stone for the tunnel), Heure-le-Romain, Kumtich 'Bath 1', Meslin-l'Évêque, Villers-le-Bouillet, or Vissoul. In some cases, the bricks or tiles were placed vertically in the soil, e.g. in Haillot (tunnel floor), Kumtich 'Bath 1' and 'Bath 2' (furnace tunnel), Maillen – Al Sauvenière (using *bessales*), Merbes-le-Château 'Bath 1', Oberüttfeld and Vechmaal. In Hoogeloon, the hearth and tunnel floor were made with inverted *tegulae* (Hiddink 2014, 207), while in Bruyelle and Vesqueville the rims of the *tegulae* were broken off and placed in a mortar bedding (Ansieau and Bausier 2018, 261; Matthys 1974, 11, respectively). In Gerpinnes, the hearth and tunnel floor were laid out in *opus spiccatum* (De Glymes, Henseval, and Kaisin 1875,

cviii). In a small number of cases, the hearth simply consisted of a mortar patch, e.g. in Maillen – Arches (Mahieu 1892, 362) or Neerharen-Rekem (Van Neuss and Bamps 1888, 335) or, even more uncommonly, only of a slab of schist in Hamois (Van Ossel 1980, 78) or just the virgin soil in Broekhem (as a pit in the loam), Haccourt 'Bath 3', Haillot, Marchienne-au-Pont or Merbes-le-Château 'Bath 2' (with a pit just in front, possibly for the stoker; Authom and Paridaens 2015, 85). In Matagne-la-Petite, the furnace was cut out of the bedrock (Rober 1984, 66). The presence of a furnace tunnel in the *praefurnium* probably points to the presence of a boiler and can be found in numerous baths (see Table 5). In several baths the tunnel also protruded into the hypocaust, presumably to create additional support underneath pools (see Table 5). The furnace of Grumelange is quite exceptional, as it seems to have been placed within the heated room (Malget and Malget 1912, 417). The elliptical shape outlined by the tunnel is also uncommon.[2] The furnace of Meerssen is even more enigmatic. The keyhole-shaped furnace does not seem to be connected to a hypocaust, and is flanked by two pools. The excavator suggested the furnace only heated a boiler supplying the pools (Habets 1871, 387). The furnace mouth was between 0.3 m (e.g. Gesves or Saint-Jean-Geest) and 0.9 m wide (e.g. Anthée 'Bath 3'), as was the case in the public baths. A width between 0.4 and 0.6 m seems most common. The length of the tunnel was obviously quite variable, reaching up to 2.6 m when continuing into the hypocaust (e.g. Mettet 'Bath 1', Oberüttfeld).

The Hypocaust

The term hypocaust is used as a shorthand by scholars to denote the system of floor heating consisting of pillars supporting a raised floor (*suspensura*). The hypocaust floor often rested on a preparation layer of uncut rocks or alternatively a layer of clay or loam, on which mortar was then poured or stacked. Once the mortar was levelled and dried out, the hypocaust pillars could be placed. These were often constructed by piling round or square terracotta tiles, bonded by clay or mortar, to an average height of 40–60 cm (Adam 1984, 290; Degbomont 1984, 98–104). Pillars made of stone monoliths or a single terracotta column were more exceptional (Degbomont 1984, 104–06; Schiebold 2010, 17). The pillars were then topped by square *bipedales* tiles (side *c.* 59 cm), meaning each pillar stood about 30 cm apart. On top of the *bipedales*, layers of hydraulic mortar were then laid, which could eventually by topped by mosaics or

---

2   In the Terme del Filosofo in Ostia, a similar boiler platform with an oval opening has been found (Boersma 1985).

Table 5. Baths with furnace tunnels extending into the *praefurnium* and/or into the hypocaust.

Site	Furnace tunnel in *praefurnium*	Furnace tunnel in hypocaust
Aiseau 'Bath 2'	×	×
Anderlecht	×	
Autre-Église		×
Basse-Wavre	×	×
Bierbeek	×	×
Broekhem	×	
Bruyelle	×	×
Emptinne-Champion (phase 1)	×	
Emptinne-Champion (phase 2)	×	×
Emptinne-Champion (phase 3)	×	×
Chastrès	×	×
Clermont-sous-Huy	×	×
Évelette – Clavia	×	
Flostoy	×	
Gesves (phase 1)	×	×
Graux	×	
Haccourt 'Bath 1'	×	
Haccourt 'Bath 2'	×	
Haccourt 'Bath 3'	×	×
Hamois	×	
Jemelle	×	
Liège	×	
Maillen – Al Sauvenière	×	
Marchienne-au-Pont	×	
Mettet 'Bath 1'	×	
Mettet 'Bath 2'		×
Miécret 'Bath 1'	×	
Miécret 'Bath 2'	×	×
Rognée	×	
Sauvenière		×
Treignes		×
Vechmaal	×	×
Villers-le-Bouillet	×	×
Vodelée	×	
Waha	×	×

slabs of decorative stone (Adam 1984, 291). Underneath pools or heavy elements (walls, *labra*) or near unstable walls, hypocaust pillars could be placed closer together to carry more weight (Lehar 2012, 62). The quest for building materials in Roman and post-Roman times, stripping baths to their foundations, as well as an indifference of early excavators to record the specific type of building materials used, has unfortunately resulted in a high number of hypocausts with no further information on the type of pillars. This was the case in three out of fourteen public baths, five out of nineteen baths with unknown accessibility, and twenty-nine out of 110 private baths (or 26 per cent; see Table 12 in the Appendix).

In the baths in the research area, the majority of hypocausts were constructed with square tiles (sixty-eight in total, see Table 12). The hypocausts in the public baths almost exclusively made use of these (nine and another eleven in baths of unknown accessibility), but also in the private baths the majority of hypocausts were made with square tiles (forty-eight of 110 sites or in 44 per cent).[3] Round tiles for the pillars are found less often in public baths (only one example) and baths with unknown accessibility (three examples), but more frequently in private baths (twenty-seven out of 110 baths, or 25 per cent). In several hypocausts, both round and square tiles were found, sometimes even in the same pillar (one in a public bath, two in baths with unknown accessibility, and seventeen in private baths, see Table 12). The mix of both types of tiles within the same hypocaust may point to a restoration phase, in which an insufficient number of tiles of one type was complemented by (newly acquired) tiles of the other type. Several baths also have heated rooms with pillars made of square tiles and heated rooms with pillars made of round tiles. This mainly occurs when a heated room was added to the original layout, e.g. in Autre-Église, Boirs, Emptinne-Champion, Gesves, Namur, Neerharen-Rekem, or Saint-Jean-Geest. In all cases, the original hypocausts were made with square tiles, while the later rooms made use of the round type. In the cases of Gesves and Namur, the added hypocaust rooms made use of a mix, perhaps revealing that a stock of the original hypocaust tiles had to be complemented by newly acquired tiles. As for the questions if one type preceded the other, it seems that in the early baths discovered in the research area, the square type of tiles was used, e.g. in Haccourt 'Bath 1', Heestert, and Tienen. Both types remain in use until Late Antiquity. In exceptional cases, several tiles were grouped together to form sturdier pillars, e.g. in the phase 1-*caldarium* in Bruyelle (Ansieau and Bausier 2018, 102), in the *caldarium* of Flostoy (Lefert 2015, 271) or in 'Bath 2' in Kumtich (Cramers 1984, 120), probably to support heavier structures such as a partition wall on the walking level.

The separate tiles of a pillar are mainly bonded by clay, although mortar could also be used (e.g. in Kortrijk). In what seems to be an ingenious solution to a lack of tiles, a hypocaust in the last phase of the villa bath of Gesves was repaired by constructing pillars made of two adjoined *tubuli* filled with mortar (Lefert 2007, 200). In the villa baths of Mettet 'Bath 1' (Mahieu 1919, 86), Miécret 'Bath 1' (Materne 1969, 81), and perhaps in Mont-lez-Houffalize – Sommerain (Dubois 1952, 5),

column drums were used to replace broken pillars in the hypocaust. Such makeshift repairs of hypocausts, sometimes also using stone monoliths, as in Modave (Anonymous 1896, 187) or Flostoy (Lefert 2015, 271), are also known from other parts of the Empire and are often linked to a lack of ceramic building material (Adam 1984, 290; Schiebold 2010, 14–17). The height of pillars is often impossible to reconstruct, as the actual walking levels of the heated rooms are unknown. For the rare cases in which a height could be reconstructed (see Table 12), we can remark important differences, with pillars attaining only 30 or 40 cm (Grumelange and Marcinelle, respectively) and pillars reaching 80 cm (Saint-Jean-Geest) or 120 cm (Fontaine-Valmont). However, the quantity of sites is too low to draw any general conclusions.

There are also some more exceptional forms of hypocaust that make use of channels under the floor instead of using pillars to create a hollow space. The channels, laid out as for example an X or Y, are connected to a furnace on one end and to chimneys on the other ends (Degbomont 1984, 121–27; Lehar 2012, 17–22). Sometimes, these channels could be combined with a small space that did have pillars (Degbomont 1984, 127–31), as can be seen in the room south-east of the bathing rooms of Maillen – Ronchinne. In our research area, only three examples of such channel hypocausts were found (see Table 12), all in private baths: Mont-lez-Houffalize – Fin de Ville 'Bath 1' (Y-shaped), Neerharen-Rekem (+-shaped), and Tourinnes-St-Lambert (Y-shaped). Only the bath at Neerharen-Rekem is uncontested (De Boe 1982, 73). Both other baths have sometimes been interpreted as drying spaces for wheat, which also made use of channel hypocausts (Meunier 1964, 156; De Ruyt 1986, 65, respectively). There is a single example of a combined channel-and-pillar hypocaust, but it pertains to the possible private baths of Tongeren Vermeulenstraat 3 (Borgers, Steenhoudt, and Van de Velde 2008). However, in the second phase of the alleged *caldarium* in Merbes-le-Château 'Bath 1' the furnace tunnels were prolonged by short channels before leading into the actual hypocaust (Authom and Paridaens 2015, 55). A fully functional mixed system may have been used in the badly published villa bath of Heer (Habets 1895, 273). In Latinne, the room with semicircular *exedra* also had a mixed channel hypocaust (Renard 1903, 90–91), but it was probably a reception hall or dining room rather than a room of the baths.

Wall Heating

The earliest traces of wall heating date back to the early second century BC, when a type of 'proto-*tubulus*' is used in a small hypocausted room in the public bath

---

3   For the measurements of the hypocaust tiles, both square and round, see Chapter 6.

of *Fregellae* (Italy) (Tsiolis 2013).[4] Until the mid-first century AD, the walls were mainly heated by placing large tiles with protruding knobs, known as *tegulae mammatae*, against the walls, so creating a hollow space that stood in direct contact with the hypocaust underneath the floor (Schiebold 2010, 19–20; Lehar 2012, 182–84). By the end of the first century AD, this system was largely replaced by a system of superimposed, vertically connected box tiles, or *tubuli*, which was much more efficient (Adam 1984, 292). Other forms of wall heating existed (Fig. 13), including systems using T-shaped iron nails, terracotta spacers, and tiles to create a hollow wall, but these are rather rare in the north-western provinces (Yegül 1992, 363–65).

The baths in the research area mainly made use of *tubuli* to heat the walls (see Table 13 in the Appendix). This system was used in fifty-two of the 110 private baths (or 47 per cent), in eight of the fourteen public baths, and in eleven of the nineteen baths of unknown accessibility.[5] *Tegulae mammatae* were only discovered in three private baths and in two baths of unknown accessibility (see Table 13). In the bath of Amay-Ombret, which may have been public, the *tegulae mammatae* date from the first phase of the baths, dated to the late first century AD (Witvrouw 1986, 88). No specifications about context are provided for the fragments found in Braives (Brulet 1981, 54) and in the integrated and freestanding baths of Aiseau (Kaisin 1878, 210). In the villa bath of Bierbeek, only the protruding knobs were found. According to the excavator, these knobs were removed so the *tegulae* could be reused for other purposes (De Clerck 1987, 99). The villa was dated on the basis of the few materials between the late first and early third century. In Amay-Ombret, Braives, and Aiseau, *tubuli* were also found. A first phase of wall heating by *tegulae mammatae* was replaced by a second phase with *tubuli*.

As has been mentioned before, most bathhouses have been heavily spoliated for building materials, sometimes stripping the building down to its foundations. In addition, ceramic building materials were often not deemed worthy of mention in early excavation reports, or fragments of *tegulae mammatae* or *tubuli* were not recognized. The description of the finds in 'Bath 2' in Anthée is a good example: the excavator mentions 'des tuyaux plats en poterie' (flat terracotta conduits), which may well have been *tubuli* (Del Marmol 1877, 174). The number of sites where the presence of wall

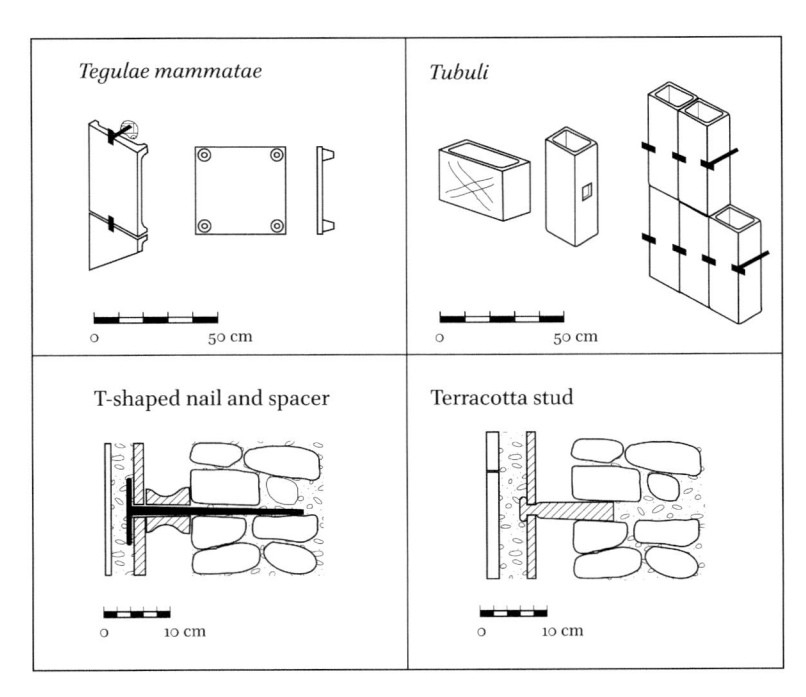

Figure 13. Schematic overview of the types of wall heating frequently encountered in Roman baths. Figure by author after Yegül 1992, 364, fig. 455.

heating can be assumed, but is further unknown, is again quite high: sixty-eight sites in total, including five public baths, eight baths of unknown accessibility, and fifty-five villa baths (or 50 per cent). In four cases, however, there is reason to believe that no wall heating was present (see Table 13). In the private baths of Diekirch and Lemiers, the absence of *tubuli* and the presence of chimney flues starting in the hypocaust seems to indicate that no wall heating was present (Paulke 2010; Braat 1934). In Mont-lez-Houffalize – Fin de Ville 'Bath 1', the channel hypocaust did not permit the use of wall heating (Meunier 1964, 156).[6] In the rather well-preserved bath of Marchienne-au-Pont, the total absence of *tubuli* seems to exclude wall heating (De Waele 1984, 205).

Water Management

Water Supply

There were several manners of supplying a bathhouse with water: by means of an aqueduct, by a well, or by collecting rain water. The first option was obviously

---

4 The thesis that the hollow walls insulated rather than heated the rooms has been debunked elsewhere in detail, see Yegül and Couch 2003, Grassmann 2011 and Lehar 2012. For a critical overview of older experiments into the functioning of hypocausts, see Degbomont 1984, 201–04.

5 For the dimensions of these *tubuli*, see below, Chapter 6.

6 In the villa of Tourinnes-St-Lambert, however, many *tubuli* were found in the room with channel hypocaust (De Ruyt 1986, 66), favouring an interpretation of a heated room rather than a room for drying corn.

preferable, as water was taken directly at a source and hence was less exposed to pollution by soil, leaves, insects, etc. (Manderscheid 2000, 484). Perennial sources also ensured a continuous water supply throughout the year. However, the construction of an aqueduct, especially over a long distance, could be quite expensive, there was a need for constant maintenance, and there was danger of illegal tapping (Manderscheid 2000, 490–91; Vladu 2017). Wells or rain water catchment systems (in reservoirs or basins) were easier to construct, but supply depended on precipitation and the volumes of water were smaller compared to a continuous supply through an aqueduct (Manderscheid 2000, 484). The quality of ground water was also variable, depending on the soil type, while rain water could be muddy and polluted if not properly stored. The assumption that public baths were always supplied by an aqueduct and that private baths were not is incorrect. In smaller towns, modest public baths may have relied on wells or rain water catchment, or a combination of both, while the presence of an aqueduct at several (larger) villas has been attested.

The water supply of public baths in the research area is quite problematic, as nothing is known for important sites such as Clavier-Vervoz, Grobbendonk, Macquenoise, Tienen, or Tourinnes-St-Lambert. The same problem is encountered for the relay bath at Outrelouxhe and the possible baths of the road station at Wyompont. The 'Vicus Bath' in Liberchies was probably supplied by a nearby source, but no pipes to connect it to the bath were found (Brulet and Demanet 1997, 12). Wells have been found near the 'Vicus Bath' of Oudenburg (Creus 1975, 9) and the bath of Aardenburg (only 6 m south-west of the baths; van Dierendonck and Vos 2013, 105), but again contemporaneity and the direct link with the baths is difficult to prove without the water supply pipes. The use of a well for these sites on the sandy soils close to the coastline, should not come as a surprise, as the ground water level could be (and still is) quite high and natural sources are less abundant than for example in the Ardennes. A direct supply by an aqueduct could be identified for Famars and Fontaine-Valmont. In Famars, the aqueduct could be traced to a source some 15 km outside of the city (Beaussart 1980, 815). The aqueduct (or perhaps only a branch of it) reached the baths from the south, entering the *praefurnium* to supply water to the boilers of the *alvei* and then continuing north underneath the courtyard where its trace was lost. It must also have supplied the nearby *piscina*, perhaps by first being stored in a reservoir just east of it (Beaussart 1980, 815). In Fontaine-Valmont, the aqueduct linked a source 2.4 km outside the centre directly to the bath (Faider-Feytmans 1995, 70). Just before it reached the bathhouse, the water was collected in a *castellum*

aquae, from which two branches departed, one to the *natationes* in the *palaestra* and one the *praefurnium*. The water supply channels were constructed in stone and mortar (Faider-Feytmans 1976, 19). A third bathhouse that may have been supplied by an aqueduct, was the possibly public bath of Tongeren – Schaetzengaerde. The large pool certainly would have required a continuous water supply (Vanderhoeven and others 2007, 165). The site was located close to the point where the aqueduct entered the city. The water supply of the military baths of Furfooz and Liberchies, both probably constructed in the fourth century AD, is unknown. However, late antique military forts had to be self-reliant when it came to water. Under siege, aqueducts could be easily cut off by the enemy. Both the Furfooz and Liberchies *castella* lay on promontories, making it also likely that water supply relied on rain water catchment or wells rather than on an aqueduct. In the late antique *castellum* of Oudenburg, a water reservoir was identified north of the baths, close to the furnace. In a later phase, a well was constructed here. In an even later phase, a water basin with a surface of 4.5 m² was constructed south of the bathhouse (Vanhoutte 2018, 168).

Several villa sites have yielded evidence of a water supply by aqueduct, even if the exact connection to the baths is not always clear. Such aqueducts were not necessarily constructed in mortar and stone. Many traces of wooden adduction pipes have survived. Often, only the iron rings that held the different parts of the pipes together survived, although these rings could also be replaced by simple ropes, which unfortunately rarely survive (Fig. 14). The large villa domain of Anthée was supplied by two aqueducts, coming from sources at a distance of 3.3 km and 2.2 km to the south (Del Marmol 1877, 167–69). The aqueduct (41 cm wide and deep) ended in a square basin (s.: 1.75 m; min. 0.43 m deep). The adduction channels to the baths were made of inverted *imbrices* and wooden pipes, of which only the iron rings to hold the different parts together have survived (Del Marmol 1877, 170). 'Bath 2' may have had a reservoir on its east side, with a water channel in one of the walls partially preserved. West of 'Bath 3', a cistern (1.7 m deep) with a lead outlet was excavated (Del Marmol 1877, 186). The villa of Mettet was supplied by a source at *c.* 2 km distance through an aqueduct made of stone, tiles, and mortar (Mahieu 1919, 70). Five inspection holes were identified along the trajectory. The aqueduct ended in a *piscina limaria*, in which dirt could settle. The distribution to the baths was ensured by wooden pipes, as the iron rings that were found seem to suggest (Mahieu 1892, 146–55). Such iron rings were also found in Emptinne-Champion (east of the bath; Van Ossel and De Poorter 1992, 200) and Modave (Anonymous 1896, 187). In Treignes, possibly supplied by a source at 2 km, the pipes were made of wood and terracotta

Figure 14. Fragment of a wooden aqueduct found in the rural settlement of Wortegem – Diepestraat (eastern Flanders, Belgium), dated by radiocarbon between AD 130–350. Cross-section (top right) and detail of the rope holding together the different parts (bottom right). Photo courtesy of SOLVA.

(Doyen 1987, 269). Terracotta adduction pipes were also found in Gerpines (De Glymes, Henseval, and Kaisin 1875, cix). The type of pipes is unknown for Haillot, but it seems the aqueduct headed towards the *piscina* (Lefert 2002, 244). For Élouges (Debove 1865, 123), Nouvelles (source at 1.5 km; Leblois and Leblois 1968, 57), and Thirimont (Van Bastelaer 1891a, 376), the link to the baths in unclear.

The villa of Liège – Place St-Lambert was supplied by an aqueduct tapping into a local source in the immediate vicinity of the villa (Otte and Degbomont 1990, 74). For a lot of sites, nearby sources have been mentioned as potentially supplying the baths: Aiseau, Anderlecht, Bierbeek (150 m south of the baths), Boussu-lez-Walcourt, Broekhem (30 m west of the baths), Clermont-sous-Huy, Jemelle, Kumtich 'Bath 2', Latinne, Marcienne-au-Pont, Mont-lez-Houffalize – Sommerain (couple of metres south of the baths), and Vellereille-les Brayeux. The presence of a source was obviously very important when choosing the location of a villa site. When natural sources were not present, wells or rain water catchment could offer a solution. Wells have been located at the sites of Bras-Haut, Bruyelle, Hamois, Heer, Hollain, Hoogeloon, Kumtich 'Bath 1', Roly, 's Gravensvoeren (three wells), Tournai – Vieux Marché aux jambons (two wells), and Vechmaal (some 10 m south-east of the baths). Only at Roly, traces of a (broken out?) water channel and iron rings of wooden pipes were found between baths and the well, located some 10 m to the north (Robert 1980, 90).

It is difficult to find direct evidence for rain water catchment, as this would have been collected on roofs and the standing remains are never preserved to a sufficient height. In 'Bath 2' at Mettet, recesses in the wall of the alleged *piscina* may point to the presence of water pipes in the walls, coming from rooftop cisterns (Mahieu 1919, 100). In the last phase of the bath of Bruyelle, a basin was constructed next to the *piscina*, which was interpreted as a second *piscina* by the excavators (Ansieau and Bausier 2018, 118), but may well have been a reservoir, perhaps to store rain water. Open-air basins probably collected run-off rain water and have been found at Basse-Wavre (600 m north of the baths; Dens and Poils 1905, 323), Évelette 'Clavia' (40 m east of the baths; Lefert 2013, 254), Froyennes (Coulon 1977, 16), Graux (1.3 × 0.75 m; 0.8 m deep; Mahieu 1910, 140), Neerharen-Rekem (De Boe 1982, 73), and perhaps Maillen – Ronchinne. In Rognée, a circular 'cistern' (3 m deep) was found in the centre of the court of the villa (Kaisin 1897, 40). However, it cannot be ascertained that such basins had anything to do with the water supply of the baths. Very few actual cisterns have been discovered. Besides the above-mentioned examples at Anthée and Bruyelle, a rectangular structure (2 × 2.75 m) in the *praefurnium* of Hoogeloon (Hiddink 2014, 220) and the two small reservoirs placed opposite each other that supplied the pools of Meerssen (Habets 1871, 387) can be mentioned.

Waste Water Disposal

The water of the pools and *labra* was discarded from the baths by underground drains, often constructed in stone, tile, and mortar, or more rarely by open-air channels. These would obviously make use of the natural slope of the terrain to channel the waste waters away from the baths. *Labra* never had an outlet: bathers scooped out the water with bowls to douse themselves. The water ended up on the floors from where it was evacuated through the drainage holes (Garbrecht and Manderscheid 1994, 50–51). For the cold pools, the water could be renewed quite frequently, as it could be directly supplied by the aqueduct. These were drained by an outlet in the bottom of the pool or an outlet piercing one of the sides, draining directly in a drainage channel that ran underneath the bath room floors, in the service corridors, or outside the bath (Maréchal 2017, 179–80). These outlets often consisted of lead pipes (*fistulae*) that could be opened or closed with a bronze valve (Fig. 15). Some *piscinae* or *natationes* with a copious and continuous water supply possibly had no plugged outlet, but a continuous overflow (Manderscheid 2000, 503). The hot pools were similarly drained by an outlet in the bottom or in one of the sides, but due to the hypocaust, the drain only seldomly ran underneath the heated rooms. Rather, it ran in the service corridors or outside of the baths (Maréchal 2017, 180–82). Therefore, the main drainage channel collecting the water from both the hot and the cold pools rarely ran inside of the baths, but rather outside of it. As the water for the hot pools had to be heated in boilers, a continuous flow was obviously not an option (Manderscheid 2000, 509). If no outlets are present in a heated pool, it may have been emptied through an outlet in the *testudo* or simply by bathers exiting the pool (Maréchal 2017, 181). The outlets of both cold and hot pools could also spill directly onto the bath room floors, on the condition that the bottom of the pool did not lie lower than the bath room floors. Such drainage had the advantage of cleaning the floors, which had to be slightly sloping towards a drainage hole in the *frigidarium* floor or in one of its walls (Garbrecht and Manderscheid 1994, 72).

In several public baths in the research area, the drainage channel(s) could not be identified. In Famars, a large open channel (1.5 m width) passed west of the bath. The later pool (west side of the building) emptied in it through a terracotta pipe (Beaussart 1980, 810). Traces of a shallow drainage channel starting at the *piscina* were discovered in the Grobbendonk bath (De Boe 1977, 37). In the badly preserved bath of Tienen, traces of channels ran along the north and south side of the bats, but these probably collected rain water from the roof (Vanderhoeven and Vynckier 1997, 12). A separate channel started at the northern *exedra* of the

Figure 15. Lead *fistula* for draining a pool with a valve, Thermenmuseum Zülpich (Germany), inv. nr 78.469, 2019. Part of the hydraulic mortar is still attached. Photo by author.

caldarium, reinforcing the hypothesis that it housed an *alveus* (Vanderhoeven, Vynckier, and Wouters 1998, 144). A different channel started in the centre of the presumed *frigidarium* and joined the *alveus*-channel east of the bath (Vanderhoeven, Vynckier, and Wouters 1998, 144). The drainage channel of the cold pool in the possibly public bath of Tournai – Quai Vifquin emptied directly into the river Scheldt (Verslype 1997, 66), while the drain of the bath in the Quai Luchet d'Antoing also headed towards the river (Amand 1968, 41). In the 'Vicus Bath' of Liberchies, the drainage channel of the *piscina* was constructed in tiles and mortar and headed towards the public latrine some 25 m north of the baths, while the heated pools were possibly drained by wooden pipes (Brulet and Demanet 1997, 19–20). In the possibly public bath of Maastricht, the *piscina* was emptied by a lead *fistula* in a drainage channel that could not be followed (Leemans 1843, 42). In Amay-Ombret, the drain (30 × 40 cm) was made out of limestone blocks. The *alveus* had a separate drain made of tiles (Witvrouw 1986, 92–93). In the very modest road relay Outrelouxhe, the pool emptied in an open-air ditch (Witvrouw 2014, 53). Little is known about the drainage of the pools in the military baths. In the 'Castellum Baths' of Liberchies, a channel made of wooden beams, stone blocks, and covered with tiles started at the presumed *alveus* (Mertens and Brulet 1974, 40).

In some of the private baths, the lead *fistulae* that drained the *piscinae* escaped the hands of those searching for building materials and metals, be it in Roman or post-Roman times. In the bath of Arquennes, a *fistula* led into a sewage channel made of local stone (Cloquet 1875, 75), in Bruyelle (Ansieau and Bausier 2018, 102) and Wancennes (Devillers 1971–1972, 104) it led into a wooden pipe. In the bath of the Oberüttfeld villa, the *fistula* emptied into a drainage channel that flushed the adjoining latrine (Faust 1999, 158), while in Treignes the *fistula* led into a drainage channel made of stone and covered with slabs of schist (Doyen 1987, 269). Other lead *fistulae* were found in the cold pools of Emptinne-Champion, Évelette – Résimont, Flostoy, and Gerpines. The *fistula* of the *piscina* in Tournai – Couvent des Frères mineurs was made in iron (Ingels 1999, 55). In Boirs, it was the *fistula* of an *alveus* that survived the spoliation (Peuskens and Tromme 1979, 387). Fragments of *fistulae* were also found at Jemelle, Mont-lez-Houffalize – Sommerain, and 's Gravensvoeren. A terracotta pipe drained the *piscina* in Maillen – Al Sauvenière (Mahieu 1892, 351). In Vechmaal, the outlet was a simple small opening (diam.: 6 cm) in the mortar (Vanvinckenroye 1997, 190). Most publications of private baths only mention one or more drainage channels, without further specifying how they were built, e.g. in Boirs, Clermont-sous-Huy, Gesves (phase 2), Graux, Heer, Hoogeloon, Jemelle (where it flushed a latrine), Limerlé, Maillen – Arches, Meerssen, Merbes-le-Château 'Bath 2', Mettet (0.5 m wide and stretching 55 m), Miécret 'Bath 2', Neerharen-Rekem, Rognée, 's Gravensvoeren (where it headed towards a well), Saint-Gérard, Soignies, Val-Meer, and Vellereille-les-Brayeux. Some drainage channels were built with stone, mortar, and tiles, the latter covering both the bottom and the top, e.g. in Anthée 'Bath 3', Basse-Wavre, Boussu-lez-Walcourt (only the *alveus* drain, made only with tiles), Emptinne-Champion (in mortar only, leading into an open channel), Chastrès (only in mortar), Grumelange (only in mortar), Latinne (only in tiles), Maillen – Al Sauvenière, Meslin-l'Évêque (only in tiles), Thirimont (in mortar covered by stone slabs), Tournai – Vieux Marché aux Jambons (in tiles and *bessales*), Villers-sur-Lesse, and Willemeau 2. A recurrent building material for sewers seems to have been *imbrices*, which were inverted to create a gutter, e.g. in Aiseau 'Bath 2' (*alveus*), Arquennes (for rain water from the roof?), Aubechies, Autre-Église (*tepidarium* and *caldarium*), Flostoy, Gesves (phase 1), Hamois (leading into a channel made of stone slabs), Mettet 'Bath 1', Mettet 'Bath 2', and Treignes. In Emptinne-Champion, one of the drainage channels was made of *tubuli* of which the lateral openings were filled with mortar (Van Ossel and De Poorter 1992, 237). In Waha, the main drain was cut out of the bedrock (Corbiau 2006, 209). Some of the ditches that seem to have evacuated waste waters might once have contained wooden pipes, which was probably the case in Bruyelle (Ansieau and Bausier 2018, 139–40). Some of the drainage channels ended in a sump, e.g. in Kumtich 'Bath 2', Meslin-l'Évêque, Gesves (phase 2), Maillen – Al Sauvenière, or Vellereille-les-Brayeux. In the open space east of 'Bath 1' in Mettet, the floor level seems to have sloped towards a sump, at the bottom of which a greasy substance (mix of dirt and oils from the baths?) was found (Mahieu 1919, 86). For 'Bath 2' at the same site, the drainage channels of cold and heated pools first collected in a basin (1.4 × 1 m; 0.56 m deep), before heading as one drain to a sump outside the villa complex (Mahieu 1919, 101). In Mont-lez-Houffalize – Fin de Ville 'Bath 2', the *piscina* emptied directly into an adjoining well (Meunier 1964, 162). The reason for collecting the waste waters in a sump or well was probably linked to reuse, for example for gardening. The agrarian author Palladius (late fourth or fifth century, Italy?) hints at such a reuse: 'If possible, the baths should be placed so that all the grey water from them runs through the gardens' (*de re rust.* 1.39.4; trans. by Fitch 2013, 66). Such water containing oil, sands, dead skin, and perhaps some other decoctions applied to the skin (often based on animal fat) may indeed have been quite fertilizing.[7] However, the majority of drains seem to have emptied into a stream.

---

7   It is unknown if the use of *nitrum*, a Latin shorthand to designate different salt compositions which were used as soap, was widespread in north-west Gaul (Blonski 2014b). However, late antique literature refers to *sapo* as a type of detergent using ashes and having a Gallic-Celtic origin (Blonski 2014a, 283–84).

CHAPTER 6

Building Material and Decoration

Vernacular building traditions in the study area relied on perishable but readily available materials such as timber and loam (Brulet 2008, 131–32; De Clercq 2011). Even after the Roman conquest, most buildings in small towns as well as in the countryside only had stone bases with the higher walls made of timber framing and wattle and daub. The availability of stone building materials obviously influenced local building techniques. Especially in the north-western part of the research area, in modern Flanders, good quality building stone was scarce, as no natural outcrops were present (Dusar, Dreesen, and De Naeyer 2009). The use of ceramic building materials in the research area was often limited to the roof (*tegulae* and *imbrices*), to elements coming into direct contact with fire and heat (hearths, kilns, furnaces, hypocausts) and as part of the wall, for constructing arches, and as levelling layer. However, due to moisture and fire hazard, bathing rooms had to be constructed entirely in stone or ceramic building materials (Brulet 2008, 149–52). Ceilings could potentially be constructed using planks, provided these were protected from moisture by layers of plaster.[1]

Building Stone

It is only in the last decades that excavation reports have started to pay attention to the provenance of building stones, even if this is often limited to macroscopic observations while chemical analysis combined with cross-referencing remains the exception.[2] Older pub-lications sometimes mention locally quarried building stone, without further detail. It is mainly limestone or sandstone or a combination of both, cut into regular small blocks and bonded with mortar, the so-called '*petit appareil*' in French literature (Adam 1984, 137). Several layers of such blocks could be alternated by one or two layers of tiles, which created a building technique called *opus vittatum mixtum* (Adam 1984, 154), e.g. in Autre-Église, Emptinne-Champion, Famars, Maastricht, or Waha. Stones that break along thin *laminae* to form flat sheets of stone such as schist, shale, or slate were mainly used as roof tiles (see above) and for covering drains. Due to their irregular shape, flint boulders and local river boulders were only used in foundations.

Limestone was the main building material in the public bath of Fontaine-Valmont (locally quarried; Faider-Feytmans 1976, 9), Liberchies (Brulet and Demanet 1997, 18), Clavier (also slate; Willems 1965, 75), and in the military baths of Furfooz (Brulet 1978, 48). At Tournai (Amand 1946, 101) and nearby Kortrijk (*c.* 25 km to the north; Despriet 1997), local Tournai limestone was used. It was also found at more remote northern sites such as Oudenburg *vicus*, where local boulders and tufa from the Rhine area were also used (Creus 1975, 9) and even at Aardenburg, some 75 km to the north of Tournai (van Dierendonck and Vos 2013, 105). All three sites were linked to the military. Tournai limestone was also used in the nearby villas of Willemeau, some 5 km to the south-west (Amand and Soleil 1988, 51), and Heestert (Janssens 1984, 11) and Tiegem (De Cock 1988, 78), both *c.* 21 km to the north of Tournai. In other private baths, (local) limestone was also used, although no further information is available on provenance, e.g. in Aiseau, Amay, Arquennes, Boirs (with tufa), Boussu-lez-Walcourt, Broekhem, Emptinne-Champion, Clermont-sous-Huy, Évelette – Résimont (with schist), Gesves (with sandstone), Haillot, Hamois, Jemelle (from Givet, some 30 km to the west), Leignon, Lemiers (on a foundation of boulders), Maillen – Al Sauvenière, Marchienne-au-Pont, Matagne-la-Petite, Mettet (locally quarried), Miécret, Montignies-Saint-Christophe, Namur, Neerharen-Rekem, Thirimont,

---

1 As proposed by Palladius (*Agr.* 1.39.4). The use of timber to construct bathing rooms, including for the heated section, is exceptional, but has been attested in Augustan/Tiberian-period military baths in the Netherlands (Velsen), Switzerland (*Vindonissa*), Czechia (Mušov), and Germany (Anreppen, Marktbreit, Dangstetten) (Bidwell 2002). Martial's epigram (ix.75) on the wooden baths of a certain Tucca may not have been a mere joke after all.

2 A good example of such attention to stone provenance in post-excavation strategy is the study of the 'Kerkakkers' villa at Hoogeloon (Hiddink 2014).

Tourinnes-St-Lambert, Villers-sur-Lesse, Vissoul, Vodelée, and Waha.

Sandstone was less frequently used and often in combination with limestone, as for example in the presumably public bath of Amay-Ombret (Witvrouw 1986, 88) and in most baths in Tongeren, where the walls rested on a foundation of flint boulders (Pauwels, Vanderhoeven, and Vynckier 2005, 76). For the small alleged public bath of Tourinnes-St-Lambert, the provenance of the sandstone was studied. The sandstone was discovered to hail from Gobertange, some 17 km to the north, or Genappe, some 20 km to the east. Slate from Villers-la-Ville, 18 km to the south-west of the *vicus*, or perhaps from the Ardennes was also found (De Maeyer 1940, 28). In Macquenoise, a small town known for its quarries of arkose, a sandstone containing at least 25 per cent feldspar, the local stone was the only type of building stone used in the public bath (Brulet 1985, 37). The so-called 'kolenzandsteen', a sandstone with small pieces of coal embedded in it, used in the public (?) baths of Maastricht is quarried in the western Rhineland (Eschweiler area). Blocks of tufa and marl (for the foundations) were also identified (Bogaers 1963, 161). In the Castellum Bath of Liberchies, locally quarried sandstone was used on a foundation of wooden posts to stabilize the soggy virgin soil (Mertens and Brulet 1974, 35). Sandstone was also primarily used in the private bath in Anderlecht, presumably quarried at Laken, some 7 km to the north-east (Dens 1906, 242). The sandstone used in the bath of the villa of Basse-Wavre was probably quarried in Landen, *c.* 30 km to the east (Dens and Poils 1905, 326). Sandstone of unknown provenance was reported for the baths at Attenhoven, Bierbeek, Flostoy, Kumtich ('Bath 1' and 'Bath 2'), Machelen, Merbes-le-Château, Mont-lez-Houffalize – Sommerain, Soignies, Vechmaal, Vesqueville, and Vorst.

Other types of stone could also be used to construct the walls. Again, it mainly concerns locally quarried material. Marl is used in Heer (Habets 1895, 270–71) and Val-Meer (De Boe 1971a, 8), schist in the road station of Wyompont (Geubel 1887, 203). In the public bath of Grobbendonk, boulders of limonite were used (De Boe 1977, 36). Tufa was found in the walls in Autre-Église, Heure-le-Romain (together with flint boulders), Marcinelle, Modave, Nouvelles, and Hoogeloon (from the Eifel). As already mentioned flint boulders were mainly used for foundations, e.g. in Ambresin (but also for walls), Autre-Église, Neerharen-Rekem, Tongeren, Val-Meer, Vechmaal, and Willemeau 2. Although mainly used as roof tiles, schist was also used for the walls in the (public?) bath of Braives, and the villa baths of Bras-Haut and Limerlé.

Wood and Timber

Wood would certainly have been used for *mobilia* such as benches, stools, cupboards, buckets, etc., which have rarely survived due to reuse and post-depositional decay. But wood could also be used for 'fixed' elements such as stairs, steps, doors, shelves (to store clothes or bath utensils), or latrine seats.[3] Timber beams and planks were used in the upper parts of walls in combination with loam or clay, and in roof construction (see above, Chapter 4), but also in wells and water reservoirs (see above, Chapter 5). Tree trunks were hollowed out and held together by rope and/or iron rings, serving as subterranean water supply channels or drainage channels (see above, Chapter 5). In wet or sandy areas, wooden posts were driven into the ground to stabilize stone foundations, as could be noted in Aardenburg (van Dierendonck and Vos 2013, 101–03), Tournai – Quai Vifquin (Verslype 1997, 66), and Liberchies 'Castellum Baths' (Mertens and Brulet 1974, 34).[4] Sometimes, timber elements could also be visible parts of the construction. In the villa of Vechmaal, two column bases were found in front of the bath entrance to create a porch (Vanvinckenroye 1997, 191). As no stone or ceramic column drums were found, the columns might have been made of wood. Similarly, in the public baths of Fontaine-Valmont, the portico might have been created using wooden columns. It cannot be ruled out that other porticos connected to baths, e.g. to connect the villa to the baths (in Haccourt 'Bath 3', Merbes-le-Château 'Bath 2', etc.), also made use of (painted or plastered?) wooden columns. Some *praefurnia* also seem to have been protected by an awning resting on wooden posts, e.g. in Soignies (Deramaix and Sartieaux 1995, 52), Haccourt 'Bath 2' (De Boe 1974, 23), and possibly Haccourt 'Bath 3' (phase 1 in the *praefurnium* of the *caldarium* and phase 2 in the *praefurnium* for the room west of the *caldarium*, De Boe 1976, 6, 18). Some of the bath rooms in which no mortar floor, tiles, or flagstones were identified may have had wooden floors. It often concerns room at the beginning of the bathing sequence, *frigidaria* or *apodyteria*, or rooms with a peripheral position vis-à-vis the main bathing rooms (*frigidarium-tepidarium-caldarium*). In at least three examples, evidence for such a wooden floor was discovered. In the small central room (*frigidarium?*) in the villa baths of Graux, a burned wooden floor was discovered (Mahieu 1910, 140). In the north-eastern

---

3   A rare example of such a wooden latrine seat was discovered in the waterlogged context of the *Vindolanda* camp (UK), see <https://www.vindolanda.com/toilet-seat> [accessed 20 September 2022].

4   Additionally, in the 'Castellum Bath' in Liberchies, some of the walls also rested on wooden beams.

room of the villa baths of Maillen – Al Sauvenière, interpreted as *apodyterium*, three large wooden beams at an interval of around 1 m crossed the room from north to south, acting as joists to support east–west oriented floorboards (Mahieu 1892, 351, 371). In the central room of the 'Castellum Bath' of Liberchies, two parallel wooden beams crossed the centre of the dirt floor, possibly to support floorboards and perhaps frame a water pipe (Mertens and Brulet 1974, 37).[5] In other cases, only a dirt floor was discovered., e.g. in the public bath of Grobbendonk (*frigidarium*) and the villa baths of Arquennes (*frigidarium*), Broekhem (*apodyterium?*), Haccourt 'Bath 3' (*apodyterium*), Saint-Gérard (*apodyterium?*), Soignies (*frigidarium*), or Vorst (part of the *frigidarium* and a room of unknown function). This would not have been an ideal combination with the water of the baths, so it is highly likely that these floors were once covered by a wooden floor, which decayed or was removed afterwards.

Up till now, no evidence of wooden baths has been found in the research area. Such baths, of which only a small number are known (in Germany, the Netherlands, Switzerland, and Czechia), seem to have been built in pre-Flavian forts (Bidwell 2002; Lehar 2015). However, some buildings made entirely out of wood, and found in the vicinity of baths, may have been used by the bathers (if contemporaneous). A small building made entirely out of perishable materials (timber and loam) stood some 40 m west of the bath of Chastrès (Bequet 1900, 31), while a small wooden building was also found west of the 'Castellum Bath' in Oudenburg (Vanhoutte 2018, 167). It is difficult to interpret these wooden buildings. An example in Germany can give us a clue. Near the military bath of Krefeld-Gellep (destroyed in AD 86), a small wooden building could be interpreted as a latrine. Other functions for these buildings, such as a temporary shed used during the construction of the baths (as proposed by Vanhoutte 2018, 167 for Oudenburg or De Boe 1976, 6 for a construction in the *praefurnium* of Haccourt 'Bath 3'), cannot be excluded.

Ceramic Building Materials

As has already been discussed in Chapter 5 on technology, different types of ceramic building materials were used to create the hypocaust system, the wall heating, and the water supply and disposal. Unfortunately, most old

publications did not pay any attention to the specifics of these bricks and tiles. More recent excavation reports do include separate sections on (ceramic) building materials, even if thorough studies are scarce. For a few of the ceramic pipes that have been found, even basic information such as dimensions is provided. Below, only the specific building materials for baths (hypocaust tiles, *tubuli*, and *tegulae mammatae*) are discussed in more detail. A discussion of more general building materials such as *lateres*, *tegulae*, and *imbrices* falls beyond the scope of this study.

The *bessales* used to construct the hypocaust pillars could be round or square in section. The dimensions of these tiles differ from site to site (see Table 12 in the Appendix). The square *bessales* have sides varying from 14 cm to 30 cm, although most have sides between 18 cm and 22 cm. The average thickness of these *bessales* is 3 to 5 cm. The round hypocaust tiles have a diameter between 12 cm and 32.5 cm, and are 3 to 5 cm thick. On average, these round tiles have a diameter between 20 cm and 23 cm.

There are very few (intact) examples of *tegulae mammatae* mentioned in the excavation reports (see Table 13 in the Appendix). Only in the first phase of the presumably public bath in Amay-Ombret, a complete square *tegula mammata* with a side of 27 cm was found (Witvrouw 1986, 101). The dimensions of the *tubuli* also vary between sites (see Table 13 in the Appendix). No two sites seem to have had the same *tubuli*. Even within the same bathhouse, *tubuli* of different sizes could be used, e.g. in Hoogeloon (Hiddink 2014, 659). The lengths and widths of the *tubuli* seem to have averaged 20 to 25 cm, while the depth was often between 10 and 16 cm. This resulted in quite broad *tubuli*, compared to for example Italian examples, which were more elongated, e.g. 14 × 32 × 12 cm for certain *tubuli* in Ostia (Maréchal forthcoming). Only in Rognée, one example of a more elongated type (40 × 11 × 13 cm) has been found (Kaisin 1897, 86). Most *tubuli* also had lateral openings, mainly round in shape with a diameter averaging 3.5 to 5 cm or more exceptionally square or rectangular, e.g. in Mettet 'Bath 1' (9 × 8 cm; Mahieu 1919, 85). Preliminary observations on some of the *tubuli* found in the research area has pointed to a production technique by which four different slabs of clay seem to have been pressed around a core (Maréchal, De Haan, and Clerbaut 2021). The reason why this technique was used instead of a technique by which a single slab was wrapped around a core, creating only a single seam, as identified in Ostia (Maréchal, De Haan, and Clerbaut 2021), is unclear. Four seams, one in each corner, present a higher risk of cracking, both during the drying process and during the actual baking (both encountered during the experimental reconstruction of the *chaîne opératoire*, see Maréchal,

---

5 A wooden beam outside of the bathhouse walls but in line with the two beams of the central room, is interpreted by the excavators as part of a drainage channel (Mertens and Brulet 1974, 40). A drainage channel of wooden beams, tiles, and stone blocks, also seems to have headed towards the presumed *caldarium*.

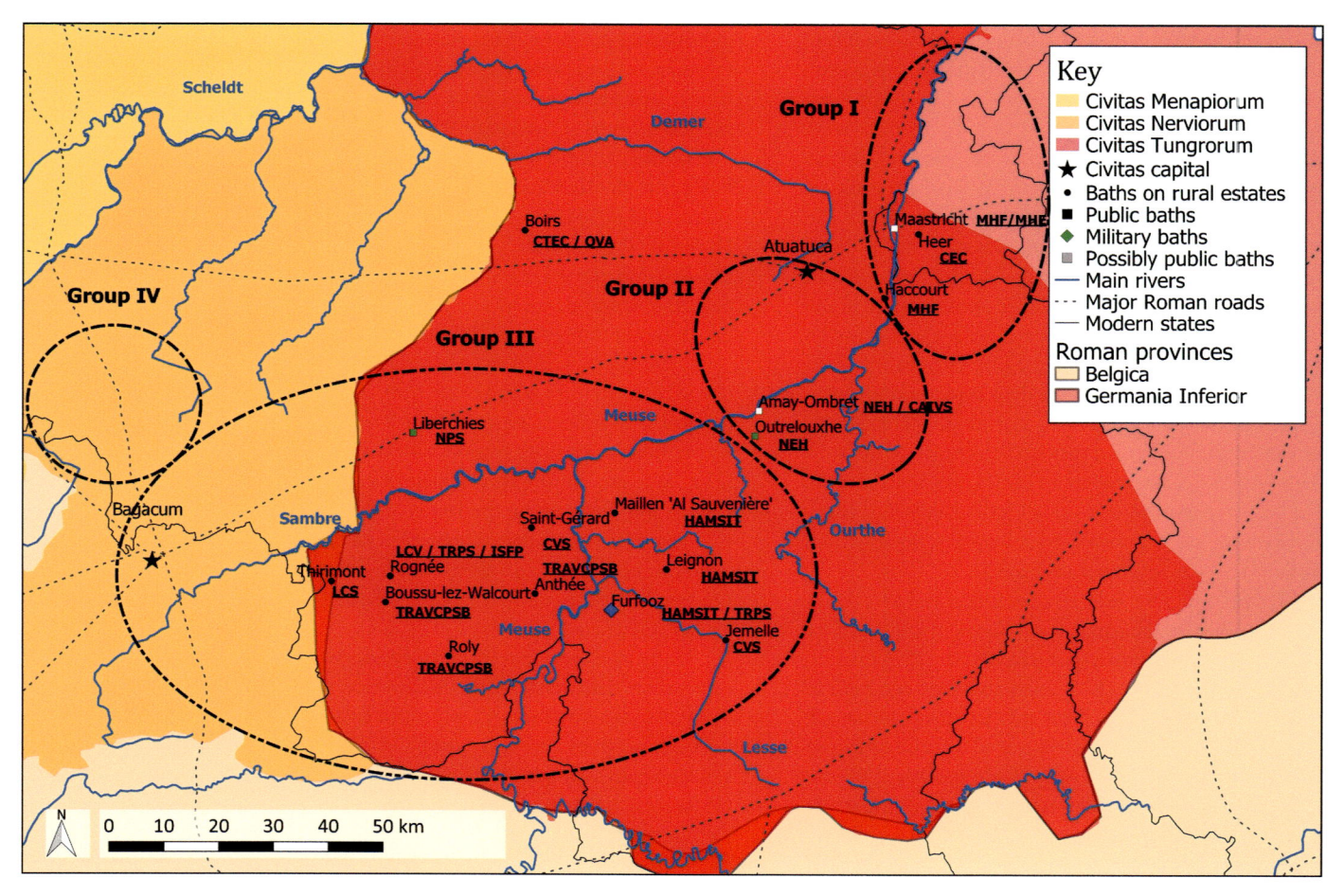

Map 6. Occurrence of tile stamps within the baths of the research area, with delimitation of the groups of stamps frequently found together (Group I: AAF, CC, CEC/CTEC/CETC, MHF-MHE; Group II: ADF/ADI, BP, CISSI, GFP, NEH, QVA/OVA; Group III: ATAB, ATII/ATIL, CVS/GVS, FAL, HAMSIT, ISFP, LCS, NSS, SABT, TRAVCPSB, TRP, TRPOIS/IRPOIS, TRPOS, TRPS, TRPOT; Group IV: CANTI/CAVTI, GABIN). Map by author; groups after Brulet 2008, 207, fig. 299.

de Haan and Clerbaut 2021). The numerous fragments of *tubuli* found throughout the research area seem to confirm that this 'four slab' technique must have been frequent, as the fragments show that the *tubuli* broke in the corners, where the seams would have been. Besides their use in wall heating, *tubuli* were sometimes used in absence of other specific building materials, e.g. to create drainage channels (see above, Chapter 5, on waste water disposal) or hypocaust pillars (see above, Chapter 5, on heating). In Tongeren – Sint-Truiderstraat a thin wall made entirely out of *tubuli* was used to separate two rooms at *suspensura* level, whereas the hypocaust underneath was not divided (Huybrigts 1904, 313).

Up till now, no examples of so-called *tubuli cuneati* or voussoir tiles have been identified in bathhouses in the research area. Few archaeologists possibly recognized this special type of wedge-shaped *tubulus*, used to create 'hollow' barrel vaults that enabled the circulation of hot gasses in ceilings. However, a recent re-examination of ceramic building materials in the research area has in fact discovered the presence of such tiles, namely at Hoogeloon, Maastricht, Tongeren, Kontich, and Dilbeek (Clerbaut 2021), but none of the finds could be linked to bathhouses. Nonetheless, *tubuli cuneati* were mainly used in baths, as the evidence in neighbouring regions seems to indicate,[6] making it likely that such building materials will be recognized in future excavations or re-examinations of older contexts.

The ceramic building materials were manufactured in regional production centres, some of which are known through excavations (Brulet 2008, 205–08). Sometimes, a *tegula* or *bessalis* was stamped with an abbreviation (Map 6). In several baths, mainly of private villas, such stamps have also been identified.

---

6   For voussoir tiles in baths in southern *Britannia*, see Lancaster 2012. For baths in *Gallia Lugdunensis*, see Ferdière and Jaffrot 2015. Some examples have also been found in *Coriovallum* (Heerlen) and surroundings in *Germania Inferior*, see Clerbaut 2021.

The stamp CTEC in Boirs (Peuskens and Tromme 1979, 387) and the variation CEC in Heer, some 15 km to the north-east (Habets 1895, 271), is frequently found in the Meuse valley east of Tongeren (Brulet 2008, 207). Similarly, the stamps MHF/MHE, found in Maastricht (Bogaers 1963, 213) and Haccourt 'Bath 3' (De Boe 1976, 12), and AAF and CC, which have not been found in baths yet, appear with some frequency in this area. The stamp TRAVCPSB has been found in Anthée 'Bath 3' (Del Marmol 1877, 188), Boussu-lez-Walcourt (Bayet 1891, 66) and Roly (Robert 1980, 92), all three sites located within a radius of 15 km of each other (Map 6). This stamp is often encountered in a large area between Bavay and Braives, where we also find other stamps. This includes CVS, identified in the villa bath of Jemelle (Mahieu 1897, 419) and Saint-Gérard (Brulet 1970, 79) which lie c. 40 km apart. The stamp HAMSIT is also found in the same area, for example in the fort baths of Furfooz (Brulet 1978, 48) and the villa bath of Leignon (Hauzeur 1851, 381) and Maillen – Al Sauvenière (Mahieu 1892, 357), which all lie within a 10 km radius. The stamps TRPS, found at the fort bath of Furfooz (Brulet 1978, 48) and the villa bath of Boussu-lez-Walcourt (Bayet 1891, 66), which lie 40 km apart and LCS at the villa of Thirimont (Van Bastelaer 1891a, 387) also appear here. In the villa bath of Rognée, some 10 km and 6 km from Boussu-lez-Walcourt and Thirimont respectively, the stamps LCV, TRPS, and (I?)SFP were found on hypocaust tiles (Kaisin 1897, 87–88). The stamps ATAB, ATII (or ATIL), FAL, NSS, SABT, TRP, TRPOIS (or IRPOIS), TRPOS, and TRPOT can be found in the same area, but for now no examples of these have been found in baths. A third group of stamps is found mainly between Tongeren and Braives (Brulet 2008, 207). It includes the stamp NEH, found in the (possibly) public baths Amay-Ombret (Witvrouw 1986, 93) and road relay bath of Outrelouxhe (Witvrouw 2014, 78), both within a 15 km radius, but also QVA, identified in the villa bath of Boirs (Peuskens and Tromme 1979, 400). Both stamps have also been found in the public building near the public bath of Clavier, rather than in the bath itself (Willems 1968, 189 correcting Willems 1965, 75). The stamps ADF (or ADI), BP, CISSI, and GFP, also belong to this third group, but have not been found in baths. Similarly, a fourth group including the stamps CANTI (or CAVTI) and GABIN occurs in the area between Tournai and Bavay, but has not been identified yet on building materials of baths. Other stamps such as NPS on a *bessales* in the 'Vicus Bath' of Liberchies (Brulet and Demanet 1997, 16) or CAIVS in phase 1 of the presumably public bath of Amay-Ombret (Witvrouw 1986, 87) are more exceptional.

Marble and Other Decorative Stone

Marble, limestone, and to a lesser degree sandstone was used for plinths, thresholds, sills, and flagstones. As there are no outcrops of marble in the study area, we must be very careful when consulting old excavation reports identifying 'marble' among the finds. The stones are often local limestones and breccias, which were conveniently grouped under the shorthand 'marble' to indicate decorative stone. Such valuable slabs of decorative stone were consistently recuperated once a building fell out of use and often only the imprints of flagstones in the mortar remain.

One would expect to find marbles and local limestone in public baths, as wealthy patrons who commissioned bathhouses, whether they acted as members of a local council or on their own behalf, would have wanted to impress bathers with the best possible decorations (Fagan 1999, 176–88; de Haan 2006). In the public bath of Famars, the *frigidarium* floor and the lower part of its walls were clad with tiles of bluish limestone, while the *caldarium* floor was tiled with black and white limestone slabs in a checkered pattern (Beaussart 1980, 810). In the *vicus* of Liberchies, the *piscina* floor was embellished with flagstones of green schist (Brulet and Demanet 1997, 19). In the possibly public baths of Bavay – Rue Saint-Maur, the *suspensura* was embellished with slabs of 'noir français' (Biévelet 1956, 574), while in the nearby 'Église Notre-Dame-de-l'Assomption', similar slabs and slabs of *marbre rouge belge* were found against the lower part of a heated room (Biévelet 1953, 43). In the other known public baths, no traces of decorative stone were recovered during the excavations, although we can imagine that these buildings must have been prime 'quarries' for later spoliation.

There are numerous attestations of the use of decorative stone in villa baths, and not only in the more luxurious sites. These are often labelled 'marble', although as mentioned above, this term could easily have been used as a shorthand to describe all sorts of decorative stone. A case in point is the so-called *marbre de St-Anne*, which is actually a limestone, and has unsurprisingly been identified in the *piscina* of the villa bath in Gerpinnes, where the stone was quarried (De Glymes, Henseval, and Kaisin 1875, cx). In most cases, only the general term 'marble' is used, without specifying the provenance and only seldomly the colour, e.g. Aiseau 'Integrated Baths', Anthée 'Bath 1', Bois-et-Borsu, Melsbroek (white marble), Mettet 'Bath 2', Neerharen-Rekem, Nouvelles, Tongeren – Boudewijnlaan (white and green marble), Tongeren – Vemeulenstraat 3, Villers-le-Bouillet, Willemeau 'Bath 2' (white marble), or Meersen. In general, it seems that stone quarried in the (immediate) vicinity was used. In Bruyelle, several fragments of more 'exotic' stone

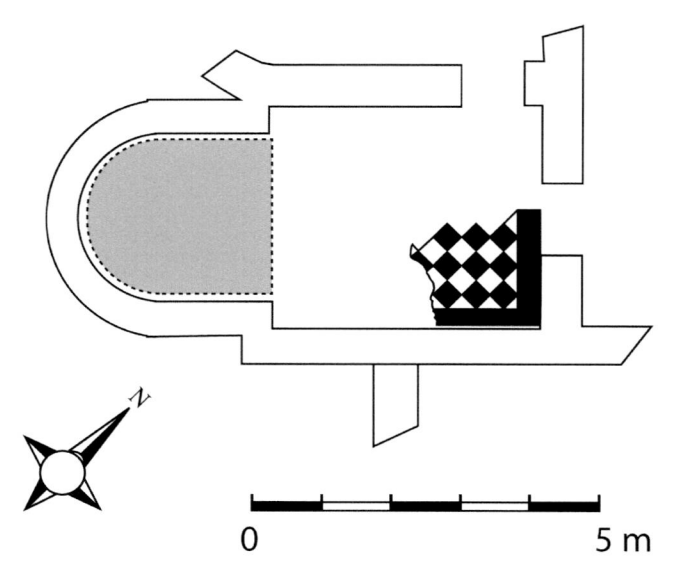

Figure 16. Drawing of the checkered *opus sectile* floor in the *frigidarium* of the baths at Boirs. Figure by author after Peuskens and Tromme 1979, 410, pl. II.

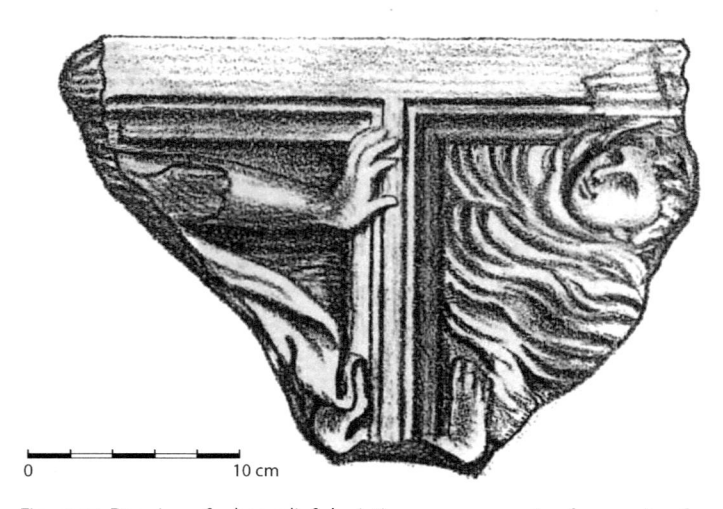

Figure 17. Drawing of a bas-relief depicting a man emerging from water, found in the villa bath of Meerssen. Figure by author after Habets 1871, pl. VIII.

were found, including Numidian *giallo antico, porfido rosso, porfido verde di Grecia,* and unspecified white marbles from the Mediterranean (Ansieau and Bausier 2018, 264). Decorative stones were mainly used in the *frigidarium* and the *piscina*. Just as for mosaics, the *piscina* probably filled in rather quickly after abandonment, hence increasing the chance of survival of its paving. Flagstones have been preserved in the *piscinae* of Basse-Wavre, Emptinne-Champion, Clermont-sous-Huy, Gerpinnes, Mettet 'Bath 2', Tongeren – Boudewijnlaan' Tournai – Couvent des Frères mineurs, Tournai – Vieux Marché aux Jambons, and Vellereille-les-Brayeux. In Arquennes, only the imprint of the slabs in the mortar

floor of the *piscina* could be discerned (Cloquet 1873, 75). In Grumelange, a bluish limestone was used in the square heated room, which may not have been part of the actual bathhouse (Malget and Malget 1912, 417). *Opus sectile* floors are attested at Anthée 'Bath 2', where slabs of red 'marble' were included (Del Marmol 1877, 174). At both Boirs (Peuskens and Tromme 1979, 390) and Boussu-lez-Walcourt (Bayet 1891, 55), the *opus sectile* consisted of a checkered pattern of black and white square limestone slabs (Fig. 16) in respectively the *frigidarium* and the *caldarium*.

Decorative stone was also used in statues and architectural elements, such as columns and capitals, entablatures, etc. Bathhouses, both public and private, were often adorned with statues of divinities linked to water (Neptune, nereids, nymphs), health and good fortune (Hygieia, Asclepius, Fortuna), or beauty (Venus, three Graces, Amor) (Manderscheid 1981, 30–34; Brödner 1983, 132–35; Dunbabin 1989, 21–30). Unfortunately, many statues and architectural elements were reused as building material, often in foundations. Limestone, be it statues or architectural elements, vanished in (post-Roman) limekilns to obtain unslaked lime, a necessary component of mortar. In the villa bath of Vodelée, a column base and part of a capital in blue limestone of Givet, located 8 km to the south-east, were found (Rober 1987, 162). In the excavations at Bovigny, a hand of a statue in limestone was found next to the pool (Mignot 1994b, 111). In the villa bath of Meerssen, a life-size finger in white marble was recovered, as well as a figurative bas-relief depicting a man emerging from water (Fig. 17; Habets 1871, 388). In Thirimont, a chiselled cornice and a column drum in limestone survived (Van Bastelaer 1891a, 386). In Haccourt 'Bath 1', a drain cover was made out of marble or limestone (De Boe 1971b, 19). In a well near the bath of Bruyelle, fragments of a limestone palmette and part of a *cornucopia* were found, which possibly came from the baths according to the excavators (Ansieau and Bausier 2018, 274, 281).[7] The bath of Famars is the only public bath to have yielded decorative stone ornaments: column drums, a composite capital, and bas-reliefs (Delmaire and others 1996, 222). At the relay station of Outrelouxhe, an arm and a leg of a limestone statue were discovered outside the building (Witvrouw 2014, 76–78). In the presumed baths underneath the Église Notre-Dame-de-l'Assomption in Bavay, a chiselled cornice in *noir français* was found (Biévelet 1953, 45).

---

7   The *cornucopia* was an attribute of the goddess Fortuna. As a goddess warding off evil, statues of Fortuna were sometimes found in bathhouses (eight examples listed by Manderscheid 1981, 139).

Mosaics

Before the Roman conquest, there was no local tradition of mosaic-laying in the north-western part of Europe so the technique had to be introduced by immigrant craftsmen (Dunbabin 1999, 73). Mosaics were a very popular form of decoration in bathhouses, not only to embellish floors, but also for the inside of pools, on walls, and on ceilings. The separate small stones (*tesserae*) made mosaics especially fitted to use on floors because adaptation to the form of the rooms was quite easy (Manderscheid 1994, 62–63). In the Mediterranean, marine and water-related themes in particular were found in bath mosaics (Manderscheid 1994, 64; Weber 1996, 140). Figurative scenes were mainly used in the most important bathing rooms, especially in the *frigidarium*, which was often a spacious and bright-lit room that could accommodate larger compositions. Non-figurative mosaics, including geometric and floral patterns, were more often confined to less important passages, corridors, and smaller rooms. The themes do not seem to have differed in public or private baths (Manderscheid 1994, 65).

Very few intact mosaics have been found in bathhouses in the research area. Often only loose *tesserae* are collected, which could have adorned floors as well as walls and ceilings. For baths integrated in houses or villas, such *tesserae*, especially if found in small numbers, might have moved from other rooms. In the public baths, only the *frigidarium* in Tienen has yielded some black and white *tesserae* (Vanderhoeven, Vynckier, and Wouters 1998, 144). A uniform blue mosaic was discovered in the possible public bath of Bavay – Rue Saint-Maur (Biévelet 1956, 578). Few examples of floor mosaics *in situ* survived from private baths. In Haccourt 'Bath 1', the *frigidarium* floor was embellished with a mosaic of black and white lozenges (Fig. 18; De Boe 1971b, 19) and in the north-east corner, a mosaic made of red terracotta fragments seems to have contained a text, of which only a single letter (R) survives (De Boe 1974, 18). In 'Bath 3' at Anthée dark blue geometric patterns with a 'Maltese cross' on a white background were found in what may be identified as a cold room (Fig. 19; Del Marmol 1877, 185; Stern 1960, 28). In Kumtich 'Bath 1' a mosaic with a black and white geometric pattern was found in the *frigidarium* (Cramers 1984, 118). At Saint-Jean-Geest a plain white mosaic was discovered in presumably a cold room south of the room with a hypocaust (Remy 1977, 14). Loose *tesserae* were found in Anthée 'Bath 2' (Del Marmol 1877, 174) and 'Bath 3' (Del Marmol 1877, 185), Basse-Wavre (Dens and Poils 1905, 319), Haccourt 'Bath 2' (De Boe 1971b, 20), Kumtich 'Bath 2' (Cramers 1984, 120), Montignies-Saint-Christophe (context unknown; Brulet 1973b, 178), and Namur (Lauwerijs 1972, 99), unsurprisingly sites

Figure 18. Mosaic floor in the *frigidarium* in 'Bath 1' at the villa of Haccourt, with stone drain cover in the northern corner. Photo in De Boe 1971b, 20, fig. 4.

Figure 19. Drawing of the geometric mosaic found in the presumed cold section of 'Bath 3' at the villa of Anthée. Figure in Stern 1960, pl. VIII, 156c.

with more luxurious baths. Figurative scenes have not been identified yet. This fits with an overall scarcity of figured scenes in the continental north of the Empire, in favour of geometric designs (Dunbabin 1999, 79). A pre-Roman preference for more abstract designs in art may well have continued in large parts of northern Europe (Millett 1990, 117). More in general, mosaics were a type of decoration that was quite uncommon for baths in the research area, perhaps only available to those who could afford to hire specialist mosaic craftsmen from other regions. For north-western continental Europe, the wider Rhineland region, especially the Mosel valley and its two main cities *Augusta Treverorum* (Trier) and

Colonia Claudia Ara Agrippensium (Cologne), was the epicentre of mosaic art (Dunbabin 1999, 79). However, the number of mosaics found in bathhouses is generally low in the province of *Germania Inferior* (Dodt 2003, 160). The only examples were found in the *frigidarium* and *apodyterium* of the public bath of Heerlen (Peterse 2020, 53–55), in a heated room of the villa baths at Vlengendaal (Goossens 1916, 5), and in the *tepidarium* of a suburban *domus* in the Benesissstraße in Cologne (Carroll-Spillecke 1997, 267). It is also important to note that mosaics were not only rare in baths, as very few examples have been found in the entire study area, even in the larger centres such as Tongeren (Stern 1960, 21–33). In the capital of the *civitas Tungrorum*, only one private house has yielded an *in situ* mosaic, consisting mainly of geometric patterns in black and white (Vanderhoeven, Vynckier, and Vynckier 1992).

Wall Paintings

Roman wall painting techniques and styles had already gone through a long evolution before they reached the study area. There is some evidence of pre-Roman forms of wall decoration in greater Gaul, including clay 'stucco' which was likely painted (Barbet 2008, 35–36). In Britain, the wattle-and-daub walls of pre-Roman houses were sometimes finished with a plaster that was decorated with geometric patterns (Perring 2002, 123). The influence might well have come from Gaul, and there is no reason to doubt that similar forms of decoration might also have been present in the research area. The fragments of burned loam which are frequently encountered in excavations, are often very fragmentary and in a bad state of preservation. Furthermore, incisions or reliefs in such loam fragments are consistently interpreted as features that ensured a better fixation of the loam to the walls (or as the negative imprints of the wattle), making it extremely difficult to distinguish actual decorative motifs. One of the earliest examples of Roman-style wall painting in the northern part of the Empire, was found in the *oppidum* of the Titelberg (G.D. Luxembourg). The red and white fragments imitating bossage were dated on the basis of dendrochronology of their context to 37 BC (Barbet 2008, 48).

In contrast to mosaics, wall paintings are frequently found in the study area, both in urban and in rural contexts. For the majority of baths, both public and private, wall paintings have been discovered during the excavations. Unfortunately, the evidence is often limited to strongly fragmented material. Furthermore, sandy (acidic) soils offer poor preservation conditions for the plaster on which the paintings were made. We find predominantly plain white fields bordered by coloured lines (red, green, ochre), geometric and floral-vegetal patterns. Few excavation reports, especially those of the late nineteenth or early twentieth century, mention the exact find location of the different fragments. As for mosaics, the dominance of geometric and floral designs may be linked to a continued preference for non-figurative, abstract themes of the pre-Roman societies.

In the public baths of Grobbendonk (De Boe 1977, 39), Tienen (Vanderhoeven, Vynckier, and Wouters 1998, 145), and Aardenburg (van Dierendonck and Vos 2013, 106), fragments of wall paintings have been found, but there is no further information available on the patterns, nor on the find spots. In the presumably public bath of Amay-Ombret (Witvrouw 1986, 106), Tongeren – Schaetzengaerde (Vanderhoeven and others 2007, 166–70), Tournai – Quai Luchet d'Antoing (Amand 1968, 41), and Tournai Quai Vifquin (Verslype 1997, 67) fragments of plain red wall painting were recovered. In Maastricht, wall paintings were found in the heated rooms (Leemans 1843, 40). In the bath of Clavier-Vervoz, the wall paintings depicted water plants and imitated marble (Willems and Lauwerijs 1973, 169). In the 'Vicus Bath' of Oudenburg, black and pink lines were drawn on a white background (Creus 1975, 9). The 'Castellum Bath' of Oudenburg also had wall paintings to embellish the interior (Vanhoutte 2018, 167–68), but no such decoration is mentioned for the fort baths of Furfooz or Liberchies.

For the private baths, most excavation reports only mention polychrome wall paintings among the finds, without further specifications, e.g. in Aiseau 'Integrated Bath', Ambresin, Anthée 'Bath 3', Boussu-lez-Walcourt, Bruyelle, Gerpinnes, Graux, Haccourt 'Bath 1' and 'Bath 2', Hollain, Leignon, Meersen, Mont-lez-Houffalize – Fin de Ville, Namur, Roly, Saint-Jean-Geest, Tiegem, Tongeren – Sint-Truiderstraat, and Tourinnes-St-Lambert. Red, yellow/ochre, and green are most commonly mentioned, blue quite rarely. Bluish-grey is the dominant colour in all of the bath rooms in Basse-Wavre (Dens and Poils 1905, 319), but it has also been found in Bruyelle (Ansieau and Bausier 2018, 268–74) and Heestert (Janssens 1984, 20). If a find spot is mentioned, it is usually in the *piscina*, which obviously offered better chances of survival as it lay lower than the floor levels. In Emptinne-Champion, a colourful round motif with vegetal motifs adorned the ceiling of the *frigidarium* (Fig. 20; Delplace 1991–1992; Delplace and Van Ossel 1991). In Marchienne-au-Pont green vegetation was depicted on a black background (De Waele 1984, 204). Several fragments of unspecified wall paintings were found in the *frigidarium* of 'Bath 2' in Mettet (Mahieu 1919, 101). In the heated rooms, wall paintings also had a better chance of survival if the hypocaust had already collapsed. In Boirs, wall

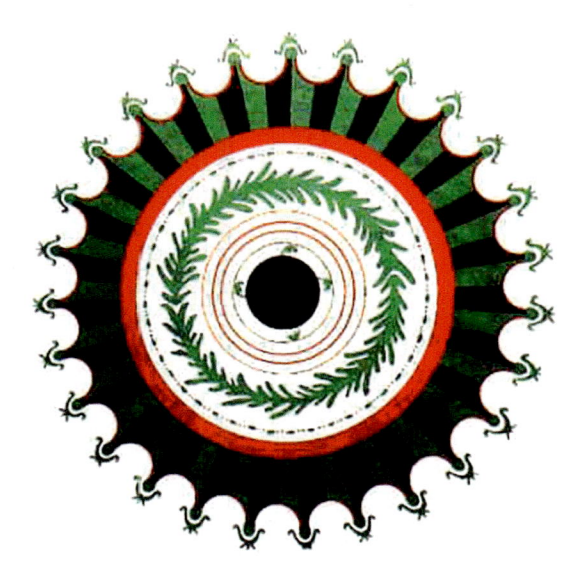

Figure 20. Reconstruction drawing of the geometric and floral wall pa nting adorning the ceiling of the *frigidarium* in the villa bath of Emptinne-Champion. Figure in Van Ossel and De Poorter 1992.

Figure 22. A *piscina* coated on the inside with a polished hydraulic mortar, Viehmarkt Thermen, Trier, 2012. Photo by author.

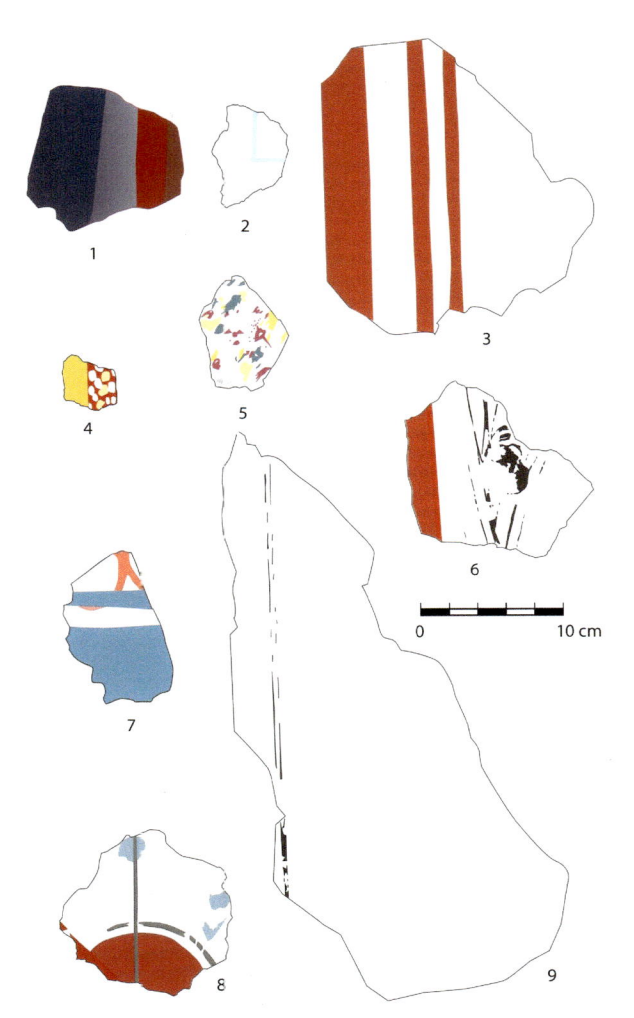

Figure 21. Fragments of polychrome wall painting found in the villa bath of Bruyelle. Nos 4 and 5 possibly imitated marble. Figure in Bausier, Bloch, and Pigière 2018, 271, fig. 199.

paintings with geometric and floral designs were found in the *tepidarium* (Peuskens and Tromme 1979, 394). In Clermont-sous-Huy (Witvrouw 1988, 37), Limerlé (Brulet 2008, 467), and Vellereille-les-Brayeux (Rahir 1928, 134) wall paintings were also found in the *tepidarium*. In the bath of Graux (Mahieu 1910, 140) and Maillen – Ronchinne (Bequet 1897, 194) fragments were found in the *caldarium*. In both 'Bath 1' and 'Bath 2' at Kumtich (Cramers 1984, 128), at Hamois (floral designs; Van Ossel 1980, 78), and in 'Bath 1' at Mettet (Mahieu 1919, 90), wall paintings were discovered in several heated rooms. In the villa bath of Oberüttfeld floral and geometric patterns adorned the walls in the *frigidarium* and *caldarium* (Faust 1999, 159). However, we must remember that these rooms are also the easiest to identify and that archaeologists will hesitate to attribute a function to a room with wall paintings but no specific features.

Besides geometric patterns, vegetal and floral designs are most commonly found, often in combination with geometric motifs, e.g. in Boirs (see above), Bruyelle (see above), Hamois (see above), Montignies-Saint-Christophe (Brulet 1973b, 178), Neerharen-Rekem (one fragment also 'engraved', Van Neuss and Bamps 1888, 349), Oberüttfeld (see above), and Thirimont (Van Bastelaer 1891, 376). Very few examples of figurative paintings have been found: a person in *tunica* in the bath in Melsbroek (De Maeyer 1940, 19–20), probably also figures in the bath of Hoogeloon (Hiddink 2014, 593), and an agrarian calendar depicting figures, animals, and carts in the possible bath of Tongeren – Vermeulenstraat 3 (Borgers, Steenhoudt, and Van de Velde 2008, 32–33). In Grumelange, paintings imitating marble were found in the *frigidarium* (Malget and Malget 1912, 417). Some fragments of flecked polychrome paintings in Hoogeloon (Hiddink 2014, 594) and Bruyelle (Ansieau and Bausier 2018, 274) have also been interpreted as marble imitation (Fig. 21).

Other Decoration

Stucco mouldings may have been more common than the evidence suggests. Well-preserved baths in the Mediterranean, including the baths in the Vesuvian cities, but also in for example North Africa, reveal that this type of decoration was widely used in the upper parts of bath rooms, for cornices, intrados of arches and vaults, etc. (Brödner 1983, 133–36). However, due to the fragility of this type of decoration, it only seldomly survives the ravages of time, shattering in numerous fragments when falling from the higher parts of the wall and dissolving in wet and acidic soils. In our research area, chances for survival are minimal. Only in the 'Integrated Bath' of Aiseau (Kaisin 1878, 189) and in the

bath of Arquennes (Cloquet 1873, 84) have fragments of such decorative stuccos been found. In Bruyelle, part of a semicolumn made of mortar was found in the bathhouse (Ansieau and Bausier 2018, 263).

A very basic way of embellishing the bath room floors, was simply polishing the pink(ish) hydraulic mortar. This type of floor was found in the *apodyterium* of the first phase of villa bath of Emptinne-Champion (Van Ossel and De Poorter 1992, 201) or in the *frigidarium* of Oberüttfeld (Faust 1999, 156). Especially for the inside of pools, this was the basic finish, in absence of more luxurious stone tiles or mosaics (Fig. 22). Alternatively, the larger *piscinae* could have a flooring of *bipedales* tiles, as has been found in Assenois (Sulbout 1868, 286), Jemelle (Mahieu 1897, 420), Machelen (Mertens 1955, 7–9), and even in the presumably public bath of Tongeren – Schaetzengaerde (Pauwels, Vanderhoeven, and Vynckier 2005, 76). In the villa bath of Heure-le-Romain, these tiles covered the *frigidarium* floor, although the excavators did not exclude that a final layer of flag stones may have been present (Peuskens and Tromme 1979, 402).

CHAPTER 7

Bathing and Society

The Introduction of Bathhouses in the Continental North-West

We have very few literary sources to inform us about the daily habits and social practices of the indigenous people inhabiting the research area before the arrival of the Romans. Caesar mainly informs us about the lands in which the conquered peoples lived (Caes. *B Gall.*) and Strabo (*Geogr.* IV.3.4–5) also gives us an account of the geography of the region, without focusing on its inhabitants. Some anecdotal information by Caesar nevertheless seems interesting. In comparing the Gauls to the Germans, Caesar (*B Gall.* VI.24) noticed how the former had grown soft: 'Gallis autem provinciarum propinquitas et transmarinarum rerum notitia multa ad copiam atque usus largitur, paulatim adsuefacti superari multisque victi proeliis ne se quidem ipsi cum illis virtute comparant' (Upon the Gauls, however, the neighbourhood of our provinces and acquaintance with oversea commodities lavishes many articles of use or luxury; little by little they have grown accustomed to defeat, and after being conquered in many battles they do not even compare themselves in point of valour with the Germans; trans. by Edwards 1917, 351). According to Caesar (Caes. *B Gall.* VI.29), the Gauls had developed a taste for Roman products and luxury. A further interesting remark concerns the social habits of the Germans, who organized banquets in which drinking seems to have played an important role. A similar remark is made by Tacitus (*Germ.* XXII.2–3) some decades later: 'Diem noctemque continuare potando nulli probrum. crebrae, ut inter vinolentos, rixae raro conviciis, saepius caede et vulneribus transiguntur. Sed et de reconciliandis invicem inimicis et iungendis adfinitatibus et adsciscendis principibus, de pace denique ac bello plerumque in conviviis consultant' (To make day and night run into one in drinking is a reproach to no man: brawls are frequent, naturally, among heavy drinkers: they are seldom settled with abuse, more often with wounds and bloodshed; nevertheless the mutual reconciliation of enemies, the forming of family alliances,

the appointment of chiefs, the question even of war or peace, are usually debated at these banquets; trans. by Hutton and Peterson 1914, 165). A sentence directly relevant for the bathing habits of these Germans, is found at the start of this same passage (*Germ.* XXII.1): 'Statim e somno, quem plerumque in diem extrahunt, lavantur, saepius calida, ut apud quos plurimum hiems occupat' (In waking from sleep, which they generally prolong into the day, they wash, usually in warm water, since winter bulks so large in their lives; trans. by Hutton and Peterson 1914, 165). Rather than washing with the cold water of a river, stream, or well, Tacitus claims the Germans heated their water if they wanted to wash. It is, however, nearly impossible to find archaeological evidence for this, as we can presume that water was simply heated in a cauldron.

In contrast to the Mediterranean region, which had been introduced to bathhouses by the spread of the Greek-Hellenistic type of bath (DeLaine 1989; Fagan 2001; Yegül 2013), in the northern part of Gaul these specific buildings only appeared after the Roman conquest. The first Roman-style baths to be built in the region may have been the baths of more permanent military camps acting as outposts in newly conquered regions and permanently manned during winter. Such camps are known from passages in Caesar (e.g. *B Gall.* IV.38), but have not been identified in the archaeological record. Temporary camps of legions on the move (e.g. Caes. *B Gall.* II.18) would not have had permanent structures (Hanel 2000, 23). For this first phase of the conquest, no bathhouses, military, private, or public, have been discovered. The earliest evidence of military baths in the wider region dates from the Neronian period (Hanel 2000, 24). In the research area, the first bathhouses date from the middle of the first century AD and did not belong to military camps. But as the earliest settlements in newly conquered regions are often linked to a military presence (Brulet 2008, 36, fig. 39), it is not inconceivable that the first public and private baths were inspired by military baths (Nielsen 1993a, 74). Several baths seem to date from the second half of the first century AD. One of the earliest examples and more or less securely dated by stratigraphic excavations, is the first phase of the bath at the villa of Emptinne-Champion. By the end of the first or the early second century, the original plan was altered, mainly in its heated part. The plan is remarkable because of the round *caldarium*. This round shape seems reminiscent of the *laconicum*, found in early Roman baths in Italy as well. Such rooms were initially heated by a portable brazier, as in the Republican baths in Pompeii (Pesando 2002), but by the late first century AD, examples heated by a hypocaust were also constructed, such as in the Central Baths in Pompeii, under construction in AD 79 (Bargellini 1991). It is interesting to note that such round rooms were often found in baths in military contexts (Nielsen 1993a, 78), perhaps because this type of sweat room was linked to Spartan customs, hence the name *laconicum*. No dated examples were found in the research area, although the 'Vicus Bath' near the *castellum* of Oudenburg had such a round room. In *Britannia* and *Germania Inferior*, however, such round rooms seem to date from the earliest phases of the baths, in the second half of the first century or early second century AD (Fair 1927, 220; Perring 2002, 175). At *Coriovallum* (Heerlen), the first phase of the public bath (Neronian or Flavian), presumably of military character, had such a round *laconicum* (see Fig. 10; Jeneson, Vos, and White 2020, 173). Perhaps the plan of the early bath at Emptinne-Champion was inspired by the military examples. Other bathhouses with such round rooms (see above, Chapter 4), such as Ambresin and Rognée, could unfortunately not be dated. The villa of Rognée, however, has a peristyle plan, which is quite exceptional for the region. It could well have been one of the first villas of which the plan was directly imported from the Mediterranean.[1] By the early second century, 'Bath 2' at Haccourt also had a round *caldarium*. The larger 'Bath 3' of the new villa at Haccourt also had a round *laconicum*, supplementing a similar room in the villa itself.

The round heated room could indicate that private baths may have been inspired by early military baths (as has also been suggested for *Britannia*, see Perring 2002, 173). If we look at other baths of the second half of the first century AD, such as the Vicus Bath of Tienen or 'Bath 1' of the villa of Haccourt, the most notable feature is their simple linear plan. Such a succession of the basic rooms of a bath, the *frigidarium*, the *tepidarium*,

and the *caldarium*, was frequently encountered in military contexts because of its simplicity (Nielsen 1993a, 76). The military baths discovered in the research area (Furfooz, Oudenburg, and possibly Liberchies) indeed present such an axial linear plan, even though these all date from Late Antiquity. Just outside the research area in *Coriovallum* (Heerlen), the first phase of the public bath (Neronian or Flavian) had a similar axial linear plan (Fig. 10; Jeneson, Vos, and White 2020, 172–73). The first phase of the public baths of Virton/Saint-Mard (second half of the first century AD?) had a similar linear plan, with a characteristic 'Vitruvian' *caldarium* (mirrored by the *frigidarium*) (Fig. 23; Defosse and Mathieu 1983–1984). However, because this layout is the simplest plan for a Roman bath, enabling the heating of both the *caldarium* and *tepidarium* with a single furnace, we cannot assume that the earliest public and private baths simply copied the plan of military baths.

Mobility of Ideas

The introduction of this new habit and this new type of building must have made an impact on the local population. The incorporation of the region into the wider Roman cultural sphere not only resulted in the spread of new items such as ceramics — the so-called 'objects in motion' (Versluys 2014, 16) — but also of new ideas. The introduction of bathhouses introduced new ways of thinking about the human body, about health, and about appearance. Each culture has its own concept about the body, called 'l'imaginaire du corps' by Georges Vigarello (1985, 11) — and whenever such a concept is confronted with a different concept, three reactions can occur: the concept may meet resistance, acceptance, or adaptation (Burke 2009, 79–99).

As discussed in Chapter 1, Roman bathhouses looked and functioned the way they did because they reflected a specific bathing habit. In Italy and the Mediterranean, the bathhouse therefore had to meet certain expectations of the people using it. In studies on the interaction of humans with their built environment and in sociology of architecture, buildings are therefore not considered to be static 'reflections of culture', but more as an integral part of and actively contributing to culture, acting as a form of non-verbal communication (Gutman 1976, 10; Rapoport 2000, 187). Hence a cold, tepid, and hot room with pools of different temperatures were expected to be present in each bathhouse, because these were a prerequisite to take care of one's health and appearance as 'dictated' by Roman bathing culture. This bathing culture was inspired

---

1   Similarly, the palatial villa at Fishbourne in Sussex (UK) has also been interpreted as the work of Mediterranean immigrant craftsmen, erecting a peristyle villa for a Roman owner or a client-king with Roman aspirations (Perring 2002, 32–33).

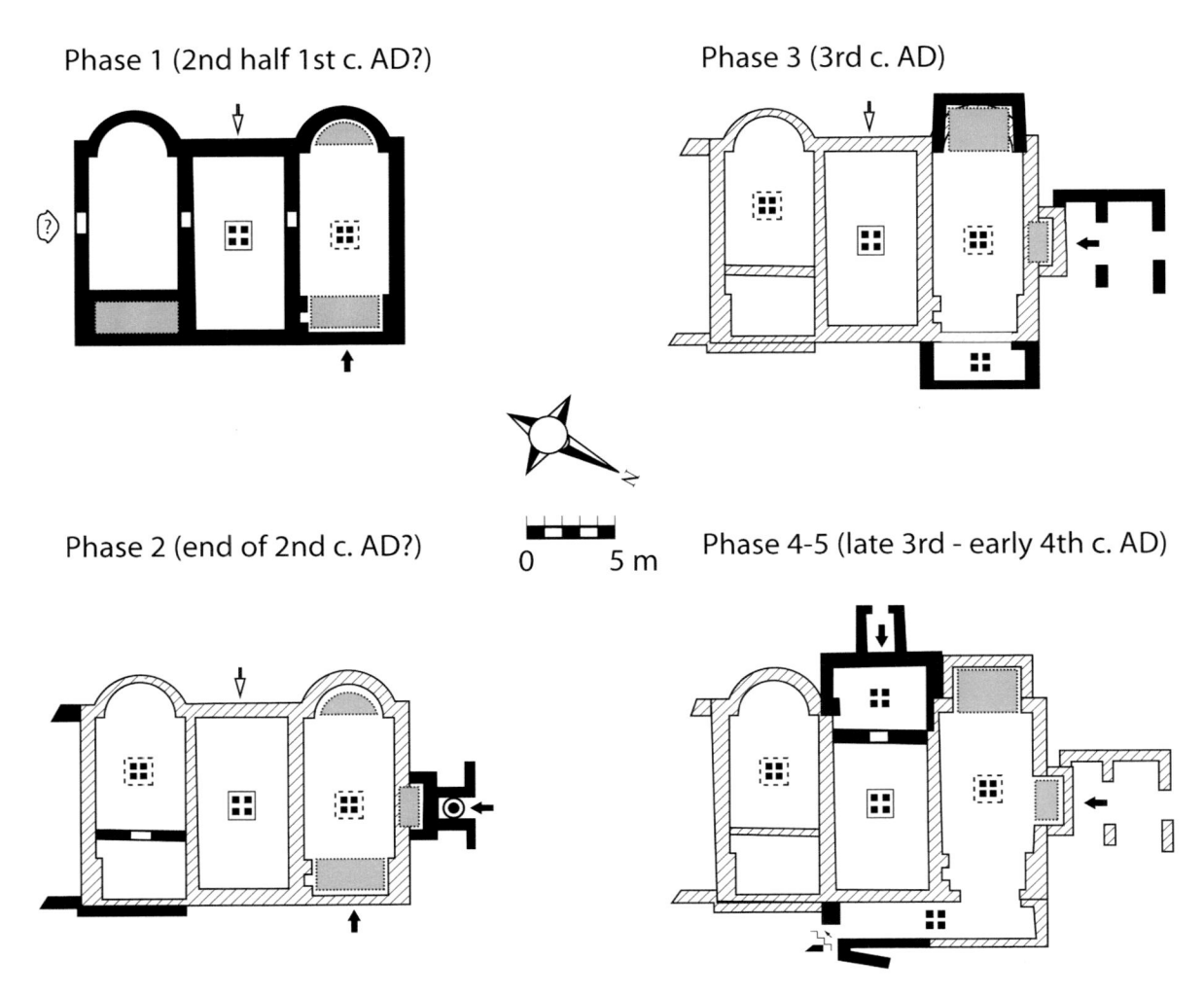

Figure 23. Evolution of the public bath of Virton/Saint-Mard (Belgium).
Figure by author after Defosse and Mathieu 1983–1984, 56–57, figs 7–8.

by medical theories about the human body: the different humours had to be kept in good balance by sweating out the bad fluids, relaxing in hot water and then restrengthening the body with cold water. So if buildings represent ideas and social practices, creating cues for behaviour for their users and acting as an enabling rather than determining environment (Gutman 1976, 38–47), archaeologists can then try to distil the specificity and variability of the bathing habit within a region through the architecture of the bathhouses. In this manner we may detect possible resistance, acceptance, or adaptation of this typically Mediterranean phenomenon in regions previously unacquainted with it. Private architecture seems more suited to study such culturally inspired choices (Kent 1993, 2). Public baths were usually paid for by the (local) government or members of the urban elite, their plans and architecture closely following 'standard' Roman prototypes. It is mainly

in the individual choices (by human agency) of the (wealthy) local population, whether or not to build a bath and how to do this, that we might be able to detect an attitude towards Roman bathing habits. Furthermore, the focus should lie on the first generation after the conquest, in this case the first century AD, as resistance seems to subside in the second and third generations (Burke 2009, 90–93).

Identifying outright resistance to the introduction of Roman bathing habits is quite difficult, as the absence of bathhouses does not necessarily imply a deliberate rejection. Without written sources, it is difficult to discern active resistance from simply a lack of interest in a very specific building type that would have cost a small fortune. Such active opposition to Roman baths is in fact attested in other parts of the Empire during Late Antiquity. Joshua Stylites (sixth century AD) recounts how the brother of the Persian king Peroz was hated by his own priests because he wanted to build Roman-style baths in Persian cities (Josh. Styl. 19). Epiphanius and Augustine inform us that the Manicheans prohibited bathing altogether (Epiph. *Adv. haeres.* LXVI.28.5; August. *De moribus manichaeorum* 19). In the archaeological record, we can observe that very few bathhouses are discovered in settlements with exclusively indigenous buildings. Especially in the *civitas Menapiorum*, where very few stone villas seem to have been built, Roman-period settlements were still made up of indigenous farmhouses (De Clercq 2011, 245). However, the discovery in the *civitas Tungrorum* of a bathhouse at Évelette – Clavia, as the only stone structure (together with a cellar) that had been built at some distance from the main building which was built in the local vernacular architecture, reminds us that some baths may have been missed due to the limited size of the excavations. Other baths, especially in areas where building material was scarce, could have been dismantled down to the foundation levels, such as the baths at Aardenburg, making it difficult to identify these as baths. The overall distribution pattern of baths (see Chapter 3) makes it clear that the bathing habit probably never spread widely in the north-western part of the research area. But the absence of baths is perhaps not surprising in a landscape inhabited by self-sustaining communities with little surplus production and probably little interest in new forms of foreign luxury. Rather than resistance, there might have been indifference to Roman baths.

The acceptance of the Roman bathing habit might seem obvious in the public baths of cities and other centres, but there is no evidence of who actually made use of these. After the initial foundation, such baths were probably 'imposed' upon the city by the local council and members of the elite, but may only have been frequented by Roman colonists, not by first generation natives who sought work and settled here. No bath-related inscriptions have been found in the research area, making it difficult to identify who built and restored these baths.[2] The same problem arises for the early villa baths discussed above: Who actually owned these villas? Wealthy natives who wanted to show off their Roman way of life by building a bath or rather Roman settlers for whom it was quite normal to have such a bath? The only archaeological clue might be provided by the architecture of the villa and the material culture found on site. A villa with strong roots in the vernacular architecture, or a finds assemblage on site made up mainly of local shapes and local production, lacking imported table wares, might point to an indigenous background of the residing elite. However, most villa sites had long phases of use, making it difficult to identify both the layout and the material culture of the earliest phase. An additional difficulty is that many baths were added during a later phase to the villa and that baths themselves could have been in use for a long time, altering the original layout. The chronology of the building phases is often poorly understood as a result of the early excavations of most sites. None of the early baths with a standard plan can be linked to a villa with clear indigenous roots. On the contrary, such baths belong to villas with a clearly 'Roman' layout. The villa of Emptinne-Champion was clearly a new Roman settlement (Brulet 2008, 541). It was implanted in the mid-first century AD on a different location than the older Iron Age habitation in the area. The first bathhouse can be dated to this oldest phase and has a plan that shows similarities to military baths (see above). Neither the plan of the villa nor the material culture provides indications that the first owner of this villa had an indigenous background. The same problem arises from the first villa at Haccourt. The first-phase bath, dated to the second half of the first century AD, had all the basic rooms, but there is no evidence that the owner was an indigenous 'early adopter'. On the contrary, the fact that an inscription was included in the *frigidarium* mosaic indicates that the person commissioning the baths was literate in Latin and so perhaps more likely to be a 'colonist' than a native. As mentioned above, the peristyle plan of the villa of Rognée (first century AD?) also rather points to colonist owners of the villa.

There is some evidence that bathhouses were adopted and adapted by indigenous elites. At least five villa baths, most of which could not be securely dated, only consisted of one heated room with an *alveus* (Maréchal 2020b). No *frigidarium* or *piscina* could be discovered. The bath at Attenhoven was part of a larger estate that consisted mainly of 'rural buildings' and a main villa of the hall-type (Piton 1939, 12). On the site of Évelette – Clavia the small freestanding bath and a cellar were the only elements made of stone and ceramic building materials (Lefert 2014, 111). The site was in use since pre-Roman times and the main buildings of the Roman-period site may still have been constructed in perishable materials. The modest villa of Heestert was built around the middle of the first century AD on top of an earlier farm in the vernacular building tradition with the same orientation (Janssens 1984, 9). The oblong structure with a stone-base wall set over the previous post-holes, can be seen as the stone version of the earlier farm. The material culture was mainly local production (Janssens 1984, 23–38). The bathhouse was

---

2   Just outside the research area an inscription was found in the public baths in *Orolaunum* (Arlon; Loes 1909, 266), in southern part of the Belgian province of Luxembourg. The text (CIL XIII.11342) is only partially preserved: '------]cuncta | sunt d[ign] a vict[ore deo virtute peracta] | excipim[u]r ther[mis pelluntur corpore sordes] | nec satis es[t sordes datur his et peller]e fat[a]'.

located some 73 m east of the villa. The villa of Bierbeek was probably also implanted on top of an earlier Iron Age farm. The Roman-period villa was constructed in the mid-first century AD, but the freestanding bath (39 m south-east of the villa) was probably added at a later date (middle of the second century AD?) (De Clerck 1987, 99). The material culture found on site contained very few imports and consisted mainly of locally produced ceramics. At Vissoul, the freestanding bath also consisted of one large heated room, possibly with one or two *alvei* in the *exedrae*, but the villa itself was not identified. The villa of Anderlecht, where the freestanding bathhouse seems to have lacked a *piscina*, was also characterized by an absence of imports and a majority of locally produced ceramics (Dens 1906, 247). Besides these five villas with a strong local background, several other villas seem to have had baths that only consisted of a heated part. For the villa bath of Froyennes, Gooik, Mabeuge, Matagne-la-Petite, Merbes-le-Château 'Bath 1', Tiegem, and Vesqueville, the remains are unfortunately too badly preserved to exclude the presence of a cold section. An apparently freestanding building with hypocaust and embellished with wall paintings, found some 28 m east of the villa of Muizen is too summarily published to identify it as a bath (De Cock 1987). The freestanding heated building in the *vicus* of Tourinnes-St-Lambert is sometimes interpreted as a public bath (Deru 1994, 56; Brulet 2008, 296), which would mean that this bath was the only public bath without a cold section, but the context of the building is unclear. The bath may well have been the freestanding bath of an unidentified villa. The bathing suites of the relay station of Outrelouxhe and of the road station at Wyompont also consisted exclusively of a heated section. At Outrelouxhe the simple rectangular building was constructed on an earlier Iron Age site (Witvrouw 2015, 263).

The absence of a *frigidarium* is remarkable, especially as this room already belonged to the 'standard set' of rooms of a bathhouse when baths started to be built in the research area. The comparison with the late Republican and early Imperial private baths in urban contexts in Italy, which often only consisted of a heated room, cannot stand, as these predate the introduction of the cold room in the classic layout of Roman baths (Nielsen 1993a, 35; Nielsen 1999). By the time baths were 'exported' to northern Gaul, the *frigidarium* with *piscina* was already a standard part of the baths, which is also confirmed by the oldest military examples found in the area (Hanel 2000). Furthermore, the technological know-how and the building materials were less challenging for the cold section than for the heated part, which seems to preclude the possibility that a lack of skilled labour or resources were the reason behind such an omission. The fact that several modest villas were equipped with a small bath that did have a *frigidarium*, e.g. Soignies, Modave, Grumelange, Maillen – Arches, Gesves (phase 1), Miécret, Graux, Haillot, and Chastrès, seems to indicate that financial constraints did not necessarily result in a bath without cold section. A bath with only a heated section might well have been a deliberate choice by the owner. This hypothesis has more importance than it might seem, because a deliberate omission of the cold room implies a deviation of the underlying bathing routine. The cold pool was an indispensable part of the Roman bathing routine because it enabled the bathers to close the pores of the skin, shutting out bad substances, and restrengthen the body after the weakening effect of the hot rooms (Blonski 2014a, 117). This is why a Roman bathhouse always offered the possibility to cool down the body, even in small baths. There is still the possibility that a portable tub with cold water was placed in such single room baths. These could be in wood, metal, or in stone. An example of such a limestone monolith bath tub was found in the villa of Alt-Inden in *Germania Inferior* (Dodt 2005). However, the fact still remains that the commissioner of the baths only invested in the heated part, which was also the most expensive part in terms of construction, operation, and maintenance. Considering the architecture and material culture of the sites where such single-room baths were found, it is possible that these belonged to indigenous people who had accumulated sufficient wealth to invest in a fashionable Roman luxury, but did not necessarily adopt the accompanying bathing culture. Furthermore, similar small baths with only a heated section have also been in discovered Britain, just south of Hadrian's Wall, in the rural settlements of Faverdale and Ingleby Barwick. The bath in Faverdale (late second century AD), with two fully functional hypocausts with *tubuli* and embellished with frescos, is the only stone building on a site characterized by indigenous round houses (Proctor 2012). The *caldarium* at Ingleby Barwick possibly predates the Roman villa and may well have been one of the earliest Roman-style buildings on a site with pre-Roman occupation (Willis 2013a, 177). The material culture at Ingleby Barwick is mainly local with few imports (Willis 2013b, 162–63). Both British examples could demonstrate that the preference for such 'reduced bathhouses' was not just a local phenomenon in the research area, but perhaps a more widespread approach to Roman bathing habits among indigenous societies in the North. Remembering also the quote by Tacitus about the Germans (see above), it is not surprising that in the cold northern climate, a heated bath and a warm-water pool must have been the luxury *par excellence* to display wealth and knowledge of Roman know-how. The popularity of heated rooms is also clear from the heated living room in villas of the

Roman North. Installing a hypocaust might not mean that the villa owner adopted the full Roman 'culture of the body' or tried to imitate an urban lifestyle, but it may well suggest that he chose to invest in revolutionary and comfort-giving technology (Maréchal 2020b).

Elite Self-Fashioning and Intra-Elite Competition

The Roman conquest started an administrative organization of a region previously ruled by several kindred chieftains. To the Romans, annexing new territory was not about conquering land, but about incorporating local populations (Millett 1990, 44). With this new administrative structure also came new ways of attaining or consolidating power. Under Roman control, traditional mechanisms of displaying power and wealth disappeared. The halt of intra-clan warfare meant the redistribution of war booty ceased, while imported Roman prestige goods became mundane objects due to the influx of Roman material culture. Rather than at traditional banquets or well-established communal activities such as drinking, as mentioned by Tacitus for the Germans (see above), high standing and wealth could now be expressed through domestic buildings (Perring 2002, 5). Even if the *habitus* of the indigenous population ensured that some local traditions filtered through in layout and architecture, the new stone domestic buildings were a radical change from pre-Roman building traditions. This is not to say that local elites tried to meticulously emulate Mediterranean villas in an effort to appear Roman. The important differences between Roman villas in Italy and the northern provinces make clear that there was certainly not an organized imposition of a new building form into the newly conquered regions, but rather that local elites tried to upgrade their houses with new amenities and comforts, clearly developing Roman tastes in domestic building (Woolf 1998, 155–57). And the construction of a bathhouse, the Roman luxury *par excellence*, could certainly help in this process of continuous 'elite self-redefinition' (Wallace-Hadrill 2008, 28). Scholars traditionally considered villa baths as personal and small copies of public baths, built by an elite that wanted to import city life to the countryside (Nielsen 1993a, 60). Recent research, however, demonstrated the important role private baths played in elite self-fashioning and intra-elite competition (de Haan 2010, 130–36). Such studies mainly examined competition in Italy and in secure urban contexts, with Pompeii as prime focus (de Haan 1997). Far less research has been conducted on villa baths.

Several ancient authors make clear that private baths were a symbol of wealth and power. The passages in the letters of Pliny the Younger (*Ep.* 2.17.26), Seneca (*Ep.* 86.6–7), and Sidonius Apollinaris (*Ep.* 2.2.4–9) already mentioned above reveal how private baths were real prestige projects, to impress peers and the lower classes alike (de Haan 2010, 130–31). The size and decoration of the baths obviously played an important part in this. Just as in the urban *domus*, *luxuria* was not just the result of a taste for extravagance by the elite, it was a 'social necessity in a highly competitive society' (Wallace-Hadrill 1988, 45). When hearing of his friend Atticus paying him a visit, Cicero wrote he would give orders to heat the baths (Cic. *Att.* 2.3). A good host was expected to offer his guests a bath when they arrived after their journey. The wealth and status of the owner, and subsequently the size and splendour of his villa, must have created certain expectations about the private baths as well. Seneca eloquently voiced such concerns:

> Pauper sibi videtur ac sordidus, nisi parietes magnis et pretiosis orbibus refulserunt, nisi Alexandrina marmora Numidicis crustis distincta sunt, nisi illis undique operosa et in picturae modum variata circumlitio praetexitur, nisi vitro absconditur camera, nisi Thasius lapis [...] piscinas nostras circumdedit.
>
> (We think ourselves poor and mean if our walls are not resplendent with large and costly mirrors; if our marbles from Alexandria are not set off by mosaics of Numidian stone, if their borders are not faced over on all sides with difficult patterns, arranged in many colours like paintings; if our vaulted ceilings are not buried in glass; if our swimming-pools are not lined with Thasian marble.) (*Ep.* 86.6; trans. by Gummere 1920, 313)[3]

It is therefore not surprising that the large and opulent villas had bathhouses that could surpass some public baths in size and luxury. At Basse-Wavre, Bruyelle (phase 3), Emptinne-Champion, Gesves, or Haccourt ('Bath 3', phase 2–3) the private baths were larger than some of the public baths found in modest central places such as Grobbendonk, Macquenoise, or Tienen (Table 6).

Furthermore, the facilities on offer in these villa baths could be quite impressive. In Basse-Wavre, Bruyelle, Emptinne-Champion, Gesves, Haccourt 'Bath 3', or Kumtich 'Bath 1' and 'Bath 2', the number of heated rooms allowed for more than just a *tepidarium*, *caldarium*, and perhaps *sudatorium*. The additional warm rooms might have been heated *apodyteria*, *unctoria*, *solaria*, *districtaria*, or other specialized rooms that were not on offer in the smaller public baths. The baths of Emptinne-Champion and Haccourt 'Bath 3' even had heated swimming pools (*calidae piscinae*),

---

3 For the entire passage, see above, Chapter 1.

Table 6. Sizes of the largest villa baths in comparison to some of the public baths in the research area.

Villa Bath	Size in sq.m
Basse-Wavre (2nd c. AD)	300
Bruyelle (phase 3, late 2nd or early 3rd c. AD)	230
Emptinne-Champion (phase 3, 3rd c. AD)	340
Gesves (phase 2, late 2nd or 3rd c. AD)	250
Haccourt 'Bath 3' (phase 3, late 2nd or early 3rd c. AD)	665
Public bath	**Size in sq.m**
Grobbendonk (2nd c. AD)	250
Macquenoise (late 2nd or early 3rd c. AD)	200
Tienen (late 1st c. AD)	200

Table 7. Evolution of the size of some villa baths over time.

Site	Phase 1		Phase 2		Phase 3	
	Chron.	Size	Chron.	Size	Chron.	Size
Autre-Église	2nd c.?	Min. 80 m²	3rd c.?	Min. 350 m²	/	/
Bruyelle	1st c.?	193 m²	2nd–3rd c.	220 m²	2nd–3rd c.	230 m²
Emptinne-Champion	1st c.	70 m²	2nd c.	230 m²	2nd–3rd c.	340 m²
Gesves	2nd c.?	70 m²	2nd–3rd c.	250 m²	/	/
Haccourt 'Bath 3'	2nd c.	390 m²	2nd c.?	658 m²	2nd–3rd c.?	665 m²
Meslin-l'Évêque	1st c.?	?	2nd c.	250 m²	/	/

an exceptional and expensive facility in construction, operation, and maintenance (see above, Chapter 4).

The increased importance of private baths is also visible in the fact that several baths were enlarged over time (Table 7). The baths of Autre-Église (perhaps public?), Bruyelle, Emptinne-Champion, Gesves, Haccourt 'Bath 3', and Meslin-l'Évêque were enlarged at least once. At Haccourt, Kumtich, and Merbes-le-Château, the original baths were even replaced by a new and larger bathhouse. For villas with two bathhouses, such as at Aiseau, Anthée, Mettet, Miécret, or Mont-lez-Houffalize – Fin de Ville, the additional bathhouse, often freestanding, may have been built because the original integrated bath was deemed too small, too modest, or out-of-date. Even if the old excavations make it difficult to untangle the exact chronological relation, it seems that for most of these sites, both baths functioned at the same time, in contrast to for example Merbes-le-Château, where the older internal bath was clearly dismantled when the new attached bath was constructed (Authom and Paridaens 2011, 61). Larger new baths may have been used when the master of the house received friends or clients, while internal baths could still be used by the members of the household.

Besides the size and the facilities on offer, a private bath could also impress with the quality of its embellishments. As already mentioned above (see Chapter 6), wall paintings were quite common in private baths. In contrast, the use of mosaics does seem to be limited to the larger baths of impressive villas. The only examples come from Anthée, Basse-Wavre, Haccourt, Kumtich, Montignies-Saint-Christophe, and Saint-Jean-Geest. Even more exceptional is the presence of 'exotic' decorative stone, such as Mediterranean marbles or porphyry. Unfortunately, few provenance studies have been carried out on such stone discovered in the more luxurious baths, such as Anthée, Boirs, Haccourt, or Mettet. Only for Bruyelle, macro-and microscopic analysis have revealed that some fragments were imported from North Africa (*giallo antico*), Greece (*porfido verde*), and perhaps Egypt (*porfido rosso*) and Italy (possibly Cararra marble). More modest baths often had to settle for more local materials, such as slabs of local limestone in the region around Tournai, or even paintings imitating marble, e.g. in Grumelange and possibly Hoogeloon. A very basic and recurrent finishing of floors and insides of pools, was polished hydraulic mortar, e.g. in Oberüttfeld, or simple terracotta tiles, e.g. in Jemelle, Machelen, and Heure-le-Romain. Plaster mouldings were also a modest form of decoration, probably as an alternative to architectural elements in stone, and were found in Aiseau 'Integrated Baths' and Arquennes. It is difficult to find evidence for upgrades of the decoration, as most baths are not sufficiently preserved to identify different phases of floors or wall decoration and decorative stones would have been torn out when the baths fell out of use. Some rooms may even have had extreme makeovers, with hypocausts and wall heating being torn out entirely. This could certainly be the case in public baths as the baths in Amay-Ombret seem to suggest, so rich proprietors might well have done the same for their private baths, keeping them up-to-date.

It is interesting to note how both wall paintings and mosaics mainly consisted of polychrome geometric patterns on plain white backgrounds. Floral, vegetal, and figurative scenes, demanding more artistic skill, were more exceptional, but do not necessarily appear in the larger and more luxurious baths. Perhaps an absence of skilled artists or simply little interest in figurative topics as decoration might explain why so few baths, and villas more generally, were embellished with figurative designs. It is possible that the classical iconographical themes, such as classical mythology, were not adopted by local elites. What would be the point of having a splendid painting of Aeneas when neither the owner nor his peers would know the story? And even if the owner did know his gods and myths, he may have chosen not to depict them on paintings and mosaics because his peers might have been ignorant. In contrast to the Mediterranean region, the research area had no tradition in the form of classical realism encountered in Greek and Roman art. In north-western Europe, the 'Celtic' art tradition was much more abstract than realist, while the system of symbols focused much more on war-related topics (weapons, equipment, horses). The absence of figurative art might thus be interpreted as the result of a continuity of local traditions, rather than as a strict opposition to or a failure of classical art (Millett 1990, 122–17). Local elites may well have accepted the new medium (wall paintings, mosaics), but perhaps preferred patterns bearing closer resemblance to traditional designs.

To find examples of possible intra-elite competition at work on a local scale can be quite difficult, as we need a region with several excavated villa baths that were in use at the same time. Within the research area, several clusters of baths can be found, yet often the remains of the baths are too poorly preserved and chronological information is too scanty to make any comparison, e.g. the baths of Bovigny, Mont-lez-Houffalize – Fin de Ville, and Mont-lez-Houffalize – Sommerian, all within a 7 km radius, or the two villas at Willemeau and Bruyelle and Hollain, all within a 5 km radius

just south of *Turnacum*. However, to the west of the *vicus* of Clavier-Vervoz, eleven villa sites have been excavated within a 10 km radius (Map 7; discussed in more detail in Maréchal 2021a). For only one of these villas, no bathhouse has been discovered (yet).[4] All villas lie in the lower valley, often at the foot of south-facings slopes near a stream, with their façades oriented towards the south (Map 7). The baths seem roughly contemporaneous in use during the second century AD, could be as small as 22 m² or as large as 250 m², and could take up between 5 and 15 per cent of the ground level of the villa (Table 8). Some of the baths had very similar plans and sizes, such as Évelette – Résimont and Miécret 'Bath 1' (compare Fig. 56 and Fig. 107 and see Table 8), or Flostoy, Haillot, Hamois, and Modave (compare Figs 58, 72, 73, and 110 and see Table 8) (Maréchal 2021a). The baths of Gesves and Emptinne-Champion, located some 8 km from each other, were both originally freestanding and around 60 m² in size, but were later attached to the villa by a corridor and enlarged to *c*. 250 m². Besides similarities in plans (Fig. 52 and Fig. 64) and roughly equal surface sizes, the size of the pools seems to imply that the envisaged number of bathers was also the same. Other similarities in building techniques, such as the *caldarium* in both Modave and Flostoy that was probably separated at floor level by a thin wall (made out of *tubuli*?), or the use of stone monoliths as pillars in the hypocausts at Miécret 'Bath 1' and Évelette – Résimont, can hardly be considered hard evidence for the same contractor.

A second area of interest lies in continuation with the area described above, but closer to the valley of Sambre, along the tributary rivers Bocq and Lesse (Map 8). All five villas lie within a 10 km radius (Table 9). The three villas found around modern Maillen even lie within a 2 km radius of each other, with the villas of Arches and Al Sauvenière perhaps depending on the largest villa at Ronchinne. No other villas have been found in this area, although some smaller buildings with stone foundations at Braibant-Halloy could possibly be the artisanal buildings of a larger and yet undiscovered villa site (Brulet 2008, 513–14). All villa baths seem to have been in use during the second century. The villas are located on south-facing slopes, near streams, with their façades oriented to the south (Map 8). The larger villas (e.g. Maillen – Al Sauvenière, Maillen – Ronchine, and probably also Gemechenne) had larger baths, between 120 and 200 m², while the modest villa of Maillen – Arches had a basic bath (50 m²). Again, the size of the pools, pointing to the maximum number

---

4 The villa of Haltinne has not been fully excavated yet (Brulet 2008, 535). Therefore, it is still possible that a freestanding bathhouse remains unidentified.

Table 8. Date, baths' size, pool sizes with maximum numbers of bathers, and location of the baths in the microregion west of Clavier compared to the size of the main villa building. F: freestanding, I: internal, A: attached (in Maréchal 2021a, table 2).

Site	Timespan	Baths' size	*Piscina* size (no. of bathers)	*Alveus* size (no. of bathers)	Loc. of baths	Villa size	Baths surface in %
Bois-et-Borsu	Unknown	Unknown	1.2 m² (1)	Unknown	Unknown	Unknown	Unknown
Emptinne-Champion (phases 1–3)	1st–4th c. AD?	70–230–340 m²	5 m² and 1.6 m² (5 and 2)	2.6 m² (2)	F?–A	800+ m²	Unknown
Évelette – Clavia	1st–3rd c. AD?	58 m²	Unknown	Unknown	F	Unknown	Unknown
Évelette – Resimont	2nd–3rd c. AD?	22 m²	2.2 m² (2)	2.3 m² and 2.3 m² (2 and 2)	I	460 m²	5%
Flostoy	2nd c. AD–?	55 m²	6 m² (6)	2 m² and 1.5 m² (2 and 1)	I	960 m²	6%
Gesves (phases 1–2)	2nd–4th c. AD?	70–250 m²	4.8 m² (5)	4.2 m² (4)	F–A	800+ m²	Unknown
Haillot	2nd–3rd c. AD?	60 m²	4 m² (4)	1.8 m² and 2 m² (2 and 2)	I	390 m²	15%
Hamois	2nd c. AD–?	77 m²	2.8 m² (3)	2.3 m² and 0.8 m² (2 and 1)	I	840 m²	9%
Miécret 'Bati 1'	1st–2nd c. AD	25 m²	1.8 m² (2)	1.8 m² and 1.1 m² (2 and 1)	I	Unknown	Unknown
Modave	2nd–3rd c. AD?	60 m²	4 m² (4)	3.6 m² and 2.4 m² (3 and 2)	A	Unknown	Unknown

Table 9. Date, baths' size, pool sizes with maximum numbers of bathers, and location of the baths in the microregion around Maillen compared to the size of the main villa building. F: freestanding, I: internal, A: attached; N/A: not applicable.

Site	Timespan	Baths' size	*Piscina* size (no. of bathers)	*Alveus* size (no. of bathers)	Loc. of baths	Villa size	Baths surface in % (if internal)
Gemechenne	2nd–3rd c. AD	120 m²	Unknown	3.1 m² and 3.6 m² (3 and 4)	F	Min. 610 m²	N/A
Leignon	2nd?–3rd c. AD	145 m²	2.25 m² (2)	2.9 m² and 1.7 m² (3 and 2)	F	Unknown	N/A
Maillen – Al Sauvenière	2nd?–4th c. AD?	150 m²	3.7 m² (4)	2 m² and 3.36 m² (2 and 3)	A	1000 m²	N/A
Maillen – Arches	1st?–4th c. AD?	50 m²	1.3 m² (1)	1.87 m² (2)	A	212 m²	N/A
Maillen – Ronchine	2nd c. AD?	120–200 m²	Unknown	7.6 m² (8)	I	1572 m²	12%

of bathers, is in line with the size of the baths and the size of the villa (Table 9).

The plans of the baths of Gemechenne, Leignon, and Maillen – Al Sauvenière (mirrored) strongly resemble each other. The three baths are presented as a freestanding block (even if a portico connected the baths of Maillen – Al Sauvenière to the villa), with the *caldarium* and the *frigidarium* on one axis and two other rooms on a parallel axis (in Gemechenne and Maillen – Al Sauvenière a *tepidarium* lay next to the *caldarium*). The *caldarium* was an oblong room which may have been divided at floor level in two parts.

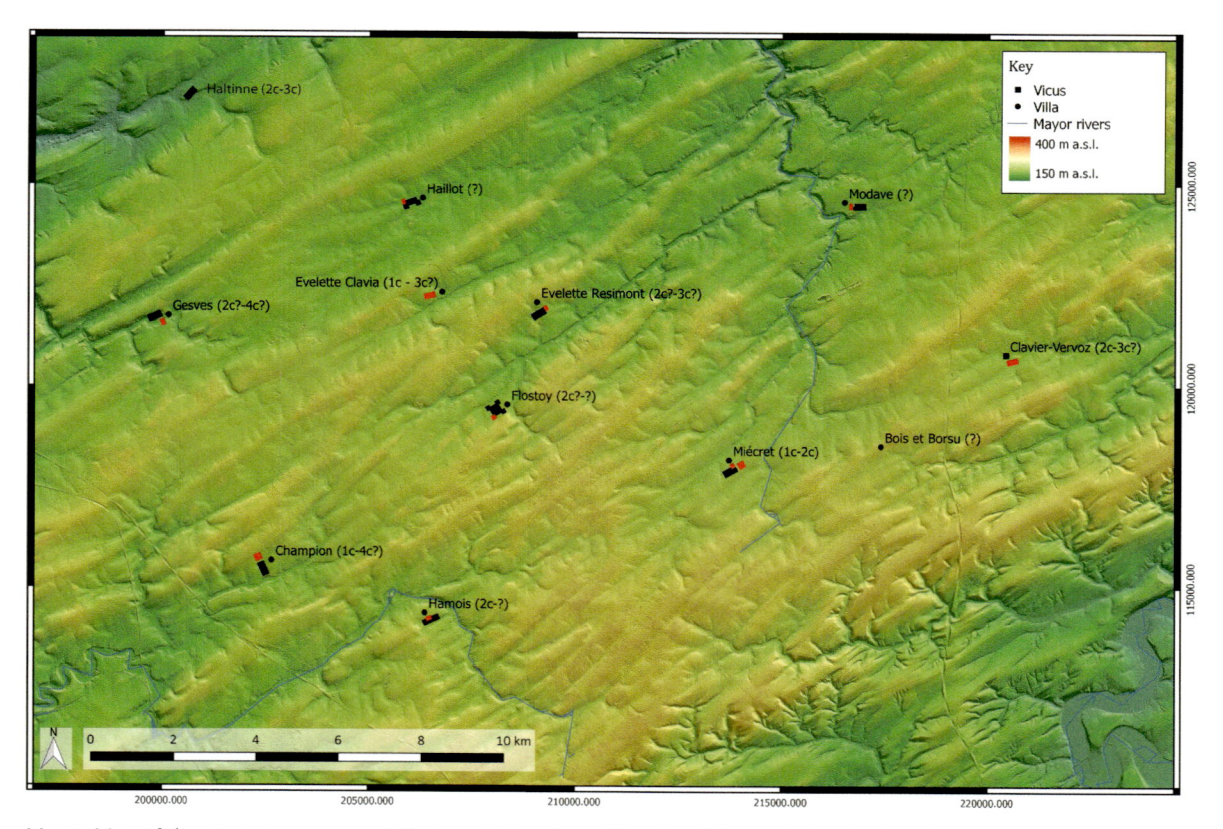

Map 7. Map of the microregion west of Clavier with location of the villas (lifespan in brackets) and their orientations (baths in red), on the DEM. Map by author; DEM by DGSPW – Département de la Géomatique du Service Public de Wallonie; EPSG: 31370 – Belgian Lambert 72.

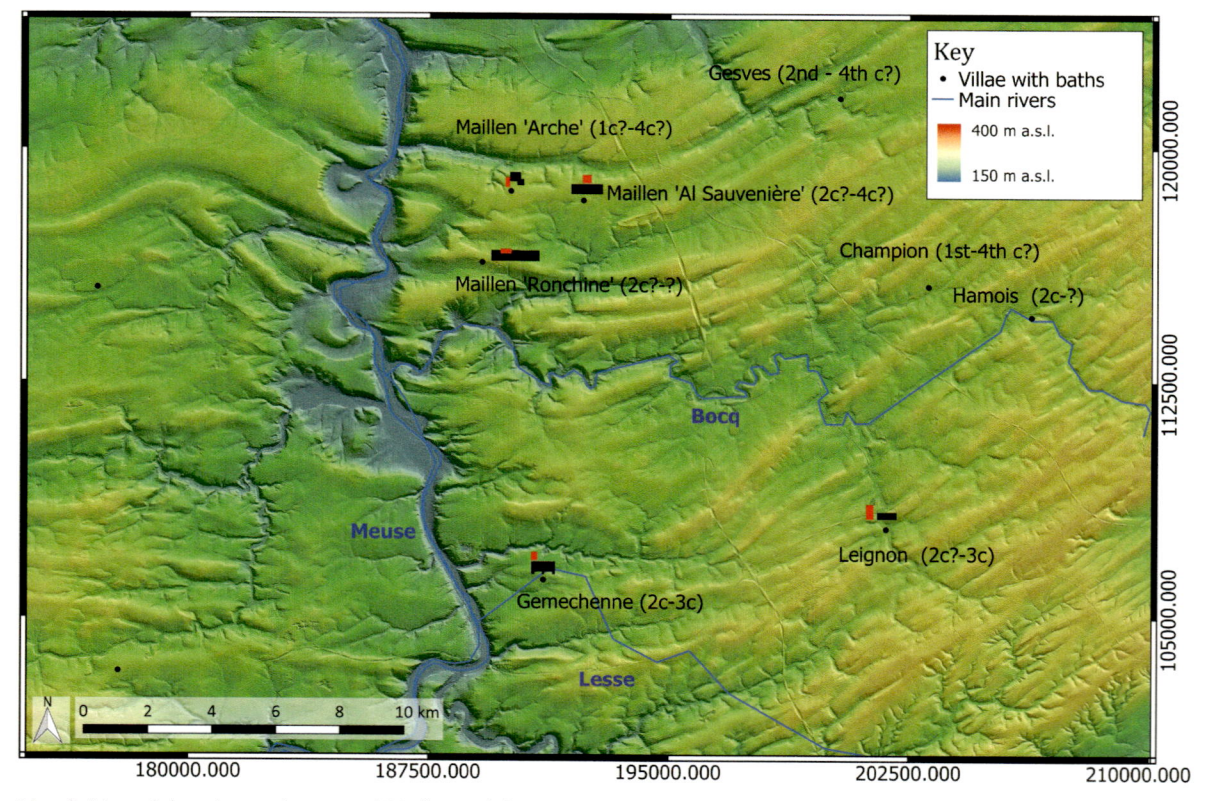

Map 8. Map of the microregion around Maillen with location of the villas (lifespan in brackets) and their orientations (baths in red), on the DEM. Map by author; DEM by DGSPW — Département de la Géomatique du Service Public de Wallonie; EPSG: 31370 — Belgian Lambert 72.

The *alvei* lay perpendicular to each other. The *alveus* along the length of the *caldarium* and the *piscina* of the *frigidarium* lay on the same axis. Besides the similarities in plan, in both Leignon and Maillen – Al Sauvenière, tiles with the stamp HAMSIT were found, indicating that the same manufacturer at least supplied both baths with ceramic building materials. The decorative schemes of the baths were unfortunately too damaged to identify possible resemblances between the sites.

The similarities in plan and size, however, are not necessarily evidence for one building influencing another, let alone copycat behaviour. Even if the existence of 'bath catalogues' by architects or contractors are attested in Latin literature (see Chapter 4), it has already been stressed that simple linear plans with a furnace heating both *caldarium* and *tepidarium* and an overlying *alveus* are so frequent because of their simplicity and efficacity. The similarities of some plans, such as at Flostoy and Haillot, may also have been the logical result of a bathhouse being added at a later date to one side of the villa. But the fact that almost all of these villas within the same limited area had baths, clearly points to the importance that such a facility must have had for the villa owners. In a region where the closest public baths probably lay more than a day's walk away (15 km), each villa owner wanted the comfort of his own bath, as a marker of wealth and civilization, especially if the neighbouring villas had one. The larger and more luxurious villas obviously had to be equipped with decent baths, but it is especially interesting that some of the smaller villas, such as Maillen – Arches, also added a fully functional bathhouse to the modest dwelling. Rather than trying to outclass neighbours with ever bigger and better baths, the real competitive aspect perhaps lies more in the fact that each villa owner invested in a bath, no matter how large or luxurious, in an effort to keep up with a civilized way of life.

That the elite was willing to invest considerable sums in the construction, embellishment, and enlargement of private baths can be understood in the context of conspicuous spending and intra-elite competition. Top-end facilities such as heated swimming pools and exotic stones such as porphyry would have dazzled friends and colleagues coming to visit. As mentioned above, second and third generations of indigenous descent might even have made an extra effort to underline their success and civilized way of life. We can recall the quote from Tacitus about how the Britons succumbed to alluring vices such as baths and dinner parties (*Agr.* XXI.2), but we might also recall the passage by Seneca mentioned above (see Chapter 1), who claimed that freedmen had the most extravagant baths of all (Sen. *Ep.* 86.7–8):

Et adhuc plebeias fistulas loquor; quid, cum ad balnea libertinorum pervenero? Quantum statuarum, quantum columnarum est nihil sustinentium, sed in ornamentum positarum inpensae causa! Quantum aquarum per gradus cum fragore labentium! Eo deliciarum pervenimus, ut nisi gemmas calcare nolimus.

(I have so far been speaking of the ordinary bathing-establishments; what shall I say when I come to those of the freedmen? What a vast number of statues, of columns that support nothing, but are built for decoration, merely in order to spend money! And what masses of water that fall crashing from level to level! We have become so luxurious that we will have nothing but precious stones to walk upon.) (trans. by Gummere 1920, 315)

Enlarging and embellishing the baths might also have been a way to contribute to the family legacy (Maréchal 2021a).

Accessibility and Social Exclusion

As we know from the literary sources, the private baths on villa estates in the Mediterranean were often accessible to friends and colleagues of the master of the house. The archaeological evidence investigated above makes clear that such private baths in the continental north-west were also important tools for elite self-representation: the size and decoration of the baths were aimed at impressing the guests invited into it. If we look at the location of the bathhouses in relation to the main villa building, we can see that three options existed. The bath could be integrated into the main building of the villa, it could be attached to the main building by a corridor or a single room, or it could be a completely freestanding building (Maréchal 2021b). The location of the bathhouse obviously had implications for its accessibility. This ranged from more restricted access for the baths integrated into the main building, which probably was reserved for its inhabitants, to the possibility of easier access for outsiders in the freestanding bathhouses and those only attached to the main building on one side. A closer examination of the location could shed light on who could make use of these baths, and who could not.

To examine the use and accessibility of the baths, it is important to understand who actually owned, worked, and lived on the villa estates. Ancient literary sources pertain mainly to (late Republican and early Imperial) Italy and point to a land-owning urban elite that entrusted the daily working of their estate to a tenant and a workforce of labourers and slaves permanently residing there (Cato, *Agr.* 11; Varro, *Rust.* 1.7; Columella, *Rust.* 1.7–9). It is commonly assumed that the villas in north-western Europe were mainly inhabited by an indigenous elite that had gradually adopted Roman architectural styles (Hingley 1989, 149–52; Smith 1997, 233–53; Brulet 2008, 129–30). The share of Roman colonists, such as army veterans, who were awarded a piece of land in newly conquered regions, is difficult to identify, although some evidence for this has come to light in the form of (funerary) inscriptions and bronze tablets/tokens on villa sites (Derks 2011), e.g. in Broekhem (Remouchamps 1924). The family household that inhabited the main villa building possibly included the master of the house, his wife and children, as well as his servants. J. T. Smith (Smith 1978, 170–72; 1997, 278–82) has argued that several kinship groups might have inhabited the same residence, which he saw as a remnant of an indigenous tradition of living in extended families. His hypothesis, however, has been criticized, as the notion of extended families is itself a controversial theory, not backed by hard archaeological evidence (Rippengal 1993).

Vitruvius mentions how the more intimate rooms of the house, including the baths, the bedrooms, dining rooms, and other apartments were only accessible to guests on invitation by the master of the house (Vitr. Arch. VI.5.1). The first-century architect stresses which parts of the house would have been accessible to guests and friends ('communia cum extraneis') and which parts were reserved for the master of the house (and the household) ('propria loca patribus familiarum'). This was necessary, because in contrast to our modern homes, the Roman home (of the better classes) was not only a private dwelling, but also a representational building in which to welcome peers and clients. The deeper one penetrated into the house, the more exclusive the access would have become (Wallace-Hadrill 1988, 45–55). Baths that were located well within the house, may therefore have had more restricted access, possibly only for the inhabitants of the house. This seems to have been the case for the baths at Ambresin, Diekirch, Évelette – Résimont, Flostoy, Graux, Haillot, Hamois, Hoogeloon, Liège, Merbes-le-Château 'Bath 1', Miécret 'Bath 1', Mont-lez-Houffalize – Sommerain, Roly, Treignes, Villers-le-Bouillet, or Wancennes. But the integration of the bath into the main building did not necessarily exclude more open access. In several villas, the baths lay in a peripheral position that could easily be accessed by going through a minimal number of rooms. Where the bath was located inside an angular pavilion, it could easily be reached by the portico running along the front of the villa, e.g. in Oberüttfeld, Vodelée, and possibly in Vellereille-les-Brayeux. The bath at Landen – Betzveld was also conceived as an angular pavilion, but may have been accessed directly from the outside or by a corridor running along the side of the villa. In Broekhem and Clermont-sous-Huy, the baths were attached to the angle pavilion in a later phase. For villas with a row plan, the baths were often attached to one of the ends, e.g. at Basse-Wavre, Emptinne-Champion, and possibly Bruyelle, Haccourt 'Bath 1', and Heer. Another way of ensuring the baths could be reached without going through several rooms, was by locating them along or at the end of a corridor, as was the case in Aiseau 'Bath 1', Jemelle, Latinne, Meslin-l'Évêque, or Saint-Gérard. Integrated baths had the obvious advantage that the inhabitants of the house did not have to leave the house if they wanted to bathe. Locating the baths within a remote part of the house did not only enable restriction of access to outsiders, the bath itself could also be 'hidden' from sight, so as not to disrupt the visual unity of the façade of the villa (Maréchal 2021b). A peripheral position along the side or at the back of the villa would also have ensured easy access to the service rooms for the supply of firewood and easier water supply and disposal, without pipes and sewers having to pass through or underneath other rooms.

Baths that were attached to the villa or were completely freestanding may have been used by a larger group of people, not only including the household and invited friends, but perhaps also tenants and labour force working and living on the lands (Perring 2002, 177; de Haan 2010, 123–24). The agrarian writer Columella (first century AD) mentions how the villa owners should provide separate baths ('rusticis balneis') in the rural part of the villa ('in parte rusticae villae') in which the *familia* could bathe on holidays (Columella, *Rust.* I.6.19–20; see also de Haan 2010, 123). The word *familia* seems to imply the household at its largest extent, including people living in the rural part of the estate. If we look at the evidence in our research area, there are several freestanding baths that could easily have been accessible to people living on the larger estate.[5] At Mettet, the larger 'Bath 1' was integrated in what seems to have been the main residence, while the smaller 'Bath 2' was located in what the excavators labelled the *pars fructuaria* (Mahieu 1919, 99). At Nivelles, the freestanding bath lay in front of, but at some distance from the largest residential building (A on Fig. 117). The proximity to the baths may have underlined the social hierarchy of the different residences, with the largest house closest to the bathhouse. However, there is no reason to doubt the residents of the smaller houses (B and C) could use the baths. Other freestanding baths, such as those at Anderlecht, Attenhoven, Bierbeek, Chastrès, Évelette – Clavia, Gooik, Heestert, Heure-le-Romain, Kumtich, Lemiers, Limerlé, Milmort, and

---

5 Such 'communal use' of a facility at the main villa has also been recognized in the presence of several large corn-drying ovens (Percival 1976, 130).

Schieren may also have been accessible to inhabitants of the estate, but in most cases the exact extent of the estates and the number of residences are unknown. Some scholars have suggested that baths were built as freestanding buildings to minimize fire hazards (Ferdière 1988, 187), or to have an optimal water supply and waste water disposal. While such concerns were most certainly taken into account when choosing the location of a bathhouse, we must remember that most villas in the north also had heated living rooms, which posed as great a fire risk as baths. Furthermore, some of the attached baths were linked to the villa by their *praefurnium*, e.g. at Gesves, Maillen – Al Sauvenière, Maillen – Arches, or Vechmaal. The fire hazard was obviously not the most important factor here in the choice of the location of the baths. The water supply in the research area was certainly not problematic, with an abundance of natural springs in the stony plateaus of the Condroz, Fagne, and Famenne and the Ardennes (see above, Chapter 5). Both villa and baths were often supplied by the same well or aqueduct.

Unlike in *Britannia*, where freestanding baths are claimed to have been the oldest baths (Perring 2002, 177), the examples in the research area are not necessarily early constructions, e.g. Aiseau 'Bath 2', Bierbeek, Heure-le-Romain, Kumtich, Lemiers, Miécret 'Bath 2', Milmort, Nivelles, Soignies. Freestanding or attached baths were often built in addition to an already existing integrated bath, suggesting a more public use may have been intended. At Aiseau, the freestanding bath seems to have been contemporaneous with the integrated bath, which was certainly not dismantled, in contrast to the integrated bath at Merbes-le-Château, which seems to have been abandoned when the attached bath was built (Authom and Paridaens 2011, 61). At the large villa of Anthée, two rather larger baths ('Bath 2' and 'Bath 3') were integrated in the main building. A third bathhouse ('Bath 1') was constructed in a separate wing that lay in both the *pars urbana* and the *pars rustica*. The early excavations could not determine the exact chronological relation between the different baths (Del Marmol 1877), but it seems that none was dismantled, which may point to a contemporaneous use at some point. The same situation occurred with the integrated and freestanding bath at Miécret (Materne 1969). At Mont-lez-Houffalize – Fin de Ville, the freestanding bath, although its interpretation is problematic, does seem to have been connected to the integrated bath by a water supply pipe (Meunier 1964, 161), pointing to a contemporaneous use. In the third villa of Haccourt, a round *laconicum* was integrated in the main building (De Boe 1971, 25), possibly for a more restricted use, in addition to the opulent bath attached to the villa. The corridor that connected the villa to the bath had a doorway from which 'outsiders' could enter the bath

directly, without even entering the villa. In addition to an easier 'public' access to the bath, a further advantage of a freestanding bath building for some of the proprietors of impressive villas may have been the available building space. This made it possible to build bigger and more architecturally complex baths, rather than fitting all the rooms of a bath into a pre-existing space in the villa.

Even if the location of the baths in relation to the main building seems to point to different degrees of accessibility, it remains difficult to ascertain whether some private baths could indeed be used by (for instance) the tenants of the proprietor. It is questionable whether the large and luxurious baths such as at Basse-Wavre, Emptinne-Champion, or Haccourt 'Bath 3' would have been accessible to lower social classes. Such lavish baths at some distance from the main building — whether attached to it on one side or completely freestanding — were more likely built to impress (groups of) peers, invited for extended stays at the estate. Going to the baths was probably a regular activity during such social events, after returning from hunting and in preparation for dinner. The smaller baths inside the main building would then have been used by the proprietor's direct family, such as the women and children, who would have been unwelcome at these quite male social events of the elite.[6] If a landlord indeed invested in a bathhouse for the larger *familia*, as recommended by Columella, one would expect it to be rather modest, perhaps mainly utilitarian.[7] It is probably not a coincidence that Columella writes about 'rustic' baths ('rusticis balneis'). However, the examples of freestanding baths complementing integrated baths in the study area are not exactly smaller or more modest. On the contrary, the additional baths seem to have been built because the integrated baths were possibly deemed too small or too modest for the increased wealth of the owner (see above). Only in the case of Mettet, the baths in the alleged *pars fructuaria* may have been built specifically for the workforce. For sites such as Nivelles or Milmort, it is more tempting to interpret the modest freestanding baths to have been accessible to tenants and labourers. Especially in the absence of civic centres and their public baths in this part of the Empire, such attached or freestanding baths on villa estates would have been the only possibility of enjoying a Roman-style bath for the majority of the rural population (Maréchal 2021b). In this way, granting access to private baths could have

6   The author would like to thank one of the anonymous reviewers for commenting on this aspect.

7   In the large late antique villa of Piazza Armerina (Sicily), a smaller and more modest bathhouse, interpreted to be the baths for the people living on the estate, was discovered near the larger and luxurious baths attached to the villa (Pensabene and Barresi 2018).

been a way for the owner to tie his labour force to his estate, as recommended by several agrarian authors (Cato, *Agr.* 142; Varro, *Rust.* 1.16.5; Columella, *Rust.* 11.1.23; Palladius *de re rust.* 1.6.2). Such benevolence towards the labour force has also been recognized in hosting occasional markets or constructing shrines on the estate, to create an 'estate-inspired community' (Bowes 2008, 36). Perhaps this could even be interpreted as the rural equivalent of the euergetism so often encountered in cities, where the same rich elite paid for the construction or embellishment of public baths, or paid the entrance fee for a year, in order to earn the favour of the people and gain political support (Fagan 1999, 167). Controlling access to such a typically Roman and 'civilized' activity was a way of controlling social stratification and it is very likely that large portions of the rural population which were denied access to baths were thus in a way socially excluded from the 'civilized' Roman way of life.

Conclusions

This study has presented an important corpus of Roman bathhouses (145 catalogued) in a relatively understudied corner of the Roman Empire. The fact that the majority of the sites were excavated in the nineteenth and early twentieth century and that the results were only published (if at all) in local bulletins, may seem an important obstacle when using the dataset for anything more than a simple architectural synthesis. However, the combination of these old sources with the high-resolution data generated by recent archaeological excavations, drawn together by modern research tools such as GIS-analysis, provides a solid dataset that can be questioned in order to investigate wider socio-cultural phenomena. The very characteristic and archaeologically recognizable bathhouses not only embodied Roman architecture and decor, but also communicated Roman ideas about health, the human body, and a civilized way of life. The reception and evolution of these buildings in newly conquered regions can thus help us understand how indigenous and Roman cultural spheres interacted.

The majority of baths in the study area were private baths (*c.* 81 per cent), whereas the number of public baths was very limited (*c.* 9 per cent). Such a pattern can also be noted for the neighbouring *civitates* in *Germania Inferior* (Dodt 2006, 64–66). Furthermore, it seems that only a single bathhouse was present in most central places, in contrast to the Mediterranean where even small towns could have several baths. This limitation to the bare necessities of civilized life has also been noted for other types of public buildings and public space and may well have been the result of a more modest form of elite euergetism. Unlike the rivalry between families vying for political power in the Mediterranean cities and towns, the perpetuation of pre-Roman social hierarchies concentrating power in the hands of the same elite families residing in the countryside probably made it less necessary for the elite to compete and hence invest in public infrastructure in the civic centres. The high number of villa baths may in fact point to a preference to invest resources in their private centres of power, namely their villas. The spread of the baths throughout the research area is therefore obviously linked to the spread of villas and central places. If we define villas as the rural residential buildings with evidence for the investment of a considerable level of surplus wealth in its construction (see Introduction), then the location of these villas was not automatically linked to the best agricultural lands, as villas are seen as manifestations of expenditure, not production (following Millett 1990, 94). Rather, the spread of villas reflects the occurrence of an elite that wished to invest their resources in a Roman-style way of living. In the *civitas Menapiorum*, the number of baths is limited and the number of central places and of villas is equally low. Nevertheless, the evidence for Roman-era occupation is abundant, with both settlements and small towns found in all corners of the *civitas*. However, these towns and villages were not Roman-style centres with public and residential buildings built from stone, but rather villages and towns built from the traditional timber-framed houses. Besides the fact that building stone was hard to come by, the local elites possibly chose to express their wealth through other forms, rather than building their houses in a Roman fashion. The few villas in this *civitas* were found mainly on the more fertile sandy loam soils. A similar pattern has been noted for the spread of villas (and baths) in the northern (sandy) parts of *Germania Inferior*, where local architectural traditions persisted (Dodt 2006, 67). The agricultural societies that developed in Menapian territory, just as in the *civitas Nerviorum* and *civitas Tungrorum*, had already evolved into a settlement type and social organization that facilitated the transition to Roman rural domestic architecture. The percentage of villas that were equipped with a bath (*c.* 25 per cent) was a bit lower than those in neighbouring *civitates* with more villas (*c.* 30–40 per cent), but still slightly higher than what has been recorded for certain regions in central Italy (*c.* 18 per cent), underlining that baths certainly found their way to this corner of the Empire. If we zoom in on the location of villas with baths, the proximity of traffic arteries (navigable rivers, roads) seems more important than the proximity of central places. In fact, the number of villas with baths is surprisingly low in the immediate hinterland of the *civitas* capitals *Atuatuca Tungrorum*, *Castellum Menapiorum*, or *Bagacum Nerviorum*. Even if we cannot rule out a bias in the archaeological data as a result of less research or poor visibility, this low number of villa baths may be explained by the availability of (larger) public baths in these cities. Villa owners might not have felt the need to have their own baths, as they mainly conducted business in the city and met their peers in the public baths. Or perhaps they felt that private baths could not compete with the facilities and luxury on offer in the public baths. Conversely, villa owners in areas with no cities or even central places within a day's travelling distance (but nevertheless connected to other villas through the road network) might have felt a greater need for baths, in the absence of public baths to meet their peers, or because their private residence was the only forum in which to display their wealth, in the absence of the civic centre as 'middle ground' for social competition.

On an architectural and functional level, both public and private baths were not fundamentally different from baths in other parts of the Empire, even if some trends and recurrent features can be noted. The public baths are often modest in size. No large imperial *thermae* such as in nearby *Augusta Treverorum* could be identified. This has also been remarked for the public baths in other parts of Gaul with few large cities, such as in *Gallia Narbonnensis* (Bouet 2003a, 717–19). The average public bath in the modest central places such as Tienen, Clavier, of Grobbendonk is between 100 and 500 m². Only the baths in Famars and Fontaine-Valmont surpassed 1000 m², although the main public baths in the *civitas* capitals Tongeren, Cassel, and Bavay still need to be located. The plans of the known public bathhouses are quite unremarkable, making use of mainly rectangular rooms, occasionally with a pool with an apsidal ending. Round rooms are quite rare and can probably be linked to *laconica*, while experimental room shapes (hexagonal, octagonal) do not occur. Linear row types and block types are by far the most common layouts, while the ring type is extremely rare. Just as in the other parts of Gaul, symmetrical plans are non-existent or extremely rare (Bouet 2003a, 716). The absence of *palaestrae* and *natationes*, which has already been remarked on for the northern (cold and wet) provinces in general, can also be mentioned, but should not come as a surprise for modest baths. The same remarks on architecture can also be made for the private baths. The large majority have a surface between 100 and 500 m², with outliers at opposite ends of the scale below 50 m² and above 600 m², making the latter larger than some public baths. The plans are of the linear row type or the block type and the rooms are rectangular in plan, sometimes with apsidal endings. Some pools were also semicircular

in plan, but other polygonal plans are non-existent. The scarcity of such more experimental room shapes has also been noted for other northern regions of the Empire, such as *Britannia*, where the only examples date from the fourth century. It is possible that this trend in architecture, which evolved in the Mediterranean core from the time of Trajan and especially Hadrian onwards, only reached the North in Late Antiquity. In the research area, however, no new villa baths were constructed at this time and so the absence of more 'experimental' plans and room shapes should not surprise. The only new late antique constructions can be linked to forts and in a single case probably to an urban *domus*, at Tongeren – Vrijthof. These baths are characterized by their small size and simple (linear) layout. Such very functional late antique military facilities have also been found in neighbouring *civitates* of *Germania Inferior* (Hanel 2000, 30). A more original feature of villa baths, which has been identified in *Gallia Belgica* and *Germania Inferior*, is the presence of a heated room, with its own furnace, in connection to the *frigidarium* but unconnected to the other heated rooms. It has been interpreted as a heated *apodyterium*, which may well have had additional functions (anointing, massages). While the *apodyterium* as a room was of course also known in the Mediterranean, the fact that it was occasionally heated may point to a preference for additional heated rooms in the colder northern climate. The presence of *calidae piscinae* in some of the luxurious baths of larger villas, a rare feature in Roman bath architecture, even in public baths in more Mediterranean regions of Gaul (Bouet 2003a, 713), also points to this fondness for the heated part of the baths. The decoration of both the public and the private baths followed the trends of domestic architecture: walls were often adorned with wall paintings, mainly with geometric and vegetal patterns on a single-colour background, while floors could be embellished with flagstones (often quarried in the research area or nearby regions) or, more exceptionally with mosaics. Again, geometric designs were omnipresent. Figurative themes were rare in both mosaics and wall paintings, possibly as a result of continuing pre-Roman tastes. Imported decorative stones from the Mediterranean are quite rare, but do appear in the larger and more luxurious baths. Unfortunately, few provenance studies have been published.

On a technological level, both public and private baths closely matched the bath-related technology that was developed in the Mediterranean. The baths were heated with traditional hypocaust systems, consisting of brick-built pillars supporting a suspended floor of tiles and hydraulic mortar. Constructional skills such as doubling the pillars beneath the pools, or reinforcing the walls at the location of the pools, were also used. The occurrence of channel hypocausts or a mixed channel and pillar system is exceptional in the Mediterranean, but certainly not restricted to the research area. The scarce evidence of *tegulae mammatae* for heating the walls is unsurprising, as this type of wall heating was already being replaced by *tubuli* when baths were introduced in the research area. The water supply of both public and private baths was often ensured by aqueducts, often (partially) made with wooden pipes, although evidence for wells is also encountered. Especially in areas where natural sources were less abundant, wells and rain water catchment must have been more important. Clues for identifying rain water catchment are more problematic to identify in the archaeological record, especially as so few cistern have been found. Waste water disposal is also unremarkable, with drains made of ceramic or wooden pipes, drains made with ceramic building materials or stone, or uncovered ditches running towards lower lying parts of the landscape (often leading into waterways), or, in cities and centres, linked to the sewer network. The use of hollowed-out tree trunks as water pipes was possibly adopted as an easy and economical alternative to terracotta pipes or channels built in mortar, stone, and tile. The building material for the walls of the baths consisted mainly of locally quarried stone (limestone, sandstone), with flint boulders often used for the foundations, and bricks and tiles for furnaces and hypocausts. Occasionally, layers of bricks were also used in wall construction (*opus vittatum*). Foliated stones such as slate were used as roof tiles or to cover drains. For some baths, mainly in regions with few building stone available, only the base of the walls seems to have been erected in stone, while the upper parts were made of a timber and loam framework. There is some evidence that thin walls were erected (with *tubuli*?) on the *suspensura* to partition larger rectangular *caldaria* into a *caldarium* and a *tepidarium*. This more original architectural feature had already been remarked upon for public baths in northern Gaul by Alain Bouet (2003a, 720), but was obviously also used for private baths. The high number of *caldaria* with an oblong plan, in both public and private bathhouses, could even indicate that this division into a *tepidarium-caldarium* by thin walls at *suspensura* level was quite common in the research area. Some examples have also come to light in *Germania Inferior* (Dodt 2006, 76), which would suggest this form of *caldarium-tepidarium* was widespread in the Roman continental north.

The introduction of bathhouses in the research area was not only important because it launched new architectural concepts (vaults, *exedrae*) and new technology (heating systems, hydraulic mortar, sewage systems), but also because it introduced Roman concepts of health, bodily hygiene, and self-representation. In the first phase of the conquest, the early adoption of Roman baths could therefore be seen as a marker for adopting a Roman way of life. However, it is difficult to identify such 'early adopters', as we cannot discover the background of those commissioning the bath. If we consider buildings as forms of non-verbal communication conveying their intended use, which in turn reflected socio-culturally embedded habits (following Rapoport 1976), evidence of divergence from the original form of a culturally charged building could point to a cultural deconstruction and recontextualization within a new cultural setting. In the research area, a number of very small baths consisting of a single heated room with a single heated pool, often constructed in the early phase of the Roman period (second half of the first century AD), could point to an adaption of the Roman bathhouse and hence also to a very selective adoption of Roman bathing habits. The absence of a *frigidarium*, a crucial room for Roman bathing practices, may well reveal how the local elite only invested in a specific element of the building which suited their taste. Similar baths in rural settlements with a strong indigenous tradition in *Britannia* suggest that this adaptation of the Roman bath and selective adoption of Roman bathing habits was not limited to the research area, but may be linked to the individual agency of local elites. The preference for geometric and vegetal patterns in wall paintings and mosaics may also point to a deliberate choice of continuing pre-Roman traditions, and only adopting some elements of Roman culture, rather than copying a new model. In the absence of written evidence of ownership, it is difficult to link the construction of these baths with any certainty to an elite with an indigenous background, although the pre-Roman origins of most settlements, continuing vernacular architectural elements, and indigenous material culture on the sites sometimes give strong indications. The adaption of the bathhouse (in all its aspects) according to local tastes would then stress that Roman baths were not simply imported as a 'package deal', nor that local elites would blindly emulate the habits of 'foreign' peers. This also supports the hypothesis that the penetration of Roman culture into newly conquered regions was not a deliberate policy, but a very gradual process driven by local elites, who negotiated their own place of power within a local framework, yet within the larger cultural language of the Roman Empire. The fact that baths were not simple 'washing facilities', but represented a Roman way of life can also explain why the baths disappeared as suddenly as they appeared. When the majority of the villas were abandoned, the private baths had also fallen out of use. Subsequent reoccupation often did not result in the restoration of the baths.

Due to a lack of well-dated early examples of Roman baths, we are still uncertain where the first baths were built. The early permanent military camps would certainly have been equipped with a bathhouse, but it is difficult to link the appearance of baths in towns and villas to these military baths. Did the first public baths copy the layout of military baths, or was the army perhaps even involved in their construction? The similarity in plans of early public baths and military baths can hardly be seen as hard evidence, as the linear row type is one of the most frequent plans due to its simplicity and efficiency. The first villa baths may also have been constructed by army veterans, but again there is hardly any evidence to support such a hypothesis. Considering the data at our disposal, we can only note how the earliest baths, both public and private, appear around the mid-first century AD. We can only speculate about the impact that the construction of baths in army camps, civic centres, and villas had on one another, but given the preponderance of villa baths in the following centuries, it is possible that private baths became the driving force in bath architecture and bathing habits in the research area, rather than the urban public baths. Within two or three generations, Roman baths and bathing habits seem to have been well integrated in both the private and public sphere. Most villa baths were constructed during the second century, often as an addition to an existing villa. The construction and maintenance of a bathhouse obviously demanded an important investment of resources, and can thus be seen as an important marker of wealth and status, and perhaps even as leaving a mark on the family legacy. In absence of cities and other central places with their public baths and public spaces, private baths in the countryside possibly played an important role as social hubs for elite interaction. Examples of very large, well-equipped, and lavishly decorated baths were obviously made to impress. The freestanding villa baths, baths attached to the villa, and internal baths which could be easily reached by visitors, also point to an accessibility beyond just the inhabitants of the house. For some villas, the occurrence of several baths could even point to a separation in use, with the internal baths for the family and their guests, and a separate bath for perhaps tenants and labourers of the lands. As public baths may not have been easily reached by a majority of rural inhabitants, such villa baths may have represented the only opportunity for large parts of the population to partake in such a 'civilizing' habit. The control of access to baths could hence also be a tool in maintaining social hierarchies, reinforcing elite status on the one hand, and possibly excluding social inferiors on the other. Having a private bath may even have become a social obligation in elite circles. Instead of the intra-elite competition encountered in the cities of the Mediterranean, local elites may have competed in their peer network of the countryside. However, this elite competition through baths should perhaps not be seen as families always trying to surpass each other with larger and more splendid baths, but rather as 'keeping up with the Joneses'.

When cultures meet, shifts in architectural design can help understand changes in the structure of the social and cultural fabric on both sides thanks to the intricate links that exist between architecture and underlying socio-cultural ideas of the people that produced and used it. Roman bath buildings not only embodied Roman architecture, technology, and decoration, they also offered a community the chance to lead a Roman way of life, taking care of their health and appearance while simultaneously engaging in public life. The way in which these buildings were received in newly conquered regions can thus also help us understand how indigenous communities engaged with these Roman socio-cultural values. This promising new line of research can move bath studies away from mere cataloguing and describing the architectural remains, and focus on the way these buildings actually impacted the lives of the people using them. This book will hopefully have underlined the potential of baths as proxies to study wider societal transformations, especially in regions unacquainted with specific buildings for communal bathing.

Catalogue

Introduction

This catalogue presents the sample of baths, both public and private, taken into account for the discussion in this book. As (development-led) excavations are continuously presenting new data and some excavated sites may have remained hidden in old excavation reports or grey literature, this corpus of bath sites cannot be considered an exhaustive catalogue of all baths in the research area. Especially for northern France, unpublished data was difficult to consult, and the apparent scarcity of sites may hence be a reflection of modern research practices rather than an historical reality. Some sites with clear evidence of baths have been included, even though the data that has been published is extremely concise or incomplete. The author has attempted to trace and consult unpublished data to the best of his ability, but unfortunately some excavation data remained nonetheless inaccessible.

The different bathhouses are arranged alphabetically following the modern topographical location where the baths were found. The name of the site is also given, as certain place names have yielded several baths. Each bath is also attributed an ID-number, which forms the link to the database system and a GIS-environment used for this research. This number was assigned following the time of database entry (first public baths, then possibly public baths, then private baths), so these ID-numbers do not follow the alphabetical order of the catalogued baths. This system enables new entries to the database in the future without needing to change ID-numbers. These ID-numbers also link the separate baths to the location as shown in Map 1. For each bathhouse, a data sheet is compiled, loosely based on the catalogues found in Nielsen (1993), Thébert (2003), or Fournet, Redon, and Vanpeene (2017). Important information on current location (1), research history (2), type of baths (3), dating (4), level of confidence to interpret as baths (5), plan and rooms (6), technology (7), decoration (8), figures (9), and relevant bibliography (10) are thus concisely presented. In the data sheet texts, the numbers in between brackets refer to the numbers on the plans of the baths.

For each catalogued bath, the following data sheet is given:

Location, site name (ID)

1. 1.1 Modern country, province, municipality
   1.2 GPS location (approximative to protect the sites from illegal digs, exact when not in danger)
2. 2.1 Year of excavations
   2.2 Conditions of the remains when excavated; present condition
3. Private or public baths and location (freestanding, integrated in or attached to a house)
4. 4.1 Construction date (type of evidence used for dating)
   4.2 Date of abandonment (type of evidence used for dating)
   4.3 Possible reuse of the bathhouse
5. Level of confidence for interpretation as a bathhouse (A, B, or C; see p. 21)
6. 6.1 Approximate size of the bath
   6.2 Type of plan
   6.3 Rooms without bath-related function belonging to the bathhouse
   6.4 Concise description of the cold rooms
   6.5 Concise description of the heated rooms
7. 7.1 Concise description of the heating system (furnaces, hypocaust)
   7.2 Concise description of the wall heating
   7.3 Concise description of the water supply
   7.4 Concise description of the waste water disposal
8. Concise description of the decoration
9. Figures in the book pertaining to the bath
10. References to the excavation report (ER) and relevant secondary sources

When available, each datasheet is followed by a general plan of the site indicating the location of the bathhouse and the plan of the bath itself. All plans have been restudied by the author, taking into account new data or new insights presented by subsequent studies, and redrawn on the basis of the original excavation plan, but following a special key and in relation to a 10 m scale bar for the general plans and a 5 m scale bar for the baths. The key to these plans can be found at the start of this book (p. 15). The numbers on the plans link the different rooms to the description in the data sheets. This uniform corpus of plans should allow for an easy comparison between plans.

Sites and Plans

Aardenburg, Glasfabriek (ID 1)

1. 1.1 The Netherlands, Zeeland, Sluis.
   1.2 51°16′11.64″N; 3°27′4.18″E (exact).
2. 2.1 1965 and 1967.
   2.2 Badly preserved when excavated, now destroyed.
3. Public bathhouse near a military fort (*extra muros*).
4. 4.1 Unknown. No ceramics or other finds were properly contextualized during the excavations. Ceramics from nearby trenches date between the last quarter of the second and the last quarter of the third century.
   4.2 Unknown.
   4.3 The bathhouse was probably dismantled during the eleventh century. Large parts of the building (especially the northern part) were destroyed during seventeenth-century construction works.
5. A (hypocaust and strong evidence for pool; overall plan).
6. 6.1 Min. 150 m² (partial plan).
   6.2 Linear or angular row type (partial plan).
   6.3 To the west of the main north-east–south-west axis of the bath, a room (1) was identified by a 6 m long part of a wall and fragments of roof tile and building stone (Tournai limestone). The room may have been an *apodyterium*.
   6.4 On the basis of its location at the northern end of the main axis, the northernmost room (2) has been interpreted as the *frigidarium*. The remains were heavily disturbed here, so there is no trace of a possible *piscina*.
   6.5 The central room (3) on the main axis (8 × 3.6 m) seems to have been heated by a hypocaust, although no furnace could be identified. Therefore, this was probably the *tepidarium*. The southernmost room (4) (3.6 × 2.3 m) had its own furnace to the south, identifying it as the *caldarium*. Even if the hypocaust were broken out for reuse in a post-Roman phase, the dense clustering of wooden pegs supporting the foundations of the building show that the south-eastern end of the room possibly housed an *alveus*.
7. 7.1 Only one *praefurnium* (5) could be discerned, protruding out of the southern end of the main bathing block (2.2 × 1.7 m). No information on hypocaust tiles or parts of the *suspensura* has been published.
   7.2 Unknown.
   7.3 A well, constructed out of wood, was discovered some 6 m south-west of the bathhouse.
   7.4 Unknown.
8. Several fragments of wall painting were recovered during the early excavations. As some contexts got mixed with other excavations, there is no information on patterns or colours.
9. Fig. 24.
10. van Dierendonck and Vos 2013, 101–06, 300 (ER).

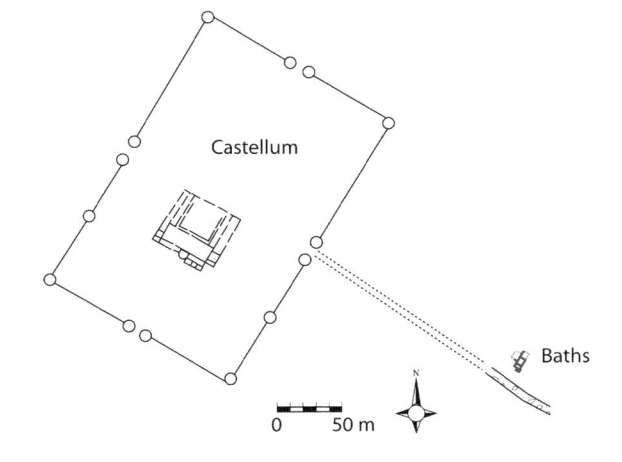

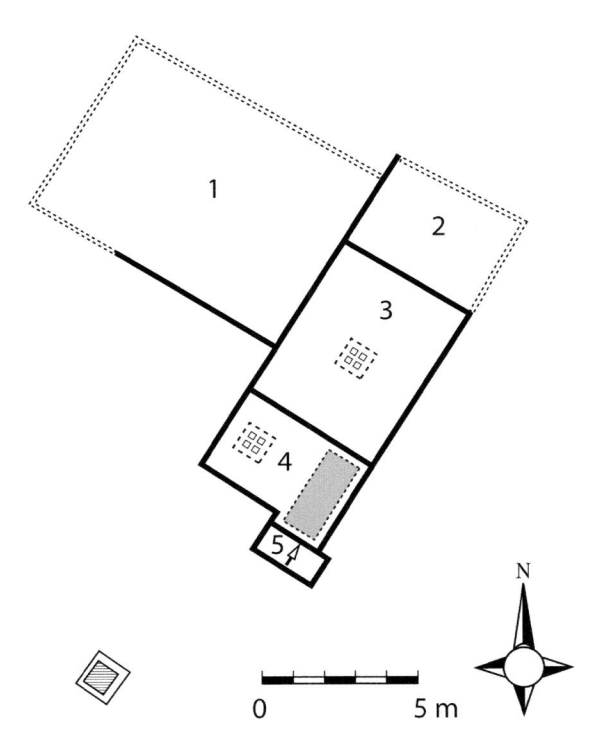

Figure 24. Location (top) and plan (below) of the bath of Aardenburg. Figure by author after van Dierendonck and Vos 2013, 104, fig. 6.9 and 300, fig. 8.9.

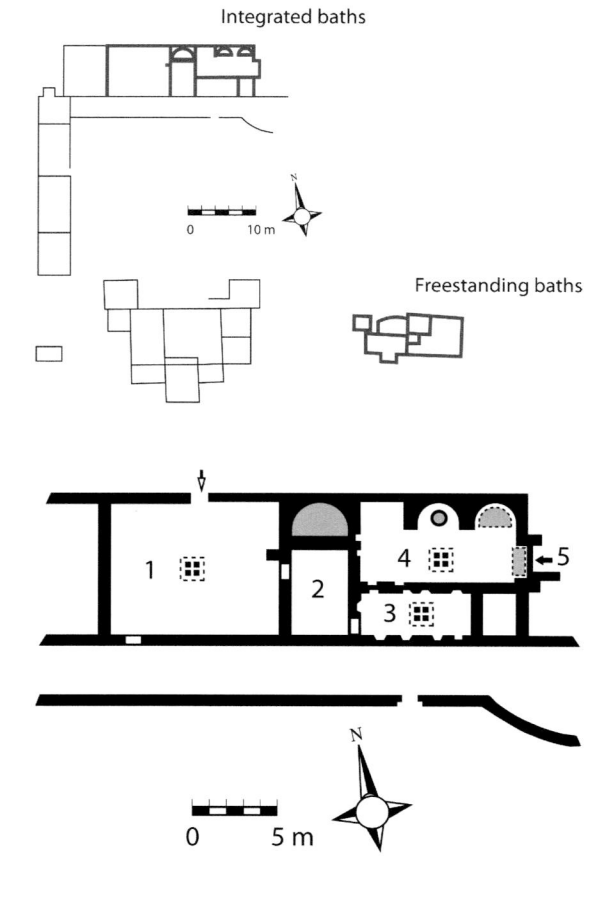

Integrated baths

Freestanding baths

Figure 25. Location (top) and plan of the 'Integrated Bath' of Aiseau. Figure by author after Kaisin 1878, pl. II.

Aiseau, Villa d'Aiseau-Presles, Integrated Baths (ID 29)

1. 1.1 Belgium, Hainaut, Aiseau-Presles.
   1.2 50°24'35.18"N; 4°35'8.94"E (approx.).
2. 2.1 1875.
   2.2 Well preserved when excavated, now destroyed.
3. Private bathhouse integrated in a villa.
4. 4.1 Second century (small finds).
   4.2 Third century (small finds).
   4.3 Unknown.
5. A (pools, hypocausts).
6. 6.1 *c.* 170 m².
   6.2 Block type.
   6.3 A large room (1) (8 × 9 m) on the western end of the bathing part was heated by a hypocaust. The alleged door to the outside of the villa is more likely to have been the furnace mouth. The room was interpreted as a winter apartment (social room), but was probably part of the bathhouse (a heated multifunctional *apodyterium?*).
   6.4 The *frigidarium* (2) (6.4 × 2.5 m) had a semicircular *piscina* (diam.: 3.3 m; 0.7 m deep). It probably connected to the *tepidarium* to its south-east.
   6.5 The *tepidarium* (3) (4.8 × 3.3 m) was wrongfully interpreted as a pool by the excavators. It was probably indirectly heated. The *caldarium* (4) (8.9 × 4.3 m) had three apses in its northern side, one rectangular (2.70 × 1.15 m) and two semicircular (diam.: 2.7 and 2.8 m), possibly for two *alvei* and a *labrum*.
7. 7.1 The *praefurnium* (5) was located east of the *caldarium*. The hypocaust pillars were made with square hypocaust tiles (s.: 19–21 cm; h.: 4–5 cm), bonded by clay, reaching 50–60 cm in height.
   7.2 Fragments of *tegulae mammatae* were found, as well as *tubuli* (box type, 22 × 23 × 10 cm, circular lateral openings with diam. 3.5 cm).
   7.3 Unknown. The stream Biesme is located 200 m from the villa.
   7.4 Unknown.
8. Fragments of polychrome wall paintings, fragments of glass (windowpane?), small slab of syenite marble, and stucco mouldings were recovered.
9. Fig. 25.
10. Kaisin 1878 (ER); Brulet 2008, 303.

Aiseau, Villa d'Aiseau-Presles, Freestanding Baths (ID 30)

1. 1.1   Belgium, Hainaut, Aiseau-Presles.
    1.2   50°24'35.18"N; 4°35'8.94"E (approx.).
2. 2.1   1875.
    2.2   Well preserved when excavated, now destroyed.
3.   Freestanding bathhouse of a villa.
4. 4.1   Second century (small finds).
    4.2   Third century (small finds).
    4.3   Unknown.
5.   A (pools, hypocaust).
6. 6.1   c. 80 m².
    6.2   Block type.
    6.3   A room with a rounded northern side (1) was built in dry stone. It may have functioned as an entrance porch or a dressing room.
    6.4   It is difficult to recognize a *frigidarium*. The northern room with curved wall in dry stone (1) seems inappropriate. According to the excavators, a small square *piscina* (s.: 1.45 m; 0.6 m deep) was attached to the building on the north-western corner. It is unclear how this pool connected to the other rooms of the bathhouse. It may have been a cistern.
    6.5   Two rooms were heated by the same *praefurnium*. The southernmost (2) (4.5 × 2.4 m) had a rectangular *exedra* on its south side, probably to lodge an *alveus*. A second *alveus* may well have been present along the east side, just above the furnace channel. This room can be interpreted as the *caldarium*. The smaller heated room (3) to the north-east (2.6 × 3.2 m) might have been a *tepidarium* or *sudatorium*. A small square space between the two heated rooms and the *praefurnium* was not interpreted by the excavators. It may have been a water tank or structure to lodge a boiler.
7. 7.1   The *praefurnium* (4) was located east of the *caldarium*. The hypocaust pillars were made with square hypocaust tiles (s.: 19–21 cm; h.: 4–5 cm), bonded by clay, reaching 50–60 cm in height. Large quantities of ash and a severely crackled hypocaust floor suggest that this bathhouse was frequently used over a long period of time.
    7.2   Fragments of *tegulae mammatae* were found, as well as *tubuli* (box type, 22 × 23 × 10 cm, circular lateral openings with diam. 3.5 cm).
    7.3   Unknown. The stream Biesme is located 200 m from the villa.
    7.4   A drainage channel made of *imbrices* ran from west to east through the *praefurnium*. It obviously collected the waste water from the *alvei*.
8.   Unknown.
9.   Figs 25–26.
10.   Kaisin 1878 (ER); Brulet 2008, 303.

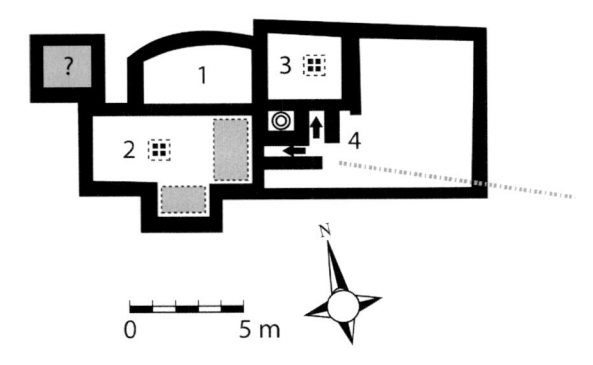

Figure 26. Plan of the 'Freestanding Bath' of Aiseau. Figure by author after Kaisin 1878, pl. II.

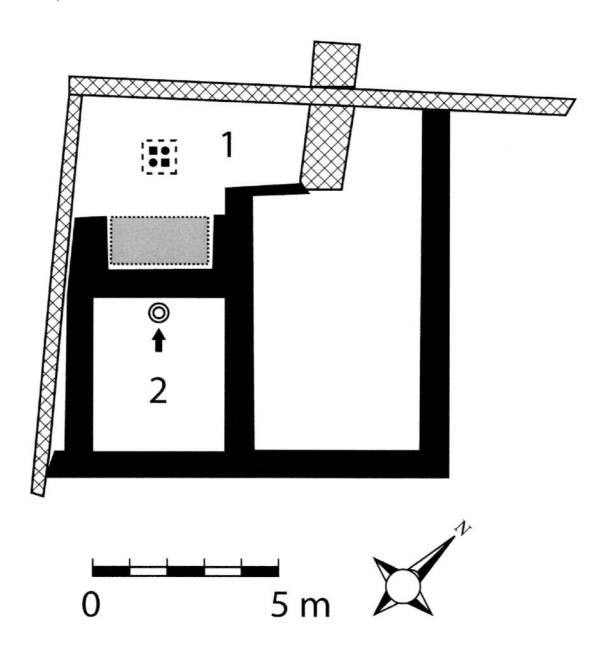

Figure 27. Plan of the bath of Amay 'La collégiale'. Figure by author after Willems, Dandoy, and Thirion 1969, unnumbered page, fig. 12.

Amay, Villa de la Collégiale (ID 31)

1.   1.1   Belgium, Liège, Amay.
      1.2   50°32'55.77"N; 5°19'3.93"E (exact).
2.   2.1   1962.
      2.2   Badly preserved at the time of excavations, now covered or destroyed.
3.   Private bath integrated in a villa.
4.   4.1   Early second century? (ceramics on site).
      4.2   Fourth century? (coins and ceramics on site).
      4.3   Graveyard in the eighth century.
5.   B (hypocaust, strong indication of a pool).
6.   6.1   Min. 60 m² (partial plan).
      6.2   Unknown (partial plan).
      6.3   Unknown (partial plan).
      6.4   Unknown (partial plan).
      6.5   Only one heated room could be identified (1). The cruciform room was possibly a *caldarium*, with perhaps *alvei* in the *exedrae*. The *praefurnium* (2) lay to the south-east.
7.   7.1   The hypocaust pillars were 65 cm high and consisted of round (diam.: 22 cm) and square (s.: 22.5 cm) tiles. Sometimes, both types were used in the same pillar. The hypocaust seems to have been reconstructed many times.
      7.2   Unknown.
      7.3   Unknown.
      7.4   Unknown.
8.   Fragments of wall paintings were found in the villa (e.g. depicting a horse).
9.   Fig. 27.
10.   Willems, Dandoy, and Thirion 1969; Brulet 2008, 387.

Amay-Ombret, bains du lieu-dit Rausa (ID 19)

1. 1.1 Belgium, Liège, Amay.
   1.2 50°32'34.31"N; 5°20'8.58"E (exact).
2. 2.1 Discovered and partially excavated in 1969–1970, further excavated in 1985.
   2.2 Well preserved at the time of excavations, now destroyed.
3. Public baths or private bath integrated in villa?
4. 4.1 Late first–early second century (ceramics in foundation trench), second phase in the middle of the second century.
   4.2 Middle of the third century (filling of the sewer) or fourth century (coin in the *praefurnium*).
   4.3 Reuse of the *praefurnium* (part of squatter occupation)?
5. A (pools, hypocausts).
6. 6.1 Min. 125 m² (partial plan).
   6.2 Linear row type? (partial plan).
   6.3 Unknown (partial plan).
   6.4 The *frigidarium* (1) has been partially excavated and may have had a rectangular *piscina* to the south-west.
   6.5 The *caldarium* (2) (5.8 × 12.6 m) had two rectangular *exedrae* (south-west and north-west), presumably to accommodate *alvei*. Both *exedrae* lay directly above a furnace. Two steps could be identified in the north-western *alveus* (min. 0.4 m deep). According to the excavators, a *tepidarium* (3) (4.5 × 3.3 m), or perhaps more likely a *sudatorium* (following A. Bouet), was located at the northern end of the *caldarium*. It was heated by a separate furnace in the north-eastern corner.
7. 7.1 The hypocaust pillars underneath the *alvei* were made with square tiles bonded with clay, although several round tiles (diam.: 20.5–22 cm; 3.8–4.5 cm thick) have also been found in the destruction layer (first phase?). The furnace channel piercing the western wall was 0.4 m wide. The south-western furnace in the *praefurnium* (4) had small reinforced walls which possibly supported a boiler.
   7.2 From the first phase of the baths, several square *tegulae mammatae* were found (s.: 27 cm; 3–4.5 cm thick). From the second phase, some *tubuli* (20 × 20 cm, 14 cm high; or 10 × 25 cm, 25 cm high; both with round lateral openings, diam.: 4.5 cm) were found *in situ* lining the north-western *alveus*.
   7.3 Unknown.
   7.4 The alleged *piscina* was drained by drainage channel (40 × 30 cm) made out of limestone blocks, running south of the *caldarium*. The water from the *alvei* possibly discharged in the latter as well. A latrine, probably flushed by the waste waters of the pools, was discovered some 15 m north of the bath. The north-western *alveus* was drained by a channel made out of *tegulae*. Some tiles had the stamp NEH or CAIVS (first phase).
8. Several fragments of wall painting and windowpane were found.
9. Fig. 28.
10. Witvrouw 1986 (ER); Bouet 2003a, 666–67; Brulet 2008, 385.

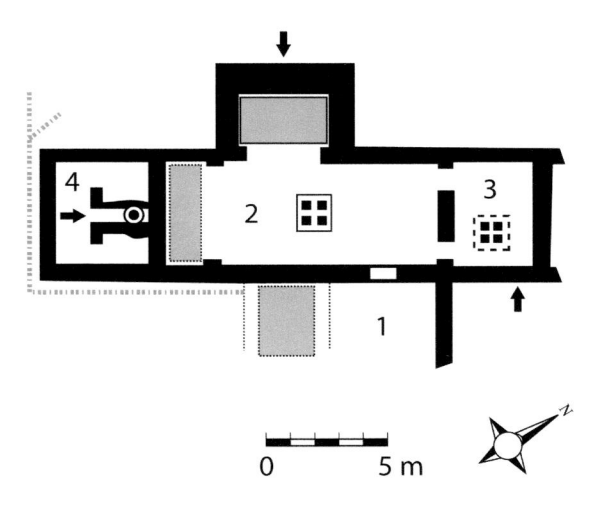

Figure 28. Plan of the bath of Amay-Ombret. Figure by author after Witvrouw 1986, 104, fig. 9.

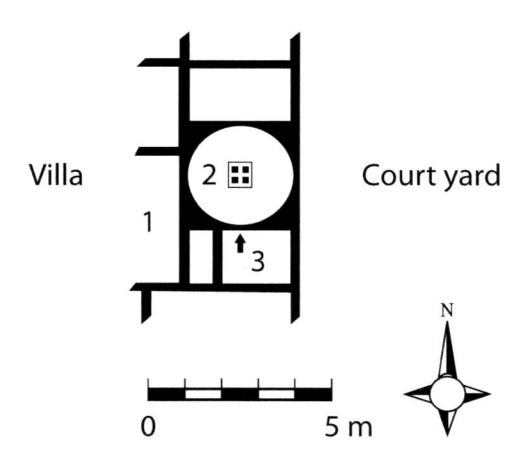

Figure 29. Location (top) and plan of the alleged bath of Ambresin. Figure by author after De Looz 1876, pl. II.

Ambresin, Villa d'Ambresin (ID 32)

1.	1.1	Belgium, Liège, Wasseiges.
	1.2	50°37'45.95"N; 5°1'48.84"E (approx.).
2.	2.1	1875.
	2.2	Well preserved when excavated, now reburied or destroyed.
3.		Private bath integrated in a villa.
4.	4.1	Second century? (ceramics and coins on site).
	4.2	Unknown.
	4.3	Unknown.
5.		C (presumed *laconicum*).
6.	6.1	*c.* 11 m².
	6.2	The room(s) immediately north or west (1) (with tile floor) of the heated room may have functioned as cold rooms.
	6.3	None.
	6.4	None.
	6.5	A single round room (2) was heated by a hypocaust (diam.: 2.75 m). It may have been a stand-alone *laconicum*.
7.	7.1	Fragments of pillar tiles found (shape unknown). The room directly south of the round room (3) was filled with ash and charcoal. It should probably be identified with the *praefurnium*. The opening on the south side of the round room was probably the furnace (rather than a door).
	7.2	Fragments of *tubuli* found (type unknown).
	7.3	Unknown (no wells found near the villa).
	7.4	Unknown.
8.		Fragments of polychrome wall painting found near the bath suite.
9.		Fig. 29.
10.		De Looz 1876 (ER); Brulet 2008, 438–39.

Anderlecht, Champ Sainte-Anne (ID 33)

1. 1.1 Belgium, Brussels, Anderlecht.
   1.2 50°49'29.37"N; 4°16'50.07"E (approx.).
2. 2.1 1890s.
   2.2 Well preserved when excavated, now covered or destroyed.
3.   Freestanding bathhouse of a villa.
4. 4.1 Unknown. The villa was in use in at least the first and second century (ceramics and coins).
   4.2 Unknown.
   4.3 The villa site was reused as burial site in the early Middle Ages. No tombs were discovered in the baths.
5.   A (hypocaust, strong evidence for pool).
6. 6.1 *c.* 32 m².
   6.2 Block type.
   6.3 The bathhouse was entered through a large doorway (1.75 m in width), leading into a first room (1). This was probably the *apodyterium*. No special features could be identified.
   6.4 A second small room (2) east of the entrance room may have been the *frigidarium*, although no traces of a *piscina* were found.
   6.5 A single heated room (3), the *caldarium* (4 × 2.7 m), had a rectangular *exedra* to the south, probably to lodge an *alveus*. Alternatively, a pool lay just above the furnace, on its eastern side, where the hypocaust pillars were doubled for extra stability.
7. 7.1 The hypocaust pillars were made with large square tiles (s.: 30 cm). The furnace channel was paved with tiles and was framed by two parallel walls. A small wall north of the furnace probably delimited the *praefurnium* (4) and may have offered protection from the weather by enabling the construction of a slanted roof.
   7.2 Fragments of *tubuli* were found amongst the debris.
   7.3 Unknown. No traces of water pipes were found in the vicinity of the baths. However, the baths lay downhill of the villa, near the Senne stream.
   7.4 Unknown.
8.   Unknown.
9.   Fig. 30.
10.   Dens 1906 (ER); De Maeyer 1940, 4–6.

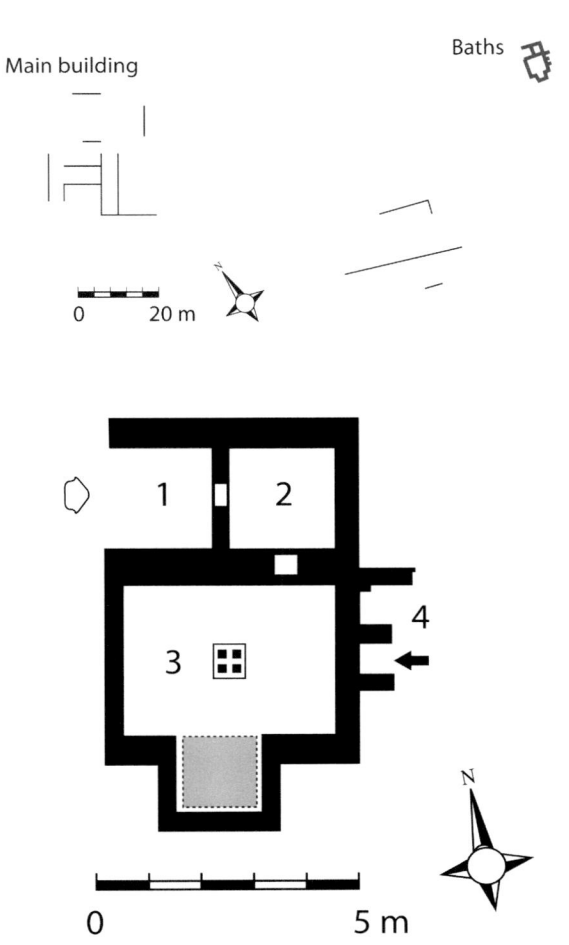

Figure 30: Location (top) and plan of the bath of Anderlecht. Figure by author after Dens 1906, pl. VII.

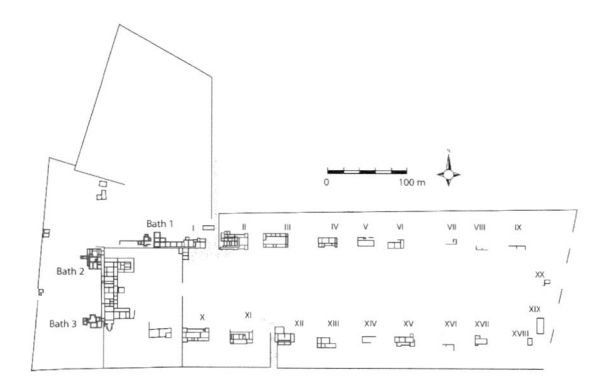

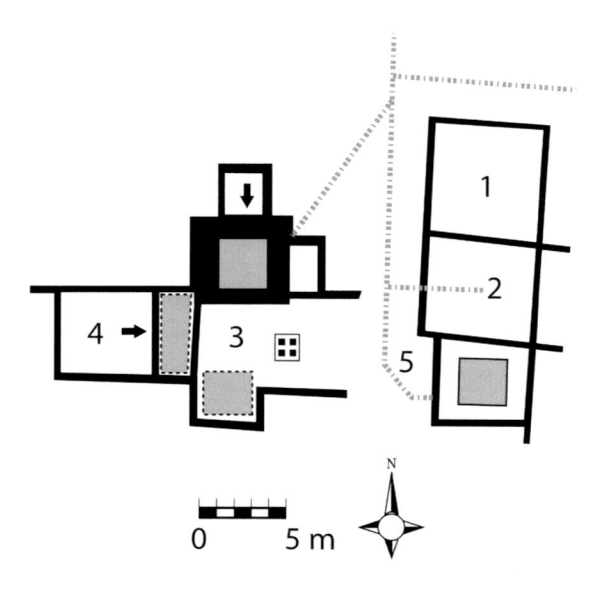

Figure 31. Location (top) and plan of Bath 1 at Anthée. Figure by author after Del Marmol 1877, pl. II.

Anthée, Villa du Grand Bon Dieu — Bath 1 (ID 34)

1. 1.1 Belgium, Namur, Onhaye.
   1.2 50°14'23.87"N; 4°45'35.90"E (approx.).
2. 2.1 1863.
   2.2 Partially preserved at the time of excavation, now covered.
3. Private bath integrated in a villa.
4. 4.1 The villa may have been late Neronian or Flavian in date (ceramics and coins on site). The construction date of the baths is unknown.
   4.2 The villa was abandoned in the fourth century, although the bath may have fallen out of use at an earlier date.
   4.3 Unknown.
5. A (hypocausts, strong evidence for pools, sewage channels).
6. 6.1 Min. 150 m².
   6.2 Unknown (partial plan).
   6.3 The eastern part of the baths was poorly preserved. A room with a mortar floor may have been an *apodyterium* (1).
   6.4 The room with a drainage channel cutting through its mortar floor (2) may have been the *frigidarium*. The *piscina* was located to the south.
   6.5 The alleged *caldarium* (3) had a rectangular *exedra* (possibly for an *alveus* or *labrum*) to the south, and an *alveus* to the north, which had a low bench running along its northern, eastern, and western sides. It was directly heated by a furnace to the north. The main *praefurnium* (4) of the *caldarium* lay to the west. The area between the *caldarium* and the *frigidarium* was heavily disturbed. There may have been a *tepidarium* (5) just west of the *piscina*, where several hypocaust tiles were found.
7. 7.1 The pillars of the *caldarium* hypocaust were made of square tiles (s.: 20 cm) bonded with clay. The furnaces of both the northern *alveus* and the of main *praefurnium* (4) were made of bricks placed on their small side, on top of a layer of small stones.
   7.2 The walls were heated by *tubuli*, some of which were still *in situ*.
   7.3 The water for the entire villa was supplied by two springs nearby (*Fontaine des Noisettes* at 3317 m and *Fontaine Al Tavienne* at 2142 m). It was channelled to the site by an aqueduct made of inverted *imbrices* and one made of wooden pipes (of which only the iron rings holding the different parts together were found).
   7.4 The *alveus* and *piscina* were drained by drainage channels, which joined together underneath the cold section and continued northwards and then eastwards. The alleged *frigidarium* also seems to have had a drain.
8. Fragments of marble were found in the area west of the alleged *apodyterium* (1).
9. Fig. 31.
10. Del Marmol 1877 (ER); Del Marmol 1881; Brulet 2008, 561–64.

Anthée, Villa du Grand Bon Dieu — Bath 2 (ID 35)

1. 1.1 Belgium, Namur, Onhaye.
   1.2 50°14'23.87"N; 4°45'35.90"E (approx.).
2. 2.1 1863.
   2.2 Partially preserved at the time of excavation, now covered.
3. Private bath integrated in a villa.
4. 4.1 The villa may have been late Neronian or Flavian in date (ceramics and coins on site). The construction date of the baths is unknown.
   4.2 The villa was abandoned in the fourth century, although the bath may have fallen out of use at an earlier date.
   4.3 Unknown.
5. A (hypocaust rooms, evidence for pools, water pipes).
6. 6.1 Min. 280 m² (plan unclear).
   6.2 Unknown (partial plan).
   6.3 The two westernmost rooms could be interpreted as an entrance vestibule (1) (with hydraulic mortar floor) and a heated *apodyterium* (2) (with hypocaust). An oblong north–south corridor (3) connected to a small square room (4) (s.: 2.35 m) with a concrete floor, perhaps an *apodyterium*.
   6.4 It is difficult to identify the *frigidarium*. According to Del Marmol, it was the large room to the north (5), although no traces of a *piscina* were recognized.
   6.5 A first room with a hypocaust in the middle of the building (6) may have had a pool in its south-eastern corner. The excavators mention how the floor was 30 cm lower here, and walled off with tufa blocks. This may have been the *tepidarium*. A second heated room to the south (7) had a semicircular *exedra*, probably lodging the *alveus*. To the west of this *exedra*, a large quantity of ash was found, pointing to the location of the furnace. The eastern side of the room was slightly raised (8), which could also point to the location of a larger rectangular *alveus*. This room should be seen as the *caldarium*.
7. 7.1 The hypocaust pillars of the first heated room were made of square tiles, those of the second with round tiles.
   7.2 The excavation report only mentions terracotta pipes (*tubuli?*) in the first heated room.
   7.3 The water for the entire villa was supplied by two springs nearby (*Fontaine des Noisettes* at 3317 m and *Fontaine Al Tavienne* at 2142 m). It was channelled to the site by an aqueduct made of inverted *imbrices* and one made of wooden pipes (of which only the iron rings holding the different parts together were found). A cistern may have been located east of the bath rooms (sturdy construction), while the location of a water channel may have been identified in the walls east of the baths.
   7.4 Unknown.
8. Fragments of marble were found in the first heated room (allegedly part of an *opus sectile* according to the excavators). Many mosaic *tesserae* were found in the second heated room. Near the baths, fragments of 'red marble' and 'une sorte de fût de colonne' (base of a *labrum?*) were found.
9. Fig. 32.
10. Del Marmol 1877 (ER); Del Marmol 1881; Brulet 2008, 561–64.

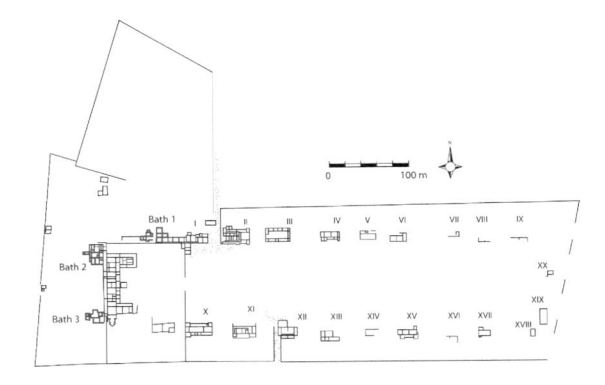

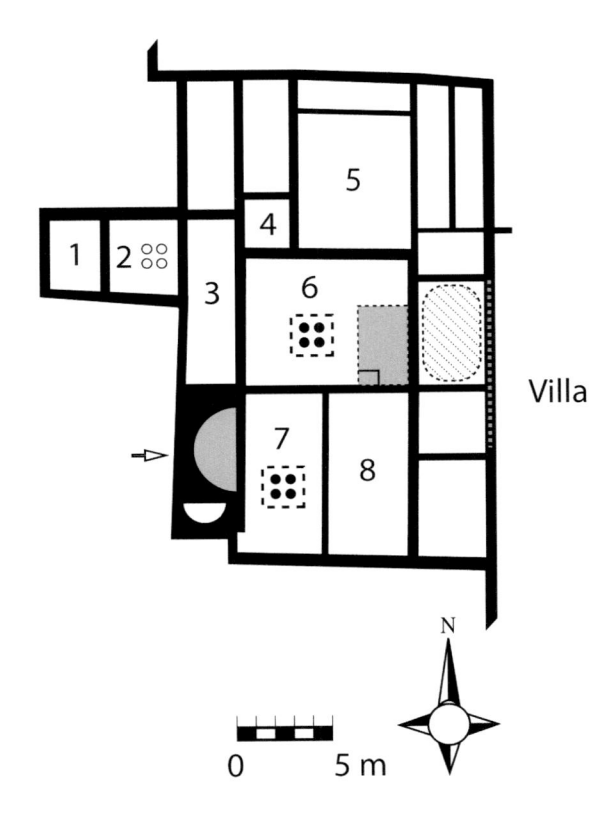

Figure 32. Location (top) and plan of Bath 2 at Anthée. Figure by author after Del Marmol 1877, pl. II.

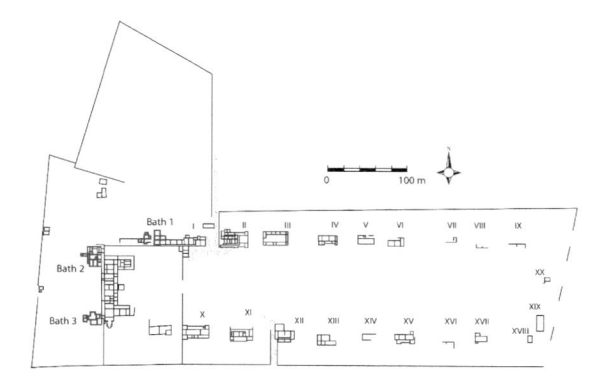

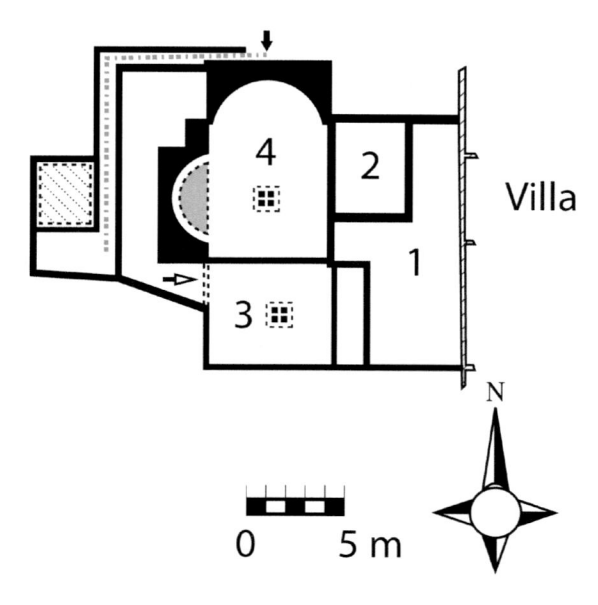

Figure 33. Location (top) and plan of Bath 3 at Anthée. Figure by author after Del Marmol 1877, pl. II.

Anthée, Villa du Grand Bon Dieu — Bath 3 (ID 36)

1. 1.1 Belgium, Namur, Onhaye.
    1.2 50°14'23.87"N; 4°45'35.90"E (approx.).
2. 2.1 1863.
    2.2 Partially preserved at the time of excavation, now covered.
3. Private bath attached to a villa.
4. 4.1 The villa may have been late Neronian or Flavian in date (ceramics and coins on site). The construction date of the baths is unknown.
    4.2 The villa was abandoned in the fourth century, although the bath may have fallen out of use at an earlier date.
    4.3 Unknown.
5. A (hypocaust rooms, strong evidence for a pool, water conduits).
6. 6.1 Min. 350 m² (plan unclear).
    6.2 Unknown (plan unclear).
    6.3 The plan is unclear. The area (1) between the villa and the bathhouse may have been used as *apodyterium-unctorium*.
    6.4 It is difficult to identify the *frigidarium*. Possibly it was the room in the centre (2), perhaps with a *piscina* to the north.
    6.5 A first room with a hypocaust (3) and two water conduits (no further information) might have been the *tepidarium* or *sudatorium*. The large room with two semicircular *exedrae* (4) was undoubtedly the *caldarium*. The western *exedra* was 1.1 m deep (from the surface?) and must have been an *alveus*, while the northern had its floor slightly raised in comparison to the *caldarium*, pointing to a *schola labri*.
7. 7.1 The hypocaust pillars were made with square tiles. The furnace mouth to the north was 0.9 m wide. On a tile found in a room with hypocaust nearby, the stamp TRAVGPSB could be recognized.
    7.2 Fragments of *tubuli* (box type) were found (no further information available).
    7.3 The water for the entire villa was supplied by two springs nearby (*Fontaine des Noisettes* at 3317 m and *Fontaine Al Tavienne* at 2142 m). It was channelled to the site by an aqueduct made of inverted *imbrices* and one made of wooden pipes (of which only the iron rings holding the different parts together were found). A branch of an aqueduct (wood) was found south of the bath. A cistern (1.7 m deep) with a lead *fistula* still in place, was located west of the *caldarium*.
    7.4 A drainage channel for collecting the waste waters of the *alvei* was found west and north (also for the *piscina*?) of the *caldarium*. It was constructed with blocks of tufa and tiles (bottom and cover).
8. Fragments of marble and wall painting (of the ceiling?) were found in the southern heated room. Mosaic *tesserae* were found among the debris.
9. Fig. 33.
10. Del Marmol 1877 (ER); Del Marmol 1881; Brulet 2008, 561–64.

Arquennes, Villa de Maleville (ID 37)

1. 1.1 Belgium, Hainaut, Seneffe.
   1.2 50°33'49.56"N; 4°16'50.02" (approx.).
2. 2.1 1872.
   2.2 Well preserved at the time of excavations, now covered or destroyed.
3. Private bath attached to a villa.
4. 4.1 Unknown.
   4.2 Fourth century? (coins in furnace).
   4.3 Unknown.
5. A (pools, hypocausts).
6. 6.1 Min. 87 m² (plan unclear).
   6.2 Angular row type? (plan unclear).
   6.3 A corridor (8 m long, 1.9 m wide) connected the bath to the villa. The first two rooms following the corridor (3 × 3.8 m and 5.4 × 3 m) possibly served as *apodyterium* (1) and perhaps *unctorium* or *districtarium* (2). It is unclear whether the rooms to the north-east of the bathing rooms belonged to the bath.
   6.4 The *frigidarium* (3) (3 × 3.45 m) had no concrete floor, suggesting wooden floorboards might have been used. The *piscina* (2.49 × 2.14 m) was accessible through some brick-built steps in its southern corner.
   6.5 A first heated room (4) (5.73 × 3.9 m) with hypocaust must have been accessed from the *frigidarium*. It could thus be interpreted as *tepidarium*, even if it was heated by its own furnace (*praefurnium* to the north-west). A second heated room (5) had an irregular shape (max. 6.7 × 2.8 m) and should be identified as the *caldarium*. The location of an *alveus* is problematic, as the *praefurnium* is somewhat strangely positioned in the south-east. The reinforced hypocaust pillars at the south-eastern side of the room possibly served to sustain an *alveus*.
7. 7.1 All the hypocaust pillars were made with square tiles (s.: 20 cm), bonded by layers of clay. The *praefurnium* of the *caldarium* was filled with ashes and charcoal when discovered. The furnace opening was closed off by a large tile with a protruding knob, enabling it to be moved.
   7.2 Several intact *tubuli* (box type) were found in the *tepidarium* (27 × 26 × 27 cm, with round lateral openings, diam. 5 cm).
   7.3 Unknown.
   7.4 The *piscina* was drained by a lead *fistula*, still *in situ*, flowing into a covered drainage channel (30 cm wide, 45 cm deep) made out of local stone. A construction of *imbrices* embedded upside-down in mortar possibly collected rain water from the roof and also led into this drainage channel. After 12 m, the channel led into an uncovered ditch.
8. The imprint of torn-out stone slabs was still visible in the *piscina*'s mortar floor. Fragments of wall painting and stucco mouldings were also found. The high quantities of charcoal, burned daub, and iron nails reveal that at least some rooms of this wing of the villa had walls in wattle and daub (auxiliary rooms?).
9. Fig. 34.
10. Cloquet 1873 (ER); Cloquet 1875, LV; Brulet 2008, 365–66.

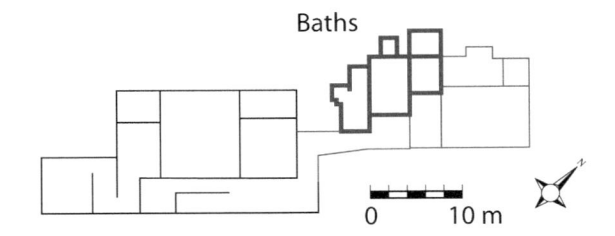

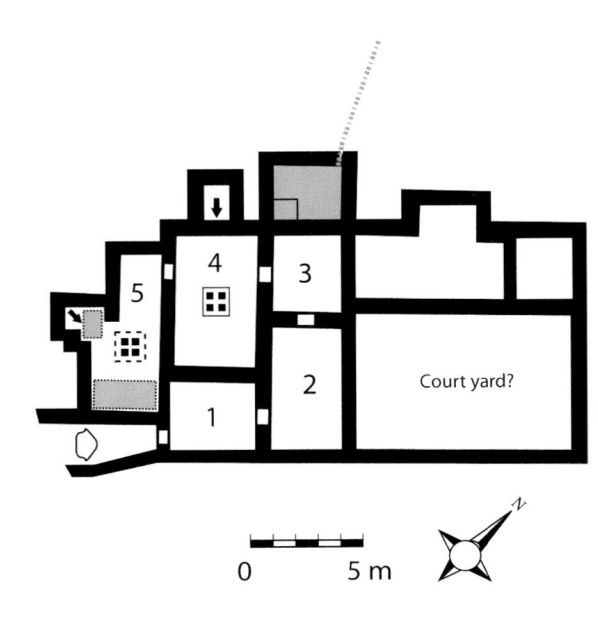

Figure 34. Location (top) and plan of the bath at Arquennes. Figure by author after De Maeyer 1937, 72, fig. 15a and Cloquet 1873, pl. II.

Assenois, La Chappelle (ID 145)

1. 1.1 Belgium, Luxembourg, Vaux-sur-Sûre.
   1.2 49°57'59.52"N; 5°40'50.00"E (approx.).
2. 2.1 1867.
   2.2 Well preserved when excavated, now reburied.
3. Private bath integrated in a villa.
4. 4.1 Unknown.
   4.2 Unknown.
   4.3 Unknown.
5. A (pool, hypocaust).
6. 6.1 Unknown (no dimensions given).
   6.2 Unknown (partial plan).
   6.3 Unknown (partial plan).
   6.4 Unknown. The excavation report does not mention whether the pool was heated by a hypocaust or not (*alveus* or *piscina*?). The inside of the pool was clad with terracotta tiles.
   6.5 At least one room was heated by a hypocaust. A bench finished in terracotta tiles ran along the walls of this room.
7. 7.1 Unknown.
   7.2 Unknown.
   7.3 Unknown.
   7.4 Unknown.
8. Unknown.
9. No plan available.
10. Sulbout 1867 (ER).

Attenhoven, Villa La Bruyère (ID 38)

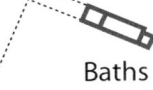
Baths

1.   1.1   Belgium, Flemish Brabant, Landen.
      1.2   50°46'2.82"N; 5°5'36.67"E (approx.).
2.   2.1   1884.
      2.2   Well preserved at the time of excavations, now covered or destroyed.
3.   Private bath integrated in villa (?).
4.   4.1   Unknown.
      4.2   Unknown.
      4.3   Unknown.
5.   A (pool and hypocaust room).
6.   6.1   Min. 82 m² (partial plan?).
      6.2   Single room.
      6.3   Unknown.
      6.4   Unknown.
      6.5   It seems that the bathing suite of the villa consisted of only one heated room (6.6 × 2 m) with a small *alveus* (1.25 × 1 m). Fragments of a *labrum* were also found. Apparently, the surrounding rooms were too badly preserved to identify whether these belonged to the bathhouse or not.
7.   7.1   Round hypocaust tiles were found among the debris. The *praefurnium* had a brick-built furnace channel (1 × 1.3 m).
      7.2   Unknown.
      7.3   Unknown.
      7.4   Unknown.
8.   Unknown.
9.   Fig. 35.
10.   Lefèvre 1887 (ER); Piton 1939.

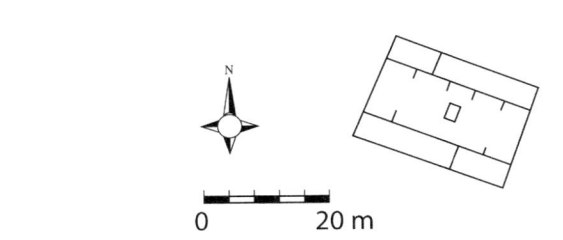

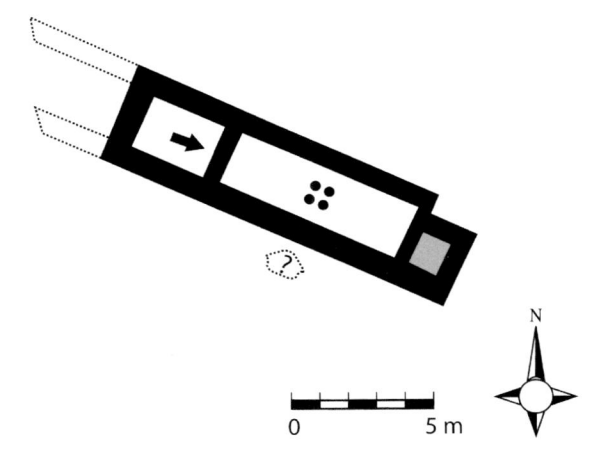

Figure 35. Location (top) and plan of the bath of Attenhoven. Figure by author after Lefèvre 1887, pl. III.

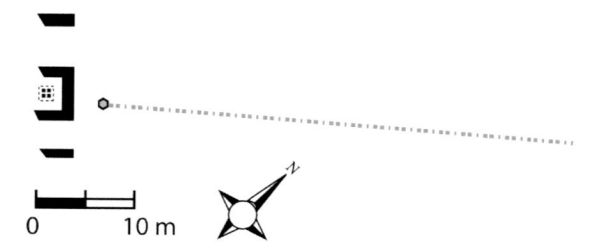

Figure 36. Partial plan of the basin and hypocausts found in Aubechies. Figure by author after Demarez and Henton 1995, 110, pl. xxxiii, fig. 3.

Aubechies, Villa d'Aubechies (ID 39)

1. 1.1   Belgium, Hainaut, Belœil.
    1.2   50°34'27.35"N; 3°40'34.72"E (exact).
2. 2.1   1958 and 1968.
    2.2   Well preserved when excavated, pool and northern hypocaust still preserved.
3.   Private bath suite integrated in a villa?
4. 4.1   Between the first and third century.
    4.2   Unknown.
    4.3   Unknown.
5.   C (possible pool, nearby hypocaust).
6. 6.1   Min. 10 m² (partial plan).
    6.2   Unknown (partial plan).
    6.3   Unknown (partial plan).
    6.4   A small hexagonal basin (diam.: 1 m; min. 39 cm deep) was found in a test pit in the crypt of the church of Saint-Géry. Interpreted by the excavators as a *nymphaeum*, it may have been a basin of a bathhouse.
    6.5   To the west of the basin, a room with a hypocaust was discovered (just outside the present church), reinforcing the idea of a bathhouse. Some 50 m to the north, two rooms with a hypocaust and a *praefurnium* were also discovered, although it cannot be confirmed whether these rooms were part of a bath suite or were simply heated rooms.
7. 7.1   There is no description of the hypocaust pillars.
    7.2   Unknown.
    7.3   Unknown.
    7.4   The hexagonal basin was drained by an orifice at the bottom (north-eastern side). The channel, made of interlocking *imbrices*, was also identified east of the present church.
8.   Unknown.
9.   Fig. 36.
10.   Demarez and Henton 1995; Brulet 2008, 311–12.

Autre-Église, Thermes du Prieuré (ID 17)

1. 1.1   Belgium, Walloon Brabant, Ramillies.
    1.2   50°39'39.33"N; 4°55'35.26"E (exact).
2. 2.1   1977–1984, 2006.
    2.2   Well preserved in parts, demolished in others when excavated, now destroyed.
3.   Freestanding bath of a villa or public bath of a small settlement?
4. 4.1   Unknown. The bathhouse had at least two construction phases. Ceramics on site point to a lifespan between the second and third century.
    4.2   Unknown, but probably not after the third century (ceramics on site).
    4.3   Unknown.
5.   A (pools, hypocausts).
6. 6.1   First phase: min. 80 m² (incomplete plan); second phase: min. 350 m² (incomplete plan).

6.2 First phase: linear row type; second phase: angular row type? (incomplete plan).

6.3 None in the first phase. In the second phase, the northernmost (1) and southernmost (2) heated rooms might have been respectively a *sudatorium* and a heated *apodyterium*. Two rooms on the east side of the bathhouse may have been service rooms. The southernmost (3) had a mortar floor.

6.4 In the first phase, the *frigidarium* was located on the eastern end of the suite of east–west oriented rooms in the centre of the building (4). During the second phase, it was transformed into a heated room. The *piscina* of the first phase, has not been identified.

6.5 In the first phase, there were two rooms (5 and 6) with a hypocaust, heated by a single furnace to the west. We can recognize the *caldarium* (6) and *tepidarium* (5). The former had a semicircular *exedra* on its northern and southern side, probably lodging *alvei*. In a second phase, the original *frigidarium* was transformed into a heated room (*tepidarium*?). The two semicircular *exedrae* of the *caldarium* were abandoned, possibly in favour of a rectangular *alveus* just above the furnace channel to the west, which was reinforced at this time. To the north of the original *frigidarium*, a square heated room (s.: 5.1 m) with a hypocaust (1) may have been a new *sudatorium*. As its hypocaust was not connected to the other hypocausts, it must have had its own furnace. On its north side, there seems to have been a semicircular *exedra* with a pink mortar floor (without hypocaust). A second new heated room (2) (4.75 × 6.55 m) was added south of the original *frigidarium*. It may have been a heated *apodyterium*. However, as it had its own furnace to the south, it might also have been a *sudatorium*.

7. 7.1 The hypocaust pillars were made of square tiles (s.: 19–21.5 cm). Only in the southernmost heated room, round tiles were used. The *praefurnium* of the east–west oriented suite of heated rooms lay to the west. In a second phase, the furnace channel was reinforced with parallel walls protruding into the hypocaust of the *caldarium*. The *praefurnium* (3.85 × 4.70 m) of the second-phase southern heated room had a furnace channel made of bricks, but no walls to support a boiler.

7.2 The excavation reports do not mention evidence for *tubuli*. In the southernmost heated room, each wall was equipped with two chimney flues.

7.3 Unknown.

7.4 In the *caldarium*, a drainage channel lay on the hypocaust floor, possibly to drain the first-phase semicircular *alvei*. In the original *tepidarium* to the east, there also ran a drain on the hypocaust floor. These channels were made with tiles or *imbrices*. Underneath the hypocaust floor of the second-phase southern heated room, a drainage channel ran south to the *praefurnium*.

8. Unknown.

9. Fig. 37.

10. Bodson and De Reymaeker 1980 (ER); Van Hove, De Waele, and Van Buylaer 2008a (ER); Van Hove, De Waele, and Van Buylaer 2008b (ER).

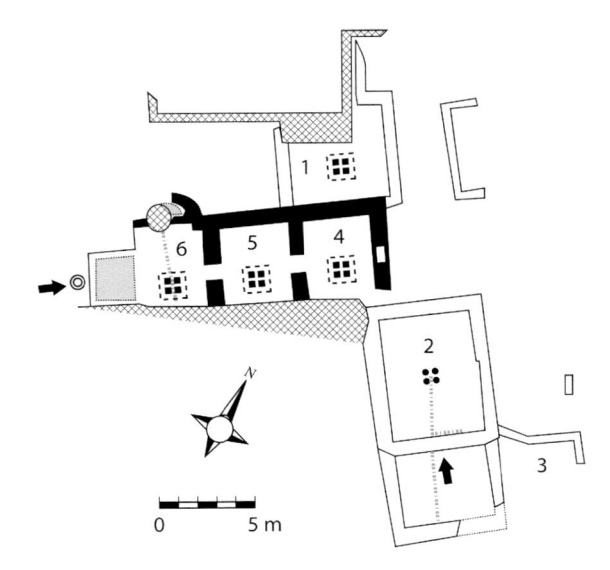

Figure 37. Plan of the bath in Autre-Église. Figure by author after Van Hove, De Waele, and Van Buylaer 2008a, 16, unnumbered fig.

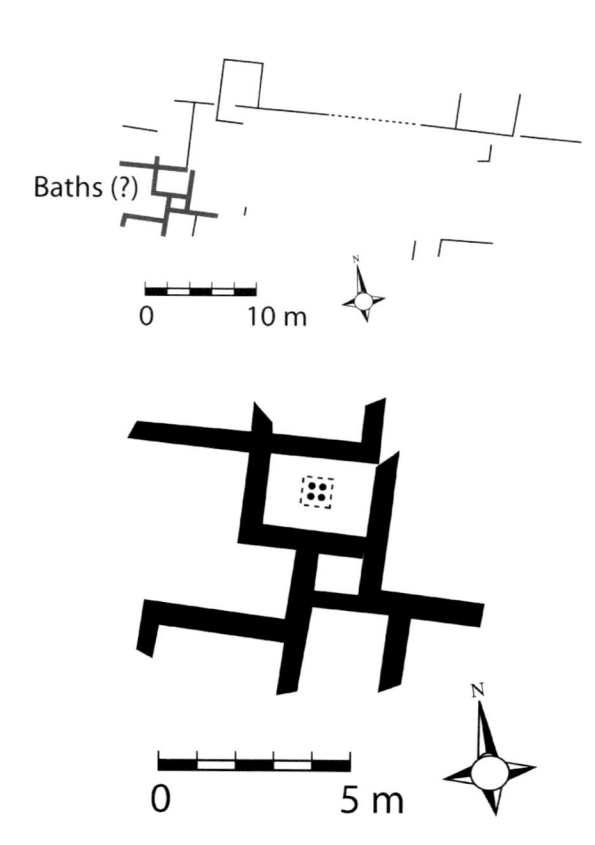

Figure 38. Location (top) and plan of the possible bath in Ave-et-Aufe. Figure by author after Plumier 1996, 26, unnumbered fig.

Baths (?)

0   10 m

0   5 m

Ave-et-Aufe, villa romaine (ID 40)

1. 1.1 Belgium, Namur, Rochefort.
    1.2 50°7'25.42"N; 5°8'42.51"E (approx.).
2. 2.1 1994.
    2.2 Badly preserved when excavated, now destroyed.
3.   Private bathhouse integrated in a villa.
4. 4.1 Unknown. Late first-century ceramics were found in the drain of the villa's cellar. The baths, however, may have been a later addition to the villa.
    4.2 Unknown. The last attested activity on the villa site dates to the late third century.
    4.3 Unknown.
5.   C (evidence for a pool, hypocaust).
6. 6.1 Min. 36 m² (partial plan).
    6.2 Unknown (partial plan).
    6.3 Unknown (partial plan).
    6.4 Unknown (partial plan).
    6.5 At least one room was heated by a hypocaust. A small almost square room to its south may have housed an *alveus*.
7. 7.1 The hypocaust pillars were made with round tiles.
    7.2 Unknown.
    7.3 Unknown.
    7.4 Unknown.
8.   Unknown.
9.   Fig. 38.
10.   Plumier, Dupont, and Van Neer 1995 (ER); Plumier 1996; Brulet 2008, 568.

Basse-Wavre, Villa de L'Hosté (ID 41)

1. 1.1 Belgium, Walloon Brabant, Wavre.
    1.2 50°43'27.98"N; 4°37'31.75"E (approx.).
2. 2.1 1904.
    2.2 Well preserved in parts at the time of excavation, now covered.
3.   Private bath attached to a villa. A small private bath may have been integrated in the villa.
4. 4.1 Second century? (second phase of the villa).
    4.2 Middle of the third century? (destruction of the villa by fire).
    4.3 An apsidal room, interpreted as 'chapel' by the early twentieth-century excavators, was built over the alleged integrated bath room.
5.   A (pools, hypocausts).
6. 6.1 Large baths *c.* 300 m², alleged integrated bath only a single room (< 10 m²).
    6.2 Angular row type.

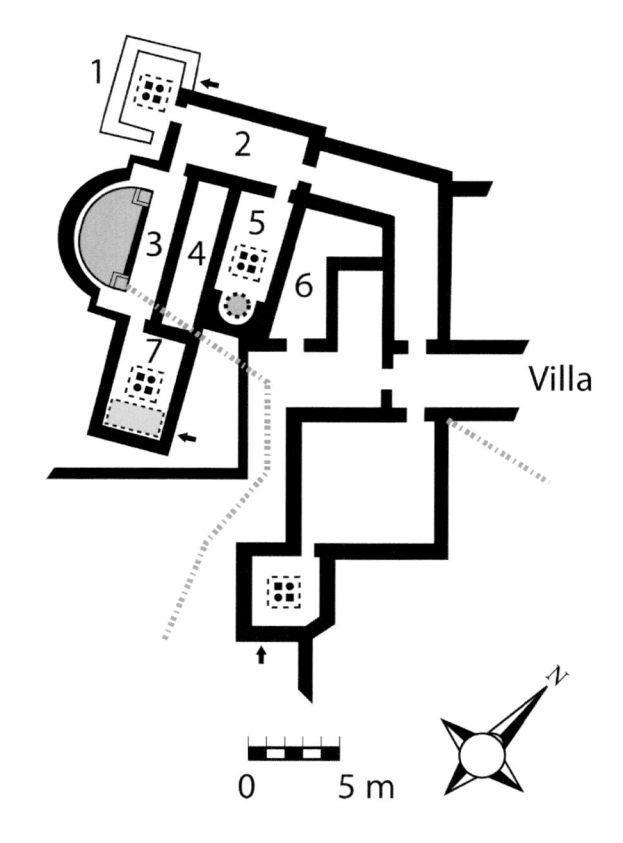

Baths

0   20 m

6.3 A small independently heated room (1) to the north-west of the large bath possibly functioned as a *sudatorium*. It had a door leading to the outside and may have been a later addition. The heated and cold section were preceded in the north by an oblong room (2) possibly functioning as *apodyterium*. The large bath could be reached by a long corridor running along the entire front of the villa.

6.4 The *frigidarium* (3) had a large semicircular *piscina* (diam.: 6 m) to the west and an oblong courtyard (4) functioning as light well to the east. The small alcoves flanking the *piscina* possibly housed benches (judging from a protruding rim).

6.5 A small heated room to the north-west (1) may have been a *sudatorium* (see 6.3). A second heated room with an apsidal ending to the south (5) was interpreted as a *caldarium*. The location of an *alveus* is problematic. However, the inverted L-shaped room to its east (6) may have been part of the *caldarium*, but the remains were too poorly preserved to understand the exact layout. A third room (7) south of the *frigidarium* may have been used as *tepidarium*, *solarium*, or *sudatorium*.

7. 7.1 Each heated room had its own furnace. The hypocausts were made with square (s.: 30 or 20 cm) or round (diam.: 25 cm) tiles and could reach 70 cm in height. In the access corridor to the large baths, two separate channels connected to the hypocausts to the south-west, crossed the corridor.

7.2 The excavators describe 'fume tiles' (10 × 15 cm; *tubuli* or chimney pipes?).

7.3 Unknown. 600 m to the north of the villa, a man-made pond may have served as reservoir for rain water.

7.4 A terracotta pipe drained the integrated bath room (disposing the water of an *alveus* or portable bath tub). The *piscina* of the large bath was drained by a drainage channel (0.5 m wide) in its south-east corner, passing underneath the 'light well' opposite the *piscina* and the *praefurnium*. The drain of the conjectured *alveus* in the *caldarium* also emptied in this channel.

8. The floor and the internal sides of the *piscina* were embellished with 'marble' slabs. In all of the rooms in the large baths, fragments of polychrome wall painting were found (mainly bluish-grey colours). Some patterns in mosaic may also have adorned the walls.

9. Fig. 39.

10. Dens and Poils 1905 (ER); Severs 1980; Brulet 2008, 297–99.

Villa

0   5 m

Figure 39. Location (top) and plan of the baths of Basse-Wavre. Figure by author after Dens and Poils 1905, pl. XIII.

Bavay, Rue Saint-Maur (ID 20)

1.   1.1   France, Département du Nord, Bavay.
       1.2   50°17'55.34"N; 3°47'36.61"E (exact).
2.   2.1   1830, 1950s.
       2.2   Well preserved when found, partially destroyed when investigated, now still visible.
3.   Possibly part of a public bathhouse.
4.   4.1   Unknown.
       4.2   Unknown.
       4.3   Unknown.
5.   C (large hypocaust).
6.   6.1   Unknown (partial plan).
       6.2   Unknown (partial plan).
       6.3   Unknown (partial plan).
       6.4   Unknown (partial plan).
       6.5   A large heated room was discovered underneath the house of a private proprietor. By the time archaeologists could inspect the find, it had already been partially destroyed. The large size of the room (111 pillars were counted) points to a public bath. Some metres to the south, underneath the church Notre-Dame-de-l'Assomption, more rooms on hypocaust were discovered (ID 21). These probably belonged to the same building, although some scholars oppose this hypothesis, as the orientation and the type of ceramic building material differs.
7.   7.1   The hypocaust pillars were made with square hypocaust tiles.
       7.2   The room was heated by *tubuli*.
       7.3   Unknown.
       7.4   Unknown.
8.   The floor of the room was embellished with slabs of black limestone (*noir français*). Parts of a uniform blue mosaic were also found.
9.   No plan available.
10.   Biévelet 1950; Biévelet 1956.

Bavay, Église Notre-Dame-de-l'Assomption (ID 21)

1. 1.1 France, Département du Nord, Bavay.

   1.2 50°17'54.78"N; 3°47'35.53"E (exact).

2. 2.1 1953.

   2.2 Well preserved when found, now reburied.

3. Possibly part of a public bathhouse. Probably related to the hypocaust found in the Rue Saint-Maur (ID 20).

4. 4.1 The excavator suggested a second-century date on the basis of wall construction, decoration, and comparison with other buildings.

   4.2 Unknown.

   4.3 Unknown.

5. B (evidence for a pool, hypocausts).

6. 6.1 Unknown (partial plan).

   6.2 Unknown (partial plan).

   6.3 Unknown (partial plan).

   6.4 Five test pits were dug in the modern church. In the test pit underneath the choir, evidence of pink hydraulic mortar was found.

   6.5 In the four other test pits, evidence of a hypocaust system was found. In the largest test pit, two sides of a room were found, one heated by hypocaust and one without. In the south-western test pit, a doubling of the hypocaust pillars was perceived (as reinforcement underneath a pool?).

7. 7.1 The hypocaust pillars were made with square hypocaust tiles (s.: 21 cm; 5 cm thick).

   7.2 Rows of *tubuli* were still *in situ* along one of the walls (16 × 31 × 44 cm and 16 × 44 × 31 cm; with round lateral openings).

   7.3 Unknown.

   7.4 Unknown.

8. The wall of the heated room without *tubuli* was clad with slabs of *noir français*. A fragment of a decorative cornice in the same black stone was also recovered, as well as fragments of 'red Belgian marble'.

9. No plan available.

10. Biévelet 1953 (ER).

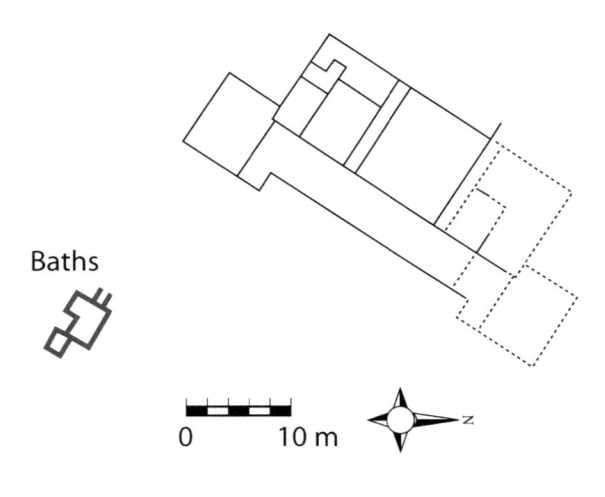

Baths

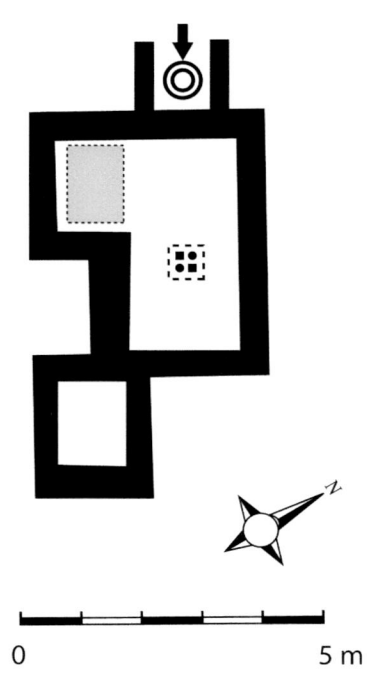

0   10 m

0   5 m

Figure 40. Location (top) and plan of the bath of Bierbeek.
Figure by author after De Clerck 1987, plan 4 and 7.

Bierbeek, Stenen Kruis (ID 42)

1.   1.1   Belgium, Flemish Brabant, Bierbeek.
    1.2   50°51'11.47"N; 4°44'54.47"E (approx.).
2.   2.1   1982.
    2.2   Well preserved when excavated, now covered.
3.   Freestanding bathhouse of a villa.
4.   4.1   Due to the absence of easily datable ceramics or coins, only a general timespan between the middle of the second and middle of the third century can be proposed.
    4.2   Unknown, but before the middle of the third century (general abandonment of the villa site).
    4.3   Unknown.
5.   A (strong evidence for pool, hypocaust).
6.   6.1   *c.* 36 m².
    6.2   Only two rooms.
    6.3   None.
    6.4   There does not seem to have been a cold section. The excavator tentatively identified the small rectangular south-east room (2 × 2.5 m) as *frigidarium*, although he admits there is no evidence to support this hypothesis (no hydraulic mortar). The small room only abuts the larger heated room. The area north of it may have been constructed in perishable materials, but no traces were encountered during the excavation.
    6.5   The L-shaped heated room must be identified as the *caldarium* (max. l.: 3.5 m: max. w.: 3 m). It was heated by a furnace in its north-west corner. An *alveus* might have been present in the southern *exedra* or alternatively took up the entire western side of the room.
7.   7.1   The furnace channel was made with bricks and protruded into the hypocaust, possibly in support of a pool. The hypocaust pillars were made with square (s.: 18–19.5 cm; 3.5–5 cm thick) or round tiles (diam.: 22 cm; 3–3.5 cm thick).
    7.2   Several terracotta knobs were found in a heap, interpreted as the 'nipples' of *tegulae mammatae* which were removed so that the *tegulae* could be used for different purposes. A single fragment of box-type *tubulus* was discovered in the villa (39 m to the north-west).
    7.3   Unknown. A small stream (Herpendaalbeek) was located some 150 m south of the villa site.
    7.4   Unknown.
8.   No decoration was found during the excavations.
9.   Fig. 40.
10.   De Clerck 1987, 97–99 (ER).

Boirs, Balneum (ID 42)

1. 1.1 Belgium, Liège, Bassenge.
   1.2 50°45'3.34"N; 5°34'47.80"E (approx.).
2. 2.1 1955.
   2.2 Well preserved when excavated, now destroyed or reburied.
3. Freestanding bath of a villa.
4. 4.1 Second century? (ceramics on site).
   4.2 (Late) third century? (ceramics on site).
   4.3 Unknown (fourth-century and Merovingian ceramics nearby).
5. A (pools, hypocausts).
6. 6.1 Min. 216 m² (partial excavations).
   6.2 Block type?
   6.3 An almost square room (4.8 × 4.2 m) with hypocaust (1) was built south of the original bath rooms. It may have functioned as *sudatorium* or heated *apodyterium*. To the east of the bathing rooms, a large room (2) (7.2 × 3.6 m), connected to the *frigidarium* and possibly the *caldarium*, probably functioned as *apodyterium*.
   6.4 The *frigidarium* (3) (6.25 × 2.45 m) had an apsidal *exedra* which possibly contained a *piscina* (a drain pierced the wall).
   6.5 Two rooms were heated by a hypocaust. The middle room (4) with an apsidal western side (4.75 × 2.72 m) without a pool, can be identified as *tepidarium*. It may have been heated by a furnace in its eastern side. The northernmost room (5) (partially excavated) with a semicircular *alveus* in the apse must have been the *caldarium*. The furnace was not located, but was probably located on the northern side.
7. 7.1 Square pillar tiles in the *tepidarium* and *caldarium*, round tiles in the southernmost heated room. Some tiles had the stamp CTEC or QVA.
   7.2 Fragments of *tubuli* found in the *tepidarium* and *caldarium* (type unknown).
   7.3 Unknown.
   7.4 The *alveus* was drained by a lead *fistula* (still *in situ* at the time of excavations), the *piscina* probably as well (only a hole in the wall was found). Both drains emptied into a drainage channel, covered by *tegulae*, running west of the bathhouse.
8. Fragments of polychrome wall paintings (geometric and floral patterns) were found in the *tepidarium* and the southern additional heated room. The *frigidarium* had a floor of black and white limestone laid in a chequerboard pattern, and a plinth of blue limestone.
9. Figs 16, 41.
10. Peuskens and Tromme 1979, 385–401 (ER); Brulet 2008, 388–89.

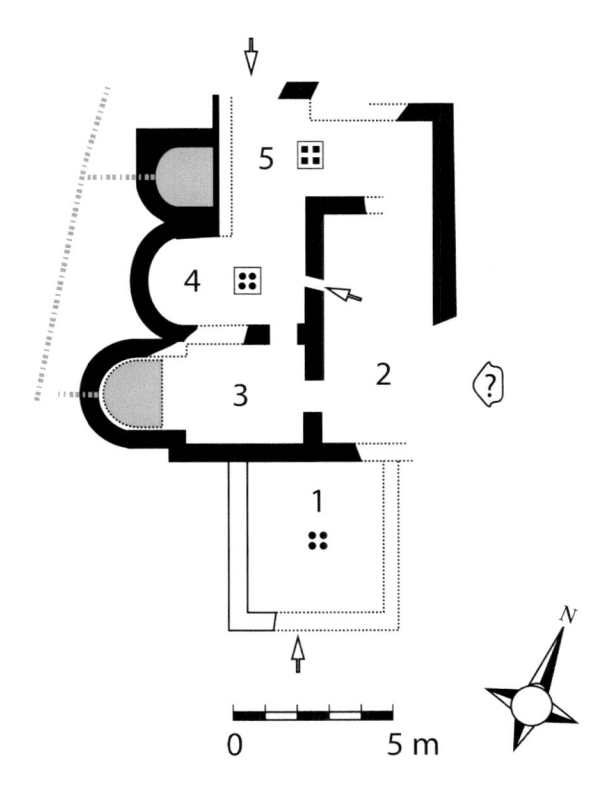

Figure 41. Plan of the bath of Boirs. Figure by author after Peuskens and Tromme 1979, 410, pl. II.

Bois-et-Borsu, Villa de Thier-Laurent (ID 44)

1. 1.1 Belgium, Liège, Clavier.
   1.2 50°22'51.39"N; 5°20'19.98"E (approx.).
2. 2.1 1895–1910.
   2.2 Well preserved when discovered, now destroyed or reburied.
3. Private bath integrated in a villa.
4. 4.1 Unknown.
   4.2 Unknown.
   4.3 Unknown.
5. A (pool, hypocaust).
6. 6.1 Unknown.
   6.2 Unknown.
   6.3 Unknown.
   6.4 A pool (1.2 × 1 m; 0.7 m deep) made out of tufa blocks and mortar, and with an internal step, might be interpreted as a *piscina*.
   6.5 At least one room seems to have been heated by a hypocaust (*caldarium*?). No further information is available.
7. 7.1 The hypocaust pillars were made with round tiles (no dimensions given).
   7.2 Unknown.
   7.3 Unknown.
   7.4 The pool was drained by a drainage channel.
8. Several slabs and fragments of 'marble' were found on the site, as well as a column drum and a capital. Windowpanes were also identified. The context of all these finds is uncertain.
9. No plan available.
10. De Maeyer 1940, 133.

Boussu-lez-Walcourt, Villa du Champ des Metz (ID 45)

1.   1.1   Belgium, Hainaut, Froidchapelle.

      1.2   50°13'24.64"N; 4°22'29.87"E (approx.).

2.   2.1   1888.

      2.2   Well preserved when excavated, now reburied or destroyed.

3.   Private bath integrated in villa.

4.   4.1   Unknown (High Empire).

      4.2   Unknown.

      4.3   Unknown.

5.   A (pools, hypocausts).

6.   6.1   Min. 100 m² (partial plan).

      6.2   Unknown.

      6.3   A square heated room to the north (1) might have functioned as a *sudatorium* or heated *apodyterium*.

      6.4   Unknown. The rooms (2 and 3) located to the east of the heated rooms might have been part of the cold or tepid section.

      6.5   The *caldarium* (4) (5.5 × 2.7 m) had a rectangular apse (1.6 × 1.26 m) for the *alveus*. A second *alveus* might have been present along the north-west wall, above the furnace channel, necessitating the blocking of an opening in the eastern hypocaust wall. Both heated rooms were serviced by the same *praefurnium* (5).

7.   7.1   The hypocaust pillars were made of square tiles (s.: 20.5 cm; h.: 2.75 cm). The furnace of the northern heated room had small walls leading gasses into the hypocaust. Some *tegulae* had the stamp TRAVCPSB. Besides the centrally located *praefurnium* (5), a service room (6) lay south of the *caldarium*.

      7.2   Fragments of *tubuli* were found in the *caldarium* (type unknown).

      7.3   Unknown (the villa was located near the stream Vivrets).

      7.4   The *alveus* was drained by a drainage channel made of tiles, heading west underneath an almost square room of unknown use.

8.   The floor of the *caldarium* was in *opus sectile* of black and white stone slabs laid out in a chequerboard pattern. Fragments of wall painting and glass panes (window glass?) were found in the *caldarium* and the northernmost room.

9.   Fig. 42.

10.   Bayet 1891 (ER); Brulet 2008, 334–35.

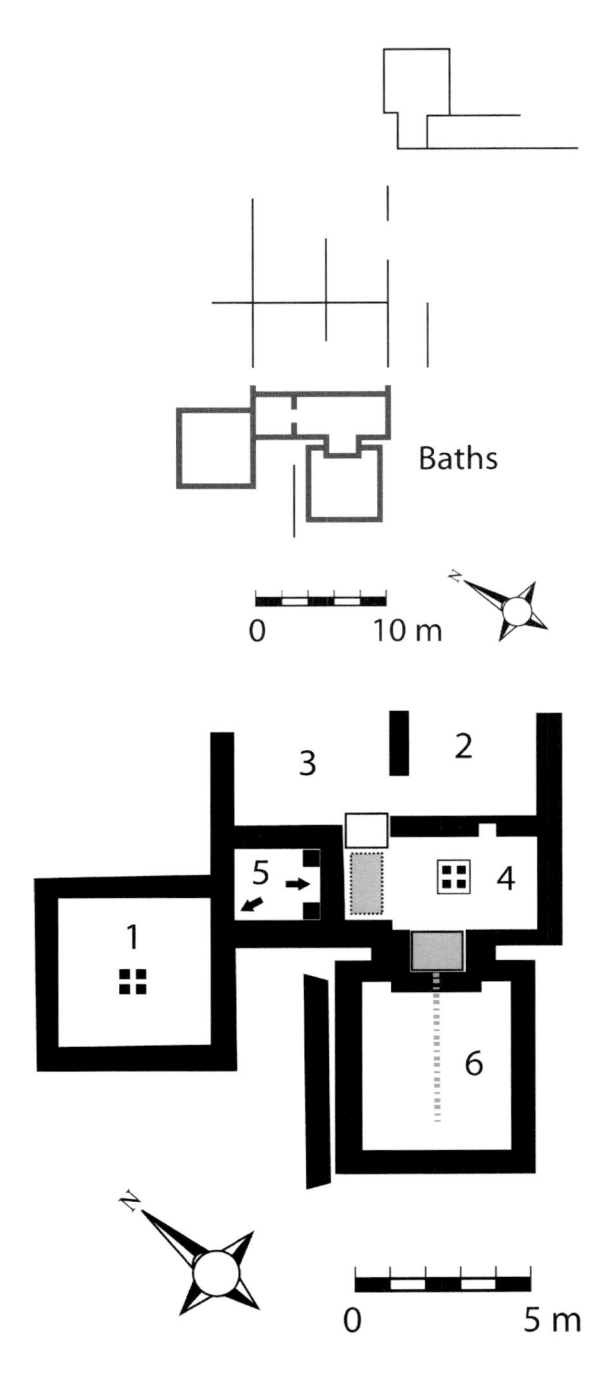

Figure 42. Location (top) and plan of the bath of Boussu-lez-Walcourt. Figure by author after Bayet 1891, 56, fig. 1 and 57, fig. 2.

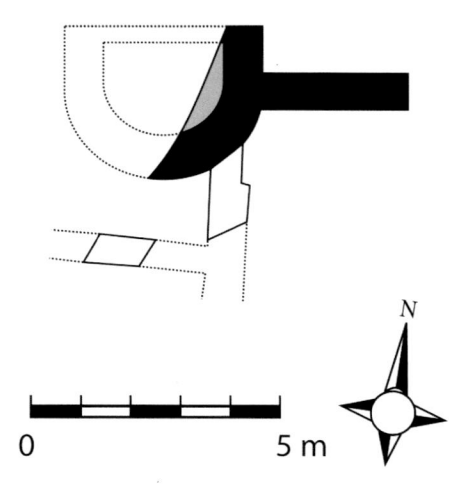

Figure 43. Partial plan of the bath of Bovigny. Figure by author after Mignot 1994b, 111, unnumbered fig.

Bovigny, Bois des Concessions (ID 46)

1. 1.1 Belgium, Luxembourg, Gouvy.
    1.2 50°13'29.52"N; 5°55'3.61"E (approx.).
2. 2.1 1992.
    2.2 Well preserved when excavated, now covered.
3.   Private bath of a villa?
4. 4.1 Unknown.
    4.2 Unknown.
    4.3 Unknown.
5.   A (pool).
6. 6.1 Min. 10 m² (partial plan).
    6.2 Unknown (partial plan).
    6.3 Unknown (partial plan).
    6.4 Only part of a semicircular pool, accessible from the north, was found. As it was not heated by a hypocaust, it was probably a *piscina* of the *frigidarium*, which must have been located north of the pool.
    6.5 Unknown. A room with a mortar floor seems to have been located west of the bath. Its connection to the bathing rooms cannot be discerned. No traces of a hypocaust or building material associated with it, was found.
7. 7.1 Unknown.
    7.2 Unknown.
    7.3 Unknown.
    7.4 Unknown.
8.   Part of a limestone statue (hand) was found in the small test pit that uncovered the pool. It cannot be ascertained that the statue once adorned the alleged bathhouse.
9.   Fig. 43.
10.   Mignot 1994b (ER); Brulet 2008, 465.

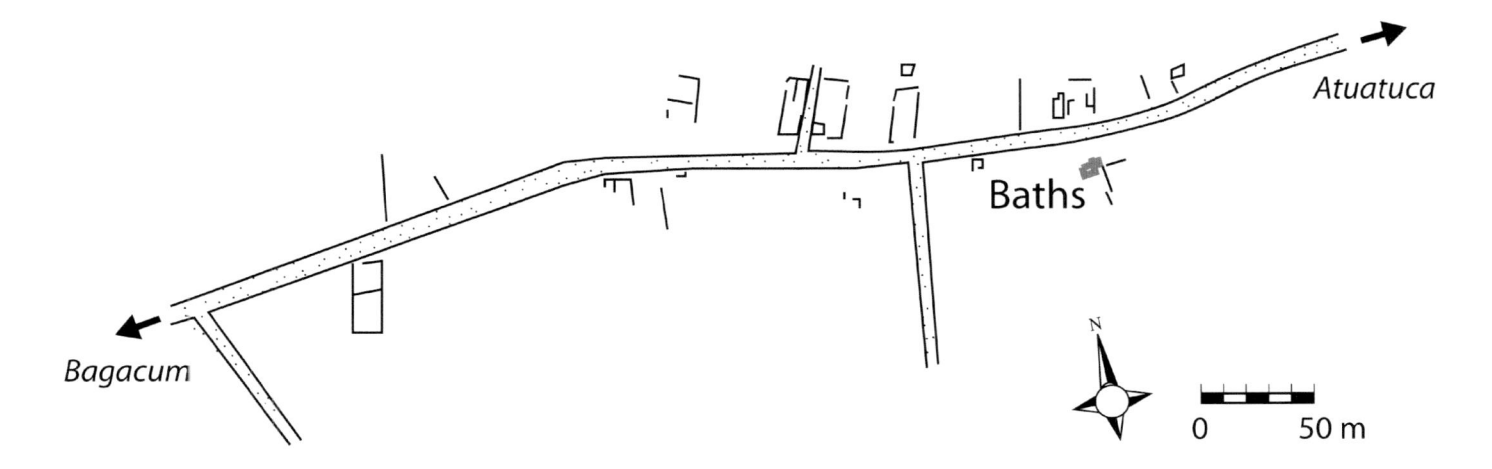

Braives, Thermes (ID 16)

1. 1.1 Belgium, Liège, Braives.
    1.2 50°37'57.85"N; 5°8'30.03"E (approx.).
2. 2.1 1977–1978.
    2.2 Mainly destroyed by modern construction.
3.   Possibly part of a public bathhouse (oriented on the street).
4. 4.1 The walls of the eastern room (belonging to the baths?) were built on top of a pit that was filled in the Flavian period and partially on top of a wall that was constructed after the middle of the second century. Archaeomagnetic analysis of the bricks of the furnace channel point to a date around AD 200. It cannot be excluded that the furnace channel was repaired and that the construction date should actually be placed before this date.
    4.2 Unknown.
    4.3 The building was heavily spoliated and partially destroyed in modern times.
5.   A (strong evidence for a pool; hypocaust).
6. 6.1 Min. 35 m² (partial plan).
    6.2 Unknown (partial plan).
    6.3 Unknown (partial plan).
    6.4 Unknown (partial plan).
    6.5 At least one room was heated by a hypocaust (*caldarium*?). Floors and hypocaust were torn out after the building fell out of use. Part of an east–west oriented wall abutting the eastern wall of the heated room may point to the delimitation of an *alveus*, which would then be located just above the furnace.
7. 7.1 The *praefurnium* (4.8 × 4.2 m) lay just south of the heated room. Only the channel floor, made of vertically placed bricks, could be identified. Fragments of square hypocaust pillar tiles were found among the debris of the heated room.
    7.2 Fragments of *tubuli* (rectangular in section) were found in the heated room.
    7.3 Unknown.
    7.4 Unknown.
8.   Unknown.
9.   Fig. 44.
10.   Brulet 1981, 52–59 (ER); Brulet 2008, 396.

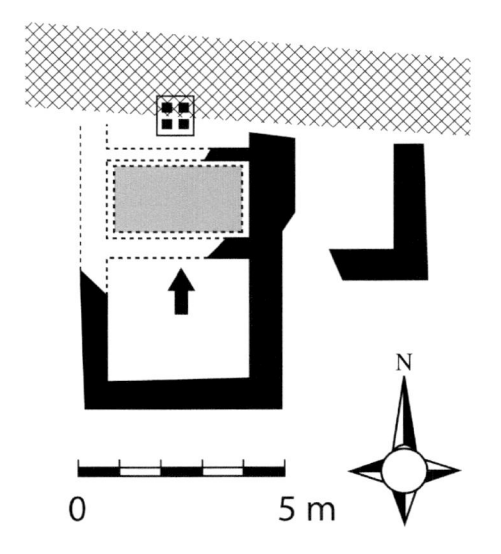

Figure 44. Location (top) and plan of the bath of Braives. Figure by author after Brulet 2008, 87, fig. 104 and Brulet 1981, pl. II.

Brakel, villa van Michelbeke (ID 47)

1. 1.1 Belgium, East Flanders, Brakel.
   1.2 50°49'54.51"N; 3°45'49.19"E (approx.).
2. 2.1 1985.
   2.2 Well preserved when excavated, now destroyed.
3. Private bath integrated in a villa?
4. 4.1 Unknown.
   4.2 Unknown.
   4.3 Unknown.
5. C (hypocausts).
6. 6.1 Unknown (plan unclear).
   6.2 Unknown (plan unclear).
   6.3 Unknown (plan unclear).
   6.4 Unknown (plan unclear).
   6.5 At least one room was heated by a hypocaust.
7. 7.1 Unknown.
   7.2 Unknown.
   7.3 Unknown.
   7.4 Unknown.
8. Unknown.
9. No plan available.
10. De Cock, Rogge, and Velghe 1985 (ER).

Brakel, villa van Zegelsem (ID 48)

1. 1.1 Belgium, East Flanders, Brakel.
   1.2 50°47'53.23"N; 3°45'30.60"E (approx.).
2. 2.1 1983–1984.
   2.2 Well preserved when excavated, now reburied or destroyed.
3. Private bathhouse integrated in a villa.
4. 4.1 Unknown. The site was already inhabited in the Iron Age.
   4.2 The villa was (partly?) destroyed by the early second century (ceramics on site).
   4.3 Unknown.
5. B (hypocaust, evidence for a pool).
6. 6.1 Min. 35 m² (plan unclear).
   6.2 Unknown (partial plan).
   6.3 Unknown (partial plan).
   6.4 Unknown (partial plan).
   6.5 At least one room (7 × 4.8 m) was heated by a hypocaust. A rectangular *exedra* (1.4 × 1 m) in the south-east side of this room probably housed an *alveus*.
7. 7.1 The *praefurnium* was located to the west of the heated room.
   7.2 Unknown.
   7.3 Unknown.
   7.4 Unknown.
8. Fragments of wall plaster were identified.
9. No plan available.
10. Rogge 1984 (ER).

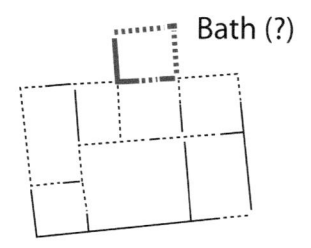

Bath (?)

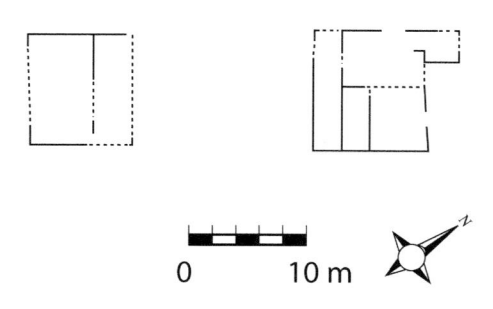

0   10 m

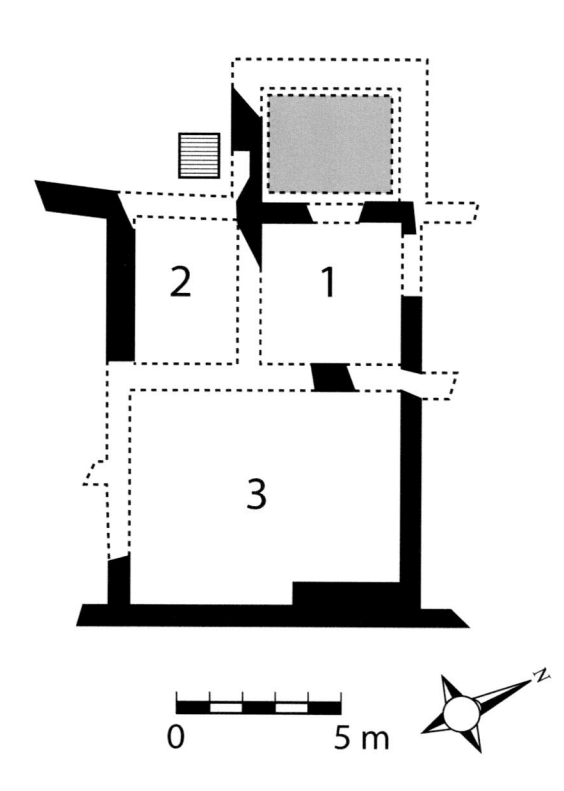

2   1

3

0   5 m

Figure 45. Location (top) and plan of the alleged bath of Bras-Haut. Figure by author after Hossey 1983, 55, fig. 25.

Bras-Haut, Villa de Toray (ID 49)

1. 1.1 Belgium, Luxembourg, Libramont-Chevigny.
    1.2 49°58'53.71"N; 5°23'22.86"E (approx.).
2. 2.1 1982.
    2.2 Badly preserved when excavated, now reburied or destroyed.
3.   Private bath integrated in a villa.
4. 4.1 Unknown. The artefacts recovered during the excavations of the villa indicate a timespan between the end of second century and the middle of the third century.
    4.2 Unknown. The villa was abandoned in the first half of the third century.
    4.3 The villa was heavily spoliated and suffered from modern agricultural activity.
5.   C (evidence for a pool, associated well).
6. 6.1 Min. 34 m² (plan unclear).
    6.2 Unknown (plan unclear).
    6.3 It is difficult to interpret which rooms belonged to the bathing suite. Most walls, made of local schist and a greenish mortar, were dismantled down to the foundations.
    6.4 An almost square *piscina* (s.: 5.8 m) protruded out of the main building block. The bottom was covered by a layer of pinkish hydraulic mortar. It would be logical to interpret the room directly to the east as the *frigidarium* (1), but no mortar floor was discovered here.
    6.5 The heated rooms could not be identified and no elements of the hypocaust system were discovered. The room (2) directly south of the alleged *frigidarium* and the large oblong room to the east (3) had mortar floors and may have been bath rooms.
7. 7.1 Unknown. No elements of the heated rooms nor a *praefurnium* were discovered.
    7.2 Unknown.
    7.3 A square well (s.: 1.2 m) cut out of the schist bedrock to a depth of 5.5 m was located directly south of the pool. The walls of the *piscina* were too badly damaged to reconstruct the connection from the well to the pool (only robber trenches remained).
    7.4 Unknown.
8.   Unknown.
9.   Fig. 45.
10.   Hossey 1983 (ER); 1984 (ER); Brulet 2008, 482.

Broekhem, Villa Ravenbosch (ID 50)

1. 1.1 The Netherlands, Limburg, Valkenburg aan de Geul.
   1.2 50°52'30.57"N; 5°49'16.94"E (approx.).
2. 2.1 1922–1923.
   2.2 Well preserved when excavated, now covered or destroyed.
3. Private bathhouse attached to a villa.
4. 4.1 Unknown. The villa was probably constructed in the early second century (ceramics on site), but the baths were added at a later date.
   4.2 Unknown. The villa site was probably out of use by the late second or early third century (ceramics on site).
   4.3 Unknown.
5. A (strong evidence for pools, hypocaust).
6. 6.1 *c.* 75 m².
   6.2 Angular row type.
   6.3 The north-east room of the baths (1), which must have connected to the room above the cellar of the villa, was probably the *apodyterium*. No floor level was found here (pointing to a wooden floor?).
   6.4 The *frigidarium* (2) should be located in the small almost square room (2.5 × 2.65 m) in the north-west corner of the building. The remains were badly damaged here. It had a semicircular *exedra* (diam.: 2 m), which probably housed a *labrum* (according to the excavator) or a *piscina*.
   6.5 The oblong north-west–south-east oriented room (3) (6 × 2.5 m) must have been the *caldarium*. It had a rectangular *exedra* (1.2 × 2 m) protruding into the alleged *apodyterium* in the north-west corner. The floor of hydraulic mortar lay 29 cm lower than the hypocaust floor of the room, suggesting this *exedra* housed a small pool. Two short walls on the north-eastern end of the room seem to have delimited the location of the *alveus*. The furnace channel lay just below it.
7. 7.1 The hypocaust pillars were made with round tiles. No dimensions are specified, but if these were the same as in the heated rooms of the villa, they had a diameter of 21 cm (4–5 cm thick). The *praefurnium* (4) (2.04 × 2.9 m) lay north-east of the *caldarium*. The furnace channel took the form of a shallow pit dug out in the virgin loam soil, bordered by walls made of *tegulae* and tiles. In a later phase, the *praefurnium* seems to have been extended by a small room (2.75 × 1.7 m).
   7.2 Fragments of *tubuli* (box type?) were found in the *caldarium*.
   7.3 Unknown. Some 30 m to the west of the villa, a small stream (Straatbeek) was located.
   7.4 Unknown.
8. Several fragments of windowpane were found in the villa (no further context given).
9. Fig. 46.
10. Remouchamps 1924 (ER).

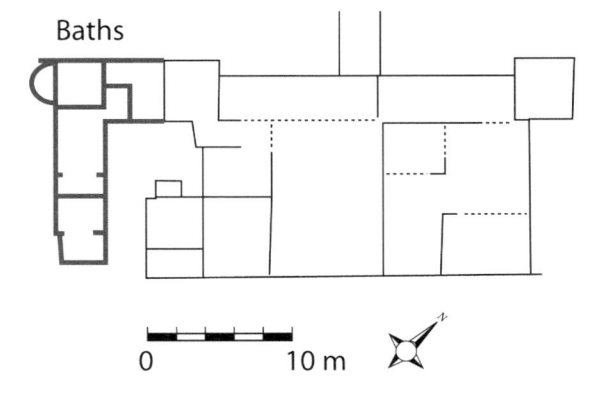

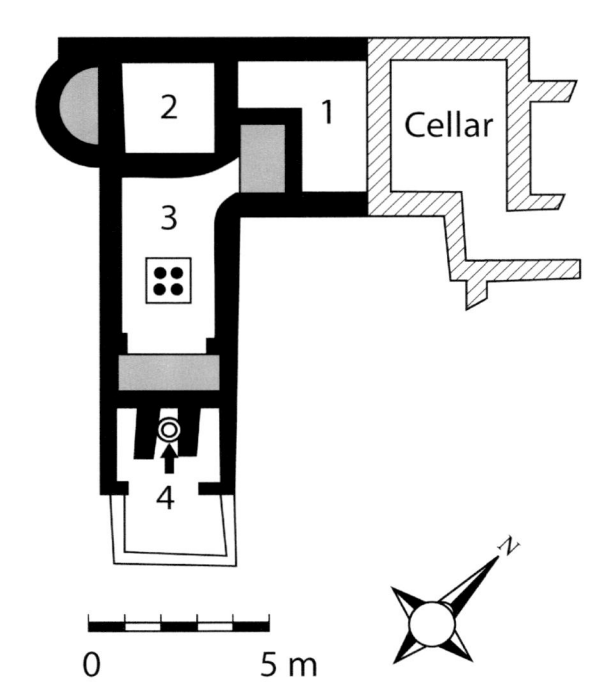

Figure 46. Location (top) and plan of the bath of Broekhem. Figure by author after Remouchamps 1924, unnumbered page, fig. 41.

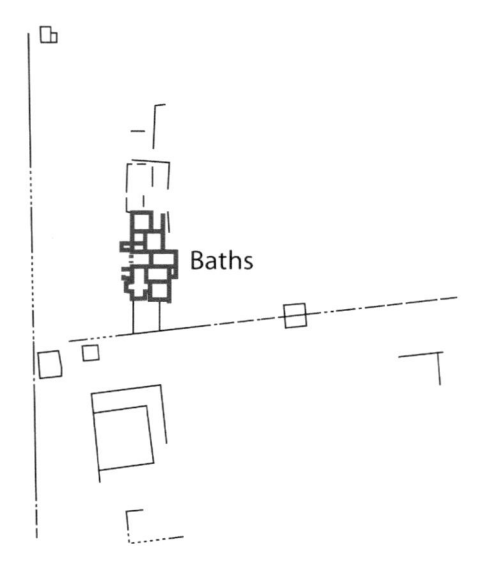

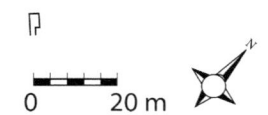

0   20 m

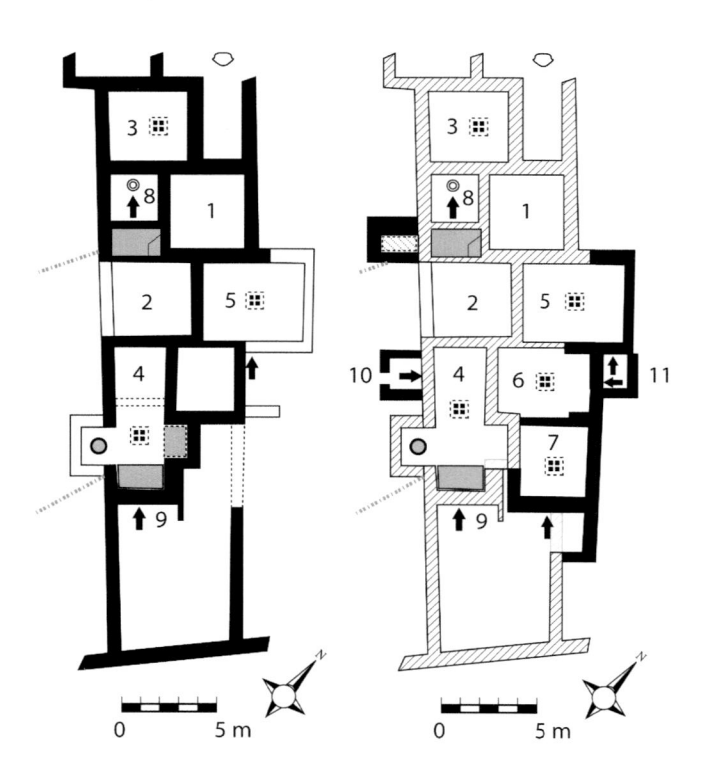

0   5 m   0   5 m

Figure 47. Location (top) and plans (left: phase 1; right: phase 2–3) of the bath of Bruyelle. Figure by author after Bausier, Bloch, and Pigière 2018, 104, fig. 45.

Bruyelle, Villa de la Haute Éloge (ID 51)

1. 1.1 Belgium, Hainaut, Antoing.
    1.2 50°33'27.74"N; 3°25'38.67"E (approx.).
2. 2.1 Partially excavated in 1932 and full excavation of the baths in 1993–1994.
    2.2 Well preserved in parts when excavated, now destroyed (new train line).
3.   Private bath attached or integrated in a villa.
4. 4.1 The first phase of the baths was probably erected at the same time of the villa, between the Flavian period and the early second century.
    4.2 At least three phases could be discerned. The original plan was altered in the course of the second half of the second century, and then again in the late second or early third century (largest extension).
    4.3 The destruction layer of baths points to abandonment in the first half of the fourth century. Some minor squatter occupation seems to have occurred during the fourth century.
5.   A (pools, hypocausts).
6. 6.1 Phase 1: 193 m²; phase 2: *c.* 220 m²; phase 3: *c.* 230 m².
    6.2 Phase 1: linear row type; phase 2 and 3: ring type? (plan unclear).
    6.3 The corridor that presumably linked the baths to the villa ended in a room without hypocaust (1). This was probably the *apodyterium*.
    6.4 The *piscina* (2.6 × 1.5 m) had a trapezoidal step in its eastern corner (transformed in a triangular step in phase 3). This implies that it was accessible from the room to its south-east (2), which can hence be interpreted as the *frigidarium* (4.3 × 3.8 m). A second 'pool' was allegedly added west of the *piscina* after phase 3 according to the excavators, but as this basin had no internal steps nor an outlet at its bottom, it might well have been a reservoir to supply the *piscina*.
    6.5 In phase 1, only two rooms were heated by a hypocaust. The north-western room (3) (4.2 × 3.7 m), heated by its own furnace, might have been a *sudatorium* or a *heated apodyterium*. The fact that it was directly heated and in connection to the *apodyterium* might favour the former interpretation, even if it is quite large. The excavators suggest that a boiler might have been present above its furnace, which would be unusual for both a *sudatorium* or heated *apodyterium*. There is no evidence that this room might have been a *calida piscina* (no water outlet or drainage channel nearby). The southernmost heated room (4) (7.55 m in length) originally only had one rectangular *exedra* on its eastern side. A second rectangular *exedra* was added on its western side shortly after its construction, giving the room a cruciform shape. Presumably the eastern *exedra* and space above the furnace to the south housed *alvei* (sturdier walls), while the western *exedra* (of slightly lighter construction) may have housed a *labrum*. Two bases of what seem to be larger pillars on the hypocaust level of the room seem to imply that a wall was raised here on the walking level, thus possibly delimiting a *tepidarium* at walking level. In phase 2, a third heated room (5) (5.5 × 4.5 m) with its own furnace was added to the east

of the *frigidarium*. The excavators suggest it might have been an *unctorium* or *districtarium*, although other possibilities could include a *sudatorium* or heated *apodyterium*. In phase 3, two more heated rooms (6 and 7) (N: 4.9 × 3.5 m; S: 3.5 × 3.75 m) were added to the east of the *caldarium*. Again, the interpretation is difficult and could include a *tepidarium*, an *unctorum/districtarium*, or *sudatorium*. The careful suggestion of a *calida piscina* in the south-eastern room (7) by the excavators is unconvincing, as the authors also admit that there is no proof for a boiler. The connection between the new rooms and the original *caldarium*, which may no longer have been subdivided to form a *tepidarium* at this point, is unclear. Possibly the eastern *exedra* with presumed *alveus* was transformed into a doorway in this phase.

7. 7.1 The north-western room was heated by its own furnace. The *praefurnium* (8) (2.4 × 1.4 m) had a dirt floor. The furnace tunnel was flanked by sturdy piers, which may have supported a boiler according to the excavators. In phase 1, the *caldarium* was heated by a furnace to its south-east (9). A platform points to the presence of a boiler. Archaeomagnetic dating of the last firing suggests it was abandoned in the (early) second century, perhaps when a new *praefurnium* (10) (1.75 × 1.75 m) was added on the west side of the *caldarium* in phase 3. Its walls were dug in and constructed directly against the virgin soil. The furnace channel was made of bricks. The furnace of the alleged phase 2-*unctorium/districtarium* was blocked up in phase 3, only to create a new *praefurnium* heating both this room and the phase 3-room to its south (11). The furnace of the south-eastern phase 3-room had a simple concrete floor. The hypocaust pillars were all made of square tiles (s.: 17 or 21 cm), bonded with clay, and standing 35 to 40 cm from each other. The floors of the phase 1 and 2 heated rooms slightly inclined towards the furnaces.

   7.2 Several fragments of *tubuli* were found (different dimensions: 25.6 × 18.4 cm; 24 × 21.5 cm; 21.8 × 14.5 cm; 18.6 × 15.5 cm), some with round or rectangular lateral openings.

   7.3 The *piscina* was drained by a lead *fistula* in its western side. This led into a ditch which probably contained wooden pipes. One such pipe fragment was discovered near the lead outlet. The ditch ran towards a north-west–south-east oriented ditch that presumably served as a collector for draining all drainage channels of the villa and ensured a good drainage of the villa site. A second drainage ditch, possibly also containing wooden pipes, led from the western *exedra* of the *caldarium* to the collector and must have evacuated the waste waters (*alvei*, perhaps *labrum*) of the *caldarium*.

   7.4 Unknown. A deep well (diam. 1.6 m) located some 20 m north-west of the baths may have provided water.

8. Several fragments of painted wall plaster were found throughout the baths. It mainly concerns polychrome geometric patterns (lines, circles) on a white background, but marble imitation, fragments of vegetal decoration, and a candelabra were also recovered. A fragment of moulded mortar in the shape of a semi-column was also found in the debris of the bath. Among the fragments of decorative stone, imported marbles (*giallo antico*, *porfido rosso*, *porfido verde di Grecia*, and white Mediterranean marbles) stand out, even if the majority is made up of greyish limestone, some of Tournai (so-called *noir de Tournai*). A sculpted fragment of white limestone depicting part of a *cornucopia* and a fragment of a palmette were found in the well close to the bath. Other statue fragments, including parts of two heads, of a ram, and of a *Fortuna* statue were discovered in the *pars rustica* of the villa and could not be linked to the bath.

9. Figs 21, 47.

10. Bausier 1994 (ER); Ansieau, Bausier, and Pigière 1998 (ER); Bausier 1998; Brulet 2008, 305–09; Ansieau and Bausier 2018.

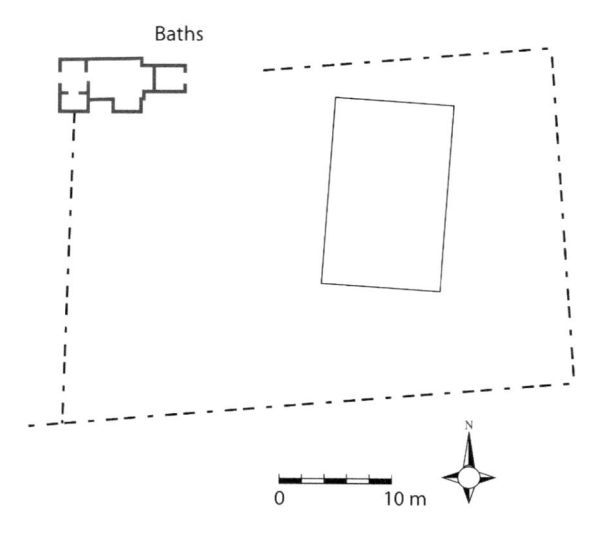

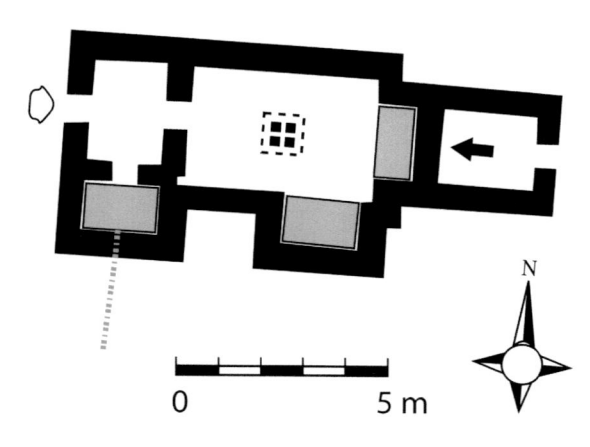

Figure 48. Location (top) and plan of the bath of Chastrès.
Figure by author after Bequet 1900a, pl. III.

Chastrès, Bains de 'Pucenevau' (ID 54)

1. 1.1 Belgium, Namur, Walcourt.
   1.2 50°16'15.26"N; 4°27'22.98"E (approx.).
2. 2.1 1899.
   2.2 Well preserved when excavated, now destroyed.
3. Freestanding bathhouse (near villa or settlement?).
4. 4.1 Second century? (ceramics on site).
   4.2 Unknown.
   4.3 Unknown.
5. A (pools, hypocaust).
6. 6.1 *c.* 50 m².
   6.2 Linear row type.
   6.3 None.
   6.4 The *frigidarium* doubles as *apodyterium* and has one rectangular *piscina* (1.8 × 1.2 m; 0.6 m deep).
   6.5 *Caldarium* (4.2 × 5.6 m) with two possible rectangular *alvei* in the apses (one above the furnace). The excavator supposes tubs in wood, but gives no further explanation. Possibly the apse above the furnace could be fended off by a curtain.
7. 7.1 Type unknown.
   7.2 Unknown.
   7.3 Unknown.
   7.4 The *piscina* is drained by a channel in concrete.
8. Unknown.
9. Fig. 48.
10. Bequet 1900a (ER); Brulet 2008, 579–80.

Clavier-Vervoz, Thermes du vicus (ID 7)

1. 1.1 Belgium, Liège, Clavier.
   1.2 50°23'42.88"N; 5°22'2.50"E (approx.).
2. 2.1 1964.
   2.2 Fairly well preserved at the time of excavation, now covered or destroyed.
3. Freestanding public bathhouse.
4. 4.1 Unknown (ceramics on site suggest a phase of use in the second and third century). Several building phases are attested (but not dated).
   4.2 Unknown.
   4.3 Unknown.
5. A (pools, hypocaust).
6. 6.1 *c.* 880 m².
   6.2 Linear row type.
   6.3 Several rooms of unknown function lie west and south of the bathing rooms. The oblong rooms nearest to the entrance (1 and 2) might have been the dressing rooms and massage rooms. The large open space south of the bathing rooms is sometimes interpreted as a *palaestra* (6). The oblong room between the cold and the heated section may have been a 'heat trap' (4), or alternatively, was a later *praefurnium* servicing the heated section to the east.
   6.4 The *frigidarium* (3) had an oval *piscina* (4.5 × 2 m; 1 m deep). The floor was paved with terracotta tiles. An east–west oriented wall may have been of a later date to delimit a new *praefurnium* (4) heating a new *sudatorium* (former *tepidarium*?).
   6.5 A large rectangular room (5) was heated by a hypocaust. The *praefurnium* (7) lay to the east. The rectangular *exedra* housed an *alveus*. The eastern end of the room could be closed off, judging from the protruding jambs. The enclosed space, just above the furnace channel, may have been used as a sweat cabin (*sudatorium*) or perhaps housed an *alveus*. The large heated room may well have been divided into two heated rooms by a thin wall at walking level (*tepidarium* to the west, *caldarium* to the east). The addition of a furnace (in 4) to the west may have transformed the *tepidarium* into a *sudatorium*.
7. 7.1 The hypocaust pillars were made of square tiles. Several *tegulae* with the stamp NEH or QVA were found near the bath, although these may have belonged to the adjacent apsidal building.
   7.2 Fragments of *tubuli* were found in the heated room.
   7.3 Unknown.
   7.4 The *piscina* was drained by an outlet in its north-eastern corner, the *alveus* by one in its eastern side. Both drainage channels joined up east of the bath and continued south.
8. Fragments of polychrome wall paintings depicting aquatic plants and marble imitation were found.
9. Fig. 49.
10. Willems 1965 (ER); Willems 1968; Willems and Lauwerijs 1973; Bouet 2003a, 673; Brulet 2008, 401.

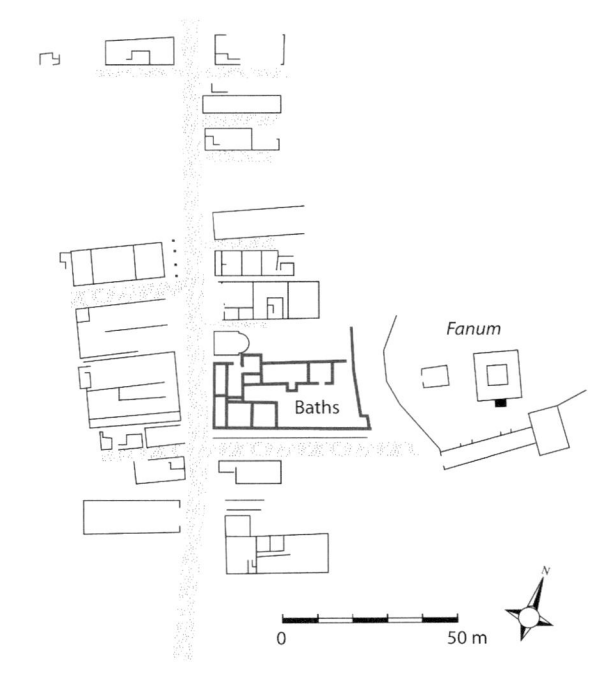

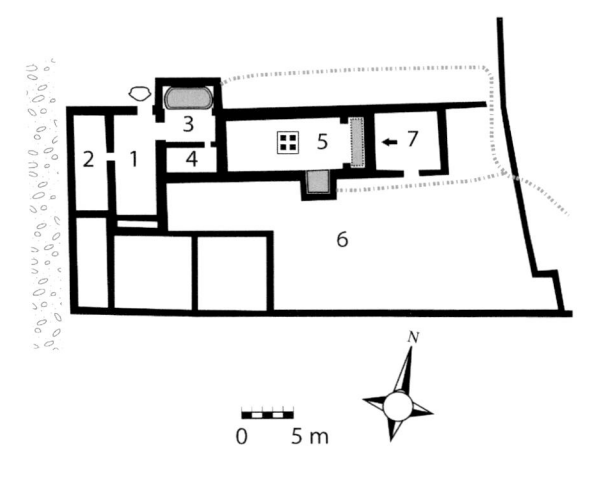

Figure 49. Location (top) and plan of the bath of Clavier-Vervoz. Figure by author after Brulet 2008, 89, fig. 106 and 401, fig. 206.

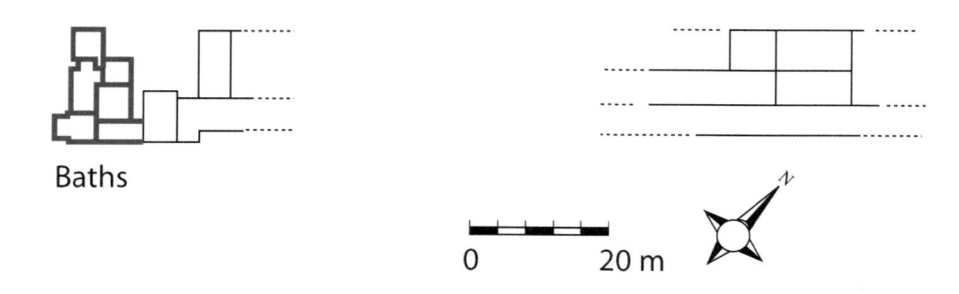

Baths

0   20 m

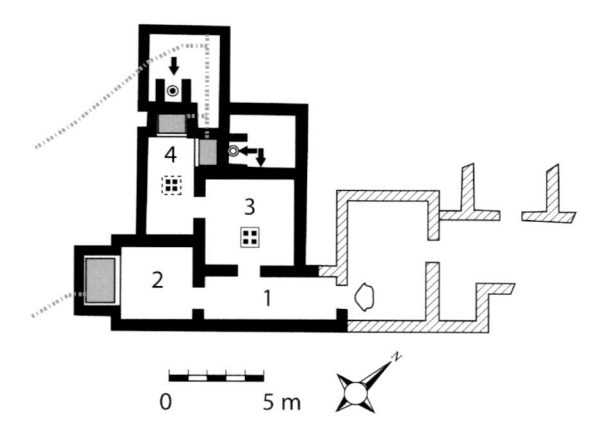

0   5 m

Figure 50. Location (top) and plan of the bath of Clermont-sous-Huy. Figure by author after Witvrouw 1987–1988, 30, fig. 2 and 48, fig. 12.

Clermont-sous-Huy, Villa d'Arvy (ID 56)

1.	1.1	Belgium, Liège, Engis.
	1.2	50°32'37.56"N; 5°26'33.82"E (approx.).
2.	2.1	1972.
	2.2	Well preserved at the time of excavations, now covered or destroyed.
3.		Private bath integrated in a villa.
4.	4.1	Middle of the second century? (ceramics on site).
	4.2	Middle of the third century (filling of drains and hypocaust).
	4.3	Reuse of building materials for medieval farm nearby.
5.		A (pools, hypocausts).
6.	6.1	*c.* 230 m².
	6.2	Block type.
	6.3	An oblong room (1) in connection to the *frigidarium* and *tepidarium* could have served as *apodyterium* (and was labelled *vestibulum* by the excavators). Alternatively, the room to the east of the latter may have served as *apodyterium*.
	6.4	The square *frigidarium* (2) (s.: 4 m) had a rectangular *piscina* (2.6 × 1.6 m) in a south-western *exedra*. There was no door connecting to the heated section.
	6.5	A first heated room (3) (s.: 4.8 m) had a hypocaust heated by its own furnace (to the west). It was interpreted as *tepidarium*, even if a function as *sudatorium* cannot be ruled out. The second heated room (4) (5.4 × 2.5 m) had two rectangular *exedrae* for *alvei* (1.6 × 1.3 m). These pools lay directly above the two furnaces heating this *caldarium*.
7.	7.1	The hypocaust of the first heated room had pillars made of square tiles. The hypocaust of the *caldarium* had pillars made of round or square tiles. The pillars were sturdier in the *exedrae* to support the weight of the *alvei*.
	7.2	*Tubuli* of the box type were found in the debris of the first heated room.
	7.3	Unknown. Several streams and sources are to be found in the vicinity.
	7.4	The *piscina* was drained by a drainage channel in its south-western wall. The ditches of the wooden building preceding the villa were partially reused as drainage channels to drain the *alvei*. Both channels headed south.
8.		Fragments of marble slabs and windowpanes were found in the debris of the *piscina*. Fragments of wall painting (red and yellow colours) were found in the first heated room.
9.		Fig. 50.
10.		Witvrouw 1987–1988; Brulet 2008, 405–06.

Diekirch, Rue de l'Esplanade (ID 57)

1. 1.1 Luxembourg, Diekirch.
   1.2 49°52'8.80"N; 6°9'43.41"E (exact).
2. 2.1 1939, 1999.
   2.2 Well preserved when excavated, now destroyed.
3. Private bathhouse (?) integrated in a villa.
4. 4.1 Unknown. The mosaics of the villa (last phase?) were dated in the third quarter of the second century.
   4.2 Unknown. The main residential building seems to have been destroyed in the third century.
   4.3 Unknown.
5. C (two rooms with hypocaust, drainage channel).
6. 6.1 Min. 50 m² (partial plan).
   6.2 Unknown (partial plan).
   6.3 Unknown (partial plan).
   6.4 Unknown (partial plan).
   6.5 At least two rooms were heated by a hypocaust. The largest room, only partially excavated, was possibly the *caldarium*. Recesses for chimney flues in the southern part of the room suggest that the furnace was located at the opposite end, i.e. the northern side. An opening in the east wall here, possibly connecting to the nearby drainage channel, could point to the presence of a pool here. South-west of this room, there seems to have been a second heated room (*tepidarium?*).
7. 7.1 The hypocaust pillars in the alleged *caldarium* were made with round tiles. The *praefurnium* possibly lay on the northern (unexcavated) side of the *caldarium*.
   7.2 The presence of chimney flues could suggest that the walls were not heated.
   7.3 Unknown.
   7.4 A drainage channel ran east of the main heated room. A breach in the wall possibly suggests that a drain pipe of a pool pierced the wall and led into this drainage channel.
8. Unknown.
9. Fig. 51.
10. Krier 2005 (ER); Paulke 2010 (ER).

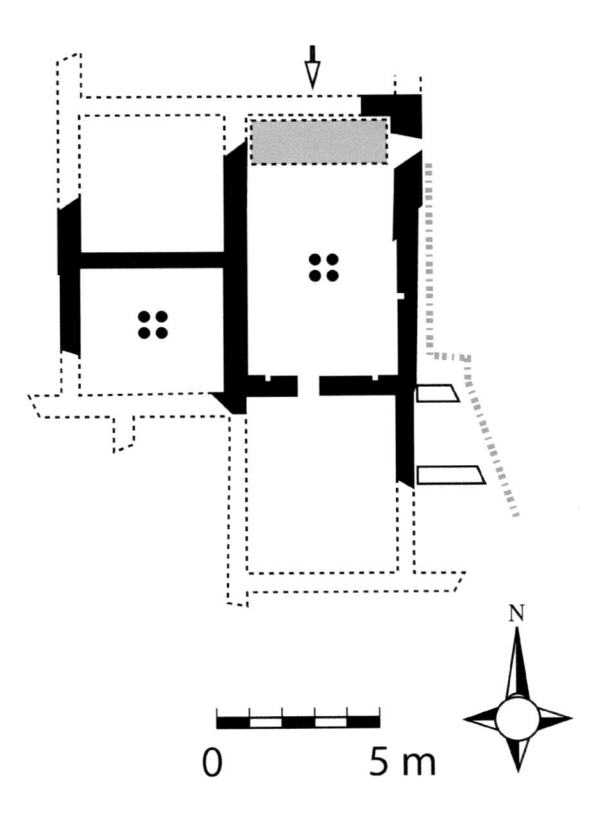

Figure 51. Plan of the alleged bath of Diekirch. Figure by author after Paulke 2010, 62, fig. 8.

Élouges, Villa d'Élouges (ID 58)

1. 1.1 Belgium, Hainaut, Dour.
   1.2 50°24'26.28"N; 3°45'12.76"E (exact).
2. 2.1 1864.
   2.2 Badly preserved when excavated, now destroyed.
3. Private bath integrated in a villa?
4. 4.1 Second century? (ceramics on site).
   4.2 Unknown (coin from the second half of the third century found on site).
   4.3 The villa site was reused as a burial ground in the Middle Ages.
5. C (hypocaust, water supply).
6. 6.1 Unknown (no plan available).
   6.2 Unknown (no plan available).
   6.3 Unknown (no plan available).
   6.4 Unknown (no plan available).
   6.5 At least one room heated by a hypocaust was discovered. A water pipe from an aqueduct ended close by, possibly to supply the boiler/pools.
7. 7.1 Unknown. The hypocaust was broken out, possibly in recent times.
   7.2 Several fragments of *tubuli* (with lateral openings) were found.
   7.3 Three aqueducts were found in the wide surroundings of the alleged villa. One of these ended near the aforementioned hypocaust.
   7.4 Unknown.
8. The villa was richly decorated: fragments of polychrome wall painting and fragments of columns and architectural elements were found.
9. No plan available.
10. Debove 1865; 1875; Brulet 2008, 327–28.

Emptinne-Champion, Villa du Rosdia (ID 52)

1. 1.1 Belgium, Namur, Hamois.
   1.2 50°20'54.15"N; 5°6'51.18"E (approx.).
2. 2.1 1983 and 1989.
   2.2 Well preserved at the time of excavations, now covered.
3. Freestanding bath connected to a villa.
4. 4.1 Phase 1 around middle of the first century AD, expansions in the second and third century, partially dismantled in the second half of the third century (ceramics on site).
   4.2 Late third or early fourth century (filling of the hypocaust and *piscina*).
   4.3 Possible squatter occupation in the fourth century.
5. A (pools, hypocausts).
6. 6.1 *c.* 340 m².
   6.2 Phase 1: angular row type; phase 2 and 3: double angular row type.
   6.3 In phase 1 the *frigidarium* (2) was preceded by a rectangular room (1), possibly the *apodyterium*. In phase 2, a large square heated room (4) south of the *frigidarium* may have been used as heated *apodyterium*. The enclosed area east of the bathhouse seems to have been used as service courtyard during phase 1, but could be entered from the access corridor during phase 2, when it was also enlarged to the east (10).

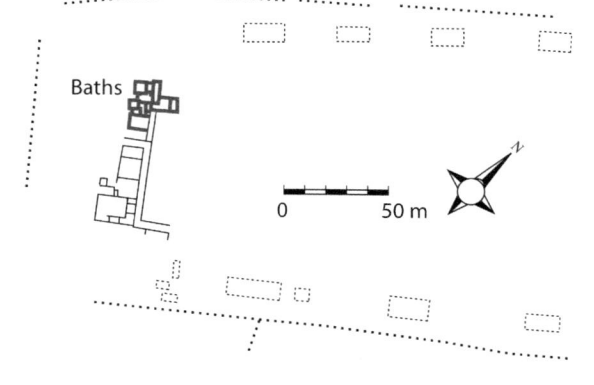

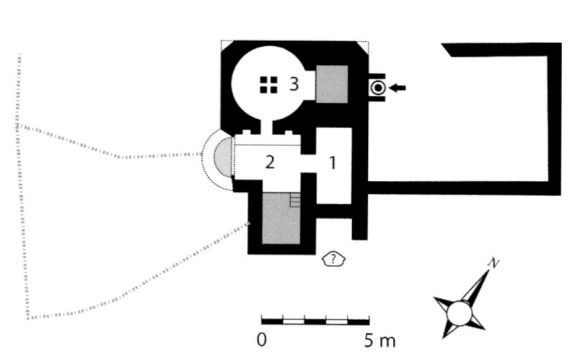

Figure 52. Location (top) and plan of phase 1 of the bath of Emptinne-Champion. Figure by author after Brulet 2008, 541, fig. 472 and Van Ossel and De Poorter 1992, 202, fig. 4.

6.4 In phase 1, the rectangular *frigidarium* had two *piscinae*, one large rectangular one (*c.* 2 × 2.5 m) and one small semicircular one (diam.: *c.* 2 m). In phase 3, the semicircular *piscina* was replaced by a large almost square *piscina* (s.: 3.5 m; 1.3 m deep).

6.5 In phase 1, only a large round room (3) heated by a hypocaust and with a rectangular *exedra* above the furnace (to accommodate an *alveus*) was identified. In phase 2, this round room was replaced by an L-shaped *caldarium* (5), possibly with an *alveus* above the furnace and a *labrum* in the niche. A square heated swimming pool (6) (s.: 6.5 m; 0.8 m deep), or *calida piscina* (6), was added to the west. It is a remarkable and quite exceptional feature. South of the *frigidarium*, a large heated room (4) and a smaller apsidal room (7) could be interpreted respectively as heated *apodyterium/tepidarium* and *sudatorium* (with separate furnace). In phase 3, the L-shaped *caldarium* was replaced by a rectangular space (11) with a rectangular *alveus* and a single-person *alveus* with apsidal endings to the west. The recess in the north-west wall may also have housed an *alveus*. The small *sudatorium* to the south-west of the cold section was probably abandoned at this time.

7. 7.1 The southern heated room (4) had its own *praefurnium* (8), which also serviced the small *sudatorium* (7). The phase 2-*caldarium* (5) also had a separate *praefurnium* (9). The furnace channel was lined by parallel walls, possibly to support a boiler. The phase 2-*caldarium* was transformed into the *praefurnium* of the phase 3-*caldarium* (11). The furnace was also delimited by parallel walls to support a boiler. The *calida piscina* (6) was heated by its own furnace. The hypocaust pillars of the phase-1 round *caldarium* were made with square or rectangular tiles. In the *frigidarium*, an east–west oriented channel with chimney flues at its ends communicated with this hypocaust. The hypocaust pillars of the *calida piscina* were made of round or square tiles. The pillars of the two southern heated rooms (4 and 7) added during the second-century transformations were made with round or round and square tiles.

7.2 The walls of the *calida piscina* were heated by *tubuli* (box type) with round or square lateral openings.

7.3 East of the bathhouse, several metal rings were found in a darker soil feature, pointing to the existence of a wooden aqueduct held together with these rings.

7.4 Each *piscina* was drained by a separate drainage channel, constructed in mortar, but both ending in an open-air ditch to the west of the baths. The lead *fistula* of the large *piscina* was still *in situ*, flowing into a channel made of *tubuli* (with the lateral openings cemented shut). The *calida piscina* (and possibly also the *alveus* of the *caldarium*) had separate sewage drains, heading north-west.

8. The *apodyterium* had a simple floor in *opus signinum*. A similar floor in the *frigidarium* was possibly finished with blue limestone slabs, as was the case for the small rectangular *piscina*, where fragments of these slabs survived. In several rooms fragments of wall painting were discovered. Most notable is a large green and red medallion that adorned the ceiling of the large *piscina*.

9. Figs 20, 52–54.

10. Van Ossel and De Poorter 1992 (ER); Brulet 2008, 540–46.

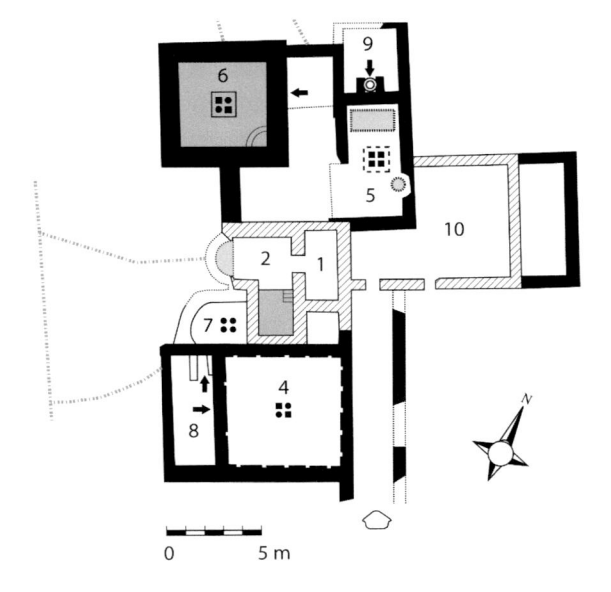

Figure 53. Plan of phase 2 of the bath of Emptinne-Champion. Figure by author after Van Ossel and De Poorter 1992, 208, fig. 9.

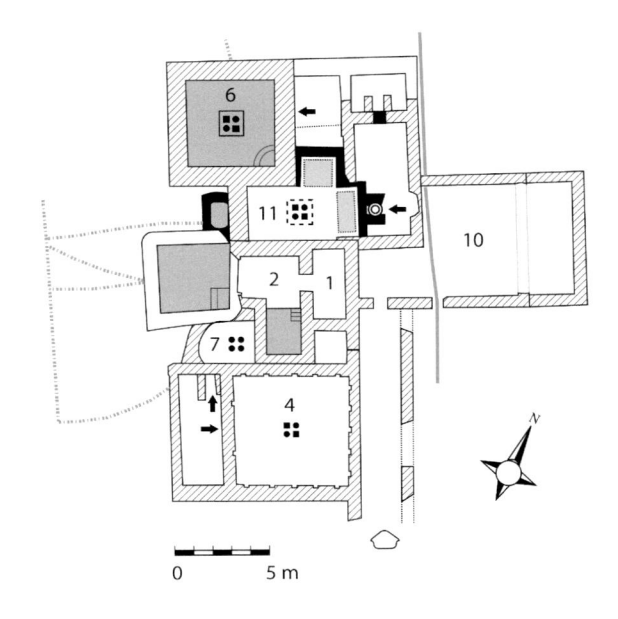

Figure 54. Plan of phase 3 of the bath of Emptinne-Champion. Figure by author after Van Ossel and De Poorter 1992, 213, fig. 14.

Post-built buildings

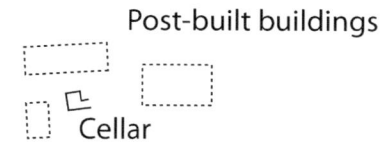

Cellar

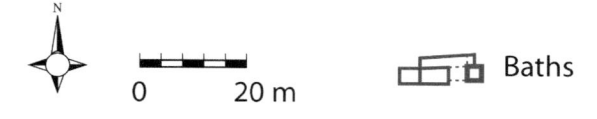

Baths

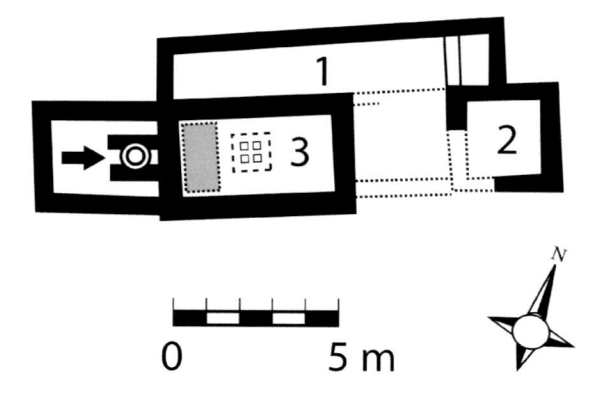

Figure 55. Location (top) and plan of the bath of Évelette – Clavia. Figure by author after Lefert 2014, 112, fig. 1.

Évelette, Villa du Clavia (ID 59)

1.	1.1	Belgium, Namur, Ohey.
	1.2	50°24'35.29"N; 5°10'11.89"E (approx.).
2.	2.1	2011.
	2.2	Badly preserved when excavated, now covered.
3.		Freestanding bathhouse of a villa.
4.	4.1	Unknown, but at least two building phases (the site was in use between the first and third century).
	4.2	Unknown.
	4.3	Unknown.
5.		C (evidence for pool, evidence for hypocaust).
6.	6.1	*c.* 58 m².
	6.2	Linear row type.
	6.3	A corridor (1) along the north side of the building was added in a second phase. Its function is unknown (*apodyterium*? *Tepidarium*?).
	6.4	The easternmost room (2) has been identified as the *frigidarium*. It may have had a *piscina*, but the remains are too badly preserved for interpretation.
	6.5	At least one room (3) was heated by a hypocaust. It can hence be labelled as the *caldarium*. Its *praefurnium* was to the east. An *alveus* most probably lay above the furnace.
7.	7.1	No hypocaust tiles were recovered during the excavation, as the site was badly damaged and possibly spoliated for building materials in post-Roman times. The furnace channel was made with bricks.
	7.2	No evidence of wall heating was found during the excavations, but this may be due to spoliation of the building.
	7.3	Some 40 m east of the bathhouse, a small pond fed by springs was discovered. It probably supplied the bathhouse. The villa, some 60 m north of the baths, had its own well.
	7.4	Unknown.
8.		Unknown.
9.		Fig. 55.
10.		Lefert 2013 (ER); 2014 (ER).

Évelette, Villa de Résimont (ID 60)

1. 1.1 Belgium, Namur, Ohey.
   1.2 50°24'33.28"N; 5°11'42.03"E (approx.).
2. 2.1 1961.
   2.2 Good at the time of excavations, now covered or destroyed.
3. Private bath integrated in a villa.
4. 4.1 Second century (ceramics and coins).
   4.2 Third century? (ceramics and coins).
   4.3 Unknown.
5. A (pools, hypocaust).
6. 6.1 Min. 20 m² (plan unclear).
   6.2 Linear row type? (plan unclear).
   6.3 Unknown. Two rooms (1 and 2) might have been part of the bath (dressing room?). A drainage channel seems to have serviced the northernmost room (2).
   6.4 Only a small *piscina* (1.25 × 1.72 m) could be identified. The actual *frigidarium* (3) should probably be located south of it.
   6.5 A single room (4) was heated by a hypocaust and had two square *exedrae* (s.: 1.5 m), possibly to accommodate *alvei*. To the south, there may have been other heated rooms (5 and 6) and/or the *praefurnium*.
7. 7.1 The hypocaust floor was made of a pinkish hydraulic mortar. The pillars were made with round tiles. The furnace was not located (south of the heated room?).
   7.2 No traces of wall heating were described.
   7.3 Unknown.
   7.4 A drainage channel ran north and south of the bath suite. The water of the *piscina* discharged into it through a lead *fistula* still *in situ* at the time of excavation.
8. Several fragments of glass windowpanes were found in and near the baths.
9. Fig. 56.
10. Willems 1966 (ER); Brulet 2008, 559.

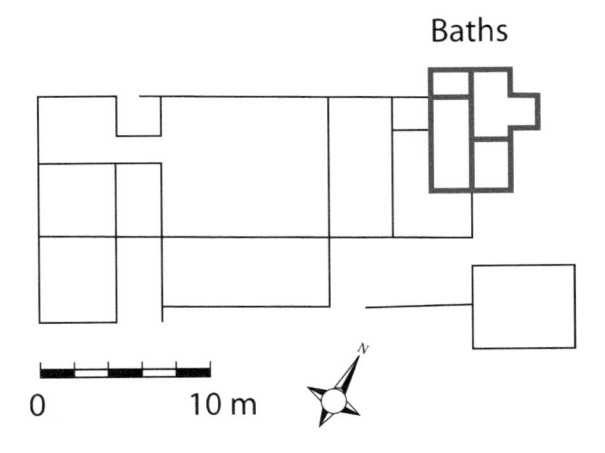

Baths

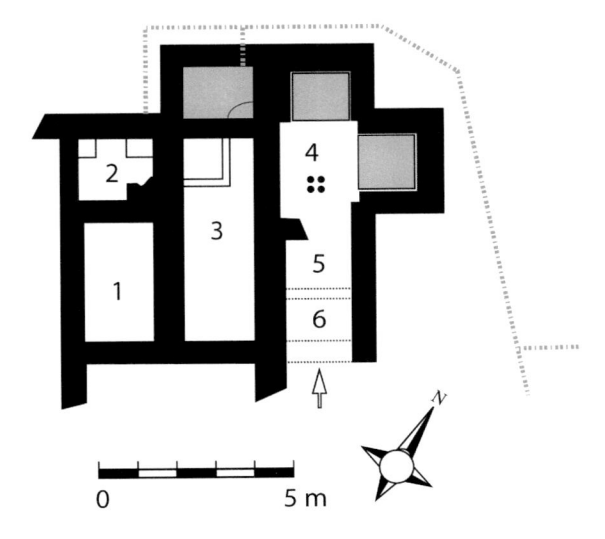

Figure 56. Location (top) and plan of the bath of Évelette – Résimont. Figure by author after Willems 1966, general plan.

Famars, Thermes (ID 9)

1. 1.1 France, Département du Nord, Famars.
   1.2 50°19'3.48"N; 3°31'4.59"E (exact).
2. 2.1 1771, 1823–1826, 1908, 1917, 1957.
   2.2 Well preserved when excavated, now covered.
3. Public bathhouse of a small town.
4. 4.1 Unknown (possibly early second century, the period of largest expansion of the settlement). The baths seem to have been enlarged westwards.
   4.2 Several coin treasures were found inside the cold section of the baths. Presumably, the baths were already out of use when these treasures were buried here. The most recent coins date to the reign of Constance, giving a *terminus ante quem* for the abandonment of the early fourth century.
   4.3 The western part of the baths was overbuilt by the fourth-century fort.
5. A (pools, hypocausts).
6. 6.1 *c.* 2600 m².
   6.2 Angular row type.
   6.3 The north-eastern part of the building consisted of a courtyard (1) with a covered gallery along its north side. An L-shaped portico (2) ran along the north and east side of the bath building. A storage cellar was added at the north side of this portico. The south-eastern part of the building (3) probably did not have a bath-related function (storage facilities? Inn?). A *palaestra* (4) might have been present south of the bathing block.
   6.4 The *frigidarium* (5) (9.4 × 11.7 m) was located in the north-western corner of the building. It had a rectangular *piscina* (3.5 × 7.15 m) along its north side, which could be accessed by two flights of steps in the south-east and south-west corners. A second (earlier?) *piscina* (6) might have been present west of the building. It seems to have been heated in a later phase from a small *praefurnium* (7).
   6.5 The heated section consisted of a large north–south oriented room (8) (*tepidarium*) and an east–west oriented central room (9) (8.5 × 12.5 m), interpreted as the *caldarium*, with two identical rooms to the north (10) and south (11) of the latter (*sudatoria*?). The *caldarium* might have had an *alveus* along its east side (above the furnace). The two rooms north (10) and south (11) of the *caldarium* each had a small annex room, only indirectly heated. Alternatively, the central east–west oriented room (9) was a *tepidarium* with *caldaria* to the north (10) and the south (11), and *alvei* in the annex rooms (according to A. Bouet). In the *piscina* west of the bathhouse (6), a hypocaust was added in a later phase.
7. 7.1 The *caldarium*'s main *praefurnium* (12) protruded into the service court east of the heated rooms. The small annex rooms of the *caldarium* were heated separately by subterranean *praefurnia* accessible through the service court. These *praefurnia* had furnaces to heat the annexes, but also to heat the *caldarium*. However, the small annex rooms were only indirectly heated through the hypocaust of the 'sudatoria'. The hypocaust pillars were made with square tiles.

7.2 *Tubuli* were found *in situ* against the west wall of newly added western room.

7.3 An aqueduct from a spring some 15 km outside Famars has been traced to the bath. The aqueduct entered the bathhouse from the south and ran along the eastern wall of the *caldarium*, where it presumably fed the water boiler(s) in the *praefurnium*. It continued north, underneath the courtyard. Here, its course became unclear. The aqueduct possibly turned west, to feed the *piscina*. Alternatively, this channel was not an aqueduct, but a drainage channel, starting from the *piscina* and collecting the waste waters of the *alvei*. A small room (4.2 × 5.2 m) east of the cold pool has been interpreted as a cistern.

7.4 The main drainage channel of the bath (1.2 m wide) ran along its western side. The alleged aqueduct supplying the *alvei* and *piscina* might actually have been a drainage channel. Only the drain of the western (early?) *piscina*, made of terracotta pipes, was identified.

8. The *frigidarium* floor was paved with square tiles of blue limestone. The lower part of the wall, to a height of around 60–70 cm, was also embellished with such slabs. Above, the walls were covered in a dark red plaster. The *caldarium* floor was paved with a chequerboard pattern of bluish black and white stone tiles. In the northern annex of the *caldarium*, a graffito containing the word *amati* was found. Several fragments of bas-reliefs, column drums, mouldings, and a composite capital were also found.

9. Fig. 57.

10. Beaussart 1980; Delmaire and others 1996, 216–25; Bouet 2003a, 676–78.

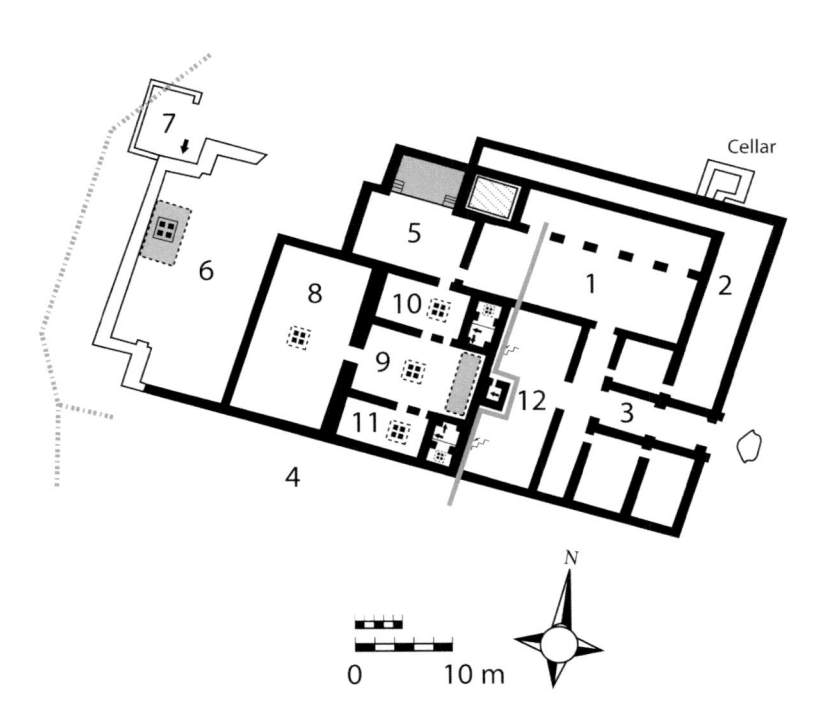

Figure 57. Plan of the bath of *Fanum Martis* (Famars). Figure by author after Beaussart 1980, 807, fig. 1.

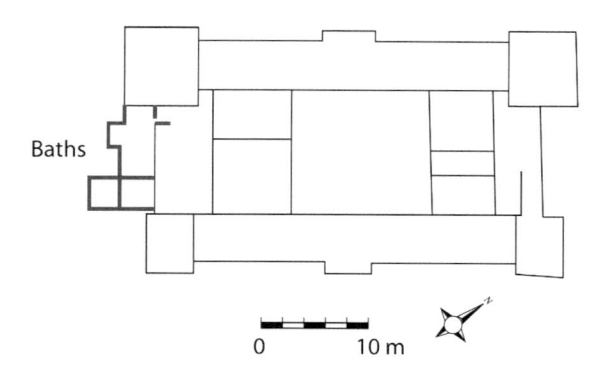

Baths

0   10 m

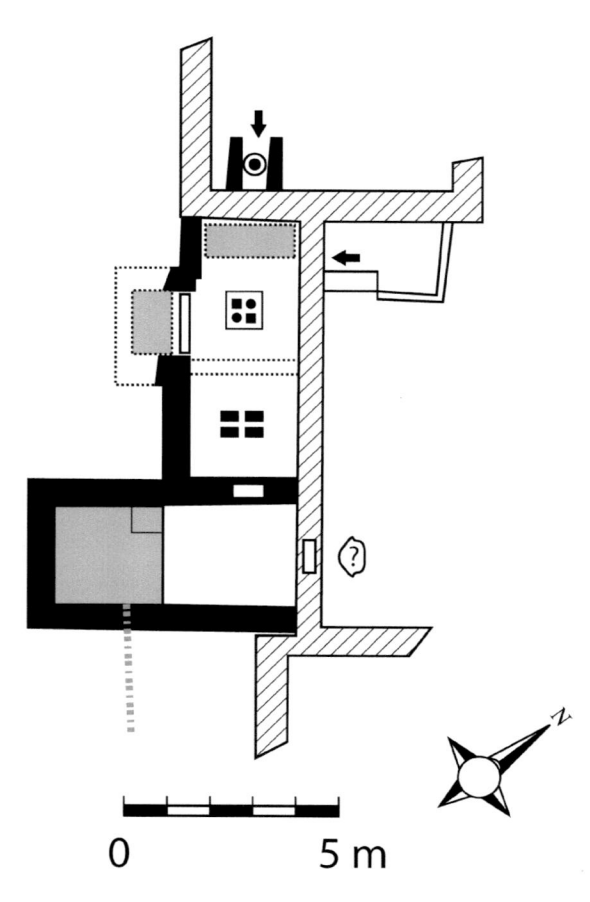

0   5 m

Figure 58. Location (top) and plan of the bath of Flostoy. Figure by author after Lefert and Hanut 2017a, 174, unnumbered fig.

Flostoy, Villa de Lizée (ID 61)

1. 1.1 Belgium, Namur, Havelange.
   1.2 50°23'1.09"N; 5°11'25.88"E (approx.).
2. 2.1 1975–1982, 2014–2016.
   2.2 Well preserved when excavated, excavations ongoing.
3. Private bathhouse integrated in a villa.
4. 4.1 Unknown. The bathhouse was added to the original villa plan (*terminus post quem* of the first century AD, based on ceramics in the nivellation layer of the site). The bathhouse seems to have had at least three phases of construction.
   4.2 Unknown. The villa site was still in use in the second half of the third century, when a pottery kiln was installed in the courtyard north of the bath.
   4.3 Unknown.
5. A (pools, hypocaust).
6. 6.1 *c.* 55 m².
   6.2 Linear row type.
   6.3 None.
   6.4 The *frigidarium* (2.7 × 2.5 m) had a mortar floor and a square *piscina* (s.: 2.45 m) on its southern side. This pool's floor, originally in reused tiles, was restored at some point, with a covering of mortar and a new finishing of tiles. The walls were also covered with *tegulae* (l.: 40 cm).
   6.5 There was one large heated room, which might have been divided into two separate parts (*caldarium* to the west, *tepidarium* to the east) by a north–south partition wall. Indeed, on the level of the hypocaust, the western part of the *suspensura* was supported by pillars, while the eastern part was supported by pillars and benches made out of brick. A rectangular *exedra* to the south (w.: 1.5 m) probably housed an *alveus* or *labrum*. It was blocked up in a later phase. An *alveus* might also have been located just above the original furnace channel (north-west side).
7. 7.1 The hypocaust pillars were made of round tiles on a base of square tiles. The eastern end of the room had broader brick pillars to support the *suspensura*. The original *praefurnium* was located west of the *caldarium*. It was abandoned and blocked up in a later phase, when a new furnace mouth was pierced through the northern wall of the room, and a *praefurnium* installed in the courtyard of the villa.
   7.2 Fragments of *tubuli* were found among the debris west of the bathhouse.
   7.3 Unknown.
   7.4 A water channel made of *imbrices* was found in the south-west corner of the *frigidarium*. The *piscina* was drained by a square hole in one of the *tegulae*. The lead *fistula* piercing the eastern wall, leading into a ditch, was still present.
8. Unknown.
9. Fig. 58.
10. Lefert 2015 (ER); 2016 (ER); Lefert and Hanut 2017a (ER); 2017b.

Fontaine-Valmont, Thermes Publics (ID 6)

1. 1.1 Belgium, Hainaut, Merbes-le-Château.
   1.2 50°18'36.03"N; 4°12'34.44"E (approx.).
2. 2.1 1961–1962, 1970.
   2.2 Well preserved when excavated, now reburied.
3. Public baths of a (religious) centre.
4. 4.1 The baths were constructed during the reign of Domitian (stratigraphic evidence). No important restorations or alterations seem to have been made.
   4.2 The baths probably fell out of use by the end of the third century (ceramics and coins in the drainage channels).
   4.3 Unknown.
5. A (pools, hypocausts).
6. 6.1 *c.* 1500 m² (including the *palaestra*).
   6.2 Linear row type.
   6.3 As the excavator passed away before the publication of the building, many rooms are not described, making interpretation extremely difficult. The large *palaestra* (1) was preceded by a gallery (2) (23.5 × 8 m), which may have had a latrine (3) attached to its eastern end. Two large *natationes* were present on the western side of the *palaestra*. The eastern *piscina* was allegedly covered, while the western *piscina* was in open air. The northernmost room might have been an *apodyterium* (5). The actual bath wing may have been entered through a corridor (4) (8.5 × 2 m), giving access to the presumed *frigidarium* (6).
   6.4 No actual *frigidarium* with *piscina* could be identified within the bathing block. It may have followed the northernmost room (5, *apodyterium*?).
   6.5 Two rooms were heated by hypocaust, both heated from the same *praefurnium*. The largest to the south (8) (*c.* 32 m²) had two *alvei* and is hence interpreted as the *caldarium*. The smaller heated room to the west (10), perhaps with a small pool along its west side, may have been a *sudatorium*. The *tepidarium* (7) may have been located to the north of the alleged *caldarium*.
7. 7.1 The *praefurnium* (9) heated both the *caldarium* and the *sudatorium*. The hypocaust pillars were made with square tiles, which stood to a height of 1.2 m.
   7.2 Some *tubuli* were still *in situ* when excavated. Recesses in the walls of both heated rooms point to the presence of chimneys.
   7.3 The water for the baths was supplied by an aqueduct fed by a natural source and stream (Rin-Wé) some 2.4 km south-west of the bath. Parts of the aqueduct were made of concrete and hydraulic mortar and others by terracotta pipes. The aqueduct ended in a *castellum divisorium* located on the high point west of the bathhouse. From the *castellum* two separate branches headed towards two *piscinae limariae*. The conduit heading north supplied both *natationes*, while the pipe heading south must have supplied the *alvei* (and perhaps *piscina*).
   7.4 The *natationes* were emptied by a drainage channel heading east (downhill). There is no information about the drainage of the *alvei*.
8. No information on the decoration was published.
9. Fig. 59.
10. Faider-Feytmans 1976 (ER); Faider-Feytmans 1995; Bouet 2003a, 678–79; Brulet 2008, 345–46.

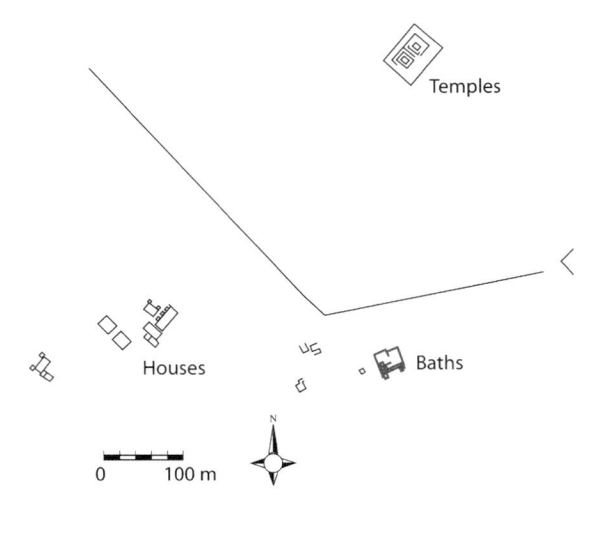

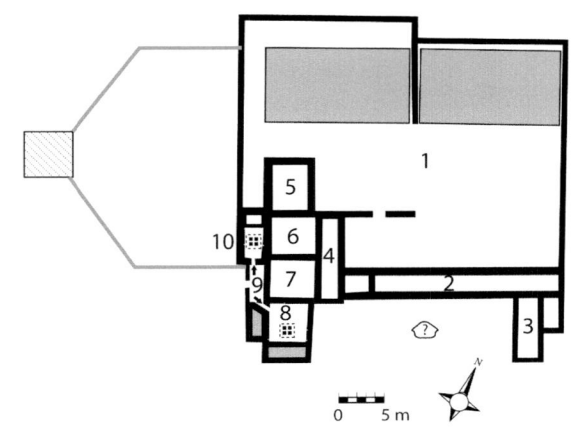

Figure 59. Location (top) and plan of the bath of Fontaine-Valmont. Figure by author after Faider-Feytmans 1995, general plan and Faider-Feytmans 1976, 18, fig. 13.

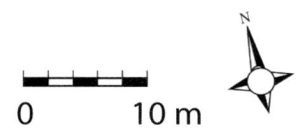

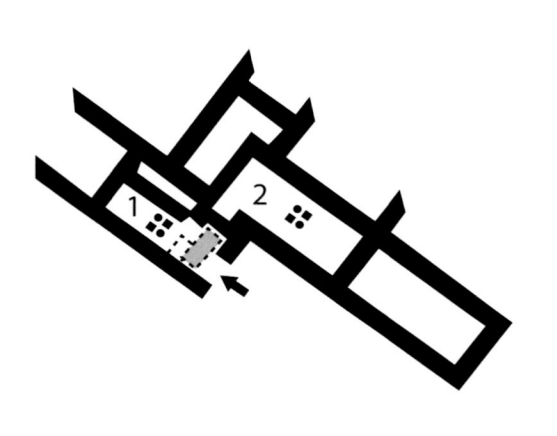

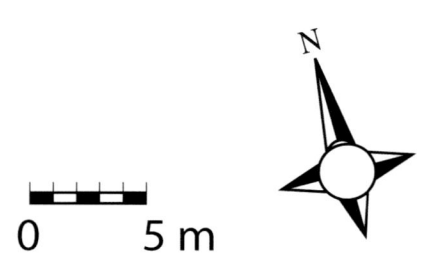

Froyennes, Villa (ID 55)

1. 1.1   Belgium, Hainaut, Tournai.
       1.2   50°37'17.38"N; 3°20'59.46"E (approx.).
2. 2.1   1966.
       2.2   Partially preserved when excavated, now covered or destroyed.
3.   Bathhouse (?) integrated in villa.
4. 4.1   There is some evidence that the site was already in use in the first century AD (ceramics on site). However, the bath seems to belong to a later phase. Two coins, one of Septimius Severus and one of Marcus Aurelius, were found near the hypocaust.
       4.2   Unknown (possibly not later than the third century).
       4.3   Unknown.
5.   C (hypocausts).
6. 6.1   Min. 32 m², max. 72 m² (plan unclear).
       6.2   Single room or two rooms in angular row?
       6.3   Unknown.
       6.4   Unknown. Several rooms connected to the heated rooms, but no pool or a mortar floor was found in these.
       6.5   Two rooms in the south-east corner of the villa were heated by a hypocaust. Their articulation is unclear. Only the western smaller room (1) was directly heated by a hypocaust, which could mean that this was a *caldarium*. The rectangular recess above the furnace could have housed an *alveus*. The eastern room (2) was indirectly heated through an opening in the dividing wall between the two rooms. This may have been a *tepidarium*. Alternatively, the rooms did not have a bathing function and were simple heated living rooms.
7. 7.1   Unknown.
       7.2   Unknown.
       7.3   A well was located south of the villa. Nearby, a small cistern was discovered. The presence of the latter could reinforce the hypothesis that the two heated rooms were in fact a small bathhouse.
       7.4   Unknown.
8.   Some rooms of the villa seem to have been plastered and embellished with wall paintings. There is no information about the heated rooms.
9.   Fig. 60.
10.   Coulon 1977 (ER); Brulet 2008, 366–67.

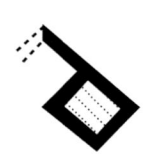

Figure 60. Location (top) and plan of the alleged bath of Froyennes. Figure by author after Coulon 1977, 16, fig. 4.

Furfooz, Bains de la fortification de Hauterecenne (ID 12)

1. 1.1 Belgium, Namur, Dinant.
   1.2 50°12'40.96"N; 4°57'20.65"E (exact).
2. 2.1 1932.
   2.2 Well preserved at the time of excavation, afterwards reconstructed.
3. Bath of a military fort (*extra muros*).
4. 4.1 Contemporaneous with the construction of the second containing wall (fourth century?).
   4.2 Before the last quarter of the fourth century (burials inside the bathhouse).
   4.3 Reused as graveyard (most burials belonged to men and had weapons as grave goods).
5. A (pools, hypocaust).
6. 6.1 *c.* 75 m².
   6.2 Linear row type.
   6.3 None.
   6.4 The *frigidarium* (3.25 × 2.4 m) had a *piscina* with apsidal ending (diam.: 2.4 m).
   6.5 The *caldarium* (6.2 × 2.87 m) had two *alvei*: one semicircular (diam.: 2.2 m) and one trapezoidal (2.75 and 1.6 × 1.1 m).
7. 7.1 The hypocaust pillars were made of square tiles. The furnace channel, north-east of the *caldarium* and directly underneath the semicircular *alveus*, was 0.5 m wide. Several *tegulae* were stamped with TRPS or H]AM[SIT.
   7.2 Several fragments of *tubuli* (box type) were found.
   7.3 Unknown.
   7.4 The *piscina* was drained by an outlet in the south-east corner.
8. Unknown.
9. Fig. 61.
10. Brulet 1978, 46–51 (ER); 2008, 519.

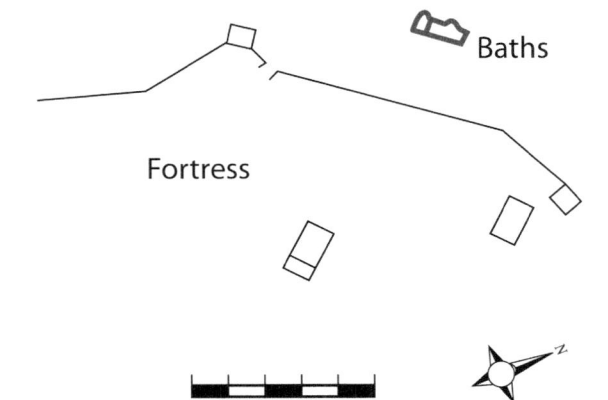

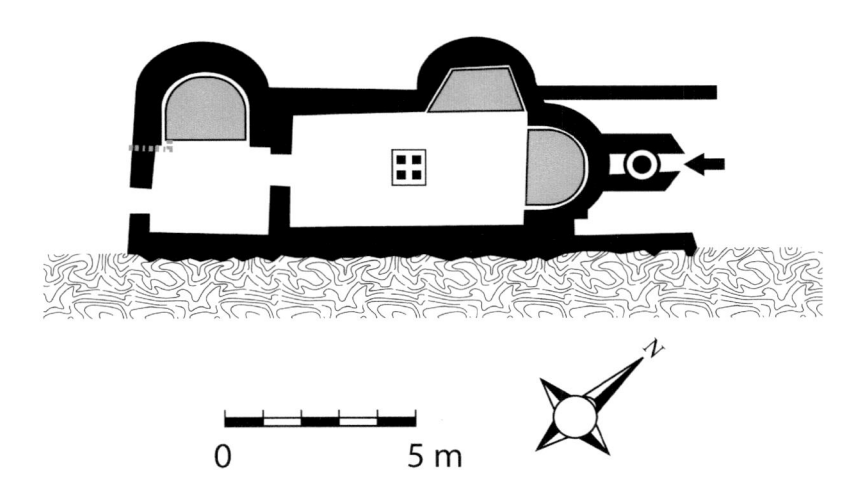

Figure 61. Location (top) and plan of the bath of Furfooz. Figure by author after Brulet 1978, general plan and 48, fig. 38

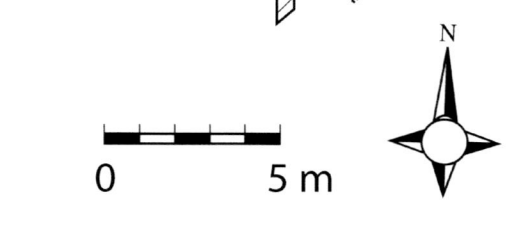

Baths

0   10 m

N

Gemechenne, Villa de Chiautes (ID 62)

1. 1.1 Belgium, Namur, Dinant.
   1.2 50°16'1.38"N; 4°56'29.80"E (approx.).
2. 2.1 Late 1970s.
   2.2 Well preserved when excavated, now covered or destroyed.
3.   Freestanding bathhouse of a villa (possibly there was a connecting corridor between the two buildings).
4. 4.1 Possibly second century (postdating the late first-century villa).
   4.2 Middle of the third century (ceramics on site).
   4.3 Reused for housing in the fourth century.
5.   A (pools, hypocausts).
6. 6.1 *c.* 120 m².
   6.2 Ring type.
   6.3 The first room when entering the bath (1) must probably be interpreted as an *apodyterium*. It was connected to the *frigidarium* and *tepidarium*.
   6.4 The *frigidarium* (2) had an oblong shape and connected to the *apodyterium*, *tepidarium* and the *caldarium*. No evidence of a pool was recorded, but it was probably located on the western side of the room.
   6.5 Two rooms were heated by a hypocaust. The almost square room (3) north of the *apodyterium* was indirectly heated by the furnace of room to the west, identifying it as the *tepidarium*. A doorway to the west gave access to the oblong room (4) heated by its own furnace to the north. This must have been the *caldarium*. The rectangular *exedra* on its west side probably accommodated an *alveus*. A second *alveus* may have been located above the furnace. The oblong shape could indicate that this room was divided into two rooms (*caldarium-tepidarium*) on the *suspensura* level. A doorway in the south-western corner gave access to an almost square room of unknown function (5), which also connected to the outside (*latrina*?).
7. 7.1 Unknown.
   7.2 Unknown.
   7.3 Unknown.
   7.4 Unknown.
8.   Unknown.
9.   Fig. 62.
10.   Gabriel 1989; Van Ossel 1992, 306–07; Brulet 2008, 516–17.

0   5 m

N

Figure 62. Location (top) and plan of the bath of Gemechenne. Figure by author after Brulet 2008, 517, fig. 429.

Gerpinnes, Villa d'Augette (ID 63)

1. 1.1 Belgium, Hainaut, Gerpinnes.
   1.2 50°20'6.97"N; 4°31'21.88"E (approx.).
2. 2.1 1875.
   2.2 Well preserved when excavated, now covered or destroyed.
3. Private bath integrated in a villa.
4. 4.1 Unknown (villa site in use in the second and third century).
   4.2 Unknown.
   4.3 The villa site was reused as a burial ground in the early medieval period (one burial in the furnace channel of the bathhouse).
5. A (pools, hypocausts).
6. 6.1 Min. 100 m² (partial plan).
   6.2 Unknown (plan unclear).
   6.3 The heated room in the north-eastern corner (1) (4.15 × 3.8 m) may have been a heated *apodyterium* or even a *sudatorium*. Alternatively, this room did not belong to the bathhouse.
   6.4 It is unclear if the pool(s) should be interpreted as *piscina(e)* or *alveus(-i)*. Therefore it is also difficult to identify a *frigidarium*.
   6.5 Two rooms with a hypocaust, each heated by its own furnace, were found. The northernmost room (2) could be a *sudatorium* (small, with its own furnace), or *tepidarium*, while the southernmost (3) was possibly the *caldarium*. The latter, which was only partially excavated, may have had an *alveus* to the north. The room east of the pool (4), in between both hypocaust rooms, was interpreted as *tepidarium* or *sudatorium*, although the description could easily fit that of a pool (floor 30 cm lower, water outlet at the bottom, terracotta pipe in the wall). Alternatively, we have here the *frigidarium*, with water supply for a *labrum*.
7. 7.1 Part of the furnace channel and the hypocaust floor were made in *opus spiccatum*. The pillar tiles were bonded with clay.
   7.2 Several fragments of *tubuli* (s.: 20 cm; box type) were found. In the northernmost heated room, four flues in each corner ensured the draught.
   7.3 Several streams now pass near the villa site, but no traces of an aqueduct were found. The 'bouche de chaleur, fait en potterie' mentioned by the excavation report, and connecting the *praefurnium* with the alleged *tepidarium/sudatorium* was possibly a water supply channel.
   7.4 The pool was drained by a lead *fistula* in its western side. An outlet was found at the bottom of the alleged *tepidarium/sudatorium*.
8. Several fragments of windowpane and wall painting were found. Especially the oblong room connecting the north-eastern heated room with the bathhouse was apparently luxuriously painted. Marble slabs (*marbre de Sainte-Anne*) adorned the upper parts of the pool.
9. Fig. 63.
10. De Glymes, Henseval, and Kaisin 1875 (ER); Brulet 2008, 335–36.

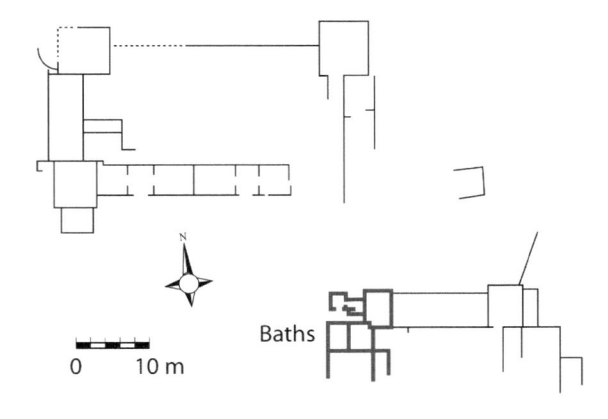

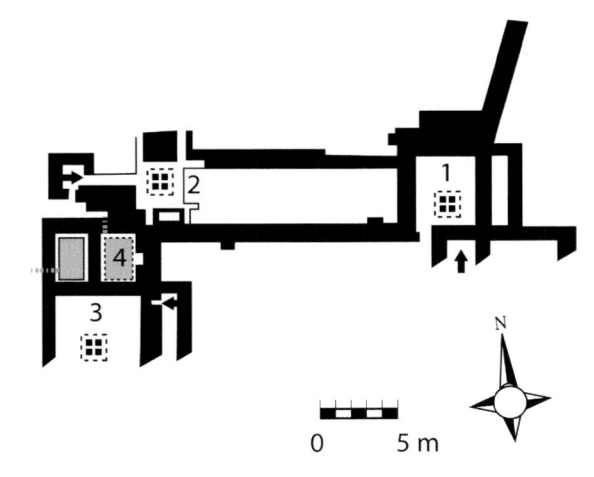

Figure 63. Location (top) and plan of the bath of Gerpinnes. Figure by author after De Glymes, Henseval, and Kaisin 1875, pl. I.

Gesves, Villa du Corria (ID 64)

1. 1.1 Belgium, Namur, Gesves.
   1.2 50°24'15.60"N; 5°4'38.64"E (approx.).
2. 2.1 2005–2006.
   2.2 Well preserved in parts when excavated, now covered.
3.   Private bathhouse attached by a 56 m long corridor to a villa.
4. 4.1 Unknown. The villa site was in use between the first and fourth century AD. The baths belong to a later phase (second century?).
   4.2 Unknown. A fourth-century coin was found in the sump collecting the waste waters of the baths.
   4.3 Unknown. The villa site was reused as a burial ground in the early Middle Ages.
5.   A (pools, hypocausts).
6. 6.1 First phase: *c.* 70 m^2; last phase: *c.* 250 m^2.
   6.2 First phase: linear row type; last phase: angular row type?
   6.3 In the first phase, the *frigidarium* (1) probably doubled as *apodyterium*. In the last phase, a large square heated room (3) (s.: 5.5 m) might have been used as heated *apodyterium*. Alternatively, the latter was a *tepidarium* and the original *frigidarium* was preceded by an *apodyterium* (4). In the second phase, an unpaved, almost square room (5) (s.: 5.3 m) on the east side of the baths may have been a service room or *frigidarium* (with wooden floor?).
   6.4 In the first phase, the *frigidarium* (3.14 × 3.5 m) had a rectangular *piscina* (1.76 × 2.7 m) in an *exedra* on its south side. In the last phase, this *frigidarium* might still have been in use, or a square room on the east side of the bath (5) may have acted as the cold room. The large basin (?) south of it (7) was perhaps a *piscina*.
   6.5 In the first phase, the *caldarium* (2) (2.85 × 3.05 m) had a rectangular *exedra* on its east side, undoubtedly to lodge an *alveus* (1.85 × 2.26 m). In the last phase, the large square room in the north-west corner was heated (3) (*tepidarium* or heated *apodyterium*), as well as a new *caldarium* (6) (5.6 × 2.85 m) to the south. The latter possibly had *alvei* in the northern apse (1.75 × 2.85 m) and the western *exedra* (2 × 3 m). The southern *exedra* seems rather small (1 × 2.7 m) to lodge a pool, but may have accommodated a *labrum*.
7. 7.1 The first-phase *caldarium* had a hypocaust made of square tiles. The pillars were double along the west side of the room. The *praefurnium* (3 × 3.14 m) lay to the east and had a long furnace channel (4 m; 50–60 cm wide) made of brick and stone. The parallel walls flanking the furnace could have supported a boiler. The hypocaust of the last phase *caldarium* and of the square heated room were made of round or square tiles. In the latter, some pillars seem to have been restored by placing two *tubuli* upright against each other and filling these with mortar. The *praefurnium* (6 × 3.1 m) of the *caldarium* was located south of it, while the *praefurnium* of the square room was located to the north.
   7.2 In the last phase, *tubuli* seem to have been used (see the restoration of the hypocaust).

7.3 Two channels north of the baths may have been used to supply water.

7.4 The first-phase *piscina* was drained by a sewage channel made of inverted *imbrices*. Two possible sewage channels were found south-east of the baths. These ended in a sump cut out of the natural bedrock.

8. Unknown.

9. Fig. 64.

10. Lefert 2007 (ER); Brulet 2008, 532–34; Lefert 2008 (ER).

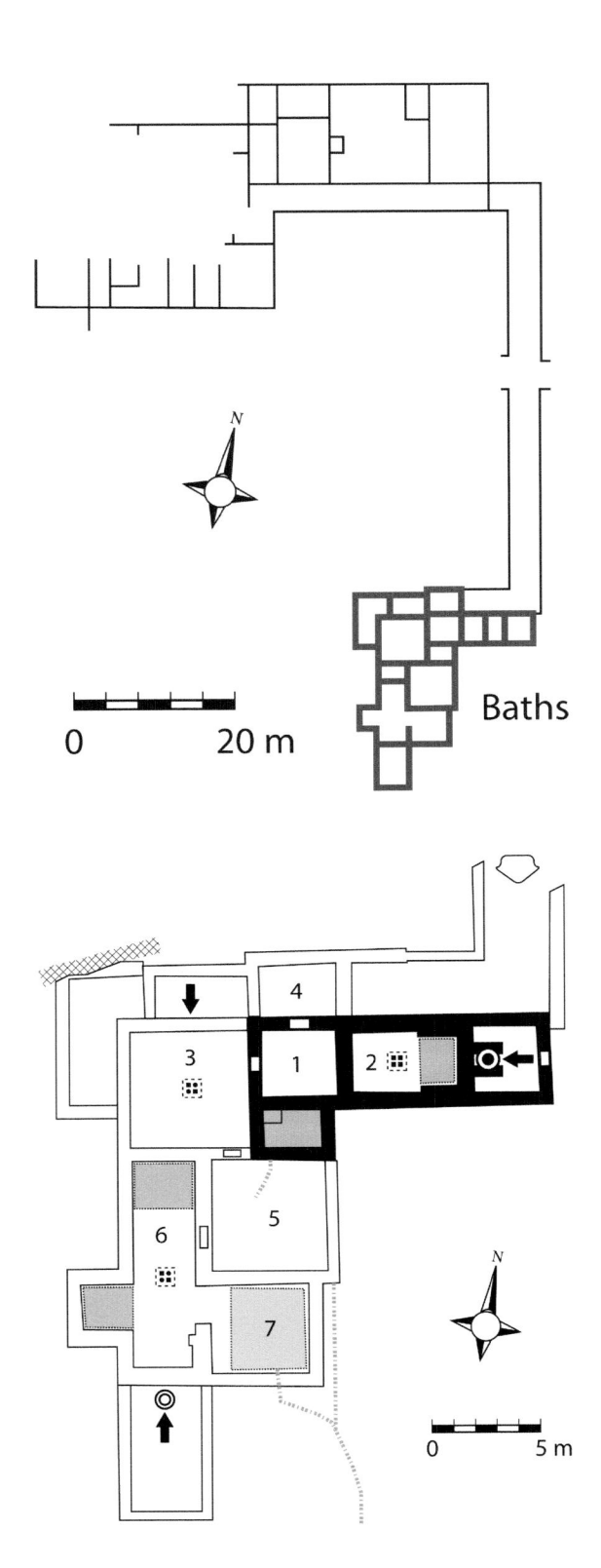

Figure 64. Location (top) and plan of the bath of Gesves. Figure by author after Lefert 2007, 201, unnumbered fig.

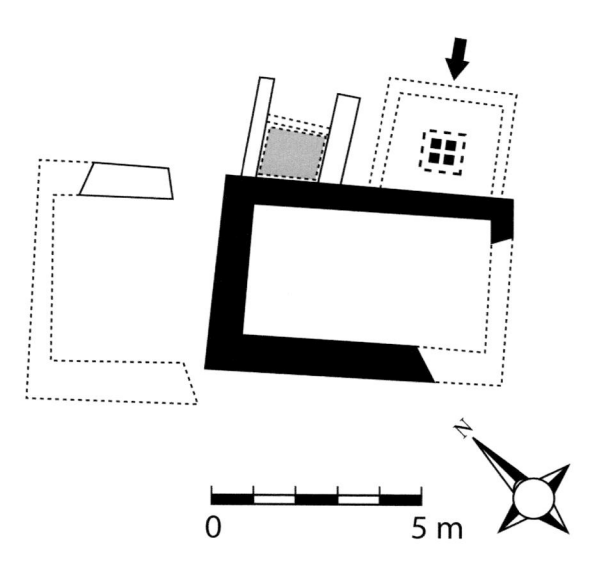

Figure 65. Plan of the alleged bath of Gooik. Figure by author after unpublished plan KMKG/MRAH archives.

Gooik, Lombergveld (ID 66)

1. 1.1   Belgium, Flemish Brabant, Gooik.
    1.2   50°47'10.75"N; 4°6'18.95"E (approx.)
2. 2.1   1972–1975, 1978.
    2.2   Well preserved when excavated, now covered.
3.   Freestanding bathhouse (?) of a villa.
4. 4.1   Unknown.
    4.2   Unknown.
    4.3   Unknown.
5.   C (hypocaust, evidence for a pool).
6. 6.1   Unknown (unpublished).
    6.2   Unknown (unpublished).
    6.3   Unknown (unpublished).
    6.4   The alleged bathhouse seems to have consisted of two rooms. Only one of these could be measured (3.2 × 2.4 m). It had two rectangular *exedrae* on its north-eastern side. The western *exedra* (2.2 × 1.7 m) may have housed a pool. The slightly different orientation of both *exedrae* and the fact that their walls abut the north-eastern wall of the room indicate that these were built at a later date.
    6.5   The eastern *exedra* (2.8 × 2.3 m) was heated by a hypocaust. The *praefurnium* was located on its north-eastern side.
7. 7.1   The hypocaust pillars were made with square tiles, of which only the imprints in the hydraulic mortar were preserved.
    7.2   Unknown.
    7.3   Unknown.
    7.4   Unknown.
8.   Unknown.
9.   Fig. 65.
10.   KMKG/MRAH archives.

Graux, Villa 'Al Ronce' (ID 67)

1. 1.1 Belgium, Namur, Mettet.
   1.2 50°19'29.49"N; 4°42'57.91"E (approx.).
2. 2.1 1899.
   2.2 Covered or destroyed.
3. Private bath integrated in a villa.
4. 4.1 Unknown (High Empire).
   4.2 Unknown.
   4.3 Unknown.
5. A (pools, hypocausts).
6. 6.1 *c.* 100 m².
   6.2 Linear row type.
   6.3 The layout of the bath rooms is unclear. A room heated by its own furnace (1) may have been a heated *apodyterium* (or *sudatorium?*).
   6.4 The square *frigidarium* (2) was quite small, had a wooden floor and a small *piscina* (0.7 m deep).
   6.5 Two rooms were heated by a hypocaust. The southernmost (3) can be identified as a *caldarium*, heated by its own furnace and possibly with *labrum* or small *alveus* in southern apse. The northernmost room (1) (3.6 × 4.75 m) was possibly a heated *apodyterium* or *sudatorium*, directly heated by its own furnace.
7. 7.1 The *caldarium* had a *praefurnium* to the west. A platform probably supported a boiler. The hypocaust pillars were made with square tiles (s.: 24 cm; h.: 4 cm).
   7.2 Fragments of *tubuli* were found, but exact dimensions were not specified.
   7.3 Unknown. A small reservoir (1.3 × 0.75 m; 0.8 m deep) was identified.
   7.4 The *piscina* was drained by a channel in the west wall of the bathing suite, crossing the northern *praefurnium*.
8. Fragments of polychrome wall paintings were found in the *caldarium*.
9. Fig. 66.
10. Mahieu 1910 (ER); Brulet 2008, 549–50.

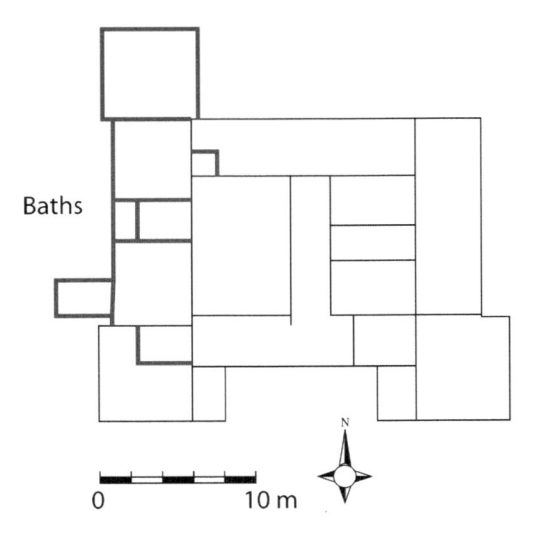

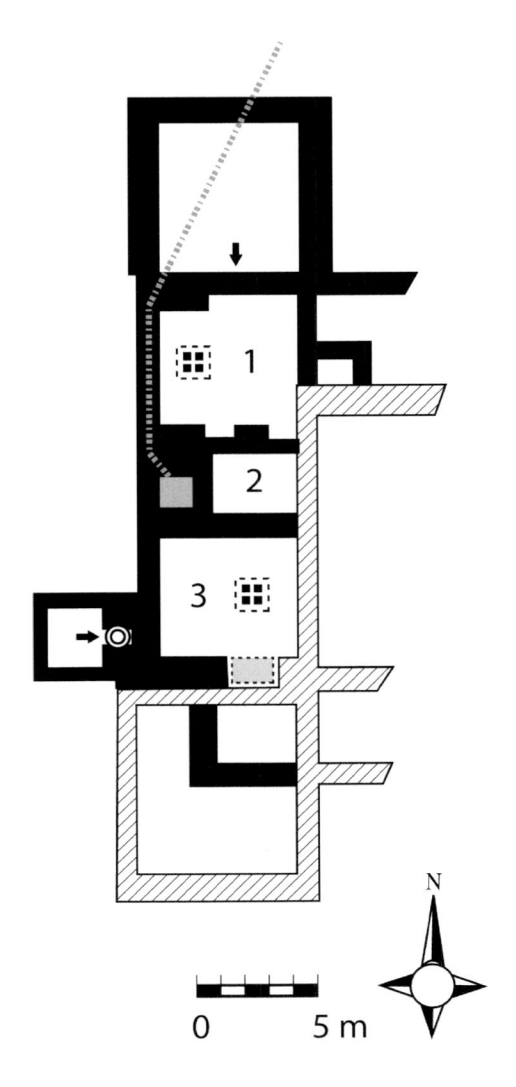

Figure 66. Location (top) and plan of the bath of Graux. Figure by author after Mahieu 1910, unnumbered page, unnumbered fig.

Grobbendonk, Vicus Bath (ID 3)

1. 1.1 Belgium, Antwerp, Grobbendonk.
   1.2 51°11'46.21"N; 4°44'14.21"E (exact).
2. 2.1 1977.
   2.2 Badly preserved when excavated, now destroyed.
3. Public bath.
4. 4.1 Early second century (ceramics in the foundation trenches).
   4.2 First half of the third century at the latest (ceramics in the destruction layer).
   4.3 Building materials were recuperated in the medieval or post-medieval period.
5. A (pools, hypocaust).
6. 6.1 Min. 250 m² (partial plan, last phase).
   6.2 Angular row type.
   6.3 One entered the baths by a small entrance vestibule (1). The protruding room to the north (8.9 × 6.75 m) was possibly the *apodyterium*. It had no special features.
   6.4 The *frigidarium* (3) was almost square (3.9 × 4.1 m) and had a rectangular *exedra* to lodge the *piscina* (4.2 × 2.3 m) on its southern side. The floor of the room may have been broken out (spoliated) or was possibly in wood.
   6.5 The only heated room (4), cruciform with possibly two or three *alvei* in the arms, must be interpreted as the *caldarium*. The oblong shape could indicate that this room was divided at *suspensura* level into a *tepidarium* (east) and *caldarium* (west). The northern *exedra* might have contained a *labrum*, as no waste water outlet was found. To the west, the *praefurnium* (5) must have been located (ash and charcoal were found here). The parallel walls flanking the furnace may have supported a boiler.
7. 7.1 Both square and round pillar tiles were found in the debris of the *caldarium*. This room was very badly preserved and almost entirely spoliated for building material at a later date.
   7.2 Unknown.
   7.3 The *piscina* was emptied through a shallow drainage channel in its south-western corner.
   7.4 Unknown.
8. Fragments of wall painting were found.
9. Fig. 67.
10. De Boe 1977 (ER).

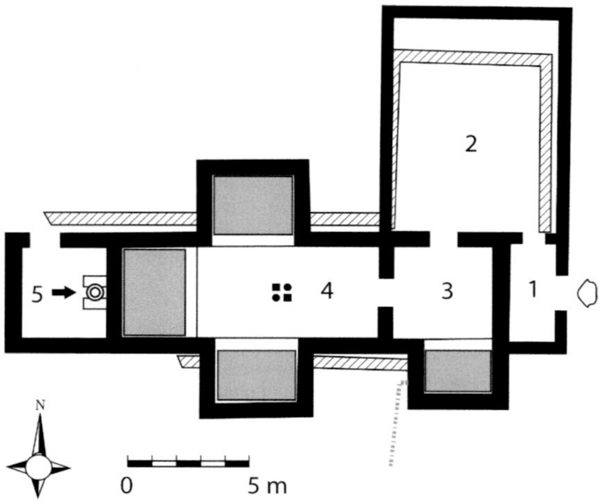

Figure 67. Location (top) and plan of the bath of Grobbendonk. Figure by author after De Boe 1984, 77, fig. 40 and De Boe 1977, 40, fig. 22.

Grumelange, villa in Lavend (ID 68)

1. 1.1 Belgium, Luxembourg, Martelange.
   1.2 49°50'39.17"N; 5°44'48.27"E (approx.).
2. 2.1 1910–1912.
   2.2 Well preserved when excavated, now covered or destroyed.
3. Private bathhouse integrated in a villa.
4. 4.1 Unknown.
   4.2 Unknown.
   4.3 Unknown.
5. A (pool, hypocaust).
6. 6.1 *c.* 43 m².
   6.2 Angular row type?
   6.3 The large square room (s.: 4 m) in the south-east corner (1) and the heated room (2) north of it (3 × 4 m) may have belonged to the bath. These could have had the function of respectively *apodyterium* and *tepidarium* or *sudatorium*. In the square room an area of 3 by 1 m and 1 m deep was dug out along the north wall. It was interpreted as a storage pit by the excavators, although human remains found inside could point to a later burial.
   6.4 The *frigidarium* (3 × 1.3 m) lay west (3) and was connected to the courtyard by a narrow doorway (0.6 m). It had a semicircular *piscina* (diam.: 1.5 m) which was accessible by steps.
   6.5 The heated room (4) connected to the *frigidarium* (3) and the square room (1). Its north-western corner was taken in by an elliptical furnace, possibly added at a later date (according to the original excavation plan). It is unclear if and where an *alveus* might have been present (north side of the room?).
7. 7.1 The northern heated room had hypocaust pillars made of square tiles (s.: 16 cm). The furnace was possibly located west, in the courtyard. The hypocaust pillars of the second heated room were made with round tiles. Both hypocausts had a height of around 30 cm. The elliptical furnace had a small square *praefurnium* (s.: 1 m) located in the courtyard.
   7.2 In both heated rooms, fragments of *tubuli* were found (dimensions unknown).
   7.3 Unknown.
   7.4 The *piscina* was drained by an orifice in the south side, leading into a drainage channel made of mortar.
8. The floor of the square room was paved with slabs of blue limestone. In the *frigidarium*, the lower part of the wall was painted brown with a horizontal yellow and black line, while the upper part was painted in a white marble imitation.
9. Fig. 68.
10. Malget and Malget 1912 (ER); Brulet 2008, 484.

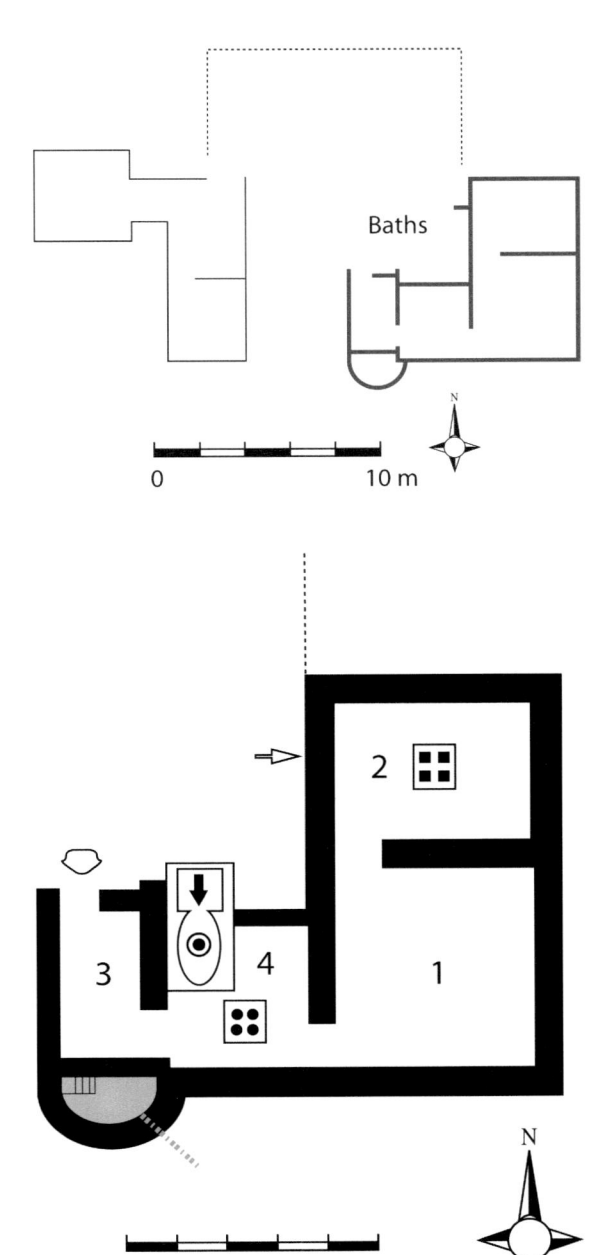

Figure 68. Location (top) and plan of the bath of Grumelange. Figure by author after Malget and Malget 1912, 416, unnumbered fig.

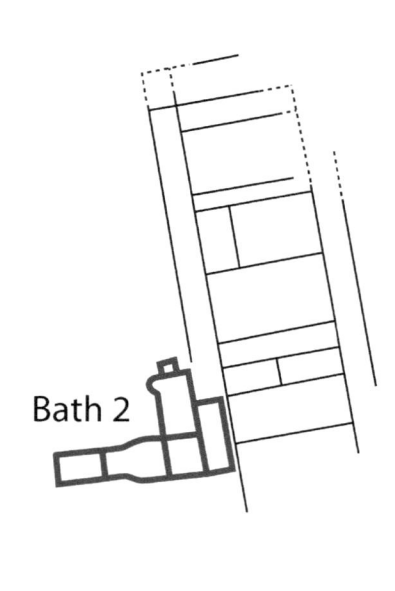

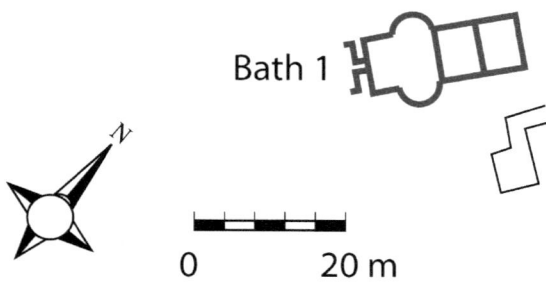

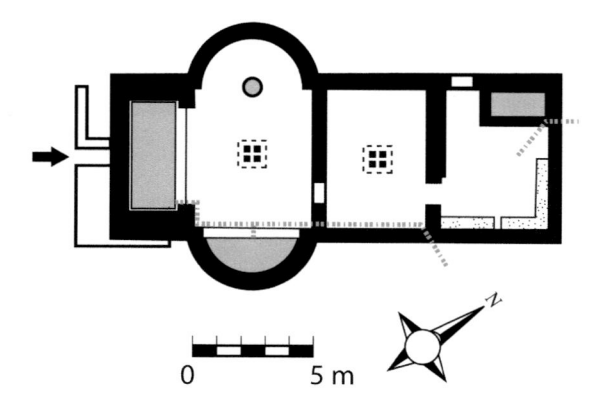

Figure 69. Location (top) and plan of 'Bath 1' at Haccourt. Figure by author after De Boe 1971b, 18, fig. 2 and De Boe 1974, 17, fig. 6.

Haccourt, Villa Bath 1 (ID 69)

1. 1.1 Belgium, Liège, Oupeye.
    1.2 50°43'48.89"N; 5°39'53.65"E (exact).
2. 2.1 1967.
    2.2 Well preserved when excavated, now destroyed.
3. Private bath of a villa. As the oldest phase of the villa has been partially destroyed by the later phase, it could not be determined whether the bathhouse was integrated, attached, or freestanding.
4. 4.1 A *terminus post quem* (ceramics) of AD 70 is proposed for the oldest stone building phase. The villa to which the baths belonged, probably replaced this oldest building before the end of the first century AD. The baths seem contemporaneous or slightly later than this second stone building.
    4.2 There seem to have been at least two phases. In a second phase, the *piscina* was dismantled, perhaps implying that the bath changed function (when a new bathhouse was built?). The old villa, as well as its bath, was dismantled in the first half of the second century.
    4.3 When the old villa was abandoned, the remains were filled in to create an artificial platform on which the new villa was built.
5. A (pools, hypocausts).
6. 6.1 *c.* 180 m².
    6.2 Linear row.
    6.3 The cold room doubled as *apodyterium*, as benches (added in a second phase) ran along north-eastern and eastern side of the room.
    6.4 The *frigidarium* (4.38 × 4.45 m) had a *piscina* in its north-western corner (external: 1.5 × 3 m) and benches along its north-eastern and eastern sides.
    6.5 Two rooms were heated by a hypocaust. The central room (4.2 × 6 m) was indirectly heated, as its hypocaust connected through three openings to the hypocaust of the southernmost room. It can be interpreted as the *tepidarium*. The southernmost room (4.9 × 6 m), directly heated by a furnace to the south, was the *caldarium*. It had a rectangular pool (4.8 × 2.1 m) right above the furnace and two semicircular *exedrae* (r.: 2.05 m). The eastern *exedra* housed an *alveus*, while the western *exedra* possibly served as *schola labri*.
7. 7.1 The *praefurnium* (5 × 5.75 m) was located south of the *caldarium* and partially dug into the virgin soil. In a later phase, the sides of the pit were reinforced with a thin wall. The furnace itself was lined by brick-built walls protruding both into the *praefurnium*, possibly to support a boiler, and into the *caldarium*-hypocaust (for 55 cm). The furnace floor was made in tiles, covered with a layer of clay. The hypocaust pillars were made with square tiles (s.: 20–21 cm), bonded with clay, standing some 40 cm apart and reaching a height of *c.* 65 cm. The *suspensura*, of which fragments were reused as building material in Bath 2, was 12–13 cm thick.
    7.2 No fragments of wall heating are mentioned in the excavation reports. Two chimney flues made of *imbrices* were housed in the north-eastern wall of the *tepidarium*.

7.3 Several iron rings, used to hold together wooden water pipes, were found in the debris of the bath. A channel connecting to the western semicircular *exedra* of the *caldarium*, might have been a water supply channel (according to the excavators). If this *exedra* held a *labrum* and the water pipe came directly from a source (rather than from the *praefurnium*), the *labrum* must have provided cold water.

7.4 A drain was integrated in the mosaic floor of the *frigidarium*. The drainage channel passed underneath the *piscina* to drain its waste water, and pierced the northern wall of the *frigidarium*. A second drainage channel, perhaps originally in mortar, started from the north-eastern corner of the *tepidarium* and may have collected the waters from the heated rooms.

8. The *frigidarium* floor was embellished with a black and white mosaic (6 × 4.3 m). A central panel of lozenges (2.42 × 2.43 m) was bordered by a plain white band. The *piscina* in the north-western corner of the room was dismantled in a later (non-bath?) phase and the void in the floor was filled in with a mosaic of terracotta *tesserae*. A text seems to have been laid out in *tesserae*, although only an R could be identified. In all of the rooms, fragments of windowpanes and painted wall plaster were found. In the *caldarium*, these wall paintings were mainly plain white panels bordered by coloured lines. Other fragments had geometric or floral designs, and some marble imitation was also identified.

9. Fig. 69.

10. De Boe 1971b (ER); 1974 (ER); Brulet 2008, 425–29.

Haccourt, Villa Bath 2 (ID 70)

1. 1.1 Belgium, Liège, Oupeye.
   1.2 50°43'48.89"N; 5°39'53.65"E (exact).
2. 2.1 1967.
   2.2 Well preserved when excavated, now destroyed.
3. Private bath attached to a villa.
4. 4.1 Bath 2 was built during a restructuration of the villa, probably when Bath 1 was transformed. A lack of pottery and coins makes it difficult to date these alterations. A general time frame of the early second century is proposed, taking into account the dismantling of the baths.
   4.2 The bath was dismantled in the course of the first half of the second century AD or around the middle of that same century at the latest (ceramics in the infill of the hypocausts, serving as foundations for the new larger villa).
   4.3 The bath was dismantled and filled in to create a terrace on which a new larger villa was built.
5. A (pools, hypocausts).

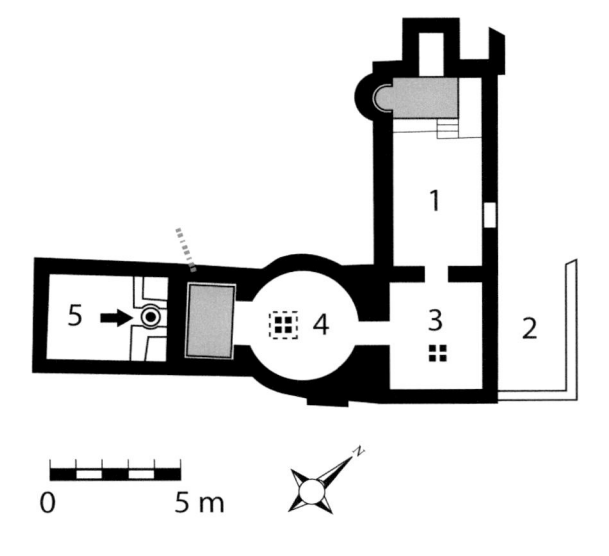

Figure 70. Plan of Bath 2 at Haccourt. Figure by author after De Boe 1974, 49, fig. 20.

6.   6.1   *c.* 73 m² (or 86 m² including the later *apodyterium*).

     6.2   Angular row type.

     6.3   In the original layout, the *frigidarium* (1) probably doubled as *apodyterium*. In a later phase, an oblong room (2) (2.6 m wide) was added north of the *tepidarium*, which may have been used as an *apodyterium*.

     6.4   The walls of the *frigidarium* (4.9 × 3.5 m) were broken out, so only the negative traces remained. A rectangular area (2.5 × 1.4 to 1.7 m) with a semicircular niche in its south-western side, can probably be identified as the *piscina*. On its western side, a square *exedra* (s.: 1 m) remains unexplained.

     6.5   Two rooms were heated by a hypocaust. The northernmost rectangular room (3) (3.6 × 4.2 m), in connection with the *frigidarium* to its west, can be interpreted as the *tepidarium*. It was indirectly heated by the furnace of the *caldarium*, the round room (diam.: 4.2 m) to its south (4). This *caldarium* had a rectangular *exedra* to the south, just above the furnace channel, lodging an *alveus* (1.95 × 3 m).

7.   7.1   The *praefurnium* (5) (3.35 × 4.65 m) was originally dug out of the virgin soil, covered by an awning resting on two posts, of which the postholes were identified. In a later phase, a small room was created, using fragments of hypocaust tile and *suspensura* of Bath 1 to create its walls. Two raised platforms were also created flanking the furnace mouth, perhaps to support a boiler. The furnace channel (50 cm wide) was flanked by walls made out of brick and covered with a barrel vault, and the furnace floor was made out of tiles. The hypocaust pillars were made of square tiles (s.: 21–23 cm), bonded with clay, standing 20 to 40 cm apart, and resting directly on the virgin soil. Their height possibly reached 51 cm.

     7.2   No (fragments of) wall heating is mentioned in the excavation reports. Two chimneys were housed in the northern wall of the *tepidarium*.

     7.3   No aqueducts or wells were found. The water may have been piped from the natural springs located uphill near the villa.

     7.4   Unknown.

8.   The sides of the *alveus* were embellished with a plain white mosaic, while the *caldarium* floor had a black-and-white mosaic. Several fragments of windowpane and painted wall plaster were found in the debris that filled in the baths after their dismantling. Two phases could be identified for the wall paintings. The first layer consisted of floral motifs on plain panels and marble imitation (in the *caldarium*). The second layer, superimposing the first layer, consisted of white and red panels, bordered by black, red, and occasionally green lines.

9.   Figs 69–70.

10.   De Boe 1971b (ER); 1974 (ER); Brulet 2008, 425–29.

Haccourt, villa Bath 3 (ID 71)

1. 1.1 Belgium, Liège, Oupeye.
   1.2 50°43'48.89"N; 5°39'53.65"E (exact).
2. 2.1 1913, 1962, 1967–1970.
   2.2 Well preserved when excavated, now destroyed.
3. Originally a freestanding private bath that was later attached to the villa.
4. 4.1 Second quarter of the second century or mid-second century AD (ceramics in nivellation layers of the site).
   4.2 Second half of the third century AD (ceramics and coins in destruction layer).
   4.3 Some small-scale metal smelting and forging took place in- and outside the baths after these had fallen out of use.
5. A (pools, hypocausts).
6. 6.1 Phase 1: 390 m²; phase 2: 658 m²; phase 3: 665 m².
   6.2 Row type.
   6.3 A small oblong room (2.57 × 5.10 m) to the north (1), where the later portico attached to the baths, probably acted as a vestibule. The larger room (2) to its west (9.10 × 7.40 m), may have acted as *apodyterium*. In phase 3, a small room (19) with a mortar floor (1.9 × 2.5 m) lying below the walking level of this alleged *apodyterium*, may have been a pool attached to this room. During phase 2, a cellar (14) (4.25 × 4.60 m; fuel storage?) was constructed directly east of the *caldarium*, but it fell out of use by the late second or early third century. When the bathhouse was connected to the villa by a portico (17) during phase 2, a porch (18) was also created along the north side of the bathhouse, perhaps to serve as *ambulatio* offering a vista over the valley below. In phase 3, several small rooms were added in the angle formed between the portico and this porch, perhaps functioning as some sort of resting pavilion (20). The area between the western *calida piscina* and the *piscina* was paved with a mortar floor (12) and perhaps covered by an awning. It may have been an exercise yard or some sort of terrace.
   6.4 The cold room was located at the centre of the baths (4). It had a rectangular plan (4.50 × 6.60 m) with a semicircular niche (diam.: 2.35 m) in its north side. In this niche, there was probably a doorway connecting to the round heated room (3). A large *piscina* (5.6 × 7.14 m internally; 1.30 to 1.40 m deep) was located to the west of the *frigidarium*. In phase 2, a small *piscina* (2 × 1.5 m) was added on top of the existing floor in the south-eastern corner of the room.
   6.5 A round room (3) (diam.: 5.07 m) with four semicircular niches (diam.: 1.61 to 1.72 m), heated by hypocaust, can be interpreted as a *laconicum*, due to its form and location between the *apodyterium* and *frigidarium*. It was originally heated by a *praefurnium* (8) to its south, but when the latter was transformed into a heat trap (9) in phase 2, it was heated by a newly created *praefurnium* to its west (16). The rectangular room (5) (3.3 × 4.05 m) immediately south of the *frigidarium* was interpreted as a *tepidarium* by the excavators, but its size and the fact that it was heated by its own furnace (in 8) could also identify it as a *sudatorium*. Immediately to the south of this room, a large rectangular room (6) was divided

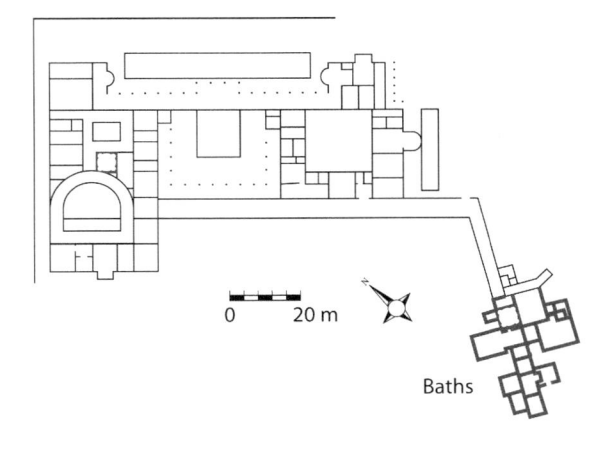

Baths

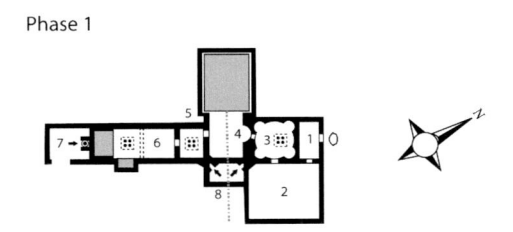

Phase 1

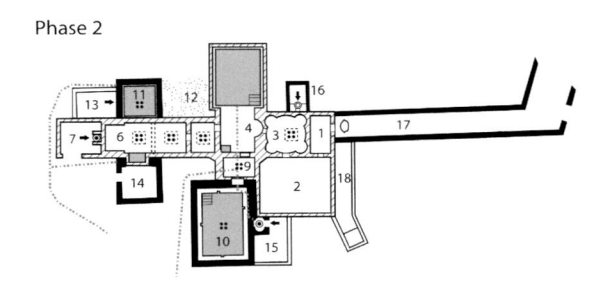

Phase 2

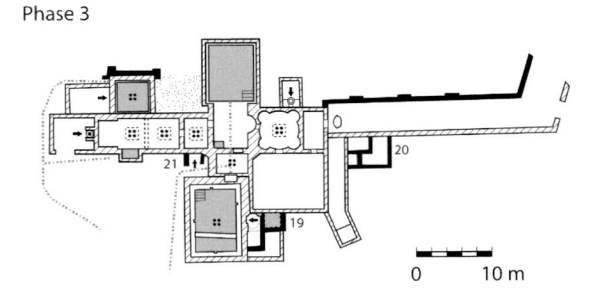

Phase 3

Figure 71. Location (top) and plan of Bath 3 at Haccourt. Figure by author after De Boe 1976, 32, fig. 15.

at hypocaust level into two parts. The excavator argued that it probably formed one large room (*caldarium*) at walking level, with a large bay dividing it into two rooms. However, we could then argue that the northern part of this room (3.27 × 4.05 m), furthest away from the furnace, acted as *tepidarium*, if it was actually divided from the *caldarium* (3.25 × 4.05 m) by an open bay or by a solid wall with a doorway. The *caldarium* had two rectangular *exedrae*, both lodging *alvei*. The southern *exedra* (2.6 × 3.4 m) was located directly above the furnace, the eastern *exedra* was quite small (2.01 × 1.22 m). In phase 2, a large pool (5.35 × 8.35 m; 0.70 m deep) heated by a hypocaust and supplied by a boiler, a so-called *calida piscina*, was added to the east of the original suite of bathing rooms (10). It had a bench at least 45 cm wide running along the sides. The *praefurnium* that heated the rooms north and south of the *frigidarium* was therefore transformed into a heat trap (9), connecting the *frigidarium* to this new heated pool. It was indirectly heated by the hypocausts of the heated rooms north and south of the *frigidarium*. A second *calida piscina* (11) (4.50 × 4.65 m; max. 1.15 m deep) was also added to the west of the *caldarium*, heated by its own furnace to the south (13). At this point, the southern *alveus* of the *caldarium* was probably dismantled. In phase 3, the eastern *calida piscina* probably fell out of use, or was perhaps transformed into a new heated room, as the pool was cut by a new wall and the boiler was obliterated.

7. 7.1 The *praefurnium* (7) (5.37 × 4.28 m) of the *caldarium* had a simple earth floor, and was accessible by a large doorway (2.57 m wide) in its eastern side. The furnace channel was flanked by two parallel walls protruding into the *praefurnium* for 1.2 m. A second *praefurnium* (8) (4.55 × 2.55 m) to the east of the *frigidarium*, also with an earth floor, heated the rooms north and south of the *frigidarium*. The furnace channels (55 cm wide) were paved with square tiles (s.: 20 cm). In phase 2, when the latter *praefurnium* was transformed into a heat trap (9), a new *praefurnium* (16) (2.20 × 3.65 m) heated the round *laconicum*. The furnace channel was flanked by two walls made of brick protruding into the *praefurnium* (1.15 m) and the fire was lit directly on the earth floor. The eastern *calida piscina* also had its own *praefurnium* (15) (5.85 × 4.25/4.40 m), with a platform constructed above the furnace channel (78 cm wide; tiled) which must have carried a cylindrical boiler. In phase 3, this *praefurnium* was reduced to a small room (1.80 × 4.50 m) without boiler. The western *calida piscina* had its own furnace (60 cm wide) to the south. It was directly dug as a pit into the virgin soil. Two walls (each 45 cm wide) flanked the furnace channel, protruding into the hypocaust for 1 m. In phase 2, the stoking area was probably an open space covered by an awning, of which two postholes have been found. In phase 3, this furnace area was transformed into a *praefurnium* (13) (5.3 × 3.6 m). Also in phase 3, the room directly south

of the *frigidarium* received its own *praefurnium* (21). The fire was lit on a small platform made of bricks. The hypocaust pillars were made of round tiles (diam.: 24 cm; larger underneath the *exedrae*: 28 cm). The pillar tiles in the *laconicum* had different dimensions (diam.: 22 cm to 32 cm). The round pillar tiles of the eastern *calida piscina* (diam.: 28 cm) rested on larger square (s.: 29 cm) or round (diam.: 38 cm) tiles. Some of the tiles used in the construction of the *piscina* had the stamp MHF (in a circle).

7.2 Unknown. The walls were not preserved to a sufficient height. No mention is made of *tubuli* or other types of wall heating in the debris. Four chimney flues (31/37 × 17 cm) in the four sides of the eastern *calida piscina* point to the absence of wall heating for this pool.

7.3 No aqueducts were found, although several iron rings used to hold together wooden water pipes were identified. The water may have been piped from the natural springs located uphill, some 2 km south-east or 1.5 km west of the villa. The combined volume of water needed to fill all the pools has been calculated to surpass 100 m³.

7.4 The *piscina* was drained by a lead *fistula* in its eastern side, flowing into a sewage channel made of mortar (30 cm wide). This channel originally passed underneath the *frigidarium* and the small *praefurnium* to its east. When the *calida piscina* was constructed, the channel bent north around the pool and seems to have ended above the boiler of the heated pool. Rather than supplying this boiler with water, as hinted at by the excavator, the water was probably used to flush the furnace after use. In a second phase, the channel was diverted to the south, bending around the south side of the *calida piscina*. Its walls were constructed of tiles, while its bottom was made out of mortar. The western *calida piscina* was drained by a drainage channel (34–42 cm wide) starting in its south-western corner. After running along the western side of the *praefurnium*, the channel led into a ditch that ran south of the bathhouse, heading east, where it connected to another ditch possibly collecting the waste water of the small eastern *alveus* of the *caldarium*.

8. In phase 2, the *frigidarium* was paved with flagstones, although only the imprints of the tiles in the mortar remain. The walls of the large *piscina* were finished with a hydraulic mortar, painted in a purple red. The additional small *piscina* was embellished with slabs of greyish marble, some of which were still *in situ*. Other fragments of local white Visé 'marble' were found throughout the bath. Several fragments of painted wall plaster were also found. Some possibly imitated marble (grey-white on white background), others depicted green leaves on a white background. Coloured lines and a circular motif on a white background were also found.

9. Fig. 71.

10. De Boe 1971b (ER); 1976 (ER); Brulet 2008, 425–29.

Haillot, Villa de Matagne (ID 72)

1. 1.1   Belgium, Namur, Ohey.
   1.2   50°26'11.52"N; 5°9'13.61"E (approx.).
2. 2.1   2001.
   2.2   Partially preserved when excavated, now covered or destroyed.
3.   Private bath integrated in a villa.
4. 4.1   Unknown.
   4.2   Unknown.
   4.3   Unknown.
5.   A (pools, hypocaust).
6. 6.1   *c.* 53 m².
   6.2   Linear row type.
   6.3   None.
   6.4   The *frigidarium* was an almost square room with a *piscina* on its west side (2.9 × 2.75 m external). The latter had a floor of hydraulic mortar.
   6.5   A single room was heated by a hypocaust and must hence be interpreted as the *caldarium* (3.9 × 6.2 m external). It had a rectangular *exedra* (2.4 × 1.4 m) on its western side, presumably to lodge an *alveus*. A second *alveus* might have been present above the furnace channel located at the north end of the room. The room may have been divided at *suspensura* level into a *tepidarium* (south) and a *caldarium* (north).
7. 7.1   The *praefurnium* (3.4 × 2.86 m external) was heavily disturbed. A spot of burnt clay soil (1.15 × 0.4 m) points to the location of the furnace. The furnace channel was made of square brick placed sideways (1.7 × 0.5 m). The hypocaust tiles were all recuperated.
   7.2   Unknown due to heavy spoliation of the site.
   7.3   Traces of an aqueduct were found coming from the north-east and turning at the *praefurnium* to continue west of the bath, probably to supply the *piscina*.
   7.4   Unknown.
8.   In the *praefurnium*, several fragments of windowpane were found, which possibly came from the *caldarium*.
9.   Fig. 72.
10.   Lefert 2002 (ER); Brulet 2008, 560.

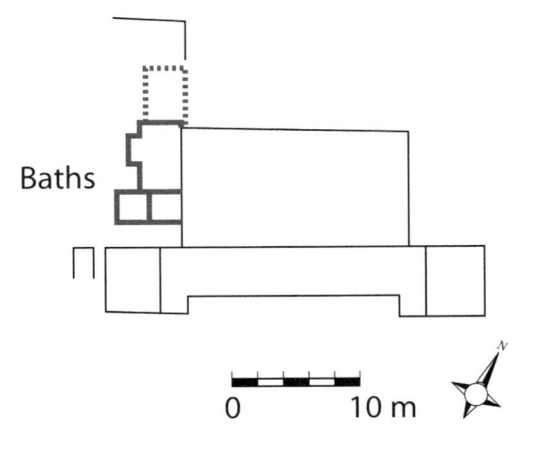

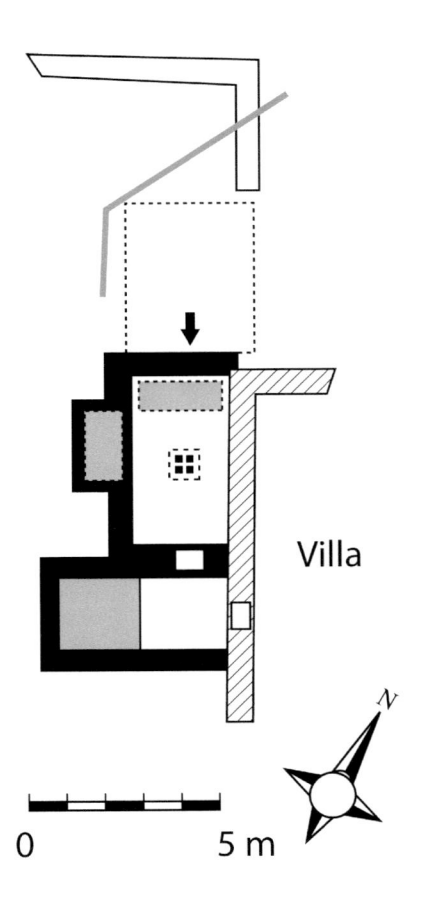

Figure 72. Location (top) and plan of the bath of Haillot. Figure by author after Lefert 2002, 244, unnumbered fig.

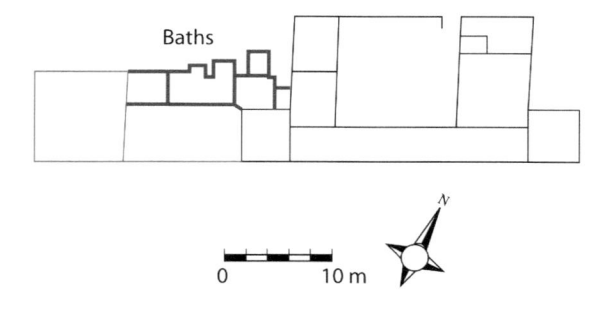

Baths

0   10 m

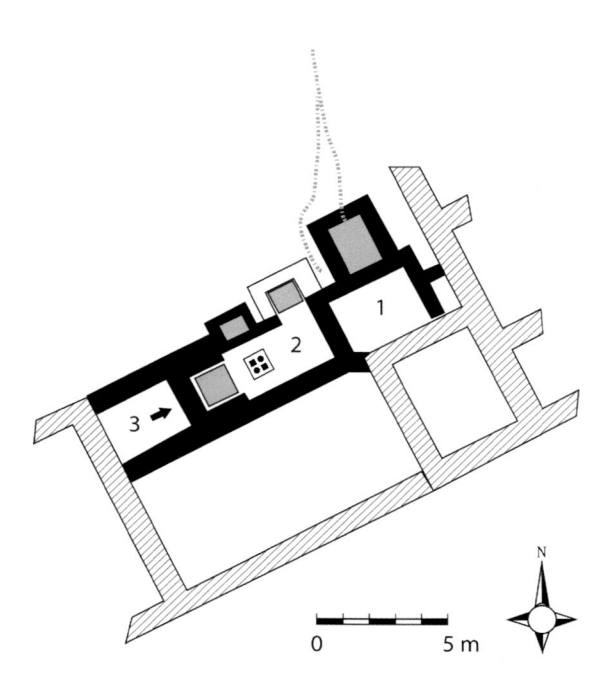

0   5 m

Figure 73. Location (top) and plan of the bath of Hamois. Figure by author after Van Ossel 1981, 134, fig. 96.

Hamois, Villa sur le Hody (ID 73)

1. 1.1 Belgium, Namur, Hamois.
    1.2 50°20′23.80″N; 5°9′33.27″E (approx.).
2. 2.1 1979–1980.
    2.2 Well preserved when excavated, now covered.
3.   Private bathhouse integrated in a villa.
4. 4.1 Possibly late second century (relative chronology of the building). A coin of Septimius Severus was found in the filling of the drain.
    4.2 Unknown.
    4.3 Unknown.
5.   A (pools, hypocausts).
6. 6.1 *c.* 77 m².
    6.2 Linear row type.
    6.3 None.
    6.4 The *frigidarium* (1) (3 × 2.5 m) had a small rectangular *piscina* (1.85 × 1.50 m) on its northern side. This pool showed at least two different phases: its bottom was deepened and repaired with hydraulic mortar.
    6.5 The only room with a hypocaust (2) had one square and one rectangular *exedra* to lodge *alvei*. The latter was added at a later date by piercing the northern wall. On the west side, above the furnace channel, a third *alveus* might have been present.
7. 7.1 The *praefurnium* (3) (3.4 × 2.2 m) lay west of the heated room. The furnace channel was delimited by two narrow parallel walls. The actual fire was probably lit on the slab of schist just in front of the furnace channel. The hypocaust pillars were made with round tiles (diam.: 23 cm), with the exception of those underneath the later *alveus*, which were square (s.: 25 cm).
    7.2 Several fragments of *tubuli* were found (no dimensions given).
    7.3 No traces of water pipes were discovered. South of the villa, a large well was identified. Two small sources in the vicinity of the site lay on lower grounds.
    7.4 The *piscina* was drained by an outlet in its northern side. A channel of inverted *imbrices* led to a drainage channel heading north, made of stone slabs. The water of the second later *alveus* was also discharged in this drainage channel.
8.   Many fragments of painted wall plaster, some with floral design, were found in the debris of the heated room.
9.   Fig. 73.
10.   Mertens 1968 (ER); Van Ossel 1980 (ER); 1981 (ER); Lefert, Bausier, and Nachtergael 2002 (ER); Brulet 2008, 536.

Heer, Bakkerbos (ID 74)

1.   1.1   The Netherlands, Limburg, Maastricht.
      1.2   50°50'15.16"N; 5°45'19.03"E (exact).
2.   2.1   1879.
      2.2   Partially preserved when excavated, now covered or destroyed.
3.   Private bathhouse (?) integrated in a villa.
4.   4.1   Unknown. The villa site was in use between the second half of the first and at least the late second century (ceramics and coins on site).
      4.2   Unknown.
      4.3   None. The villa seems to have been destroyed by a fire.
5.   C (hypocaust, possible pools).
6.   6.1   Min. 10 m² (plan unclear).
      6.2   Single room? (plan unclear).
      6.3   Unknown (plan unclear).
      6.4   According to the excavators, the bathroom may have had a cold and a hot pool. However, they do not present clear evidence to support this interpretation.
      6.5   The alleged bathroom (1) seems to have had a channel hypocaust, taking the form of an H. The excavators placed one heated and one cold pool above the 'arms' of the H, i.e. on the north and south side of the room. However, the only evidence for the presence of a pool consists of a drainage channel running southwards from the centre of the room.
7.   7.1   The excavation report mentions many round tiles for the construction of hypocaust pillars, but it is unknown in which room this hypocaust was located. A furnace was located west of the alleged bathroom.
      7.2   Several fragments of *tubuli* (box tiles) were found.
      7.3   Unknown. A well was located west of the villa, but no water pipes were found.
      7.4   A sewage channel ran underneath the alleged bathroom to the south.
8.   Several fragments of wall painting (polychrome, floral scenes) were found throughout the villa site (no exact location of the finds mentioned).
9.   Fig. 74.
10.   Habets 1895 (ER).

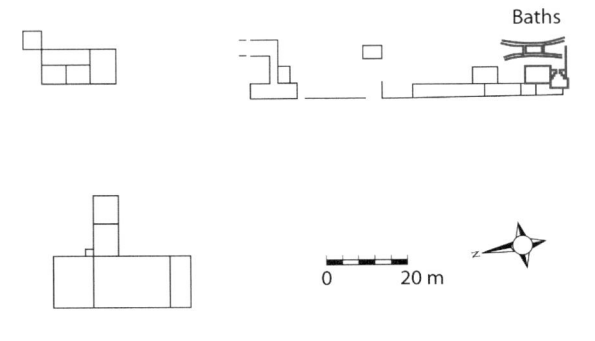

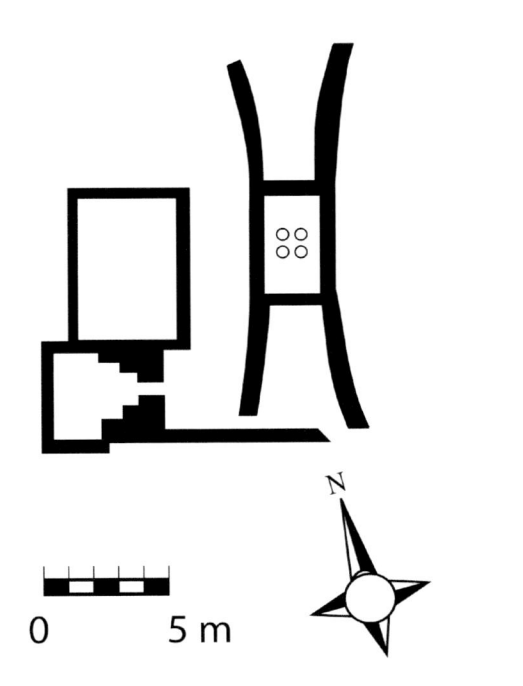

Figure 74. Location (top) and plan of the bath of Heer. Figure by author after Habets 1895, pl. II.

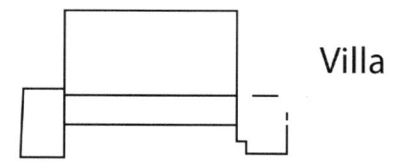

Villa

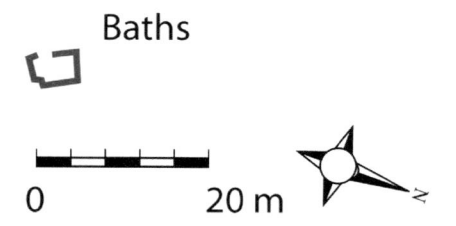

Baths

0   20 m

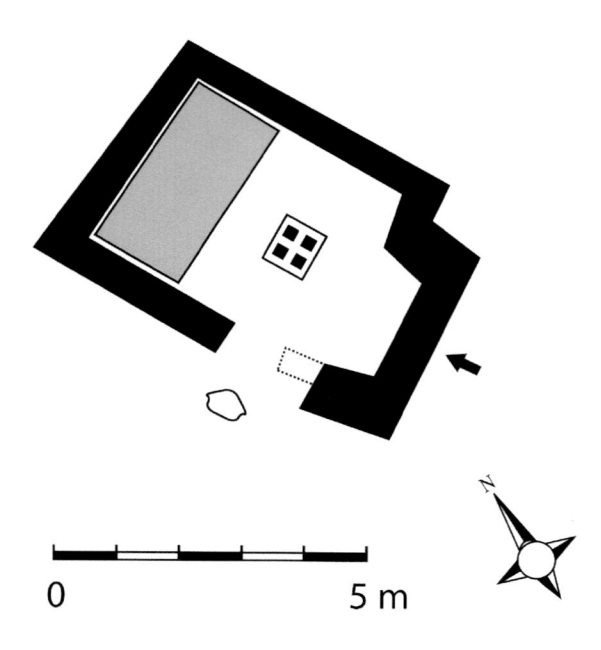

0   5 m

Figure 75. Location (top) and plan of the bath of Heestert.
Figure by author after Janssens 1984, 19, fig. 12.

Heestert, Blinde Kapel Villa (ID 75)

1.	1.1	Belgium, West Flanders, Zwevegem.
	1.2	50°47'43.55"N; 3°24'43.76"E (approx.).
2.	2.1	1980.
	2.2	Badly preserved at the time of excavations, now covered.
3.		Freestanding bathhouse of a villa.
4.	4.1	First century (contemporary or slightly later than villa; ceramics in older ditch underneath the baths).
	4.2	Second half of the second century (ceramics and coin in destruction layer).
	4.3	The shell of the baths was probably reused as a shed or stable in the Roman period. The restoration was carried out using wooden posts, including one blocking the furnace. In the early Middle Ages, the villa site was reused as a burial ground.
5.		A (strong evidence of a pool, hypocaust).
6.	6.1	c. 26 m².
	6.2	Single room.
	6.3	Not present.
	6.4	Not present.
	6.5	The bathhouse consisted of a single heated room. The north part of the room (around half of the surface) was a pool, built into the hypocaust. The southern half of the room was heated by a hypocaust. The southern niche may have housed a bench.
7.	7.1	No hypocaust pillars were recovered from the excavations. The furnace pierced the southern wall of the baths.
	7.2	Several fragments of *tubuli* were found in the destruction layer of the bath.
	7.3	Unknown.
	7.4	Several ditches ran along the building, possibly serving as a drainage channel for the pool.
8.		Fragments of wall painting (bluish-grey) and windowpane were found in the destruction layer.
9.		Fig. 75.
10.		Janssens 1980 (ER); 1984 (ER).

Heure-le-Romain, Bains Sur les Moulins (ID 76)

1.   1.1   Belgium, Liège, Oupeye.
     1.2   50°43′24.55″N; 5°37′49.97″E (approx.).
2.   2.1   1956.
     2.2   Well preserved when excavated, now covered or destroyed.
3.   Freestanding bathhouse of a villa.
4.   4.1   The bath was in use during the second and third century (ceramics on site).
     4.2   Unknown (third century?).
     4.3   Unknown.
5.   A (pools, hypocaust).
6.   6.1   Min. 21 m² (partial plan).
     6.2   Linear row type? (partial plan).
     6.3   A rectangular room (1) (2.2 × 1.6 m), possibly with a rounded northern side, gave access to the heated room. Besides a mortar floor, it had no specific amenities. It was interpreted by the excavators as an *apodyterium*.
     6.4   A rectangular room (2) with a floor of hydraulic mortar and an apsidal end on the south-east side of the building, can probably be interpreted as the *frigidarium*. It had a mortar consolidation in its southern corner, possibly to support a *labrum*. Its walls, made of flint and porous tuff, abutted the walls to the north, showing that this part of the building was added later.
     6.5   One room with a hypocaust (3) was excavated (3.3 × 3.1 m). Its walls were sturdier than the other rooms, undoubtedly for better insulation. The two rectangular recesses probably contained *alvei*. The south-western one was directly heated by the furnace.
7.   7.1   The hypocaust pillars were made with round tiles. The *praefurnium* (4) was located south-west of the *caldarium*. The floor of the furnace channel was made of bricks, bonded with clay. There was a considerable gap between this furnace floor and the wall of the *caldarium*, which remains unexplained. A base made of brick against the southern wall may have supported a boiler.
     7.2   Fragments of *tubuli* were found in the heated room.
     7.3   Unknown.
     7.4   Unknown.
8.   The floor of the cold room was made of several layers of mortar topped with terracotta tiles. Perhaps these were covered with mosaics or flagstones.
9.   Fig. 76.
10.   Peuskens and Tromme 1979, 402–06 (ER); Brulet 2008, 429–30.

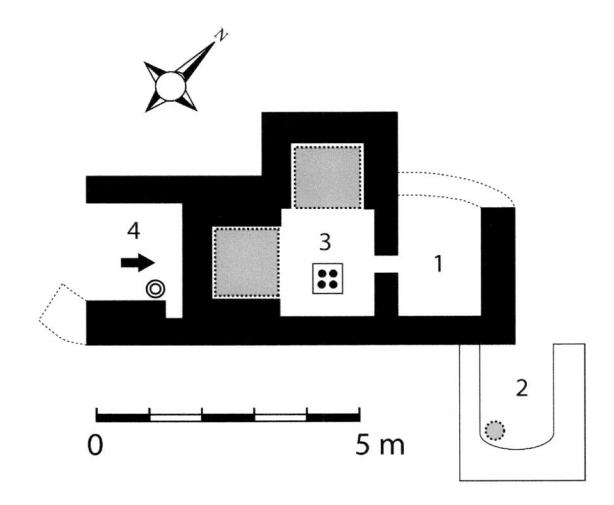

Figure 76. Plan of the bath of Heure-le-Romain. Figure by author after Peuskens and Tromme 1979, 411, pl. III.

Hollain, Les Bas de Bléharies (ID 77)

1. 1.1 Belgium, Hainaut, Brunehaut.
    1.2 50°32'24.92"N; 3°24'40.62"E (approx.).
2. 2.1 1952–1960 (mainly prospection).
    2.2 Well preserved when discovered, now covered or destroyed.
3.   Part of a bathhouse?
4. 4.1 High Empire (ceramics and small finds on site).
    4.2 Unknown (site is still in use in the fourth century, based on the finds assemblage).
    4.3 Unknown.
5.   C (hypocaust, evidence for pool).
6. 6.1 Min. 25 m² (partial plan).
    6.2 Unknown (partial plan).
    6.3 Unknown (partial plan).
    6.4 Unknown (partial plan).
    6.5 At least two rooms were heated by a hypocaust. The northernmost was slightly smaller (3 × 3.6 m) than the southern room (3 × 4.6 m). There was a space of 2.8 m between both rooms. The connection between the rooms is unclear. Further to the north, a third room with hypocaust (3.6 × 4.8 m) was identified. It had a *praefurnium* to the north-west (2.45 × 1.85 m), in which a piece of lead was found (part of a *fistula* or pool?). This room probably belonged to a separate building or part of the building (villa?).
7. 7.1 The hypocaust pillars of the separate room to the north were made with square tiles (s.: 17 cm; 2–3 cm tick). The hypocausts to the south had pillars made of almost square tiles (16 × 18.5 cm; 3 cm thick).
    7.2 In the southernmost hypocaust, several fragments of *tubuli* were found.
    7.3 A well (5 m deep) was discovered north-east of the two southern heated rooms.
    7.4 Unknown.
8.   In the southernmost room, several fragments of polychrome wall painting were found.
9.   Fig. 77.
10.   Amand 1962 (ER); Brulet 2008, 319–20.

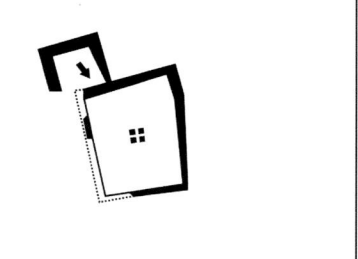

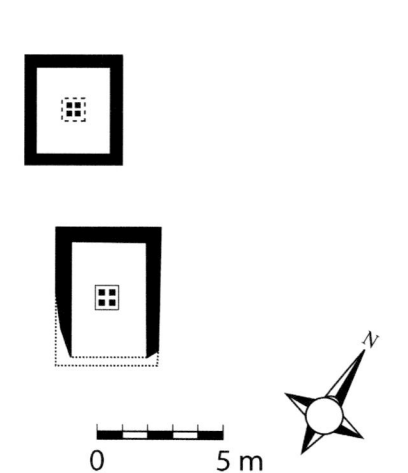

Figure 77. Plan of hypocaust found in Hollain. Figure by author after Amand 1962, 108, pl. VIII, fig. 3; 110, pl. IX, fig. 4 and 111, pl. X, fig. 5.

Hoogeloon, Kerkakkers (ID 78)

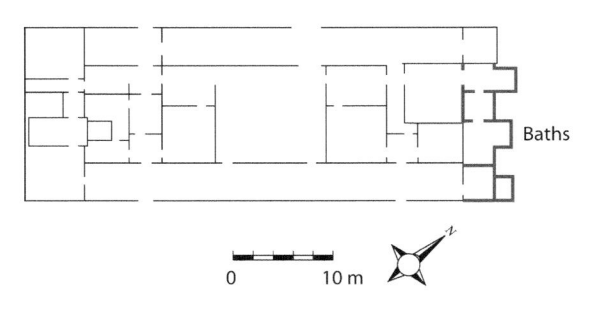

1. 1.1 The Netherlands, north Brabant, Bladel.
    1.2 51°23'53.31"N; 5°16'16.45"E (approx.).
2. 2.1 1980–1987.
    2.2 Partially preserved when excavated, now destroyed.
3. Private bathhouse integrated in a villa.
4. 4.1 Possibly second half of the second century (relative chronology of the site). The baths were added in a later phase to the original villa plan.
    4.2 The villa fell out of use in the third century (ceramics in destruction layers).
    4.3 Large parts of the villa, including the baths, were dismantled for building material after abandonment.
5. A (pools, hypocausts).
6. 6.1 *c.* 120 m².
    6.2 Angular row type.
    6.3 A large room (1) (6 × 6.15 m) lying in an angle to the main north-west–south-east axis of the bath, may have been a multipurpose *apodyterium* (room for undressing, anointing, massages). It may have been (indirectly?) heated by a hypocaust. The function of the room (2) on the north-west end of the bathhouse is unknown (*apodyterium*? *Unctorium*?).
    6.4 The *frigidarium* (3) had a rectangular *exedra* to lodge the *piscina* (1.95 × 1.7 m; 0.8 m deep). Few other features of the room (i.e. the type of floor) were preserved.
    6.5 The bathhouse had a single heated room (4) which may have been subdivided into a *tepidarium* (north) and a *caldarium* (south). On the south-eastern end of the room, above the furnace channel, an *alveus* must have been present (the walls are also sturdier here). A rectangular *exedra* on the north-eastern side may have housed a second pool or a *labrum*.
7. 7.1 No hypocaust pillars were found *in situ*, but several (fragments of) round hypocaust tiles (diam.: 20–23 cm) were found throughout the site. The *praefurnium* (5) (2.8 × 3.3 m) lay south of the *caldarium*. The furnace channel was made of inverted *tegulae*. A rectangular structure on the east side of the *praefurnium* (2 × 2.75 m) may have been a water reservoir.
    7.2 Several fragments of *tubuli* were found (box type). Two types could be identified (11–14 × 21–23 × 16–18 cm and 24–35 × 8–12.5 × 26–32 cm). Both types were used in the heated room(s) of the baths.
    7.3 The excavators suggest that the water was supplied by a well north of the villa. Iron rings support the thesis that wooden water pipes were used. Rain catchment from the roof would also have been an option. A bronze water tap, making it possible to mix hot and cold water, was also found near the bath.
    7.4 Two ditches ran from the baths to the south. One started at the *piscina* and the other at the *caldarium*.
8. Fragments of window glass were found throughout the site. The vast majority (*c.* 85 per cent) of the painted wall plaster (polychrome plains and lines, floral designs, figures, possible marble imitation) was found in or near the bath.
9. Fig. 78.
10. Slofstra 1982 (ER); Hiddink 2014 (ER).

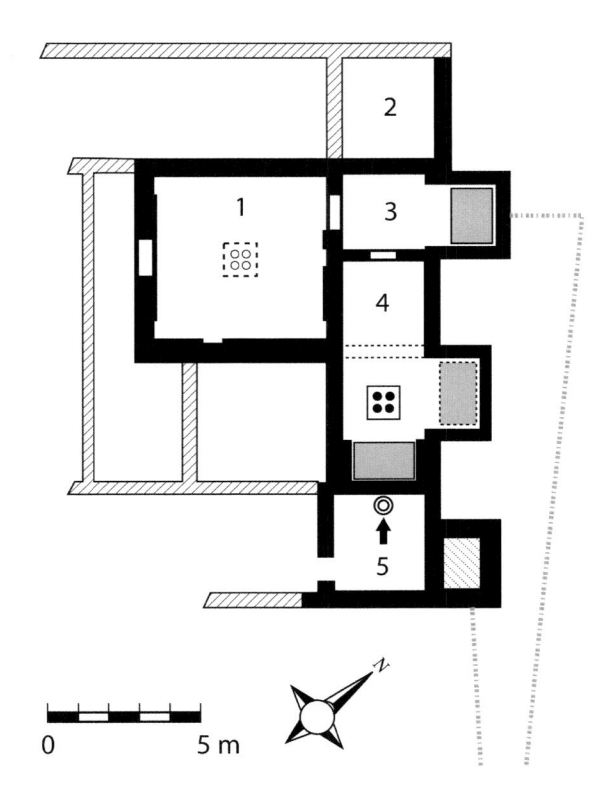

Figure 78. Location (top) and plan of the bath of Hoogeloon. Figure by author after Hiddink 2014, 1145, pl. 35 and 1146, pl. 36.

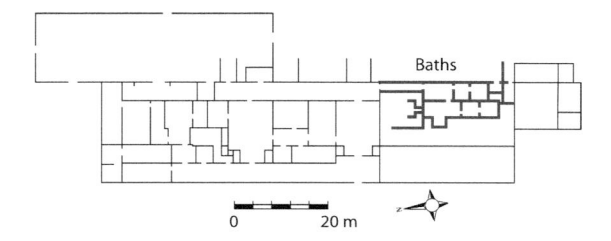

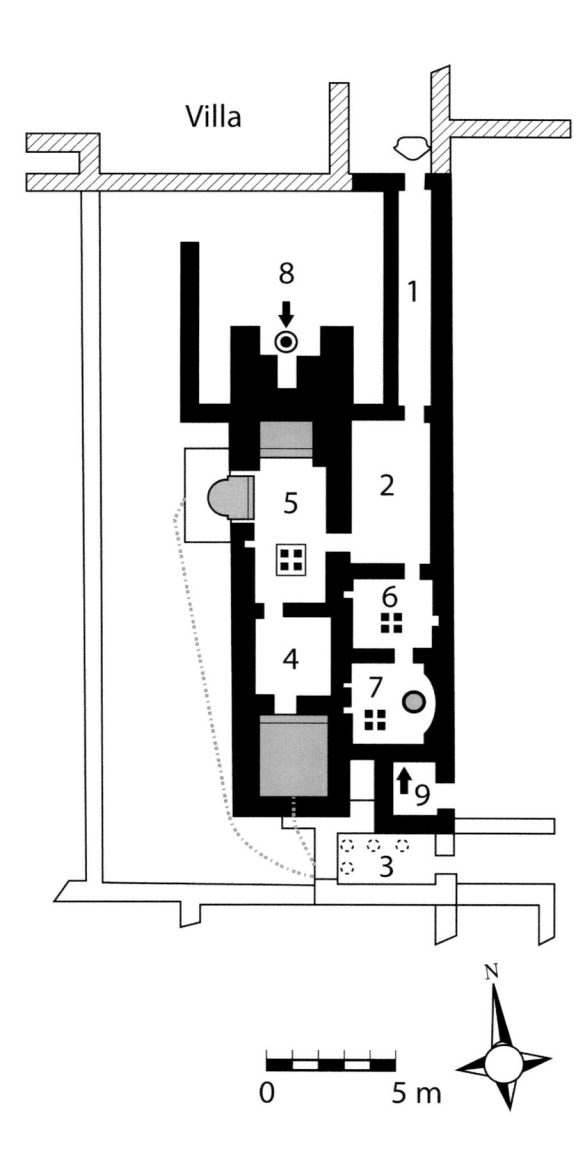

Figure 79. Location (top) and plan of the bath of Jemelle.
Figure by author after De Maeyer 1937, 88, fig. 21a.

Jemelle, Villa de La Malagne (ID 79)

1. 1.1 Belgium, Namur, Rochefort.
   1.2 50°9'41.11"N; 5°14'25.60"E (exact).
2. 2.1 1894, 1993.
   2.2 Well preserved when excavated, now restored and open to the public.
3. Private bathhouse integrated in a villa.
4. 4.1 Unknown. The villa was built after the first century, but the baths were added during a later phase. The baths were restored in a second phase.
   4.2 The villa was destroyed by a fire during the third century.
   4.3 Unknown. Some smaller buildings on the villa estate were reoccupied during the (early) fourth century.
5. A (pools, hypocausts).
6. 6.1 c. 250 m².
   6.2 Block type.
   6.3 A corridor (1) with a mortar floor connected the villa to the bathhouse. The first room (2) was identified as apodyterium (5.7 × 3.27 m) by the excavator. It gave access to two heated rooms to the south and a heated room to the west. A latrine (3) was added in a later phase south of the baths. It could be entered from the outside of the villa.
   6.4 The frigidarium (4) (3.3 × 3.4 m) was oddly located at the centre of the baths, and had a piscina (3.1 × 2.8 m) to the south. This pool had a single step (24 cm wide, 50 cm high) along its north side, from which it was entered.
   6.5 The caldarium (5) (6.55 × 2.75 m) connected to the 'apodyterium' (2) and the frigidarium (4). It had a rectangular exedra on its west side to lodge a pool (bottom at 40 cm below the floor level). During the restoration phase, the shape of the alveus was altered to form a semicircular apse on its western side. Presumably there was a second alveus above the furnace on the north side of the room. The two heated rooms connecting to the apodyterium have been identified as tepidarium (6) (3.27 × 2.85 m; indirectly heated) and sudatorium (7) (3.42 × 3.65 m; directly heated). A labrum was found near the latter, which probably stood in the apse on the east side.
7. 7.1 The caldarium had a spacious praefurnium (8) to the north, with the actual furnace lying at a lower level than the room. The sudatorium was heated from its own small praefurnium to the south (9). A small space to its west has been interpreted as fuel storage. The hypocaust pillars were made with square tiles (24 × 24 cm; 5 cm thick).
   7.2 Some tubuli (box type, no dimensions given) were found in situ along the semicircular alveus. The tepidarium and sudatorium had flue channels housed in the walls, which points to an absence of wall heating.
   7.3 Unknown. Several sources are found in the vicinity of the villa, as close as 250 and 500 m from the main building. A fragment of a lead fistula was found near the bath.
   7.4 The piscina was drained by an outlet (diam. 10 cm) in its south wall. The semicircular alveus was equipped with a new drain during the restoration phase (20 cm wide). It connected to the drainage channel of the piscina and then flushed the

latrines (wrongly identified as the slaves' baths by the original excavation report).

8. The *piscina* had a floor of terracotta tiles.
9. Fig. 79.
10. Mahieu 1897 (ER); Mignot 1994c (ER); Mignot, Van Neer, and Toussaint 1995 (ER); Brulet 2008, 572.

Kortrijk, Onze-Lieve-Vrouw Kerk (ID 80)

1. 1.1 Belgium, West Flanders, Kortrijk.
   1.2 50°49'45.39"N; 3°16'3.00"E (exact).
2. 2.1 1995–1997.
   2.2 Partially preserved when excavated, now destroyed.
3. Public bathhouse?
4. 4.1 Possibly late antique. The coins and ceramics found on site point to a phase of use between the fourth and possibly early fifth century.
   4.2 Early fifth century? (ceramics on site).
   4.3 The present church was later built over the Roman remains. A burial was found inside the former bathhouse.
5. C (hypocaust, evidence of a pool).
6. 6.1 Min. 7 m² (partial plan).
   6.2 Unknown (partial plan).
   6.3 Unknown (partial plan).
   6.4 Unknown (partial plan).
   6.5 At least one room was heated by a hypocaust. As the furnace was not located and no other rooms were found, it is difficult to assign a function. Heavy fragments of hydraulic mortar could point to the presence of an *alveus*. The room could then be interpreted as the *caldarium*.
7. 7.1 The hypocaust pillars were made with square tiles (s.: 17.4 cm; 3.8 cm thick), bonded with mortar.
   7.2 Several fragments of *tubuli* were found (box type). These had round lateral openings (diam.: 4.8 cm).
   7.3 Unknown.
   7.4 Unknown.
8. Fragments of wall painting were found among the debris of the heated room (red, light green, and ochre planes).
9. Fig. 80.
10. Despriet 1997 (ER).

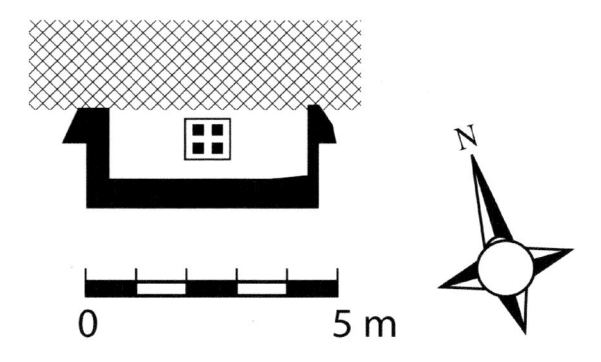

Figure 80. Plan of the hypocaust of Kortrijk O.L.V. Kerk. Figure by author after Despriet 1997, unnumbered page, unnumbered fig.

Kumtich, Villa Mellenberg Bath 1 (ID 122)

1.   1.1   Belgium, Flemish Brabant, Tienen.

     1.2   50°48'19.51"N; 4°54'46.68"E (approx.).

2.   2.1   1981.

     2.2   Partially preserved when excavated (through trenches), now reburied.

3.   Freestanding bathhouse of a villa.

4.   4.1   Unknown.

     4.2   The bathhouse was dismantled at the end of second or early third century (stratigraphy).

     4.3   The bathhouse was replaced by a larger bathhouse on the same location (Villa Mellenberg 'Bath 2').

5.   A (pools, hypocausts).

6.   6.1   *c.* 100 m².

     6.2   Linear row type.

     6.3   One of the heated rooms might have been a heated *apodyterium*. The excavators interpreted the southernmost room as such, locating the entrance to the baths here as well. This would mean the *frigidarium* was located at the end of the bathing itinerary, directly next to the *caldarium*, which is very unlikely.

     6.4   The *frigidarium* (4.2 × 3.7 m) should be located on the north-eastern end of the baths (1). Together with the *praefurnium* to its north (2), it was the only room without hypocaust. The location of a possible *piscina* is unknown. The excavators reconstructed it in the southern corner, where a fragment of mosaic floor was found *in situ*. This floor lay 13 cm lower than the hypocaust floors, which prompted the excavators to place a pool here. However, there is still the possibility that the heated rooms lay higher than the outdoor walking level. Bathers should then mount a few steps to access the part of the baths on hypocaust. Furthermore, the mosaic floor is not embedded in a hydraulic mortar, making it unlikely it was the floor of a *piscina*.

     6.5   A suite of three north-east–south-west oriented rooms (3–4–5) west of the *frigidarium* was heated by a hypocaust, as well as a smaller room to the north (6), which was directly heated by the only furnace. The excavator interpreted this entire northern room (6) (2.6 × 3.1 m) as a heated pool. The location of such an *alveus* would be quite strange, as this would mean the *caldarium* should be placed directly next to the *frigidarium*, in the middle of the building, and would not be heated by its own furnace. Perhaps the small room (6) was a *sudatorium* which could be accessed from the *tepidarium or* heated *apodyterium* (4.15 × 2.35 m) to its south (3). On the hypocaust level, the small northern room was also connected to the middle of the three heated rooms (4), perhaps a *tepidarium* (4.2 × 2.85 m). The south-western room (5) might have been the *caldarium* (4.15 × 2.15 m), if a furnace was located to its south-west. The limited excavations and the construction of the second bath impede a clear understanding of this side of the building, which was heavily disturbed and was not excavated.

7.   7.1   The only *praefurnium* (2) that was discovered heated the small northern room. The furnace floor was made with tiles placed in rowlocks, while the furnace channel, protruding

75 cm into the hypocaust, was made with tiles and *tegulae*. From a technical point of view, it is questionable whether this would have been the only furnace, as the suite of north-east–south-west oriented rooms could only have been mildly heated by this furnace. A second furnace in the axis of these three rooms would make more sense. The hypocaust pillars of the suite of three rooms were made with square tiles (s.: 23.5 cm; 4 cm thick) bonded by loam. In the northern room, round tiles (diam.: 21.5 cm; 4 cm thick) were also used.

7.2   Unknown.

7.3   A well with an almost square plan was located south-west of the bathhouse. It was filled in when the bath was dismantled and was subsequently covered by the second bathhouse. Fragments of terracotta water pipes and iron rings of wooden pipes were found.

7.4   Unknown.

8.   Several fragment of greenish windowpane were discovered in the small northern room, as well as fragments of purple wall painting. The *frigidarium* had a black-and-white mosaic floor with geometric designs. Fragments of *suspensura* with mosaics still attached confirm that some if not all of the heated rooms also had mosaic floors.

9.   Fig. 81.

10.   Mertens 1981 (ER); Cramers 1984 (ER); Depraetere 2017.

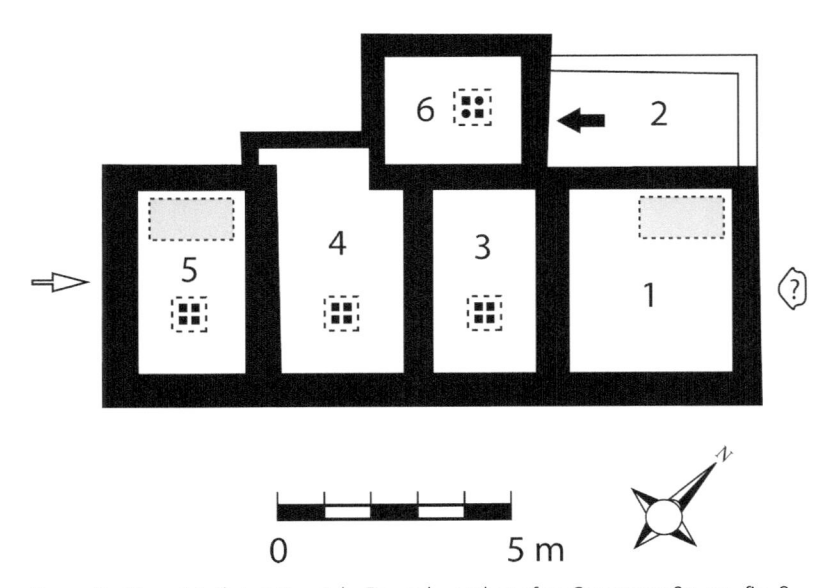

Figure 81. Plan of Bath 1 at Kumtich. Figure by author after Cramers 1984, 131, fig. 8.

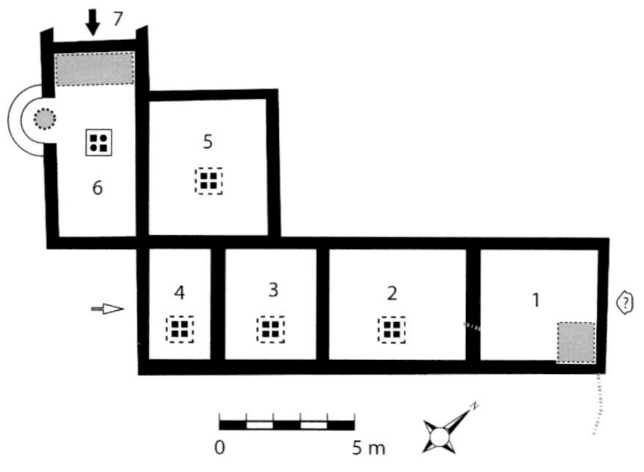

Figure 82. Plan of Bath 2 at Kumtich. Figure by author after Cramers 1984, 131, fig. 8.

Kumtich, Villa Mellenberg Bath 2 (ID 123)

1. 1.1 Belgium, Flemish Brabant, Tienen.
    1.2 50°48'19.51"N; 4°54'46.68"E (approx.).
2. 2.1 1981.
    2.2 Partially preserved when excavated (through trenches), now reburied.
3.   Freestanding bathhouse of a villa.
4. 4.1 The bath was constructed on top of the older Bath 1 (ID 122), which was dismantled in the late second or early third century (ceramics in debris).
    4.2 The bath was destroyed by a fire in the second half of the third century (no fourth-century material was found on site).
    4.3 The bath was partially spoliated for building materials and severely damaged in the nineteenth and twentieth century.
5.   A (pools, hypocausts).
6. 6.1 c. 225 m².
    6.2 Linear row type.
    6.3 The large rectangular heated room (5) (5.45 × 4.75) west of the suite of four north-east–south-west oriented rooms was interpreted by the excavators as heated *vestibulum*. By its position next to the *caldarium* (6) (to the south), an interpretation as *tepidarium* is perhaps more likely.
    6.4 The *frigidarium* should probably be located in the only room not heated by a hypocaust (1). The room at the north-eastern end of the suite of four rooms had a drainage channel starting in its eastern corner, presumably to drain an unidentified *piscina*.
    6.5 The oblong room with semicircular apse on the south-western end of the building was probably the *caldarium* (6) (7.45 × 3.3 m). It was heated by a furnace in its western side. Presumably, a heated pool was located against this side. The apse (diam.: 1.7 m) might have housed a *labrum*. The large room immediately to the north-east (5), indirectly heated, was probably the *tepidarium*. To the east, the three north-east–south-west oriented heated rooms (2–3–4) are difficult to interpret. The lack of any additional furnaces makes it unlikely that one of these functioned as *sudatorium*. Only if a furnace was present in the south side of the smallest of these rooms, which was not fully excavated and very badly preserved, this room might have been a *sudatorium* (4). In the middle of the three rooms (3), parts of 'benches belonging to the *suspensura*' were found. This may point to a function as heated *apodyterium*, or alternatively, these 'benches' should be interpreted as the steps of a pool. The easternmost heated room (2) could be interpreted as a heated *apodyterium* on the basis of its location next to the *frigidarium*. The north-eastern side of the hypocaust was fended off by a wall made of tiles and a drain pierced the wall to the *frigidarium*, perhaps pointing to the presence of a pool.
7. 7.1 The only *praefurnium* that was discovered (7) heated the *caldarium*. Parallel walls flanked the furnace channel inside the *praefurnium*. The furnace floor was made with tiles placed in rowlocks. The hypocaust pillars of the different heated rooms were made with almost square tiles (22.1 × 21.5 × 3.4 cm

and 25.5 × 25.0 × 4.5 cm). Round tiles (diam.: 29 cm; 4.2 cm thick) were only used in the apse, which may have been a later addition.

7.2   Several fragments of *tubuli* were found (with rectangular lateral openings).

7.3   The well that probably supplied the older Bath 1 was filled in and disappeared underneath the *caldarium*. The water was perhaps supplied by a source at some 1 km distance.

7.4   A shallow ditch (20 cm deep) ran from the east corner of the alleged *frigidarium* to a square sump (s.: 3.8 m). The drain that pierced the wall between the *frigidarium* and the easternmost heated room was constructed with tiles.

8.   Fragments of painted wall plaster were found throughout the bathhouse. In the middle room of the north-east–south-west oriented rooms, these wall paintings were a uniform red. Other wall paintings had a white background and coloured lines (in blue, brown, red). Hundreds of black and white tesserae made of local sand- and limestone, were found in the heated rooms. Fragments of windowpanes were also recovered.

9.   Fig. 82.

10.   Mertens 1981 (ER); Cramers 1984 (ER); Depraetere 2017.

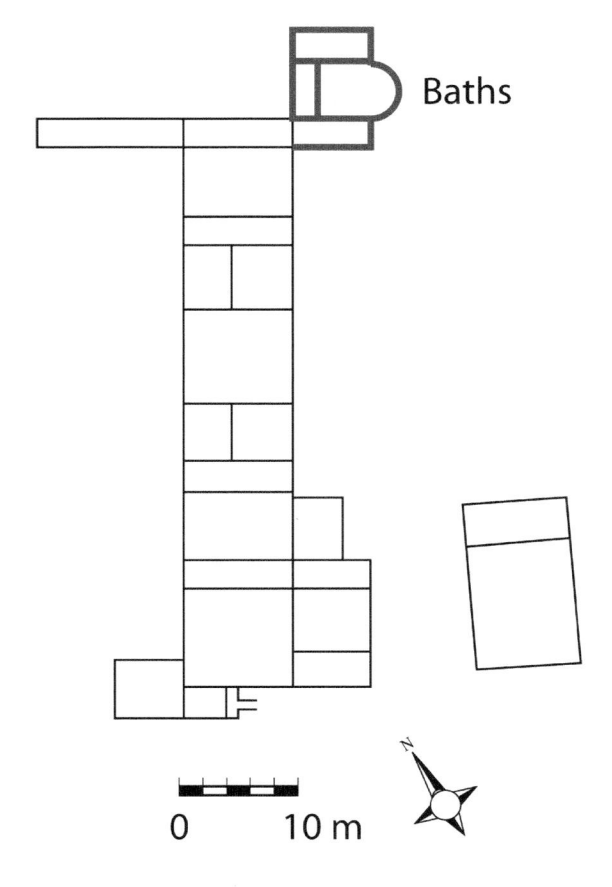

Landen, Villa Betzveld (ID 81)

1.   1.1   Belgium, Flemish Brabant, Landen.
     1.2   50°44'54.24"N; 5°5'28.00"E (approx.).

2.   2.1   1871.
     2.2   Well preserved when excavated, now reburied or destroyed.

3.   Private bath attached to a villa.

4.   4.1   Unknown.
     4.2   Unknown.
     4.3   Unknown.

5.   C (hypocausts, evidence for a pool).

6.   6.1   *c.* 94 m².
     6.2   Block type.
     6.3   An oblong room (1) that connected the bath to the villa may have been an *apodyterium*.
     6.4   Unknown.
     6.5   The largest central room of the bath (2), possibly the *caldarium*, had a semicircular *exedra* in its eastern side, possibly to lodge a pool.

7.   7.1   Unknown.
     7.2   Unknown.
     7.3   Unknown.
     7.4   Unknown.

8.   Unknown.

9.   Fig. 83.

10.   De Maeyer 1937, 68–70.

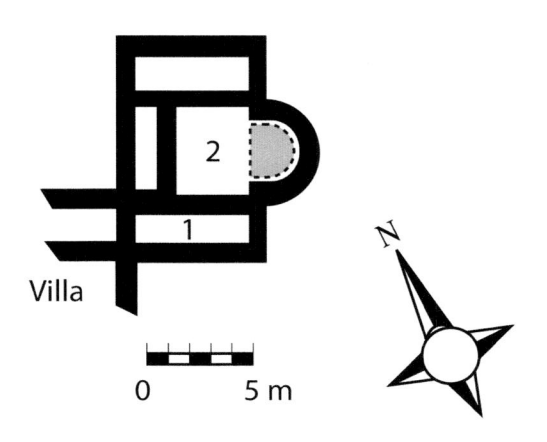

Figure 83. Location (top) and plan of the bath of Landen 'Betzveld'. Figure by author after De Maeyer 1937, 69, fig. 13.

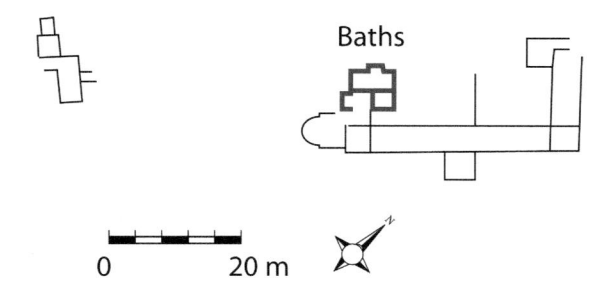

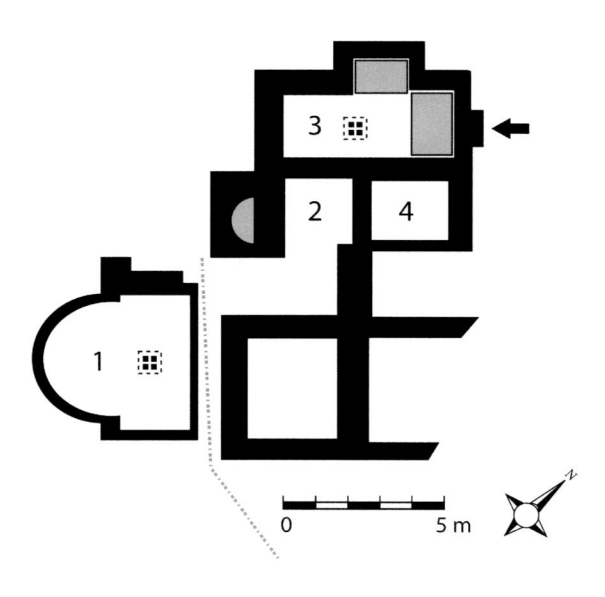

Figure 84. Location (top) and plan of the bath of Latinne.
Figure by author after Plumier 1984, 70, fig. 40.

Latinne, Villa des Grandes Pièces (ID 82)

1. 1.1 Belgium, Liège, Braives.
   1.2 50°37'40.51"N; 5°10'19.94"E (approx.).
2. 2.1 Partially excavated in 1903 and again in 1970 and 1979.
   2.2 Badly preserved when excavated, now destroyed or reburied.
3. Private bath integrated in a villa.
4. 4.1 The villa was constructed during the second century (ceramics on site).
   4.2 The villa was abandoned at the beginning of the third century (ceramics on site).
   4.3 The site was probably reoccupied during the fourth century (coins on site), but the bath was probably left in ruins.
5. A (pools, hypocausts).
6. 6.1 *c.* 45 m².
   6.2 Block type.
   6.3 Unknown. The plan is unclear. A room with a semicircular *exedra* (1) and heated by a hypocaust, taking the form of a channel hypocaust underneath the *exedra*, may have belonged to the bathing wing, but could also have been an audience hall or dinner room.
   6.4 The cold room (2) should probably be reconstructed south-west of the *caldarium*, where a semicircular apse within a rectangular *exedra* probably housed a *piscina*.
   6.5 Only one heated room could be identified (3), on the northern end of the bathing wing. It had two rectangular *alvei*, one in the axis of the room, above the furnace on the eastern end, and one in the northern rectangular *exedra*. The room (4) to the south-east of this *caldarium* might have been a *tepidarium*, but no hypocaust was discovered.
7. 7.1 The *praefurnium* was located east of the *caldarium*. The hypocaust pillars were made with square tiles.
   7.2 Unknown.
   7.3 Unknown. A natural spring was located some 500 m from the villa.
   7.4 A drainage channel made of *tegulae* seems to have started from the *piscina* and passed the heated apsidal room.
8. Several wall paintings, column drums, and mosaics were found in the villa, but the context is unfortunately unknown.
9. Fig. 84.
10. Renard 1903 (ER); Moureau 1979 (ER); Plumier 1984 (ER); Brulet 2008, 398–99. The old excavations are being re-examined by F. Vilvorder.

Leignon, Villa de Barcenne (ID 83)

1.   1.1   Belgium, Namur, Ciney.
     1.2   50°16′45.85″N; 5°5′42.05″E (approx.).
2.   2.1   1850.
     2.2   Fairly well preserved at the time of excavation, now destroyed.
3.   Freestanding bathhouse of a villa.
4.   4.1   Unknown (occupation of the site from at least in the late first century AD).
     4.2   Middle of the third century?
     4.3   Unknown.
5.   A (pools, hypocaust).
6.   6.1   *c.* 145 m².
     6.2   Linear row type? (plan unclear).
     6.3   Two rooms of unknown function (1 and 2) are located on the eastern side of the bathhouse. To the south-west, a separate room (3) may have acted as *apodyterium*.
     6.4   The *frigidarium* (4) had a rectangular *piscina* housed in a western *exedra*.
     6.5   A rectangular north–south oriented heated room (5) with two adjacent rectangular *exedrae* on its western side (for *alvei*?) could be interpreted as *caldarium*. An *alveus* might also have been present at the northern end of the room. The oblong shape could indicate that this room was divided at *suspensura* level into a *tepidarium* (south) and *caldarium* (north); each with an *exedra*.
7.   7.1   The hypocaust pillars were made of square tiles, bonded by clay. Some *tegulae* had the stamp HAMSIT.
     7.2   Several *tubuli* (box type, no dimensions given) with lateral openings were found.
     7.3   Unknown.
     7.4   The *piscina* was drained by an outlet in its northern side.
8.   Fragments of polychrome wall painting were found.
9.   Fig. 85.
10.   Hauzeur 1851 (ER); Brulet 2008, 514–15.

Baths

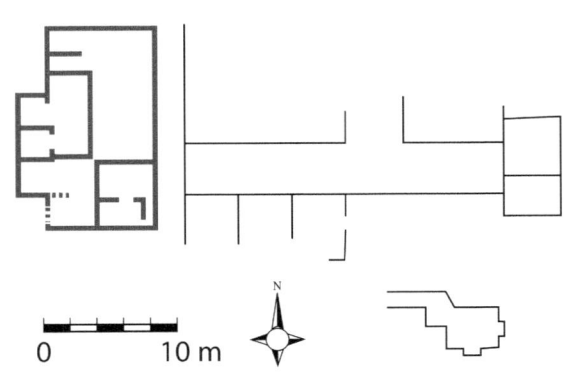

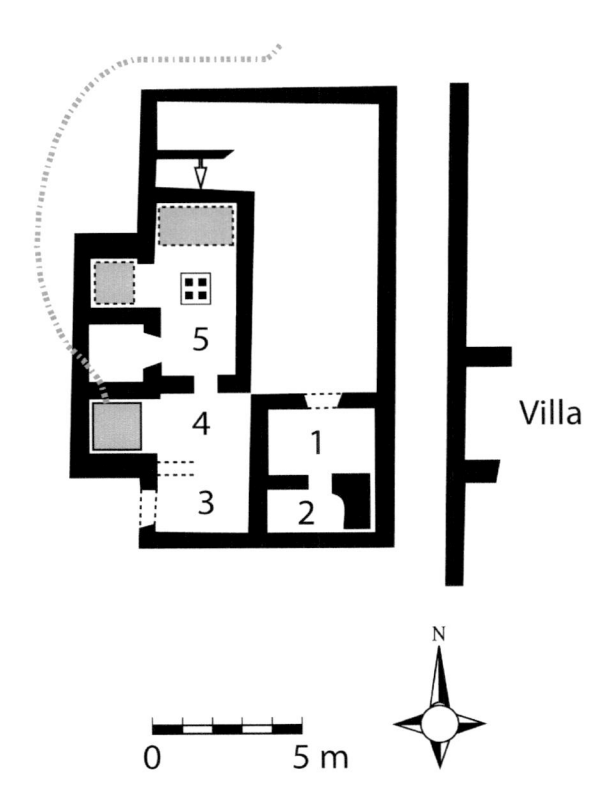

Villa

Figure 85. Location (top) and plan of the bath of Leignon. Figure by author after Brulet 2008, 515, fig. 426.

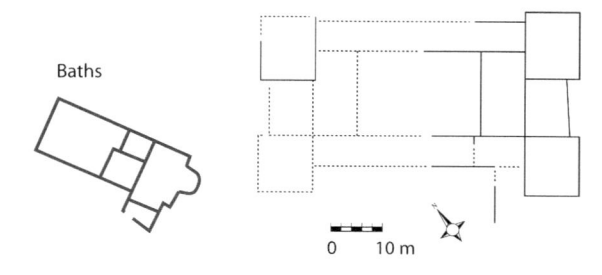

Baths

0   10 m

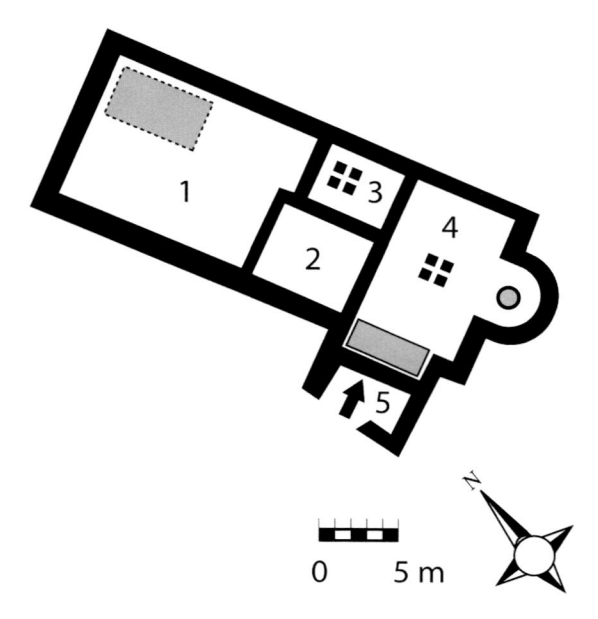

1

3

2

4

5

0   5 m

Figure 86. Location (top) and plan of the bath of Lemiers. Figure by author after Braat 1934, 19, fig. 12.

Lemiers, Villa van Lemiers (ID 84)

1. 1.1 The Netherlands, Limburg, Vaals.
    1.2 50°47'4.29"N; 5°59'42.14"E (approx.).
2. 2.1 1930.
    2.2 Well preserved when excavated, now covered.
3.   Freestanding bathhouse of a villa.
4. 4.1 The villa was constructed in the early second century (ceramics on site).
    4.2 The entire site seems to have been abandoned by the late second or early third century (ceramics on site).
    4.3 Unknown.
5.   A (strong evidence for a pool, hypocaust).
6. 6.1 *c.* 132 m².
    6.2 Angular row type.
    6.3 A small almost square room (2) on the west side of the building was interpreted by the excavator as *apodyterium*.
    6.4 The large room (1) (13.5 × 9.5 m) on the north end of the building was interpreted as the *frigidarium*, with part of a mortar floor seen as base for a cold pool. However, there is no other indication of a paved floor.
    6.5 Two rooms were heated by a hypocaust. The smallest (3) (3.2 × 3.8 m) was indirectly heated and has been interpreted as the *tepidarium*. The larger room on the southern end of the building (4) must have been the *caldarium*. It had a small semicircular *exedra*, undoubtedly for a *labrum*, as suggested by the horseshoe-shaped base of stones lying underneath it. Along the western end of the room, where the hypocaust pillars were reinforced and the furnace channel was located, an *alveus* must have been present.
7. 7.1 The *praefurnium* (5) was located west of the *caldarium*. The limestone walls of the hypocaust were protected by a facing of *tegulae*. The pillars were made with square tiles. The hypocaust of the *caldarium* connected through an arched opening with the hypocaust of the *tepidarium*. The hypocaust pillars were made with *tegulae* instead of square tiles, topped by other *tegulae*. The draught inside the hypocaust was ensured by a chimney made of *imbrices* in the north wall.
    7.2 The presence of chimneys in both rooms suggests that there was no wall heating. However, in the heated room of the villa, fragments of *tubuli* were found.
    7.3 Unknown.
    7.4 Unknown.
8.   Unknown.
9.   Fig. 86.
10.   Braat 1934 (ER).

Liberchies, Les Bons-Villers (ID 5)

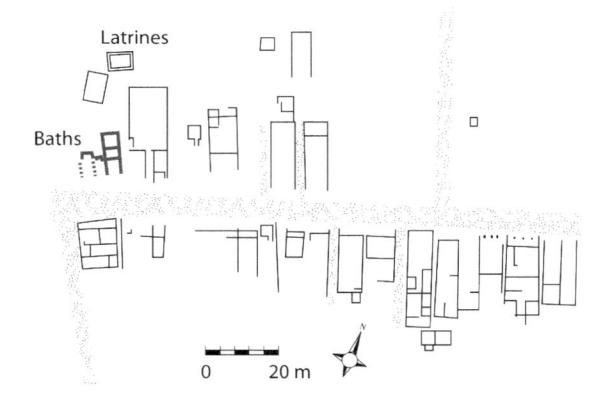

1.   1.1   Belgium, Hainaut, Pont-à-Celles.
       1.2   50°30'17.65"N; 4°26'2.93"E (approx.).
2.   2.1   1973, 1989–1990.
       2.2   Some parts badly preserved when excavated, now covered or destroyed.
3.   Public bathhouse of a small town.
4.   4.1   The baths were constructed on top of older structures during the second century (ceramics and coins in destruction layer of the older structure), and remained in use throughout the third century.
       4.2   Unknown.
       4.3   Unknown.
5.   A (pools, hypocausts).
6.   6.1   Min. 400 m²–max. 600 m².
       6.2   Unknown (partial plan).
       6.3   Unknown (partial plan). The southern part of the bathhouse was destroyed by the modern road.
       6.4   The *frigidarium* (1) (3 × 4.5 m) had a floor of hydraulic mortar, and a large *piscina* (5 × 5.2 m) on its northern side. It was accessible through some steps in its south-east corner. The cold section might have been added in a second phase (according to A. Bouet).
       6.5   Two rooms, each one heated by its own furnace, were discovered. The westernmost room (3) had a large *exedra* (2.4 × 3.4 m), possibly to lodge an *alveus*. The central room (2) also had an *exedra* on its north side (2.4 × 3.2 m), perhaps also for an *alveus*. It was later transformed into a *praefurnium*.
7.   7.1   The *exedra* of the westernmost room was heated by a furnace on its west side. The *exedra* of the central room had a furnace to the north. The hypocaust pillars were made with almost square tiles (20 × 21 cm; 5 cm thick). On one of these tiles, a stamp NPS was identified.
       7.2   Unknown.
       7.3   A source north-west of the bathhouse probably supplied the water. No traces of the water pipes were discovered.
       7.4   The water of the *piscina* was discarded through a drainage channel made of tiles and mortar. It headed north-west and possibly had a separate branch heading towards the public latrines, located some 25 m north of the baths.
8.   The *piscina* floor was paved with neatly cut, tightly fitting slabs of greenish schist from the Belgian Ardennes.
9.   Fig. 87.
10.   Brulet 1973a (ER); 1975, 25–27; Brulet and Demanet 1997, 12–36; Bouet 2003a, 682–83; Brulet 2008, 355.

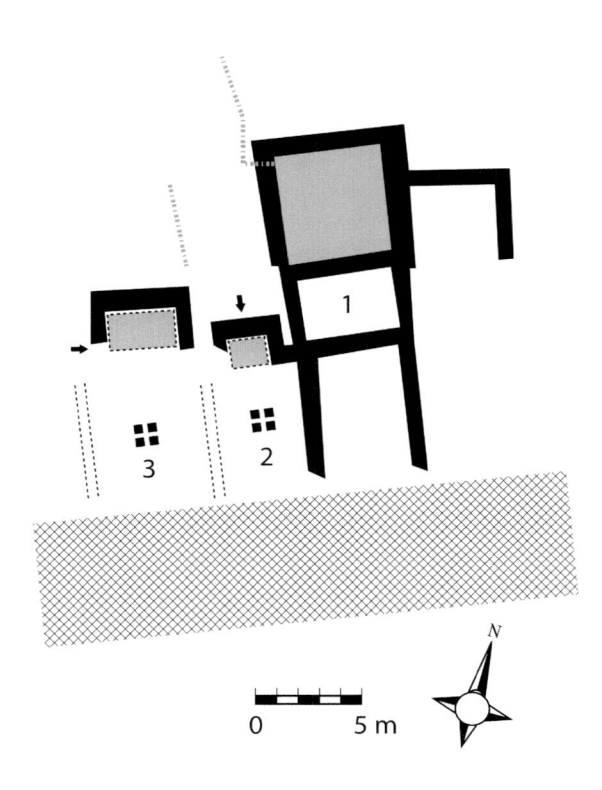

Figure 87. Location (top) and plan of the Vicus Bath of Liberchies. Figure by author after Brulet 2008, 355, fig. 127 and Brulet and Demanet 1997, 15, fig. 4.

Baths

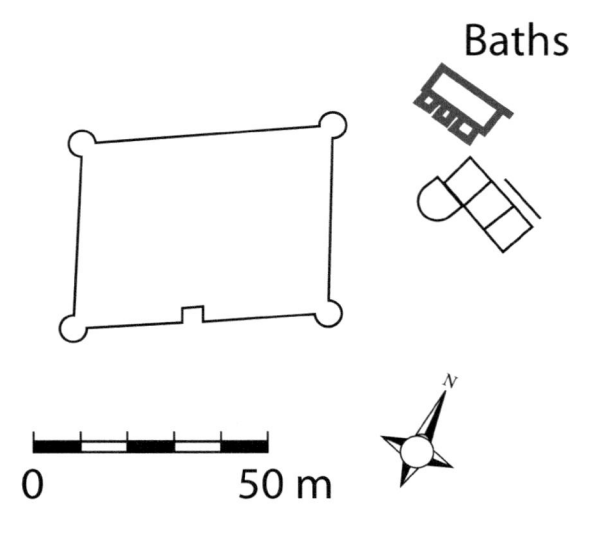

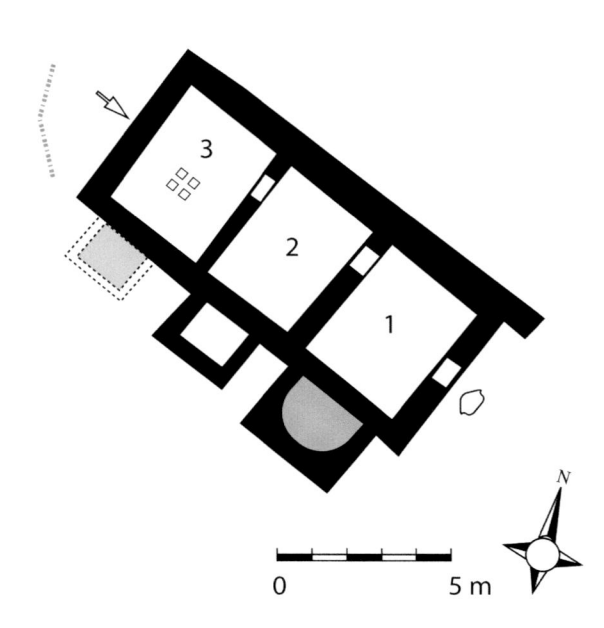

Figure 88. Location (top) and plan of the alleged fort bath of Liberchies. Figure by author after Brulet 2008, 243, fig. 357 and Mertens and Brulet 1974, pl. V.

Liberchies, Castellum de Brunehaut (ID 13)

1.	1.1	Belgium, Hainaut, Pont-à-Celles.
	1.2	50°30'2.84"N; 4°25'5.66"E (approx.).
2.	2.1	1968–1971.
	2.2	Partially preserved when excavated, now covered.
3.		Probable bathhouse of the late antique fort. A separate building with semicircular *exedra* to the south (see general plan) may have been a second bathhouse (according to A. Bouet), but the evidence is too scanty to make a clear identification.
4.	4.1	Early fourth century (a coin of Constantine underneath the baths gives a *terminus post quem*).
	4.2	Unknown. The fort was probably abandoned before the end of the fourth century.
	4.3	The building was heavily spoliated for building materials.
5.		C (evidence for pools, evidence for hypocaust, general plan).
6.	6.1	*c.* 123 m².
	6.2	Linear row type.
	6.3	None.
	6.4	The easternmost room (1) had a semicircular apse (diam.: 2.9 m) built in a rectangular *exedra*. Its floor of hydraulic mortar points to a *piscina*, even if the excavators have doubts due to the absence of water supply or drains. However, the walls are levelled to the walking level, making identification of such drainage pipes impossible. There was no trace of a mortar floor in the *frigidarium* itself, which could mean that there were wooden floors.
	6.5	The central room (2) had a rectangular *exedra* (2 × 1.5 m) paved with reused hypocaust tiles. No traces of mortar were discovered, excluding its use as pool. There was no evidence of a mortar floor in the room either. However, two wooden beams crossed the centre of the room from north to south. The excavators interpret this as a possible base for a dividing wall, but this would inconveniently 'cut' the *exedra* in half. Perhaps these beams supported wooden floorboards running east–west? The westernmost room (3) (*caldarium*?) also had a rectangular *exedra* (ext.: 2.75 × 2 m; for an *alveus*?), which was completely dismantled after the baths fell out of use. A small part of a mortar floor was still preserved in the south-eastern corner of the room. Several slabs of tuff formed a small paved zone abutting the western external wall. This may have been the floor of the furnace channel.
7.	7.1	Besides the reused hypocaust tiles in the central *exedra*, no traces of a hypocaust system have been preserved. The building was heavily spoliated for building materials, which apparently included the mortar floors.
	7.2	Unknown.
	7.3	Unknown.
	7.4	A drainage channel made of two parallel wooden beams and stones, covered with tiles, was found west of the bath. The channel seems to have curved towards the dismantled *exedra* of the westernmost room. This reinforces the hypothesis that an *alveus* was located there. A large wooden beam found north of the baths may also have been part of a drain.
8.		Unknown.
9.		Fig. 88.
10.		Mertens and Brulet 1974, 34–40 (ER); Bouet 2003a, 684–85; Brulet 2008, 360–61.

Liège, villa de la Place St-Lambert (ID 85)

1. 1.1 Belgium, Liège, Liège.
    1.2 50°38'41.89"N; 5°34'24.49"E (exact).
2. 2.1 1907, 1977–1984, 1990–1995.
    2.2 Badly preserved when excavated, now restored and open to the public.
3. Private bath integrated in a villa.
4. 4.1 The bath suite was a later addition to the villa in the late second century AD (ceramics on site).
    4.2 The bath probably fell out of use in the first half of the third century AD (ceramics on site).
    4.3 Unknown. The villa was inhabited until the fourth or fifth century.
5. A (pool, hypocausts).
6. 6.1 Min. 65 m² (partial plan, plan unclear).
    6.2 Block type?
    6.3 The rooms east of the cold pool may have belonged to the bath (1), acting as cold rooms (*apodyterium*? *Frigidarium*?).
    6.4 The room (2) to which the semicircular *piscina* (diam.: 3 m) opened, was probably the *frigidarium*, although the elongated shape is quite uncommon.
    6.5 To the north-west of the *piscina*, two small heated rooms (3 and 4) may have been part of the *caldarium* or *sudatorium*. The remains of the bathhouse are too damaged here to attempt identification. Another larger almost square room (6) in the north-eastern corner of the bath may have been a *tepidarium*. It was heated by its own furnace, located in the north-western corner, which was a later addition. Alternatively, this heated room did not belong to the baths, but was a heated living room. The rectangular room (5) that separated this heated room from the rest of the baths was apparently not heated by a hypocaust. Its function is unclear.
7. 7.1 A *praefurnium* (7) was located north of the two small heated rooms. The furnace channel, paved with bricks, prolonged into the *praefurnium*, pointing to the presence of a boiler. The furnace which heated the larger almost square room to the north-east, was pierced through the wall at a later date. The hypocaust pillars in this room were made with round tiles (diam.: 20–22 cm; 4 cm thick) and bonded by clay. At least one pillar was made with both round and square tiles (s.: 22 cm). The pillars reached a height of 60 cm.
    7.2 Unknown.
    7.3 A water channel arrived from the north into the *praefurnium* (possibly filling a boiler here). According to the excavators, the water was taken from a local source near the villa.
    7.4 The *piscina* was emptied by an orifice in its western side. The supply channel arriving at the *praefurnium* seems to have continued in the direction of the *piscina*.
8. Several fragments of windowpanes and fragments of Belgian and Italian 'marble' were found in the debris. The inside of the *piscina* was clad with slabs of stone.
9. Fig. 89.
10. Otte and Degbomont 1990 (ER); Léotard and Coura 1996; Brulet 2008, 422–23; Henrard, van der Sloot, and Léotard 2008.

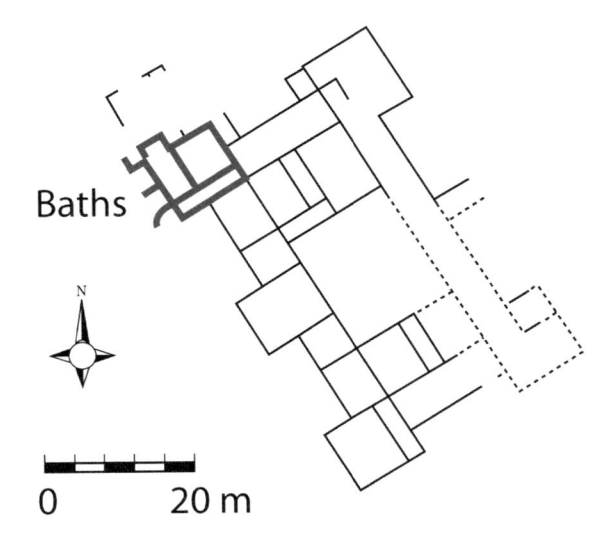

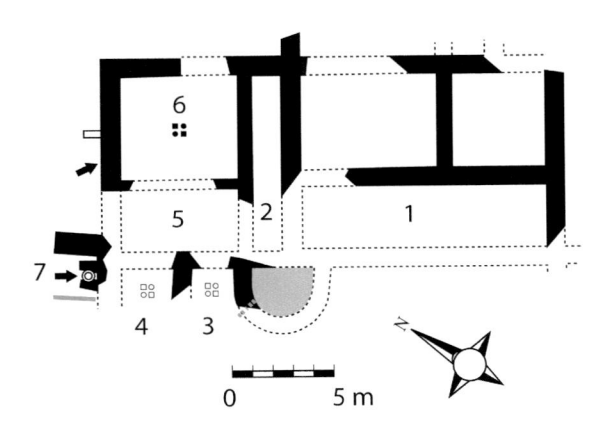

Figure 89. Location (top) and plan of the bath of Liège. Figure by author after Henrard, van der Sloot, and Léotard 2008, 106, unnumbered fig. and Otte and Degbomont 1990, unnumbered page, fig. 66.

Baths

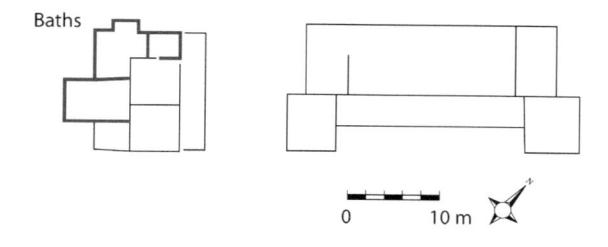

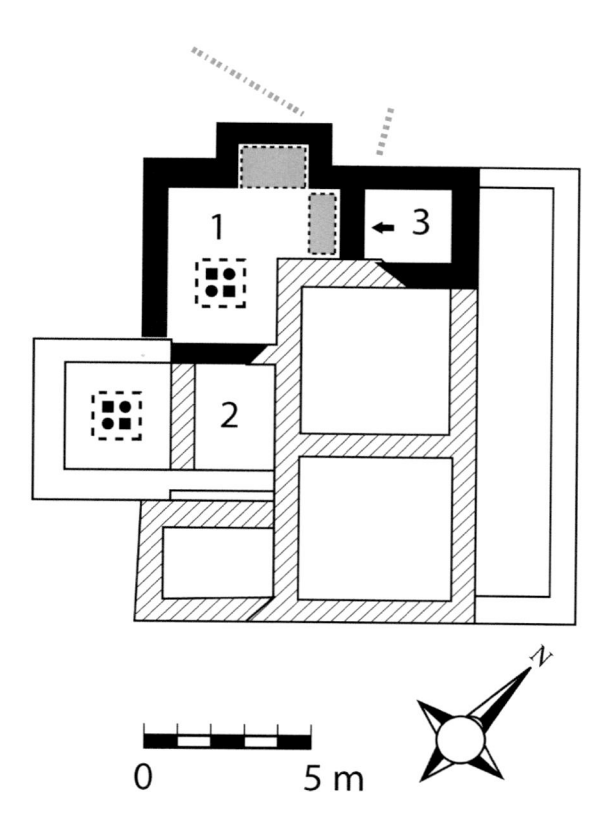

Figure 90. Location (top) and plan of the bath of Limerlé.
Figure by author after Brulet 2008, 467, fig. 342.

Limerlé, Villa de Rouvroy (ID 86)

1. 1.1 Belgium, Luxemburg, Gouvy.
    1.2 50°6'16.54"N; 5°53'41.37"E (approx.).
2. 2.1 1974–1976.
    2.2 Well preserved at the time of excavations, now covered or destroyed.
3. Freestanding bathhouse of a villa.
4. 4.1 Unknown (site in use between late first and third century), at least four phases.
    4.2 Unknown (before the third century).
    4.3 Unknown.
5. A (strong evidence for pools, hypocausts).
6. 6.1 *c.* 195 m².
    6.2 Angular row or ring type?
    6.3 The bathhouse had a long corridor running along its north-eastern side.
    6.4 No traces of a *piscina* were discovered.
    6.5 Two rooms with a hypocaust were added to the original plan of the western building. The north-western room (1) with its rectangular *exedra* was possibly the *caldarium* with an *alveus*. A *praefurnium* (3) was located north-east of it. The south-western heated room (2) may have been the *tepidarium*, as there are no indications that it was heated by a separate furnace.
7. 7.1 The type of hypocaust pillars is unknown.
    7.2 Unknown.
    7.3 Unknown.
    7.4 A drainage channel led westwards from the rectangular *exedra* (reinforcing the hypothesis that an *alveus* was located here).
8. In the alleged *tepidarium*, several fragments of wall painting were found.
9. Fig. 90.
10. Mertens 1974 (ER); 1975 (ER); Brulet 2008, 467–68.

Maastricht, Stokstraat (ID 14)

1.   1.1   The Netherlands, Limburg, Maastricht.
      1.2   50°50'54.03"N; 5°41'37.67"E (exact).
2.   2.1   Discovered and partially excavated in 1840, new excavations in 1963–1965.
      2.2   Partially preserved when excavated, now destroyed or covered.
3.   Public bath or baths of an urban *domus* (?).
4.   4.1   The baths were built on top of an earlier (domestic) structure, which was filled in with material dating from around AD 100. The baths must have been built in the (early) second century.
      4.2   Some coins, the latest dating from the reign of Claudius Gothicus (AD 268–270), were found on the *frigidarium* floor. By the end of the third or the beginning of the fourth century, the rooms were filled with debris.
      4.3   Unknown.
5.   A (pools, hypocausts).
6.   6.1   Min. 100 m² (partial plan).
      6.2   Block type?
      6.3   Unknown (partial plan).
      6.4   The *frigidarium* (1) lay north of the heated rooms and possibly doubled as an *apodyterium*. In a later phase, the cold room was enlarged with a small semicircular *piscina*, which could be accessed by three internal steps.
      6.5   At least two rooms heated by a hypocaust were found. The *caldarium* (3) had a semicircular *alveus* on its northern side and a rectangular *alveus* above the furnace (east side). The indirectly heated room (2) west of the *caldarium* must be interpreted as the *tepidarium* (*c.* 6.6 × 5.15 m). It connected to the *frigidarium* to the north.
7.   7.1   The furnace channel was made of tiles and measured 1.8 m in length and 0.66 m to 0.9 m in width. Above the furnace mouth, the remains of an iron grate, possibly to support a boiler, were still visible when excavated in the nineteenth century. The hypocaust pillars were made with square (s.: 22 cm; 5.5 cm thick) and round tiles (diam.: 22 cm; 4.2 cm thick).
      7.2   The *tepidarium* had wall heating by box-type *tubuli* (22 × 12.5 cm; 25 cm high) with circular lateral openings. These were found *in situ* up to a height of 1.8 m. In the *caldarium*, only three rows of *tubuli* were housed in a recess in the eastern wall.
      7.3   A water supply channel made out of bricks was found in the wall of the *frigidarium* to supply the *piscina*.
      7.4   The rectangular *alveus* was drained by a lead *fistula* in its south side.
8.   Several fragments of painted wall plaster were found in the heated rooms.
9.   Fig. 91.
10.   Leemans 1843, 38–61 (ER); Bogaers 1963 (ER); Bloemers 1973; Bouet 2003a, 685–86.

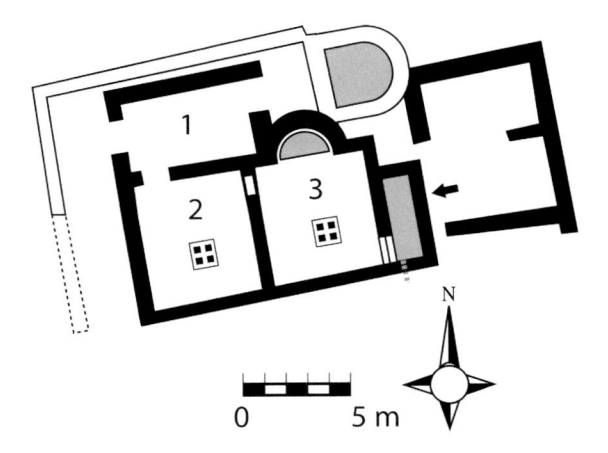

Figure 91. Plan of the bath at Maastricht. Figure by author after Bloemers 1973, 239, fig. 3.

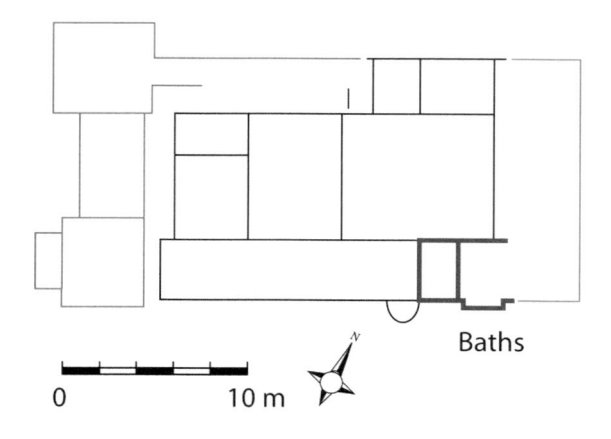

Baths

0   10 m

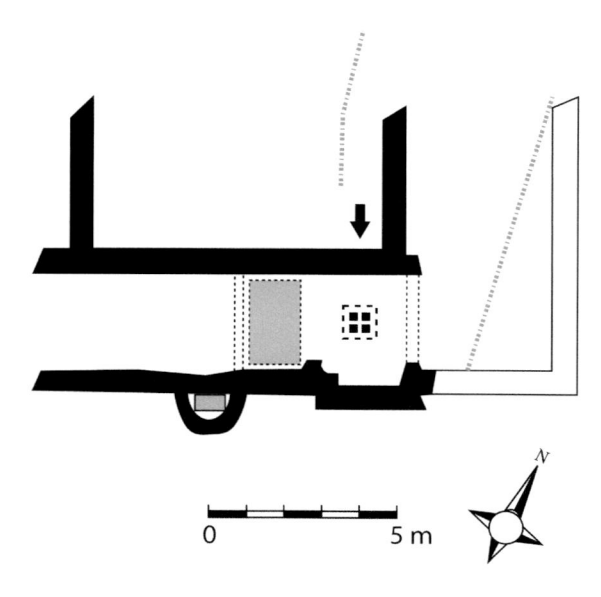

0   5 m

Figure 92. Location (top) and plan of the bath at Mabeuge.
Figure by author after Leman 1977, 286, fig. 8.

Mabeuge, Villa du Bois Brûlé (ID 87)

1.	1.1	France, Département du Nord, Mabeuge.
	1.2	50°17'52.31"N; 3°58'52.39"E (exact).
2.	2.1	1974.
	2.2	Partially preserved when excavated, now reburied or destroyed.
3.		Private bathhouse integrated in a villa.
4.	4.1	Unknown. The bath was added during a later phase of the (late first century?) villa. A construction date during the second century is probable.
	4.2	The villa was in use between the late first and the third century.
	4.3	Unknown.
5.		A (pool, hypocaust, sewage).
6.	6.1	Min. 17 m² (partial plan).
	6.2	Unknown (partial plan).
	6.3	Unknown (partial plan).
	6.4	Unknown (partial plan).
	6.5	At least one room heated by a hypocaust was discovered. It had a heated pool on its south-western side, which would identify this room as the *caldarium* with its *alveus*.
7.	7.1	The *praefurnium* was located on the north-western side of the *caldarium*, protruding into the large central space of the villa. The hypocaust pillars were made of square tiles (no dimensions given, although the pillar tiles from the heated angular pavilion were 20 × 20 cm).
	7.2	Unknown.
	7.3	Unknown.
	7.4	A drainage channel ran north-east of the baths, but the link between the two is unclear. It may have been a drainage channel for a cold pool. A second drainage channel ran from the *praefurnium* towards the north. It possibly drained the *alveus*.
8.		Unknown.
9.		Fig. 92.
10.		Leman 1975, 277; 1977, 285–86.

Machelen, Villa de Heuf (ID 88)

1. 1.1 Belgium, Flemish Brabant, Machelen.
    1.2 50°55'6.38"N; 4°26'44.74"E (exact).
2. 2.1 1954 (discovered during construction works).
    2.2 Badly damaged even before the excavations, now destroyed.
3.   Private bath integrated in a villa.
4. 4.1 Middle of the second century? (small finds).
    4.2 Unknown.
    4.3 Unknown.
5.   A (pool).
6. 6.1 Only a pool was identified.
    6.2 Unknown.
    6.3 Unknown (partial plan).
    6.4 A *piscina* (1.5 × 1.4 m) consisting of layers of pinkish hydraulic mortar on a bed of fieldstones and finished with a layer of *tegulae* is the only part that could be identified.
    6.5 Unknown.
7. 7.1 Unknown.
    7.2 Unknown.
    7.3 Unknown.
    7.4 Unknown.
8.   Unknown.
9.   Fig. 93.
10.   Mertens 1955.

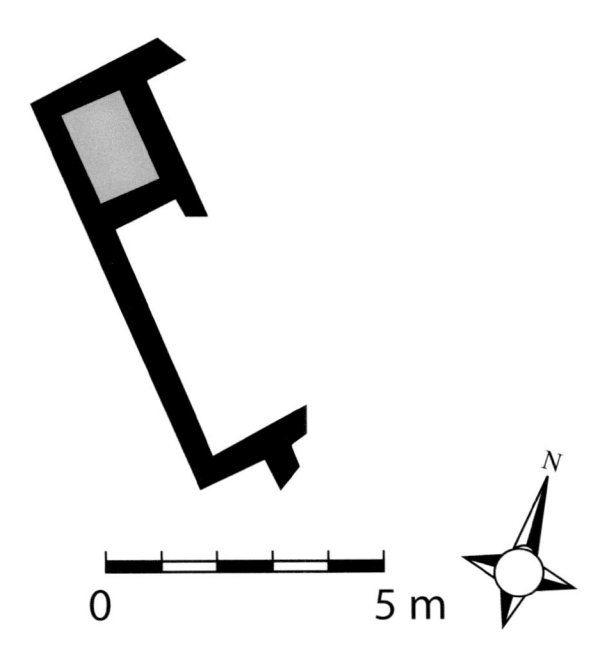

Figure 93. Plan of the bath at Machelen. Figure by author after Mertens 1955, 7, fig. 1.

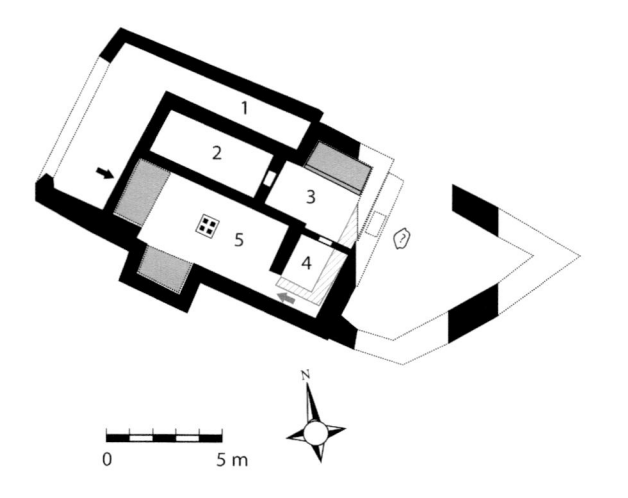

Figure 94. Plan of the bath of Macquenoise. Figure by author after Brulet 1985, 38, fig. 6.

Macquenoise, Balneum (ID 8)

1. 1.1 Belgium, Hainaut, Momignies.
   1.2 49°58'32.53"N; 4°10'47.38"E (approx.).
2. 2.1 1979–1980.
   2.2 Badly preserved in parts (north side) when excavated, now covered or destroyed.
3. Freestanding public bathhouse.
4. 4.1 Second half of the second or early third century (ceramics and coins found on site).
   4.2 Second half of the third century (ceramics in the abandonment layer).
   4.3 Unknown.
5. A (pools, hypocausts).
6. 6.1 *c.* 200 m².
   6.2 Angular row type?
   6.3 To the east and west of the bath, several walls in dry stone were identified. These might have formed annexes of the bath (fuel storage?). The L-shaped corridor (1), ending in the *praefurnium* to the south, may have had the function of an *apodyterium*, provided there was an entrance in the north-east side of the bathhouse. The rectangular room (2) (2.5 × 5 m) at the centre of the bath may also have been a cloakroom or room for massages, anointing, etc.
   6.4 The *frigidarium* (3) (2.2 × 3.6 m) had a *piscina* (1.4 × 2.8 m) on its north-eastern side. The room may have been accessed from the east. Unfortunately, this area was not excavated.
   6.5 Only one room (5) was heated by a hypocaust (5.5 × 10.25 m). It possibly had a pool in the southern rectangular *exedra* (1.5 × 2.2 m) and another one above the furnace to the west (1.5 × 2.4 m). This room was the *caldarium*. Just to its east, a small room (4) which covered the first phase *praefurnium*, might have been a *tepidarium* or a simple heat trap.
7. 7.1 The tiles of the hypocaust pillars were square (s.: 21 cm; 4 cm thick), having a smaller size in the corners of the room (s.: 14 cm). The *praefurnium* lay west of the hypocaust and was part of the corridor that encompassed the north side of the bathhouse. The furnace channel had a floor made of tiles, and small walls extending into the hypocaust.
   7.2 Fragments of *tubuli* were found (max. width 15.5 cm).
   7.3 Unknown.
   7.4 Unknown.
8. Fragments of glass (window?) panes were found.
9. Fig. 94.
10. Brulet 1980 (ER); 1985 (ER); 2008, 347–48.

Maillen, Villa Al Sauvenière (ID 89)

1. 1.1 Belgium, Namur, Assesse.
    1.2 50°22'30.96"N; 4°57'57.05"E (approx.).
2. 2.1 1889.
    2.2 Well preserved when excavated, now covered or destroyed.
3.   Private bathhouse attached to a villa.
4. 4.1 Unknown (villa site was in use from the second century).
    4.2 Unknown (villa site was abandoned in the fourth century).
    4.3 Unknown.
5.   A (pools, hypocausts).
6. 6.1 c. 150 m².
    6.2 Block type.
    6.3 A corridor (1) (8.15 × 2.7 m) led from an open courtyard to the *praefurnium* (north). The bath rooms lay to the east. A room (2) in the south-eastern corner of the bath (3.3 × 4.9 m) had no mortar floor. Instead, three charred east–west oriented wooden beams were discovered, which may have supported a raised wooden floor. This room may be interpreted as *apodyterium*.
    6.4 The room in the north-eastern corner (3) had a concrete floor and *piscina* (1.85 × 2 m) on its northern side. The floor of this pool was covered with terracotta tiles, while its walls were made of bricks covered in hydraulic mortar. The room can be identified as the *frigidarium*.
    6.5 Two rooms were heated by a hypocaust. The northernmost (5) was directly heated by its own furnace to the west. It had two *exedrae*, one rectangular (1.8 × 1.1 m) with mortar coating on the inside and one semicircular (diam.: 2 m). This must have been the *caldarium* with an *alveus* in the rectangular *exedra* and possibly a *labrum* in the semicircular *exedra*. A second *alveus* may have been located just above in the furnace. The second room (4) on a hypocaust (s.: 4.8 m) was only indirectly heated, and can thus be interpreted as *tepidarium* or heated *apodyterium*.
7. 7.1 The hypocaust pillars were made with square tiles (s.: 21 cm, 5 cm thick) bonded by clay. The furnace channel (60 cm wide) was lined by sturdy walls made of bricks, and had a floor made of hypocaust tiles placed on their small side and bonded by mortar. In the *praefurnium*, a thick layer of ash and charcoal was found.
    7.2 In the *caldarium*, fragments of *tubuli* (10 × 6 cm) were found.
    7.3 Unknown.
    7.4 An orifice in the north-eastern corner of the *frigidarium* drained the water into a drainage channel heading north. Its sides were constructed of mortar and field stones, while the bottom was made of tiles. The *piscina* was drained by a terracotta pipe. The *alveus* was drained by an orifice in its north-western corner. The drainage channel led to a sump north of the baths.
8.   Among the debris of the *caldarium*, fragments of wall painting were found.
9.   Fig. 95.
10.   Mahieu 1892 (ER); Brulet 2008, 510.

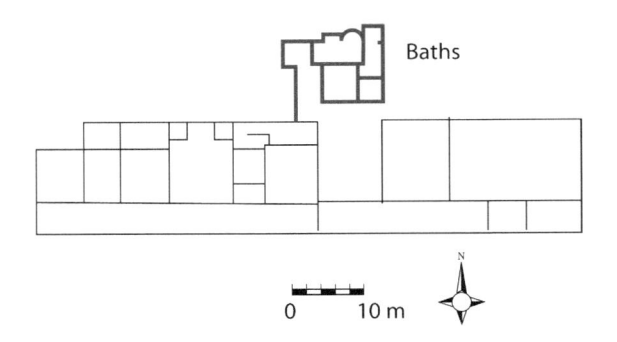

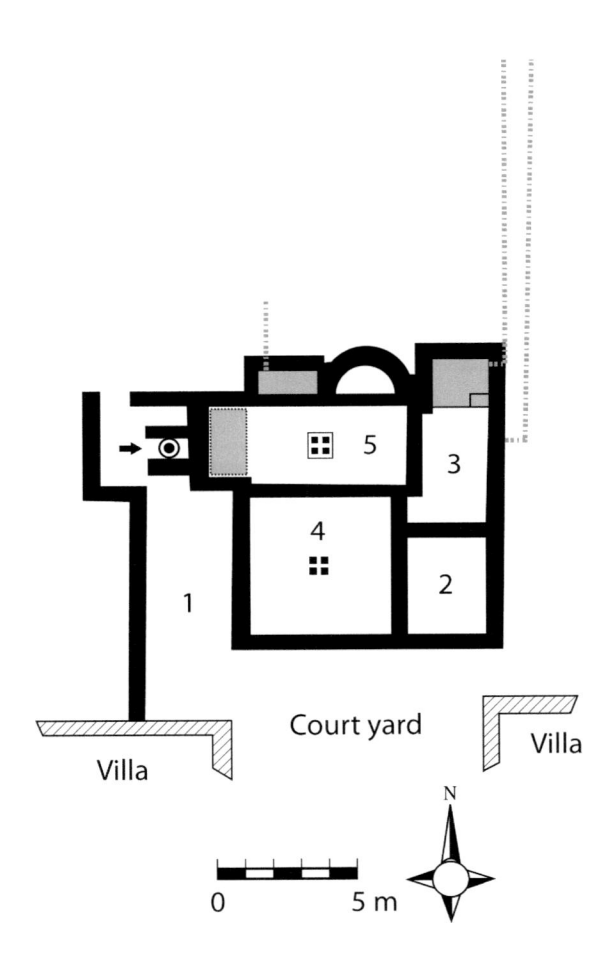

Figure 95. Location (top) and plan of the bath of Maillen – Al Sauvenière. Figure by author after Mahieu 1892, pl. I, fig. 2.

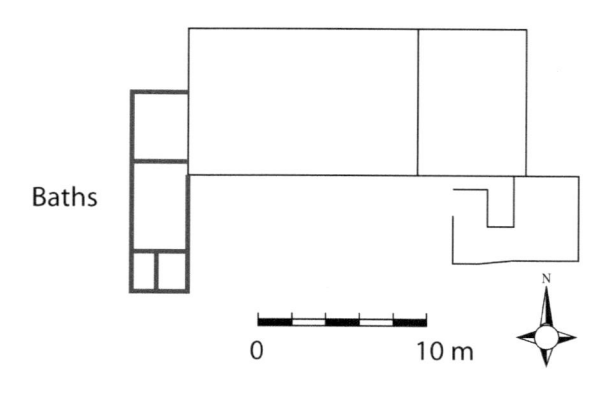

Baths

0   10 m

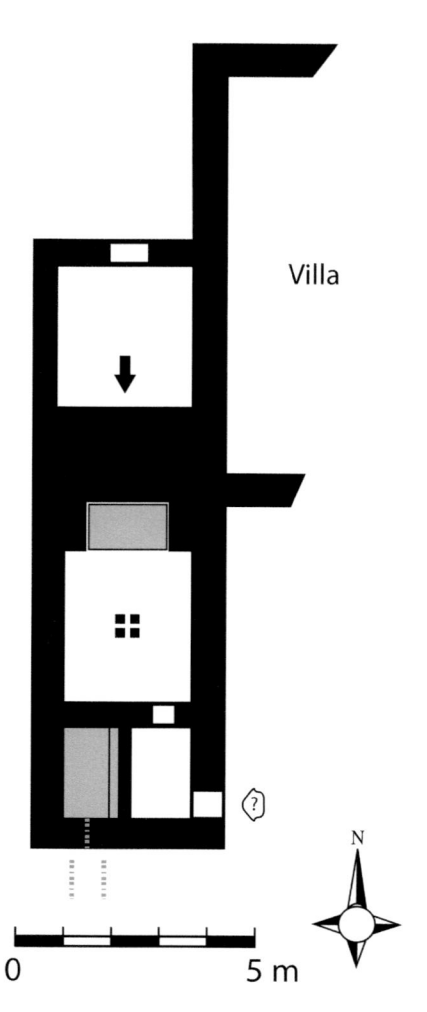

Villa

0   5 m

Figure 96. Location (top) and plan of the bath of Maillen –
Arches. Figure by author after Mahieu 1892, pl. 5.

Maillen, Villa d'Arches (ID 90)

1.   1.1   Belgium, Namur, Assesse.
       1.2   50°22'35.56"N; 4°56'41.52"E (approx.).
2.   2.1   1889.
       2.2   Well preserved when excavated, now covered or destroyed.
3.   Private bathhouse attached to a villa.
4.   4.1   Unknown (the earliest occupation of the villa site was in the first century AD).
       4.2   Unknown (villa site was abandoned in the fourth century).
       4.3   Unknown.
5.   A (pools, hypocaust).
6.   6.1   c. 50 m².
       6.2   Linear row type.
       6.3   None.
       6.4   The bath was entered from outside the villa. The first room (1.9 × 1.3 m) had rectangular *piscina* to the west (1 × 1.3 m). It must have had the function of both *frigidarium* and *apodyterium*.
       6.5   The bathhouse only had one heated room (3.3 × 2.7 m). In the recess to the north, just above the furnace channel, an *alveus* (1.1 × 1.7 m) must have been located.
7.   7.1   The hypocaust pillars were made with square tiles. The furnace channel (40 cm wide) had a mortar floor. The *praefurnium* (2.85 × 3 m) had slanting sides.
       7.2   Unknown.
       7.3   Unknown.
       7.4   The *piscina* was drained by a drainage channel piercing its southern side. Outside the building, two gutters heading south were found.
8.   Unknown.
9.   Fig. 96.
10.   Mahieu 1892 (ER); Brulet 2008, 511.

Maillen, Villa de Ronchinne (ID 91)

1.   1.1   Belgium, Namur, Assesse.
       1.2   50°21'23.88"N; 4°55'8.22"E (approx.).
2.   2.1   1894.
       2.2   Well preserved when excavated, now covered or destroyed.
3.   Private bath integrated in a villa.
4.   4.1   Unknown.
       4.2   Unknown.
       4.3   Unknown.
5.   A (strong evidence for pools, hypocausts).
6.   6.1   Min. 120 m² (plan unclear).
       6.2   Linear row type? (plan unclear).
       6.3   A small square room (1) and a rectangular room (2) to the west might have been part of the bathhouse (vestibule and *apodyterium*?). Both rooms seem to have had a doorway to the outside. The north–south oriented room (3) with a semicircular *exedra* on its west side connected the bath to the long corridor running along the entire south side of the villa.

6.4   The *frigidarium* (4) seems strangely positioned in the centre of the bath flanked on both east and west sides by a heated room. Fragments of a large limestone *labrum* were found in the semicircular apse on the north side. According to the excavators, who wrongly interpreted this room as the *caldarium*, a pool might have been present along the south wall. However, it is more likely that there was a doorway here to the small square heated room (5) (*sudatorium?*).

6.5   If the room with a *labrum* was the *frigidarium*, this would make the heated room west of it (6) a heated *apodyterium*. The room (5) south of the *frigidarium* could have been a *sudatorium*, while the room east of it was the *caldarium* (7) (called the guest's bath in the excavation report). Two rectangular recesses must have housed *alvei*.

7. 7.1   The 'heated *apodyterium*' had its own *praefurnium* (8) to the north. The square *sudatorium* (5) had a separate furnace in its east side. The *caldarium* was heated from a small *praefurnium* to the north-west (9), which also heated the *sudatorium* through a channel running underneath the *frigidarium*, and a larger *praefurnium* to the east (10), which also heated a nearby non-bath related room (11). An additional furnace might have been used under the eastern *alveus*. There is no information on the type of hypocaust pillars.

    7.2   Unknown. For the possible heated *apodyterium*, two chimney flues were identified, which could mean that there was no wall heating here.

    7.3   Unknown. The sturdy square room (12) north of the easternmost *praefurnium*, interpreted by the excavators as the *fornacator*'s lodging, might actually have been a cistern.

    7.4   An outlet in the semicircular apse of the *frigidarium* drained the water of the *labrum*.

8.   Fragments of wall painting were found in the *caldarium*.

9.   Fig. 97.

10.   Bequet 1897 (ER); Brulet 2008, 509.

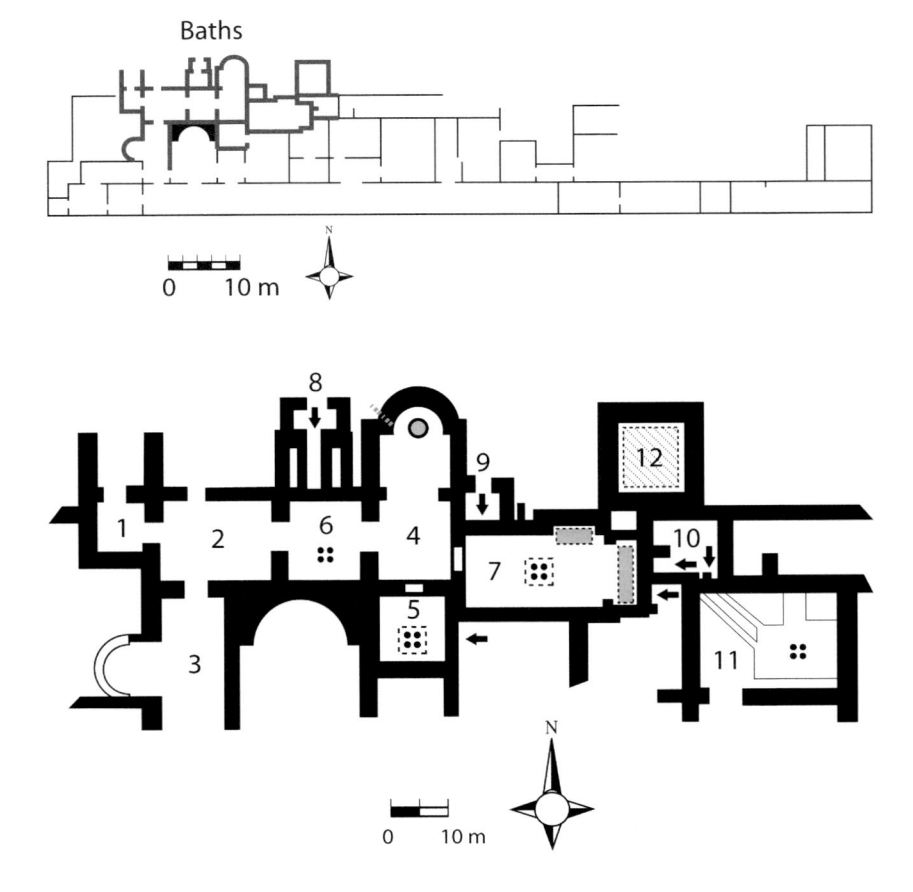

Figure 97. Location (top) and plan of the bath of Maillen – Ronchinne. Figure by author after De Maeyer 1937, fig. 22a.

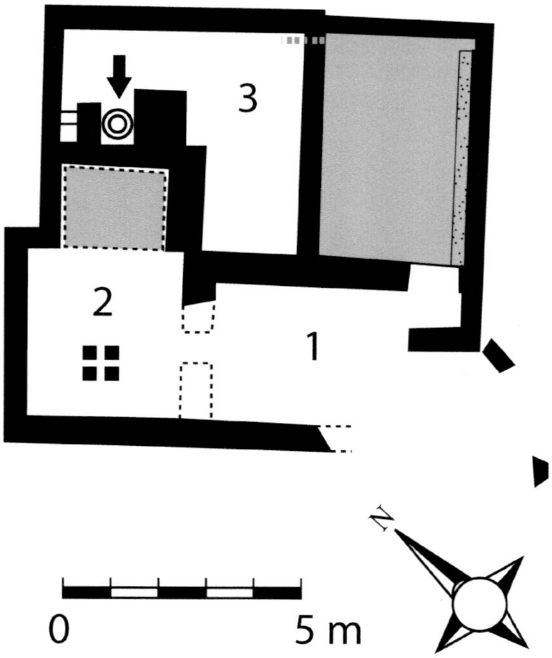

Figure 98. Plan of the bath of Marchienne-au-Pont. Figure by author after De Waele 1984, 203, fig. 151.

Marchienne-au-Pont, Pachi al Cave (ID 22)

1. 1.1 Belgium, Hainaut, Charleroi.
   1.2 50°24'21.59"N; 4°23'53.93"E (exact).
2. 2.1 1981.
   2.2 Well preserved when excavated, now destroyed.
3. Bathhouse of a villa?
4. 4.1 The ceramics and wall paintings point to a phase of use between AD 100 and 150.
   4.2 The bath seems to have fallen out of use in the second half of the second century (ceramics on site).
   4.3 None.
5. A (pools, hypocaust).
6. 6.1 Min. 111 m² (partial plan).
   6.2 Linear row type? (partial plan).
   6.3 The south-eastern part of the bath has been destroyed by two medieval cellars. Two mortar floors confirm that at least two rooms were to be found here (dressing room, cold room?).
   6.4 The *frigidarium* (1) was badly preserved, with only small parts of its mortar floor still visible. A large rectangular *piscina* (3 × 4.8 m) to its north was accessed by an angular corridor. The pool itself had a bench along its south-eastern wall. The floors, the walls, and the bench were covered in a fine pinkish hydraulic mortar.
   6.5 Only one heated room (2) has been found. The rectangular *caldarium* (3.3 × 3.6 m) had a rectangular *exedra* to the north (2.2 × 1.8 m), just above the furnace channel, which must have housed the *alveus* (rather than just before the *exedra* as suggested by the excavators). Several fragments of tile and fragments of hydraulic mortar indicate the presence of such a pool.
7. 7.1 The L-shaped *praefurnium* (3) was located north of the *caldarium*. It had an earthen floor. The furnace channel must have been unpaved, as was suggested by the red scorched clay, but had two parallel walls made of tiles, slightly projecting into the hypocaust. The pillars were made of square tiles (s.: 21.5 cm; 6 cm thick). The large tiles (5–8 cm thick) resting on top of the pillars had conical recesses, according to the excavators for a better circulation of the hot gasses.
   7.2 No fragments of *tubuli* were found, indicating no wall heating was present.
   7.3 Unknown. However, the stream *Eau d'Heure* was situated nearby.
   7.4 The *piscina* was drained by an outlet in its north-western corner. This drainage channel ran through the *praefurnium* heading north-west.
8. Several fragments of polychrome wall painting (including mainly dark red, ochre, white and black colours) were found throughout the bathhouse. Above the *piscina*, these wall paintings were still *in situ*, depicting green-yellow vegetal motifs on a black background. The black field was separated from a red and ochre field by white lines.
9. Fig. 98.
10. De Waele 1984 (ER); Brulet 2008, 322–23.

Marcinelle, Villa de Marcinelle (ID 53)

1. 1.1 Belgium, Hainaut, Charleroi.
   1.2 50°23'29.72"N; 4°25'38.67"E (exact).
2. 2.1 1973.
   2.2 Well preserved at the time of excavation, now destroyed.
3. Private bath integrated in a villa.
4. 4.1 Unknown.
   4.2 Third century? (destruction layer by fire).
   4.3 Unknown.
5. C (evidence for pools, hypocausts).
6. 6.1 Min. 30 m² (partial plan).
   6.2 Unknown (partial plan).
   6.3 Unknown (partial plan).
   6.4 Unknown (partial plan).
   6.5 At least two heated rooms were found. Only one (1) has been fully excavated (2.75 × 3.2 m). It had its own furnace, but its hypocaust was not connected to the second heated room (2), which could point to a use as heated *apodyterium* or *sudatorium*. The second heated room had a rectangular and a semicircular *exedra*, possibly to lodge *alvei*. An interpretation as *caldarium* seems plausible.
7. 7.1 Both hypocausts were heated by their own furnace. The pillars were made with square tiles, standing to a height of 40 cm.
   7.2 In the fully excavated heated room, five recesses in the walls point to the presence of chimney flues. No information is available about *tubuli*.
   7.3 Unknown.
   7.4 Unknown.
8. Fragments of blue windowpane were found.
9. Fig. 99.
10. Lejeune 1973 (ER); Brulet 2008, 323.

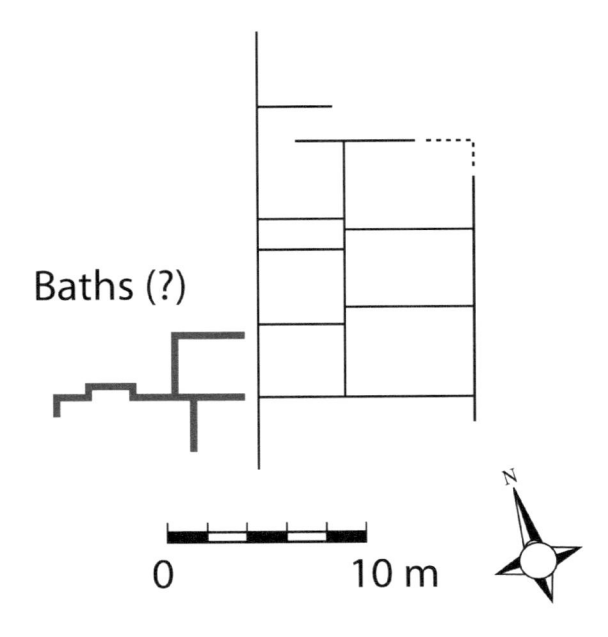

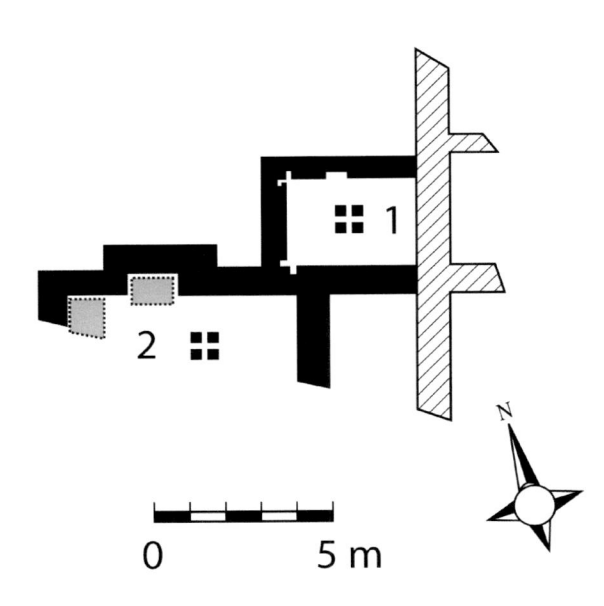

Figure 99. Location (top) and plan of the alleged bath at Marcinelle. Figure by author after Lejeune 1973, 118, fig. 1.

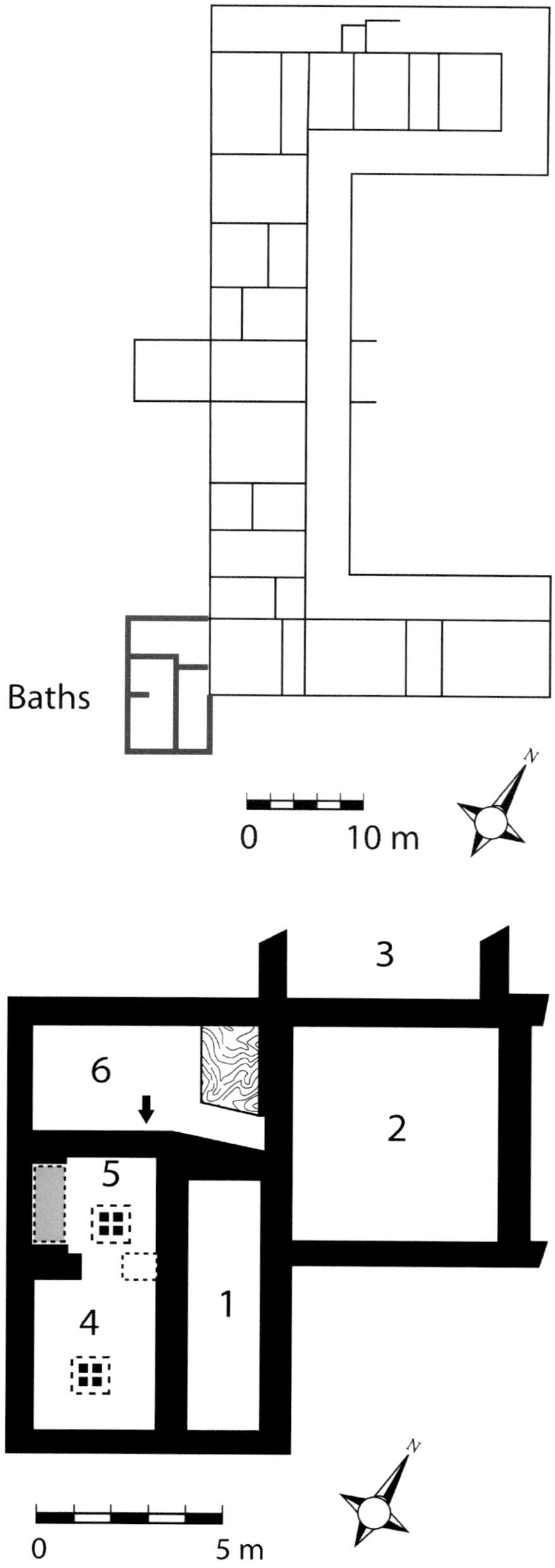

Baths

0   10 m

N

Matagne-la-Petite, Villa aux Murets (ID 92)

1. 1.1   Belgium, Namur, Doische.
    1.2   50°7'3.13"N; 4°38'30.24"E (approx.).
2. 2.1   Discovered in the early twentieth century, but excavated in 1982–1983.
    2.2   Well preserved when excavated, now destroyed.
3.   Private bath integrated in a villa.
4. 4.1   The villa seems to have been built during the second century and the bath was contemporaneous with this first building phase.
    4.2   The villa was destroyed by a fire at the end of the third century (ceramics on site).
    4.3   Some rooms of the villa were reused for living during the fourth century, but the bath seems to have been abandoned.
5.   B (evidence for pool, hypocausts).
6. 6.1   Min. 87.5 m² or max. 124 m² (plan unclear).
    6.2   Block type.
    6.3   The oblong room (1) to the east of the heated room(s) may have been an *apodyterium*. If the almost square room (2) east of the bathing block also belonged to the bath, this may have been an *apodyterium* and/or *frigidarium*. The oblong room to the north (3) may have served as entrance vestibule or dressing room.
    6.4   The excavator suggested that the almost square room (2) (6 × 5.4 m) north-east of the protruding bathing block may have been the *frigidarium*. Its floor was made of a pink hydraulic mortar, but there is no indication of a *piscina*. The walls were made with regularly cut limestone blocks.
    6.5   The bath had one heated room, heated by a *praefurnium* on its western side, which may have been divided into a *caldarium* (5) and *tepidarium* (4). In the south-western corner, a recess is created by a protruding wall, probably to lodge an *alveus*.
7. 7.1   The *praefurnium* (6) was a rectangular room in the south-western corner of the bathing block. The furnace itself was directly cut out of the bedrock. No hypocaust tiles were found, but the imprints of square tiles could still be seen on the mortar floor of the hypocaust.
    7.2   Unknown.
    7.3   Unknown.
    7.4   Unknown.
8.   Unknown.
9.   Fig. 100.
10.   Rober 1984 (ER); Brulet 2008, 523–24.

0   5 m

N

Figure 100. Location (top) and plan of the bath of Matagne-la-Petite. Figure by author after Rober 1984, 65, fig. 32.

Meerssen, Villa Herkenberg (ID 93)

1. 1.1 The Netherlands, Limburg, Meerssen.
   1.2 50°53'2.09"N; 5°45'38.56"E (approx.).
2. 2.1 1865.
   2.2 Partially preserved when excavated, now covered.
3. Private bathhouse integrated in a villa.
4. 4.1 Unknown. The site seems to have been in use between the second half of the first century and at least the second half of the second century.
   4.2 Unknown.
   4.3 A human skeleton was found in the *praefurnium* of the bath. As the body was found facing the ground, with the left hand resting on the skull, and the lower spine shattered by a stone block, the excavators interpreted this person as a member of the household being killed while the building collapsed in a fire.
5. B (pools, boiler).
6. 6.1 Min. 62 m² (partial plan).
   6.2 Unknown (partial plan).
   6.3 Unknown (partial plan).
   6.4 Unknown (partial plan).
   6.5 The only part of the bathhouse that was found (or recognized) during the nineteenth-century excavations, consisted of two pools, each with a semicircular apse, and a bottle-shaped furnace channel with two facing water reservoirs at its end. According to the excavators, a boiler stood in between the two pools, heated by the channel. Such a boiler in the middle of the room seems rather unlikely. If this interpretation were to be correct, we should imagine that the pools were not accessed from the centre of the room, but rather from the apse-sides through an unidentified room encompassing the pools.
7. 7.1 According to the excavation report, neither the pools, nor the room had hypocaust pillars. However, several round and square hypocaust tiles were found throughout the villa.
   7.2 Unknown.
   7.3 The source of the water supply is unknown. The furnace mouth seems to have been flanked on each side by a water reservoir.
   7.4 The pools had no outlets. Outside of the villa, remains of plastered water channels were found in the direction of the nearby stream the Geul.
8. The bathhouse was richly decorated. Several fragments of decorative stone (called 'marble') in diverse colours were found inside the baths, as well as fragments of translucent 'spar' (probably gypsum). The walls or ceilings were adorned with wall paintings (white plains with lines in different colours). At least one fragment depicted a plant. A life-size white marble finger was also found inside one of the pools. Several fragments of bas-reliefs in a hard white limestone were even recovered (one depicting the head of a man surfacing from water).
9. Figs 17, 101.
10. Habets 1871 (ER).

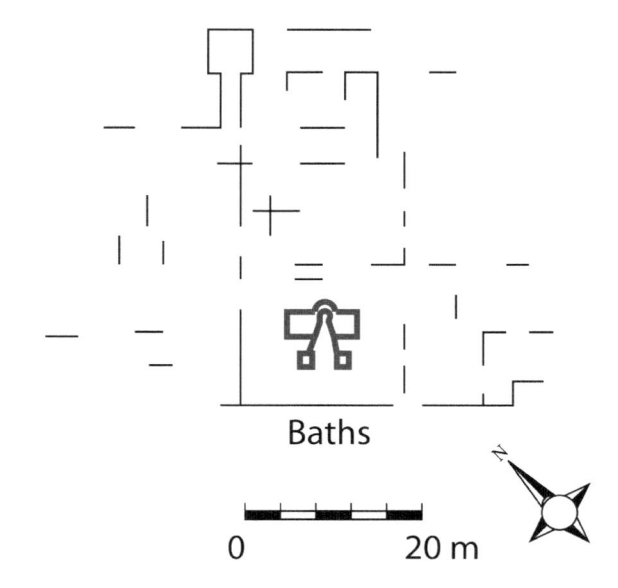

Baths

0   20 m

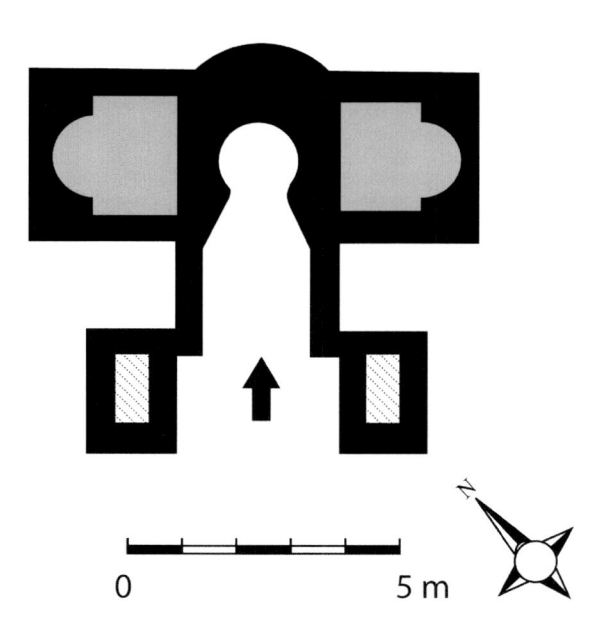

0   5 m

Figure 101. Location (top) and plan of the bath of Meerssen. Figure by author after Habets 1871, pl. VII.

Melsbroek, Hof ten As (ID 94)

1.	1.1	Belgium, Flemish Brabant, Steenokkerzeel.
	1.2	50°55'0.11"N; 4°29'16.43"E (approx.).
2.	2.1	1856.
	2.2	Well preserved when excavated, now destroyed.
3.		Private bathhouse integrated in a villa.
4.	4.1	Unknown.
	4.2	Unknown.
	4.3	Unknown.
5.		C (hypocaust, evidence for a pool?).
6.	6.1	Unknown (no dimensions given).
	6.2	Single room?
	6.3	Unknown.
	6.4	None?
	6.5	According to the description of the site, the villa was equipped with a bath (pool?) and a room with hypocaust. It is unknown whether the entire 'bathhouse' was excavated.
7.	7.1	The hypocaust pillars were made with round tiles of odd dimensions (diam.: 12 cm; 5 cm thick).
	7.2	Unknown.
	7.3	Unknown.
	7.4	Unknown.
8.		Several fragments of (white) marble were found, as well as painted wall plaster (one depicting the tunic of a figure). A bronze *strigilis* was also recovered.
9.		No plan available.
10.		Galesloot 1859; De Maeyer 1940, 19–20.

Merbes-le-Château, Champ de Saint-Eloi Bath 1 (ID 95)

1. 1.1 Belgium, Hainaut, Merbes-le-Château.
   1.2 50°19'5.93"N; 4°9'57.04"E (exact).
2. 2.1 2005–2006.
   2.2 Badly preserved in parts when excavated, now covered.
3. Private bathhouse integrated in a villa.
4. 4.1 The baths were added in the second phase of the villa (second century AD).
   4.2 At least two distinct phases of use were recognized. The villa site fell out of use in the last third of the third century (money treasure and ceramics in the abandonment layer).
   4.3 Unknown.
5. A (strong evidence for a pool, hypocausts).
6. 6.1 Min. 35 m² (plan unclear).
   6.2 Block-type? (plan unclear).
   6.3 Some of the smaller rooms east of the heated rooms might have been part of the bathhouse, but the lack of specific features makes any interpretation difficult.
   6.4 The cold room could not be identified with certainty, but should probably be located east of the heated rooms. The large room (1) lying on the same east–west axis as both heated rooms might have been the *frigidarium*, but no water supply or disposal channel to help locate a *piscina* has been preserved.
   6.5 Three rooms were heated by a hypocaust. The easternmost room (3) was rectangular in plan (4.2 × 2.3 m), but had a slightly curved southern side. It was directly heated by a furnace in its south-western corner. It may have been a *tepidarium* or a *sudatorium*. The westernmost room (4) had a square plan in its last phase (s.: 3.65 m; *caldarium*?) and connected to the third small heated room on its southern side. The latter may have originally been the *alveus*, heated by its own furnace. In the second phase of the baths, the surface of the westernmost heated room was reduced and the furnace of the small third 'room' (or *alveus*?) was abandoned, perhaps to construct a new (larger) *alveus* on the south side.
7. 7.1 A single *praefurnium* (2.25 × 1.7 m) was located south of the heated rooms, and had originally three furnaces, one for each heated room. The furnace channels (to the '*tepidarium*' 1.75 m long; to the '*caldarium*' 0.40 m long) were made with bricks placed vertically in the loess soil and bonded with whitish mortar. The hypocaust pillars were made with square tiles (s.: 20 cm).
   7.2 Both rooms were probably equipped with *tubuli*, although none were found *in situ*. The examples found together with a buried treasure were rectangular in section (29 × 24.3 × 12 cm and 45.4 × 13.2 × 11.9 cm) and had rectangular lateral openings.
   7.3 Unknown.
   7.4 Unknown. If the small room south of the alleged *caldarium* was in fact an *alveus*, the drain should probably be reconstructed in its south-western corner.
8. Unknown.
9. Fig. 102.
10. Authom and Paridaens 2008 (ER); 2009 (ER); 2015, 52–55 (ER).

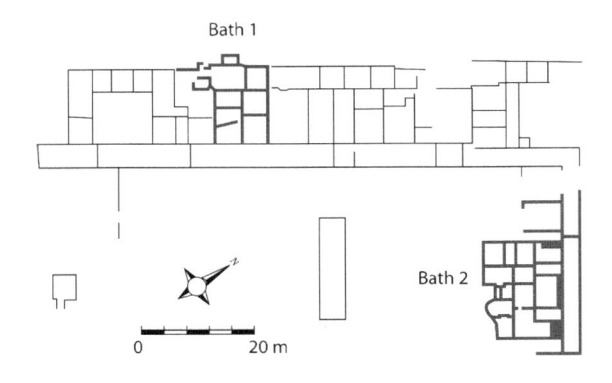

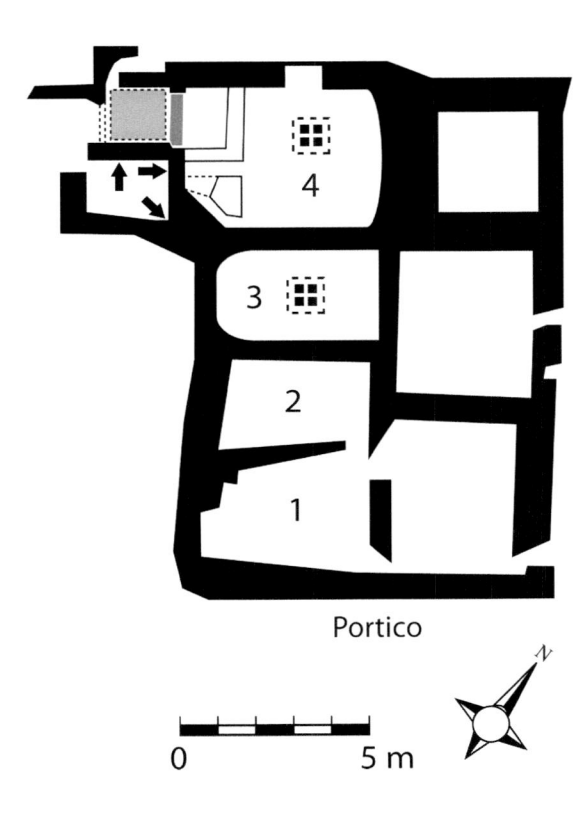

Figure 102. Location (top) of the baths at Merbes-le-Château and plan of Bath 1. Figure by author after Authom and Paridaens 2011, 58, unnumbered fig. and Authom and Paridaens 2015, 54, figs 27 and 31.

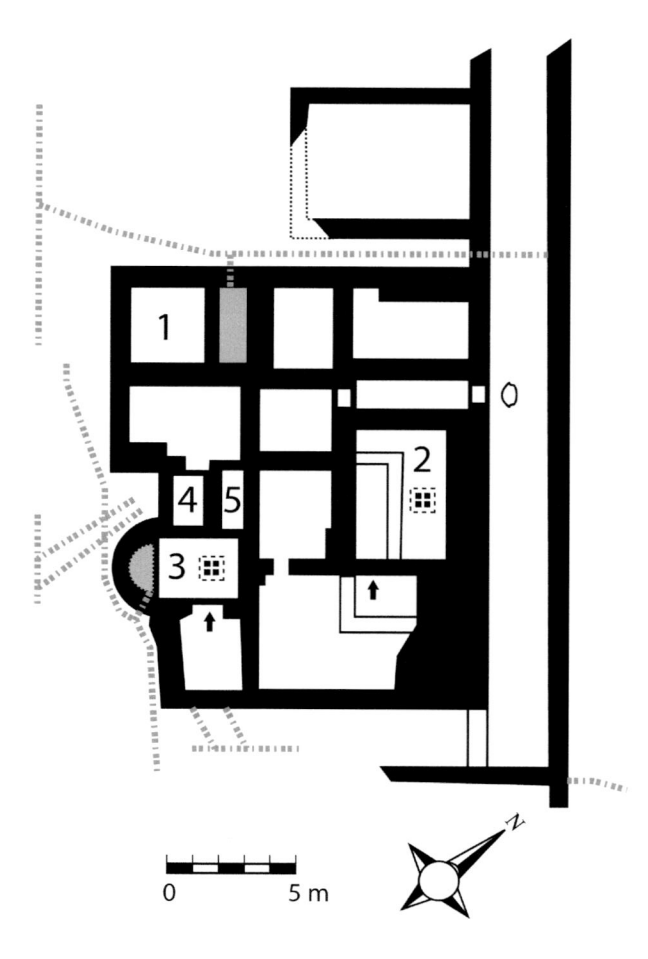

Figure 103. Plan of Bath 2 at Merbes-le-Château. Figure by author after Authom and Paridaens 2015, 79, fig. 84.

Merbes-le-Château, Champ de Saint-Eloi Bath 2 (ID 96)

1. 1.1 Belgium, Hainaut, Merbes-le-Château.
   1.2 50°19′5.93″N; 4°9′57.04″E (exact).
2. 2.1 2009.
   2.2 Badly preserved in parts when excavated, now covered.
3. Private bathhouse attached to a villa (possibly replacing Bath 1 integrated in the villa).
4. 4.1 The bath was probably added to the villa when the latter was enlarged in the second half of the second century (ceramics on site). A small bath suite (Bath 1, ID 95) was present in the centre of the villa before the larger Bath 2 was built.
   4.2 The villa site fell out of use in the last third of the third century (money and ceramics in abandonment layer). There are no indications that the bath was reused after the villa was destroyed.
   4.3 Unknown.
5. A (pools, hypocausts).
6. 6.1 *c.* 257 m².
   6.2 Unknown (plan unclear).
   6.3 Several rooms without mortar floor or pool were excavated, although it is difficult to interpret their function (*apodyterium, unctorium, districtarium,* etc.). The bath was connected to the villa by a long corridor (130 m).
   6.4 A room with a pinkish mortar floor (1) was identified as *frigidarium* in the south-west corner of the building. To the north, a rectangular room with a concrete floor lying 80 cm below the *frigidarium*'s level, must have been the *piscina* (2.6 × 1.2 m).
   6.5 At least two rooms with a hypocaust were identified. To the north-east, a room (2) was equipped with a hypocaust only in a second phase, adding a *praefurnium* to the east. In a third phase, this heated room was reduced and a new *praefurnium* was created. The absence of water supply or drainage channels points to a function as heated *apodyterium* or *sudatorium*. The second heated room to the south, the *caldarium*, had an apsidal ending in which the *alveus* was probably housed (3.8 × 2.4 m). To its west, two small rooms (4 and 5), badly preserved, seem to have had drains, pointing to a bath-related use.
7. 7.1 Only a few hypocaust pillars escaped the later spoliation of the site. The pillars were made of square tiles. The *caldarium*'s *praefurnium* was located on its eastern side. The furnace channel, unpaved, was preceded by a dug-out area for the *fornacator*. The *praefurnium* of the northern heated room was created inside an existing room of unknown function.
   7.2 Unknown. The third-century treasure in the villa was supported by two *tubuli* (from the baths?).
   7.3 Unknown.
   7.4 A sewage channel started in the villa complex, possibly at a latrine, and headed east, downhill towards the baths. Near the *frigidarium*, it split up in a branch heading north, to collect the waste water from the *piscina*, and east, to meet the drain of the *alveus*. Near the apse of the *caldarium*, two parallel drainage channels crossed the large sewer, heading south-east. To the east of the baths, a separate drainage channel starting with two parallel drains, headed north. To the north-east of the

corridor, a drainage channel headed north, possibly to dispose of the rain water from the roof.

8. Unknown.
9. Figs 102–03.
10. Authom and Paridaens 2011 (ER); 2015.

Meslin-l'Évêque, Villa de Preuscamps (ID 65)

1. 1.1 Belgium, Hainaut, Ath/Ghislenghien.
    1.2 50°39'6.33"N; 3°51'27.04"E (exact).
2. 2.1 Prospections in 1983, excavations in 1993.
    2.2 Badly preserved when excavated, now destroyed.
3.   Private bathhouse integrated in a villa.
4. 4.1 First phase possibly slightly later than the construction of the villa (middle of the first century AD?), second phase possibly in the second century.
    4.2 End of the second century? (abandonment of the villa).
    4.3 Building materials were recuperated during the Middle Ages.
5.   A (pools, hypocausts).
6. 6.1 First phase min. 225 m² (partial plan), last phase min. 250 m².
    6.2 Unknown (plan unclear).
    6.3 Unknown (plan unclear). In a first phase, the bathhouse had a semicircular *exedra* (1) on its western end.
    6.4 In the last phase, the *frigidarium* had a rectangular *piscina*.
    6.5 At least two rooms were heated by a hypocaust. The easternmost heated room (2) might have been the *caldarium*, with two rectangular *alvei* and a *praefurnium* to the north. A second heated room (*tepidarium* or *sudatorium*) had a *praefurnium* that was accessible through the courtyard to the south of the baths.
7. 7.1 The hypocaust pillars were torn out to be reused as building material in the Middle Ages. The furnace channel of the *caldarium* was paved with tiles.
    7.2 Unknown.
    7.3 Unknown.
    7.4 The *piscina* was drained by a channel made of tiles, dumping the waste waters in a sump.
8.   Unknown.
9.   Fig. 104
10.   Deramaix and Sartieaux 1994 (ER); 1998 (ER); Brulet 2008, 309–10.

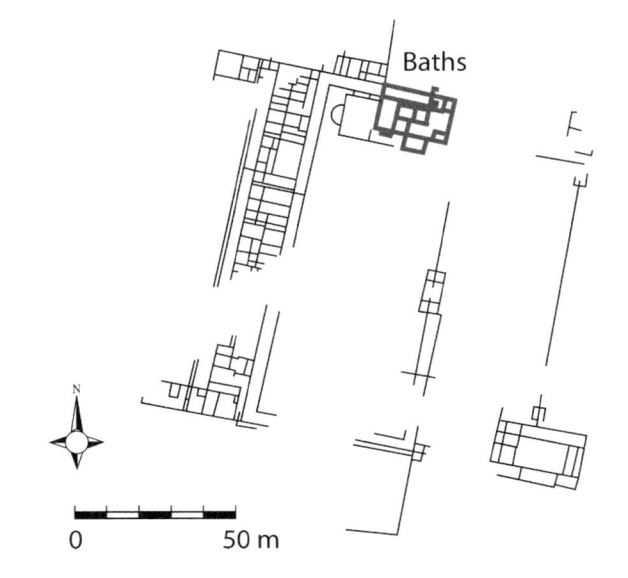

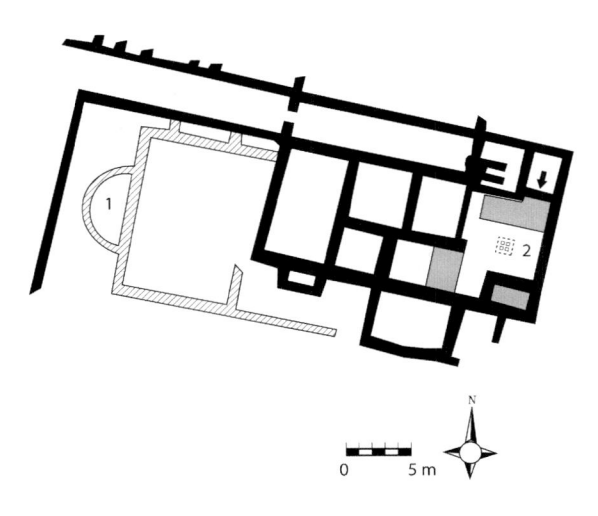

Figure 104. Location (top) and plan of the bath of Meslin-l'Évêque. Figure by author after Deramaix and Sartieaux 1998, 316, unnumbered fig.

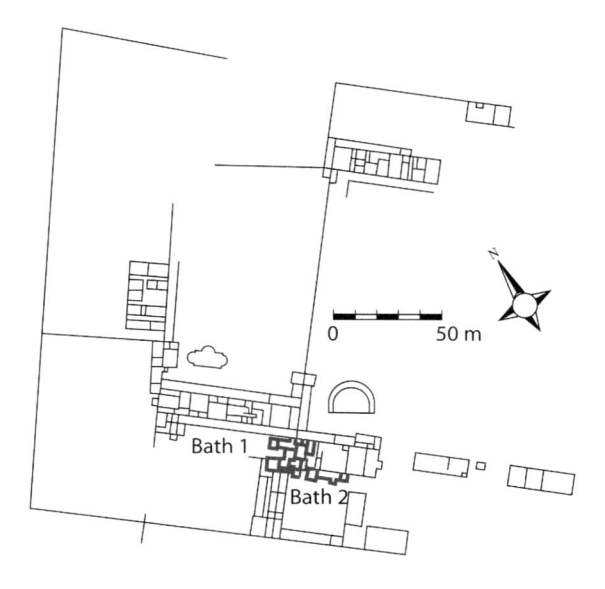

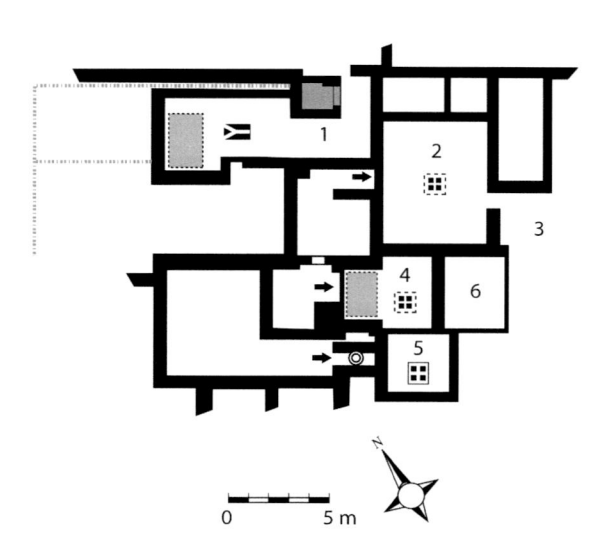

Figure 105. Location (top) of the baths and Mettet and plan of Bath 1. Figure by author after Mahieu 1919, general plan.

Mettet, Villa de Bauselenne, Bath 1 (ID 97)

1. 1.1 Belgium, Namur, Mettet.
   1.2 50°19'33.37"N; 4°39'6.92"E (approx.).
2. 2.1 1903 and following years.
   2.2 Some parts badly preserved.
3. Private bath integrated in a villa.
4. 4.1 Unknown (villa site in use from first century AD onwards, based on ceramics on site).
   4.2 Unknown (villa probably abandoned in late fourth century, based on ceramics on site).
   4.3 Unknown.
5. A (pools, hypocausts).
6. 6.1 *c.* 200 m².
   6.2 Angular row type?
   6.3 One of the rooms connected to the north-west–south-east oriented corridors was probably an *apodyterium*.
   6.4 The north-western part of the bathhouse (1) was badly preserved, making an interpretation difficult. It seems at least two pools were located here. One almost square pool (1.55 × 1.6 m) had an internal step/bench. The other pool must have been located to the north-west, where a drain was found. This part of the baths had a type of channel hypocaust according to the excavators, although its furnace is not located.
   6.5 A large room (6.6 × 5.35 m) in the centre of the bath (2) was heated by a hypocaust and could be interpreted as the *tepidarium*. It seems to have had a doorway leading into the courtyard to the south (3). To the west, two rooms also had a hypocaust. The north-western room (4) may have been the *caldarium*. A large bay separated the northern part, which was unpaved. It had a doorway leading into the *praefurnium* to the east. Perhaps the latter was the location of a broken-out *alveus*? To the south-east, a room (6) with mortar floor had very thin southern and western walls (*heliocaminus*?). The westernmost room (5) (3.1 × 3 m) had its own large furnace (to the north) and may have been a *sudatorium*.
7. 7.1 The only preserved tiles of the hypocaust pillars were square (s.: 16 cm). Drums of columns may have been used as pillars as well. In the large L-shaped *praefurnium* of the *sudatorium*, an oval pit in the floor (l.: 0.5 m; 0.3 m deep) was filled with ashes and charcoal. So was the space next to the furnace. The furnace channel (l.: 2.55 m; w.: 0.6 m) was lined by two sturdy walls, possibly to support a boiler (for the *alveus* of the *caldarium* lying north-east of it?). The *praefurnium* of the central room also had a furnace with sturdy walls. Through two terracotta pipes in recesses in the east wall, this furnace may have heated the 'channel hypocaust' under the north part of the baths.
   7.2 Several *tubuli* (13 × 10 × 42 cm, rectangular lateral openings of 9 × 8 cm) were found on the villa site, although it is not specified if these came from the baths. Two examples were found in the possible *sudatorium*.
   7.3 The water for the villa site was captured at a source some 2 km to the west and transported through an impressive aqueduct (stone, tile, and mortar) with five inspection holes. It ended

in a *piscina limaria*, a cistern in which impurities would settle, before being distributed throughout the villa by a network of wooden supply pipes (of which only the iron rings holding the segments together were found).

7.4 In the northern cold section of the bathhouse, the pools were drained by separate drainage channels made of *imbrices* and mortar. Both drains flowed into a drainage channel (0.5 m wide) north-west of the baths which ran 55 m west to a sump (diam.: 1.75 m; 3 m deep), filled with debris and charcoal. In the courtyard south-east of the baths, another sump was found (diam.: 1.2 m; 2.5 m deep). A greasy black substance, perhaps linked to products (e.g. oil?) used in the baths, was found at the bottom. A stone paving slumped towards this sump, acting as a catchment basin, possibly for the waste waters of the *alveus* and perhaps from rain water from the roof.

8. Fragments of wall painting and windowpanes were found in the large central room. From the channel hypocaust of the northern part, fragments of wall painting (mainly with red colours) and fragments of marble slabs were retrieved.

9. Fig. 105.

10. Mahieu 1919 (ER); Brulet 2008, 547–48.

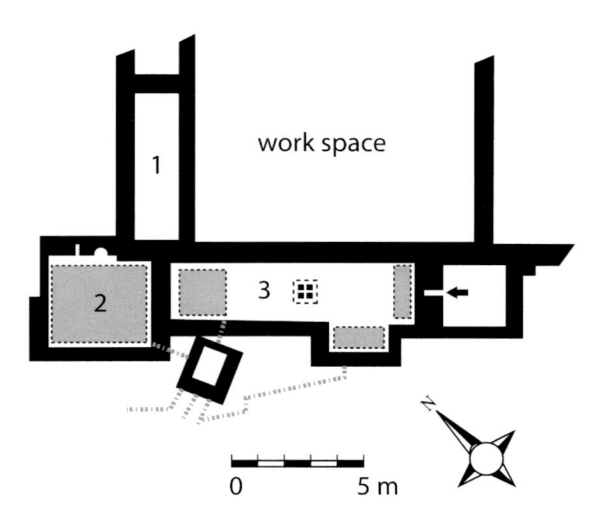

work space

Figure 106. Plan of Bath 2 at Mettet. Figure by author after Mahieu 1919, general plan.

Mettet, Villa de Bauselenne, Bath 2 (ID 98)

1.	1.1	Belgium, Namur, Mettet.
	1.2	50°19'33.37"N; 4°39'6.92"E (approx.).
2.	2.1	1903 and following years.
	2.2	Some parts badly preserved, now covered or destroyed.
3.		Private bath integrated in a villa.
4.	4.1	Unknown (villa site in use from the first century AD onwards, based on ceramics on site).
	4.2	Unknown (villa probably abandoned in the late fourth century, based on ceramics on site).
	4.3	Unknown.
5.		A (pools, hypocaust).
6.	6.1	*c.* 80 m².
	6.2	Angular row type?
	6.3	The oblong north-east–south-west oriented room (1) to the west of the bathing rooms has been interpreted as an *apodyterium*.
	6.4	The almost square room (3.92 × 3.75 m) in the north-west corner (2) was a *piscina*, or at least partially. The internal walls were covered in hydraulic mortar and finished with a marble veneer. There is no indication of a proper *frigidarium*, although the supposed *apodyterium* might have had a double function.
	6.5	The only heated room (3) (9 × 2.8 m) had a rectangular *exedra*, undoubtedly containing an *alveus* (judging from the outlet). The furnace was located at the southern end of the room. The reinforced walls here also point to the presence of a pool. According to the excavators, a tepid pool was located at the northern end of the room (2.8 × 2.35 m).
7.	7.1	There is no information on the hypocaust pillars in the original excavation report, although the accompanying plan (pl. III in Mahieu 1919) shows square tiles. The *praefurnium* (2.9 × 2.5 m) was accessible through the courtyard to the east. The furnace channel (l.: 1.35 m; w.: 0.4 m) was delineated by two sturdy walls (w.: 0.7 m), possibly to support a boiler.
	7.2	Unknown.
	7.3	The water for the villa site was captured at a source some 2 km to the west and transported through an impressive aqueduct (stone, tile, and mortar) with five inspection holes. It ended in a *piscina limaria*, a cistern in which impurities would settle, before being distributed through the villa by a network of wooden supply pipes (of which only the iron rings holding the segments together were found). Evidence for one of these wooden pipes was found west of the bathhouse. A hole in the east wall of the heated room may have been used for a pipe supplying the alleged tepid pool. Two recesses in the east wall of the *piscina* possibly housed water pipes, perhaps connected to a water catchment system on the roof.
	7.4	Three drainage channels made of *imbrices* and mortar, coming from the *piscina*, the tepid pool, and the *alveus*, led into a water basin (1.4 × 1 m; 0.56 m deep). From here, a drainage channel headed west to a sump outside the villa's domain.
8.		In the *piscina* several fragments of wall painting and marble slabs were found.
9.		Figs 105–06.
10.		Mahieu 1919 (ER); Brulet 2008, 547–48.

Miécret, Villa de Saint-Donat Bath 1 (ID 99)

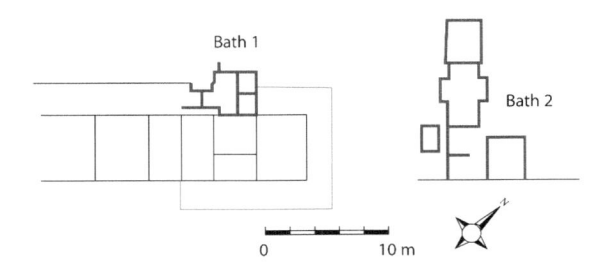

1. 1.1 Belgium, Namur, Havelange.
    1.2 50°22′6.97″N; 5°15′10.03″E (approx.).
2. 2.1 1968–1968.
    2.2 Poorly preserved at the time of excavation, now covered or destroyed.
3. Bath suite integrated into a villa.
4. 4.1 Unknown.
    4.2 Unknown.
    4.3 Unknown.
5. A (pools, hypocaust).
6. 6.1 *c.* 25 m².
    6.2 Block type.
    6.3 None.
    6.4 The bath suite had a small almost square *piscina*, while the space to the south-east possibly acted as *frigidarium*.
    6.5 The bath had an almost square *caldarium* with two rectangular *exedrae* for *alvei* (or a *labrum*).
7. 7.1 The hypocaust pillars were made with square and round tiles. Several column drums seem to have been reused as hypocaust pillars.
    7.2 Unknown.
    7.3 Unknown.
    7.4 Unknown.
8. Unknown.
9. Fig. 107.
10. Materne 1969 (ER); Brulet 2008, 546–47.

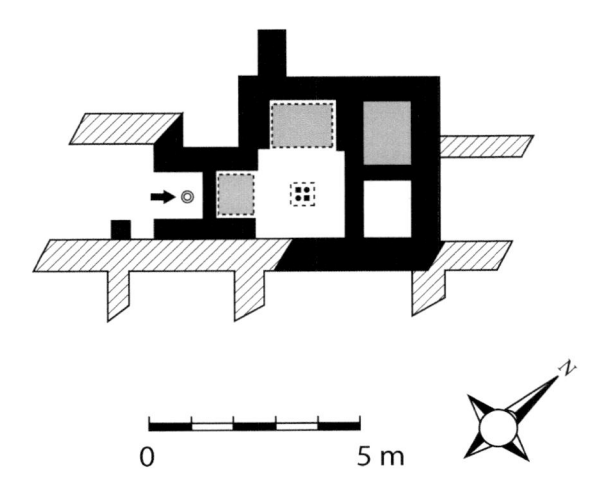

Figure 107. Location (top) of the baths at Miécret and plan of Bath 1. Figure by author after Materne 1969, general plan.

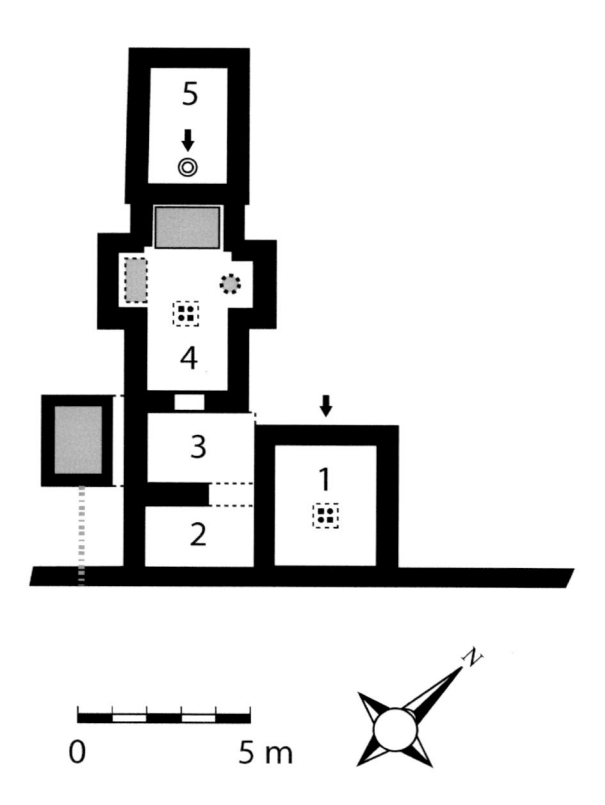

Figure 108. Plan of Bath 2 of Miécret. Figure by author after Materne 1969, general plan.

Miécret, Villa de Saint-Donat Bath 2 (ID 100)

1. 1.1 Belgium, Namur, Havelange.
    1.2 50°22'6.97"N; 5°15'10.03"E (approx.).
2. 2.1 1968–1968.
    2.2 Poorly preserved at the time of excavation, now covered or destroyed.
3. Freestanding bathhouse of a villa.
4. 4.1 Late first or early second century AD (coin of Domitian in the drainage channel).
    4.2 Unknown.
    4.3 Unknown.
5. A (pools, hypocaust).
6. 6.1 *c.* 75 m².
    6.2 Angular row type? (plan unclear).
    6.3 The bathhouse had a separate heated room (1) which may have functioned as a *sudatorium* (it had a separate furnace) or a heated *apodyterium*. The southernmost room (2) may have been an *apodyterium*.
    6.4 Only a rectangular *piscina* could be identified. The actual *frigidarium* possibly lay to the east (3).
    6.5 The *caldarium* (4) was cruciform in shape, with possibly *alvei* and a *labrum* in the *exedrae*. The southern part of this room may have served as *tepidarium*, perhaps separated from the *caldarium* part to the north by a thin wall at *suspensura* level. The *praefurnium* (5) lay to the north.
7. 7.1 The hypocaust pillars were made with square and round tiles.
    7.2 Unknown.
    7.3 Unknown.
    7.4 The *piscina* was drained by a drainage channel heading south-east.
8. Several fragments of windowpanes were recovered from the filling of a drainage channel.
9. Figs 107–08.
10. Materne 1969; Brulet 2008, 546–47.

Milmort, Hauts-Sarts (ID 101)

1. 1.1 Belgium, Liège, Herstal.
   1.2 50°41'1.22"N; 5°34'29.43"E (exact).
2. 2.1 2014.
   2.2 Badly preserved when excavated, now destroyed.
3. Freestanding bathhouse (of a villa?).
4. 4.1 Unknown (ceramics on site point to a phase of use between the second and fourth century).
   4.2 End of the third century (ceramics in destruction layer).
   4.3 The building was entirely dismantled for building material (including the foundations).
5. A (pools, hypocaust).
6. 6.1 *c.* 75 m².
   6.2 Linear row type.
   6.3 None.
   6.4 The northernmost room can be interpreted as the *frigidarium*. It had a semicircular *exedra* on its western side, probably lodging a small *piscina*.
   6.5 The middle room of the building was heated by a hypocaust and had two semicircular *exedrae* on its western side. It can be identified as the *caldarium*, with possibly an *alveus* above the furnace (south) and one or two in the *exedrae*. In one of the *exedrae* a *labrum* might have stood. It cannot be ruled out that this room was split into two separate rooms by an east–west oriented wall, hence creating a *tepidarium* in the northern part. Such a partitioning was not visible in the hypocaust, meaning such a wall must have been very light (examples made of *tubuli* are known). The wall separating the *caldarium* from the *praefurnium* was likewise invisible on the hypocaust level.
7. 7.1 Only the imprints of the square hypocaust tiles could be discerned. No actual tiles were found. The *praefurnium* was located south of the *caldarium*.
   7.2 Fragments of *tubuli* were found (type unknown).
   7.3 Unknown.
   7.4 Unknown.
8. Unknown.
9. Fig. 109.
10. De Bernardy de Sigoyer and others 2016 (ER).

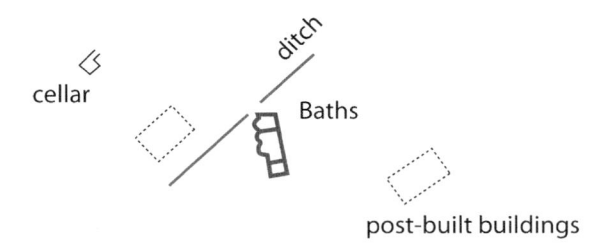

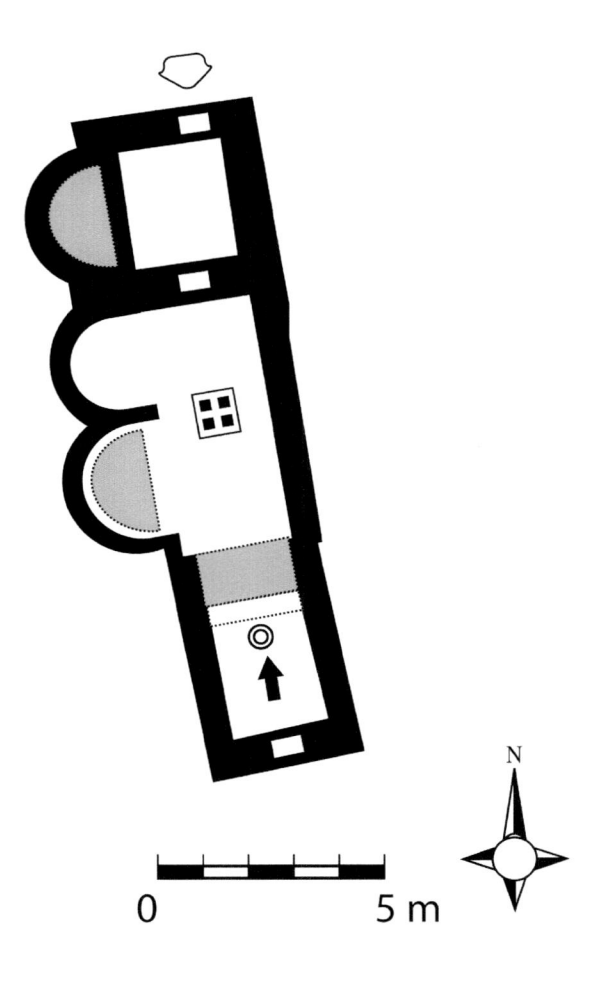

Figure 109. Location (top) and plan of the bath of Milmort. Figure by author after De Bernardy de Sigoyer and others 2016, 159, unnumbered fig.

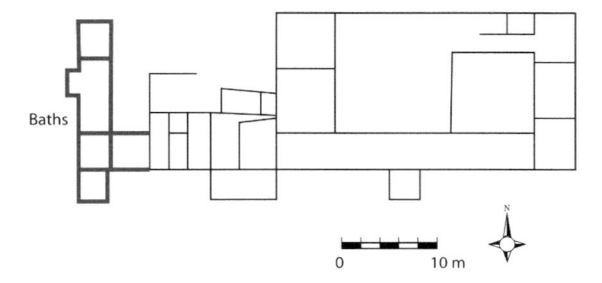

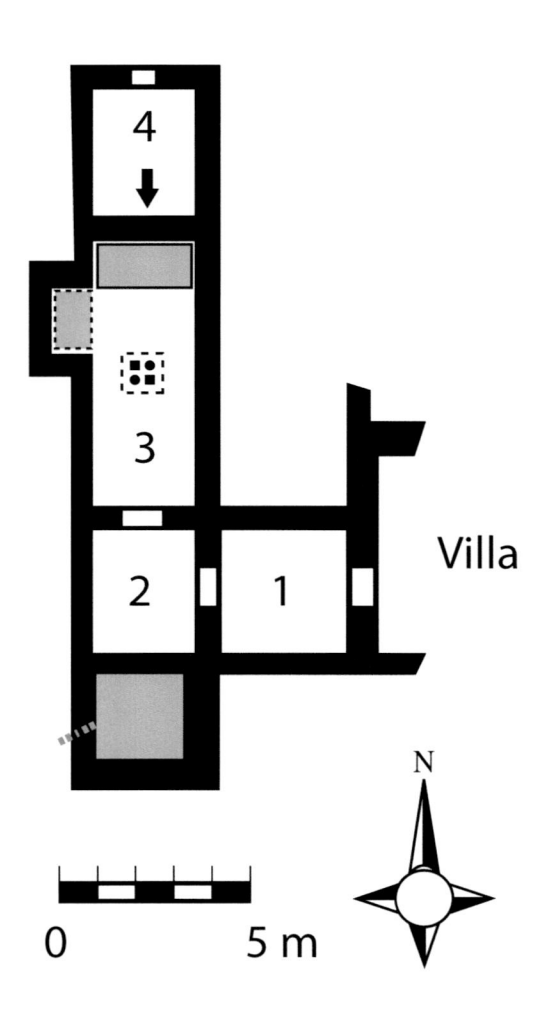

Figure 110. Location (top) and plan of the bath of Modave.
Figure by author after Anonymous 1896, 181, fig. 1.

Modave, Villa de Survillers (ID 102)

1. 1.1 Belgium, Liège, Modave.
   1.2 50°25'30.78"N; 5°18'29.74"E (approx.).
2. 2.1 1889.
   2.2 Well preserved at the time of excavations, now covered or destroyed.
3. Bath attached to a villa.
4. 4.1 Unknown.
   4.2 Unknown.
   4.3 Unknown.
5. A (pools, hypocaust).
6. 6.1 *c.* 60 m².
   6.2 Linear row type.
   6.3 The room (1) that connected the bathing rooms to the villa may have been used as *apodyterium* (s.: 3.55 m).
   6.4 The rectangular *frigidarium* (2) (3.5 × 2.8 m) had a square *piscina* (s.: 2 m) to the south.
   6.5 The rectangular *caldarium* (3) (7.4 × 2.8 m) had an *exedra* (2 × 1.2 m) in which an *alveus* was probably located. The very elongated shape of the *caldarium* makes it likely that the room was actually divided into a *tepidarium* and *caldarium* by a partitioning wall at floor level.
7. 7.1 The *praefurnium* (4) (3.6 × 2.8 m) lay north of the *caldarium*. There is no information on the hypocaust. The heated rooms of the villa had pillars made with round tiles (diam.: 22 cm).
   7.2 There is no information for the bath suite, but the heated rooms in the villa had wall heating by *tubuli* (box type).
   7.3 There is no direct evidence for the type of water supply, although several metal rings that were used to hold wooden pipes together were found outside the villa (pointing to a possible aqueduct).
   7.4 The south wall of the *piscina* was pierced, undoubtedly for an outlet.
8. Several fragments of wall painting (mainly red and yellow colours) were found. Outside the villa, mosaic *tesserae* were also identified, although their original location could not be ascertained.
9. Fig. 110.
10. Anonymous 1896 (ER); Brulet 2008, 424–25.

Montignies-Saint-Christophe, Terre d'Au Village (ID 103)

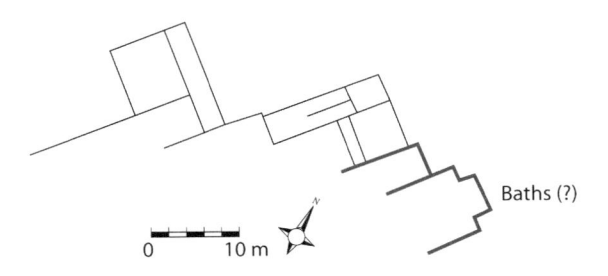

1.
   1.1   Belgium, Hainaut, Erquelinnes.
   1.2   50°17'3.16"N; 4°11'50.04"E (approx.).

2.
   2.1   1878–1879 (partial excavations), 1971.
   2.2   Well preserved when excavated, now covered or destroyed.

3.   Private bath suite (?) integrated in a villa.

4.
   4.1   Unknown (the villa site was in use in the High Empire; ceramics on site).
   4.2   Unknown.
   4.3   Unknown.

5.   C (hypocausts, evidence for a pool).

6.
   6.1   Min. 105 m² (partial plan).
   6.2   Linear row type? (partial plan).
   6.3   Unknown (partial plan).
   6.4   Unknown (partial plan).
   6.5   At least two rooms were heated by a hypocaust. The southernmost room had a rectangular *exedra* on its east side, possibly lodging a pool or *labrum*.

7.
   7.1   According to the nineteenth-century excavation report, the *praefurnium* was located to the west of the heated rooms. The hypocaust pillars were made of rectangular and round tiles. The alternation of pillars with a square and round cross-section could point to different phases/restorations.
   7.2   The excavation report mentions fragments of *tubuli*.
   7.3   Unknown.
   7.4   A drainage channel was discovered west of the villa. Its connection to the presumed bath rooms is, however, unclear.

8.   Several fragments of polychrome wall painting (geometric and vegetal designs), as well as black and white mosaic *tesserae* were found.

9.   Fig. 111.

10.   Van Bastelaer 1891b (ER); Brulet 1973b; 2008, 329.

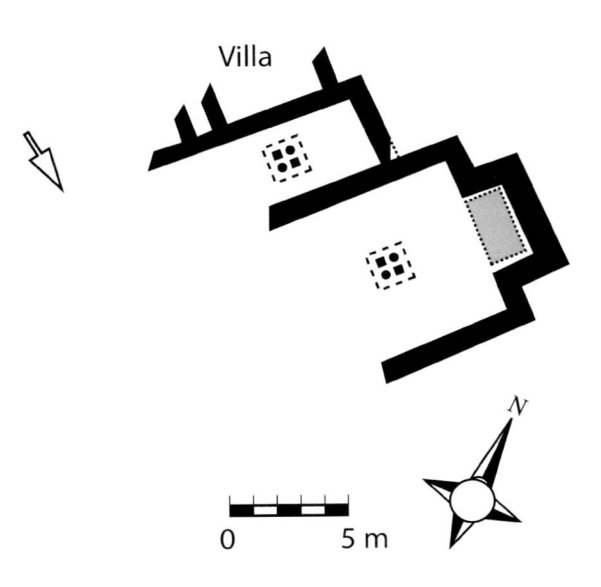

Figure 111. Location (top) and plan of the alleged bath of Montignies-Saint-Christophe. Figure by author after Brulet 1973b, 177, fig. 2.

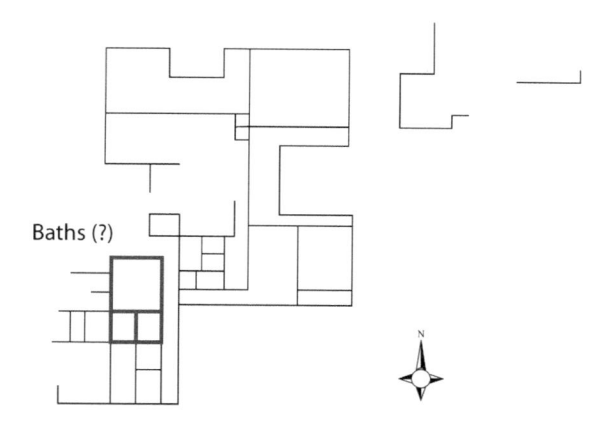

Baths (?)

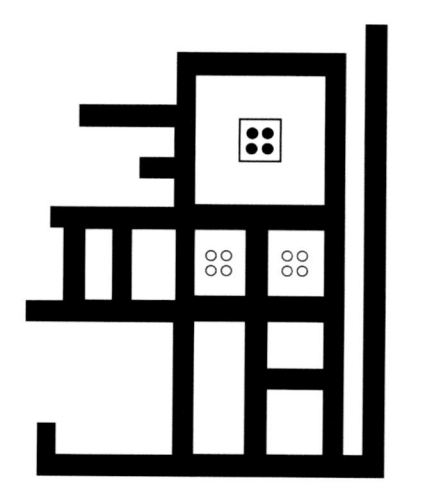

Figure 112. Location (top) and plan (without scale) of the alleged bath of Mont-lez-Houffalize – Sommerain. Figure by author after Brulet 2008, 477, fig. 358.

Mont-lez-Houffalize, Villa de Sommerain (ID 104)

1. 1.1 Belgium, Luxembourg, Mont.
   1.2 50°9'44.30"N; 5°48'57.61"E (approx.).
2. 2.1 1834–1835.
   2.2 Well preserved when excavated, now covered.
3. Private bath integrated in a villa.
4. 4.1 Unknown (ceramics and coins on site point to a phase of use between the first and fourth century).
   4.2 Unknown.
   4.3 Unknown.
5. C (hypocausts, *fistula*).
6. 6.1 Unknown (plan unclear).
   6.2 Unknown (plan unclear).
   6.3 Unknown (plan unclear).
   6.4 Unknown (plan unclear).
   6.5 Several rooms seem to have been heated by a hypocaust. In one of these, lead *fistulae* were found (no further information given), pointing to the existence of pools.
7. 7.1 The hypocaust pillars were made of round tiles (diam.: 15 cm). A long limestone column found near the heated rooms, might actually have been reused as a hypocaust pillar in a restoration phase of the baths.
   7.2 *Tubuli* of 12–13 cm diameter with lateral openings were found.
   7.3 The villa site may have been supplied by a spring a couple of metres south of the remains. Inside the bathhouse, lead *fistulae* were found *in situ*.
   7.4 Unknown.
8. Several fragments of wall painting (white, red, and polychrome lines) were found, as well as fragmented panes of (window?) glass.
9. Fig. 112.
10. Dubois 1952; Brulet 2008, 477.

Mont-lez-Houffalize, Villa de Fin-de-Ville Bath 1 (ID 105)

1. 1.1 Belgium, Luxemburg, Houffalize.
   1.2 50°8'17.59"N; 5°46'37.18"E (approx.).
2. 2.1 1957, 1960–1962.
   2.2 Badly preserved in parts when excavated, now covered or destroyed.
3. Freestanding private bathhouse of a villa.
4. 4.1 Unknown. The villa was built around the middle of the second century (ceramics on site), but the freestanding bath may have been older (according to the excavator, building material from the bath was used in the villa).
   4.2 Unknown. The villa was abandoned in the second quarter of the third century (ceramics on site).
   4.3 Unknown.
5. A (pool, hypocaust).
6. 6.1 *c.* 125 m².
   6.2 Angular row type.
   6.3 Unknown.
   6.4 An oblong room (1) on the eastern end of the bath had an almost square *piscina* (3 × 3.6 m), identifying it as the *frigidarium*. The large room to its west (2), in the centre of the bathhouse may have been an *apodyterium* or a *tepidarium*.
   6.5 Only the northern room (3) was heated by a hypocaust (*caldarium*). There is no evidence for an *alveus*.
7. 7.1 The *caldarium* had a Y-shaped channel hypocaust. The *praefurnium* lay to the south. The northern channels ended in recesses in the wall, lodging chimney flues.
   7.2 Unknown. The fact that a channel hypocaust was used, points to the absence of wall heating.
   7.3 An aqueduct was found between the bathhouse and the villa, although the actual source for the water is unknown.
   7.4 Unknown.
8. Unknown.
9. Fig. 113.
10. Meunier 1964 (ER); Brulet 2008, 477–78.

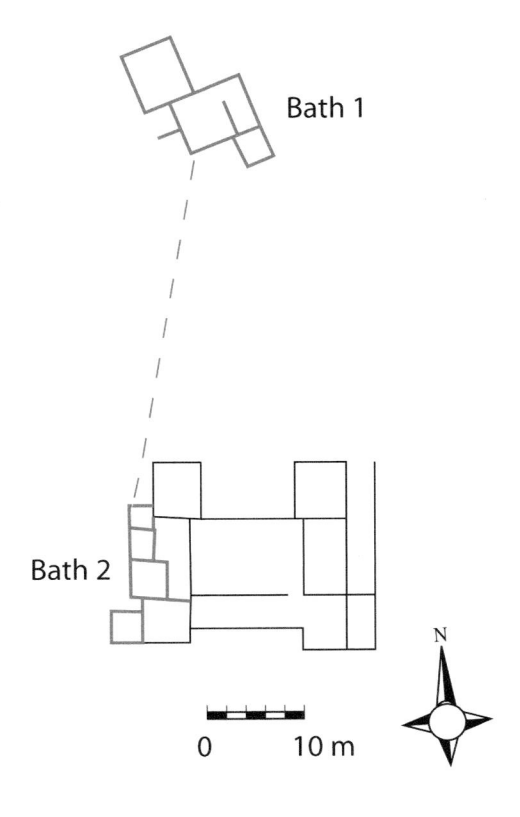

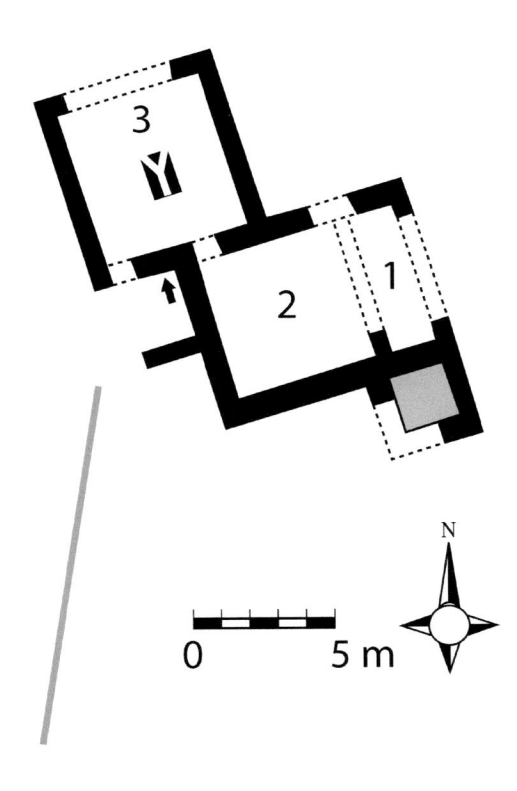

Figure 113. Location (top) of the baths at Mont-lez-Houffalize – Fin de Ville and plan of Bath 1. Figure by author after Meunier 1964, 157, fig. 3 and pl. I.

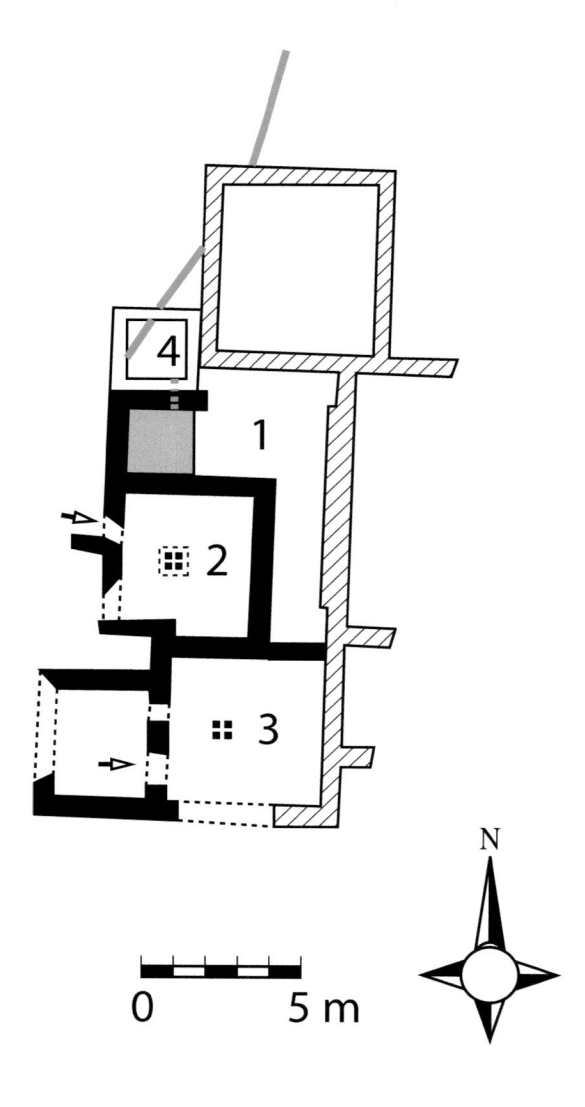

Figure 114. Plan of Bath 2 of Mont-lez-Houffalize – Fin de Ville. Figure by author after Meunier 1964, pl. I.

Mont-lez-Houffalize, Villa de Fin-de-Ville Bath 2 (ID 106)

1. 1.1 Belgium, Luxemburg, Houffalize.
   1.2 50°8'17.59"N; 5°46'37.18"E (approx.).
2. 2.1 1957, 1960–1962.
   2.2 Badly preserved in parts when excavated, now covered or destroyed.
3. Private bathhouse integrated in a villa.
4. 4.1 Unknown. The villa was built around the middle of the second century (ceramics on site).
   4.2 Unknown. The villa was abandoned in the second quarter of the third century (ceramics on site).
   4.3 Unknown.
5. A (pool, hypocausts).
6. 6.1 Min. 90 m² (plan unclear).
   6.2 Linear row type?
   6.3 Unknown.
   6.4 A small cold pool was accessible by a step along its east side. The elongated room (1) in connection to this pool must have been the *frigidarium*, which possibly also acted as an *apodyterium*.
   6.5 There seem to have been two rooms heated by a hypocaust (2 and 3), south of the cold pool. There is no evidence for warm water pools, making it difficult to identify the *caldarium*.
7. 7.1 The hypocaust pillars were broken out. There is no further information about the type of pillars.
   7.2 Several fragments of *tubuli* were found in the northernmost heated room.
   7.3 An aqueduct was found between the freestanding bathhouse and the villa, although the actual source for the water is unknown. It ended near the cold pool of the integrated bath, which it probably supplied directly.
   7.4 The cold pool was drained by an outlet in its northern side, flowing directly into a sump (1 m deep) in a small square room (4) (s.: 1.89 m). It was filled with ashes, charcoal, and debris when excavated.
8. Fragments of glass windowpanes and wall painting were found.
9. Figs 113–14.
10. Meunier 1964 (ER); Brulet 2008, 477–78.

Namur, Rue des Echasseurs (ID 23)

1.   1.1   Belgium, Namur, Namur.
        1.2   50°27'45.22"N; 4°51'56.89"E (exact).
2.   2.1   1931, 1967–1969.
        2.2   Partially preserved when excavated, now destroyed.
3.   Private bath of a *domus*?
4.   4.1   The presumed bathhouse is one of the oldest stone buildings in Namur, possibly dating back to the middle of the first century AD (ceramics on site).
        4.2   The main room with hypocaust was dismantled and a new sewer cut through it. A coin of AD 260–270 was found in this sewer, giving a *terminus ante quem* for the abandonment of the baths.
        4.3   The hypocaust pillars were reused and the shell of the building was probably reoccupied.
5.   C (hypocausts).
6.   6.1   Min. 225 m² (partial plan).
        6.2   Unknown (partial plan).
        6.3   Unknown (partial plan). One of the rooms was not heated by a hypocaust (3) and may have been a cold room.
        6.4   Unknown (partial plan).
        6.5   The building had at least three rooms heated by a hypocaust, although none of the furnaces have been found. The northernmost room (1) had a semicircular *exedra*, perhaps to lodge a *labrum*. It may have been a *caldarium*. The rooms to the south (2–4) could perhaps be interpreted as *tepidaria* and *sudatoria*.
7.   7.1   The hypocaust pillars of the northernmost room were made with square or round tiles. The *praefurnium* of this room most probably lay to the north (under the modern street), as it has not been found west, east, or south of the room.
        7.2   Unknown.
        7.3   Unknown.
        7.4   Unknown.
8.   Fragments of polychrome wall painting (linear patterns) and fragments of a mosaic floor were found in the south-western heated room. *Tesserae* were also found, perhaps belonging to wall mosaics.
9.   Fig. 115.
10.   Lauwerijs 1969 (ER); 1972; Bouet 2003a, 690–91; Brulet 2008, 555.

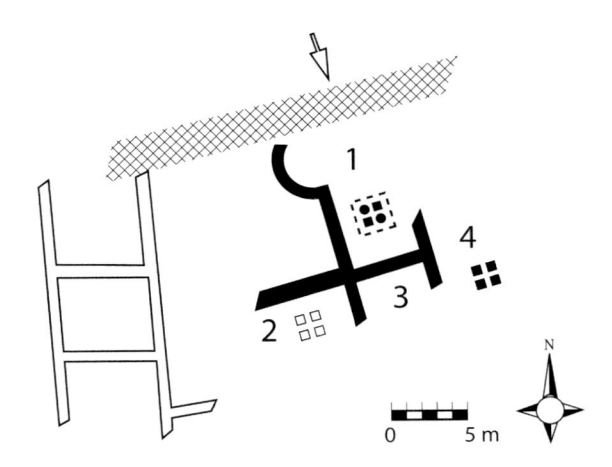

Figure 115. Plan of the bath of Namur. Figure by author after Lauwerijs 1969, 68, fig. 1.

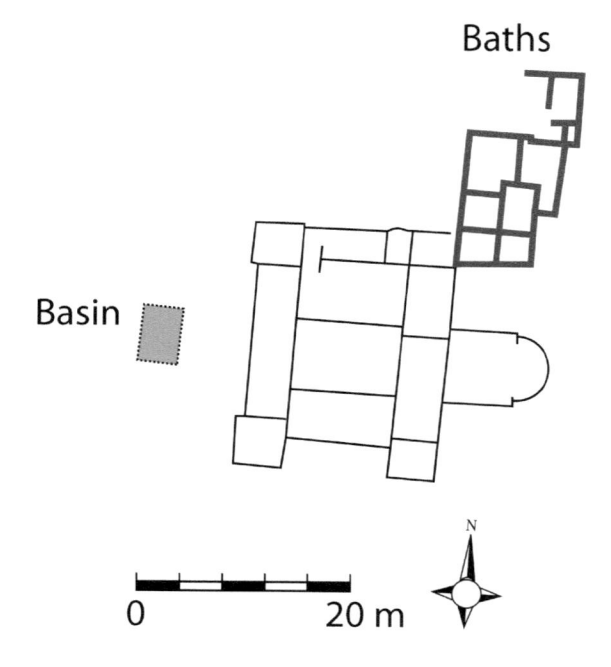

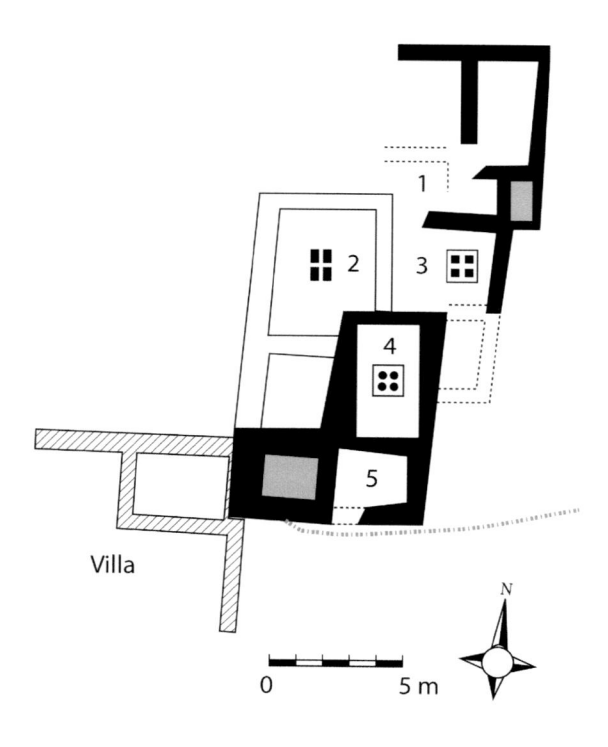

Figure 116. Location (top) and plan of the bath of Neerharen-Rekem. Figure by author after De Boe 1982, plan.

Neerharen – Rekem, Roman villa (ID 107)

1. 1.1 Belgium, Limburg, Lanaken.
   1.2 50°54'42.45"N; 5°41'7.12"E (approx.).
2. 2.1 1886 and 1981.
   2.2 Badly preserved when excavated, now destroyed.
3. Private bath attached to a villa.
4. 4.1 Unknown. The villa seems to have been erected in the second half of the first century AD, but the bathhouse was added at a later date. There seem to have been at least three phases.
   4.2 The villa was abandoned before the end of the third century (ceramics in destruction layers).
   4.3 The bathhouse was largely dismantled for building materials in the Middle Ages.
5. A (pools, hypocausts).
6. 6.1 c. 120 m².
   6.2 Block type? (plan and phasing unclear).
   6.3 Unknown.
   6.4 The cold section may have been located in the northern or southern part of the bathhouse (1 or 5). A northern location of the cold rooms would make more sense, as the heated section would get sun exposure in the south. However, the larger pool, presumably the *piscina*, was located south, attached to an unheated room (5) and close to the villa.
   6.5 Three rooms were heated: two by a traditional hypocaust with pillars (3 and 4) and one (to the west) by an X-shaped channel hypocaust (2). The latter may have been the *tepidarium*. The northern heated room (3) had a small pool. The pool (1.9 × 1.45 m) in the south-western corner of the bathhouse may have been a *piscina* (locating the *frigidarium* south) or an *alveus* (locating the *caldarium* here). It had an internal step on its east side, making this the side where one entered.
7. 7.1 The hypocaust pillars of the central heated room (4) were made with round tiles (diam.: 22 cm, 4 cm thick). The pillars of the northernmost heated room (3) consisted of square tiles (s.: 20 cm). The channel hypocaust was made of concrete.
   7.2 Several fragments of *tubuli* were found among the debris (h.: 23.5 cm; with round lateral openings, diam.: 4–5 cm).
   7.3 Unknown. In front of the villa, a large water basin was found, which was reinforced on the sides by wooden planks and made waterproof by loam coating.
   7.4 The southern pool was drained by an outlet in its south-eastern corner. The drainage channel ran to the east, joining up with a second drain coming from the northern part of the bathhouse.
8. Several fragments of marble veneer, glass panes (window glass?), and wall paintings (geometric and floral patterns) were found in the debris of the bath.
9. Fig. 116.
10. Van Neuss and Bamps 1888 (ER); De Boe 1981 (ER); 1982.

Nivelles, Villa La Tournette (ID 108)

1. 1.1 Belgium, Walloon Brabant, Nivelles.
   1.2 50°36'16.33"N; 4°18'39.69"E (approx.).
2. 2.1 1989.
   2.2 Badly preserved when excavated, now destroyed.
3. Freestanding bathhouse of a rural estate.
4. 4.1 Unknown. The site was in use from the beginning of the second century.
   4.2 Unknown. The cellar of the main building was destroyed after AD 260 (coin in the destruction layer).
   4.3 The site was heavily spoliated during the Middle Ages (several kilns found on site).
5. A (hypocausts, overall plan).
6. 6.1 *c.* 142 m².
   6.2 Angular row type?
   6.3 Unknown (plan unclear).
   6.4 Unknown (plan unclear).
   6.5 At least two rooms had mortar floor. These were possibly equipped with a hypocaust system.
7. 7.1 Unknown. A large *praefurnium* was identified.
   7.2 Unknown.
   7.3 Unknown. A well was located nearby.
   7.4 Unknown.
8. Unknown.
9. Fig. 117
10. Dewert, Osterrieth, and Severs 1992, 34–37; Dewert and others 1997; Brulet 2008, 290–91.

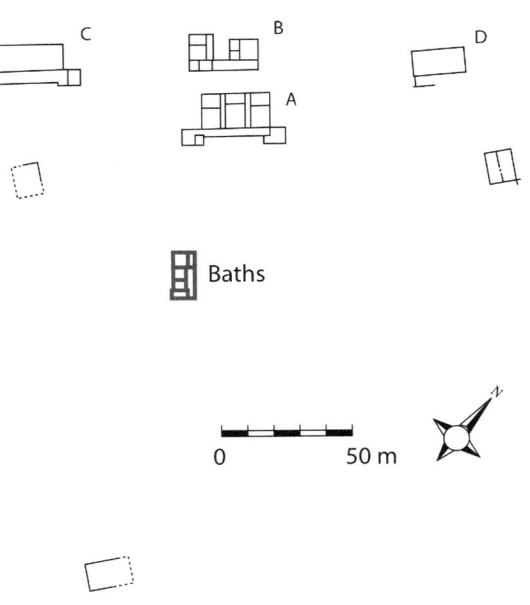

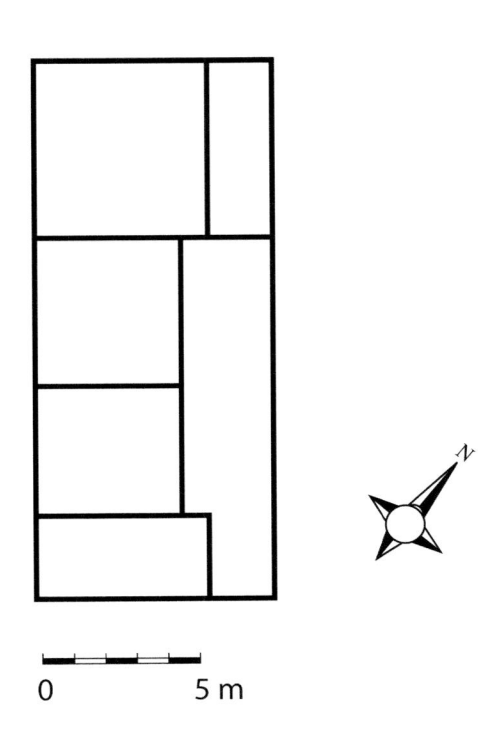

Figure 117. Location (top) and sketch plan of the bath of Nivelles. Figure by author after Dewert and others 1997, 343, unnumbered fig.

Nouvelles, Villa de Grande Boussue (ID 109)

1.	1.1	Belgium, Hainaut, Mons.
	1.2	50°24'37.68"N; 3°58'1.47"E (approx.).
2.	2.1	The bathhouse, lying in the north-east corner of the villa complex, has been identified, but has not been fully excavated.
	2.2	Unknown.
3.		Bathhouse of a villa.
4.	4.1	Unknown (the villa site was in use from the middle of the first century AD until the second half of the third century).
	4.2	Unknown.
	4.3	Unknown.
5.		C (hypocausts).
6.	6.1	Min. 40 m² (no plan available).
	6.2	Unknown (no plan available).
	6.3	Unknown (no plan available).
	6.4	Unknown (no plan available).
	6.5	At least one heated room was discovered some 40 m south of a large room of the villa. A second room to the south (6.75 × 5 m) had a mortar floor on the same level as the hypocaust floor, possibly pointing to a second hypocaust.
7.	7.1	Unknown.
	7.2	Fragments of *tubuli* (some with square lateral openings) were found.
	7.3	The villa was supplied by a 1.5 km long aqueduct (channel in mortar), probably tapping water from the stream Asquillies.
	7.4	Unknown.
8.		The bath was luxuriously decorated, with different types of marbles. In the villa, *giallo antico* and cipollino fragments were found, as well as pieces of mosaic floor. Fragments of glass windowpane were also amongst the debris of the hypocaust.
9.		No plan available.
10.		(Villa) Leblois and Leblois 1968 (ER); 1970 (ER); Hanut, Leblois, and Leblois 2000; Brulet 2008, 348–49.

Oberüttfeld, Villa (ID 110)

1. 1.1 Germany, Rheinland-Pfalz, Bitburg-Prüm.
   1.2 50°8'30.39"N; 6°15'38.42"E (approx.).
2. 2.1 1991.
   2.2 Partially preserved when excavated, now covered.
3. Private bathhouse integrated in a villa.
4. 4.1 The villa site was in use between the middle of the first and the fourth century (ceramics and coins on site). The bath, which had at least two phases, may have been added at a later date (material in the sewer is mainly second and third century). It possibly replaced an existing corner pavilion of the villa.
   4.2 The sewage channel under the latrine contained material of the third century.
   4.3 Part of the walls were heavily spoliated once the bath fell out of use.
5. A (pools, hypocaust).
6. 6.1 *c.* 60 m² (67 m² including the latrine).
   6.2 Linear row type.
   6.3 The cold room (1) must have doubled as *apodyterium*. A latrine (3) was located just north of the cold room.
   6.4 The cold room (1) (3.4 × 2.6 m) had a *piscina* (1.65 × 2.6 m; at least 65 cm deep) on its eastern end. The floor and the lower part of the walls were covered in hydraulic mortar. A low base in mortar in the north-western corner might have been used to support a small *labrum* or a locker for clothes. A shallow gully in the floor along the south wall presumably collected water (from condensation and exiting the *piscina*).
   6.5 The *caldarium* (2) was the only heated room (6 × 2.6 m), and was accessible through a narrow door opening (67 cm) from the *frigidarium*. The *alveus* was located on the eastern end, where the hypocaust was reinforced by a mortar base. It lay directly above the furnace channel.
7. 7.1 The hypocaust pillars were made with round tiles. The *praefurnium* (3 × 2.9 m) was located east of the *caldarium*. The furnace channel was 2.6 m long and had a floor made of tiles placed on their small sides. Two parallel walls possibly lined this channel.
   7.2 Several fragments of *tubuli* were found among the debris of the *caldarium*.
   7.3 Unknown.
   7.4 The *piscina* was drained by a lead *fistula* in its north-western angle (6 cm above the floor). This outlet gave directly into the sewage channel running underneath the latrine (3). The waste waters were then channelled north.
8. The lower part of the *frigidarium* wall was covered with pinkish hydraulic mortar. Several fragments of painted wall plaster (white background with lines and motifs in red, yellow, and blue) were found in the *frigidarium* and *caldarium*, which must have adorned the upper parts of the walls. One design consisted of four petals forming an X within a circle. The outside of the bathhouse was, at least in the lower part, covered in a red plaster.
9. Fig. 118.
10. Faust 1999 (ER); Goethert 1999.

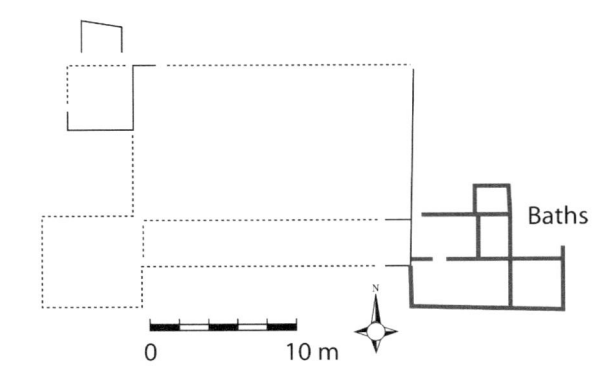

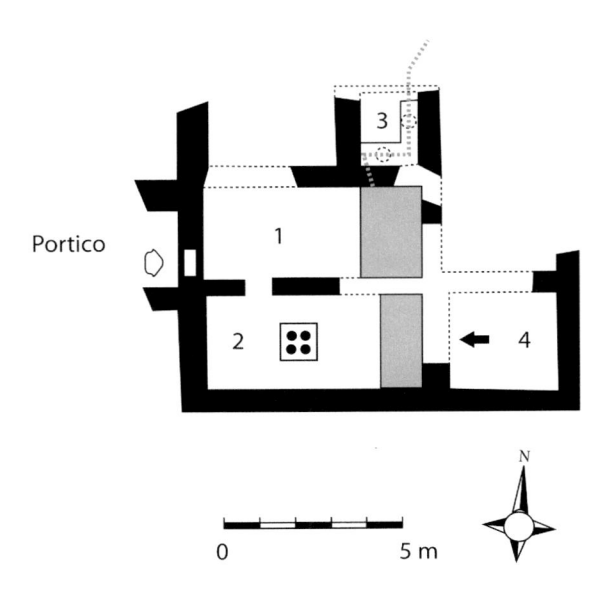

Figure 118. Location (top) and plan of the bath of Oberüttfeld. Figure by author after Faust 1999, 156, fig. 1 and 157, fig. 2.

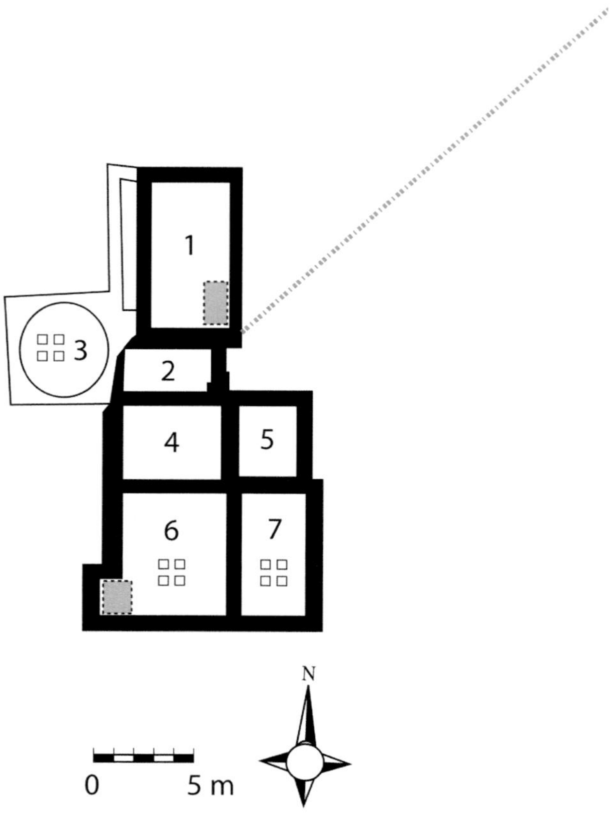

Figure 119. Plan of the 'Vicus Bath' of Oudenburg. Figure by author after Creus 1975, pl. II.

Oudenburg, Vicus Bath (ID 2)

1. 1.1   Belgium, West Flanders, Oudenburg.
    1.2   51°10'58.41"N; 3°0'7.19"E (approx.).
2. 2.1   1962–1968.
    2.2   Badly preserved when excavated, now destroyed.
3.   Public bathhouse outside of a military fort.
4. 4.1   Unknown.
    4.2   The baths were out of use and covered by sands before the site was reused for burials in Late Antiquity.
    4.3   The building was heavily spoliated during Antiquity: the walls were dug out to their foundation levels. After the bath was covered with sand, the site was used as a burial ground during Late Antiquity.
5.   C (plan, sewage channel).
6. 6.1   c. 244 m².
    6.2   Linear row type? (plan unclear).
    6.3   Unknown.
    6.4   The unheated part of the bath would be expected on the north side of the building, so that the heated part could benefit from the afternoon sun. A drainage channel started from the large room (1) in the north (7.5 × 3.75 m), which could point to the presence of a *piscina*. The size of this room, which could also have served as *apodyterium*, fits well with a cold room.
    6.5   The heated rooms of the bath are to be expected on the south side of the building, exposed to the afternoon sun. The room in the south-west corner (6) had a rectangular *exedra* in its south-western corner, which may have housed an *alveus*. No traces of furnaces were identified. The room to its east might have been a *tepidarium* or *sudatorium*. The rooms in the middle of the building (2–4–5) might have been tepid rooms. The almost square construction (3) (5.5 × 5 m) added in a later phase to the west side of the building, had an internal round space. This may have been a *laconicum*, although no traces of a hypocaust were discovered.
7. 7.1   No *praefurnia* were identified. By their location, we could imagine rooms 5 and/or 7 as *praefurnia* servicing rooms 4 and 6. It seems that all the ceramic building material was recuperated after the building fell out of use. Only fragments of hydraulic mortar floor were discovered.
    7.2   Unknown.
    7.3   Unknown. Three wells were discovered in the vicinity of the bath, although there is no evidence of a direct connection.
    7.4   A drainage channel ran from the south-eastern corner of the northernmost room towards the north-east. It probably drained a *piscina*.
8.   Several fragments of painted wall plaster were found in the destruction layer of the bath, mainly in the south-eastern room. The fragments had a white background crossed by pink and black lines.
9.   Fig. 119.
10.   Creus 1975.

Oudenburg, Castellum Baths (ID 113)

1. 1.1 Belgium, West Flanders, Oudenburg.
   1.2 51°11'0.37"N; 3°0'16.15"E (approx.).
2. 2.1 2001–2005.
   2.2 Badly preserved when excavated, now destroyed.
3. Bathhouse of a military fort.
4. 4.1 On the basis of the stratigraphy of the site, the construction was dated to the fourth century.
   4.2 Unknown. However, it seems that the bath-area within the fort was used for animal husbandry and grazing in the late fourth or early fifth century, making it unlikely that the bath was still in use.
   4.3 The bath may have been reused to fence off an area for grazing. During the eleventh and twelfth century, the building was dismantled down to the foundation trenches to recuperate building material.
5. A (hypocausts, evidence for pools, plan).
6. 6.1 Min. 105 m² (incomplete plan).
   6.2 Linear row type.
   6.3 Unknown (incomplete plan).
   6.4 If there was a *frigidarium*, which is highly likely, it was located to the east of the heated rooms, outside of the excavation area.
   6.5 At least two rooms were heated by a hypocaust. The westernmost room, with a rectangular *exedra* on its north and south side, can be interpreted as the *caldarium*. The *exedrae* (or at least the one on the north side) possibly housed *alvei*. To the east, and apparently indirectly heated, there was probably a *tepidarium*.
7. 7.1 One furnace was identified, to the north of the northern *caldarium exedra*. Its location directly underneath an *exedra* points to the presence of an *alveus* here. No separate furnace was identified for the second heated room, although part of this room lay beyond the limits of the excavations. The pillars were made with square tiles.
   7.2 Several fragments of *tubuli* were found (box type).
   7.3 A square water tank (3 × 3 m) to the north of the bath may have served as cistern (for rain water?). It was later converted into a well. During a later phase of the bath, a large water basin (4.5 m²) to the south may have been used as cistern.
   7.4 A drain ran from the northern *exedra* to the east, probably draining an *alveus*. It may have joined the drain of a *piscina*.
8. Several fragments of painted wall plaster were found, some showing traces of two different layers. This suggests two phases in the decorative programme inside the bathhouse.
9. Fig. 120.
10. Vanhoutte 2018 (ER).

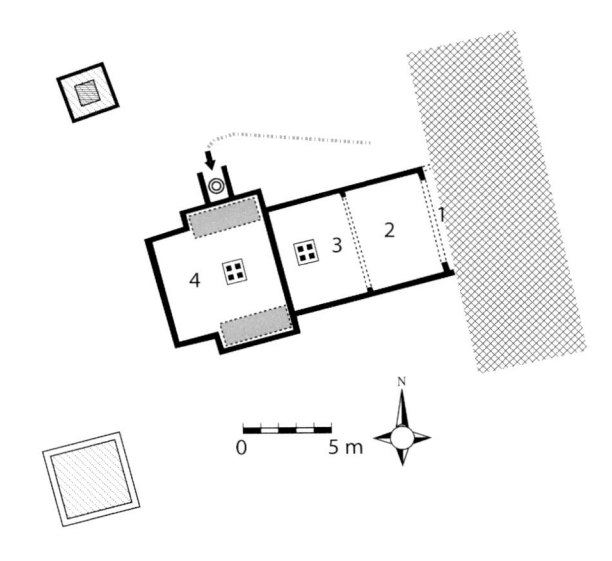

Figure 120. Plan of the Castellum Bath of Oudenburg. Figure by author after Vanhoutte 2018, 165, fig. 5.

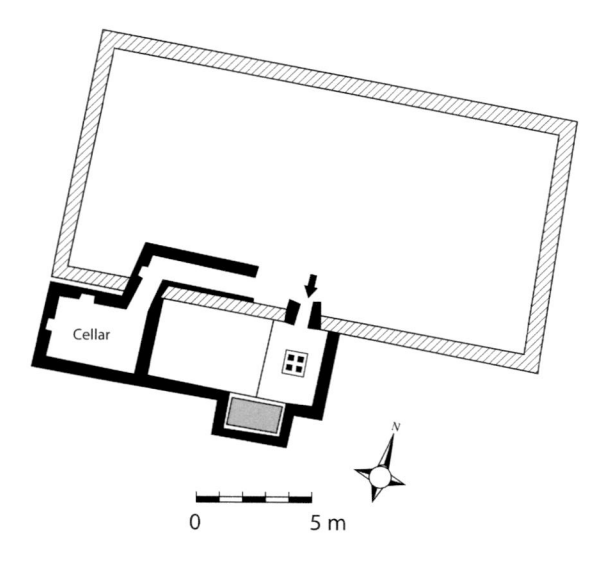

Figure 121. Plan of the relay station of Outrelouxhe with small bathing suite. Figure by author after Witvrouw 2015, 264, fig. 2.

Outrelouxhe, Relais d'Elmer (ID 10)

1.	1.1	Belgium, Liège, Modave.
	1.2	50°30'4.21"N; 5°19'33.58"E (approx.).
2.	2.1	1996.
	2.2	Badly preserved when excavated, now covered or destroyed.
3.		Bathhouse integrated in a relay station.
4.	4.1	Unknown. The ceramic material found on site points to a phase of use in the second and third century.
	4.2	Unknown, but the material evidence on site does not show occupation after the third quarter of the third century.
	4.3	Unknown.
5.		A (pool, hypocaust).
6.	6.1	c. 34 m².
	6.2	The bathhouse consists of a single large room.
	6.3	None.
	6.4	The western part of the large room was not heated (4.6 × 3 m). Hence it could have served as *frigidarium/apodyterium*. A rectangular *exedra* (2.5 × 1.5 m) on the south side of the main room housed a pool. The inside of the pool seems to have been clad with tiles. It was possibly filled with cold water, as it was not heated by a hypocaust, and there is no evidence for the support of a boiler.
	6.5	The eastern part of the large room was heated by a hypocaust (3.3 × 2.8 m). It hence served as *tepidarium/caldarium*.
7.	7.1	The furnace of the heated room could be lit from the large hall. There is no actual *praefurnium*. The furnace channel (0.5 m wide; 1.25 m long) seems to have been paved with tiles. The hypocaust pillars were made with square tiles (only fragments were found). The stamp NEH was found on a *tegula*.
	7.2	Fragments of *tubuli* (rectangular in section) were found in the heated room, but no entire example could be reconstructed (round lateral opening, diam.: 3.5 cm).
	7.3	Unknown.
	7.4	The pool was drained by an orifice in its south wall (30 cm wide), leading into an open-air drainage channel heading south (to the ditch surrounding the site).
8.		Two fragments of a statue (an arm and a leg) made of white limestone were found outside the building.
9.		Fig. 121.
10.		Witvrouw and Witvrouw 1997; 1998; Witvrouw 2014; 2015.

Rognée, Villa du Péruwelz (ID 112)

1. 1.1 Belgium, Namur, Walcourt.
   1.2 50°16'13.92"N; 4°23'22.58"E (approx.).
2. 2.1 1887, 1892, 1894–1895.
   2.2 Well preserved when excavated, now reburied or destroyed.
3. Private bathhouse integrated in a villa.
4. 4.1 Unknown. The villa site was in use between the late first and third century AD (ceramics on site).
   4.2 Unknown. The villa was abandoned during the third century.
   4.3 Unknown.
5. A (hypocausts, strong evidence for pools).
6. 6.1 Min. 150 m² (plan unclear).
   6.2 Block type.
   6.3 The description of the remains is unclear. The excavator speaks of a bathing suite, without going into much detail. It is possible that two different bathing parts were present, but not recognized.
   6.4 Unknown. The cold rooms may have been located to the north of the cluster of heated rooms. A space with a mortar floor (1) may have been part of the cold section. The location of the drainage channel close by, could indicate the presence of a (cold) pool here.
   6.5 Two distinct heated parts can be identified. A round room (2) (diam. 5.15 m) with four semicircular niches (1.80 m wide; 1.10 m deep) should probably be interpreted as a *laconicum* (rather than as a *sacrarium* as suggested by the excavator). It was heated by its own furnace to the north. If this *laconicum* formed the original bathing suite, the small rooms south of it (3) may have acted as heat trap and dressing room. A second suite of heated rooms, called 'winter apartments' by the excavator, might have been a new bathing suite added in a later phase. A large, almost square room (4) (6.70 × 6.90 m) was heated by its own furnace to the south, and may have been a *sudatorium*, a *tepidarium*, or heated *apodyterium*. A second heated room (5) (8.6 m long) had two rectangular *exedrae*, one in its east and one in its south-west side, possibly lodging *alvei*. This would identify the room as *caldarium*. The south-western *alveus* would then be located directly above the furnace. A smaller room (6) was located north of this *caldarium*. It is unclear whether it was directly heated by the *praefurnium* to the south-west, identifying it as a *sudatorium*, or if it was indirectly heated through the hypocaust of the *caldarium*, pointing to a *tepidarium*. West of these heated rooms, another *praefurnium* was discovered, but it is unclear which rooms it heated.
7. 7.1 A *praefurnium* (7) (1.40 × 1.85 m) heated the large almost square room and the presumed *caldarium*. A second *praefurnium* (8) serviced the *caldarium* and possibly the smaller room to the north. The floor of this *praefurnium* was covered with tiles, while a platform possibly supported a boiler. The third *praefurnium* (9) probably heated an unidentified room to its north-east. The hypocaust pillars, made with square tiles (s.: 22 cm; 4.5 cm thick) bonded by clay, stood 40 cm apart and reached a height of 90 cm. The stamps LCV and SFP were

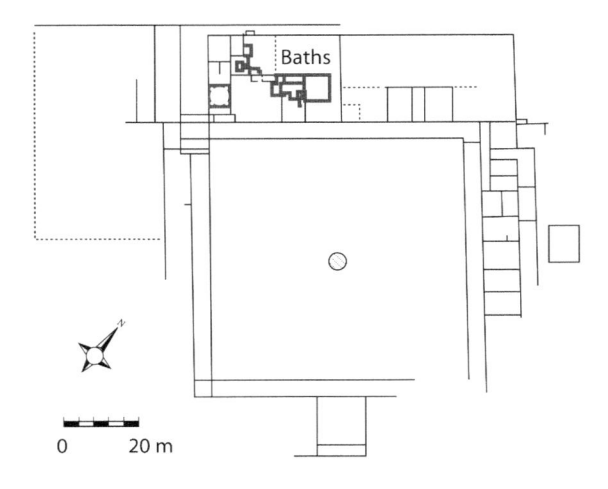

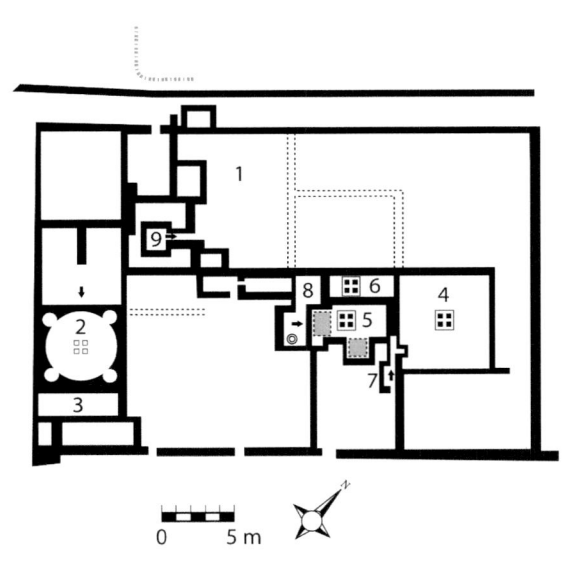

Figure 122. Location (top) and plan of the baths of Rognée. Figure by author after Kaisin 1897, pl. I.

found on hypocaust tiles (other tiles in the villa were stamped with TRPS).

7.2 The walls of the heated rooms were lined with *tubuli* (20 × 22 × 10 cm). One *tubulus* was more elongated, measuring 40 × 11 × 13 cm. It had lateral openings of 16 × 6 cm. The other *tubuli* also had rectangular lateral openings.

7.3 Unknown. A round cistern was found in the middle of the courtyard of the villa (3 m deep), possibly to collect rain water from the roofs. The excavators suggest the baths were supplied by this cistern, but no evidence for connecting pipes was discovered.

7.4 A drainage channel was located north of the baths, outside of the villa walls. It is unclear how the channel connected to the baths.

8. Unknown. Fragments of wall painting were discovered throughout the villa, including a depiction of a man and of a crocodile.

9. Fig. 122.

10. Kaisin 1897 (ER); Brulet 2008, 581–83.

Roly, Villa La Crayellerie (ID 111)

1. 1.1 Belgium, Namur, Philippeville.
   1.2 50°8'4.04"N; 4°32'12.80"E (approx.).
2. 2.1 1969–1977.
   2.2 Well preserved when excavated, now covered or destroyed.
3. Private bathhouse integrated in a villa.
4. 4.1 Second half of the second century (no further evidence given). The villa itself probably dates from the first century AD.
   4.2 Unknown.
   4.3 Unknown. The building was heavily dismantled for building materials in the post-Roman period.
5. A (strong evidence for pools, hypocaust).
6. 6.1 *c.* 65 m².
   6.2 Linear row type.
   6.3 None.
   6.4 The easternmost room (1) probably doubled as *apodyterium-frigidarium*. A *piscina* might have been present on the northern side, where the mortar floor seems to have been broken out.
   6.5 A single heated room at the centre of the bathhouse (2), the *caldarium*, had a rectangular apse on its western side, just above the furnace channel. It possibly housed an *alveus*.
7. 7.1 The hypocaust pillars were made with square tiles. On one of these, the stamp TRAVCPSB was identified. The *praefurnium* (3) was located west of the *caldarium*.
   7.2 Unknown.
   7.3 The bath was built near the well of the villa, located some 10 m north. Traces of wooden water supply pipes, held together by iron rings, were found between this well and the bathhouse.
   7.4 Unknown.
8. Both rooms had plastered walls, adorned with wall paintings.
9. Fig. 123.
10. Robert 1980 (ER); Brulet 2008, 566.

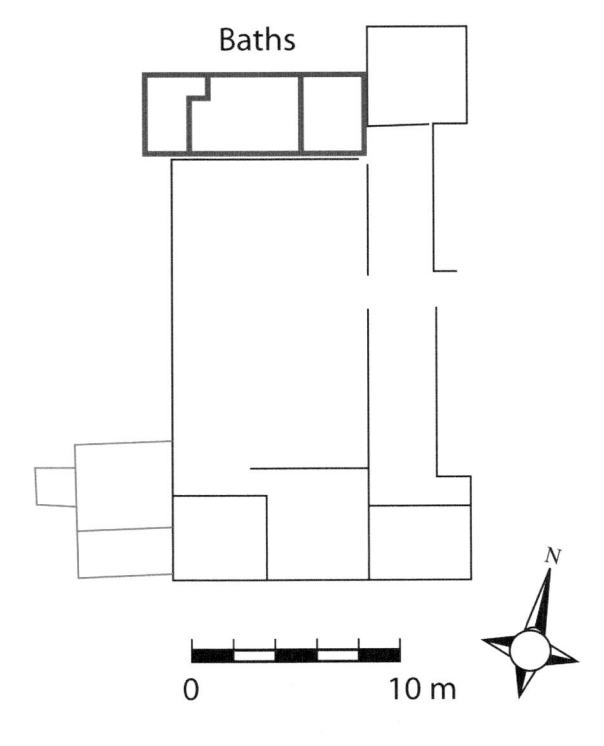

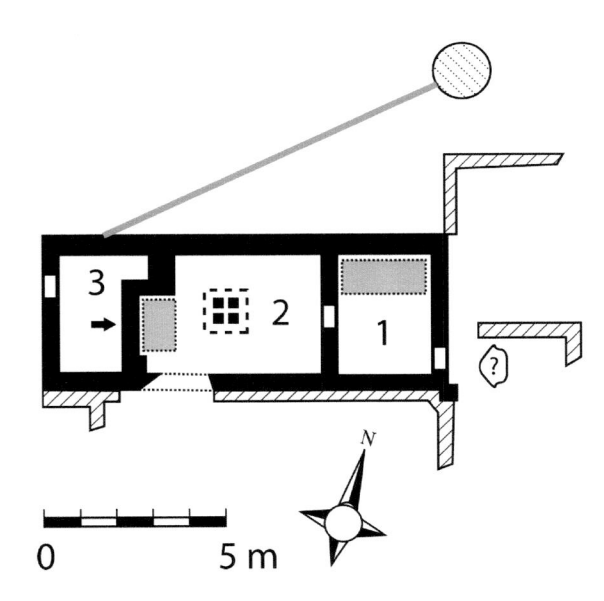

Figure 123. Location (top) and plan of the bath of Roly. Figure by author after Robert 1980, 91, fig. 27.

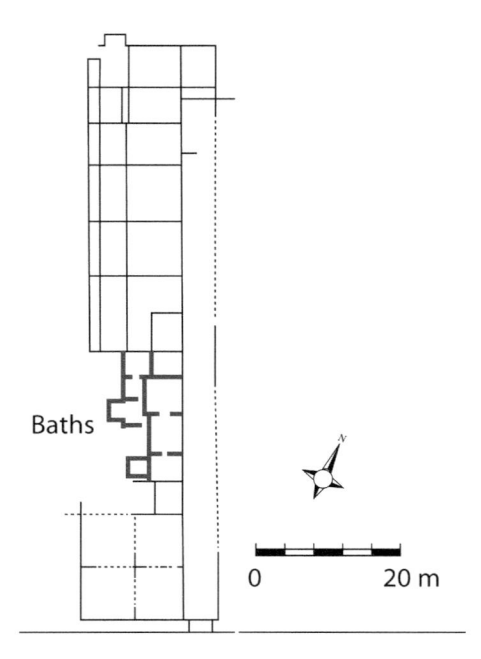

Baths

0   20 m

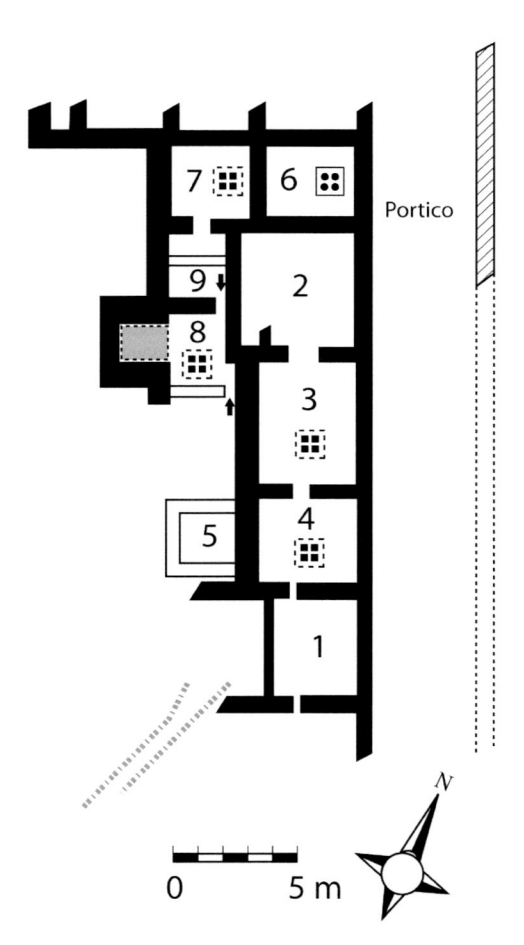

7   6   Portico

9   2

8

3

5   4

1

0   5 m

Figure 124. Location (top) and plan of the bath of Saint-Gérard. Figure by author after Brulet 1970, unnumbered page, fig. 5.

Saint-Gérard, Villa du Try-Hallot (ID 114)

1. 1.1 Belgium, Namur, Mettet.
    1.2 50°21'2.49"N; 4°45'1.60"E (approx.).
2. 2.1 Discovered in 1888, excavated in 1961.
    2.2 Well preserved at the time of excavation, now covered.
3.   Private bath integrated in a villa.
4. 4.1 The villa was in use in the second and fourth century. The bath was added after initial construction (ceramics and coins on site).
    4.2 Unknown. The villa was still occupied in the fourth century (ceramics and coins on site).
    4.3 The villa site was used as a burial ground in the Middle Ages.
5.   A (strong evidence for pools, hypocausts).
6. 6.1 Min. 225 m² (partial plan).
    6.2 Angular row type? (partial plan).
    6.3 As the rooms in the southern and western part of the bath were not excavated, it is difficult to identify auxiliary rooms.
    6.4 The proximity of two drains could point to the presence of a pool; perhaps in the southernmost room (1) (a *frigidarium*?). In the centre of the building, a room without an apparent floor (2) (4.65 × 4.55 m) may have been a cold room with wooden floor.
    6.5 Two heated rooms (3 and 4) to the south (4.1 × 3.6 m and 5 × 4 m) may have been heated rooms for massages or epilation. Alternatively, the northern room was a *tepidarium* and the southern room a *caldarium*. The doorway between these was very narrow (0.53 m). The square room (5) that was added to the west, with its two orifices in the west wall, may have been an *alveus*. In the north of the bathhouse, two more rooms (6 and 7) with hypocaust but without pools were discovered (east: 3.5 × 3.05 m; west: 3.05 × 3 m). In the central western part of the bathhouse lay a fifth heated room (8) with two *exedrae*. At some point, this room must have been a *caldarium* with two *alvei*. Its *praefurnium* (9) was located to the north.
7. 7.1 The tiles of the hypocaust pillars were square (s.: 20.5 cm; 5 cm thick). In contrast, the tiles of a heated room in the northern part of the villa were round (diam.: 22 cm).
    7.2 Only in the heated room in the northern end of the villa *tubuli* of different sizes were found.
    7.3 Unknown.
    7.4 Two drainage channels connected to the drain in the southernmost room were found (to drain a *piscina* or the *alveus* of the presumed southern *caldarium*?).
8.   Unknown.
9.   Fig. 124.
10.   Brulet 1970 (ER); 2008, 550–51.

Saint-Jean-Geest, Villa de la Seigneurie (ID 115)

1. 1.1 Belgium, Walloon Brabant, Jodoigne.
   1.2 50°44'2.10"N; 4°52'44.80"E (approx.).
2. 2.1 1915–1916.
   2.2 Badly preserved at the time of excavations, now covered or destroyed.
3. Freestanding bath of a villa?
4. 4.1 Unknown. The bath seems to have been in use during the second and third century (ceramics on site).
   4.2 Unknown.
   4.3 Unknown.
5. A (strong evidence for a pool, hypocausts).
6. 6.1 Min. 130 m² (partial plan).
   6.2 Unknown (partial plan).
   6.3 A system of intersecting drainage channels in the south-west has been interpreted as a latrine (1). A large room (2) (6.7 × 5.8 m) postdating the other rooms, was heated by a hypocaust, and may have been a heated *apodyterium* (judging from its size).
   6.4 Unknown (partial plan).
   6.5 The northernmost room (3) was heated by a hypocaust and had a semicircular *exedra*, possibly to accommodate a pool. The furnace was located to the north-west. This may have been the *caldarium*. A second heated room (4) to the south had an apsidal ending. No traces of a pool survive, perhaps identifying this room as a *sudatorium*. It had its own furnace to the east. The third heated room (2), already discussed above, may have been a *tepidarium* or heated *apodyterium*.
7. 7.1 In the northernmost room hypocaust pillars survived. They were made of square tiles (s.: 20 cm; 5 cm thick) and bonded with clay, reaching a height of 80 cm. The furnace channel of this room was only 30 cm wide. In the large southern heated room, the hypocaust pillars were made with round tiles (diam.: 32.5 cm).
   7.2 The original excavation diaries only mention several 'hot air conduits' (*tubuli*?).
   7.3 Unknown.
   7.4 The intersecting sewage channels of the alleged latrine may have been connected to the drains of the pools, although no traces of their trajectory remained.
8. Several fragments of polychrome wall painting and of window-panes were recovered from the debris. A plain white mosaic was found just south of the northernmost heated room.
9. Fig. 125.
10. Remy 1977 (ER); Brulet 2008, 289.

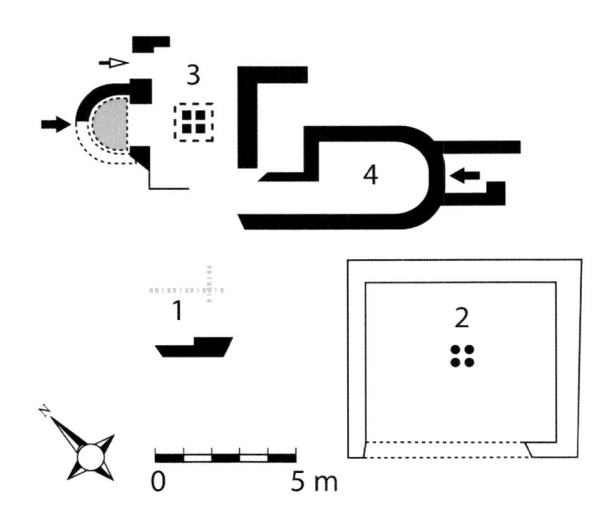

Figure 125. Plan of the bath of Saint-Jean-Geest. Figure by author after Remy 1977, 13, fig. 6.

Baths

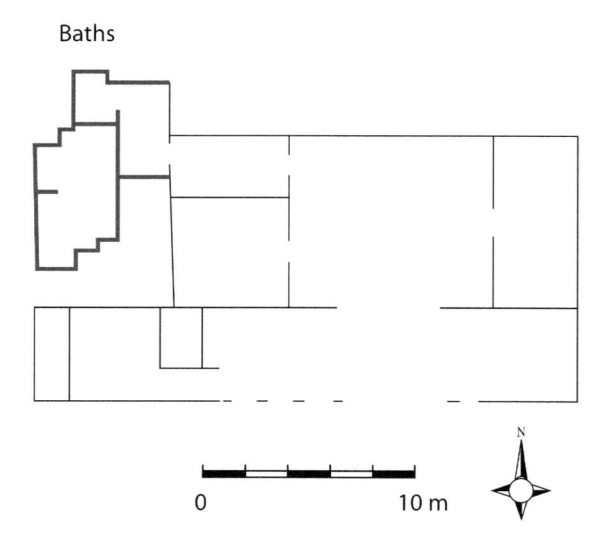

0 10 m

N

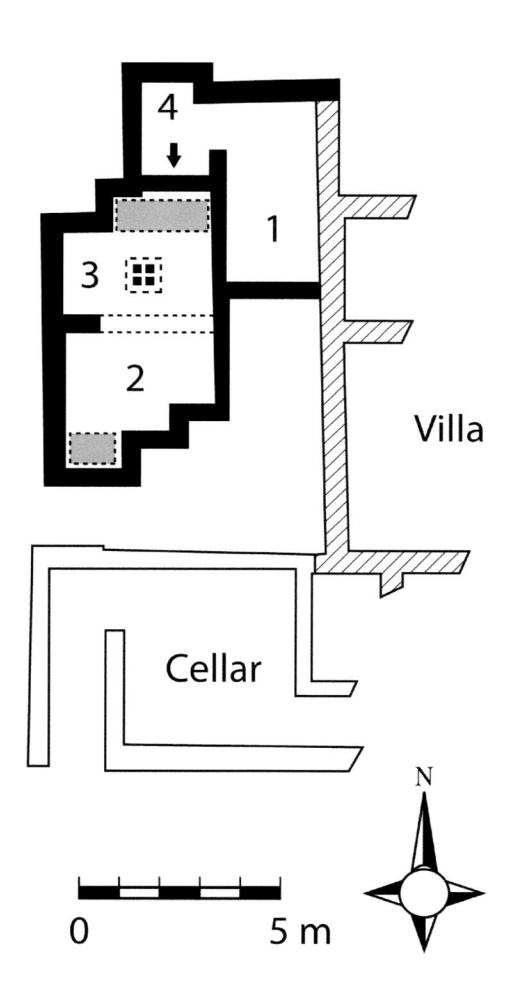

Villa

Cellar

N

0 5 m

Figure 126. Location (top) and plan of the bath of Sauvenière. Figure by author after Bequet 1900b, pl. II.

Sauvenière, Villa d'Arlansart (ID 116)

1. 1.1 Belgium, Namur, Gembloux.
   1.2 50°34'54.50"N; 4°43'31.36"E (approx.).
2. 2.1 1898.
   2.2 Badly preserved when excavated, now covered or destroyed.
3. Private bathhouse integrated in a villa.
4. 4.1 Possibly second century or early third century (tile stamp).
   4.2 The villa was destroyed by fire, possibly in the third century.
   4.3 Unknown.
5. C (hypocausts, possible pools).
6. 6.1 Min. 31 m² (plan unclear).
   6.2 Linear row type? (plan unclear).
   6.3 Unknown. The room (1) linking the bathhouse to the villa may have been part of the baths (*apodyterium*?).
   6.4 The southernmost room (2) may have been a *frigidarium*. The rectangular *exedra* in the southern side may have housed a *piscina*. The walls were too damaged here to make any conclusions about the function of the room. The wall separating it from the heated room (3) to the north was only preserved for 90 cm.
   6.5 At least one room (3) was heated by a hypocaust identifying it as *caldarium*. The rectangular *exedra* in the north side, just above the furnace, seems an ideal location for an *alveus*.
7. 7.1 The *praefurnium* (4) was located just north of the heated room. The furnace walls protruded into the hypocaust. The pillars were made with square tiles (no dimensions given).
   7.2 Unknown. The fact that the northern wall is slightly set back where the presumed *alveus* would have been located, could point to the use of wall heating.
   7.3 Unknown.
   7.4 Unknown.
8. Unknown.
9. Fig. 126.
10. Bequet 1900b (ER); Brulet 2008, 530–31.

Schieren, Villa romaine (ID 117)

1. 1.1 Luxembourg, Diekirch, Schieren.
   1.2 49°49'29.14"N; 6°5'59.51"E (exact).
2. 2.1 1991, 2016.
   2.2 Well preserved when excavated, now partially destroyed, partially covered.
3. Freestanding bathhouse of a villa.
4. 4.1 Unknown. The villa was in use in the second century AD (ceramics on site).
   4.2 Unknown. Several alterations were made to the original plan, pointing to a long phase of use.
   4.3 Unknown.
5. A (hypocausts, pool).
6. 6.1 Min. 120 m² (partial plan).
   6.2 Unknown (partial plan).
   6.3 Unknown (partial plan).
   6.4 Unknown (partial plan).
   6.5 Only the eastern part of the building was excavated, when a new road was constructed. A heated room with a hypocaust and pool can probably be interpreted as a *caldarium* with an *alveus*.
7. 7.1 Unknown.
   7.2 Unknown.
   7.3 Unknown.
   7.4 Unknown.
8. Several fragments of windowpanes were found in the debris of the *caldarium*.
9. Fig. 127 (location, no plan available).
10. Schoellen 1997; Biver and others 2016; Biver and Groetembril 2017.

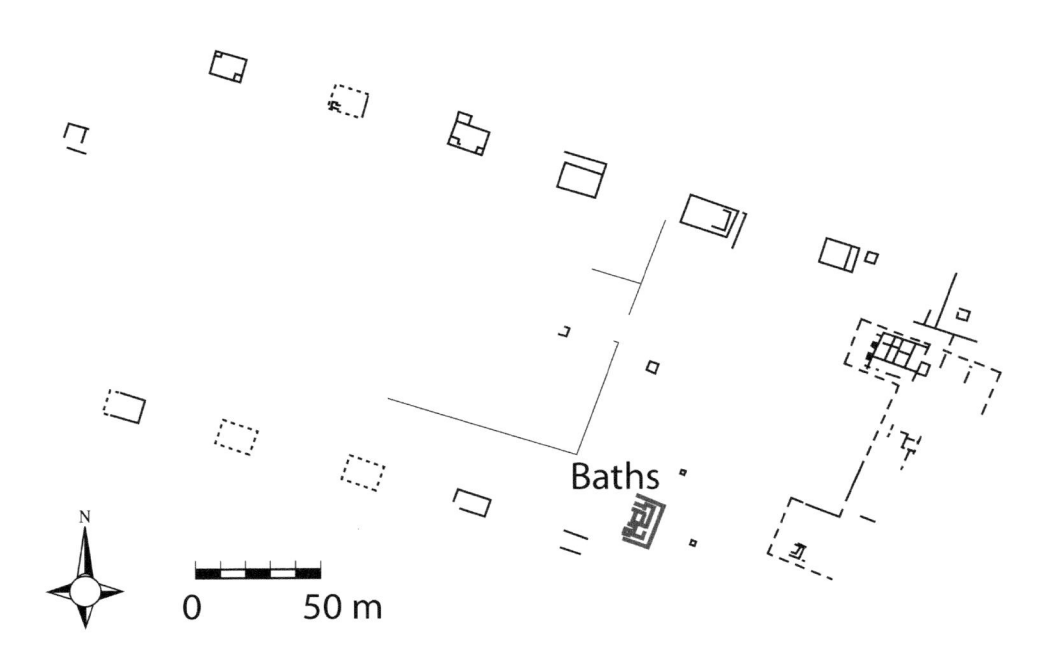

Figure 127. Location of the bath of the villa of Schieren.
Figure by author after Biver and others 2016, 48, fig. 4.

's Gravensvoeren, Villa Steenbosch (ID 118)

1. 1.1 Belgium, Limburg, Voeren.
    1.2 50°45'18.03"N; 5°46'44.80"E (approx.).
2. 2.1 1840–1846.
    2.2 Badly preserved at the time of excavations, now destroyed.
3. Private bath integrated in villa.
4. 4.1 Unknown. The villa was in use between the first and third century AD (ceramics on site).
    4.2 Unknown.
    4.3 Large parts of the villa were dismantled to recuperate building materials.
5. B (hypocausts, evidence for pools).
6. 6.1 *c.* 200 m² (plan unclear).
    6.2 Unknown (plan unclear).
    6.3 Unknown (plan unclear).
    6.4 Unknown (plan unclear).
    6.5 At least two rooms heated by a hypocaust were identified. Two rooms with very sturdy concrete floors (pinkish mortar) could possibly be interpreted as pools.
7. 7.1 The hypocaust pillars of one of the heated rooms, standing to a minimum height of 44 cm, were made of round tiles (diam.: 23 cm).
    7.2 Fragments of *tubuli* were found.
    7.3 Unknown. Fragments of lead *fistula* were found among the destruction layer of the villa. Three wells, two of which in the vicinity of the bath, may have supplied the water for the pools.
    7.4 Two drainage channels led from the bathrooms and joined a ditch to give into a well.
8. Fragments of mosaics, wall painting (geometric and floral patterns) and glass panes (window?) were discovered in the debris of the villa.
9. Fig. 128 (location, no plan available).
10. Delvaux 1851 (ER).

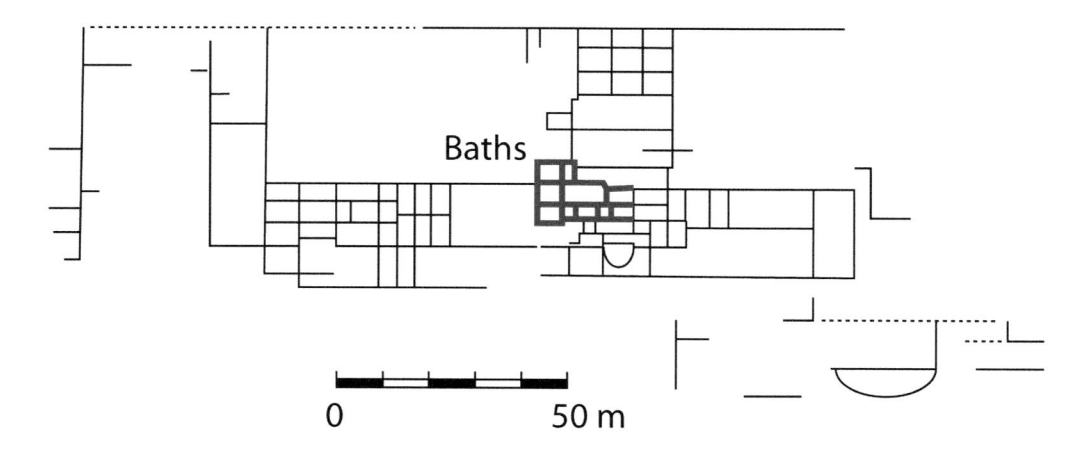

Figure 128. Location of the bath of 's Gravensvoeren. Figure by author after Delvaux 1851, general plan.

Soignies, l'Espesse (ID 119)

1. 1.1 Belgium, Hainaut, Soignies.
   1.2 50°34'36.00"N; 4°4'15.76"E (approx.).
2. 2.1 1984 and 1989.
   2.2 Badly preserved in parts when excavated, now covered or destroyed.
3. Freestanding public bath or more likely a private bath of a rural estate.
4. 4.1 Middle or second half of the second century (ceramics on site).
   4.2 Before the end of the third century (ceramics on site).
   4.3 Unknown.
5. A (pools, hypocausts).
6. 6.1 *c.* 33 m².
   6.2 Linear row type.
   6.3 None.
   6.4 The *frigidarium* (2.4 × 3.4 m) had a rectangular *piscina* (1.5 × 1.8 m) on its western side. No trace remained of this pool, except for a robber's trench, nor of the floor (in wood?).
   6.5 The *caldarium* was the only heated room. It had an *alveus* (1.25 × 1.85 m) on its northern side, above the furnace, and possibly a second *alveus* or *labrum* in the rectangular *exedra* (1.15 × 1.75 m) on the western side.
7. 7.1 The hypocaust pillars were made with square tiles, although no complete examples survived (4–5 cm thick). The *praefurnium* was located north of the bathhouse. Two square post holes found in line with the bath building, indicate that this furnace area was covered by a slanting roof.
   7.2 Several fragments of *tubuli* (25.5 × 13.5 × 20 cm) were found.
   7.3 Unknown.
   7.4 Ditches interpreted as (dismantled) drainage channels were found north and west of the baths, both heading north. These must have drained the pool (s) and/or *labrum* in the *exedrae*.
8. Fragments of glass windowpanes were found outside the western *exedra* of the *caldarium*.
9. Fig. 129.
10. Deru 1991 (ER); Deramaix and Sartieaux 1995 (ER); Brulet 2008, 366.

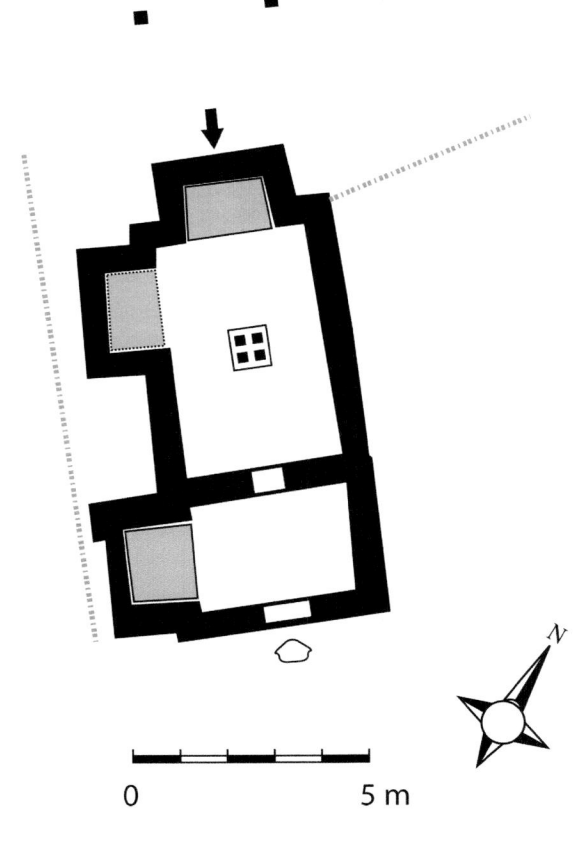

Figure 129. Plan of the bath of Soignies. Figure by author after Deramaix and Sartieaux 1995, 51, unnumbered fig.

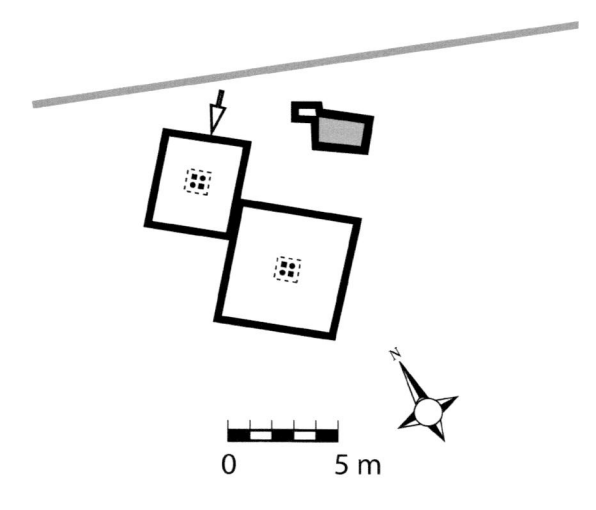

Figure 130. Plan of the bath of Thirimont. Figure by author after Van Bastelaer 1891a, 374, unnumbered fig.

Thirimont, Villa de Saint-Remy (ID 120)

1. 1.1 Belgium, Hainaut, Beaumont.
    1.2 50°15'36.65"N; 4°14'13.24"E (approx.).
2. 2.1 1886.
    2.2 Well preserved when excavated, now destroyed or reburied.
3.   Private bath (?) of a villa.
4. 4.1 Unknown.
    4.2 Unknown. Some coins dating from the third century were found on the site.
    4.3 The site was reused as a burial ground in the Middle Ages. One inhumation was found in the pool.
5.   A (pool, hypocausts).
6. 6.1 Min. 22 m² (partial plan).
    6.2 Unknown.
    6.3 Unknown.
    6.4 One pool was identified (1.3 × 2.4 m). As it was not heated by a hypocaust, it can probably be identified as a *piscina*. The actual *frigidarium* has not been found.
    6.5 Three rooms were equipped with a hypocaust. Two were almost square in shape (5 × 5 m and 4 × 4.5 m). On the basis of the brief descriptions in the excavation report, no functions (*tepidarium, sudatorium, caldarium*) can be attributed with certainty. The smaller room, which was heated by its own furnace, was most likely the *caldarium*. No *alveus* was identified.
7. 7.1 The almost square room was heated by a furnace in its north-eastern side. The hypocaust pillars were made with both square (13 × 14 cm) and round tiles (diam.: 24 cm; 5 cm thick). On one of the *bessales*, the stamp LCS was found.
    7.2 Fragments of *tubuli* were found (no dimensions given).
    7.3 The site was located some 200 m from a stream. An aqueduct (25 cm wide, 35 cm deep) with a south-east–north-west orientation ran just north of the baths. It was made out of mortar and covered with slabs of blue stone (schist?).
    7.4 Unknown.
8.   Several fragments of polychrome wall painting were found in and around the bath rooms. Some vegetal patterns could be identified. A limestone cornice and a column drum were also found.
9.   Fig. 130.
10.   Van Bastelaer 1891a (ER); De Maeyer 1940, 97–98; Brulet 2008, 311.

Tiegem, Villa Hofdries (ID 121)

1. 1.1 Belgium, West Flanders, Anzegem.
    1.2 50°47'46.33"N; 3°27'46.35"E (exact).
2. 2.1 1904 (discovery), 1982–1983 (excavations).
    2.2 Partially destroyed during construction works in 1980, now destroyed.
3.   Private bath (?) integrated in a villa.
4. 4.1 Unknown. The material remains point to a phase of use between the second and third century.
    4.2 The villa site seems to have been abandoned in the third century.
    4.3 None.
5.   C (hypocausts).
6. 6.1 Min. 22 m² (partial plan).
    6.2 Unknown (partial plan).
    6.3 Unknown (partial plan).
    6.4 Unknown (partial plan).
    6.5 At least one room, on the corner of the building (*Eckrisalit*), was heated by a hypocaust (3.3 × 3.7 m). A second room (min. 4.6 × 2.2 m) may also have been heated. The hypocaust pillars were *c.* 40 cm high. The walls were built with blocks of Tournai limestone.
7. 7.1 The heated room had a furnace (40 cm wide) in its north-western side. The hypocaust pillars were made with both square (s.: 16 cm; 3–4 cm tick) and round tiles (diam.: 17–18 cm; 3 cm thick).
    7.2 Fragments of *tubuli* were found in both rooms (with round lateral openings).
    7.3 Unknown.
    7.4 Unknown.
8.   Fragments of painted wall plaster and of windowpanes were found.
9.   Fig. 131.
10.   De Cock 1983 (ER); 1988 (ER).

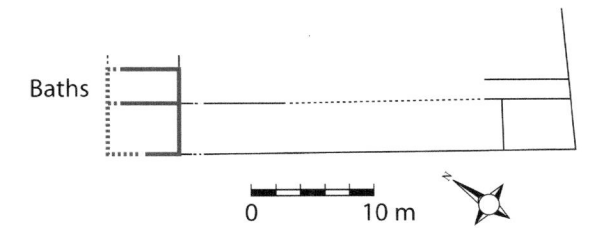

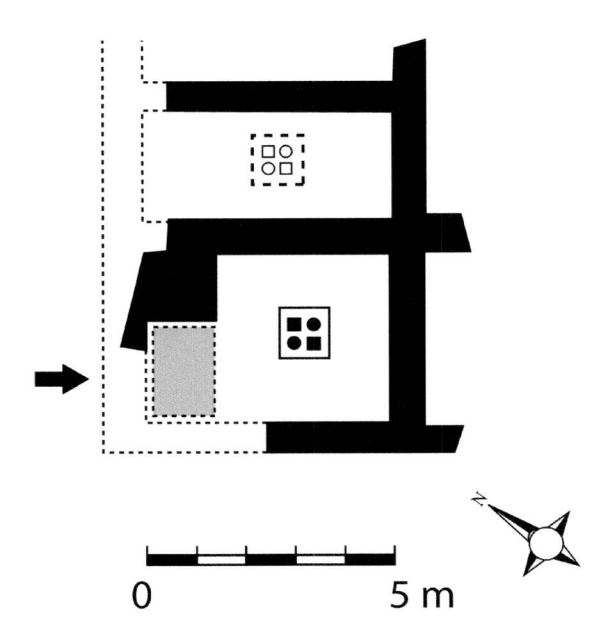

Figure 131. Location (top) and plan of the bath of Tiegem. Figure by author after De Cock 1988, 78, fig. 3.

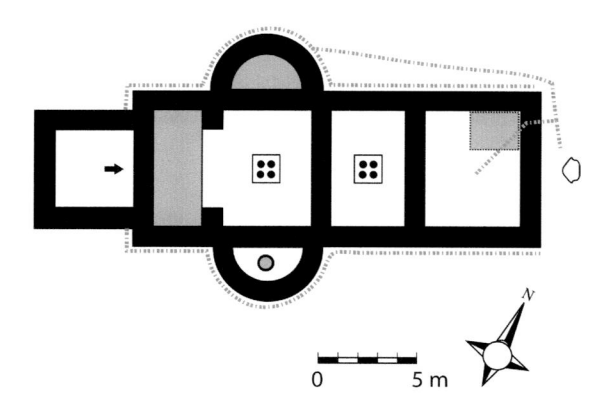

Figure 132. Plan of the bath of Tienen. Figure by author after Vanderhoeven and Vynckier 1997, 143, fig. 16.

Tienen, Vicus Baths (ID 4)

1.   1.1   Belgium, Flemish Brabant, Tienen.
    1.2   50°48'36.73"N; 4°55'28.03"E (exact).
2.   2.1   1996.
    2.2   Badly preserved when excavated (walls and foundations dug out for reuse of building material), now destroyed.
3.   Public baths of a small settlement.
4.   4.1   Flavian period (type of plan, superimposed on the same features as those under the Flavian road).
    4.2   Before the middle of the second century (dismantled before a fire).
    4.3   Used for burial (or abandonment offering) shortly after the bath fell out of use. Although the entire area was rebuilt as a domestic-artisanal quarter, no new structures were built on top of the bathhouse.
5.   A (strong evidence for pools, hypocausts).
6.   6.1   *c.* 200 m².
    6.2   Linear row type.
    6.3   None.
    6.4   The *frigidarium* (4 × 6 m) probably had a small pool in its north-eastern corner (location of a drain) and must have doubled as *apodyterium.*
    6.5   The central room (4 × 6 m) had a hypocaust which was indirectly heated, identifying it as *tepidarium.* The *caldarium* (4 × 6 m) had two semicircular and one rectangular (2 × 6 m) *exedra.* The northern and western *exedrae* possibly accommodated *alvei,* while the sturdy concrete platform in the southern *exedra* might have supported a *labrum.*
7.   7.1   Only one round tile of the hypocaust pillars was found. As no traces of concrete flooring were found in the hypocaust, the excavators suggest that the pillars were placed directly onto the virgin soil. A burned patch of loam underneath the rectangular *exedra,* near the furnace, seems to confirm this. The *praefurnium* had a furnace channel made of several layers (phases?) of tiles.
    7.2   Several fragments of *tubuli* were found in the destruction layer of the bath.
    7.3   Unknown.
    7.4   A drainage channel delimited by vertical tiles ran along the northern and southern side of the bathhouse. A separate channel ran from the northern semicircular *exedra* (*alveus*) and from the centre of the *frigidarium.*
8.   Mosaic black and white *tesserae* were found in the *frigidarium.* Several fragments of polychrome wall painting were also among the debris.
9.   Fig. 132.
10.   Vanderhoeven and Vynckier 1997 (ER).

Tongeren. Schaetzengaerde (ID 15)

1. 1.1   Belgium, Limburg, Tongeren.
      1.2   50°46'42.02"N; 5°27'29.04"E (exact).
2. 2.1   2004.
      2.2   Well preserved when excavated, now destroyed.
3.   Unknown.
4. 4.1   Second half of the second century (*terminus post quem* by older pits underneath the building).
      4.2   Before the early fourth century (*terminus ante quem* by a pit cutting through the walls of the bathhouse).
      4.3   Unknown.
5.   A (pool).
6. 6.1   Min. 60 m² (partial plan).
      6.2   Unknown (partial plan).
      6.3   Unknown (partial plan).
      6.4   The remains of a *piscina* (c. 4 × 2 m; depth unknown) were identified. The imprints of the terracotta tiles that once formed the floor could still be seen. The walls were covered with hydraulic mortar. The remains of the steps for accessing the pool were found in the south-west corner. The *frigidarium* thus might have been located south-west of the pool.
      6.5   The walls south-east of the pool, forming an angle, had a coating of mortar until a certain height. This may point to a raised floor level, which would imply the presence of a hypocaust. However, no hypocaust tiles were found *in situ* or in the debris.
7. 7.1   Unknown.
      7.2   Unknown.
      7.3   Unknown.
      7.4   A robber's trench starting south of the *piscina* floor, and heading south, might well point to the presence of a drainage channel. Furthermore, a water channel was found in the broad wall (width: 1.1 m) south of the *piscina*. It is unknown whether this channel was cut out in an existing wall, or whether it was constructed as such, being part of the drainage system of the bath.
8.   Fragments of red wall painting were found among the debris.
9.   Figs 133–35.
10.   Pauwels, Vanderhoeven, and Vynckier 2005 (ER); Vanderhoeven and others 2007 (ER); Vanderhoeven and Vynckier 2009.

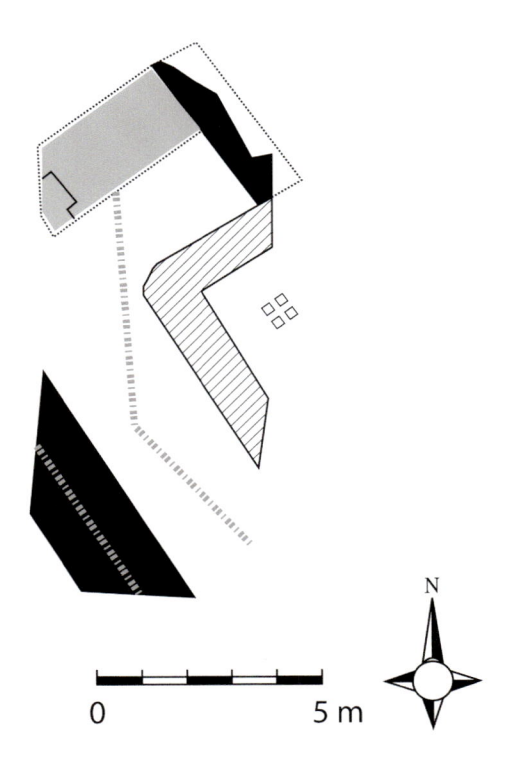

Figure 133. Plan of the remains of a pool at the Schaetzengaerde site in Tongeren. Figure by author after Vanderhoeven and others 2007, 162, fig. 4.

Figure 135. Tongeren – Schaetzengaerde, water channel in the wall south of the *piscina*. Photo by Alain Vanderhoeven, reproduced with his permission.

Figure 134. Tongeren – Schaetzengaerde, mortar floor of the alleged *piscina* with imprints of torn out slabs at the moment of excavation. Photo by Alain Vanderhoeven, reproduced with his permission.

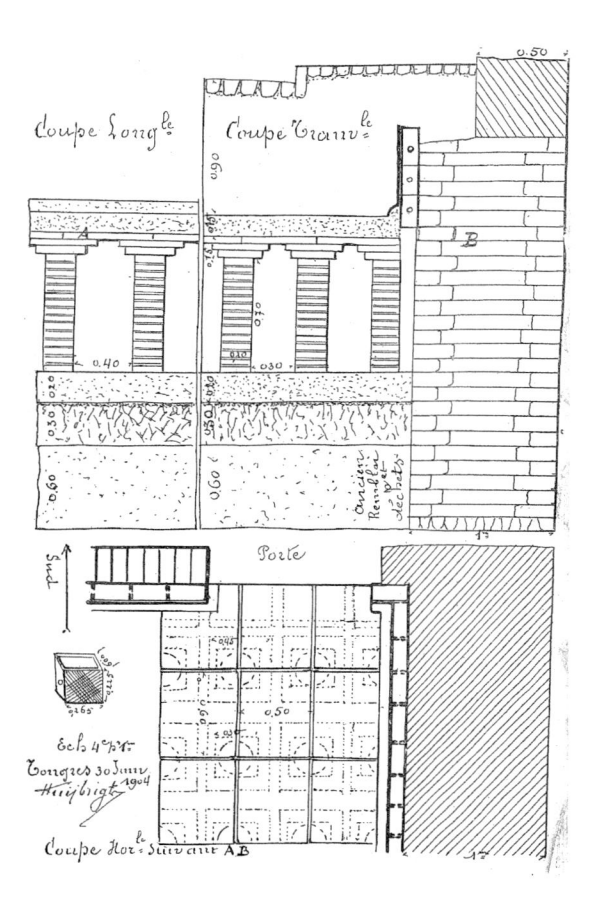

Figure 136. Original sketch plan of the hypocaust found in Sint-Truiderstraat in Tongeren. Figure in Huybrigts 1904, unnumbered plan.

Tongeren, Sint-Truiderstraat (ID 125)

1. 1.1 Belgium, Limburg, Tongeren.
   1.2 50°46'49.38"N; 5°27'42.69"E (exact).
2. 2.1 1904, 1971.
   2.2 Partially preserved when excavated, dismantled in 1971.
3. Private bathhouse of a house?
4. 4.1 The rooms were built on a rubble layer containing first- to second-century materials.
   4.2 The building fell out of use by the fourth century (coins in the destruction layer).
   4.3 Unknown.
5. C (large hypocaust).
6. 6.1 Min. 25 m² (partial plan).
   6.2 Unknown (partial plan).
   6.3 Unknown (partial plan).
   6.4 A room south of the heated room had its floor on a higher level, meaning it was not heated by a hypocaust. Its function and its dimensions are unknown. To the north, a wall made only of *tubuli* seems to have delimited another room.
   6.5 At least one room with a hypocaust was discovered (min. 7 m wide). Its western wall was 1 m wide, probably to limit heat loss (making this an outer wall of the house). No traces of a pool were discovered.
7. 7.1 The hypocaust pillars were made with round tiles (diam.: 20 cm) bonded by clay. The hypocaust floor slightly inclined to the east, possibly for a better draught of the hot gasses. The furnace could not be located, but presumably lay on the east side.
   7.2 The walls of the room were heated by *tubuli* (box type, 26.5 × 22.5 × 9 cm; with circular lateral openings).
   7.3 Unknown.
   7.4 Unknown.
8. Several fragments of polychrome wall painting were found (mainly coloured plains and lines).
9. Fig. 136; no plan available.
10. Huybrigts 1904 (ER); Smeesters 1971 (ER); Vanvinckenroye 1971; Smeesters 1975, 17–18.

Tongeren, Vrijthof-O.L.V. Basiliek (ID 127)

1. 1.1 Belgium, Limburg, Tongeren.
    1.2 50°46′50.86″N; 5°27′53.76″E (exact).
2. 2.1 1999–2001.
    2.2 Partially preserved when excavated, partially destroyed by foundation walls of the later basilica. Now visible as part of a museum underneath the present basilica.
3.   Freestanding (?) private bathhouse of a *domus*.
4. 4.1 A nearby *domus* was constructed in the second half of the second century (stratigraphy). The bath was probably added at a later date. The entire *domus* site was destroyed by a fire during the third century (stratigraphy). The bathhouse seems to date from after this fire (late third or fourth century?).
    4.2 The small bath was probably dismantled when the first basilica was built in the middle of the fourth century, as it would have been located just in front of the western side of the basilica, i.e. where the main entrance would have been located.
    4.3 Unknown.
5.   A (hypocaust, pool).
6. 6.1 *c.* 44 m².
    6.2 Linear row type?
    6.3 None.
    6.4 The bathhouse may have had a single cold room with a semicircular apse to the west. The *piscina* was then located opposite this apse. Alternatively, the bathhouse consisted of a single heated room, with an apsidal pool opposite the furnace.
    6.5 The only heated room, the *caldarium*, was heated by a furnace from the north. An *alveus* may have been constructed just above the furnace channel, on the north end of the room.
7. 7.1 Part of the furnace channel (50 cm wide) was excavated. The hypocaust pillars were mainly made with round tiles, even if square tiles were sometimes used.
    7.2 Unknown.
    7.3 Unknown. Part of a cistern (at least 3 × 3 m) was located some 8 m north of the bathhouse. It was built in the same construction technique and must have been contemporaneous with the bath.
    7.4 Unknown.
8.   Unknown.
9.   Figs 137–38.
10.   Van den Hove, Vanderhoeven, and Vynckier 2002 (ER); Vanderhoeven and others 2017, 182–86 (ER).

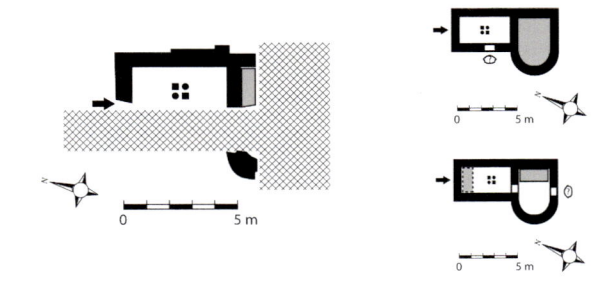

Figure 137. Excavated plan (left) and possible reconstructions (right) of the 'Vrijthof' bath in Tongeren. Figure by author after Vanderhoeven and others 2017, 184, fig. I.262.

Figure 138. Tongeren – Vrijthof, part of the hypocaust and of the pool seen from the north, preserved *in situ* in Teseum museum, 2022. Photo by author.

Tongeren, Boudewijnlaan (ID 124)

1. 1.1 Belgium, Limburg, Tongeren.
   1.2 50°46'45.52"N; 5°27'24.60"E (approx.).
2. 2.1 1975–1976.
   2.2 Well preserved when excavated, now destroyed.
3. Private bath (?) of an urban *domus*.
4. 4.1 Post-Flavian (built on earlier structures).
   4.2 The house was in use between the second and third century (scattered finds).
   4.3 Unknown.
5. A (pool, hypocaust).
6. 6.1 Unknown (partial plan).
   6.2 Unknown (partial plan).
   6.3 Unknown (partial plan).
   6.4 A pool (2 × 2.4 m), not heated by a hypocaust, may be interpreted as a *piscina*.
   6.5 At least one room with a hypocaust was found near the pool.
7. 7.1 Unknown.
   7.2 Unknown.
   7.3 Unknown.
   7.4 Unknown.
8. The floor of the pool was embellished with slabs of green and white marble.
9. No plan available.
10. Vanvinckenroye 1976 (ER).

Tongeren, Vermeulenstraat 3 (ID 126)

1. 1.1 Belgium, Limburg, Tongeren.
   1.2 50°46'56.28"N; 5°27'50.08"E (exact).
2. 2.1 2007–2008.
   2.2 Partially preserved when excavated, now destroyed.
3. Possible private bath of an urban *domus*.
4. 4.1 Coins underneath the hypocaust floor give a *terminus post quem* of the late third or early fourth century, while a destruction layer contained a fourth-century coin, giving a *terminus ante quem*.
   4.2 Late fourth century or later?
   4.3 The entire building was partially dismantled after occupation.
5. C (hypocausts).
6. 6.1 Min. 30 m² (partial plan).
   6.2 Unknown (partial plan).
   6.3 Unknown (partial plan).
   6.4 No cold section was identified in the limited excavation trench.
   6.5 At least two rectangular rooms were heated by a hypocaust. Only the westernmost (1) (24 m²) was entirely excavated. No pools could be identified, making the interpretation as a bath suite hypothetical.
7. 7.1 The westernmost room (1) was heated by a channel hypocaust. Each channel was 30 to 40 cm wide and 60 cm high. One channel was wide enough (80–90 cm) to contain a row of hypocaust pillars, made of round tiles. This mildly heated room might have been a *tepidarium*. The second heated room (2) had a standard hypocaust with pillars made of both square and round tiles.
   7.2 At the end of the north-western and south-western hypocaust channel, a single column of *tubuli* ensured the draught.
   7.3 Unknown.
   7.4 Unknown.
8. The room with channel hypocaust was embellished with wall paintings depicting an agrarian calendar. Some fragments of marble were also recovered.
9. Fig. 139.
10. Unpublished excavation report (Borgers, Steenhoudt, and Van de Velde 2008).

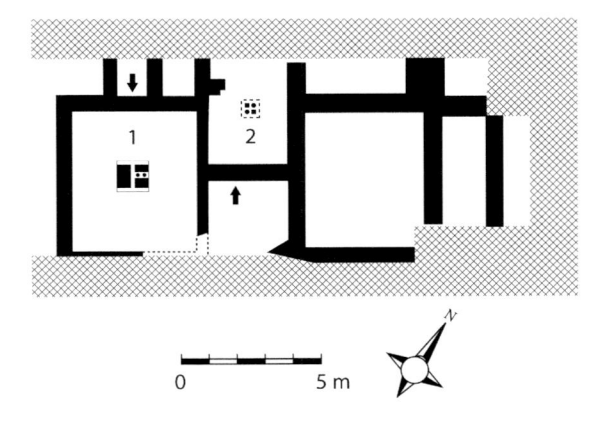

Figure 139. Plan of the hypocausts in the Vermeulenstraat in Tongeren. Figure by author after Borgers, Steenhoudt, and Van de Velde 2008, 4, fig. 3.

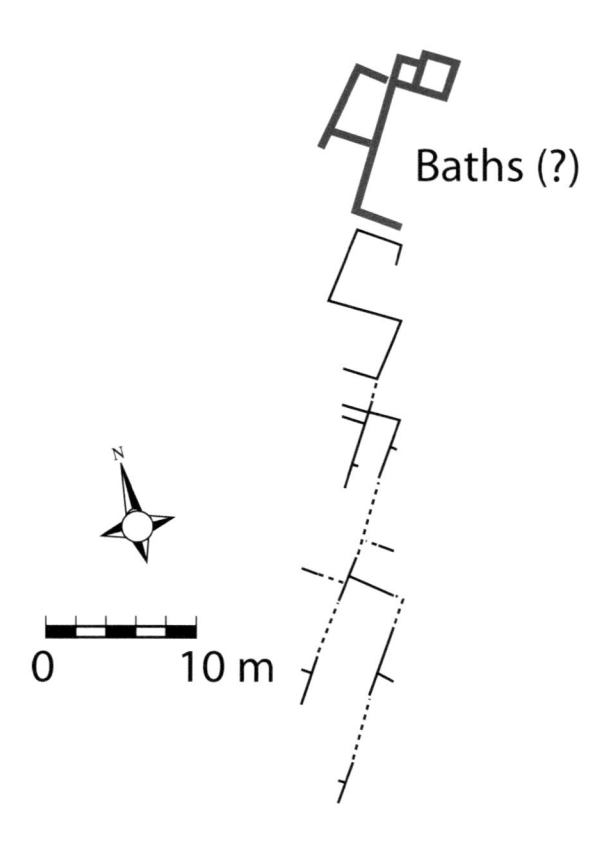

Baths (?)

0   10 m

Figure 140. Location of the alleged bath in the villa of Tourinnes-St-Lambert. Figure by author after De Ruyt 1986, 66, fig. 2.

Tourinnes-St-Lambert, villa baths (ID 128)

1. 1.1   Belgium, Walloon Brabant, Walhain.
    1.2   50°38'7.92"N; 4°43'8.63"E (approx.).
2. 2.1   1984–1985.
    2.2   Badly preserved at the time of excavations, now covered or destroyed.
3.   Bathhouse (?) of a villa (to the south of the baths).
4. 4.1   Unknown.
    4.2   Unknown.
    4.3   Unknown.
5.   C (hypocaust).
6. 6.1   Min. 70 m² (partial plan).
    6.2   Unknown (partial plan).
    6.3   Unknown (partial plan).
    6.4   Unknown (partial plan).
    6.5   At least one room seems to have been heated by a Y-shaped channel hypocaust.
7. 7.1   The only indication of floor heating was the Y-shaped channel hypocaust (bottom in concrete, walls in stone and tiles).
    7.2   In the room with the hypocaust, several fragments of *tubuli* were found (favouring the interpretation as a room rather than as a drying space).
    7.3   Unknown.
    7.4   Unknown.
8.   Fragments of polychrome wall painting were found in the north-eastern room.
9.   Fig. 140 (location, no plan available).
10.   De Ruyt 1986 (ER); Brulet 2008, 297.

Tourinnes-St-Lambert, Campagne du Préat (ID 18)

1. 1.1 Belgium, Walloon Brabant, Walhain.
   1.2 50°38'49.16"N; 4°43'38.52"E.
2. 2.1 1910.
   2.2 Well preserved when excavated, now destroyed.
3. Freestanding public bathhouse or bath of a villa?
4. 4.1 Unknown. The only chronological evidence consists of third-century coins found in the hypocaust.
   4.2 Unknown.
   4.3 Unknown.
5. B (hypocaust, strong evidence for a pool).
6. 6.1 *c.* 82 m².
   6.2 Linear row type.
   6.3 None.
   6.4 None.
   6.5 The bath consisted of two rooms heated by a hypocaust. The largest room had a rectangular *exedra* (4.1 × 2 m) on its south side and was heated by its own furnace (east). It can be interpreted as the *caldarium*, presumably with an *alveus* above the furnace. The smaller room on the west side of the building must have been indirectly heated and can thus be identified as a *tepidarium*. A 1.5 m wide path paved with small white limestone ran south of the building. A branch headed towards the *exedra*, where the main entrance of the bath must have been located.
7. 7.1 The furnace floor was made of concrete and lined by two walls of brick, possibly to support a boiler. The furnace channel was 2.25 m long and protruded into the hypocaust. The hypocaust pillars were made with square tiles (s.: 20–22 cm; 3.5–4 cm thick).
   7.2 Unknown.
   7.3 Unknown.
   7.4 Unknown.
8. Unknown.
9. Fig. 141.
10. Dens and Poils 1911 (ER); De Maeyer 1940, 27–28.

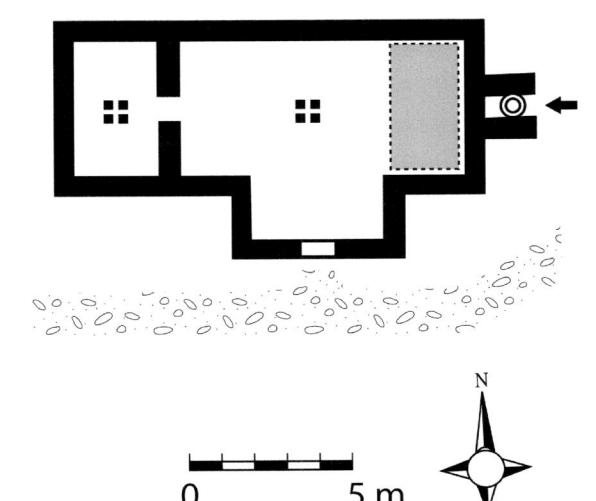

Figure 141. Plan of the possible 'Vicus Bath' in Tourinnes-St-Lambert. Figure by author after Dens and Poils 1911, 295, pl. III.

Tournai, Marché aux Jambons (ID 24)

1.   1.1   Belgium, Hainaut, Tournai.
         1.2   50°36'30.21"N; 3°23'12.38"E (exact).
2.   2.1   1943–1944.
         2.2   Well preserved when excavated, now covered or destroyed.
3.   Private bathhouse integrated in a *domus*?
4.   4.1   The oldest phase possibly dates from the late first century AD (ceramics on site).
         4.2   Late second century (ceramics in the destruction layer of the furnace).
         4.3   The room with the oval pool was transformed in the Middle Ages (function unknown).
5.   A (pool, hypocaust).
6.   6.1   Min. 26 m² (incomplete plan).
         6.2   Unknown (incomplete plan).
         6.3   Unknown (incomplete plan).
         6.4   The largest room had an oval pool (1 × 1.8 m) of min. 60 cm deep (*piscina?*). A small almost square room (3 × 2.9 m), which may have been heated once (chimney flues in the northern corners), had a nicely embellished rectangular *piscina* (2.53 × 1.42 m).
         6.5   A room of 3.75 × 3.5 m had a hypocaust, but apparently had no pools. It was heated by its own furnace to the east, which could point to a function as *sudatorium*.
7.   7.1   The hypocaust pillars were made of square tiles (s.: 17 cm; 3 cm thick) bonded with clay (2 cm thick). These reached a height of 51 cm. The *praefurnium* of the heated room lay on its eastern side.
         7.2   In the heated room, recesses in the eastern wall housed *tubuli* (20 × 25 × 12 cm; 2 cm thick; round lateral openings with diam.: 5 cm). Two such recesses were also found in the large room with the oval pool (possibly reminiscent of an earlier phase of the room).
         7.3   Two wells were found in the vicinity of the bathing rooms.
         7.4   The oval pool was drained by an orifice at the bottom (which could not be followed deeper due to rising ground water). Outside of the building, a water channel (sewer?) made of fragments of *tegula* and hypocaust tiles, was identified.
8.   The heated room had plastered walls painted in vermillion red. The rectangular pool was embellished with slabs of white marble on its walls. The floor was covered with slabs of local limestone. The walls surrounding the pool, some 1.54 m above the bottom, were plastered and adorned with painted panels of green bordered by black and white lines.
9.   No plan available.
10.   Amand 1946 (ER); Brulet 2008, 373.

Tournai, Place Paul-Emile Janson (ID 25)

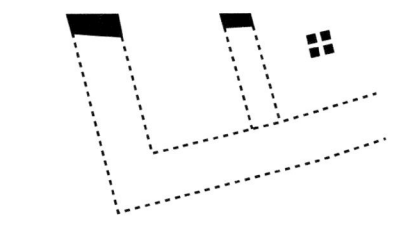

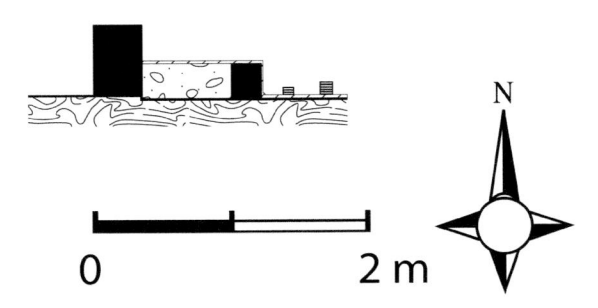

1. 1.1 Belgium, Hainaut, Tournai.
    1.2 50°36'24.92"N; 3°23'21.79"E (exact).
2. 2.1 1954.
    2.2 Partially preserved when excavated, now destroyed.
3.   Private bathhouse (?) integrated in a *domus*.
4. 4.1 Late first or early second century (ceramics underneath the hypocaust).
    4.2 Unknown.
    4.3 Unknown.
5.   B (strong evidence for a pool, hypocaust).
6. 6.1 Min. 12 m² (partial plan).
    6.2 Unknown (partial plan).
    6.3 Unknown (partial plan).
    6.4 It seems that in a first phase, the location of the hypocaust served as a cold pool. A reddish hydraulic mortar covered the floor, the wall, and what seems to be an internal step.
    6.5 The hypocaust pillars seem to have been built in an abandoned *piscina*. A second similar mortar floor was found nearby, which could also have been part of the alleged bathhouse.
7. 7.1 The hypocaust pillars were made of square tiles (s.: 18 cm). The *praefurnium* was not located.
    7.2 Unknown.
    7.3 Unknown.
    7.4 Unknown.
8.   Unknown.
9.   Fig. 142.
10.   Amand 1953 (ER); Amand and Eykens-Dierickx 1960, 116–18.

Figure 142. Plan and section of the hypocaust excavated on the Place Paul-Emile Janson in Tournai. Figure by author after Amand and Eykens-Dierickx 1960, 117, fig. 11.

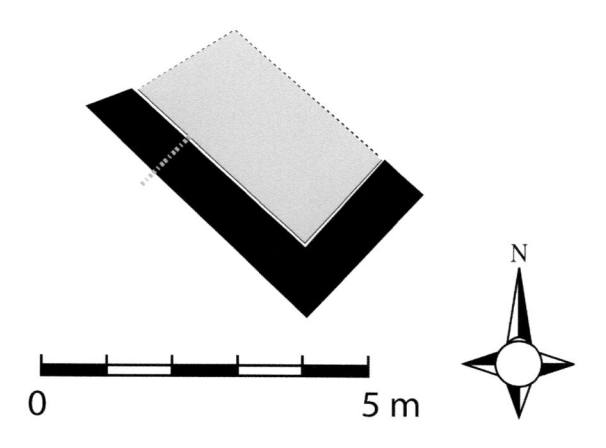

Figure 143. Plan of the pool excavated on the Quai Vifquin in Tournai. Figure by author after Verslype 1997, 67, unnumbered fig.

Tournai, Quai Vifquin (ID 26)

1.   1.1   Belgium, Hainaut, Tournai.
      1.2   50°36'21.50"N; 3°23'42.15"E (exact).
2.   2.1   1995.
      2.2   Well preserved when excavated, now destroyed.
3.   Public bathhouse (?).
4.   4.1   The bathhouse was in use in the second and third century (ceramics on site).
      4.2   Late third or early fourth century (ceramics in the filling of the *piscina*).
      4.3   After the pool was filled, a new pavement of *tegulae* was laid on top of it, pointing to a secondary use of the building. After a fire in the fourth or early fifth century, the building was abandoned, even if there are traces of squatter occupation afterwards.
5.   A (pool).
6.   6.1   Min. 10 m² (partial plan).
      6.2   Unknown (partial plan).
      6.3   Unknown (partial plan).
      6.4   Only part of the *piscina* of the *frigidarium* was discovered during the rescue excavations. The foundations of stone rubble were built on top of wooden posts, used to stabilize the marshy soils near the river Scheldt. The stone rubble was topped with tiles and a layer of hydraulic mortar.
      6.5   Unknown (partial plan).
7.   7.1   Unknown (partial plan).
      7.2   Unknown (partial plan).
      7.3   Unknown.
      7.4   The *piscina* was drained by a pipe leading directly into the river.
8.   Several fragments of wall painting were found in the filling of the pool.
9.   Fig. 143.
10.   Verslype 1995 (ER); 1997 (ER).

Tournai, Quai Luchet d'Antoing (ID 27)

1. 1.1 Belgium, Hainaut, Tournai.
    1.2 50°36'11.80"N; 3°23'55.78"E (approx.).
2. 2.1 1964.
    2.2 Badly preserved when excavated (partially destroyed by the modern river embankment), now destroyed.
3. Unknown (partial plan).
4. 4.1 Possibly third quarter of the second century (ceramics).
    4.2 Unknown.
    4.3 Unknown.
5. A (pool).
6. 6.1 Min. 10 m² (partial plan).
    6.2 Unknown (partial plan).
    6.3 Unknown (partial plan).
    6.4 A part of a *piscina* (3.5 m wide; at least 2 m long) was the only evidence of the presence of a bathhouse. A second pool (w.: 1.2 m) may have been present.
    6.5 Unknown.
7. 7.1 Unknown.
    7.2 Unknown.
    7.3 Unknown.
    7.4 A (drainage?) channel ran along the south side of the pool. Its walls were made of blocks of stone, while the bottom consisted of tiles. As the remains lay near the river Scheldt, it is likely that the waste waters were eventually dumped in the river.
8. Fragments of wall painting (vermillion red) were found among the debris.
9. Fig. 144.
10. Amand 1964 (ER); 1968 (ER); Brulet 2008; 374.

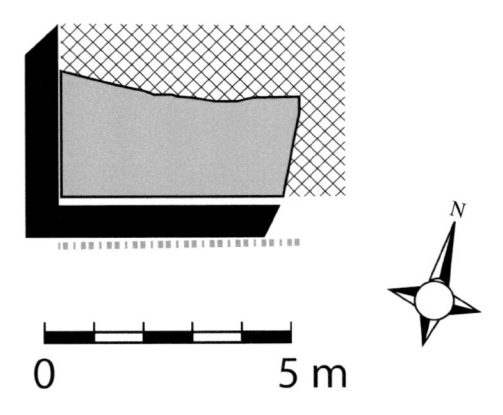

Figure 144. Plan of the pool excavated on the Quai Luchet d'Antoing in Tournai. Figure by author after Amand 1964, 42, fig. 25.

Tournai, Couvent des Frères mineurs (ID 129)

1. 1.1 Belgium, Hainaut, Tournai.
   1.2 50°36'7.72"N; 3°23'54.27"E (exact).
2. 2.1 1997.
   2.2 Partially preserved when excavated, now destroyed.
3. Private bath of an urban *domus*?
4. 4.1 Unknown.
   4.2 Unknown.
   4.3 The site was later used as a burial ground for the monastery. A burial cut through the pool.
5. A (pool).
6. 6.1 Unknown (partial plan).
   6.2 Unknown (partial plan).
   6.3 Unknown (partial plan).
   6.4 A pool (3.35 × 1.9 m; 1.25 m deep) was partially hewn out of the bedrock, partially made out of uncut stone bonded by mortar. The inside of the pool was covered with pinkish waterproof mortar. The bottom was made out limestone slabs. The small sides had opposing small benches.
   6.5 Unknown (partial plan).
7. 7.1 Unknown (partial plan).
   7.2 Unknown (partial plan).
   7.3 Unknown (partial plan).
   7.4 A fragment of a metal outlet pipe was still *in situ* at the bottom of the pool.
8. Unknown.
9. No plan available.
10. Ingels 1999 (ER).

Treignes, Villa Les Bruyères (ID 130)

1. 1.1 Belgium, Namur, Viroinval.
   1.2 50°5'15.55"N; 4°39'50.44"E (exact).
2. 2.1 1980–1987, 1995.
   2.2 Well preserved when excavated, now restored and open to the public.
3. Private bathhouse integrated in a villa.
4. 4.1 The bathhouse seems to have been included in the original layout of the villa, which was constructed in the second half of the second century (ceramics on site). A restoration phase of the *caldarium* probably dates from the third century.
   4.2 Unknown. The villa fell out of use around AD 375 (ceramics).
   4.3 Unknown.
5. A (pools, hypocausts).

6. 6.1 *c*. 130 m².

6.2 Linear row type.

6.3 None.

6.4 The *frigidarium* (1) had a rectangular *piscina* (4 × 2.5 m) on its western side. It must also have served as a dressing room.

6.5 South of the *frigidarium* lay an almost square heated room (2), protruding out of the south side of the villa and heated by its own furnace. It was probably a *sudatorium*. East of the *frigidarium* lay the *caldarium* (3), with possibly an *alveus* above the furnace to the east. In a second phase, the *caldarium* was enlarged to the east by a semicircular *exedra* in dry stone, while a semicircular *exedra* was added to the south side, probably to lodge a pool or *labrum*. The oblong shape of the room could indicate that a partitioning wall at *suspensura* level divided the room into a *tepidarium* (west) and *caldarium* (east).

7. 7.1 Both heated rooms were heated by their own furnace. The hypocaust pillars were made with square tiles.

7.2 Some *tubuli* were found in the villa.

7.3 Terracotta pipes and iron rings to hold together wooden pipes were found in the vicinity of the bath, pointing to a water supply by aqueduct. The *Fontaine Saint-Pierre* some 2 km from the villa may have been the source that supplied the villa.

7.4 The *piscina* was drained by a lead *fistula* flowing into a drainage channel running west of the villa. The latter was made of stone blocks and covered with slabs of schist. The eastern *alveus* was drained by a channel made of *imbrices*, running underneath the *caldarium* and the *sudatorium* to join the above-mentioned drainage channel. After the restoration, the newly added *exedra* had a separate drain made of *imbrices*, heading south-east.

8. Unknown.

9. Figs 145–47.

10. Doyen 1981 (ER); 1987 (ER); Bott and Cattelain 1996–1997; 1999.

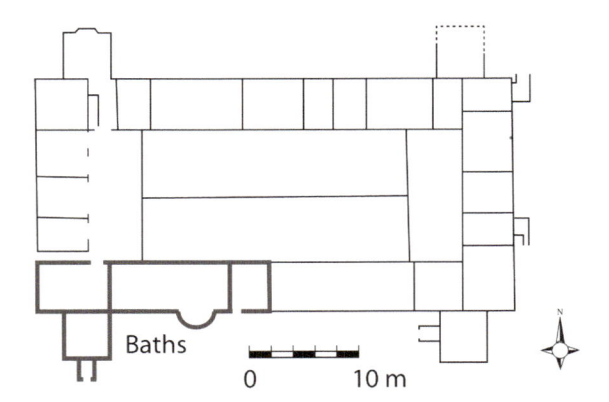

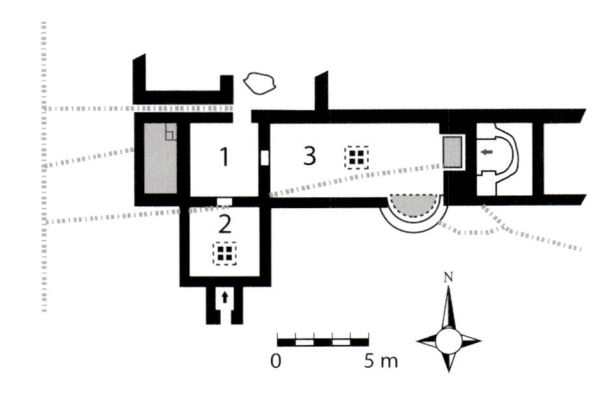

Figure 145. Location (top) and plan of the baths of Treignes. Figure by author after Bott and Cattelain 1996–1997, 186, plan.

Figure 146. Reconstructed *piscina* of the bath of Treignes seen from the south. Photo courtesy of Ghent University, Department of Archaeology.

Figure 147. Reconstructed heated section of the bath of Treignes seen from the west. Photo courtesy of Ghent University, Department of Archaeology.

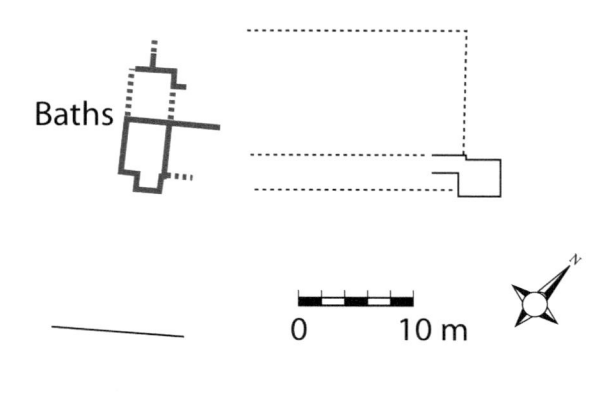

Baths

0   10 m

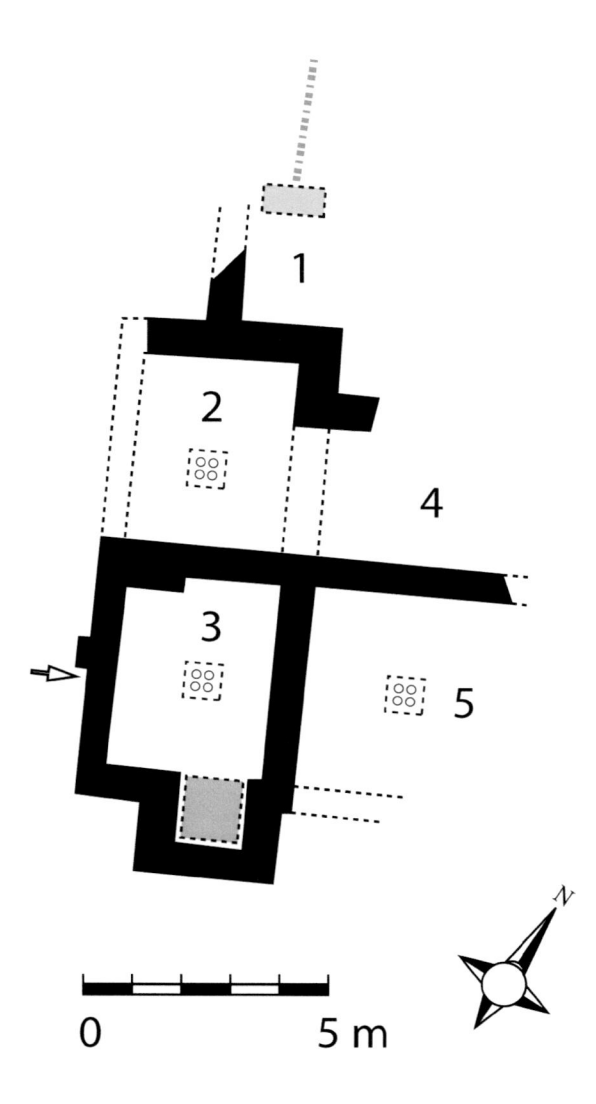

Figure 148. Location (top) and plan of the bath of Val-Meer. Figure by author after De Boe 1971a, pl. III.

Val-Meer, Villa Meerberg (ID 131)

1. 1.1 Belgium, Limburg, Riemst.
    1.2 50°47'43.77"N; 5°35'0.73"E (approx.).
2. 2.1 1966.
    2.2 Very badly preserved when excavated, now destroyed.
3. Private bathhouse of a villa (connection unclear).
4. 4.1 On the basis of the scarce datable ceramics, the villa site seems to have been in use in the second and third century. However, a first-century phase cannot be excluded. The orientation of the bath, slightly different from the orientation of the villa, points to a later construction date (integrated, attached, or freestanding?).
    4.2 There were no fourth-century ceramics found on site, which points to abandonment during the third century.
    4.3 Unknown. The site was probably spoliated for building materials in a post-Roman phase.
5. B (hypocausts, evidence for pools).
6. 6.1 Min. 54 m² (partial plan).
    6.2 Linear row type? (partial plan).
    6.3 Unknown (partial plan).
    6.4 The cold room was probably located to the north (1), where a drainage channel seems to have started. No further evidence was found, but considering the bad state of preservation of all walls above ground, this is not surprising.
    6.5 At least two rooms seem to have been heated by a hypocaust. The southernmost (3) had an almost square *exedra* (s.: *c.* 1.5 m), presumably to lodge an *alveus*. This could then be interpreted as the *caldarium*. The room to the north (2) (*c.* 3 × 4 m), between the alleged *frigidarium* and *caldarium*, would reasonably be the *tepidarium*. To the east of these two heated rooms, two more rooms (4 and 5) were identified, which may have belonged to the bath. The southernmost (5) might also have been heated (*sudatorium?*).
7. 7.1 The furnace(s) could not be located. A small protruding wall on the west side of the *caldarium* could point to a furnace channel. The hypocaust tiles were round (diam.: 20.5 cm; 3.5–4 cm thick).
    7.2 Fragments of *tubuli* were found, but no complete example survived.
    7.3 Unknown.
    7.4 A ditch, probably a drainage channel, ran from the northernmost room heading further north. It probably drained the *piscina*.
8. Several fragments of windowpanes were found.
9. Fig. 148.
10. De Boe 1966 (ER); 1971a (ER).

Vechmaal, Middelpadveld (ID 132)

1. 1.1 Belgium, Limburg, Heers.
    1.2 50°45'20.89"N; 5°21'40.41"E (approx.).
2. 2.1 1989.
    2.2 Well preserved when excavated, now covered or destroyed.
3. Private bathhouse attached to a villa.
4. 4.1 Third century? (postdating the second century-villa).
    4.2 Unknown. The villa was abandoned in the first half of the fourth century.
    4.3 Unknown.
5. A (pools, hypocausts).
6. 6.1 *c.* 44 m².
    6.2 Linear row type.
    6.3 The entrance to the bath was emphasized by a porch of two columns/posts (1).
    6.4 The *frigidarium* (2) had a rectangular *piscina* (1.6 × 1 m; min. 0.75 m deep). This pool had a floor of large terracotta tiles and an internal step/bench in the form of a quarter of a circle. As there are no rooms preceding the *frigidarium*, the latter must also have been used as *apodyterium*.
    6.5 The first room with a hypocaust (3) (2.25 × 1.25 m) was only indirectly heated by the furnace of the second heated room, and must hence be interpreted as a *tepidarium*. The fact that no pool was found here, which is quite normal for *tepidaria*, cannot justify the excavator's interpretation as a sweat room. The second heated room (4) (3.5 × 2.25 m) had its own furnace to the north-west and can thus be identified as the *caldarium*. It probably had an *alveus* above the furnace channel and a second one in the rectangular *exedra* on its southern side (1.6 × 1 m).
7. 7.1 The hypocaust pillars were made of round tiles. The *praefurnium* (5) to the west of the *caldarium* had a furnace channel made of bricks inserted on their small sides in the virgin loam soil, and two parallel walls which may have supported a furnace or a *testudo*.
    7.2 The walls of the *caldarium* were heated by *tubuli* (24 × 23 × 10 cm; round lateral openings).
    7.3 A well was located some metres south-east of the bathhouse. However, other types of water supply (rain catchment) cannot be excluded.
    7.4 The *piscina* was drained by a narrow outlet (diam.: 6 cm) in its south-eastern corner. It gave directly into a sump, in which bronze and bone hair pins, a ring, and fragments of *fibulae* were found.
8. The walls of all the rooms were embellished with wall paintings. Simple coloured panels were framed by up to three red lines, while vegetal patterns were also discovered. Several fragments of glass windowpanes were found.
9. Fig. 149.
10. Vanvinckenroye 1997 (ER).

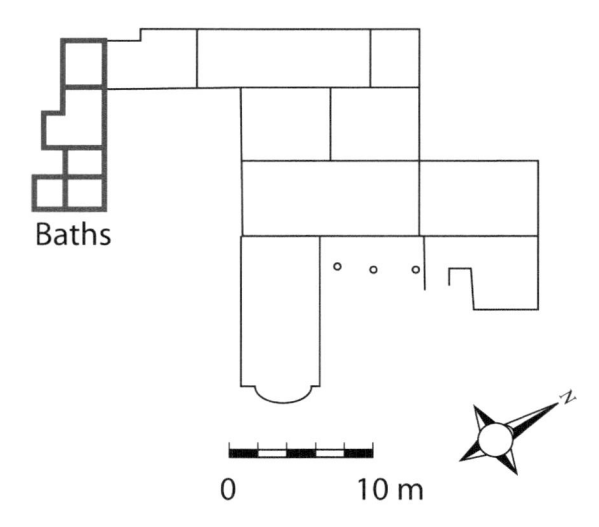

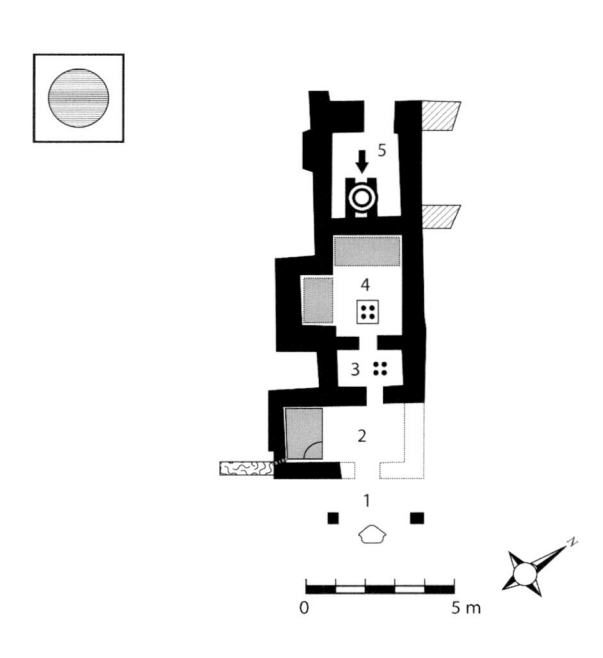

Figure 149. Location (top) and plan of the bath of Vechmaal. Figure by author after Vanvinckenroye 1997, 185, fig. 3 and 189, fig. 4.

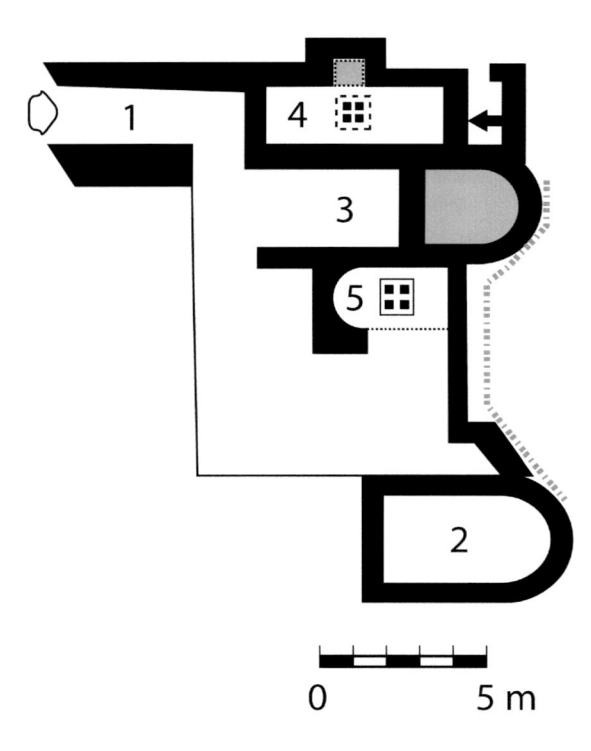

Figure 150. Plan of the bath of Vellereille-les-Brayeux. Figure by author after Rahir 1928, 133, fig. 67.

Vellereille-les-Brayeux, Villa de Pincemaille (ID 133)

1.   1.1   Belgium, Hainaut, Estinnes.
      1.2   50°22'37.15"N; 4°10'26.98"E (approx.).
2.   2.1   1909–1911.
      2.2   Badly preserved in parts when excavated, now covered or destroyed.
3.   Private bathhouse attached to a villa.
4.   4.1   Unknown.
      4.2   Unknown.
      4.3   Unknown.
5.   A (pools, hypocausts).
6.   6.1   *c.* 130 m².
      6.2   Linear row type? (plan unclear).
      6.3   The bathhouse was connected to the villa by a 30 m-long corridor (1). The apsidal room (2) on the lowest end of the bathhouse may have been added at a later date. Its function is unknown.
      6.4   It seems that the *frigidarium* (3) was located at the centre of the building. A *piscina* was identified in an apsidal *exedra* (s.: 2.8 m).
      6.5   A rectangular room (4) in line with the corridor must be interpreted as the *caldarium*. It had a rectangular *exedra*, possibly to lodge an *alveus*. A second heated room (5) (*tepidarium/ sudatorium*?) lay beyond the *frigidarium*. It had a semicircular apse. The excavator also mentions two more basins (pools?) with tiled floors.
7.   7.1   The hypocaust pillars were made with square tiles. The *praefurnium* of the *caldarium* was located in prolongation of the latter and the corridor.
      7.2   Fragments of *tubuli* were found in the *sudatorium/tepidarium*.
      7.3   The water of the bath was supplied by a diverted branch of a nearby stream (no further information given).
      7.4   The semicircular *piscina* was drained by an orifice, emptying into a drainage channel that ran along the side of the bathhouse. It ended in a sump.
8.   The bottom and the sides of the *piscina* were clad with marble slabs. In the *tepidarium/sudatorium*, fragments of wall paintings were found.
9.   Fig. 150.
10.   De Loë 1911 (ER); Rahir 1928, 132–36; Brulet 2008, 331.

Vesqueville, villa romaine de Vesqueville (ID 134)

1. 1.1   Belgium, Luxembourg, Saint-Hubert.
   1.2   50°0'22.51"N; 5°23'38.69"E (approx.).
2. 2.1   1971.
   2.2   Well preserved when excavated, now covered.
3.   Private bathroom (?) integrated in a villa.
4. 4.1   Late second or early third century (*terminus post quem* by ceramics in the foundation trenches).
   4.2   Before the third quarter of the third century (abandonment of the villa site; ceramics on site).
   4.3   Unknown.
5.   C (hypocausts).
6. 6.1   *c.* 32 m².
   6.2   Single room?
   6.3   None.
   6.4   None.
   6.5   The alleged bathroom possibly consisted of a single heated room, perhaps with an *alveus* along its south-eastern side. As the room was only partially excavated, the exact layout is unclear. There may have been an internal division in *tepidarium-caldarium*. Two parallel walls flanking the furnace channel may have been used to support a pool.
7. 7.1   The hypocaust floor was made of mortar finished with *tegulae* (with the rims trimmed off). The pillars were made with square tiles (s.: 16.5–17 cm; 3 cm thick). The *praefurnium* (2) (3 × 1.2 m) was located south-west of the heated room and also heated the south-western square angular room (3) of the villa. The furnace channel floor was covered with tiles.
   7.2   Unknown. However, in the heated living room, fragments of *tubuli* were found.
   7.3   Unknown.
   7.4   Unknown.
8.   Unknown.
9.   Fig. 151.
10.   Matthys 1974 (ER); Brulet 2008, 490.

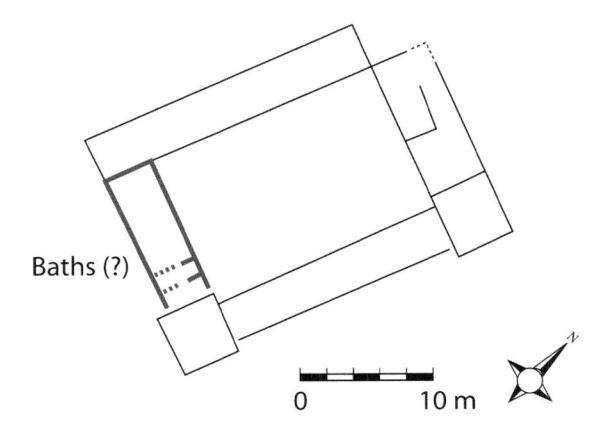

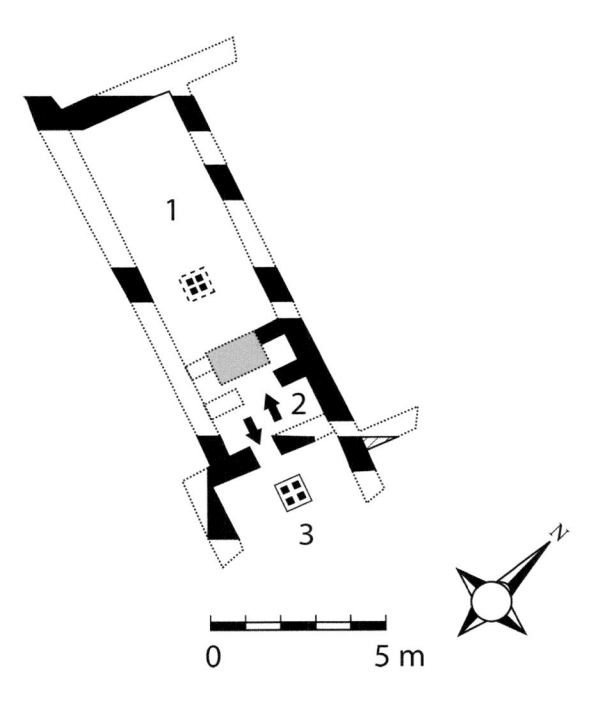

Figure 151. Location (top) and plan of the alleged bath of Vesqueville. Figure by author after Matthys 1974, pl. I and II.

Baths

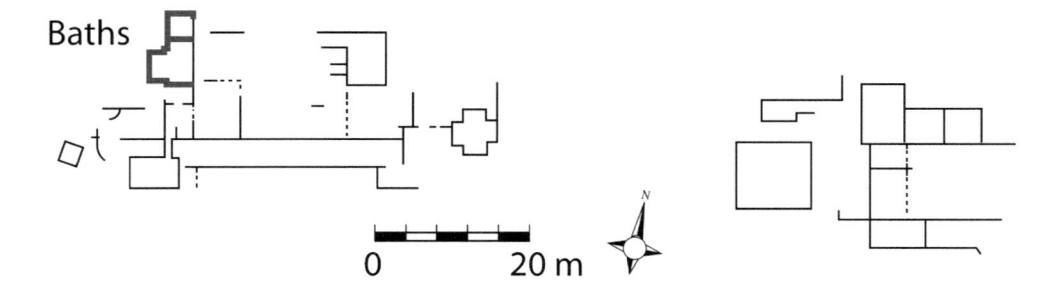

0   20 m   N

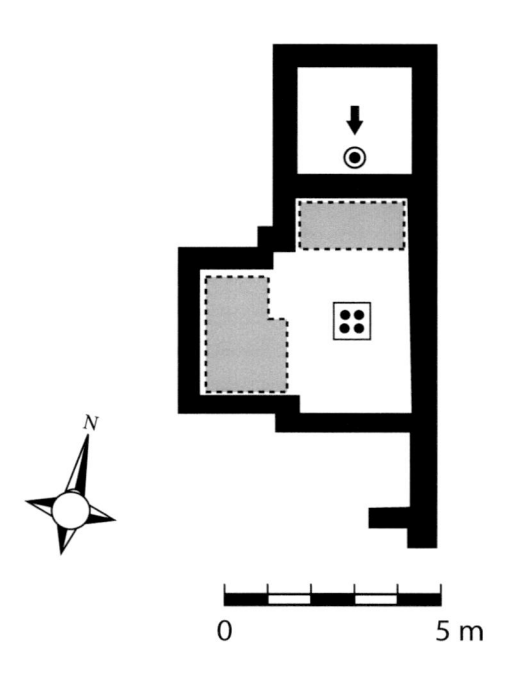

N

0   5 m

Figure 152. Location (top) and plan of the bath of Villers-le-Bouillet. Figure by author after Brulet 2008, 436, fig. 279.

Villers-le-Bouillet, Villa romaine (ID 135)

1. 1.1 Belgium, Liège, Villers-le-Bouillet.
    1.2 50°34'27.02"N; 5°15'19.63"E (approx.).
2. 2.1 1935–1937, 1970.
    2.2 Well preserved in 1930s, deteriorated because of deep ploughing in 1970.
3.   Private bath integrated in a villa.
4. 4.1 The oldest phase of the villa dates back to the first century AD, but the baths seem to have been added at a later date (ceramics on site).
    4.2 Unknown. Ceramics and coins point to continued activity at the villa site until the late fourth and possibly early fifth century.
    4.3 Unknown.
5.   A (hypocausts, strong evidence for pools).
6. 6.1 Min. 30 m² (partial plan).
    6.2 Angular row type? (partial plan).
    6.3 Unknown (partial plan).
    6.4 A small semicircular *exedra* south-west of the heated room might have housed a pool or an *alveus*, but the limited excavations cannot give conclusive evidence.
    6.5 At least three rooms in the villa were heated by a hypocaust. The northernmost room possibly had two rectangular pools: one on its north side (above the furnace) and one on its west side. This probably identifies the room as a *caldarium*.
7. 7.1 The hypocaust pillars were made with round tiles. A *praefurnium* lay north of the *caldarium*. The furnace channel was made out of bricks and had two sturdy side walls, possibly to support a boiler or a *testudo*.
    7.2 The rectangular *exedra* of the *caldarium*, possibly an *alveus*, had *tubuli* along its walls.
    7.3 Unknown.
    7.4 Unknown.
8.   Fragments of wall paintings and marble slabs were found in the debris of the villa.
9.   Fig. 152.
10.   Geubel 1938 (ER); Willems 1972 (ER); Dandoy and Willems 1995; Brulet 2008, 435.

Villers-sur-Lesse, villa de Génimont (ID 136)

1. 1.1 Belgium, Namur, Rochefort.
   1.2 50°7'17.72"N; 5°6'47.83"E. (approx.).
2. 2.1 1994.
   2.2 Well preserved when excavated, now destroyed.
3. Private bathhouse integrated in a villa.
4. 4.1 Unknown. The villa was probably built in the late first or early second century (ceramics on site). A wooden structure possibly preceded the stone villa.
   4.2 Unknown. Some fourth-century ceramics were found in the cellar of the villa.
   4.3 Unknown.
5. A (pool).
6. 6.1 Min. 34 m² (partial plan).
   6.2 Unknown (partial plan).
   6.3 Unknown (partial plan).
   6.4 Several rooms had a mortar floor. To the south of one of these, a small pool (*piscina*?) was identified.
   6.5 Unknown (partial plan).
7. 7.1 Unknown.
   7.2 Unknown.
   7.3 Unknown.
   7.4 The small pool was drained by a drainage channel made of limestone blocks and tiles, heading south-east, following the downhill slope.
8. Unknown.
9. Fig. 153.
10. Plumier, Dupont, and Van Neer 1995 (ER); Plumier 1996 (ER); Brulet 2008, 574.

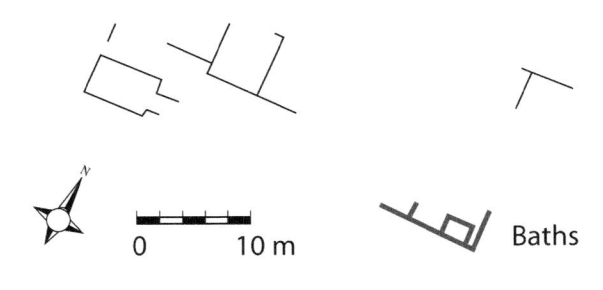

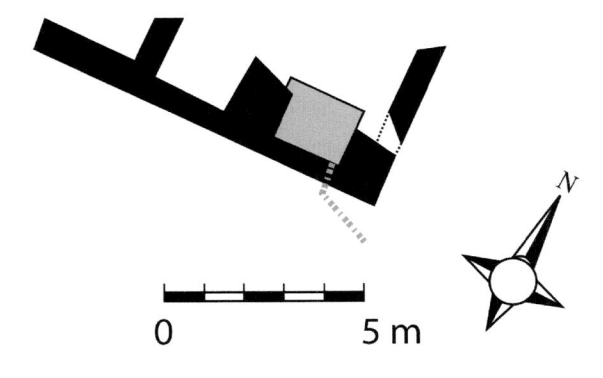

Figure 153. Location (top) and plan of the bath at Villers-sur-Lesse. Figure by author after Plumier 1996, 24, unnumbered fig.

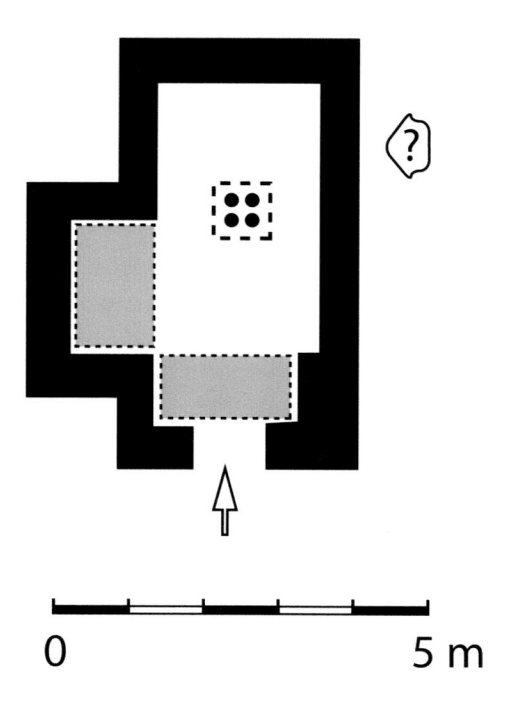

Figure 154. Sketch plan of the bath at Vissoul, no N-arrow given. Figure by author after Tihon 1900, 82, unnumbered fig.

Vissoul, Bounia (ID 144)

1.	1.1	Belgium, Liège, Burdinne.
	1.2	50°34'53.91"N; 5°6'53.91"E (approx.).
2.	2.1	1900.
	2.2	Well preserved when excavated, now reburied.
3.		Freestanding private (?) bathhouse (of a villa?).
4.	4.1	Unknown.
	4.2	Unknown.
	4.3	Unknown.
5.		C (hypocaust, overall plan).
6.	6.1	c. 13 m².
	6.2	Single room.
	6.3	None.
	6.4	None.
	6.5	The small building consisted of a single heated room (5.23 × 2.05 m) with two rectangular *exedrae* (0.95 × 2 m and 1.80 × 1.11 m). One or both *exedrae* may have housed an *alveus*. The alleged 'doorway' (1 m wide) in the *exedra* on the long axis of the building should probably be interpreted as the furnace mouth, because a floor made of tegulae could be discerned here. The walls of the building (54 cm wide) were faced with small blocks of limestone.
7.	7.1	The furnace floor was made with fragments of *tegula*. The hypocaust floor consisted of pink hydraulic mortar on a preparation layer of flint boulders. Round hypocaust tiles were found (no dimensions given).
	7.2	Unknown.
	7.3	Unknown. The building was located near a natural spring.
	7.4	Unknown.
8.		Unknown.
9.		Fig. 154.
10.		Tihon 1900 (ER).

Vodelée, villa romaine (ID 137)

1. 1.1   Belgium, Namur, Doische.
   1.2   50°10'14.56"N; 4°44'11.10"E (approx.).
2. 2.1   1986.
   2.2   Badly preserved when excavated, now covered.
3.   Private bath integrated in a villa.
4. 4.1   *Terminus post quem* of the second half of the second century (ceramics in the foundation of phase 2 of the villa).
   4.2   Middle of the fourth century at the latest (destruction of the villa by fire).
   4.3   Two possible lime kilns were found in the villa, possibly from a period when the villa was dismantled for building material.
5.   A (pools, hypocausts).
6. 6.1   *c.* 50 m².
   6.2   Block type.
   6.3   An almost square room (1) (1.9 × 1.8 m) was indirectly heated, identifying it as a heated *apodyterium* or a *tepidarium*.
   6.4   The *frigidarium* (2) (2.2 × 1.8 m) had a concrete floor. A thin wall made of fragments of *tubuli* separated the room from a semicircular *piscina* (diam.: 2 m).
   6.5   The *caldarium* (3) (4.5 × 2.1 m) had two semicircular niches (for *alvei* and/or a *labrum*) and a rectangular niche (with reinforced hypocaust) for an *alveus*. The indirectly heated room to the south-west (1) may have been a *tepidarium*.
7. 7.1   The hypocaust pillars were made of square tiles (s.: 18 cm). The *praefurnium* (4) (3.25 × 2 m) was located on the east side. The furnace channel (45 cm wide; 1.2 m long) had two parallel walls, possibly to support a boiler.
   7.2   No traces of wall heating were discovered *in situ*, but fragments of *tubuli* were reused in the *frigidarium*.
   7.3   Unknown.
   7.4   The *piscina* had an outlet piercing the bottom of the pool on the east side. No traces of a drainage channel were found outside the building.
8.   Fragments of polychrome wall paintings with geometric designs were found inside the bathhouse.
9.   Fig. 155.
10.   Rober 1987 (ER); Brulet 2008, 524–25.

Baths

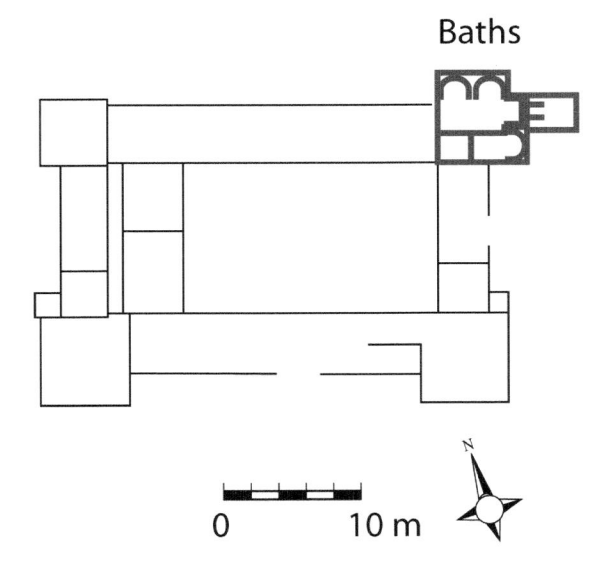

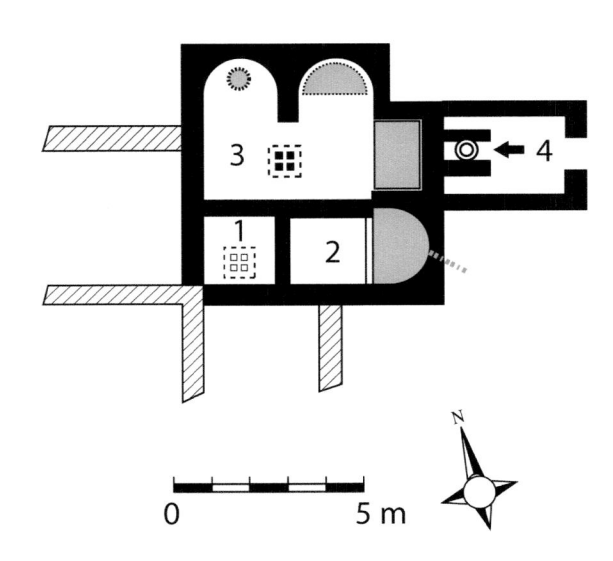

Figure 155. Location (top) and plan of the bath of Vodelée. Figure by author after Rober 1987, 155, fig. 4.

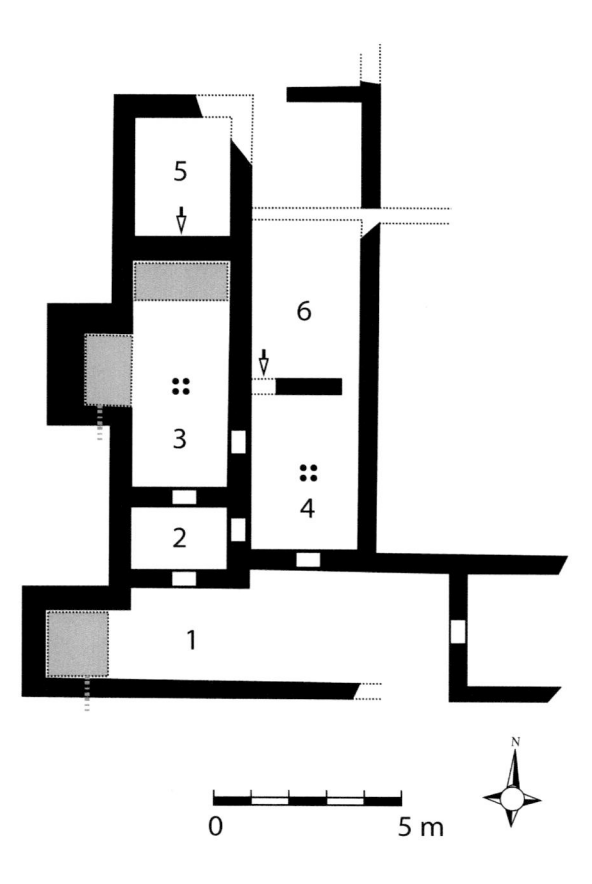

Figure 156. Plan of the bath of Vorst. Figure by author after Janssens and De Greef 1968, 16, fig. 6.

Vorst, Steenbergen (ID 138)

1. 1.1 Belgium, Antwerp, Laakdal.
    1.2 51°4′51.64″N; 5°0′43.24″E (exact).
2. 2.1 1963–1964.
    2.2 Partially preserved when excavated, now covered or destroyed.
3.   Private bathhouse integrated in a villa.
4. 4.1 Unknown (ceramics on site point to activity from the middle of the second century).
    4.2 Unknown (ceramics on site point to a third-century abandonment of the site).
    4.3 Some walls of the baths were torn out to recuperate building material. Several medieval burials were found in- and outside the baths.
5.   A (pools, hypocausts).
6. 6.1 Min. 60 m² (plan unclear).
    6.2 Linear row type? (plan unclear).
    6.3 Unknown (plan unclear).
    6.4 The southernmost room (1) had an almost square *exedra* with a mortar floor. Its southern wall was pierced, probably for a drainage channel. This could identify the *exedra* as a *piscina*, making the eastern part of this room the *frigidarium*. As there was no mortar floor here, we could imagine a wooden floor. Alternatively, the small room (2) (1.8 × 2.6 m) with a mortar floor north of the one described was the *frigidarium*, albeit without a *piscina*.
    6.5 The oblong room (3) (6.2 × 2.6 m) with a rectangular *exedra* in its west wall (2.25 × 1.25 m) was heated by a hypocaust and can be identified as the *caldarium* with *alveus* in *exedra*. A second *alveus* might have been present at the northern end of the room, where the furnace must have been located. The oblong room might have been divided by a thin wall at *suspensura* level into a *tepidarium* and *caldarium*. A second heated room (4) lay to the east (4.25 × 2.75 m). It was probably heated by a separate furnace to the north. However, it is unclear whether this room belonged to the bath (*tepidarium* or *sudatorium*?), or if it was a heated living room.
7. 7.1 Fragments of the hypocaust pillars were found. These consisted of round tiles (diam.: 19 cm; 4.5 cm thick). The furnace of the *caldarium* was not identified, but must have been located to its north. The small room (5) here was unpaved, while the walls were not bonded with mortar. The second heated room (4) was probably heated from the room north of it (6).
    7.2 No fragments of *tubuli* or other types of wall heating were reported.
    7.3 Unknown.
    7.4 An opening in the southern side of the *caldarium exedra* probably housed the outlet of the *alveus*. The southern wall of the southernmost room was likewise pierced at the level of the mortar floor. It possibly drained a *piscina*.
8.   Unknown.
9.   Fig. 156.
10.   Janssens 1963 (ER); Janssens and De Greef 1968 (ER).

Waha, Villa de Hologne (ID 139)

1. 1.1 Belgium, Luxembourg, Marche-en-Famenne.
   1.2 50°12'41.64"N; 5°21'30.48"E (approx.).
2. 2.1 1996, 2004–2005.
   2.2 Badly preserved when excavated, now covered.
3. Bathhouse attached to a villa.
4. 4.1 Unknown. At least three different phases during the lifespan of the baths were identified (the villa site was in use until the fourth century).
   4.2 Unknown.
   4.3 After the abandonment of the bath, a wooden building was erected over the dismantled shell of the building.
5. A (pools, hypocaust).
6. 6.1 *c.* 270 m².
   6.2 Linear row type.
   6.3 The rooms in the north part of the building (1) may have been used as *apodyterium*, *unctorium*, etc. The westernmost square room (2) (s.: 3.3 m) had a floor in pink hydraulic mortar.
   6.4 The *frigidarium* (3) in the last phase of the building had a rectangular shape (5.2 × 3.5 m). To the south, a rectangular *piscina* was later transformed into an apsidal pool.
   6.5 The *caldarium* (4) (6.25 × 2.15 m) was the only room with a hypocaust. Reinforced corners on the southern end, flanking the furnace channel, point to the presence of an *alveus*. The rectangular *exedra* on the western side (2.15 × 2 m), with hypocaust, must have contained a second *alveus*, as it was drained by a drainage channel. The small room (5) between the *caldarium* and the *frigidarium* must have acted as heat trap. Depending on the width of the doorway with the *caldarium*, this room might have been mildly heated, thus acting as a *tepidarium*.
7. 7.1 The building was heavily spoliated after its abandonment. Only imprints of the round hypocaust tiles survived on the mortar hypocaust floor. The *praefurnium*, south of the *caldarium*, had a furnace channel created by sturdy parallel walls, which possibly supported a boiler or a *testudo*.
   7.2 Unknown.
   7.3 Unknown.
   7.4 A drainage channel ran from the *caldarium*'s western *exedra* (presumably lodging a pool) to the north, bending underneath the heat trap/*tepidarium* and joining the drainage channel of the *piscina*. The channel, cut out in the schist bedrock, then ran along the west side of the *frigidarium* before turning west.
8. Unknown.
9. Fig. 157.
10. Corbiau 1994 (ER); 1998 (ER); 2002 (ER); 2006 (ER); 2007 (ER); Brulet 2008, 483.

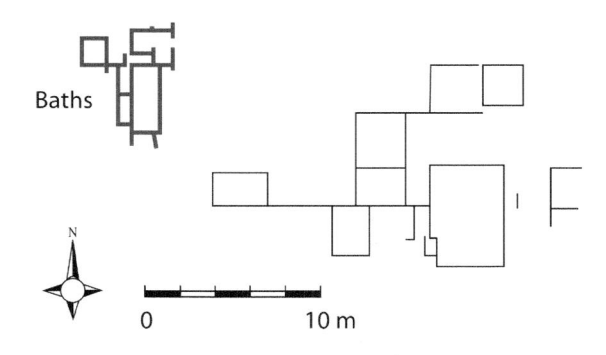

Baths

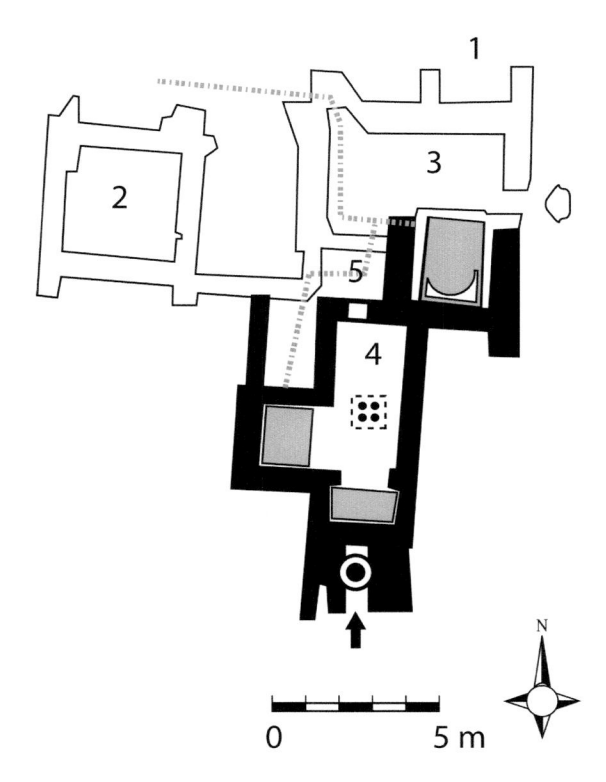

Figure 157. Location (top) and plan of the bath of Waha. Figure by author after Corbiau 2007, 166, unnumbered fig.

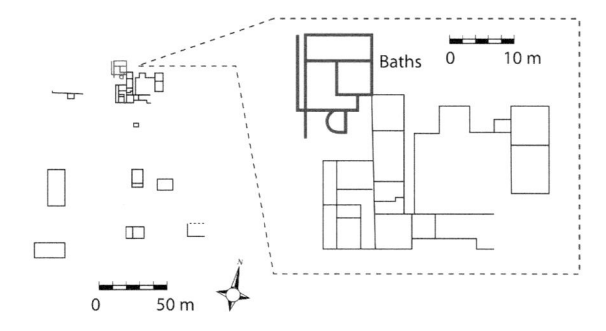

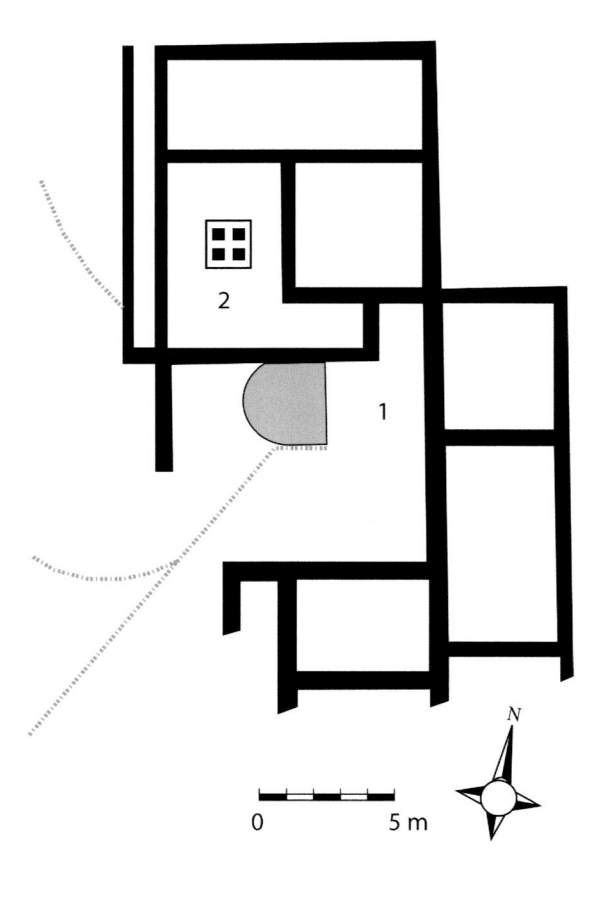

Figure 158. Location (top) and plan of the bath of Wancennes. Figure by author after Devillers 1987, 7, fig. 2 and 23, fig. 11.

Wancennes, Villa La Couterelle (ID 140)

1. 1.1 Belgium, Namur, Beauraing.
    1.2 50°5'56.14"N; 4°58'2.57"E (approx.).
2. 2.1 First discovered and partially excavated in 1882 and 1884, and again by amateur archaeologists between 1965 and 1982.
    2.2 Partially preserved when excavated, now reburied or destroyed.
3. Private bath integrated in a villa.
4. 4.1 The earliest finds on site date from the first century (coins), but the major villa development seems to have taken place in the second and early third century. The baths are probably contemporaneous with the first villa phase.
    4.2 The entire villa was destroyed by fire during the third century. The site was reoccupied after AD 275 until the end of the fourth century.
    4.3 Unknown.
5. A (pool, hypocaust).
6. 6.1 Min. 35 m² (partial plan).
    6.2 Unknown (partial plan).
    6.3 Unknown (partial plan).
    6.4 A *piscina* with apsidal ending (diam.: 3 m) and a mortar floor indicates the presence of a *frigidarium*, possibly the space to its east (1).
    6.5 Only one heated room (2) (*caldarium?*) was identified (3.9 × 6.3 m), north of the *piscina*. No pool could be identified, although a drainage channel seems to have started here. The rooms to the north and east may also have belonged to the baths.
7. 7.1 No *praefurnium* was located. The pillars of the hypocaust were made of square tiles (s.: 20 cm) bonded by clay, standing at a distance of 40 cm to each other.
    7.2 Fragments of *tubuli* were discovered among the debris of the heated room.
    7.3 The water was supplied by a natural source at some 600 m distance. A vaulted aqueduct led the water to the villa. A lead *fistula* was also found.
    7.4 The *piscina* was emptied by a lead *fistula* piercing its south-eastern corner. The drainage channel then continued as wooden pipes. A second drainage channel started from the heated room and headed north-west.
8. Unknown.
9. Fig. 158.
10. Bequet 1886 (ER); Devillers 1971–1972; 1987.

Wange, Villa van Wange (ID 141)

1. 1.1   Belgium, Flemish Brabant, Landen.
       1.2   50°47'6.82"N; 5°1'56.02"E (exact).
2. 2.1   1989–1990.
       2.2   Partially preserved when excavated, now covered or destroyed.
3.   Private bathhouse attached to a villa.
4. 4.1   The villa was erected in the early second century (ceramics on site), replacing wooden structures in indigenous building traditions. The bathhouse was a later addition.
       4.2   The villa was destroyed by a fire in the third century.
       4.3   Some squatter occupation may have occurred on site during the late third and early fourth century (coins).
5.   B (hypocaust, strong evidence for pools).
6. 6.1   Min. 17 m² (plan unclear).
       6.2   Linear row type.
       6.3   Unknown.
       6.4   Unknown. The room south of the heated room might have been a cold room.
       6.5   At least one room was heated by a hypocaust. It had two rectangular recesses, presumably to lodge *alvei*. The oblong shape of the room may indicate that it was divided by a wall at *suspensura* level into a *tepidarium* (south) and *caldarium* (north).
7. 7.1   There is little information on the type of hypocaust.
       7.2   Unknown.
       7.3   Unknown.
       7.4   Unknown.
8.   Fragments of painted wall plaster were found among the debris.
9.   Fig. 159.
10.   Lodewijckx 1991.

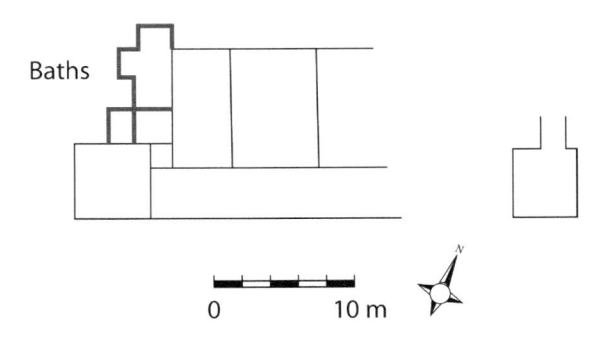

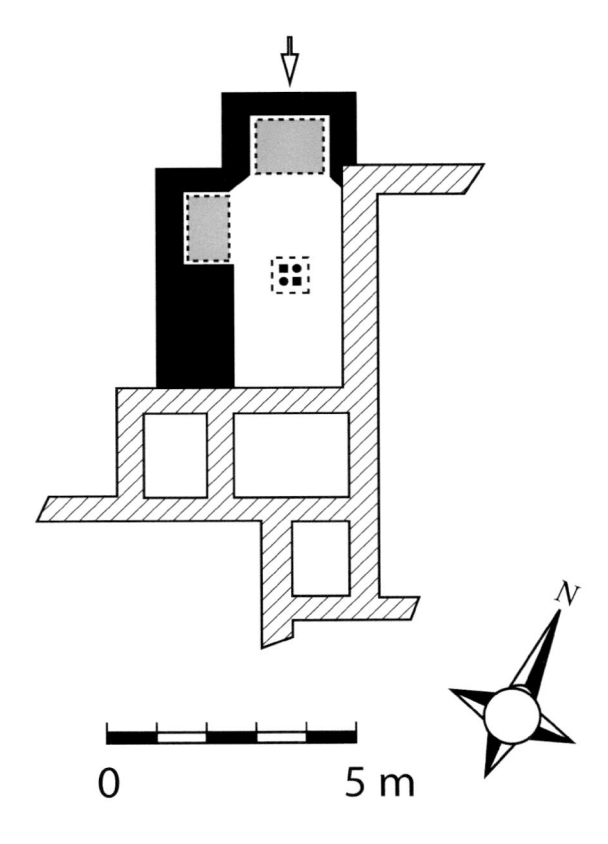

Figure 159. Location (top) and plan of the bath of Wange. Figure by author after Lodewijckx 1991, 46, fig. 5.

Waudrez, Thermes du vicus (ID 28)

1. 1.1 Belgium, Hainaut, Binche.
   1.2 50°24'45.19"N; 4°8'52.49"E (approx.).
2. 2.1 1979–1981, 1986.
   2.2 Badly preserved when excavated, now covered.
3.   Unknown. The baths have been interpreted as a public facility in the centre of the *vicus*, but there is no conclusive evidence to rule out the possibility of a private bathhouse of a house.
4. 4.1 Unknown. Coins found among the debris date back to the first half of the first century, but the contexts of these finds are not given. The site of the bathhouse had several phases.
   4.2 Unknown.
   4.3 Unknown.
5.   A (pool, hypocaust).
6. 6.1 Min. 20 m² (partial plan).
   6.2 Unknown (partial plan).
   6.3 Unknown (partial plan). Several elongated rooms south of the heated room may have been part of the bathhouse.
   6.4 A small apsidal pool might be interpreted as a *piscina*.
   6.5 At least one room (3.8 × 3 m) was heated by a hypocaust.
7. 7.1 The location of the *praefurnium* near the heated room was identified as a patch of red scorched earth.
   7.2 Several fragments of *tubuli* were found in the debris of the heated room.
   7.3 Unknown.
   7.4 Unknown.
8.   Unknown.
9.   No plan available.
10.   Dekegel 1979 (ER); 1980 (ER); Capers 1998, 14–16; Brulet 2008, 316.

Willemeau, Villa romaine 1 (ID 142)

1. 1.1 Belgium, Hainaut, Tournai.
   1.2 50°34'24.81"N; 3°20'57.25"E (approx.).
2. 2.1 1955.
   2.2 Badly preserved when excavated, now reburied or destroyed.
3. Private bathhouse integrated in a villa.
4. 4.1 Unknown.
   4.2 Unknown.
   4.3 Unknown.
5. C (hypocausts, evidence for pools).
6. 6.1 Min. 34 m² (plan unclear).
   6.2 Block type? (plan unclear).
   6.3 Unknown (plan unclear).
   6.4 Unknown (plan unclear).
   6.5 At least two rooms were heated by a hypocaust, but these were not adjacent. The smaller almost square room in the north-east is possibly a later addition (living room?). The larger room (*c.* 34 m²) in the north-western corner of the villa had two rectangular *exedrae*, one in its northern and one in its western side. These may have housed *alvei*.
7. 7.1 Unknown.
   7.2 Unknown.
   7.3 Unknown.
   7.4 Unknown.
8. The large room with hypocaust was embellished with polychrome wall paintings.
9. Fig. 160.
10. Brulet 2008, 379.

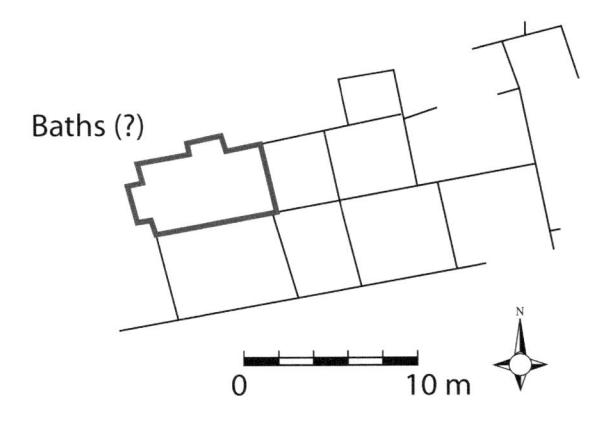

Figure 160. Location of the possible bath suite in villa 1 at Willemeau. Figure by author after Brulet 2008, 379, fig. 169.

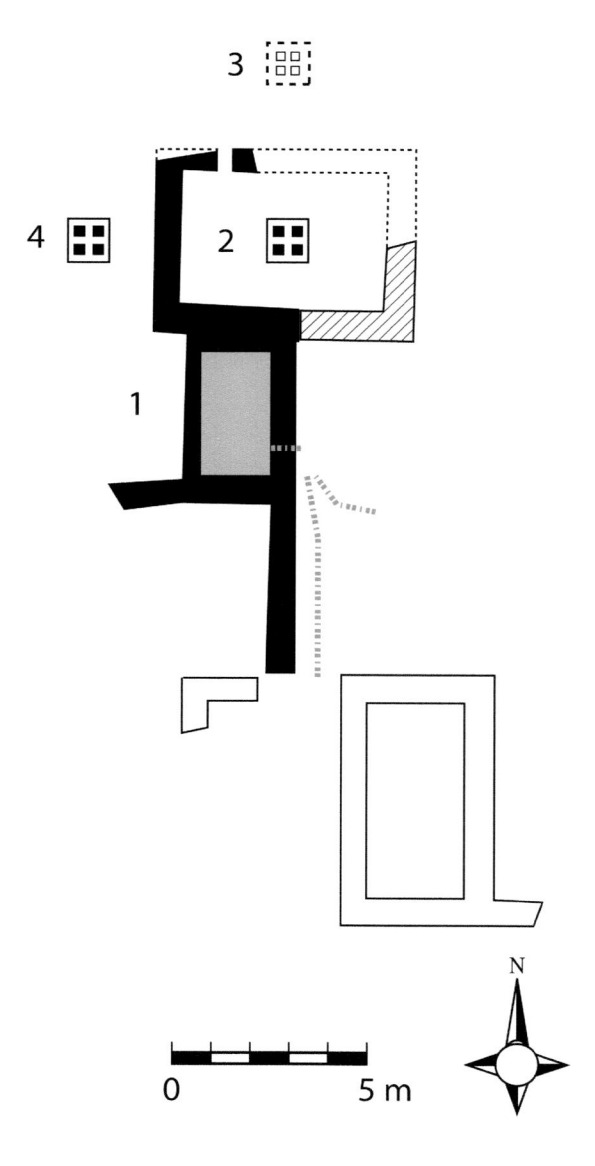

Figure 161. Plan of the bath of villa 2 at Willemeau. Figure by author after Amand and Soleil 1988, fig. 5.

Willemeau, Villa 2 (ID 143)

1. 1.1 Belgium, Hainaut, Tournai.
   1.2 50°34'24.81"N; 3°20'57.25"E (approx.).
2. 2.1 Partially excavated in 1955 and again in 1985.
   2.2 Well preserved when excavated, now destroyed.
3. Private bathhouse integrated in a villa.
4. 4.1 Unknown (few materials were recovered by the amateur archaeologists). The bathhouse seems to have had different phases.
   4.2 Unknown. A fourth-century coin of Constantine II (minted in London) is the last evidence of occupation.
   4.3 Medieval spoliation of building materials and damage of the heated section by seventh-century burials.
5. A (pool, hypocausts).
6. 6.1 Min. 24 m² (partial plan).
   6.2 Linear row type? (partial plan).
   6.3 Unknown (partial plan).
   6.4 A rectangular *piscina* (3 × 1.8 m) was restored at least two times (the original floor of marble was replaced by two separate layers of hydraulic mortar). The area west (1) or south of it might have been the actual *frigidarium*. The walls were made with regular blocks of limestone on a base of flint boulders.
   6.5 At least two rooms heated by a hypocaust were found. The northernmost room (2) had a mortar floor (*c.* 5 × 3.5 m). An opening in the northern wall possibly connected this hypocaust to a third hypocaust to the north (3). The room (4) west of the first heated room was only partially excavated. Its hypocaust lay 60 cm higher, possibly pointing a different phase of the bath. For none of these rooms, a furnace was found. This, in combination with the absence of heated pools, could identify at least the northern room as *tepidarium*. Test pits north of the northernmost room (at 1.75 m) also brought to light a wall with a coating of hydraulic mortar.
7. 7.1 No *praefurnia* were discovered. These could be located further north or west. The hypocaust pillars were made of square tiles (s.: 16 cm).
   7.2 Several fragments of *tubuli* were found in the heated rooms.
   7.3 Unknown.
   7.4 The *piscina* was drained by an orifice in its eastern wall (7 cm above the first phase floor). A shallow sump in front of it seems to have facilitated water disposal. A drainage channel made of mortar and stones and covered with terracotta tiles, headed south.
8. In its first phase, the bottom and the sides of the *piscina* were finished with slabs of white marble. Several fragments of painted wall plastered (red, ochre, olive green) were found on the northern (heated) side. A large threshold of local Tournai limestone was also found.
9. Fig. 161.
10. Amand and Soleil 1988 (ER); Soleil 1988 (ER); Brulet 2008, 379.

Wyompont, Station routière (ID 11)

1. 1.1 Belgium, Luxemburg, Tenneville.
    1.2 50°5'9.00"N; 5°34'17.73"E (approx.).
2. 2.1 1850s.
    2.2 Well preserved when excavated, now covered or destroyed.
3. Bathhouse (?) integrated in a building.
4. 4.1 Unknown.
    4.2 Unknown.
    4.3 After the abandonment, the building was reused as a burial ground.
5. C (evidence for a pool, hypocausts).
6. 6.1 *c.* 90 m².
    6.2 Linear row type?
    6.3 The eastern side of the building consisted of an L-shaped corridor (1) and a rectangular room in the north-east corner (2). It is unknown whether these rooms were part of the alleged bathhouse.
    6.4 Unknown (plan unclear).
    6.5 At least two rooms were heated by a hypocaust, making use of the same *praefurnium*. The largest northernmost room (3) had no specific features and may be interpreted as a *tepidarium*. The southern smaller room (4), the *caldarium*, had a rectangular recess in its western wall. Two parallel walls lining the furnace channel and protruding into the hypocaust (for extra stability), suggest that a pool (*alveus*) was housed in this recess.
7. 7.1 The hypocaust pillars were made with square tiles (s.: 20 cm). A single *praefurnium* (5) in the south-west corner of the excavated remains had a furnace to the north, heating the *tepidarium*, and one to the east, heating the *caldarium* (and possibly also directly an *alveus*).
    7.2 At least the *caldarium* had *tubuli* (box type) along all its walls.
    7.3 Unknown.
    7.4 Unknown.
8. In the *caldarium*, the *suspensura* was finished with a mosaic floor, consisting of white and blue *tesserae*. Contrary to the (reconstruction) drawing in the original excavation report (pl. VIII, no. 14 in Geubel 1887), only part of this mosaic floor was preserved (Geubel 1939, 34). The *tepidarium* floor was a polished hydraulic mortar. Several fragments of wall painting were also found.
9. Fig. 162.
10. Geubel 1887, 203–04; 1939; Brulet 2008, 491–92.

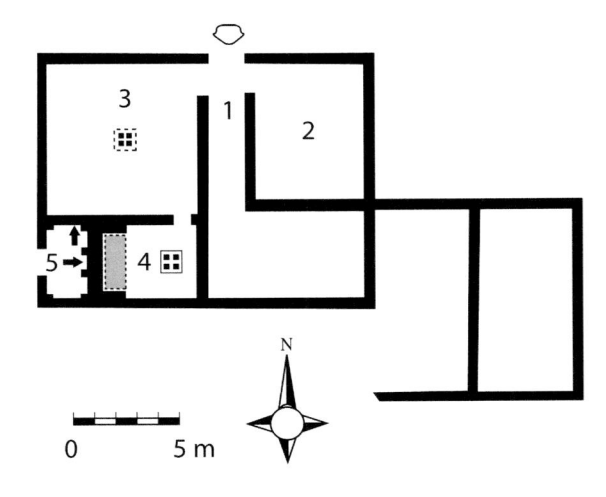

Figure 162. Plan of the road station with possible bath suite at Wyompont. Figure by author after Geubel 1887, pl. VII.

Appendices

Table 10. Sizes of the most important rooms of the baths in square meters (CM: *Civitas Menapiorum*; CN: *Civitas Nerviorum*; CT: *Civitas Tungrorum*; U: unknown; N: not present.). Values in bold are given by the excavation reports, other values are extrapolated from the published plans. Values with ? are uncertain, values with * point to an uncertain identification of the room. The baths with unknown accessibility that are underlined are likely to have been public baths due to their location within civic centres.

Site	Name	Civitas	Frigidarium	Tepidarium	Caldarium	Sudatorium
Public baths						
Aardenburg	Gasfabriek	CM	U	28.8*	8.28	N
Clavier-Vervoz	Thermes	CT	11.25	N	52.5	N
Famars	Thermes	CN	**110**	212	**106.25**	(2×) 44*
Fontaine-Valmont	Thermes	CT	U	U	18	6*
Furfooz	Fortification de Hauterecenne	CT	**7.8**	N	**17.8**	N
Grobbendonk	Vicus Baths	CT	**16**	N	**21.45**	N
Liberchies	Thermes Les Bons-Villers	CT	min. **13.5**	min. 20	U	U
Liberchies	Castellum de Brunehaut	CT	10.15	8.84	10.15	N
Macquenoise	Thermes Marchienne au Pont	CN	**7.92**	7	**56.38**	N
Oudenburg	Fort Baths	CM	U	23.2	37.2	U
Oudenburg	Vicus Baths	CM	**28***	U	45*	21*
Outrelouxhe	Relais d'Elmer	CT	N	N	26.25	N
Tienen	Vicus Baths	CT	**24**	**24**	**24**	N
Wyompont	Station routière	CT	N	49*	10.88	N
Baths with unknown accessibility						
<u>Amay-Ombret</u>	Rausa	CT	U	U	73	14.85
Aubechies	Bains sous l'église Saint-Géry	CN	U	U	U	U
<u>Bavay</u>	Rue Saint-Maur	CN	U	U	U	U
<u>Bavay</u>	Église Notre-Dame-de-l'Assomption	CN	U	U	U	U
<u>Braives</u>	Thermes	CT	U	U	U	U
Chastrès	Thermes de Puceneveau	CT	6.61	N	23.52	N
<u>Kortrijk</u>	O.L. Vrouwekerk (Fort?)	CM	U	U	U	U
<u>Maastricht</u>	Stokstraat	CT	19.14	34	34	U
Marchienne-au-Pont	Pachi al Cave	CT	U	U	11.88	U
Milmort	Balneum de Hauts Sarts	CT	5.5	N	11	N
<u>Namur</u>	Rue des Echasseurs	CT	U	U	U	U
Ramillies Autre-Église	Complexe thermale	CT	U	(2nd phase) 31.11*	U	(2nd phase) 26*
Soignies	Balneum de l'Espesse	CN	5.76	N	16.25	N
<u>Tongeren</u>	Schaetzengaerde	CT	U	U	U	U
<u>Tongeren</u>	Sint-Truiderstraat	CT	U	U	U	U
<u>Tourinnes-St-Lambert</u>	Champ de la Sainte	CT	N	12.9	45.22	N
<u>Tournai</u>	Vieux-Marché-aux-Jambons	CM	U	8.7*	U	13.13*
<u>Tournai</u>	Quai Vifquin	CM	U	U	U	U
<u>Tournai</u>	Quai Luchet d'Antoing	CM	U	U	U	U
<u>Waudrez</u>	Bains	CN	U	U	11.4*	U

Site	Name	Civitas	Frigidarium	Tepidarium	Caldarium	Sudatorium
Private baths						
Aiseau	Villa d'Aiseau Bath 1	CT	**16**	**15.84**	**38.27**	N
Aiseau	Villa d'Aiseau Bath 2	CT	U	U	**10.8**	**8.32**
Amay	Villa de la Collégiale	CT	U	U	U	U
Ambresin	Villa d'Ambresin	CT	N	U	**23.8**	U
Anderlecht	Champs St-Anne	CN	3.15	N	10.8	N
Anthée	Villa du Grand Bon Dieu Bath 1	CT	U	U	31	U
Anthée	Villa du Grand Bon Dieu Bath 2	CT	U	U	41.4	U
Anthée	Villa du Grand Bon Dieu Bath 3	CT	U	36*	47*	U
Arquennes	Villa d'Arquennes	CN	**10.35**	**22.35**	**18.76**	N
Assenois	La Chapelle	CT	**U**	**U**	**U**	U
Attenhoven	Villa de la Bruyère	CT	N	N	**13.2**	N
Ave-et-Aufe	Villa de Bois d'Ave	CT	U	U	U	U
Basse-Wavre	Villa de l'Hosté	CT	16	17	17	11*
Bierbeek	Stenen Kruis	CT	N	N	7.9	N
Boirs	Thermes de la villa	CT	15.31	12.92	U	U
Bois-et-Borsu	Villa de Thier-Laurent	CT	U	U	U	U
Boussu-lez-Walcourt	La villa du Champ des Metz	CT	U	U	**14.85**	18.92*
Bovigny	Bois des Concessions	CT	U	U	U	U
Brakel (Michelbeke)	Heksteelstraat	CN	U	U	U	U
Brakel (Zegelsem)	Kanakkendries 1	CN	U	U	35	U
Bras	Villa de Bras-Haut	CT	18.9*	U	U	U
Broekhem	Villa Ravenbosch	CT	**6.63**	N	**15**	N
Bruyelle	Villa de Haute Éloge (phase 1)	CM	**16.43**	7.8	13.76	**15.54***
Bruyelle	Villa de Haute Éloge (phase 2–3)	CM	**16.43**	**24.75***	21.43	**13.25***
Emptinne-Champion	Villa du Rosdia (phase 1)	CT	8	N	8.5	N
Emptinne-Champion	Villa du Rosdia (phase 2)	CT	8	U	18	U
Emptinne-Champion	Villa du Rosdia (phase 3)	CT	8	N	13	N
Clermont-sous-Huy	Villa d'Arvy	CT	**16**	**23**	**13.5**	N
Diekirch	Rue de l'Esplanade	CT	U	U	U	U
Élouges	Villa des Monts d'Élouges	CN	U	U	U	U
Évelette	Villa du Clavia	CT	U	N	8	N
Évelette	Villa de Résimont	CT	U	U	4.75	U
Flostoy	Villa de Lizée	CT	**6.75**	N	15	N
Froyennes	Villa de Froyennes		U	U	U	U
Gemechenne	Villa de Gemechenne	CT	12	18	21	N
Gerpines	Villa de Gerpines	CT	U	U	U	U
Gesves	Villa du Coria (phase 1)	CT	**11**	N	**8.7**	N
Gesves	Villa du Coria (phase 2)	CT	**11**	30.25	**16**	U
Gooik	Lombergveld	CN	7.68*	U	**6.44***	U
Graux	Villa romaine de Graux	CT	5.2*	17*	19	U
Grumelange	Villa	CT	**3.9**	U	6	U
Haccourt	Villa de Haccourt — Bath 1	CT	**25.8**	**25.2**	**52.4**	N
Haccourt	Villa de Haccourt — Bath 2	CT	**21.53**	**15.12**	**19.7**	N

Site	Name	Civitas	Frigidarium	Tepidarium	Caldarium	Sudatorium
Haccourt	Villa de Haccourt — Bath 3	CT	**75.94**	**13.24**	**24.45**	**13.37**
Haillot	Villa de Matagne	CT	5	N	18	N
Hamois	Villa de Hody	CT	7.5	N	8.8	N
Heer	Bakkerbos	CT	U	U	U	U
Heestert	Blinde Kapel	CM	N	N	8.9	N
Heure-le-Romain	Bains domestiques Sur les Moulins	CT	U	U	10.23	U
Hollain	Hypocaustes de Bas de Bléharies	CM	U	U	U	U
Hoogeloon	Kerkakkers	CT	6.5	7	7.2	N
Jemelle	Villa de Malagne	CT	**11.22**	**9.3**	**18**	**12.48**
Kumtich	Mettenberg 1	CT	**15.54**	**11.97***	**8.92***	**8.06***
Kumtich	Mettenberg 2	CT	19	**25.89***	24.58	U
Landen	Betzveld	CT	U	U	U	U
Latinne	Villa des Grandes Pièces	CT	4?	U	8?	N
Leignon	Villa de Barcenne	CT	7.44?	3.4*	11.7?	U
Lemiers	Villa	CT	**128.25***	**12.16**	52.25	N
Liège	Villa de la Place St-Lambert	CT	U	**31.41***	U	U
Limerlé	Villa de Rouvroy	CT	U	9*	16	U
Mabeuge	Villa au Bois Brûlé	CN	U	U	5	U
Machelen	Villa de Heuf	CN	U	U	U	U
Maillen	Villa de Ronchinne	CT	22.4?	10.24	12.8?	9
Maillen	Villa d'Arches	CT	**2.47**	N	**8.91**	N
Maillen	Villa Al Sauvenière	CT	9.2	**23**	**17.13**	N
Marcinelle	Villa de Marcinelle	CT	U	U	U	**8.8***
Matagne-la-Petite	Villa Aux Murets	CT	**32.4***	**15.75***	**6.75***	N
Meerssen	Villa Herkenberg	CT	U	U	U	U
Melsbroek	Hof ten As	CN	U	U	U	U
Merbes-le-Château	Villa de Champ St-Eloi — Bath 1	CN	U	**9.66***	**13.32***	U
Merbes-le-Château	Villa de Champ St-Eloi — Bath 2	CN	8.4*	U	7.7	17.68*
Meslin-L'Évêque	Villa de Preuscamps	CN	U	U	33	U
Mettet	Villa de Bauselenne — Bath 1	CT	U	**35.31**	13.5	**9.3**
Mettet	Villa de Bauselenne — Bath 2	CT	N	N	**25.2**	N
Miécret	Villa de Miécret — Bath 1	CT	1.7	N	4.4	N
Miécret	Villa de Miécret — Bath 2	CT	6.3	N	10.7	11*
Modave	Villa de Survillers	CT	**9.8**	N	**20.72**	N
Montignies-Saint-Christophe	Villa de la Terre d'Au	CT	U	U	U	U
Mont-lez-Houffalize	Sommerain	CT	U	U	U	U
Mont-lez-Houffalize	Villa de Fin de Ville — Bath 1	CT	7.5?	25?	27.5	N
Mont-lez-Houffalize	Villa de Fin de Ville — Bath 2	CT	14?	20.25*	17.6*	N
Neerharen-Rekem	Hangveld	CT	U	U	U	U
Nivelles	Villa La Tournette	CN	U	U	U	U
Nouvelles	Villa de Grande Boussue	CN	U	U	U	U
Oberüttfeld	Villa	CT	**8.84**	N	**15.6**	N
Rognée	Villa du Peruwelz	CT	U	**46.23***	12.5	**U**
Roly	Villa de la Crayellerie	CT	5.5?	N	12.16	N

Site	Name	Civitas	Frigidarium	Tepidarium	Caldarium	Sudatorium
Saint-Gérard	Villa du Try-Hallot	CT	U	U	7.2*	U
Saint-Jean-Geest	Villa de Saint-Jean-Geest	CT	U	U	U	U
Sauvenière	Villa d'Arlansart	CT	8?	U	7?	U
Schieren	Villa	CT	U	U	U	U
's Gravensvoeren	Villa Steenbosch	CT	U	U	U	U
Thirimont	Villa de Saint-Rémy	CT	U	25*	18*	U
Tiegem	Hofdries	CM	U	U	12.21*	U
Tongeren	Vrijthof	CT	6.25?	N	7?	N
Tongeren	Boudewijnlaan	CT	U	U	U	U
Tongeren	Vermeulenstraat	CT	U	24*	U	U
Tourinnes-St-Lambert	Villa de Tourinnes-St-Lambert	CT	U	U	U	U
Tournai	Place Paul Janson	CM	U	U	U	U
Tournai	Couvent des Récollets	CM	U	U	U	U
Treignes	Villa des Bruyères	CT	14.4	N	36	13
Val-Meer	Villa	CT	U	12	12	U
Vechmaal	Middelpadveld 3	CT	5?	2	4.4	N
Vellereille-les-Brayeux	Villa de Pincemaille	CN	9.2?	6?*	9*	U
Vesqueville	Corps de logis de Vesqueville	CT	N	N	22.2	N
Villers-le-Bouillet	Villa de Vi Tchestia	CT	U	U	12	U
Villers-sur-Lesse	Villa de Génimont	CT	U	U	U	U
Vissoul	Bounia	CT	N	N	13	N
Vodelée	Villa romaine de Vodelée	CT	**3.96**	**3.42***	**9.45**	N
Vorst	Steenbergen	CT	U	**4.68?**	13	N
Waha-Hollogne	Villa de Hologne	CT	**18.2**	3*	**13.44**	N
Wancennes	Villa romaine de Wancennes	CT	U	U	28*	U
Wange	Villa	CT	4.3*	U	9.7	U
Willemeau	Villa 1	CM	U	U	28*	U
Willemeau	Villa 2	CM	U	17.5*	U	U

Table 11. Surfaces of the pools of the baths in square metres (CM: *Civitas Menapiorum*; CN: *Civitas Nerviorum*; CT: *Civitas Tungrorum*; U: unknown; N: not present). If more than one *piscina* or *alveus* is present, a distinction is made following the location within the room (No: north; NE: north-east; NW: north-west; E: East; S: south; SE: south-east; SW: south-west; W: west). Values in bold are given by the excavation reports, other values are extrapolated from the published plans. Values with ? are uncertain, values with * point to an uncertain identification as pool.

Site	Name	Civitas	Piscinae	Alvei
Public baths				
Aardenburg	Gasfabriek	CM	U	U
Clavier-Vervoz	Thermes	CT	**9 (depth: 1 m)**	7.5
Famars	Thermes	CN	**25**	U
Fontaine-Valmont	Thermes	CT	U	S: 4; W: 3
Furfooz	Fortification de Hauterecenne	CT	**2.3**	No: **2.3**; W: **2.1**
Grobbendonk	Vicus Baths	CT	**9.7**	No: **14***; S: **12**
Liberchies	Thermes Les Bons-Villers	CT	**26**	E: **7.7**; W: **8.2**
Liberchies	Castellum de Brunehaut	CT	1.13	U
Macquenoise	Thermes Marchienne au Pont	CN	**3.92**	S: **3.3**; W: **3.6**
Oudenburg	Fort Baths	CM	U	U
Oudenburg	Vicus Baths	CM	U	U
Outrelouxhe	Relais d'Elmer	CT	N	**3.75**
Tienen	Vicus Baths	CT	U	No: 4.8; W: **12**
Wyompont	Station routière	CT	N	2.8*
Baths with unknown accesibilty				
Amay-Ombret	Rausa	CT	U	W: 7.1 (depth: min. 0.4 m); S: 6.9
Aubechies	Bains sous l'église Saint-Géry	CN	**7, 79*** (depth: min. 0.4 m)	U
Bavay	Rue Saint-Maur	CN	U	U
Bavay	Église Saint-Pierre	CN	U	U
Braives	Thermes	CT	U	7?
Chastrès	Thermes de Puceneveau	CT	2.2 (depth: 0.6 m)	S: 2.2; E: 1.6
Kortrijk	O.L. Vrouwekerk (Fort?)	CM	U	U
Maastricht	Stokstraat	CT	7	1.9
Marchienne-au-Pont	Pachi al Cave	CT	14.4	4
Milmort	Balneum de Hauts Sarts	CT	U	U
Namur	Rue des Echasseurs	CT	U	U
Ramillies Autre-Église	Complexe thermale	CT	U	U
Soignies	Balneum de l'Espesse	CN	2.7	No: 2.3; W: 2
Tongeren	Schaetzengaerde	CT	U	U
Tongeren	Sint-Truiderstraat	CT	U	U
Tourinnes-St-Lambert	Champ de la Sainte	CT	N	10.75?

Site	Name	Civitas	Piscinae	Alvei
Tournai	Vieux-Marché-aux-Jambons	CM	**3.6**; oval: **1.5** (depth: min. **0.6** m)	U
Tournai	Quai Vifquin	CM	U	U
Tournai	Quai Luchet d'Antoing	CM	min. 7.5	U
Waudrez	Bains	CN	U	U

Private baths

Site	Name	Civitas	Piscinae	Alvei
Aiseau	Villa d'Aiseau Bath 1	CT	**4.27** (depth: 0.7 m)	E: **3.1**; C: **2.9**; W: **3.1**
Aiseau	Villa d'Aiseau Bath 2	CT	**2.1***	E: **3.36**; S: 1.4
Amay	Villa de la Collégiale	CT	U	4.4
Ambresin	Villa d'Ambresin	CT	N	N
Anderlecht	Champs St-Anne	CN	N	2
Anthée	Villa du Grand Bon Dieu Bath 1	CT	U	No: 6.25; S: U
Anthée	Villa du Grand Bon Dieu Bath 2	CT	U	9.8
Anthée	Villa du Grand Bon Dieu Bath 3	CT	U	8.3 (depth: **1.1** m)
Arquennes	Villa d'Arquennes	CN	**5.33**	U
Assenois	La Chapelle	CT	U	U
Attenhoven	Villa de la Bruyère	CT	N	**1.25**
Ave-et-Aufe	Villa de Bois d'Ave	CT	U	U
Basse-Wavre	Villa de l'Hosté	CT	**14.13**	U
Bierbeek	Stenen Kruis	CT	N	U
Boirs	Thermes de la villa	CT	min. 5.3	U
Bois-et-Borsu	Villa de Thier-Laurent	CT	**1.2** (depth: 0.7 m)	U
Boussu-lez-Walcourt	La villa du Champ des Metz	CT	U	**2**
Bovigny	Bois des Concessions	CT	1.57	U
Brakel (Michelbeke)	Heksteelstraat	CN	U	U
Brakel (Zegelsem)	Kanakkendries 1	CN	U	1.4
Bras	Villa de Bras-Haut	CT	33.6*	U
Broekhem	Villa Ravenbosch	CT	**1.57**	**2.4**
Bruyelle	Villa de Haute Éloge (phase 2–3)	CN	**3.9**	E: 1.8; S: 2.86
Emptinne-Champion	Villa du Rosdia (phase 1)	CT	S: **5**; W: **1.57**	2.61
Emptinne-Champion	Villa du Rosdia (phase 2)	CT	S: **5**; W: **1.57**	U
Emptinne-Champion	Villa du Rosdia (phase 3)		S: **5**; W: **13** (depth: **1.3** m)	No: 2.9; E: 3
Clermont-sous-Huy	Villa d'Arvy	CT	**4.16**	NE: **2.08**; NW: **2.08**
Diekirch	Rue de l'Esplanade	CT	U	U
Élouges	Villa des Monts d'Élouges	CN	U	U
Évelette	Villa du Clavia	CT	N	U
Évelette	Villa de Résimont	CT	**2.15**	No: **2.25**; E: **2.25**
Flostoy	Villa de Lizée	CT	**6**	2
Froyennes	Villa de Froyennes		U	U
Gemechenne	Villa de Gemechenne	CT	U	No: 3.1; W: 3.6

Site	Name	Civitas	Piscinae	Alvei	
Gerpines	Villa de Gerpines	CT	U	4.5	
Gesves	Villa du Coria (phase 2)	CT	**4.75**	**4.18**	
Gesves	Villa du Coria (phase 1)	CT	**4.75**	W: **6**	
Gooik	Lombergveld	CN	U	U	
Graux	Villa romaine de Graux	CT	**1.1** (depth: **0.7** m)	1.5*	
Grumelange	Villa	CT	**0.88**	U	
Haccourt	Villa de Haccourt — Bath 1	CT	2.2	E: 5.08; S: 7.48	
Haccourt	Villa de Haccourt — Bath 2	CT	**4.25**	**5.85**	
Haccourt	Villa de Haccourt — Bath 3	CT	E: 3; W: **40** (depth: 1.3–1.4 m)	E: **2.45**; S: **8.84**	
Haillot	Villa de Matagne	CT	4	1.8	
Hamois	Villa de Hody	CT	**2.8**	SW: 2.25; NW: 0.8; NE: 1	
Heer	Bakkerbos	CT	U	U	
Heestert	Blinde Kapel	CM	N	5.5	
Heure-le-Romain	Bains domestiques Sur les Moulins	CT	U	S: 1.82; 1.62	
Hollain	Hypocaustes de Bas de Bléharies	CM	U	U	
Hoogeloon	Kerkakkers	CT	**3.3**	No: 2; E: 2.6	
Jemelle	Villa de Malagne	CT	**8.68**	No: 2.5; W: 2.4	
Kumtich	Mettenberg 1	CT	U	U	
Kumtich	Mettenberg 2	CT	U	3.2?	
Landen	Betzveld	CT	2.45*	U	
Latinne	Villa des Grandes Pièces	CT	1?	No: 2?; E: 2?	
Leignon	Villa de Barcenne	CT	2.25	No: 2.9; W: 1.7	
Lemiers	Villa	CT	U	8.1	
Liège	Villa de la Place St-Lambert	CT	U	U	
Limerlé	Villa de Rouvroy	CT	U	No: 0.8*; W: 2.4	
Mabeuge	Villa au Bois Brûlé	CN	U	6	
Machelen	Villa de Heuf	CN	**2.1**	U	
Maillen	Villa de Ronchinne	CT	U	7.6	
Maillen	Villa d'Arches	CT	**1.3**	**1.87**	
Maillen	Villa Al Sauvenière	CT	**3.7**	No: 2; W: 3.36	
Marcinelle	Villa de Marcinelle	CT	U	U	
Matagne-la-Petite	Villa Aux Murets	CT	U	2*	
Meerssen	Villa Herkenberg	CT	U	E: 3.3; W: 3.9	
Melsbroek	Hof ten As	CN	U	U	
Merbes-le-Chateau	Villa de Champ St-Eloi — Bath 1	CN	U	U	
Merbes-le-Chateau	Villa de Champ St-Eloi — Bath 2	CN	**3.12**	2.2?	
Meslin-L'Évêque	Villa de Preuscamps	CN	U	No: 12.5; S: 3	
Mettet	Villa de Bauselenne — Bath 1	CT	**2.48**	5.6	
Mettet	Villa de Bauselenne — Bath 2	CT	**14.7***	No: **6.58***; E: 2.5; S: 2.2	
Miécret	Villa de Miécret — Bath 1	CT	1.8	NW: 1.8; S: 1.1	

Site	Name	Civitas	Piscinae	Alvei
Miécret	Villa de Miécret — Bath 2	CT	2.8	NE: 1.2; NW: 2.7; SW: 1.2
Modave	Villa de Survillers	CT	**4**	No: 3.6; W: **2.4**
Montignies-Saint-Christophe	Villa de la Terre d'Au	CT	U	5.25*
Mont-lez-Houffalize	Sommerain	CT	U	U
Mont-lez-Houffalize	Villa de Fin de Ville — Bath 1	CT	10.8*	U
Mont-lez-Houffalize	Villa de Fin de Ville — Bath 2	CT	4	U
Neerharen-Rekem	Hangveld	CT	**2.75***	0.8*
Nivelles	Villa La Tournette	CN	U	U
Nouvelles	Villa de Grande Boussue	CN	U	U
Oberüttfeld	Villa	CT	**4.29** (depth: min. **0.65** m)	2.86
Rognée	Villa du Peruwelz	CT	U	U
Roly	Villa de la Crayellerie	CT	U	1.6?
Saint-Gérard	Villa du Try-Hallot	CT	U	3
Saint-Jean-Geest	Villa de Saint-Jean-Geest	CT	U	1.57
Sauvenière	Villa d'Arlansart	CT	U	1.84
Schieren	Villa	CT	U	U
's Gravensvoeren	Villa Steenbosch	CT	U	U
Thirimont	Villa de Saint-Rémy	CT	3.12	U
Tiegem	Kapellewijk	CM	U	U
Tongeren	Vrijthof	CT	1.9?	U
Tongeren	Boudewijnlaan	CT	4.8*	U
Tongeren	Vermeulenstraat	CT	U	U
Tourinnes-St-Lambert	Villa de Tourinnes-St-Lambert	CT	U	U
Tournai	Place Paul Janson	CM	U	U
Tournai	Couvent des Récollets	CM	**6.37** (depth: min. 1.25 m)	U
Treignes	Villa des Bruyères	CT	**10**	E: 2.4; S: 2.86*
Val-Meer	Villa	CT	U	**2.25**
Vechmaal	Middelpadveld 3	CT	**1.6** (depth: **0.75** m)	S: **1.6**; W: 2
Vellereille-les-Brayeux	Villa de Pincemaille	CN	**5.6**	0.8*
Vesqueville	Corps de logis de Vesqueville	CT	N	U
Villers-le-Bouillet	Villa de Vi Tchestia	CT	U	No: 7.5; W?: 6
Villers-sur-Lesse	Villa de Génimont	CT	3	U
Vissoul	Bounia	CT	N	2?; 1.9?
Vodelée	Villa romaine de Vodelée	CT	**1.57**	NE: 1.57*; E: 2.6; NW: 1.57*
Vorst	Steenbergen	CT	U	No: 3.25; W: **2.8**
Waha-Hollogne	Villa de Hologne	CT	4	S: 2.4; W: **4.3**
Wancennes	Villa romaine de Wancennes	CT	7	U
Wange	Villa	CT	U	No: 1.9; W: 1.5
Willemeau	Villa 1	CM	U	U
Willemeau	Villa 2	CM	**5.4**	U

Table 12. Overview of the type of hypocaust pillars used in the baths, the form of the constituent tiles and their dimensions (in cm), the reconstructed height of the pillars (until the start of the suspensura), and the number of rooms with hypocaust within the baths

Site	Name	*Civitas*	Square	Dimensions	Round	Dimensions	Mixed	Channel	Channel mixed	Unknown	Height pillars	Hyp
Public baths												
Aardenburg	Gasfabriek	CM								1		2?
Clavier-Vervoz	Thermes	CT	1									1
Famars	Thermes	CN	1									4
Fontaine-Valmont	Thermes	CT	1								120	2
Furfooz	Fortification de Hauterecenne	CT	1									1
Grobbendonk	Vicus Baths	CT					1					1
Liberchies	Thermes Les Bons-Villers	CT	1	20 × 21								2
Liberchies	Castellum de Brunehaut	CT								1		1?
Macquenoise	Thermes Marchienne au Pont	CN	1	21; 14								1
Oudenburg	Fort Baths	CM	1									2
Oudenburg	Vicus Baths	CM								1		1+
Outrelouxhe	Relais d'Elmer	CT	1									1
Tienen	Vicus Baths	CT			1							2
Wyompont	Station routière	CT	1	20								2
Sum			**9**		**1**		**1**	**0**		**3**		
Baths with unknown accessibility												
Amay-Ombret	Rausa	CT	1		1	20.5–22						2+
Aubechies	Bains sous l'église Saint-Géry	CN								1		1+
Bavay	Rue Saint-Maur	CN	1									1
Bavay	Église Saint-Pierre	CN	1	21								2?
Braives	Thermes	CT	1									1+
Chastrès	Thermes de Puceneveau	CT								1		1

Site	Name	*Civitas*	Square	Dimensions	Round	Dimensions	Mixed	Channel	Channel mixed	Unknown	Height pillars	Hyp
Kortrijk	O.L. Vrou-wekerk (Fort?)	CM	1	17.4								1
Maastricht	Stokstraat	CT		22		22	1					2+
Marchienne-au-Pont	Pachi al Cave	CT	1	21.5								1
Milmort	Balneum de Hauts Sarts	CT	1									1
Namur	Rue des Echasseurs	CT					1					3
Ramillies Autre-Église	Complexe thermale	CT	1	19–21.5	1							2
Soignies	Balneum de l'Espesse	CN	1									1
Tongeren	Schaetzen-gaerde	CT								1		U
Tongeren	Sint-Truiderstraat	CT			1	20						1
Tourinnes-St-Lambert	Champ de la Sainte	CT	1	20–22								2
Tournai	Vieux-Marché-aux-Jambons	CM	1	17							51	1+
Tournai	Quai Vifquin	CM								1		1?
Tournai	Quai Luchet d'Antoing	CM										U
Waudrez	Bains	CN								1		1
Sum			**11**		**3**		**2**	**0**		**5**		

Private baths

Site	Name	*Civitas*	Square	Dimensions	Round	Dimensions	Mixed	Channel	Channel mixed	Unknown	Height pillars	Hyp
Aiseau	Villa d'Aiseau Bath 1	CT	1	19–21							50–60	2
Aiseau	Villa d'Aiseau Bath 2	CT	1	19–21							50–60	2
Amay	Villa de la Collégiale	CT		22.5		22	1					1+
Ambresin	Villa d'Ambresin	CT								1		1
Anderlecht	Champs St-Anne	CN	1	30								1
Anthée	Villa du Grand Bon Dieu Bath 1	CT	1	20								3
Anthée	Villa du Grand Bon Dieu Bath 2	CT	1		1							3
Anthée	Villa du Grand Bon Dieu Bath 3	CT	1									2

Site	Name	*Civitas*	Square	Dimensions	Round	Dimensions	Mixed	Channel	Channel mixed	Unknown	Height pillars	Hyp
Arquennes	Villa d'Arquennes	CN	1	20								2
Assenois	La Chapelle	CT								1		1+
Attenhoven	Villa de la Bruyère	CT			1							1
Ave-et-Aufe	Villa de Bois d'Ave	CT			1							1+
Basse-Wavre	Villa de l'Hosté	CT		20; 30		25	1				70	3
Bierbeek	Stenen Kruis	CT		18–19.5		22	1					1
Boirs	Thermes de la villa	CT	1		1							2
Bois-et-Borsu	Villa de Thier-Laurent	CT			1							1+
Boussu-lez-Walcourt	La villa du Champ des Metz	CT	1	20.5								2
Bovigny	Bois des Concessions	CT								1		U
Brakel (Michelbeke)	Heksteelstraat	CN								1		
Brakel (Zegelsem)	Kanakken-dries 1	CN								1		1
Bras	Villa de Bras-Haut	CT								1		U
Broekhem	Villa Ravenbosch	CT	1	21								1
Bruyelle	Villa de Haute Éloge	CN	1	17; 21								5
Emptinne-Champion	Villa du Rosdia	CT	1				1					1
Clermont-sous-Huy	Villa d'Arvy	CT	1		1							2
Diekirch	Rue de l'Esplanade	CT			1							2+
Élouges	Villa des Monts d'Élouges	CN								1		1+
Évelette	Villa du Clavia	CT								1		1
Évelette	Villa de Résimont	CT			1							1+
Flostoy	Villa de Lizée	CT					1					1
Froyennes	Villa de Froyennes									1		1+
Gemechenne	Villa de Gemechenne	CT								1		2

Site	Name	*Civitas*	Square	Dimensions	Round	Dimensions	Mixed	Channel	Channel mixed	Unknown	Height pillars	Hyp
Gerpines	Villa de Gerpines	CT								1		3?
Gesves	Villa du Coria	CT	1				1					1
Gooik	Lombergveld	CN	1									1
Graux	Villa romaine de Graux	CT	1	24								2
Grumelange	Villa	CT	1	16	1						30	2?
Haccourt	Villa de Haccourt — Bath 1	CT	1	20–21							65	2
Haccourt	Villa de Haccourt — Bath 2	CT	1	21–23							51	2
Haccourt	Villa de Haccourt — Bath 3	CT			1	22–32						3
Haillot	Villa de Matagne	CT								1		1
Hamois	Villa de Hody	CT		25		23	1					1
Heer	Bakkerbos	CT			1							1
Heestert	Blinde Kapel	CM								1		1
Heure-le-Romain	Bains domestiques Sur les Moulins	CT			1							2
Hollain	Hypocaustes de Bas de Bléharies	CM	1	17; 16 × 18.5								3?
Hoogeloon	Kerkakkers	CT			1	20–23						2+
Jemelle	Villa de Malagne	CT	1	24								3
Kumtich	Mettenberg 1	CT	1	23.5		21.5	1					4
Kumtich	Mettenberg 2	CT	1	21.1 × 21.5; 25		29	1					5
Landen	Betzveld	CT								1		1+
Latinne	Villa des Grandes Pièces	CT	1									1
Leignon	Villa de Barcenne	CT	1									1
Lemiers	Villa	CT	1									2
Liège	Villa de la Place St-Lambert	CT			1	20–22	1				60	2+
Limerlé	Villa de Rouvroy	CT								1		2
Mabeuge	Villa au Bois Brûlé	CN	1									1
Machelen	Villa de Heuf	CN								1		U

Site	Name	*Civitas*	Square	Dimensions	Round	Dimensions	Mixed	Channel	Channel mixed	Unknown	Height pillars	Hyp
Maillen	Villa de Ronchinne	CT								1		3?
Maillen	Villa d'Arches	CT	1									1
Maillen	Villa Al Sauvenière	CT	1	21								2
Marcinelle	Villa de Marcinelle	CT	1								40	2+
Matagne-la-Petite	Villa Aux Murets	CT	1									1
Meerssen	Villa Herkenberg	CT								1		1
Melsbroek	Hof ten As	CN			1	12						1
Merbes-le-Chateau	Villa de Champ St-Eloi — Bath 1	CN	1	20								2
Merbes-le-Chateau	Villa de Champ St-Eloi — Bath 2	CN	1									2
Meslin-L'Évêque	Villa de Preuscamps	CN								1		2?
Mettet	Villa de Bauselenne — Bath 1	CT	1	16								3?
Mettet	Villa de Bauselenne — Bath 2	CT	1									1
Miécret	Villa de Miécret — Bath 1	CT					1					1
Miécret	Villa de Miécret — Bath 2	CT					1					2
Modave	Villa de Survillers	CT								1		1
Montignies-Saint-Christophe	Villa de la Terre d'Au	CT					1					2+
Mont-lez-Houffalize	Sommerain	CT			1	15						3
Mont-lez-Houffalize	Villa de Fin de Ville — Bath 1	CT						1				1
Mont-lez-Houffalize	Villa de Fin de Ville — Bath 2	CT								1		2
Neerharen-Rekem	Hangveld	CT	1	20	1	22		1				3
Nivelles	Villa La Tournette	CN								1		2

Site	Name	*Civitas*	Square	Dimensions	Round	Dimensions	Mixed	Channel	Channel mixed	Unknown	Height pillars	Hyp
Nouvelles	Villa de Grande Boussue	CN								1		U
Oberüttfeld	Villa	CT			1							1
Rognée	Villa du Peruwelz	CT	1	22							90	4
Roly	Villa de la Crayellerie	CT	1									1
Saint-Gérard	Villa du Try-Hallot	CT	1	20.5								5
Saint-Jean-Geest	Villa de Saint-Jean-Geest	CT	1	20	1	32.5					80	3
Sauvenière	Villa d'Arlansart	CT	1									1
Schieren	Villa	CT								1		1+
's Gravensvoeren	Villa Steenbosch	CT			1	23						2+
Thirimont	Villa de Saint-Rémy	CT		13 × 14		24	1					2
Tiegem	Hofdries	CM		16		17–18	1					1
Tongeren	Vrijthof	CT					1					1
Tongeren	Boudewijnlaan	CT								1		1
Tongeren	Vermeulenstraat	CT					1	1				2+
Tourinnes-St-Lambert	Villa de Tourinnes-St-Lambert	CT							1			1+
Tournai	Place Paul Janson	CM	1	18								1+
Tournai	Couvent des Récollets	CM								1		U
Treignes	Villa des Bruyères	CT	1									2
Val-Meer	Villa	CT			1	20.5						2+
Vechmaal	Middelpadveld 3	CT			1							2
Vellereille-les-Brayeux	Villa de Pincemaille	CN	1									2+
Vesqueville	Corps de logis de Vesqueville	CT	1	16.5–17								1
Villers-le-Bouillet	Villa de Vi Tchestia	CT			1							1
Villers-sur-Lesse	Villa de Génimont	CT								1		U
Vissoul	Bounia	CT			1							1

Site	Name	*Civitas*	Square	Dimensions	Round	Dimensions	Mixed	Channel	Channel mixed	Unknown	Height pillars	Hyp
Vodelée	Villa romaine de Vodelée	CT	1	18								1
Vorst	Steenbergen	CT			1	19						2?
Waha-Hollogne	Villa de Hologne	CT			1							1
Wancennes	Villa romaine de Wancennes	CT	1	20								1
Wange	Villa	CT								1		1
Willemeau	Villa 1	CM								1		1
Willemeau	Villa 2	CM	1	16	1							2+
Sum			**48**		**27**		**17**	**3**		**29**		

Table 13. Overview of the type of wall heating in the baths, their dimensions (in cm), and the number of rooms with hypocaust in each bath

Site	Name	Civ.	Tubuli	Dimensions	Lateral opening	Teg.	Mam.	Dim.	Both	None	Unknown	Hyp
Public baths												
Aardenburg	Gasfabriek	CM									1	2?
Clavier-Vervoz	Thermes	CT	1									1
Famars	Thermes	CN	1									4
Fontaine-Valmont	Thermes	CT	1		round							2
Furfooz	Fortification de Hauterecenne	CT	1									1
Grobbendonk	Vicus Baths	CT									1	1
Liberchies	Thermes Les Bons-Villers	CT									1	2
Liberchies	Castellum de Brunehaut	CT									1	1?
Macquenoise	Thermes Marchienne au Pont	CN	1									1
Oudenburg	Fort Baths	CM	1									2
Oudenburg	Vicus Baths	CM									1	1+
Outrelouxhe	Relais d'Elmer	CT	1		round: 3.5							1
Tienen	Vicus Baths	CT	1									2
Wyompont	Station routière	CT	1									2
Sum			**8**				**0**		**0**	**0**	**5**	
Baths with unknown accessibility												
Amay-Ombret	Rausa	CT	1	20 × 20 × 14; 10 × 25 × 25	round: 4.5	1		27	1			2+
Aubechies	Bains sous l'église Saint-Géry	CN									1	1+
Bavay	Rue Saint-Maur	CN	1									1
Bavay	Église Saint-Pierre	CN	1	16 × 31 × 44; 16 × 44 × 31	round							2?
Braives	Thermes	CT	1				1					1+
Chastrès	Thermes de Puceneveau	CT									1	1
Kortrijk	O.L. Vrouwekerk	CM	1		round: 4.8							1
Maastricht	Stokstraat	CT	1	22 × 12.5 × 25	round							2+
Marchienne-au-Pont	Pachi al Cave	CT								1		1
Milmort	Balneum de Hauts Sarts	CT	1									1

Site	Name	Civ.	Tubuli	Dimensions	Lateral opening	Teg. Mam.	Dim.	Both	None	Unknown	Hyp
Namur	Rue des Echasseurs	CT								1	3
Ramillies Autre-Église	Complexe thermale	CT								1	2
Soignies	Balneum de l'Espesse	CN	1	25.5 × 13.5 × 20							1
Tongeren	Schaetzengaerde	CT								1	U
Tongeren	Sint-Truiderstraat	CT	1	26.5 × 22.5 × 9	round						1
Tourinnes-St-Lambert	Champ de la Sainte	CT								1	2
Tournai	Vieux-Marché-aux-Jambons	CM	1	20 × 25 × 12	round: 5						1+
Tournai	Quai Vifquin	CM								1	1?
Tournai	Quai Luchet d'Antoing	CM								1	U
Waudrez	Bains	CN	1								1
Sum			**11**			**2**		**1**	**1**	**8**	

Private baths

Site	Name	Civ.	Tubuli	Dimensions	Lateral opening	Teg. Mam.	Dim.	Both	None	Unknown	Hyp
Aiseau	Villa d'Aiseau Bath 1	CT	1	22 × 23 × 10	round: 3.5	1		1			2
Aiseau	Villa d'Aiseau Bath 2	CT	1	22 × 23 × 10	round: 3.5	1					2
Amay	Villa de la Collégiale	CT								1	1+
Ambresin	Villa d'Ambresin	CT	1								1
Anderlecht	Champs St-Anne	CN	1								1
Anthée	Villa du Grand Bon Dieu Bath 1	CT	1								3
Anthée	Villa du Grand Bon Dieu Bath 2	CT								1	3
Anthée	Villa du Grand Bon Dieu Bath 3	CT	1								2
Arquennes	Villa d'Arquennes	CN	1	27 × 26 × 27	round: 5						2
Assenois	La Chapelle	CT								1	1+
Attenhoven	Villa de la Bruyère	CT								1	1
Ave-et-Aufe	Villa de Bois d'Ave	CT								1	1+
Basse-Wavre	Villa de l'Hosté	CT								1	3
Bierbeek	Stenen Kruis	CT					1				1
Boirs	Thermes de la villa	CT	1								2
Bois-et-Borsu	Villa de Thier-Laurent	CT								1	1+

Site	Name	Civ.	Tubuli	Dimensions	Lateral opening	Teg. Mam.	Dim.	Both	None	Unknown	Hyp
Boussu-lez-Walcourt	La villa du Champ des Metz	CT	1								2
Bovigny	Bois des Concessions	CT								1	U
Brakel (Michelbeke)	Heksteelstraat	CN								1	
Brakel (Zegelsem)	Kanakkendries 1	CN								1	1
Bras	Villa de Bras-Haut	CT								1	U
Broekhem	Villa Ravenbosch	CT	1								1
Bruyelle	Villa de Haute Éloge	CN	1	25.6 × 18.4; 24 × 21.5; 21.8 × 14.5; 18.6 × 15.5	round; rectangular						5
Emptinne-Champion	Villa du Rosdia	CT	1		round; square						1
Clermont-sous-Huy	Villa d'Arvy	CT	1								2
Diekirch	Rue de l'Esplanade	CT							1		2+
Élouges	Villa des Monts d'Élouges	CN	1		unknown						1+
Évelette	Villa du Clavia	CT								1	1
Évelette	Villa de Résimont	CT								1	1+
Flostoy	Villa de Lizée	CT	1								1
Froyennes	Villa de Froyennes									1	1+
Gemechenne	Villa de Gemechenne	CT								1	2
Gerpines	Villa de Gerpines	CT	1	20							3?
Gesves	Villa du Coria	CT	1								1
Gooik	Lombergveld	CN								1	1
Graux	Villa romaine de Graux	CT	1								2
Grumelange	Villa	CT	1								2?
Haccourt	Villa de Haccourt — Bath 1	CT								1	2
Haccourt	Villa de Haccourt — Bath 2	CT								1	2
Haccourt	Villa de Haccourt — Bath 3	CT								1	3
Haillot	Villa de Matagne	CT								1	1
Hamois	Villa de Hody	CT	1								1
Heer	Bakkerbos	CT	1								1

Site	Name	Civ.	Tubuli	Dimensions	Lateral opening	Teg. Mam.	Dim.	Both	None	Unknown	Hyp
Heestert	Blinde Kapel	CM	1								1
Heure-le-Romain	Bains domestiques Sur les Moulins	CT	1								2
Hollain	Hypocaustes de Bas de Bléharies	CM	1								3?
Hoogeloon	Kerkakkers	CT	1	11–14 × 21–23 × 16–18; 24–35 × 8–12.5 × 26–32							2+
Jemelle	Villa de Malagne	CT	1								3
Kumtich	Mettenberg 1	CT								1	
Kumtich	Mettenberg 2	CT	1		rectangular						
Landen	Betzveld	CT								1	1+
Latinne	Villa des Grandes Pièces	CT								1	1
Leignon	Villa de Barcenne	CT	1		unknown						1
Lemiers	Villa	CT							1		2
Liège	Villa de la Place St-Lambert	CT								1	1+
Limerlé	Villa de Rouvroy	CT								1	2
Mabeuge	Villa au Bois Brûlé	CN								1	1
Machelen	Villa de Heuf	CN								1	U
Maillen	Villa de Ronchinne	CT								1	3?
Maillen	Villa d'Arches	CT								1	1
Maillen	Villa Al Sauvenière	CT	1	10 × 6							2
Marcinelle	Villa de Marcinelle	CT								1	2+
Matagne-la-Petite	Villa Aux Murets	CT								1	1
Meerssen	Villa Herkenberg	CT								1	1
Melsbroek	Hof ten As	CN								1	1
Merbes-le-Chateau	Villa de Champ St-Eloi — Bath 1	CN	1								2
Merbes-le-Chateau	Villa de Champ St-Eloi — Bath 2	CN								1	2
Meslin-L'Évêque	Villa de Preuscamps	CN								1	2?
Mettet	Villa de Bauselenne — Bath 1	CT	1	13 × 10 × 42	rect.: 9 × 8						3?
Mettet	Villa de Bauselenne — Bath 2	CT								1	1

Site	Name	Civ.	Tubuli	Dimensions	Lateral opening	Teg. Mam.	Dim.	Both	None	Unknown	Hyp
Miécret	Villa de Miécret — Bath 1	CT								1	1
Miécret	Villa de Miécret — Bath 2	CT								1	2
Modave	Villa de Survillers	CT								1	1
Montignies-Saint-Christophe	Villa de la Terre d'Au	CT	1								2+
Mont-lez-Houffalize	Sommerain	CT	1	12–13 × ? × ?	unknown						3
Mont-lez-Houffalize	Villa de Fin de Ville — Bath 1	CT						1			1
Mont-lez-Houffalize	Villa de Fin de Ville — Bath 2	CT	1								2
Neerharen-Rekem	Hangveld	CT	1	? × ? × 23.5	round: 4–5						3
Nivelles	Villa La Tournette	CN								1	2
Nouvelles	Villa de Grande Boussue	CN	1								U
Oberüttfeld	Villa	CT	1								1
Rognée	Villa du Peruwelz	CT	1	20 × 22 × 10; 40 × 11 × 13	rectangular; 16 × 6						4
Roly	Villa de la Crayellerie	CT								1	1
Saint-Gérard	Villa du Try-Hallot	CT	1								5
Saint-Jean-Geest	Villa de Saint-Jean-Geest	CT								1	3
Sauvenière	Villa d'Arlansart	CT								1	1
Schieren	Villa	CT								1	1+
's Gravensvoeren	Villa Steenbosch	CT	1								2+
Thirimont	Villa de Saint-Rémy	CT	1								2
Tiegem	Kapellewijk	CM	1		round						1
Tongeren	Vrijthof	CT								1	1
Tongeren	Boudewijnlaan	CT								1	1
Tongeren	Vermeulenstraat	CT	1								2+
Tourinnes-St-Lambert	Villa de Tourinnes-St-Lambert	CT	1								1+
Tournai	Place Paul-Émile Janson	CM								1	1+
Tournai	Couvent des Récollets	CM								1	U
Treignes	Villa des Bruyères	CT	1								2
Val-Meer	Villa	CT	1								2+

Site	Name	Civ.	Tubuli	Dimensions	Lateral opening	Teg. Mam.	Dim.	Both	None	Unknown	Hyp
Vechmaal	Middelpadveld 3	CT	1	24 × 23 × 10							2
Vellereille-les-Brayeux	Villa de Pincemaille	CN	1								2+
Vesqueville	Corps de logis de Vesqueville	CT								1	1
Villers-le-Bouillet	Villa de Vi Tchestia	CT	1								1
Villers-sur-Lesse	Villa de Génimont	CT								1	U
Vissoul	Bounia	CT								1	1
Vodelée	Villa romaine de Vodelée	CT	1								1
Vorst	Steenbergen	CT								1	2?
Waha-Hollogne	Villa de Hologne	CT								1	1
Wancennes	Villa romaine de Wancennes	CT	1								1
Wange	Villa	CT								1	1
Willemeau	Villa 1	CM								1	1
Willemeau	Villa 2	CM	1								2+
Sum			52			3		1	3	55	

Works Cited

Primary Sources

August. *De moribus manichaeorum = Augustini, opera omnia*, ed. by Jacques-Paul Migne, *Patrologia Latina*, 32 (Paris: Garnier, 1844–1855), cols 1309–78

Caes. *B Gall.* = *Caesar: The Gallic War*, ed. and trans. by Henry John Edwards, Loeb Classical Library, 72 (Cambridge, MA: Harvard University Press, 1917)

Cato, *Agr.* = *Cato, Varro: On Agriculture*, ed. and trans. by William Davis Hooper and Harry Boyd Ash, Loeb Classical Library, 283 (Cambridge, MA: Harvard University Press, 1934), pp. 1–158

Cic. *Att.* = *Cicero: Letters to Atticus*, I, ed. and trans. by David Roy Shackleton Bailey, Loeb Classical Library, 7 (Cambridge, MA: Harvard University Press, 1999)

Columella, *Rust.* = *Columella: On Agriculture*, I: *Books 1–4*, ed. and trans. by Harry Boyd Ash, Loeb Classical Library, 361 (Cambridge, MA: Harvard University Press, 1941)

Edwards, Henri John. 1917. *Caesar: The Gallic Wars*, Loeb Classical Library, 72 (Cambridge, MA: Harvard University Press)

Epiph. *Adv. haeres.* = *The Panarion of Epiphanius of Salamis: De fide*, ed. and trans. by Frank Williams, Nag Hamadi and Manichean Studies, 63–79, 2 vols (Leiden: Brill, 2009–2012)

Fitch, John. 2013. *Palladius: The Work of Farming ('Opus agriculturae') and Poem on Grafting* (Totnes: Prospect)

Gell. *NA* = *Gellius: Attic Nights*, III: *Books 14–20*, ed. and trans. by John Rolf, Loeb Classical Library, 212 (Cambridge, MA: Harvard University Press, 1927)

Gummere, Richard. 1920. *Seneca: Epistles*, II: *Epistles 66–92*, Loeb Classical Library, 76 (Cambridge, MA: Harvard University Press)

Hutton, Maurice, and William Peterson. 1914. *Tacitus: Agricola; Germania; Dialogue on Oratory*, Loeb Classical Library, 35 (Cambridge, MA: Harvard University Press)

Josh. *Styl.* = *The Chronicle of Joshua the Stylite, Composed in Syriac A.D. 507*, ed. and trans. by William Wright (Cambridge: Cambridge University Press, 1882)

Palladius, *de re rust.* = *Palladius: The Work of Farming*, trans. by John Fitch (Totnes: Prospect, 2013)

Plin. *Ep.* = *Pliny the Younger: Letters*, I: *Books 1–7*, ed. and trans. by Betty Radice, Loeb Classical Library, 55 (Cambridge, MA: Harvard University Press, 1969)

Ptol. *Geog.* = *Die Geographie des Ptolemaeus: Galliae Germania Raetia Noricum Pannoniae Illyricum Italia*, trans. by Otto Cuntz (Berlin: Weidmann, 1923)

Sen. *Ep.* = *Seneca: Epistles*, ed. and trans. by Richard Gummere, Loeb Classical Library, 75–77, 3 vols (Cambridge, MA: Harvard University Press, 1917–1925)

Sid. Apoll. *Ep.* = *Sidonius: Poems; Letters*, ed. and trans. by William Blair Anderson, Loeb Classical Library, 296, 420, 2 vols (Cambridge, MA: Harvard University Press, 1936–1965)

Strabo, *Geogr.* = *Strabo: Geography*, ed. and trans. by Horace Leonard Jones, Loeb Classical Library 49, 50, 182, 196, 211, 223, 241, 267, 8 vols (Cambridge, MA: Harvard University Press, 1917–1932)

Tacitus, *Agr.* = *Tacitus: Agricola; Germania; Dialogue on Oratory*, ed. and trans. by Maurice Hutton and William Peterson, rev. by Robert Maxwell Ogilvie, Eric Herbert Warmington, and Michael Winterbottom, Loeb Classical Library, 35 (Cambridge, MA: Harvard University Press, 1914), pp. 26–118

Tacitus, *Germ.* = *Tacitus: Agricola; Germania; Dialogue on Oratory*, ed. and trans. by Maurice Hutton and William Peterson, rev. by Robert Maxwell Ogilvie, Eric Herbert Warmington, and Michael Winterbottom, Loeb Classical Library, 35 (Cambridge, MA: Harvard University Press, 1914), pp. 128–218

Varro, *Rust.* = *Cato, Varro: On Agriculture*, ed. and trans. by William Davis Hooper and Harry Boyd Ash, Loeb Classical Library, 283 (Cambridge, MA: Harvard University Press, 1934), pp. 159–530

Venantius Fortunatus, *De Praemiaco, villa Burdegalensi = Venantius Fortunatus: Miscellanea*, ed. by Jacques-Paul Migne, *Patrologia Latina*, 88 (Paris: Garnier, 1850), cols 51–596

Vitr. *Arch.* = *Vitruvius: On Architecture*, ed. and trans. by Frank Granger, Loeb Classical Library, 251, 280, 2 vols (Cambridge, MA: Harvard University Press, 1931–1934)

Secondary Works

Adam, Jean-Pierre. 1984. *La construction romaine: matériaux et techniques* (Paris: Picard)

Amand, Marcel. 1946. 'Substructions romaines du Marché-aux-Jambons', *L'antiquité classique*, 15.1: 97–105

——. 1953. 'Tournai. Travaux du Musée d'Histoire et d'Archéologie', *L'antiquité classique*, 22.2: 441–43

——. 1962. 'Nouveaux aspects de la romanisation en Pévèle belge', in *Hommages à Albert Grenier*, ed. by Marcel Renard, Collection Latomus, 58 (Brussels: Latomus), pp. 104–20

——. 1964. 'Tournai: fouilles au Luchet d'Antoing', *Archéologie*, 1964.2: 84–86

——. 1968. 'Un nouveau quartier romain à Tournai. Les fouilles du Luchet d'Antoing', *Archaeologia Belgica*, 102: 5–46

Amand, Marcel, and Irène Eykens-Dierickx. 1960. *Tournai Romain*, Dissertationes Archaeologicae Gandenses, 5 (Brugge: De Tempel)

Amand, Marcel, and Philippe Soleil. 1988. 'Willemeau, haut lieu de l'archéologie gallo-romaine et franque dans les Tournaisis', *Vie archéologique*, 29: 37–52

Angelis d'Ossat, Guglielmo. 1943. *Tecnica costruttiva e impianti delle terme*, Civiltà romana, 23 (Rome: Carlo Colombo)

Anonymous. 1896. 'Villa belgo-romaine de Survillers', *Bulletin de l'Institut archéologique liégeois*, 25: 179–89

——. 2000. *La villa de Mageroy après 14 années de fouilles*, Arc-Hab, 37 (Habay-la-Neuve: Groupe d'Archéologie de Habay)

——. 2009. *Bailleul 'La zac des collines': une villa gallo-romaine en Flandre* (Villeneuve-d'Ascq: DRAC Nord-Pas-de-Calais, Service régional de l'archéologie)

Ansieau, Cécile, and Karine Bausier. 2018. 'Les bâtiments de la villa', in *Antoing, Bruyelle: villa romaine et occupations antérieures*, ed. by Karine Bausier, Nathalie Bloch, and Fabienne Pigière, Études et documents archéologie, 23 (Namur: Agence wallonne du Patrimoine), pp. 91–129

Ansieau, Cécile, Karine Bausier, and Fabienne Pigière. 1998. 'Bruyelle (Antoing): le site de la *Haute Éloge*', *Vie archéologique*, 49: 21–34

Authom, Nicolas, and Nicolas Paridaens. 2008. 'Merbes-le-Château/Labuissière et Erquelinnes/Solre-sur-Sambre: la villa gallo-romaine du "Champ de Saint-Eloi". Bilan de la première campagne de fouille', *Chronique de l'archéologie wallonne*, 15: 44–47

——. 2009. 'Merbes-le-Château/Labuissière: la villa gallo-romaine du "Champ de Saint-Eloi". Bilan des deux premières campagnes de fouilles (2006–2007)', *Chronique de l'archéologie wallonne*, 16: 42–45

——. 2011. 'Merbes-le-Chateau/Labuissière: la villa gallo-romaine du "Champ de Saint-Eloi". Troisième campagne de fouilles (2009)', *Chronique de l'archéologie wallonne*, 18: 57–61

——. 2015. *La villa gallo-romaine du 'Champ de Saint-Éloi' à Merbes-le-Château*, Études et documents. Archéologie, 30 (Namur: Institut du patrimoine wallon)

Barbet, Alix. 2008. *La peinture murale en Gaule romaine* (Paris: Picard)

Bargellini, Paola. 1991. 'Le terme centrali di Pompei', in *Les thermes romains: actes de la table ronde de Rome (11–12 novembre 1988)*, Collection de l'école française de Rome, 142 (Rome: École française de Rome), pp. 115–28

Bausier, Karine. 1994. 'Antoing/Bruyelle: "Haute Éloge", villa romaine et occupation antérieur', *Chronique de l'archéologie wallonne*, 2: 39–40

——. 1998. 'ANTOING, Bruyelle. La villa romaine et des traces d'occupation antérieure à "Haute Éloge"', in *Le patrimoine archéologique de Wallonie*, ed. by Marie-Hélène Corbiau (Namur: Ministère de la Région wallonne), pp. 319–22

Bausier, Karine, Nathalie Bloch, and Fabienne Pigière. 2018. *Antoing, Bruyelle: villa romaine et occupations antérieures*, Études et documents. Archéologie, 23 (Namur: Agence Wallonne du Patrimoine)

Bayet, L. 1891. 'Villa belgo-romaine de Boussu-lez-Walcourt', *Documents et rapports de la Société paléontologique et archéologique de Charleroi*, 18: 53–69

Beaussart, Philippe. 1980. 'Les thermes gallo-romains de Famars d'après les fouilles anciennes', *Revue du Nord*, 62: 805–23

Bequet, Alfred. 1886. 'Nos fouilles en 1883 et 1884. Wancennes', *Annales de la Société archéologique de Namur*, 16: 363–87

——. 1897. 'La villa romaine de Ronchinne et sa brasserie (IIIe et IVe siècles)', *Annales de la Société archéologique de Namur*, 21: 177–208

——. 1900a. 'Bains publics, IIe siècle, à Chastrès (Namur)', *Annales de la Société archéologique de Namur*, 24: 27–32

——. 1900b. 'Ferme du IIe siècle à Sauvenière (Namur)', *Annales de la Société archéologique de Namur*, 24: 11–20

Bidwell, Paul. 2002. 'Timber Baths in Augustan and Tiberian Fortresses', in *Limes XVIII: Proceedings of the XVIIIth International Congress of Roman Frontier Studies Held in Amman, Jordan (September 2000)*, ed. by Philip Freeman, Julian Bennett, Zbigniew Tomasz Fiema, and Birgitta Hoffmann, British Archaeological Reports, International Series, 1084 (Oxford: Archaeopress), pp. 467–81

——. 2009. 'The Earliest Occurrences of Baths at Auxiliary Forts', in *The Army and Frontiers of Rome: Papers Offered to David J. Breeze on the Occasion of his Sixty-Fifth Birthday and his Retirement from Historic England*, ed. by William Hanson, Journal of Roman Archaeology Supplement, 74 (Portsmouth, RI: Journal of Roman Archaeology), pp. 55–62

Biévelet, Henri. 1950. 'L'exploration archéologique de Bavai. "Notes sur les hypocaustes de Bavai"', *L'antiquité classique*, 19.1: 81–92

——. 1953. 'L'exploration archéologique de Bavai. Les fouilles de l'église (juillet 1953)', in *Verbond der geschiedkundige en oudheidkundige kringen van België: Handelingen van het 35e Congres (Kortrijk, 26–30 juli 1953)*, ed. by Jean de Béthune (Gembloux: Duculot), pp. 37–48

——. 1956. 'L'exploration archéologique de Bavai. Dallages de marbres, mosaïques et peintures murales à Bavai', *Latomus*, 15.4: 567–84

Biver, Véronique, and Sabine Groetembril. 2017. 'La villa gallo-romaine de Schieren (G.-D. de Luxembourg), découverte d'enduits peints remarquables dans un contexte privilégié. Méthode et résultats de la fouille', *Signa romana*, 6: 9–19

Biver, Véronique, Alan Stead, Michel Polfer, and Foni Le Brum-Ricalens. 2016. 'Le domaine de la villa gallo-romaine de Schieren (G.-D. de Luxembourg): contexte archéologique et résultats préliminaires des fouilles récentes', *Archaeologia Luxemburgensis*, 3: 42–63

Black, Ernest. 1994. 'Villa-Owners: Romano-British Gentlemen and Officers', *Britannia*, 25: 99–110

Bloemers, Johan Hendrik Frederik. 1973. 'Twenty-Five Years of ROB Research in Roman Limburg', *Berichten van de Rijksdienst voor het Oudheidkundig Bodemonderzoek*, 23: 237–58

Blonski, Michel. 2014a. *Se nettoyer à Rome. IIe avant J.-C. – IIe s. après J.-C.: pratiques et enjeux*, Études anciennes, 77 (Paris: Les belles lettres)

——. 2014b. 'Comment définir et utiliser des détergents dans le balneum? L'exemple du "nitre" à l'époque romaine', in *25 siècles de bain collectif en Orient: Proche-Orient, Égypte et péninsule Arabique; Balaneia, Thermae, Hammam; actes du 3e colloque international Balnéorient (Damas/Syrie 2–6 nov. 2009)*, ed. by Marie-Françoise Boussac, Sylvie Denoix, Thibaud Fournet, and Bérangère Redon, Études urbaines, 9.4 (Cairo: Institut français d'archéologie orientale), pp. 883–97

Bodson, Bernadette, and Michel De Reymaeker. 1980. 'Vestiges gallo-romains à Autre-Église', *Activités du SOS Fouilles*, 1: 67–69

Boersma, Johannes. 1985. *Amoenissima civitas: Block V:ii at Ostia; Description and Analysis of the Visible Remains*, Scrinium, 1 (Assen: Van Gorcum)

Bogaers, Julianus Egidius. 1963. 'Maastricht', *Bulletin van de Koninklijke Nederlandse oudheidkundige bond*, 16: 159–234

——. 1971. 'Germania Inferior, Gallia Belgica en de civitates van de Frisiavones en de Tungri', *Helinium*, 11: 228–37

Bonenfant, Pierre. 1987. 'La villa belgo-romaine de Robelmont', in *Archéologie entre Semois et Chiers*, ed. by Gérard Lambert (Brussels: Crédit communal de Belgique), pp. 119–24

Borgers, Kristien, Michiel Steenhoudt, and Ellen Van de Velde. 2008. 'Een derde noodopgraving aan de Vermeulenstraat te Tongeren (unpublished excavation report, Rapportage Onroerend Erfgoed Vlaanderen)

Bossicard, Dominique. 1994. 'Rouvroy/Torgny: villa romaine', *Chronique de l'archéologie wallonne*, 2: 114–16

Bott, Saskia, and Pierre Cattelain. 1996–1997. 'Viroinval/Treignes: recherches récentes dans la villa gallo-romaine des "Bruyères"', *Chronique de l'archéologie wallonne*, 4–5: 185–86

——. 1999. 'Viroinval/Treignes: la villa gallo-romaine des Bruyères. Nouvelle interprétation chronologique des premières phases d'occupation', *Chronique de l'archéologie wallonne*, 7: 155–57

Boudeau, Jasmine. 2011. 'Devenir et place des thermes publics dans les *castra* du Bas-Empire du Nord-Ouest de la Gaule: étude de dix chefs-lieux de cité de Gaule Belgique et Lyonnaise', *Revue archéologique du Centre de la France*, 50: 453–99

Bouet, Alain. 2000. 'Les modèles thermaux et leur diffusion en Gaule', in *Termas romanas en el occidente del imperio: II Coloquio Internacional de Arqueología en Gijón (Gijón 1999)*, ed. by Carmen Fernández Ochoa and Virginia García-Entero, Serie Patrimonio, 5 (Gijón: VTP), pp. 35–46

——. 2003a. 'Les thermes publics d'agglomérations secondaires en Gaule', in *Thermae Gallicae: les thermes de Barzan (Charente-Maritime) et les thermes des provinces gauloises*, ed. by Alain Bouet, Aquitania. Suppléments, 11 (Bordeaux: Ausonius), pp. 589–722

——. 2003b. *Les thermes privés et publics en Gaule Narbonnaise, 1: Synthèse*, Collection de l'École française de Rome, 320 (Rome: École française de Rome)

——. 2007. 'Die öffentlichen Thermen in den "agglomerations secondaires" Galliens', in *Leben im römischen Europa: Von Pompeji nach Bliesbruck-Reinheim*, ed. by Jean-Paul Petit and Sara Santoro (Paris: Errance), pp. 221–26

——. 2018. 'Des thermes thérapeutiques dans les cités de la Gaule?', in *Thermae in Context, the Roman Bath in Town and in Life: Actes du Colloque de Dalheim, Luxembourg, du 21 au 24 février 2013*, ed. by Heike Pösche, Andrea Binsfeld, and Stefanie Hoss, Archaeologia Mosellana, 10 (Luxembourg: Centre national de recherche archéologique), pp. 267–91

Bowes, Kim. 2008. *Private Worship, Public Values, and Religious Change in Late Antiquity* (Cambridge: Cambridge University Press)

Bowman, Alan, and David Thomas. 1983. *Vindolanda: The Latin Writing-Tablets*, Britannia Monograph Series, 4 (London: Society for the Promotion of Roman Studies)

Braat, Wouter Cornelis. 1934. 'Een romeinsche villa bij Lemiers', *Oudheidkundige Mededeelingen uit 's Rijksmuseum van Oudheden te Leiden*, 15: 18–28

——. 1953. 'De groote romeinse villa van Voerendaal', *Oudheidkundige Mededeelingen uit 's Rijksmuseum van Oudheden te Leiden*, 34: 48–78

Brandt, Roel, and Jan Slofstra (eds). 1983. *Roman and Native in the Low Countries: Spheres of Interaction*, British Archaeological Reports, International Series, 184 (Oxford: BAR)

Brödner, Erika. 1983. *Die römischen Thermen und das antike Badewesen: Eine kulturhistorische Betrachtung* (Darmstadt: Wissenschaftliche Buchgesellschaft)

Broise, Henri. 1994. 'La pratique du bain chaud par immersion en Sicile et dans la péninsule italique à l'époque hellénistique', *Xenia antiqua*, 3: 17–32

Broise, Henri, and Vincent Jolivet. 1991. 'Le bain en Étrurie à l'époque hellénistique', in *Les thermes romains: actes de la table ronde, Rome, 11.11.1988–12.11.1988*, Collection de l'École française de Rome, 142 (Rome: École française de Rome), pp. 79–95

Brulet, Raymond. 1970. 'La villa romaine du Try-Hallot à Saint-Gérard. Étude topographique', *Recherches d'archéologie et de l'histoire de l'art (Antiquité)*, 1: 63–80

——. 1973a. 'Établissement de bains dans le vicus de Liberchies. Rapport preliminaire', *Documents et rapports de la Société paléontologique et archéologique de Charleroi*, 56: 113–15

——. 1973b. 'Un vase à masques à Montignies-Saint-Christophe', *Helinium*, 13: 175–90

——. 1975. *Liberchies gallo-romain: rempart de la Romanité* (Gembloux: Duculot)

——. 1978. *La fortification de Hauterecenne à Furfooz*, Publications d'histoire de l'art et d'archéologie de l'Université catholique de Louvain, 13 (Louvain-la-Neuve: Institut Supérieur d'archéologie et d'histoire de l'art)

——. 1980. 'Macquenoise: thermes gallo-romains', *Archéologie*, 1980.2: 84–85

——. 1981. *Braives gallo-romain*, I: *La zone centrale*, Publications d'histoire de l'art et d'archéologie de l'Université catholique de Louvain, 26 (Louvain-la-Neuve: Institut supérieure d'archéologie et d'histoire de l'art)

——. 1985. 'Établissement gallo-romain à Macquenoise: thermes et centre sidérurgique', *Documents et rapports de la Société paléontologique et archéologique de Charleroi*, 49: 27–55

——. 2008. *Les romains en Wallonie* (Brussels: Éditions Racine)

Brulet, Raymond, and Jean-Claude Demanet. 1997. *Liberchies*, III: *Vicus Gallo-Romain*, Publications d'histoire de l'art et d'archéologie de l'Université catholique de Louvain, 94 (Louvain-la-Neuve: Département d'archéologie et d'histoire de l'art)

Burke, Peter. 2009. *Cultural Hybridity* (Cambridge: Polity)

Busch, Stephan. 1999. *Versus Balnearum: Die antike Dichtung über Bäder und Baden im römischen Reich* (Stuttgart: Teubner)

Capers, Pierre. 1998. *Vodgoriacum: Le vicus gallo-romain de Waudrez* (Waudrez: Statio Romana)

Carlier, Omar. 2000. 'Les enjeux sociaux du corps. Le hammam maghrébin (xixe-xxe siècle), lieu pérenne, menacé ou recréé', *Annales: histoire, sciences sociales*, 55.6: 1303–33

Carroll-Spillecke, Maureen. 1997. 'An Early Bath House in the Suburbs of Roman Cologne', *Journal of Roman Archaeology*, 10: 263–70

Clerbaut, Tim. 2021. 'De *tubulus cuneatus*: een "vergeten" Romeins verwarmingselement', *ArtefActueel*, 1: 31–39

Cloquet, Norbert. 1873. 'Rapport sur la villa belgo-romaine à Arquennes, prov. du Hainaut', *Documents et rapports de la Société paléontologique et archéologique de Charleroi*, 6: 69–129

——. 1875. 'Rapport sur la villa belgo-romaine d'Arquennes, seconde fouille', *Documents et rapports de la Société paléontologique et archéologique de Charleroi*, 7: lv–lxxvii

Coquelet, Catherine. 2000. 'Les thermes publics urbains des villes de Gaule Belgique', in *Termas romanas en el occidente del Imperio: II Colloquio Internacional de Arqueología, Gijón 1999*, ed. by Carmen Fernández Ochoa and Virginia García-Entero, Serie Patrimonio, 5 (Gijón: VTP), pp. 263–70

——. 2011. *Les capitales de cité des provinces de Belgique et de Germanie: étude urbanistique*, Publications d'histoire de l'art et d'archéologie de l'Université catholique de Louvain, 103 (Louvain-la-Neuve: Presses universitaires de Louvain)

Corbiau, Marie-Hélène. 1982. 'Établissement routier romain à Anlier', *Archaeologia Belgica*, 247: 79–82

——. 1983. 'Établissement routier romain à Anlier', *Archaeologia Belgica*, 253: 50–51

——. 1994. 'Marche-en-Famenne/Waha: villa romaine', *Chronique de l'archéologie wallonne*, 2: 114

——. 1997. 'Habay, Anlier. Le relais routier, étape de la poste impériale romaine', in *Le patrimoine archéologique de Wallonie*, ed. by Marie-Hélène Corbiau (Namur: Ministère de la Région wallonne. Division du patrimoine), pp. 304–06

——. 1998. 'Marche-en-Famenne/Waha: villa romaine de Hollogne', *Chronique de l'archéologie wallonne*, 6: 131

——. 2002. 'La villa romaine de Hollogne – Waha (Marche-en-Famenne)', *Vie archéologique*, 57–58: 91–94

——. 2006. 'Marche-en-Famenne/Waha: les bains de la villa romaine de Hollogne', *Chronique de l'archéologie wallonne*, 13: 208–09

——. 2007. 'Marche-en-Famenne/Waha: les bains de la villa romaine de Hollogne', *Chronique de l'archéologie wallonne*, 14: 165–66

Coulon, G. 1977. 'Froyennes (Hain.): substructions romaines', *Archéologie*, 1977.1: 15–16

Cramers, D. 1984. 'Het badgebouw van de villa te Kumtich (Tienen)', in *Liber amicorum Paul Dewalhens: Bijdragen tot de geschiedenis van Tienen*, ed. by Staf Thomas (Tienen: Stedelijk Museum 'Het Toreke'), pp. 111–38

Creemers, Guido, Wim De Clercq, and Henk Hiddink. 2015. 'An Inventory of Roman Habitation in the Meuse-Demer-Scheldt Area', in *The Roman Villa of Hoogeloon and the Archaeology of the Periphery*, ed. by Nico Roymans, Ton Derks, and Henk Hiddink, Amsterdam Archaeological Studies, 22 (Amsterdam: Amsterdam University Press), pp. 33–44

Creus, Ingeborg. 1975. *De Gallo-Romeinse nederzetting onder het Laat-Romeins grafveld van Oudenburg*, Archaeolgia Belgica, 179 (Brussels: Nationale Dienst voor Opgravingen)

Crova, Bice. 1956. 'Le terme romane nella Campania', *Atti dell' VIII Convegno nazionale di storia dell' architettura* (Rome: Centro di studi per la storia dell'architettura), pp. 271–88

Curran, John. 1998. 'From Jovian to Theodosius', in *The Late Empire, A.D. 337–425*, ed. by Averil Cameron and Peter Garnsey, The Cambridge Ancient History, 13 (Cambridge: Cambridge University Press), pp. 78–110

Dandoy, M., and Jacques Willems. 1995. 'La villa romaine au lieu-dit "à Trou" à Villers-le-Bouillet (Lg.)', *Vie archéologique*, 44: 28–35

De Bast, Martin Jean. 1804. *Recueil d'antiquités romaines et gauloises, trouvées dans la Flandre proprement dite, avec désignation des lieux où on les a découvertes* (Ghent: Stéven)

De Bernardy de Sigoyer, Sophie, Catherine Coquelet, Claire Gouffioul, and Jean-Philippe Marchal. 2016. 'Herstal/milmort: fouille d'un établissement le long de la chaussée Brunehaut', *Chronique de l'archéologie wallonne*, 24: 155–61

De Boe, Guy. 1966. 'Val-Meer: romeinse villa', *Archéologie*, 1966.2: 69

——. 1971a. 'De Romeinse villa op de Meerberg te Val-Meer', *Acta archaeologica Lovaniensia*, 4: 5–37

——. 1971b. 'Une villa romaine à Haccourt (Liège). Rapport provisoire des fouilles 1967–1970', *Archaeologia Belgica*, 132: 15–32

——. 1974. *Haccourt, I: Vestiges d'habitat et premières périodes de la villa romaine*, Archaeologia Belgica, 168 (Brussels: Service national des Fouilles)

——. 1976. *Haccourt, III: Les bains de la grande villa*, Archaeologia Belgica, 182 (Brussels: Service national des Fouilles)

——. 1977. *De Romeinse vicus op de Steenberg te Grobbendonk*, Archaeologia Belgica, 197 (Brussels: Service national des Fouilles)

——. 1979. 'Saint-Denis: villa romaine (?)', *Archéologie*, 1979.2: 27

——. 1981. 'Noodopgravingen te Neerharen (Belgisch Limburg)', *Archeologie in Limburg*, 12: 5–7

——. 1982. 'Meer dan 1.500 jaar bewoning rond de Romeinse villa te Neerharen-Rekem', *Archaeologia Belgica*, 247: 71–74

——. 1984. 'Nieuw onderzoek in de Romeinse vicus te Grobbendonk: de steenbouwfase', *Archaeologia Belgica*, 258: 74–78

De Clerck, Marlyse. 1987. *Bierbeek 30 cm. dieper: Archeologische inventaris van 15 jaar prospectie en opgravingen* (Bierbeek: Gemeentebestuur Bierbeek)

De Clercq, Wim. 2011. 'Roman Rural settlements in Flanders. Perspectives on a "Non-Villa" Landscape in *extrema Galliarum*', in *Villa Landscapes in the Roman North: Economy, Culture and Lifestyles*, ed. by Nico Roymans and Ton Derks, Amsterdam Archaeological Studies, 17 (Amsterdam: Amsterdam University Press), pp. 235–57

De Cock, Suzie. 1983. 'Tiegem (W.-Vl.): Gallo-Romeinse bewoning', *Archéologie*, 183.2: 111

——. 1987. 'Muizen (Antw.)', *Archéologie*, 1987.1: 35

——. 1988. 'Onderzoek van een Gallo-Romeinse villa te Tiegem (Gem. Anzegem)', *Westvlaamse Archaeologica*, 4.3: 76–83

De Cock, Suzie, Marc Rogge, and Marc Velghe. 1985. 'Michelbeke-Brakel (O.-Vl.): Romeinse villa', *Archéologie*, 1985.2: 111

De Glymes, Libert, Léopold Henseval, and Joseph Kaisin. 1875. 'Rapport sur la fouille de la villa belgo-romaine de Gerpinnes', *Documents et rapports de la Société paléontologique et archéologique de Charleroi*, 7: 93–140

de Haan, Nathalie. 1996. 'Die Wasserversorgung der Privatbäder in Pompeji', in *Cura aquarum in Campania: Proceedings of the Ninth International Congress on the History of Water Management and Hydraulic Engineering in the Mediterranean Region; Pompeii, 1–8, 1994*, ed. by Nathalie de Haan and Gemma Jansen, Babesch Supplement, 4 (Leiden: Babesch), pp. 59–66

——. 1997. 'Nam nihil melius esse quam sine turba lavari. Privatbäder in den Vesuvstädten', *Mededelingen van het Nederlands Instituut te Rome: Antiquity*, 56: 205–26

——. 2006. '"…zoveel verfijning en glans". Privébaden in Romeinse woningen', *Lampas*, 39.4: 343–61

——. 2007. 'Terme Romane. Tipologie tra uso e utilità', in *Bains curatifs et bains hygiéniques en Italie de l'antiquité au moyen âge*, ed. by Marie Guérin-Beauvois and Jean-Marie Martin, Collection de l'École française de Rome, 383 (Rome: École française de Rome), pp. 37–51

——. 2010. *Römische Privatbäder: Entwicklung, Verbreitung, Struktur und sozialer Status* (Frankfurt: Lang)

De Laet, Sigfried. 1961. 'Les limites des cités des Ménapiens et des Morins', *Helinium*, 1.1: 20–34

De Loë, Alfred. 1911. 'Fouilles à Vellereille-le-Brayeux', *Bulletin des Musées royaux d'art et d'histoire*, 10: 45–46

——. 1937. *Belgique ancienne: catalogue descriptif et raisonné*, III: *La période romaine* (Brussels: Vromant)

De Looz, Georges. 1876. 'Exploration de quelques villas romaines et tumulus de la Hesbaye (1). Fouilles exécutées dans la villa romaine d'Embresin', *Bulletin des Commissions royales d'art et d'archéologie*, 15: 253–67

De Maeyer, Robert. 1937. *De Romeinsche villa's in België: een archeologische studie*, RUG. Werken uitgegeven door de Faculteit van de wijsbegeerte en letteren, 82 (Antwerp: De Sikkel)

——. 1940. *De overblijfselen der Romeinsche villa's in België* (Antwerp: De Sikkel)

——. 1979. 'De overblijfselen der Romeinse villa's in België', *Acta archaeologica Lovaniensia*, 18: 34–143

De Ruyt, Claire. 1986. 'Une villa gallo-romaine à Tourinnes-Saint-Lambert (com. de Walhain)', *Archaeologia Belgica*, n.s., 1: 65–68

De Waele, Eric. 1984. 'Bains romains et deux caves médiévales à Marchienne-au-Pont', *Activités du SOS Fouilles*, 3: 200–32

Debove, Charles. 1865. 'Antiquités gallo-romaine et franques trouvées à Élouges', *Annales du cercle archéologique de Mons*, 6: 114–27

——. 1875. 'Elouges, ses antiquités et son histoire', *Annales du cercle archéologique de Mons*, 12 (1885), 289–376

Defosse, Pol, and Sylviane Mathieu. 1983–1984. 'Les thermes du vicus gallo-romain de Saint-Mard. Rapport des fouilles (1972–1980)', *Le pays gaumais*, 44–45: 13–154

Degbomont, Jean-Marie. 1984. *Le chauffage par hypocauste dans l'habitat privé: de la place St-Lambert à Liège à l'Aula Palatina de Trèves*, Études et recherches archéologiques de l'Université de Liège, 17 (Liège: Service d'archéologie préhistorique)

Dekegel, Philippe. 1979. 'Waudrez (Hain.): fouilles dans le vicus', *Archéologie*, 1979.2: 26–27

——. 1980. 'Waudrez (Ht.): fouilles dans le vicus', *Archéologie*, 1980.2: 86

Del Marmol, Eugène. 1877. 'Villa d'Anthée', *Annales de la Société archéologique de Namur*, 14: 165–94

——. 1881. 'Villa d'Anthée (suite)', *Annales de la Société archéologique de Namur*, 15: 1–40

DeLaine, Janet. 1988. 'Recent Research on Roman Baths', *Journal of Roman Archaeology*, 1: 11–32

——. 1989. 'Some Observations on the Transition from Greek to Roman Baths in Hellenistic Italy', *Mediterranean Archaeology*, 2: 111–25

——. 1992. 'New Models, Old Modes: Continuity and Change in the Design of Public Baths', in *Die römische Stadt im 2. Jahrhundert n. Chr.: Der Funktionswandel des öffentlichen Raumes*, ed. by Hans-Joachim Schalles, Henner von Hesberg, and Paul Zanker, Xantener Berichte, 2 (Cologne: Rheinland-Verlag), pp. 257–75

——. 1999a. 'Bathing and Society', in *Roman Baths and Bathing: Proceedings of the First International Conference on Roman Baths Held at Bath, England, 30 March – 4 April 1992*, ed. by Janet DeLaine and David Johnston, Journal of Roman Archaeology, Supplementary Series, 37 (Portsmouth, RI: Journal of Roman Archaeology), pp. 7–16

——. 1999b. 'Baths. The Urban Phenomenon', in *Roman Baths and Bathing: Proceedings of the First International Conference on Roman Baths Held at Bath, England, 30 March – 4 April 1992*, ed. by Janet DeLaine and David Johnston, Journal of Roman Archaeology, Supplementary Series, 37 (Portsmouth, RI: Journal of Roman Archaeology), pp. 157–64

——. 2007. 'Historiography. Origins, Evolution and Convergence', in *Bains curatifs et bains hygiéniques en Italie de l'antiquité au moyen âge*, ed. by Marie Guérin-Beauvois and Jean-Marie Martin, Collection de l'École française de Rome, 383 (Rome: École française de Rome), pp. 21–35

Delmaire, Roland, Alain Jacques, and Jean-Alain Acquart (eds). 1994. *Le Pas-de-Calais*, Carte archéologique de la Gaule, 62 (Paris: Académie des inscriptions et belles-lettres)

Delmaire, Roland, Germaine Leman-Delerive, and Claude Seillier. 1996. *Le Nord*, Carte archéologique de la Gaule, 59 (Paris: Académie des inscriptions et belles-lettres)

Delplace, Christiane. 1991–1992. 'Les décors peints du frigidarium du complexe thermal de la villa gallo-romaine de Champion-Emptinne (Hamois). Note sur la frise de perles et pirouettes', *Annales de la Société archéologique de Namur*, 67: 257–66

Delplace, Christiane, and Paul Van Ossel. 1991. 'Les apports de l'étude des enduits peints à l'architecture du complexe thermal de la villa gallo-romaine de Champion à Emptinne (Namur) en Belgique', in *4. Internationalen Kolloquium zur römischen Wandmalerei, Köln, 20. – 23. September 1989*, ed. by Friederike Naumann-Stecker and Renate Thomas, Kölner Jahrbuch zu Uhr- und Frühgeschichte, 24 (Berlin: Mann), pp. 261–68

Delvaux, Henri. 1851. *La découverte du Steenbosch et l'origine de sa chapelle à Fouron-le-Comte* (Liège: Imprimerie de J. Desoer)

Demanet, Jean-Claude, and Fabienne Vilvorder. 2016. 'Structuration et évolution des espaces privés dans le vicus de Liberchies', *Signa romana*, 5: 53–57

Demarez, Léonce, and Alain Henton. 1995. 'Synthèse des différentes découvertes archéologiques d'Aubechies', in *Un siècle de découvertes archéologiques dans l'entité de Beloeil* (Beloeil: Association pour la sauvegarde du patrimoine de Beloeil), pp. 111–13

Dens, Charles. 1906. 'Fouilles d'Anderlecht. La villa belgo-romaine et le cimetière franc du champ de Sainte-Anne, à Anderlecht', *Annales de la Société d'Archéologie de Bruxelles*, 20: 236–56

Dens, Charles, and Jean Poils. 1905. 'L'Hosté. Villa belgo-romaine, à Basse-Wavre', *Annales de la Société d'Archéologie de Bruxelles*, 19: 303–43

——. 1911. 'Habitations et cimetière belgo-romains. Commune de Tourinnes-St-Lambert. La ville des Sarrasins', *Annales de la Société royale d'archéologie de Bruxelles: mémoires, rapports et documents*, 25: 281–305

Depraetere, David. 2017. 'Waarderend archeologisch proefsleuvenonderzoek op drie Gallo-Romeinse sites binnen het ruilverkavelingsgebied Willebringen. Site Mellenberg (Kumtich-Tienen), site Meer (Meldert-Hoegaarden) en site Wiederveld (Willebringen-Boutersem)' (unpublished archaeological report, Archeologisch Rapport VLM/Vl-Bra)

Deramaix, Isabelle, and Pierre-Philippe Sartieaux. 1994. 'Ath/Meslin-l'Évêque: sauvetage d'une villa romaine inédite dans un zoning industriel', *Chronique de l'archéologie wallonne*, 2: 43–44

——. 1995. 'Soignies: "Espesse", fouilles de prévention au *balneum*', *Chronique de l'archéologie wallonne*, 3: 50–52

——. 1998. 'ATH, Meslin-l'Évêque. La villa romaine', in *Le patrimoine archéologique de Wallonie*, ed. by Marie-Hélène Corbiau (Namur: Ministère de la Région wallonne), pp. 315–18

Derks, Ton. 2011. 'Town–Country Dynamics in Roman Gaul. The Epigraphy of the Ruling Elite', in *Villa Landscapes in the Roman North: Economy, Culture and Lifestyles*, ed. by Nico Roymans and Ton Derks, Amsterdam Archaeological Studies, 17 (Amsterdam: Amsterdam University Press), pp. 107–38

Deru, Xaxier. 1991. 'Soignies, "L'Espesse": rapport de fouilles', *Vie archéologique*, 37: 5–10

——. 1994. 'Les bains publics et domestiques dans la cité des Tongres', *Documents d'archéologie régionale*, 4: 5–63

——. 2009. 'Cadres géographiques du territoire des Nerviens', *Revue du Nord*, 91: 181–201

Despriet, Philippe. 1997. 'Jaarverslag Archeologische Stichting voor Zuid-West-Vlaanderen/ Opgravingen 1997' (unpublished excavation report, Archeologische Stichting voor Zuid-West-Vlaanderen)

Devillers, Lucien. 1971–1972. 'La villa romaine de Wancennes', *Annales de la Société archéologique de Namur*, 56: 97–132

——. 1987. 'La villa romaine de Wancennes', *De la Meuse à l'Ardenne*, 4: 5–35

Dewert, Jean-Pierre, Martine Osterrieth, Pierre-Philippe Sartieaux, and Martine Soumoy. 1997. 'Nivelles. Sauvetage d'un domaine agricole gallo-romain à "La Tournette"', in *Le patrimoine archéologique de Wallonie*, ed. by Marie-Hélène Corbiau (Namur: Ministère de la Région wallonne), pp. 342–44

Dewert, Jean-Pierre, Martine Osterrieth, and Luc Severs. 1992. *Nivelles et sa région, de la préhistoire à l'histoire* (Nivelles: Musée communal de Nivelles)

Di Capua, Francesco. 1940. 'Appunti su l'origine e sviluppo delle terme romane', *Rendiconti della R. Accademia di archeologia, lettere e belle arti*, n.s., 20: 81–160

——. 1941. *L'idroterapia ai tempi dell'impero romano*, La scienza e la tecnica ai tempi di Roma imperiale, 10–11, 2nd edn (Rome: Istituto di studi romani)

Dodt, Michael. 2003. 'Die Thermen von Zülpich und die römische Badeanlagen der Provinz Germania Inferior' (unpublished doctoral thesis, Friedrich-Wilhelms Universität zu Bonn)

——. 2005. 'Das Bad der villa rustica von Alt-Inden', *Archäologie im Rheinland*, 2005: 86–88

——. 2006. 'Bäder römischer Villen in Niedergermanien im Lichte neuer Ausgrabungen im rheinische Braunkohlerevier', *Bonner Jahrbücher*, 206: 63–85

——. 2007. 'Römische Badeanlagen in Niedergermanien. Eine Verbreitungskarte zum aktuellen Forschungsstand', *Archäologie im Rheinland*, 2006: 96–99

——. 2010. 'Bäder römischer Villen im rheinischen Braunkohlenrevier', in *Braunkohlenarchäologie im Rheinland: Entwicklung von Kultur, Umwelt und Landschaft; Kolloquium der Stiftung zur Förderung der Archäologie im rheinischen Braunkohlenrevier in Braunweiler vom 5.-6. Oktober 2006*, ed. by Michaela Aufleger, Materialien zur Bodendenkmalpflege im Rheinland, 21 (Weilerwist: Liebe), pp. 99–103

Doyen, Jean-Marc. 1981. 'Treignes (Viroinval), rapport préliminaire de la campagne 1980', *Bulletin du Club archéologique Amphora*, 23: 36–41

——. 1987. 'Villa romaine à Treignes', in *L'archéologie en Wallonie 1980–1985: découvertes des cercles archéologiques*, ed. by Anne Cahen-Delhaye, Carine de Lichtervelde, and Françoise Leuxe (Brussels: Fédération des archéologues de Wallonie), pp. 266–71

Dubois, Charles. 1952. 'La villa romaine de Sommerain (Comune de Mont, canton de Houffalize)', *Bulletin de l'Institut archéologique du Luxembourg*, 28: 3–11

Dunbabin, Katherine. 1989. '*Baiarum grata voluptas*. Pleasures and Dangers of the Baths', *Papers of the British School at Rome*, 57: 6–46

——. 1999. *Mosaics of the Greek and Roman World* (Cambridge: Cambridge University Press)

Dusar, Michiel, Roland Dreesen, and André Frans De Naeyer. 2009. *Renovatie & restauratie: Natuursteen in Vlaanderen, versteend verleden* (Mechelen: Wolters Kluwer)

Eschebach, Hans. 1979. *Die stabianer Thermen in Pompeji*, Denkmäler antiker Architektur, 13 (Berlin: De Gruyter)

Fabbricotti, Emanuela. 1976. 'I bagni nelle prime ville romane', *Cronache Pompeiane*, 2: 29–111

Fagan, Garrett. 1999. *Bathing in Public in the Roman World* (Ann Arbor: University of Michigan Press)

——. 2001. 'The Genesis of the Roman Public Bath. Recent Approaches and Future Directions', *American Journal of Archaeology*, 105: 403–26

Faider-Feytmans, Germaine. 1952. 'Les limites de la cité des Nerviens', *L'antiquité classique*, 21.2: 338–58

——. 1976. 'Fouilles du Musée Royal de Mariemont. Le site des Castellains à Fontaine-Valmont', *Cahiers de Mariemont*, 7: 6–53

——. 1995. *Le site gallo-romain des Castellains à Fontaine-Valmont*, Monographies du Musée Royal de Mariemont, 7 (Mariemont: Musée Royal de Mariemont)

Fair, Mary. 1927. 'Circular Bath-Buildings in Connexion with Cohort Forts', *Journal of Roman Studies*, 17: 220–24

Farrington, Andrew. 1995. *The Roman Baths of Lycia: An Architectural Study* (London: British Institute of Archaeology at Ankara)

Faust, Sabine. 1999. 'Ein römisches Gebäude bei Oberüttfeld (Kreis Bitburg-Prüm)', *Trierer Zeitschrift*, 62: 155–67

Ferdière, Alain. 1988. *Les campagnes en Gaule romaine*, I: *Les techniques et les productions rurales en Gaule*, Collection des Hesperides (Paris: Errance)

Ferdière, Alain, and Etienne Jaffrot. 2015. 'Tuiles en écaille et quelques autres types originaux de terres cuites architecturales de Gaule centrale et septentrionale', in *Actualité de la recherche sur les mobiliers non céramiques de l'Antiquité et du haut Moyen Âge: actes de la Table ronde européenne 'Instrumentum', Lyon (F, Rhône), 18–20 octobre 2012*, ed. by Stéphanie Raux, Isabelle Bertrand, and Michel Feugère, Monographie Instrumentum, 51 (Montagnac: Mergoil), pp. 517–52

Flemming, Rebecca. 2013. 'Baths and Bathing in Greek Medicine', in *Greek Baths and Bathing Culture: New Discoveries and Approaches*, ed. by Sandra Lucore and Monika Trümper, Babesch Supplement, 23 (Leuven: Peeters), pp. 23–32

Fontaine, Souen, and Danièle Foy. 2005. 'De pierre et de lumière: le *lapis specularis*', in *De transparentes spéculations: vitres de l'Antiquité et du Haut Moyen-Âge (Occident-orient)*, ed. by Danièle Foy, d'Antique: notions croisées d'héritage romain et d'approches contemporaines, 4 (Bavay: Musée/Site d'archéologie), pp. 159–63

Fournet, Thibaud, Bérangère Redon, and Matthieu Vanpeene. 2017. 'Catalogue of the Roman and Byzantine Baths of Egypt', in *Collective Baths in Egypt*, II: *New Discoveries and Perspectives*, ed. by Bérangère Redon, Études urbaines, 10 (Cairo: Institut français d'archéologie orientale), pp. 451–523

Gabriel, J. 1989. 'La villula de Gemechenne (commentaire)', *Metinus*, 2: 65

Galesloot, Louis. 1859. 'La province de Brabant sous l'Empire romain', *Revue d'histoire et d'archéologie*, 1: 252–84

Garbrecht, Günther, and Hubertus Manderscheid. 1994. *Die Wasserbewirtschaftung römischer Thermen: Archäologische und hydrotechnische Untersuchungen*, Mitteilungen / Leichtweiss-Institut für Wasserbau der Technischen Universität Braunschweig, 118 (Braunschweig: Leichtweiss-Institut für Wasserbau)

García-Entero, Virginia, and Raúl Arribas Domínguez. 2000. 'Los balnea de las villae y su proceso de monumentalización', in *Termas romanas en el Occidente del Imperio*, ed. by Carmen Fernández Ochoa and Virginia García-Entero, Serie Patrimonio, 5 (Gijón: VTP), pp. 83–96

Geubel, Arsène. 1887. 'Notice sur les voies romaines du Luxembourg', *Annales de la Société pour la conservation des monuments historiques et des œuvres d'art dans la Province de Luxembourg*, 1849–1850 and 1850–1851: 203–04

—— 1938. 'Notes sur la fouille d'une villa romaine à Villers-le-Bouillet', in *Fédération archéologique et historique de Belgigue XXXIme session: Congrès de Namur 1938*, ed. by Joseph Balon (Namur: Godenne), pp. 226–35

——. 1939. 'Wyompont gallo-romain', *Bulletin de l'Institut archéologique du Luxembourg*, 15.2: 33–37

Ginouvès, René. 1962. *Balaneutike: recherches sur le bain dans l'antiquité grecque*, Bibliothèque des écoles françaises d'Athènes et de Rome, 200 (Paris: De Boccard)

Goethert, Klaus-Peter. 1999. 'Der Grundriß der Villa von Oberüttfeld', *Trierer Zeitschrift*, 62: 169–80

Goossens, Willem. 1916. *Die Römische villa bei Vlengendaal: Bericht über die Ausgrabungen in den Jahren 1911 und 1913*, Internationales Archiv für Ethnographie, 24 (Leiden: Brill)

Grassmann, Hans-Christian. 2011. *Die Funktion von Hypokausten und Tubuli in antiken römischen Bauten, insbesondere in Thermen: Erklärungen und Berechnungen*, British Archaeological Reports, International Series, 2309 (Oxford: Archaeopress)

Grenier, Albert. 1960. *Manuel d'archéologie gallo-romaine: quatrième partie; les monuments des eaux, aqueducs – thermes*, Manuel d'archéologie gallo-romaine, 4 (Paris: Picard)

Gros, Pierre. 1996. *L'architecture romaine: du début du IIIᵉ siècle av. J.-C. à la fin du Haut-Empire*, Les manuels d'art et d'archéologie antiques, 2 vols (Paris: Picard)

——. 2001. *L'architecture romaine*, II: *Maisons, palais, villas et tombeaux*, Les manuels d'art et d'archéologie antiques (Paris: Picard)

Guérin-Beauvois, Marie. 2007. 'Les aquae: sujet médico-religieux ou thème littéraire', in *Bains curatifs et bains hygiéniques en Italie de l'antiquité au moyen âge*, ed. by Marie Guérin-Beauvois and Jean-Marie Martin, Collection de l'École française de Rome, 333 (Rome: École française de Rome), pp. 93–114

——. 2015. *Le thermalisme romain en Italie: aspects sociaux et culturels aux deux premiers siècles de l'Empire*, Bibliothèque des Écoles françaises d'Athènes et de Rome, 364 (Rome: École française de Rome)

Guérin-Beauvois, Marie, and Jean-Marie Martin. 2007. 'Introduction Méthodologique', in *Bains curatifs et bains hygiéniques en Italie de l'antiquité au moyen âge*, ed. by M. Guérin-Beauvois and Jean-Marie Martin, Collection de l'École française de Rome, 333 (Rome: École française de Rome), pp. 1–19

Gutman, Robert. 1976. 'The Social Function of the Built Environment', in *The Mutual Interaction of People and their Built Environment: A Cross-Cultural Perspective*, ed. by Amos Rapoport (The Hague: Mouton), pp. 37–49

Habets, Joseph. 1871. 'Exploration d'une villa belgo-romaine au Herkenbergh à Meerssen', *Publications de la société historique et archéologique dans le duché du Limbourg*, 8: 379–428

——. 1887. 'Overblijfselen van romeinse gebouwen met bad en verwarmingstoestel te Hoens-broek', *Verslagen en mededeelingen der Koninklijke akademie van Wetenschappen: Afdeeling letterkunde*, 3rd ser., 4: 315–31

——. 1895. 'De Romeinsche villa Backerbosch, onder Heer', *Publications de la société historique et archéologique dans le duché du Limbourg*, 32: 267–96

Halbardier, Benoît, and Alain Thomas. 1987. 'La villa gallo-romaine de Chaumont à Rulles', in *Archéologie entre Semois et Chiers*, ed. by Gérard Lambert (Brussels: Crédit communal de Belgique), pp. 125–33

Hanel, Norbert. 2000. 'Militärische Thermen in Niedergermanien – eine Bestandsaufnahme', in *Termas romanas en el occidente del imperio*, ed. by Carmen Fernández Ochoa and Virginia García-Entero, Serie Patrimonio, 5 (Gijón: VTP), pp. 23–33

Hanut, Frédéric, Eric Leblois, and Yves Leblois. 2000. 'Étude et interprétation chronologique du mobilier d'une fosse dépotoir de Nouvelles (Mons, Province du Hainaut)', *Revue du Nord*, 82.338: 93–113

Hartz, Cécile. 2018. 'Baths in the Great Sanctuaries of Roman Gaul: Considerations on their Use', in *Thermae in Context, the Roman Bath in Town and in Life: Actes du colloque de Dalheim, Luxembourg, du 21 au 24 février 2013*, ed. by Heike Pösche, Andrea Binsfeld, and Stefanie Hoss, Archaeologia Mosellana, 10 (Luxembourg: Centre national de recherche archéologique), pp. 231–44

Hauzeur, Nicolas. 1851. 'Établissement romain de Barcenne', *Annales de la Société archéologique de Namur*, 2: 375–82

Heinz, Werner. 1983. *Römische Thermen: Badewesen und Badeluxus im Römischen Reich*, Edition antike Welt (Munich: Hirmer)

Henrard, Denis, Pierre van der Sloot, and Jean-Marc Léotard. 2008. 'Liège/Liège: site de la place Saint-Lambert. La villa gallo-romaine, indices de chronologie relative et techniques de construction', *Chronique de l'archéologie wallonne*, 15: 103–07

Henrotay, Denis. 2011. 'Découverte d'une villa gallo-romaine à l'origine de l'abbaye de Saint-Hubert', *Romeinendag/Journée d'archéologie romaine*, 2011: 69–70

Hiddink, Henk. 2014. 'De Romeinse villa-nederzetting op de Kerkakkers bij Hoogeloon (Noord-Brabant)' (unpublished excavation report, Zuidnederlandse archeologische rapporten)

Hingley, Richard. 1989. *Rural Settlement in Roman Britain* (London: Seaby)

Höcker, Christoph. 2006. 'Architect', in *Brill's New Pauly Online* <http://dx.doi.org/10.1163/1574-9347_bnp_e132610>

Hoffmann, Michaela. 1999. *Griechische Bäder*, Quellen und Forschungen zur Antiken Welt, 32 (Munich: Tuduv)

Hoss, Stefanie. 2005. *Baths and Bathing: The Culture of Bathing and the Baths and Thermae in Palestine from the Hasmoneans to the Moslem Conquest*, British Archaeological Reports, International Series, 1346 (Oxford: Archaeopress)

——. 2010. 'Die spätantike Blüte römischer Thermen in Palästina', in *Die antike Stadt im Umbruch: Kolloquium in Darmstadt, 19. Bis 20. Mai 2006*, ed. by Nadine Burkhardt and Rudolf Stichel (Wiesbaden: Reichert), pp. 165–77

——. 2012. 'From Rejection to Incorporation. The Roman Bathing Culture in Palestine', in *Spa: sanitas per aquam; Proceedings of the International Frontinus-Symposium on the Technical and Cultural History of Ancient Baths, Aachen, March 18–22, 2009*, ed. by Ralf Kreiner and Wolfram Letzner, Babesch Supplement, 21 (Leuven: Peeters), pp. 259–64

Hossey, Guido. 1983. 'Vestiges romains à Bras-Haut', *Archaeologia Belgica*, 253: 54–55

——. 1984. 'Vestiges romains à Bras-Haut', *Archaeologia Belgica*, 258: 57–58

Hunt, David. 1998. 'The Successors of Constantine', in *The Late Empire, A.D. 337–425*, ed. by Averil Cameron and Peter Garnsey, The Cambridge Ancient History, 13 (Cambridge: Cambridge University Press), pp. 1–43

Hurard, Séverine, Luc Leconte, Aurélien Lefeuvre, and Pascal Raymond. 2016. 'A Roman *miliarium* from a Private Bath House in Northern Gaul: From Water Technology to Ritual Offering', *Antiquity*, 90.354: 1562–75

Huybrigts, François. 1904. 'L'hypocauste romain sous la rue de St.-Trond, à Tongres', *Bulletin de la Société scientifique et littéraire du Limbourg*, 22: 305–16

Ingels, Dolores. 1999. 'Tournai: recherches archéologiques dans le périmètre du couvent des Frères mineurs', *Chronique de l'archéologie wallonne*, 7: 54–55

Jacob, E. 1968. 'Notice historique sur les bains de Spa', in *Le centenaire de l'établissement des bains à Spa (1868–1968)* (Verviers: Gérard), pp. 67–86

Janssens, Dirk. 1980. 'Heestert (W.-Vl.): Romeins balneum', *Archeologie*, 1980.2: 97

——. 1984. *Een Romeinse villa te Heestert*, Archeologische en Historische Monografieën van Zuid-West-Vlaanderen, 8 (Kortrijk: Archeologische Stichting voor Zuid-West-Vlaanderen)

Janssens, Paul. 1963. 'Vorst (Antw.): Romeinse funderingen en kapel', *Archéologie*, 1963.2: 66–67

Janssens, Paul, and Hugo De Greef. 1968. 'Gallo-Romeinse en Middeleeuwse bewoningssporen te Vorst – Kempen', *Hades*, 20: 1–25

Jeneson, Karen, and Wouter Vos (eds). 2020. *Roman Bathing in Coriovallum: The Thermae of Heerlen Revisited*, Nederlandse Archeologische Rapporten, 65 (Amersfoort: Cultural Heritage Agency of the Netherlands)

Jeneson, Karen, Wouter Vos, and G. White. 2020. 'Reconstructing the History of the Public Baths of Coriovallum', in *Roman Bathing in Coriovallum: The Thermae of Heerlen Revisited*, ed. by Karen Jeneson and Wouter Vos, Nederlandse Archeologische Rapporten, 65 (Amersfoort: Cultural Heritage Agency of the Netherlands), pp. 161–87

Kaisin, Joseph. 1878. 'Villa belgo-romaine d'Aiseau. Rapport de la fouille', *Documents et rapports de la Société paléontologique et archéologique de Charleroi*, 9: 145–243

——. 1897. 'Rapport de la Commission chargée de la surveillance des fouilles faites au lieu dit Peruwelz à Rognée', *Documents et rapports de la Société paléontologique et archéologique de Charleroi*, 21: 2–97

Kent, Susan. 1993. 'Activity Areas and Architecture: An Interdisciplinary View of the Relationship between Use of Space and Domestic Built Environments', in *Domestic Architecture and the Use of Space: An Interdisciplinary Cross-Cultural Study*, ed. by Susan Kent, New Directions in Archaeology (Cambridge: Cambridge University Press), pp. 1–8

Koethe, Harald. 1940. 'Die Bäder römischer Villen im Trierer Bezirk', *Deutsches archäologisches Institut: Berichte der Römisch-Germanischen Kommission*, 30: 43–131

Köhler, Jens. 2006. 'Forschungen zu römischen Thermalbädern', in *Cura aquarum in Ephesus: Proceedings of the Twelfth International Congress on the History of Water Management and Hydraulic Engineering in the Mediterranean Region; Ephesus/Selçuk, Turkey, October 2–10, 2004*, ed. by Gilbert Wiplinger, Babesch Supplement, 6 (Leuven: Peeters), pp. 437–42

——. 2012. 'Tradition und Fortschritt in römischen Thermalbädern', in *Spa: sanitas per aquam; Proceedings of the International Frontinus-Symposium on the Technical and Cultural History of Ancient Baths, Aachen, March 18–22, 2009*, ed. by Ralf Kreiner and Wolfram Letzner, Babesch Supplement, 21 (Leuven: Peeters), pp. 57–63

——. 2016. 'Death in the Bath: From Therapeutic Hazard to a Reconstruction of Ancient Roman Bathing', in *De Aquaeductu atque aqua urbium Lyciae Pamphyliae Pisidiae: The Legacy of Sextus Julius Frontinus; Tagungsband des Internationalen Frontinus-Symposiums. Antalya, 31. Oktober – 9. November 2014*, ed. by Gilbert Wiplinger, Babesch Supplement, 27 (Leuven: Peeters), pp. 191–202

Kolodziejczyk, Kamila. 2001. 'Caractères généraux des bains privés romains en Italie', *Études et travaux*, 19: 120–25

Krencker, Daniel, and Emil Krüger. 1929. *Die Trierer Kaiserthermen: Mit einer Übersicht über die wichtigsten Thermenanlagen des römischen Reiches*, Trierer Grabungen und Forschungen, 1.1–2 (Augsburg: B. Filser)

Krier, Jean. 2005. 'Fouilles, découvertes et prospections archéologiques – époque gallo-romaine, Diekirch – 39 "Esplanade"', in *Rapports du Musée National d'Historie et d'art 1993–2002*, ed. by Paul Reiles (Luxembourg: Musée national d'histoire et d'art), pp. 290–91

Lafon, Xavier. 1991. 'Les bains privés dans l'Italie romaine au IIe siècle av. J.C.', in *Les thermes romains: actes de la table ronde, Rome, 11.11.1988–12.11.1988*, Collection de l'École française de Rome, 142 (Rome: École française de Rome), pp. 97–114

Lancaster, Lynne. 2012. 'A New Vaulting Technique for Early Baths in Sussex: The Anatomy of a Romano-British Invention', *Journal of Roman Archaeology*, 25: 419–40

——. 2015. *Innovative Vaulting in the Architecture of the Roman Empire: 1st to 4th Centuries CE* (Cambridge: Cambridge University Press)

Lauwerijs, Édouard. 1969. 'Namur – Sauvetage archéologique en 1967–69', *Bulletin du Cercle archéologique Hesbaye-Condroz*, 9: 67–74

——. 1972. 'Sauvetage archéologique à Namur', *Bulletin du Cercle archéologique Hesbaye-Condroz*, 12: 99–112

Leblois, Ch., and Yves Leblois. 1968. 'Fouilles à la villa gallo-romaine de Nouvelles', *Études régionales*, 6: 57–80

——. 1970. 'Une campagne de fouilles à Nouvelles (1968–1969)', *Études régionales*, 8: 11–46

Leemans, Conrad. 1843. *Romeinsche oudheden te Maastricht* (Leiden: Hazenberg)

Lefert, Sophie. 2002. 'Ohey/Haillot: le corps de logis et les bains de la villa de Matagne', *Chronique de l'archéologie wallonne*, 10: 243–45

——. 2007. 'Gesves/Gesves: les bains de la villa du Corria', *Chronique de l'archéologie wallonne*, 14: 199–202

——. 2008. 'Gesves/Gesves: la villa gallo-romaine du Corria', *Chronique de l'archéologie wallonne*, 15: 206–09

——. 2013. 'Ohey/Évelette: la villa du Clavia', *Chronique de l'archéologie wallonne*, 21: 253–54

——. 2014. 'La villa gallo-romaine du Clavia (Ohey/Évelette)', *Chronique de l'archéologie wallonne*, 22: 238–40

——. 2015. 'Havelange/Flostoy: la villa gallo-romaine de "Lizée"', *Chronique de l'archéologie wallonne*, 23: 271–73

——. 2016. 'Havelange/Flostoy: la villa gallo-romaine de "Lizée"', *Chronique de l'archéologie wallonne*, 24: 257–59

Lefert, Sophie, Karine Bausier, and Ingrid Nachtergael. 2002. 'Hamois/Hamois: la villa gallo-romaine "Sur le Hody"', *Chronique de l'archéologie wallonne*, 10: 200–03

Lefert, Sophie, and Frédéric Hanut. 2017a. 'Havelange/Flostoy: la villa gallo-romaine de "Lizée"', *Chronique de l'archéologie wallonne*, 25: 173–77

——. 2017b. 'Le logis de la villa de "Lizée" (Havelange/Flostoy)', *Signa romana*, 6: 69–74

Lefèvre, G. 1887. 'Rapport sur les fouilles archéologiques faites dans les environs de Landen', *Bulletin de l'Institut archéologique liégeois*, 20: 1–37

Lehar, Hannes. 2012. *Die römische Hypokaustheizung: Berechnungen und Überlegungen zu Leistung, Aufbau und Funktion* (Aachen: Shaker)

——. 2015. 'Hölzerne Hypokaustheizungen an Lippe und Main?', *Germania*, 93: 259–75

Lejeune, Bernard. 1973. 'Découverte d'une villa romaine à Marcinelle', *Documents et rapports de la Société paléontologique et archéologique de Charleroi*, 56: 117–20

Leman, Pierre. 1975. 'Circonscription du Nord', *Gallia*, 33.2: 267–90

——. 1977. 'Circonscription de Nord-Pas-de-Calais', *Gallia*, 35.2: 279–94

Léotard, Marc, and Geneviève Coura. 1996. *Place Saint-Lambert à Liège: cinq années de sauvetage archéologique* (Liège: Ministère de la Région wallonne)

Lodewijckx, Marc. 1991. 'Preliminary Report on the Roman and Early Medieval Period in the Region of the Kleine Gete at Landen and Linter (Central Belgium)', *Acta archaeologica Lovaniensia*, 30: 41–47

Loes, François. 1909. 'Découvertes romaines faites à Arlon en 1907', in *Fédération archéologique et historique de Belgique: annales du XXIᵉ congrès (Liège, 1909)*, ed. by Joseph Brassine and L. Renard-Grenson (Liège: Henri Poncelet), pp. 253–68

Lucore, Sandra. 2013. 'Bathing in Hieronian Sicily', in *Greek Baths and Bathing Culture: New Discoveries and Approaches*, ed. by Sandra Lucore and Monika Trümper, Babesch Supplement, 23 (Leuven: Peeters), pp. 151–79

Lucore, Sandra, and Monika Trümper (eds). 2013. *Greek Baths and Bathing Culture: New Discoveries and Approaches*, Babesch Supplement, 23 (Leuven: Peeters)

Mahieu, Adolphe. 1892. 'Villas belgo-romaines de Maillen', *Annales de la Société archéologique de Namur*, 19: 345–91

——. 1897. 'Villa romaine de Neufchâteau à Malagne (Jemelle)', *Annales de la Société archéologique de Namur*, 21: 403–49

——. 1910. 'Ruines belgo-romaines mises à jour dans la province de Namur', *Annales de la Société archéologique de Namur*, 29: 137–52

——. 1919. 'La villa belgo-romaine de Bauselenne à Mettet', *Annales de la Société archéologique de Namur*, 33: 49–189

Maiuri, Amedeo. 1958. *Ercolano: i nuovi scavi (1927–1958)* (Rome: Istituto poligrafico dello Stato)

Malget, Eugène, and René Malget. 1912. 'Villa de "Lavend"', *Annales de l'Institut archéologique du Luxembourg*, 47: 416–18

Manderscheid, Hubertus. 1981. *Die Skulpturenausstattung der kaiserzeitlichen Thermenanlagen*, Monumenta artis Romanae, 15 (Berlin: Mann)

——. 1994. 'Aspekte der Mosaikausstattung in öffentlichen und privaten Thermenanlagen', in *La mosaïque gréco-romaine IV (Trèves 8–14 août 1984)*, ed. by Jean-Pierre Darmon and Alain Rebourg (Paris: Association internationale pour l'étude de la mosaïque antique), pp. 61–66

——. 1996. 'Standard und Luxus in römischen Bädern. Überlegungen aus der Sicht der Hydrotechnik', in *Cura aquarum in Campania: Proceedings of the Ninth International Congress on the History of Water Management and Hydraulic Engineering in the Mediterranean Region*, ed. by Nathalie de Haan and Gemma Jansen, Babesch Supplement, 4 (Leiden: Brill), pp. 109–15

——. 2000. 'The Water Management of Greek and Roman Baths', in *Handbook of Ancient Water Technology*, ed. by Örjan Wikander (Leiden: Brill), pp. 467–538

Maréchal, Sadi. 2012. 'Research on Roman Bathing: Old Models and New Ideas', *Revue belge de Philologie et d'Histoire/Belgisch Tijdschrift voor Filologie en Geschiedenis*, 90: 143–64

——. 2015. 'Lavacrum: Just Another Word for Baths? How the Terminology of Baths May Have Reflected Changes in Bathing Habits', *Revue belge de Philologie et d'Histoire/Belgisch Tijdschrift voor Filologie en Geschiedenis*, 93: 139–77

——. 2017. 'A Note on the Drainage of Pools in Roman Baths', *Babesch*, 92: 179–86

——. 2020a. *Public Baths and Bathing Habits in Late Antiquity: A Study of the Evidence from Italy, North Africa and Palestine A.D. 285–700*, Late Antique Archaeology Supplementary Series, 6 (Leiden: Brill)

——. 2020b. 'Not your Classic Bath: Adopting and Adapting Roman Bathing Habits in NW Gaul', *Journal of Roman Archaeology*, 33: 147–68

——. 2021a. '"Quod grata lavacra nitescunt": Roman Villa Baths as Markers of Elite Competition in Continental North-Western Europe', *European Journal of Archaeology*, 24.4: 477–95

——. 2021b. 'By Invitation Only. Accessibility of Villa Baths in the Roman North-West', *Oxford Journal of Archaeology*, 40.2: 211–30

——. Forthcoming. 'The *tubuli* from Ostia', in *Roman Brick and Tile: Past, Present and Future of the Study of Roman Ceramic Building Materials*, ed. by Tim Clerbaut (Oxford: Archaeopress)

Maréchal, Sadi, Nathalie de Haan, and Tim Clerbaut. 2021. 'Manufacturing *tubuli*. An Experimental Reconstruction of the *chaîne opératoire* Based on Archaeological Evidence', in *Tracing Technology*, ed. by Marijke Gnade and Martina Revello Lami, Babesch Supplement, 42 (Leuven: Peeters), pp. 243–47

Marichal, Robert. 1992. *Les ostraca de Bu Njem*, Supplements to Libya Antiqua, 7 (Tripoli: Department of Antiquities)

Marzano, Annalisa. 2007. *Roman Villas in Central Italy: A Social and Economic History*, Columbia Studies in the Classical Tradition, 30 (Leiden: Brill)

Materne, D. 1969. 'Notes au sujet de la villa belgo-romaine de Miécret (Province de Namur)', *Bulletin du Cercle archéologique Hesbaye-Condroz*, 9: 79–82

Matthys, André. 1974. *La villa romaine de Vesqueville*, Archaeologia Belgica, 159 (Brussels: Service national des Fouilles)

Matthys, André, and Jan Wouters. 1978. 'De Gallo-Romeinse villa van Wemmel (Onder Kerkhofsveld)', in *Brussel voor 400: Romeinse aanwezigheid te Brussel en omgeving*, ed. by Frans Van Bellingen (Brussels: Geschied- en heemkundige kring van het graafschap Jette en omgeving), pp. 17–20

Medri, Maura, and Antonio Pizzo (eds). 2019. *Le terme pubbliche nell'Italia romana (II secolo a.C. – fine IV d.C.): architettura, tecnologia e società; Seminario Internazionale di Studio, Roma, 4–5 ottobre 2018*, Patrimonio culturale e territorio, 6 (Rome: Roma TrE-Press)

Mertens, Jozef. 1955. 'Gallo-Romeins uit Vlaams-Brabant', *Eigen Schoon en de Brabander*, 38: 5–13

——. 1968. 'Hamois', *Archéologie*, 17

——. 1974. 'Limerlé: villa romaine de Rouvroy', *Archéologie*, 1974.2: 79

——. 1975. 'Limerlé: villa romaine de Rouvroy', *Archéologie*, 1975.2: 80

——. 1981. 'Kumtich-Tienen (Brab.): romeins badgebouw', *Archéologie*, 1981.1: 29

Mertens, Jozef, and Raymond Brulet. 1974. 'Le castellum du Bas-Empire romain de Brunehaut-Liberchies', *Archaeologia Belgica*, 163: 1–70

Meunier, Maurice. 1964. 'La villa belgo-romaine de "Fin-de-Ville" (commune de Mont-lez-Houffalize)', *Archaeologia Belgica*, 78: 154–72

Mignot, Philippe. 1994a. 'Etalle/Sainte-Marie-sur-Semois: la villa romain du "Magenot"', *Chronique de l'archéologie wallonne*, 2: 110–11

——. 1994b. 'Gouvy/Bovigny: la villa romaine de Glain', *Chronique de l'archéologie wallonne*, 2: 111

——. 1994c. 'Rochefort/Jemelle: villa romaine', *Chronique de l'archéologie wallonne*, 2: 145–48

Mignot, Philippe, Denis Henrotay, and Dominique Bossicard. 1997. 'Florenville: villa romaine à Martué', *Chronique de l'archéologie wallonne*, 4–5: 143

Mignot, Philippe, Wim Van Neer, and Michel Toussaint. 1995. 'Rochefort/Jemelle: villa romaine de Malagne', *Chronique de l'archéologie wallonne*, 3: 135–37

Millett, Martin. 1990. *The Romanization of Britain* (Cambridge: Cambridge University Press)

Moke, Henri. 1854. *Fragments d'une histoire de la Belgique ancienne* (Ghent: L. Hebbelynck)

Mora, Gloria. 1981. 'Las termas romanas en Hispania', *Archivo español de arqueología*, 54: 37–86

Moureau, Georges. 1979. 'Hypocauste et cave belgo-romaine à Latinne', *Bulletin de la Société d'Archéologie et d'Histoire de Waremme et environs*, 10: 14–21

Nicolas, David, and Raphaëlle Chosserot (eds). 2011. *Les Ardennes*, Carte archéologique de la Gaule, 8 (Paris: Académie des inscriptions et belles-lettres)

Nieberle, Matthias. 2020. 'Das römische Baiae. Ein *otium*-Badeort *par excellence?*', in *Das Bad als Mußeraum: Räume, Träger und Praktiken der Badekultur von der Antike bis zur Gegenwart*, ed. by Hans Hubert, Anja Grebe, and Antonio Russo, Otium, 13 (Tübingen: Mohr Siebeck), pp. 25–39

Nielsen, Inge. 1985. 'Considerazioni sulle prime fasi dell'evoluzione dell'edificio termale romano', *Analecta Romane Instituti Danici*, 14: 81–112

——. 1993. 'The Baths: Problems of Terminology', *Balnearia*, 1.1: 3–4

——. 1993a. *Thermae et balnea: The Architecture and Cultural History of Roman Public Baths*, I: *Text*, 2nd edn (Aarhus: Aarhus Universitet)

——. 1993b. *Thermae et Balnea: The Architecture and Cultural History of Roman Public Baths*, II: *Catalogue and Plates*, 2nd edn (Aarhus: Aarhus University Press)

——. 1999 'Early Provincial Baths and their Relations to Early Italic Baths', in *Roman Baths and Bathing: Proceedings of the First International Conference on Roman Baths Held at Bath, England, 30 March – 4 April 1992*, ed. by Janet DeLaine and David Johnston, Journal of Roman Archaeology, Supplementary Series, 37 (Portsmouth, RI: Journal of Roman Archaeology), pp. 35–43

Nola, Josep Maria. 2000. 'Las termas republicanas en Hispania', in *Termas romanas en el occidente del imperio: II Coloquio Internacional de Arqueología en Gijón (Gijón 1999)*, ed. by Carmen Fernández Ochoa and Virginia García-Entero, Serie Patrimonio, 5 (Gijón: VTP), pp. 47–57

Nutton, Vivian. 2004. *Ancient Medicine*, Sciences of Antiquity (London: Routledge)

Otte, Marcel, and Jean-Marie Degbomont. 1990. *Les fouilles de la Place Saint-Lambert à Liège*, III: *La villa gallo-romaine* (Liège: Université de Liège. Service de préhistoire)

Papi, Emanuele. 1999. 'Il balneum nelle dimore di Roma dall'età repubblicana al I secolo D.C.', *Mélanges de l'école française de Rome: Antiquité*, 111: 695–728

Pasquinucci, Marinella (ed.). 1987. *Terme romane e vita quotidiana* (Modena: Panini)

Paulke, Matthias. 2010. 'Die römische Axialhofvilla von Diekirch – Neue Grabungen und Forschungen', *Empreintes*, 3: 54–67

Pauwels, Dirk, Alain Vanderhoeven, and Geert Vynckier. 2005. 'Vijf noodopgravingen in Romeins Tongeren', *Romeinendag/Journée d'archéologie romaine*, 2005: 75–78

Pensabene, Patrizio, and Paolo Barresi. 2018. 'Le terme meridionali e aspetti di continuità nella Villa del Casale di Piazza Armerina tra IV e VI secolo alla luce delle nuove scoperte (2012–2014)', in *Abitare nel Mediterraneo Tardoantico: atti del II Convegno Internazionale del Centro Interuniversitario di Studi sull'Edilizia abitativa tardoantico nel Mediterraneo (CISEM) (Bologna 2–5 marzo 2016)*, ed. by Isabella Baldini and Carla Sfameni (Bari: Edipuglia), pp. 407–12

Percival, John. 1976. *The Roman Villa: An Historical Introduction* (London: Batsford)

Peréx, María, Carmen Fernández Ochoa, Virginia García-Entero, Carme Miró i Alaix, and Silvia Gonzáles Soutelo. 2014. 'Thermes et balaneia en Hispanie. Un état de la question', in *25 siècles de bain collectif en Orient: Proche-Orient, Égypte et péninsule Arabique; Balaneia, Thermae, Hammam; actes du 3e colloque international Balnéorient (Damas/Syrie 2–6 nov. 2009)*, ed. by Marie-Françoise Boussac, Sylvie Denoix, Thibaud Fournet, and Bérangère Redon, Études urbaines, 9.1 (Cairo: Institut français d'archéologie orientale), pp. 67–82

Perring, Dominic. 2002. *The Roman House in Britain* (London: Routledge)

Pesando, Fabrizio. 2002. 'Le "Terme Repubblicane" di Pompei: cronologia e funzione', *Annali di Archeologia e Storia Antica*, n.s., 9–10: 221–43

Peterse, K. 2020. 'Construction History and Reconstruction', in *Roman Bathing in Coriovallum. The Thermae of Heerlen Revisited*, ed. by Karen Jeneson and Wouter Vos, Nederlandse Archeologische Rapporten, 65 (Amersfoort: Cultural Heritage Agency of the Netherlands), pp. 51–84

Peuskens, Nicolas, and François Tromme. 1979. 'Deux balnea belgo-romains: Boirs "village" et Heure-le-Romain "Sur les moulins"', *Bulletin de la Société royale belge d'études géologiques et archéologiques*, 24: 381–414

Pfretzschner, Ernst. 1909. *Die Grundrissentwicklung der römischen Thermen: Nebst einem Verzeichnis der erhaltenen altrömischen Bäder mit Literaturnachweis*, Zur Kunstgeschichte des Auslandes, 65 (Strasbourg: Heitz)

Piton, Ernest. 1939. 'Au pays de Landen. Attenhoven', *Bulletin de l'Institut archéologique liégeois*, 63: 5–64

Plumier, Jean. 1984. 'La villa gallo-romaine des "GRANDES PIECES" à Latinne', in *Archeolo-J. 15 années, 15 chantiers*, ed. by Paul Van Ossel, Jean Plumier, and Pierre Claeys (Rixensart: Service des Jeunesses archéologiques), pp. 69–74

——. 1996. 'Fouilles préventives des deux villas romaines de Génimont et Ave-et-Aufe à Rochefort', in *Cinq années d'archéologie en province de Namur, 1990–1995*, ed. by Jean Plumier, Études et documents, 3 (Namur: Institut du Patrimoine wallon), pp. 23–28

Plumier, Jean, Claude Dupont, and Wim Van Neer. 1995. 'Rochefort/Ave-et-Aufe et Génimont: deux villas romaines', *Chronique de l'archéologie wallonne*, 3: 133–35

Proctor, Jennifer. 2012. *Faverdale, Darlington: Excavations at a Major Settlement in the Northern Frontier Zone of Roman Britain*, Pre-construct Archaeology Limited Monograph, 15 (London: Pre-construct Archaeology)

Raepsaet-Charlier, Marie-Thérèse. 1994. 'La cité des Tongres sous le Haut-Empire: problèmes de géographie historique', *Bonner Jahrbücher*, 194: 43–59

——. 1995. 'Municipium Tungrorum', *Latomus*, 54: 361–69

Rahir, Edmond. 1928. *Vingt-cinq années de recherches, de restaurations et de reconstitutions* (Brussels: Musées royaux du Cinquantenaire)

Rapoport, Amos. 1976. 'Sociocultural Aspects of Man-Environment Studies', in *The Mutual Interaction of People and their Built Environment: A Cross-Cultural Perspective*, ed. by Amos Rapoport (The Hague: Mouton), pp. 7–35

——. 2000. 'Culture and Built From – A Reconsideration', in *Culture – Meaning – Architecture: Critical Reflections on the Work of Amos Rapoport*, ed. by Keith Diaz Moore, Ethnoscapes (Aldershot: Ashgate), pp. 175–216

Redon, Bérangère. 2009. 'L'armée et les bains en Égypte hellénistique et romaine', *Bulletin de l'Institut français d'archéologie orientale*, 109: 407–50

——. 2017. 'The Missing Baths of the First and Second Centuries in Egypt: A Tentative Explanation', in *Collective Baths in Egypt*, II: *New Discoveries and Perspectives*, ed. by Bérangère Redon, Études urbaines, 10 (Cairo: Institut français d'archéologie orientale), pp. 267–78

Reis, Maria Pillar. 2004. *Las termas y balnea romanos de Lusitania*, Studia Lusitana, 1 (Madrid: Ministerio de Cultura, Secretaría General Técnica)

Remouchamps, August. 1924. 'Opgraving van een romeinsche villa in het Ravenbosch (L.)', *Oudheidkundige Mededeelingen uit 's Rijksmuseum van Oudheden te Leiden*, 5: 41–79

Remy, Hélène. 1977. 'Les villas romaines de Jodoigne et Saint-Jean-Geest', *Archaeologia Belgica*, 195: 5–19

Renard, L. 1903. 'Exploration d'une villa belgo-romaine à Latinne', *Bulletin de l'Institut archéologique liégeois*, 33: 89–94

Reyes Hernando, Olivia. 2000. 'Síntesis evolutiva de las termas en las villas de Britannia', in *Termas romanas en el occidente del imperio: II Coloquio Internacional de Arqueología en Gijón (Gijón 1999)*, ed. by Carmen Fernández Ochoa and Virginia García-Entero, Serie Patrimonio, 5 (Gijón: VTP), pp. 373–82

Rippengal, Robert. 1993. '"Villas as a Key to Social Structure?" Some Comments on Recent Approaches to the Romano-British Villa and Some Suggestions toward an Alternative', in *Theoretical Roman Archaeology: First Conference Proceedings*, ed. by Eleanor Scott, Worldwide Archaeology Series, 4 (Aldershot: Avebury), pp. 79–101

Rober, André. 1984. 'La villa gallo-romaine de Matagne-la-Petite', *Archaeologia Belgica*, 258: 64–66

——. 1987. 'Une villa gallo-romaine à Vodelée (comm. de Doische)', *Archaeologia Belgica*, 3: 153–64

Robert, C. 1980. 'Roly (Nr.): Villa', in *L'archéologie en Wallonie: découvertes récentes des cercles d'archéologie* (s.l.: Fédération des archéologues de Wallonie), pp. 90–92

Rogge, Marc. 1984. 'Zegelsem-Brakel (O.-Vl.): nederzettingssporen uit de ijzertijd en de Romeinse periode', *Archéologie*, 184.2: 96

Rook, Tony. 1992. *Roman Baths in Britain*, Shire Archaeology, 69 (Princes Risborough: Shire)

Roymans, Nico (ed.). 1996. *From the Sword to the Plough*, Amsterdam Archaeological Studies, 1 (Amsterdam: Amsterdam University Press)

Russo Mailer, Carmela. 1988. 'L'acqua dall'antichità al Medioevo: le terme flegree', *Quaderni medievali*, 26: 79–98

Schaub, Andreas. 2012. 'Aachen als römische Bäderstadt', in *Spa: sanitas per aquam; Proceedings of the International Frontinus-Symposium on the Technical and Cultural History of Ancient Baths, Aachen, March 18–22, 2009*, ed. by Ralf Kreiner and Wolfram Letzner, Babesch. Supplement, 21 (Leuven: Peeters), pp. 11–20

Schayes, Antoine Guillaume Bernard. 1858. *La Belgique et les Pays-Bas, avant et pendant la domination romaine: Tableau historique, géographique, physique, statistique et archéologique de la Gaule septentrionale, jusqu'au VIe siècle*, II (Brussels: Emm. Devroye)

Schiebold, Hans. 2010. *Heizung und Wassererwärmung in römischen Thermen: Historische Entwicklung, Nachfolgesysteme, Neuzeitliche Betrachtungen und Untersuchungen*, Schriften der Deutschen Wasserhistorischen Gesellschaft, Sonderbände, 3, 2nd edn (Siegburg: Dt. Wasserhist. Gesellschaft)

Schoellen, André. 1997. 'Schieren: un village aux richesses archéologiques ignorées', in *Schiren: 1947–1997; d'Duerf, séng Musek, séng Leit*, ed. by Jean Thill (Schieren: Société de musique), pp. 147–56

Scholz, Markus. 2018. 'Reduction and Conversion of Bathhouses in the Limes Area during the 3rd Century', in *Thermae in Context, the Roman Bath in Town and in Life: Actes du colloque de Dalheim, Luxembourg, du 21 au 24 février 2013*, ed. by Heike Pösche, Andrea Binsfeld, and Stefanie Hoss, Archaeologia Mosellana, 10 (Luxembourg: Centre national de recherche archéologique), pp. 141–57

Schön, Franz. 2006. 'Belgica', in *Brill's New Pauly Online* <http://dx.doi.org/10.1163/1574-9347_bnp_e214990>

Severs, Luc. 1980. 'La villa belgo-romaine de Basse-Wavre. Étude du matériel archéologique et essai d'interprétation chronologique', *Wavriensia*, 29: 89–126

Sgobbo, Italo. 1929. 'Terme Flegree ed origine delle terme romane', *Atti del I Congresso Nazionale di Studi Romani* (Rome: Istituto di studi romani), pp. 186–94

Slofstra, Jan. 1982. 'Een inheems-Romeinse villa op de Kerkakkers bij Hoogeloon', in *Het Kempenproject: Een regionaal-archeologisch onderzoek in uitvoering*, ed. by Jan Slofstra, Herman Hendrik van Regteren Altena, Nico Roymans, and Frans Theuws, Bijdragen tot de studie van het brabants heem deel, 22 (Waalre: Stichting Brabants Heem), pp. 102–12

——. 1991. 'Changing Settlement Systems in the Meuse-Demer-Scheldt Area during the Early Roman Period', in *Images of the Past: Studies on Ancient Societies in Northwestern Europe*, ed. by Nico Roymans and Frans Theuws, Studies in Pre- en Protohistorie, 7 (Amsterdam: Amsterdam University Press), pp. 131–99

Smeesters, Jozef. 1971. 'Tongeren: rioleringswerken, hypocaustum', *Archéologie*, 1971.1: 11–13

——. 1975. *De Romeinse monumenten van Tongeren*, Publicaties van het Provinciaal Gallo-Romeins Museum te Tongeren, 20 (Tongeren: Provinciaal Gallo-Romeins museum)

Smith, John Thomas. 1978. 'Villas as a Key to Social Structure', in *Studies in the Romano-British Villa*, ed. by Malcolm Todd (Leicester: Leicester University Press), pp. 149–85

——. 1997. *Roman Villas: A Study in Social Structure* (London: Routledge)

Soleil, Philippe. 1988. 'Willemeau (Tournai): 1985 – bains d'un habitat gallo-romain', in *L'archéologie en Hainaut occidental (1983–1988)*, Amicale des Archéologues du Hainaut Occidental, 4 (Ath: Cercle royal d'histoire et d'archéologie d'Ath et de la région), pp. 62–71

Staccioli, Romolo Augusto. 1958. 'Sugli edifici termali minori', *Archeologia classica*, 10: 273–78

Stern, Henri. 1960. *Recueil général des mosaïques de la Gaule*, I.2: *Province de Belgique: Partie Est*, Supplément à Gallia, 10 (Paris: Centre national de la recherche scientifique)

Sulbout, Césaire. 1867. 'Quelques autres établissements romains de l'Ardenne. Canton de Fauvillers', *Annales de l'Institut archéologique du Luxembourg*, 5: 279–95

Thébert, Yvon. 2003. *Thermes romains d'Afrique du Nord et leur contexte méditerranéen: études d'histoire et d'archéologie*, Bibliothèque des écoles françaises d'Athènes et de Rome, 315 (Rome: École française de Rome)

Tihon, Ferdinand. 1900. 'Fouilles à Vissoul', *Annales de la Société d'Archéologie de Bruxelles*, 14: 81–83

Trümper, Monika. 2009. 'Complex Public Bath Buildings of the Hellenistic Period. A Case Study in Regional Differences', in *Le bain collectif en Égypte: Balaneia, thermae, hammam*, ed. by Marie-Françoise Boussac, Thibaud Fournet, and Bérangère Redon, Études urbaines, 7 (Cairo: Institut français d'archéologie orientale), pp. 139–79

——. 2010. 'Bathing Culture in Hellenistic Domestic Architecture', in *Städtisches Wohnen im östlichen Mittelmeerraum 4. Jh. v. Chr. – 1. Jh. n. Chr.: Akten des internationalen Kolloquiums vom 24. – 27. Oktober 2007 an der Österreichischen Akademie der Wissenschaften*, ed. by Sabine Ladstätter and Veronika Scheibelreiter (Vienna: Verlag der Österreichischen Akademie der Wissenschaften), pp. 529–67

——. 2014. '"Privat" versus "öffentlich" in hellenistischer Bädern', in *Stadtkultur im Hellenismus*, ed. by Albrecht Matthaei and Martin Zimmermann, Die hellenistische Polis als Lebensform, 4 (Heidelberg: Verlag Antike), pp. 206–49

Tsiolis, Vasilis. 2013. 'The Baths at Fregellae and the Transition from Balaneion to Balneum', in *Greek Baths and Bathing Culture: New Discoveries and Approaches*, ed. by Sandra Lucore and Monika Trümper, Babesch Supplement, 23 (Leuven: Peeters), pp. 89–111

Van Bastelaer, Désiré-Alexandre. 1891a. 'La villa belgo-romaine de Montignies-Saint-Christophe (Champ du Roi ou Terre d'au village)', *Documents et rapports de la Société paléontologique et archéologique de Charleroi*, 17: 396–406

——. 1891b. 'La villa belgo-romaine de Saint-Rémy', *Documents et rapports de la Société paléontologique et archéologique de Charleroi*, 17: 372–95

Van Bellingen, Stephan. 2011. 'Enkele nieuwe gegevens m.b.t. de Gallo-Romeinse villa van Jette (Brussels Hoofdstedelijk Gewest)', *Romeinendag/Journée d'archéologie romaine*, 2011: 129–34

Van den Hove, Peter, Alain Vanderhoeven, and Geert Vynckier. 2002. 'Het archeologisch onderzoek in de O.LV.-Basiliek van Tongeren Fase 1: 1999–2001', *Monumenten & Landschappen*, 21.4: 12–37

Van den Vonder, Igor. 2008. 'Een Gallo-Romeinse villa met grafveld te Merchtem – Dooren (Vlaams-Brabant)', *Romeinendag/Journée d'archéologie romaine*, 2008: 115–19

Van Desse, Camille, and Henri Schuermans. 1877. *Topographie des voies romaines de la Belgique: statistique archéologique et bibliographique* (Brussels: C. Mucquardt)

van Dierendonck, Robert, and Wouter Vos. 2013. *De Romeinse agglomeratie Aardenburg: Onderzoek naar de ontwikkeling, structuur en datering van de Romeinse castella en hun omgeving, opgegraven in de periode 1955-heden*, Hazenberg Archeologische Serie, 3 (Middelburg: Hazenberg Archeologie)

Van Hove, Marie-Laure, Eric De Waele, and Muriel Van Buylaer. 2008a. 'Ramillies/Autre-Église: un complexe thermal gallo-romain', *Chronique de l'archéologie wallonne*, 15: 15–18

——. 2008b. 'Ramillies/Autre-Église: un complexe thermal gallo-romain', *Romeinendag/Journée d'Archéologie romaine*, 2008: 133–35

Van Neuss, Henri, and J.-A. Bamps. 1888. 'Découverte d'une villa belgo-romaine sur la limite des communes de Neerhaeren et de Reekheim', *Bulletin des Commissions royales d'art et d'archéologie*, 27: 325–74

Van Ossel, Paul. 1980. 'La villa romaine sur le Hody à Hamois', *Activités du SOS Fouilles*, 1: 74–83

——. 1981. 'La villa romaine "sur le Hody" à Hamois', *Activités du SOS Fouilles*, 2: 117–35

——. 1992. *Établissement ruraux de l'Antiquité tardive dans le nord de la Gaule*, Gallia Supplément, 51 (Paris: Centre national de la recherche scientifique)

Van Ossel, Paul, and Alexandra De Poorter. 1992. 'Un ensemble balnéaire de l'époque romaine à Champion-Emptinne (Hamois)', *Annales de la Société archéologique de Namur*, 67: 195–242

Van Thienen, Vince, Guido Creemers, and Wim De Clercq. 2019. 'Mapping the civitas Tungrorum', *Signa romana*, 8: 181–85

Vanderhoeven, Alain, Annick Arts, Kristien Borgers, Daan Celis, Jasmine Cryns, Natasja De Winter, An Peelaerts, Peter Van den Hove, Vanessa Vander Ginst, and Geert Vynckier. 2017. 'De sporen uit de vroeg-Romeinse periode', in *Het archeologische en bouwhistorisch onderzoek van de O.L.V.-basiliek van Tongeren (1997–2013)*, III: *De vroeg-Romeinse periode*, ed. by Alain Vanderhoeven and Aanton Ervynck, Relicta Monografieën, 13 (Brussels: Agentschap Onroerend Erfgoed), pp. 15–210

Vanderhoeven, Alain, and Geert Vynckier. 1997. 'Een noodopgraving in de Romeinse vicus van Tienen', *Romeinendag/Journée d'Archéologie romaine*, 1997: 12–13

——. 2009. 'Tongeren: de Schaetzengaarde', *Limburg: Het Oude Land van Loon*, 88: 328–32

Vanderhoeven, Alain, Geert Vynckier, Brigitte Cooremans, Anton Ervynck, An Lentacker, and Wim Van Neer. 2007. 'Het oudheidkundig bodemonderzoek aan de de Schaetzengaarde te Tongeren (prov. Limburg). Eindverslag 2004', *Relicta*, 3: 159–82

Vanderhoeven, Alain, Geert Vynckier, and Patrick Vynckier. 1992. 'Het oudheidkundig bodemonderzoek aan de Hondsstraat te Tongeren (prov. Limburg). Interimverslag 1989', *Archeologie in Vlaanderen*, 2: 65–88

Vanderhoeven, Alain, Geert Vynckier, and Werner Wouters. 1998. 'Het Oudheidkundig bodemonderzoek aan de Zijdelingsestraat te Tienen (prov. Vlaams-Brabant). Interim-verslag 1995–1996', *Archeologie in Vlaanderen*, 6: 133–60

Vanhoutte, Sofie. 2018. 'The Roman Fort at Oudenburg (Belgium): A 4th Century Bathhouse *intra muros*', in *Thermae in Context, the Roman Bath in Town and in Life: Actes du Colloque de Dalheim, Luxembourg, du 21 au 24 février 2013*, ed. by Heike Pösche, Andrea Binsfeld, and Stefanie Hoss, Archaeologia Mosellana, 10 (Luxembourg: Centre national de recherche archéologique), pp. 159–74

Vanvinckenroye, Willy. 1971. 'Het "Hypocaustum" in de Sint-Truiderstraat te Tongeren', *Limburg: Het Oude Land van Loon*, 50: 192–203

——. 1976. 'Tongeren: opgraving en prospectie', *Archéologie*, 1976.1: 18–20

——. 1997. 'De Romeinse villa in het "Middelpadveld" te Vechmaal (Heers)', *Limburg: Het Oude Land van Loon*, 76.2: 179–92

Verbrugge, Arne, Hans Vandendriessche, Arne De Graeve, Véronique Guillaume, Ruben Pede, and Bart Cherretté. 2021. 'Ruien Rosalinde. Archeologisch onderzoek' (unpublished excavation report, SOLVA Archeologie Rapport)

Versluys, Miguel John. 2014. 'Understanding Objects in Motion. An Archaeological Dialogue on Romanization', *Archaeological Dialogues*, 21.1: 1–20

Verslype, Laurent. 1995. 'Thermes urbains à Tournai (Belgique)', *Balnearia*, 3: 7–10

——. 1997. 'Tournai: sondage au quai Vifquin. Un ensemble thermal public du Haut-Empire sur la rive droite de l'Escaut?', *Chronique de l'archéologie wallonne*, 4–5: 66–67

Vigarello, Georges. 1985. *Le propre et le sale: l'hygiène du corps depuis le Moyen Âge* (Paris: Seuil)

Villard, Laurence. 1994. 'Le bain dans la médecine hippocratique', in *L'eau, la santé et la maladie dans le monde grec: actes du colloque organisé à Paris (CNRS et Fondation Singer-Polignac) du 25 au 27 novembre 1992*, ed. by R. Ginouvès, Anne-Marie Guimier-Sorbets, and Jacques Jouanna, Bulletin de correspondance hellénique supplément, 28 (Athens: École française d'Athènes), pp. 41–60

Vladu, Adrian-Marius. 2017. 'The Theft of Water from the Aqueducts of the City of Rome in Frontinus' Time', *Rivista Cicsca*, n.s., 2017: 4–18

Wallace-Hadrill, Andrew. 1988. 'The Social Structure of the Roman House', *Papers of the British School at Rome*, 56: 43–97

——. 2008. *Rome's Cultural Revolution* (Cambridge: Cambridge University Press)

Walters, Bryn. 1996. 'Exotic Structures in 4th-Century Britain', in *Architecture in Roman Britain*, ed. by Peter Johnson and Ian Hayes (York: Council for British Archaeology), pp. 152–62

Weber, Marga. 1996. *Antike Badekultur*, Beck's archäologische Bibliothek (Munich: Beck)

Wightman, Edith Marie. 1985. *Gallia Belgica* (London: Batsford)

Willems, Jacques. 1965. 'Clavier Vervoz – Bains et hypocauste', *Bulletin du Cercle archéologique Hesbaye-Condroz*, 5: 75

——. 1966. 'Notes au sujet de la villa belgo-romaine d'Évelette', *Bulletin du Cercle archéologique Hesbaye-Condroz*, 6: 15–28

——. 1968. 'Les fouilles archéologiques de Clavier-Vervoz. Six années de prospections', *Latomus*, 27.1: 187–90

——. 1972. 'La villa romaine de Villers-le-Bouillet', *Bulletin du Cercle archéologique Hesbaye-Condroz*, 12: 118

Willems, Jacques, M. Dandoy, and Eugène Thirion. 1969. 'La Villa gallo-romaine de la Collégiale d'Amay', *Bulletin du Cercle archéologique Hesbaye-Condroz*, 9: 41–57

Willems, Jacques, and Edouard Lauwerijs. 1973. 'Le vicus belgo-romain de Vervoz à Clavier', *Helinium*, 13: 155–74

Willis, Steven. 2013a. 'The Iron Age and Roman Settlement at Ingleby Barwick', in *A Roman Villa at the Edge of Empire: Excavations at Ingleby Barwick, Stockton-on-Tees, 2003–04*, ed. by Steven Willis and Peter Carne, CBA Research Report, 170 (York: Council for British Archaeology), pp. 165–93

——. 2013b. 'The Later Iron Age and Roman Finds Assemblage', in *A Roman Villa at the Edge of Empire: Excavations at Ingleby Barwick, Stockton-on-Tees, 2003–04*, ed. by Steven Willis and Peter Carne, CBA Research Report, 170 (York: Council for British Archaeology), pp. 153–64

Wilson, Roger John Anthony. 1983. *Piazza Armerina* (London: Granada)

Wirtz, Rut. 1993. 'Die villa rustica von Aachen-Süsterfeld', *Archäologie im Rheinland*, 1993: 78–80

Witvrouw, Daniel, and Jacques Witvrouw. 1997. 'Modave/Outrelouxhe: vestiges au lieu-dit "Elmer"', *Chronique de l'archéologie wallonne*, 4–5: 98–99

Witvrouw, Jacques. 1986. 'Les thermes du vicus gallo-romain d'Amay-Ombret', *Bulletin du Cercle archéologique Hesbaye-Condroz*, 19: 83–115

——. 1988. 'La villa romaine d'Arvy à Clermont-sous-Huy', *Bulletin du Cercle archéologique Hesbaye-Condroz*, 20: 27–53

——. 2014. *Le relais routier romain d'Elmer à Outrelouxhe (Modave)*, Bulletin du Cercle archéologique Hesbaye-Condroz, 31 (Amay: Cercle Archéologique Hesbaye-Condroz)

——. 2015. 'Le relais routier romain d'Elmer à Outrelouxhe (Modave)', *Signa romana*, 4: 263–65

Witvrouw, Jacques, and Daniel Witvrouw. 1998. 'Modave/Outrelouxhe: vestiges gallo-romains', *Chronique de l'archéologie wallonne*, 6: 94–95

Woolf, Greg. 1998. *Becoming Roman: The Origins of Provincial Civilization in Gaul* (Cambridge: Cambridge University Press)

Yegül, Fikret. 1979. 'The Small City Bath in Classical Antiquity and a Reconstruction Study of Lucian's "Baths of Hippias"', *Archeologia classica*, 31: 108–31

——. 1992. *Baths and Bathing in Classical Antiquity* (New York: MIT Press)

——. 2010. *Bathing in the Roman World* (Cambridge: Cambridge University Press)

——. 2013. 'Thermal Matters: Intersected Legacies of Greek and Roman Baths and Bathing Culture', in *Greek Baths and Bathing Culture: New Discoveries and Approaches*, ed. by Sandra Lucore and Monika Trümper, Babesch Supplement, 23 (Leuven: Peeters), pp. 73–88

Yegül, Fikret, and Tristan Couch. 2003. 'Building a Roman Bath for the Cameras', *Journal of Roman Archaeology*, 16: 153–77

Index

THE ARCHAEOLOGY
OF NORTHERN EUROPE

All volumes in this series are evaluated by an Editorial Board, strictly on academic grounds, based on reports prepared by referees who have been commissioned by virtue of their specialism in the appropriate field. The Board ensures that the screening is done independently and without conflicts of interest. The definitive texts supplied by authors are also subject to review by the Board before being approved for publication. Further, the volumes are copyedited to conform to the publisher's stylebook and to the best international academic standards in the field.

Titles in Series

Contrasts of the Nordic Bronze Age: Essays in Honour of Christopher Prescott, ed. by Knut Ivar Austvoll, Marianne Hem Eriksen, Per Ditlef Fredriksen, Lene Melheim, Lisbeth Prøsch-Danielsen, and Lisbeth Skogstrand (2020)

In Preparation

Bear and Human: Facets of a Multi-layered Relationship from Past to Recent Times with an Emphasis on Northern Europe, ed. by Oliver Grimm (3 vols)